Existential psychology is more relevant to the contemporary world than ever before. This dynamic and provocative anthology not only presents an authoritative history and descriptions of the topic, but includes chapters by Chinese psychologists who have found ways in which existentialism both resonates and contrasts with Asian wisdom traditions. This is a cutting-edge book that needs not only to be read, but to be applied to the human condition, both East and West.

Stanley Krippner, PhD Professor of Psychology, Saybrook Graduate School
Co-Editor, *The Psychological Impact of War Trauma on Civilians*

Face-to-face interaction in China led to virtual collaboration in writing this book. With the perspectives of scholars in both the USA and China represented, a true dialogic relationship is evident in this collection. Differences and difficulties in cultural understandings of existentialism are addressed forthrightly which deepens the reflection process that is a hallmark of existential psychology. Existential Psychology East-West also serves as a bridge to Chinese/Asian traditions as they are articulated from an existential perspective. What a terrific model for cross-cultural collaboration and dialogue!

David Lukoff, PhD

In this collection of 20 chapters entitled Existential Psychology East-West, the authors have brightly limned the commonalities and differences in Eastern and Western mentalities and their respective approaches into the "vasty deep" of human joy and anxiety, pleasure and suffering, enduring human values and personal ephemerality, and the emic and personological peculiarities of individuals in the various cultures that are clustered in these two hemispheres. The indigenous existentialism they each, separately, have in common provides a bridge for readers to understand each other in both universes of discourse. The Human in its sociality and individuality is treated without sentimentality and with scholarship. This book is not an ideational blender. Free of bromides and clichés, Existential Psychology East-West respects the distinctness and beauty of stand-alone paradigms for, and cultural visions of, the Human. This book makes a significant contribution to its domain of interest.

Frank Dumont, EdD
Full Professor (retired), McGill University, Montreal, Quebec

Existential Psychology East-West will appeal to anyone with an interest in understanding themselves and the nature and nurture of the human condition. Reading EPEW is like encountering a great river. It courses through the existential terrain and draws from many tributaries. It is both mysterious and inviting, beckoning the reader: ride the currents, plumb the depths, drink from the water.

Kevin Keenan, PhD
Faculty, Michigan School of Professional Psychology

# Existential Psychology East-West
# Volume 1: Revised and Expanded Edition

Edited by
Louis Hoffman,
Mark Yang,
Francis J. Kaklauskas,
Albert Chan,
&
Monica Mansilla

University
PROFESSORS PRESS

Colorado Springs, CO
www.universityprofessorspress.com

First published in 2019. University Professors Press. United States.

ISBN 10: 1-939686-23-7
ISBN 13: 978-1-939686-23-7

University Professors Press
Colorado Springs, CO
www.universityprofessorspress.com


Cover Design by Laura Ross

First Edition of *Existential Psychology East-West* (Volume 1) was published by University of the Rockies Press. The Revised and Expanded Edition is published with permission from the University of the Rockies Press.

Chapter 22: "*Brokeback Mountain*: A Gay and Universal Love Story" by Ilene Serlin was originally published in *PsycCRITIQUES: APA Review of Books*. This chapter was reprinted with permission from the American Psychological Association.

# Table of Contents

**Part 3: Existential-Humanistic Perspectives on Culture and Myths**

# Acknowledgments

Compiling a book with contributors writing in different languages and located in different countries is an enormous undertaking. There are many people who have played a pivotal role in the idea of this book, its development, and the final product. This truly was a collaborative process that entailed the help and support of many people.

First, the editors would like to thank the many talented contributors to this book. The contributors to this volume include many prominent scholars in the United States and China, as well as a number of rising stars in the profession. We are deeply humbled by their contributions to *Existential Psychology East-West*.

The idea for this book emerged from a trip to Hong Kong and various cities throughout China in 2008 to conduct trainings in existential psychology in China. Many individuals who participated in this trip deserve our thanks, including J. Christy Thrash, Michael Dow, Elizabeth Saxon, Yang Yuchuan, Simon Chow, and Reverend David Yip. We would like to thank Steve Caruthers Emory Cowan, who helped arrange financial support for this trip. A number of organizations provided additional support in various forms. The Hong Kong Institute of Christian Counseling provided space and funding for the trip; we are deeply thankful for their generosity and hospitality. Lutheran Theological Seminary and Alliant University, Hong Kong Campus hosted talks and discussions on existential psychology. In Beijing, the China Youth University of Political Science was gracious in providing us with space and providing meals.

Al Dueck and Buxin Han also deserve a special acknowledgement for organizing a series of psychology of religion conferences in mainland China, where the editors of this book met and began formulating plans for bringing dialogues on existential psychology to China. It was at these conferences where the editors also met several of the contributors to this volume. Drs. Dueck and Han also provided a model for holding an international conference in a culturally sensitive manner. Wang Xuefu has been an invaluable contributor to this volume in many ways: making connections with contributors, providing feedback and insight, editorial support, assistance with translation, and contributing to this volume. We would also like to acknowledge a number of people who provided editorial support on particular chapters or portions of the book, including Kate Calhoon, Ed Mendelowitz, Kirk Schneider, Katie McGuire, Cheryl Deloia, John Chavis, Glen Moriarty, and Cathy Calvert. We owe special gratitude to Angela Nazworth, who was the original copy editor for the book and worked with us on a tight timeline. We also appreciate the University of the Rockies, who published the original version of this book, for granting permission for it to be republished with a new publisher.

Last, we want to thank the family and friends of all those who contributed to this volume for their support, encouragement, and generosity in sharing their loved ones with us.

Louis Hoffman would like to thank his co-editors: Mark, Francis, Albert, and Monica. It has been a terrific honor to work with the four of you. I would like to give a special thanks to Kirk Schneider, the leading contemporary scholar and advocate of existential-humanistic psychology, whose support and encouragement has been extremely meaningful. Ed Mendelowitz and Stephen A. Diamond, who I view as two of the most talented writers in psychology, deserve deep gratitude for your encouragement of my writing and contributions to existential thought. I am also deeply grateful for the encouragement of Ilene Serlin and David Elkins. I would like to acknowledge H. Newton Malony and Winston Gooden, who helped introduce me to existential psychology during my graduate school days. Several friends and family members who provided early encouragement and feedback will always deserve credit on any writing I do throughout my career; without them, I may have never found my voice or the courage to write: Robert Murney, Brittany Bowser, and John Hoffman. I would also like to acknowledge my good friend and colleague Glen Moriarty whose collaboration and friendship has been a wonderful blessing and influence, and Sandra K. Knight, whose collaborations, friendship, and encouragement has been an incredible blessing in my life. I am appreciative of two great friends, Clarence Leung and Jonathon Choi, who first introduced me to Chinese culture over dim sums during graduate school. These conversations opened my eyes to the excitement of multiculturalism and forever changed my life.

I would like to thank Emory Cowan, a wonderful mentor and friend, who modeled existential applications in many areas of life. Several colleagues also deserve acknowledgement for their support and encouragement of my writing: Jim Ungvarsky, Susan Cooper, Lorri White, Sharon Trivette, and Jean Jones. I am deeply indebted to Al Dueck and Buxin Han, who first invited me to China. There are many students who, throughout the years, helped me become a better professor and I wish to thank all those who taught me while I was in the role of teaching them; good learning is always mutual! In particular, I would like to thank J. Christy Thrash, Michael Dow, Elizabeth Saxon, and Francis Kaklauskas, who participated in my first trip to China focused on trainings in existential psychology. I'm deeply thankful to my friend and colleague, Mark Yang, who first invited me to present in Hong Kong and China on existential psychology. Mark and I have a shared passion and mission to promote existential psychology throughout Asia and have been committed to this mission ever since the inception of this book. I look forward to the opportunities to expand our mission in the many years to come. Last, and most importantly, I am thankful to my family. My parents, Clarence and Lynn, have supported me in my education and career, but also in becoming a person of compassion. You deserve credit for any and every success in my life. My brother, John, and sister-in-law, Joy, have been wonderful supports as friends and colleagues as well as family members. My wife, Heatherlyn, and sons, Lakoda, Lukaya, and Lyon: You are my motivation in life and my greatest blessing; all these years of writing and I can still never find words enough to voice my love and appreciation of you.

Mark Yang: I would like to thank his co-editors Louis, Francis, Albert, and Monica. A most special and warm gratitude is offered to Louis Hoffman who has become a friend, colleague, and even mentor of mine even though you are younger in age. You continue to model wisdom, grace, and humility for me throughout the years. Your sharing about your own faith journey encourages me to face my own existential isolation and know that the All-Mighty can be found in unexpected places that may sometimes require that I let go of my "old wineskins." I would also like to thank Wang Xuefu who, through the work of this project and other teaching collaborations, has introduced and given me deeper insights into what Lu Xun and you have to say about the Chinese psyche. The knowledge I have gained from you helps me to have a better understanding of myself and my life here in Asia. I would also like to thank Winston Gooden, the dean at the Graduate School of Psychology at Fuller Seminary. Winston, you modeled and introduced to me the field of existential psychology. You helped me to explore my own ethnic identity and your belief in me sustained me through graduate school and beyond. You made my Fuller experience worthwhile. A special thanks also goes out to Zhang Zhibin and Lucy Liu, two of my colleagues here in China whose companionship and shared sacrifice helps me to keep becoming the person and the leader that I am. I would like to thank Irvin Yalom who has become a written mentor of mine. I channel your writing and your wisdom on a daily basis. If it were not for your writing, I would not have known that I was an existential psychologist who is also interested in group and grief work.; all because of you. Even though I have yet to meet you, I feel like you have already made a significant part of yourself known to me. You are my teacher and mentor!  Finally, I wish to acknowledge the strong influence of Carl Rogers in my life.  I have always been drawn to your writings and it is only now, given my own maturation, that I've come to better appreciate the beauty of your personhood.  Your spirit lives on through this book.

Francis Kaklauskas: I wish to thank my other co-editors, Louis, Mark, Albert, and Monica whose open hearts and gracious spirits made me quickly feel as if we have always been siblings.  I would like to thank my own sister, Kathy Graber, for countless generosities of time, spirit, and scholarship, as she was responsible for me considering Leibniz's monads instead of paying attention in high school. Finally, I cannot thank my wife, Elizabeth, and my son, Levi, enough for their gift of loyalty and love.

Albert Chan: I never thought of myself as someone who was going to write a chapter on myths of Chinese culture and especially a chapter on existential psychology, although in my undergraduate years, I had written some poems and did some editorial work for a university magazine and for a church. I am grateful to Dr. Louis Hoffman who initiated my involvement in this writing project. I am also indebted to his faith and trust in my writing, even though I feared that I would most likely fail with my inexperience in writing. I am particularly grateful for Dr.

Francis Kaklauskas' editorial work on my chapter. I am thankful for his friendship and passion to make this chapter both truthful and readable. To my friend and mentor Dr. Frank Dumont, I am thankful for your kind companionship in reading my chapter before I had courage to submit it to the other editors. Dr. Mark Yang, I thank you for your comradeship in Hong Kong. Without this I would not have started this chapter in my life. With my editorial friends, I would like to show my gratitude; because of you and our meeting in Beijing, 2008, I have come to appreciate existential psychology which reminds me of my early years of studies in philosophy, theology, and literature, a long overdue revisit.

I thank my daughters Hannah and Erin who keep up my interest in writing, as they share their writings with me and their faith in me. In many ways the chapter I contributed is for you. I am inspired by my students in Hong Kong and Macau for their trust in my teaching and special thanks to Christina Leung's curiosity, which assists me not only in my teaching but also in challenging me in my writing in existential psychology. I thank Mark Lam who introduced me to learn Chinese natural philosophy. I thank my mother and my late father who gave me all their blessings in my life. My mentors/professors Drs. Claude Guldner and Andy Hum encouraged me in different stages of my life. My friends Janice Maloney and Lorena Perna have been accompanying me in my professional development and keep me as their friends, I have not thanked you sufficiently.

Father, Dr. Vincente Sanchez, we have discussed so many issues on individual and collective culture and life in general; we are set sailing into an exciting journey. Lastly, I thank Lillian Ko, who accompanied me in my life journey till now, words will not express my appreciation, love, and gratitude.

Monica Mansilla, I would like to thank my mentor Louis Hoffman for his invaluable support and continuous encouragement to expand and contribute to the field of Existential-Humanistic Psychology around the world, and also for his ever-present holding heart and unbreakable belief in me. I would also like to thank my co-editors: Mark, Francis, and Albert, who mentor me not only by their warm support and guidance, but also by the greatness of their example. Finally, I'd like to thank my grandfather, David Santa Cruz, my father, Jose Luis Mansilla, and my brother, David Mansilla for being the male pillar of my life whose strength and love guide me in their presence and their absence.

# Poetic Preface

## Tom Greening

PING

Let us now our praises sing
of a humble duck named Ping.
Dynasties may come and go,
governments put on their show,
emperors orate and strut—
All seek fame and power, but
a hundred years from now you'll see
who goes down in history

Floating with the Yangtze's flow,
he knows as only ducks can know
when to fly and when to dive,
how to keep his hope alive,
and so of wisdom he is king,
even though he's only Ping.

*This poem was inspired by the Chinese children's book,* Ping, *which was read to me in 1935.*

# Foreword

## Donadrian L. Rice

Every once in a while, we are treated with a text that adds a completely new dimension to our understanding of the world around us and the people who inhabit that world. While there is a plethora of disciplines that attempt to assist us in our understandings, psychology has emerged as the *sine qua non* among the disciplines that intend to teach us about ourselves. Of the many theoretical approaches to psychology, existential psychology has offered us the ability to illuminate and highlight the salient characteristics of human existence in ways that go beyond what psychology "as usual" has been able to achieve. While I readily admit to my bias, I am persuaded by the many volumes of literature published over the last six decades devoted exclusively to this important mission of apprehending the significant features of human existence.

The introduction of existential psychology to the United States in the 1950s was literally a breath of fresh air to those psychologists who found the dominate theories of behaviorism and psychoanalysis lacking in their abilities to address the important questions about life posed by their clients in the consulting room. Leaders in this field such as Rollo May provided a template and direction in this emerging field that has allowed others to advance further the theory and practice of Existential psychology. The present volume, *Existential Psychology East-West* is firmly grounded in the foundations of European Existentialism while at the same time advancing into what many might consider to be terra incognita.

Prior to the writings of notable figures such as Alan Watts, little was known in the West of the psychological concepts found in Eastern philosophies and religions. While some of the concepts were new and quite different from Western understandings of psychology, there were other instances of considerable overlap. However, the traditional approaches to psychology did not have a means to explore and integrate the nuances of this rich and complex tradition. To be sure, existential psychology, along with its methodological companion phenomenology, was the only theoretical position in psychology that remotely approached topics and questions found in Eastern psychologies such as, "Who am I, what is experience, and what is the nature of consciousness and Being." I am aware, of course, of the contributions made by Humanistic and Transpersonal approaches to psychology and their efforts to integrate Eastern concepts; however, I consider existential psychology as a foundation for these approaches.

While the similarities found in existential psychology and Eastern philosophies and religions have always been there; until now, no concerted effort has been made to explore in depth this relationship in a text that is both scholarly and practical. Hoffman and his colleagues have taken on the herculean task of elucidating the subject matter of two complex areas and providing the reader, whether for scholarly purposes or practical application, with a comprehensible volume that clearly advances our understanding of the subtle fabric that connects these two traditions. Scholars will find that this volume reveals new insights that are worthy of exploration apart from the theme of this text. Therapists will be delighted with the care taken to introduce the practical applications that will certainly increase their knowledge, comprehension, and effectiveness as existential psychotherapists.

Lastly, I would emphasize that this volume could not have come at a more significant time in our history. As a long-time member of the existential choir, I have always believed that our clients are best served by an existential approach to therapy. I have also recognized and explored several Eastern disciplines in scholarly and practical ways. From these experiences, I have come to appreciate the reality of how existential psychology and the Eastern disciplines both contribute to quality cross-cultural understanding. Moreover, I have come to value the importance of both of these traditions as possibly the only ways to address the angst experienced by so many in our increasingly multifaceted world. As we move even faster into a global society, only philosophies, systems, and concepts that speak to the essence of experience of all of humanity will help facilitate a better understanding among cultures that we desire while helping us navigate the inevitable travails of life. It is my contention that this volume is a gigantic step in that direction.

# Introduction to the First Edition

Louis Hoffman
Mark Yang
Francis J. Kaklauskas
Albert Chan

During a trip to China in 2008, three of us had the opportunity to visit the Great Wall. Historically, the Great Wall is a symbol of division. What is one of the most monumental human structures ever built is also one of the great symbols of division. But one of the remarkable things about symbols is that their meaning can be recreated and re-envisioned over time.

As we approached the Great Wall, we could not help being awestruck. The beauty, the power, and the emotion in the thousands of carved bricks as far as the eye can see resonated across the across time and through our beings. As we stood for a group picture, the Great Wall stretched across the many peaks behind us and the endless path in front of us. There was not enough time; you could walk the Great Wall for days, even months, and never reach its end or the end of the pondering it stimulates. Begrudgingly, we eventually realized we could not suspend a return to our lives and commitments in Beijing any longer. When leaving, we came across a decorative stone with this inscription:

> Once intended to ward off enemy attacks. Today it brings together the peoples of the world. The Great Wall, may it continue to act as a symbol of friendship for future generations.

Re-envisioning. What has kept people apart can now bring them together. While on the wall, we felt a sense of unity as we met people from all over the world. Each person displayed a friendliness and embodied openness that was inspiring. There is something magical, even transcendent, about the wall.

Existential philosophy began in Europe in the 1800s, and sometimes has been unfairly characterized as a dark philosophy. It emerged during a time when individualism reigned in Western thought and, in many ways, it took on this individualism. But, again, some of the portrayals of existentialism, as excessively individualist, are unfair and may be due to a misunderstanding of basic existential ideas. Existentialism promulgates the relational imperative. In many ways, relationships provide the container against the void in which the individual can feel, act, and exist.

Regardless, existentialism is not guilt-free; it must take responsibility for its mistakes. If it is going to reach its ideals, existential philosophy and psychology must extend beyond the limits of Western thought. This, in part, is the story of this book. Culture has served to be a barrier, much like the Great Wall, for the extension of existential thought. Although the indigenous similarities between Eastern thought and existentialism are striking, it seemed that culture, politics, and language precluded existential thought from moving beyond its Western origins. Nothing, however, could be more *unexistential* than such rigid and narrow application of existential thought! Existential thought, and of particular interest in this book, existential psychology, must transcend the cultural and temporal limitations of its origins, which surely will include some changes in existential psychology.

The four editors of this book along with J. Christy Thrash, Michael Dow, and Elizabeth Saxon had the opportunity to begin discussing existential psychology in the East on our trip in 2008. In earlier eras, where international communication and travel were more difficult and rare, it was easier for schools of thought to become stuck in a singular cultural context. Now, in postmodern times, this same stuckness is the death of any theory sophisticated enough to gain prominence. Theories, especially psychological theories, must be culturally adaptable and must remain fluid enough to adjust to the times and the contexts in which they exist. Although existential thought has not always followed this guideline, it has been implicit in its anti-dogmatic and contextual understanding of human existence.

*Existential Psychology East-West* seeks to re-envision existential thought beyond its original limited cultural context while remaining true to the core values of existentialism. Few experiences can transform a person's understanding of the world more than cross-cultural exchanges. This is very evident in the classroom. No amount of within group differences can account for the same richness that is available in cross-cultural dialogues. Different cultures see and experience the world in such radically different ways that it often hard to leave one's own culture behind long enough to truly understand the other's perspective. Similarly, we believe that there can be no better teacher about existential psychology's weakness and future needs than cross-cultural dialogue.

As is evident in the chapters in this book, there are some challenges. At times, it seems that existential psychology may have to soften on core principles in order to be culturally respectful and culturally relevant. It is our belief, however, that the core elements of existential psychology are culturally adaptable. We do not believe that there is a need to sacrifice any core principles of existential thought to be applied cross-culturally; however, many may need some re-envisioning and adaptation. It is our hope that this book is the beginning of a dialogue that will grow and develop for many years to come.

In the first part of this book, Louis Hoffman provided an overview of the practice of existential-humanistic psychology and psychotherapy. The focus of this chapter, and this book, is primarily on the existential psychology strand emerging from Rollo May and later James F. T. Bugental. This chapter introduces existential psychology's theory and practice and sets the philosophical and historical foundation for the later chapters. In chapter two, a case illustration by

Louis Hoffman and Nathaniel Granger helps to put a face to what existential psychotherapy looks like in practice.

In part 2, the focus shifts to the theoretical development of existential psychology in a cross-cultural context. The first chapter by J. Christy Thrash and colleagues sets the stage for issues examined later in the book. This chapter uses the information gathered during the 2008 trip to China to identify the major challenges of applying existential psychology in the East as well as the opportunities that can be built upon in moving toward understanding and integration. As the stage is set, these issues are addressed by a number of leading Eastern and Western scholars. A primary theme in these chapters is the religious influences. Religion often reflects the indigenous values and the indigenous psychology of a culture. The existential and religious dialogues illuminate many of the challenges and opportunities of this dialogue in a rich manner. Other chapters address the interface of Jungian and existential psychology, global authenticity, mindfulness and existential psychology, and the similarities between several Chinese theories, such as LuXun, and existential thought.

The final section of this book draws on the ideas Rollo May (1991) initiated in his book *The Cry for Myth*. In the first chapter, Hoffman examined how myths reflect the universality of the existential givens and the need for cultural specific answers to the givens. In the following chapters, various authors built upon Eastern and Western myths to illuminate the various existential givens, while at the same time illustrating the culture-specific answers which emerge.

In closing, we hope this is the beginning of a long and rich dialogue. We hope readers will join us in this journey of exploration and bring along their openness, curiosity, and critical reflections. Existential truths are rarely easily attained. They are sought after, revised, and re-envisioned over time. This is only the beginning.

## References

May, R. (1991). *The cry for myth*. New York, NY: Delta.

# Introduction to the Second Edition

Louis Hoffman, Mark Yang, Francis J. Kaklauskas,
Albert Chan, & Monica Mansilla

The decade since the publication of *Existential-Psychology East-West* has been a fruitful period for the cross-cultural dialogue on existential-humanistic psychology. This includes seven international conferences focusing on existential-humanistic psychology in Southeast Asia, a special section of *The Humanistic Psychologist* based on presentations at the first of these conferences, the formation of the International Institute on Existential-Humanistic Psychology (IIEHP) to promote training on existential and humanistic psychology in Southeast Asia, beginning systematic training programs in China, and the establishment of four training centers in China (Beijing, Chengdu, Chongging, and Changsha).

We are excited, too, that the publication of the revised and updated version of *Existential Psychology East-West* is being published concurrently with *Existential Psychology East-West,* Volume 2. The success of the first edition as well as publication of volume 2 provide a testament to the importance of the cross-cultural dialogues on existential-humanistic psychology.

## Updates in the Second Edition

The Revised and Expanded edition of *Existential-Psychology East-West* (Volume 1) includes a number of important changes, including adding Monica Mansilla as an editor. There are a number of updated chapters in the second edition as well as several new chapters. Chapter 1 has been significantly updated with three important changes. First, the chapter is more specific now, as Hoffman focused on existential-humanistic psychology, which represents the version of the existential psychology that emerged in the United States under the influence of Rollo May and James F. T. Bugental (see Hoffman, Serlin, & Rubin, in press, Schneider, in press). Second, the chapter reflects updates that identify important trends in the existential-humanistic scholarship since the original publication, particularly scholarship relevant to evidence-based practice in psychology. Third, while the primary intention of the chapter remains to provide an overview of existential-humanistic psychology as it is understood in the West, there is greater attention given to cultural issues. This serves as a starting point for future dialogue. Chapter 2, the case illustration, was updated to be more explicit in articulating how particular aspects of the case are connected to tenets of existential-humanistic therapy. A number of other chapters also have minor updates as well. The entire volume has also received a new copy-edit. In the first edition, our intentions were to try to preserve as much of the original writing style through translation; however, the feedback we received was that this was not as successful as we had hoped. The new copy-edit increases the readability of the book.

We have also added five new chapters to the book. In the first edition, our aspiration was to have a balance in chapters that reflected Eastern and Western perspectives. We also were focused on publishing the book a year in advance of the First International Conference on Existential Psychology. Partially due to the complexities of the translation process, a number of chapters in the myth section were not finished in time for publication. Therefore, as noted by Paul T. P. Wong (2009) in his review of the book, the East-West balance was lacking. Although Wong's review overall was quite positive, we took his critique seriously and worked to improve the balance in the second edition. The balance was also continued into Volume 2.

In the first section of the book, we added four new chapters. Chapter 3, which was updated for the second edition, now provides a history and overview of the development of existential-humanistic psychology in China leading up to its publication along with a discussion of some of the challenges. While we did update this chapter to reflect changes in the psychology landscape in China, we felt it was important to add a separate chapter that builds upon this initial history and overview. Chapter 4 provides an overview of the history since the original publication of *Existential Psychology East-West*. This chapter also gives consideration to the expansion of this work to Taiwan, Malaysia, and the Middle East, and is co-authored by individuals from Taiwan, China, Malaysia, Canada, and the United States.

A chapter on existential psychology in Africa by Anthony Nkyi along with a chapter on dreams by Richard Bargdill were added to the theory section. Bargdill's chapter is the one new chapter from a Western perspective. This chapter is based on Bargdill's presentation on dreams at the Third International Conference on Existential Psychology held in Guangzhou, China, and was included due to its positive reception at the conference. Nkyi's chapter is an important addition that expands the dialogue to Africa. Nkyi presented at the First International Conference on Existential Psychology held in Nanjing and was one of the few individuals from Africa who attended the First World Congress of Existential Therapy in London in 2015. Through his teaching and writing, he has been active in developing existential psychology in Ghana with unique African perspective.

In the final section, we added an African Myth discussed by Alan Vaughan, who is an important scholar of the African Diaspora. The last new chapter is a Chinese myth, written about by Bohan Zhang. This diversifies the myth section to include three Chinese myths, one of which is written from the perspective of Western scholars, and two myths from the African diaspora, as well as five myths rooted more in a Western perspective.

Finally, we updated the Annotated Bibliography. There have been numerous important publications in existential-humanistic psychology since the first edition, and the updates reflect some of the important scholarship that has occurred since this time.

## Conclusion

It has taken 8-years to complete *Existential Psychology East-West*, Volume 2, which was much longer than anticipated. While the delays were disappointing, the advantage is that we have been able to complete a revision of Volume 1 to be published concurrently with Volume 2. We are excited that these two volumes are part of a growing appreciation for multiculturalism within humanistic and existential psychology. When the original version of this book was published, humanistic and existential psychology were struggling with accepting the essential place of multicultural perspectives (see Hoffman, 2016; Hoffman, Cleare-Hoffman, & Jackson, 2014). There were even some who perceived multicultural and cross-cultural perspectives as a threat to humanistic and existential psychology. However, multicultural and cross-cultural perspectives are increasingly becoming commonplace at humanistic and existential conferences and publications. We hope these two volumes can continue to help advance this dialogue.

We are also pleased to add a number of important authors to the update of *Existential Psychology East-West* and *Existential Psychology East-West*, Volume 2. Since the first publication of this book in 2009, there have been a number of important emergent voices in existential-humanistic psychology, as well as a number of people advocating for international perspectives. Monica Mansilla has been instrumental in bringing existential-humanistic perspectives to the Middle East, Spain, and New Zealand. Anne Hsu and Rodger Broomé, along with Mark Yang, have helped bring perspectives to Teipei, and Evone Phoo has helped create interest in Malaysia. A number of other early career psychologists have participated in the international work in existential-psychology helping generate more excitement for this work. This includes Kristen Beau Howard, Jenna Noah, and Sivan Wilson. These emergent leaders are vital for the continued developing of existential-humanistic psychology and creating of a more deeply committed multicultural influence.

Although we do not anticipate a Volume three to this series, we are certain that this work is still in its infancy. We are confident that the many voices in these two volumes will continue to cultivate new ideas and energy that will carry existential-humanistic psychology forward.

## References

Hoffman, L. (2016). Multiculturalism and humanistic psychology: From neglect to epistemological and ontological diversity. *The Humanistic Psychologist, 44,* 56-71.

Hoffman, L., Cleare-Hoffman, H. P., & Jackson, T. (2014). Humanistic psychology and multiculturalism: History, current status, and advancements. In K. J. Schneider, J.

F. Pierson & J. F. T. Bugental (Eds.), *The handbook of humanistic psychology: Theory, research, and practice* (2nd edition; pp. 41-55). Thousand Oaks, CA: Sage.

Hoffman, L., Serlin, I. D., & Rubin, S. (in press). The history of existential-humanistic integrative psychology. In E. van Duerzen, K. Schneider, E. Craig, A. Langle, & D. Tatum (Eds.), *Wiley world handbook of existential therapy*. Hoboken, NJ: Wiley.

Schneider, K. J. (in press). Existential-humanistic and existential-integrative philosophy and theory. In E. van Duerzen, K. J. Schneider, E. Craig, A. Langle, & D. Tatum (Eds.), *Wiley world handbook of existential therapy*. Hoboken, NJ: Wiley.

Wong, P. T. P. (2009). An existential vision of the good life: Toward an international psychology and psychotherapy based on meaning [Review of Existential Psychology East-West]. *PsycCRITIQUES*, 54(51). doi:10.1037/a0018290

# Part 1

## Overview of Existential-Humanistic Theory and Practice

# Chapter 1

## Introduction to Existential-Humanistic Psychology in a Cross-cultural Context[1]

### Louis Hoffman

> The purpose of [existential] psychotherapy is to set people free.
> ~ Rollo May, 1981, p. 19

> Viewed from an existential standpoint, questions of choice, freedom and responsibility cannot be isolated or contained within some separate being (such as 'self' or 'other')…. Viewed in this way, no choice can be mine or yours alone, no experienced impact of choice can be separated in terms of 'my responsibility' versus 'your responsibility', no sense of personal freedom can truly avoid its interpersonal dimensions.
> ~ Ernesto Spinelli, 2001, p. 16

Existential thought is rooted in the study of what it means to exist (Bakewell, 2017). With such a vague starting point, it is no wonder much confusion exists about existential thought and existential psychology. Furthermore, while there are similarities in the writings of the people often identified as the early representatives of existential philosophy, there are also important divergences. The same is true with early figures in existential psychology.

Still, it is common for existentialists to hear questions such as, "Isn't everything really existential?" Or, on the other end of the continuum, there are some who some see existential psychology as being bound by the ideas of Sartre, Heidegger, or, perhaps, some other existential hero. These common misconceptions of existential thought—making it overly inclusive or overly restrictive—create confusion about what could be considered existential.

The label *existential* itself has a complicated history. Flynn (2006) pointed out that while Kierkegaard is most often identified as the first existentialist, Marcel was the first to use the label of *existentialist* to refer to John Paul Sartre. Many identified as existentialists do not label themselves as such and maintain deep concern about labels as overly constrictive. Even Karl Jaspers (1971), who

---

[1] Writing an introduction to existential psychology and psychotherapy today must be engaged with a certain degree of humility due to the many great introductions that already exist. In particular, the reader is encouraged to also consider Mendelowitz and Schneider (2007), Schneider (2008a), May (1958a, 1958b), and Yalom (1980).

wrote *Philosophy of Existence*, resisted the label. Therefore, many influential existential voices never referred to themselves as existentialists and many contemporary existentialists do so with some reticence. While empathizing with their concern and recognizing the need of protecting existentialism from succumbing to overly restrictive, narrow, and reified definitions, the label serves an important purpose in bringing together writers, theorists, practitioners, and students who share the basic values of existential thought.

The study of existence is only the starting point of existential thought. As with any school of thought, it must evolve beyond its starting point if it is to retain utility and meaning. Cooper (2016) identified five distinct primary schools of existential therapy: (a) Daseinsanalysis; (b) Meaning-Centered Therapies, which includes Logotherapy; (c) Existential-Humanistic Therapy; (d) Laingian approaches to existential therapy; and (e) Existential-Phenomenological Therapy. In addition to these schools, there are some smaller, emergent approaches to existential therapy, such as Zhi Mian Therapy, which originated in China (Wang, 2011, 2018). While there are some similarities and shared values across the different approaches to existential therapy, there are also important differences (Cooper, 2016, Craig, Vos, Cooper, & Correia, 2016).

The purpose of this chapter is to provide the reader with an accessible introduction and overview of existential-humanistic psychology, which is one of the schools identified by Cooper (2016). In this chapter, I have begun with the assumption that existential-humanistic therapists may not fully agree on any one aspect of this approach as essential. Instead, I understand existential-humanistic psychology as a collection of values that emerge from the beginning point of the study of human existence. Those who identify with the labeling of "existential" tend to agree with many of the key aspects identified in this chapter, but not necessarily all of them.

## A Brief History of Existentialism

The early existential writings of Blaise Pascal, Friedrich Nietzsche, and Soren Kierkegaard were connected with romanticism and the anti-enlightenment movement in Europe. Embodied in both these trends, existential thought was concerned with the dominance of rationalism and objectivism over and against other ways of knowing. These early existential writers sought more subjective and holistic ways to pursue knowledge. In many ways, the origin of existentialism is a reaction to scientific modernism,[2] which explains the many similarities between existentialism and postmodernism. Existential thought, however, is not opposed to reason; rather, it is concerned about the exclusive reliance on rationalism and devaluing of other ways of knowing. Later philosophical figures that have been connected

---

[2] "Scientific" is used as an adjective for "modernism" here to distinguish it from its use by modernist literary figures, such as Franz Kafka, Virginia Woolf, and Samuel Becket, who have greatly influenced the work of many existential writers.

with existential thought include Husserl, Heidegger, Sartre, de Beauvoir, and Camus.

A second dominant theme demonstrated in existential writing is a commitment to honesty about the entirety of the human condition, or existence. This can be seen in the writing of Nietzsche (1886/1966) in the West, and also in the writing of Lu Xun and Xuefu Wang in the East (see chapter 6), and it is illustrated in Lu Xun's (1925/1961) words:

> The world is changing from day to day; it is high time for our writers to take off their masks, look frankly, keenly, and boldly at life and write about real flesh and blood. It is high time for a brand-new arena for literature, high time for some bold fighters to charge headlong into battle! (p. 203)

With the ascendancy of scientific modernism and method, which emphasizes a study of parts over wholes, a way of studying and understanding human nature in discrete parts emerged. There also was a move toward valuing reason and science over and against the arts, emotions, and subjective experience. The existentialists, who drew heavily upon literature and the arts, sought to bring things back into balance. The central themes of existential thought emerged out of a foundation premised upon holistic methodology, a valuing of subjectivity, and brutal honesty about the human condition.

Phenomenology—focusing on the study of subjectivity and consciousness— is a third central theme in existential thought. However, not all phenomenologists are existentialists, and not all existentialists are phenomenologists (Bakewell, 2017; Flynn, 2006). Furthermore, for some existential-humanistic therapists, existential-humanistic psychology is primarily just phenomenology; however, for most, this is one aspect of a broader approach that cannot be reduced to phenomenology. The existential approach, although emphasizing subjectivity, tends to bring objective realities, including the existential givens, into dialogue with the subjective self. Even here, existentialists are more concerned with the subjective experience of the objective realities than the objective realities themselves. For example, the objectivity of the givens is that these are universal challenges or struggles that must be faced, but this does not necessitate any specific answer to these objective realities.

These three themes provide a basis for existential-humanistic thought. One could note, however, that these three themes are devoid of specific content; they are values that inform existential methodology. In other words, one would be hard-pressed to find an existential approach that does not seek a holistic understanding of what it means to be human, an appreciation for subjective experience, and the intent to be honest about the human condition. However, from this foundation, many perspectives emerge.

**The Beginning of Existential Psychology**
Existential psychology began in Europe with the writings of Ludwig Binswanger. Unfortunately, Binswanger remains relatively unknown outside of Europe, even among some existential psychologists. The primary English introduction to Binswanger is the translations of his work included in the book *Existence* (May, Angel, & Ellenberger, 1958), often cited as the origins of existential psychology in the United States. This book thrust Rollo May, the lead editor of the book, into role of the father of American existential psychology.

Shortly after the publication of *Existence*, James F. T. Bugental (1965) emerged as an influential voice in existential psychology in the United States with the publication of his book *The Search for Authenticity*. It was Bugental who began using the *existential-humanistic* label that now is applied to both May and Bugental. Although Rollo May (1982) was also active in humanistic psychology and the founding of the Association for Humanistic Psychology, he eventually favored the label existential because of key differences with Carl Rogers (1982), a leading representative of humanistic psychology. Despite his preference for the term existential, he remained involved with humanistic psychology.

The most well-known follower of Rollo May is Irvin Yalom (1980). In an international survey of existential therapists, only Viktor Frankl was identified as more influential than Yalom (Correia, Cooper, & Berdondini, 2015). Yalom's *Existential Psychotherapy* was identified as the second most influential book as well. Yalom, a former client of May, provided the most commonly used organizational structure for existential psychology through what he called the *four existential givens*: death, freedom, isolation, and meaninglessness. This continues to be the most common classification of the existential givens, though it was not the first or only classification. Yalom also popularized existential psychology through writing several novels (1993, 1997) and case study books (1989, 1999).

Despite Yalom's influence, there is not consistent agreement about where he fits within the broader landscape of existential therapy (Hoffman, Serlin, & Rubin, in press). Yalom did not see existential therapy as a distinct, free-standing therapy and, in many ways, he represented his own, unique approach to therapy. He is, however, most frequently associated with the existential-humanistic approach.

More recently, Kirk Schneider (as cited in Schneider & May, 1995), who mentored under both May and Bugental, moved into the role of the most prominent figure in existential-humanistic psychology. Schneider co-edited with Rollo May the book *The Psychology of Existence*, which served as the first introductory text on existential therapy since Yalom's (1980) *Existential Psychotherapy*. Schneider's (2008a) *Existential-Integrative Psychotherapy: Guideposts to the Core of Practice* was a ground-breaking text that positioned existential-humanistic therapy as a potential foundation for various approaches to therapy. His book *Existential-Humanistic Therapy* (2017) with Orah Krug, which is already in its second edition, was published in the American Psychological Association's Theories of Psychotherapy Series, establishing existential-humanistic therapy as one of the most influential therapy modalities in the United States.

## Existential-Humanistic Psychotherapy as a Depth Psychotherapy

Existential-humanistic psychotherapy is a depth psychotherapy. Depth psychotherapy, however, suffers from many of the same definitional problems that
plague existential psychology. Similar to what was previously discussed about
existential psychotherapy, depth psychotherapy often is assumed to be a set of approaches that takes seriously unconscious, or subconscious aspects of being
human, and self-awareness. Some existential psychologists (Wyschogrod, 1961)
take issue with the unconscious based upon critiques of Freud's conception of the
unconscious. Subconscious is sometimes used as an alternative but can bring
some of the same concerns. Within the existential-humanistic tradition, the focus
on increasing awareness justify claiming it as a depth psychotherapy.

Bugental (1987, 1990) discussed the idea of *life changing psychotherapy*,
which could be equated to depth psychotherapy. Bugental distinguished life
changing psychotherapy from forms of therapy that are solution-focused, skill
based, or centered on coping. This form of therapy was assumed to be a longer-
term therapy in most instances, often lasting 6 months or longer, as compared to
the 8-20 sessions typical of brief therapies today.

Depth psychotherapies posit that there are multiple layers of consciousness
and/or experience that are part of human existence. A complete understanding of
the human being, therefore, needs to be holistic, looking beyond the surface layers.
In other words, depth psychology embraces a complex and holistic understanding
of human nature.

Although the non-depth psychologies may also claim to embrace a complex
and even holistic understanding of what it means to be human, this is generally
understood more narrowly. Additionally, these other psychologies tend to focus
on significantly circumscribed aspects of being human as the central aspect of
their psychology. For example, the various cognitive and behavioral therapies
focus primarily on the aspects of being human bearing their name: cognitions and
behaviors. Although many acknowledge human existence is more complex than
this, they do not see the need for their psychologies or therapies to delve into these
realms in any great detail.

## Implications for Existential-Humanistic Therapy as a Depth Psychotherapy

The depth emphasis in existential psychotherapy is relevant to the therapeutic
practice. Although there have been a number of attempts at brief forms of
existential psychotherapy (Bugental, 2008; Galvin, 2008; Strasser & Strasser,
1997), the authors of these approaches acknowledge the limitations inherent in
such attempts. This should not discourage people from attempting to modify
existential therapy for short-term applications; however, it does distinguish the
brief existential approaches from the longer-term approaches.

Existential therapy maintains that many of the challenges that bring people
to therapy are inherent in the nature of being. To this end, Yalom (1989) stated:

> I believe that the primal stuff of psychotherapy is always such existence pain—and not, as is often claimed, repressed instinctual strivings or imperfectly buried shards of tragic personal past... basic anxiety emerges from a person's endeavors, conscious and unconscious, to cope with the harsh facts of life, the "givens" of existence. (p. 4-5)

This quote distinguishes existential from other depth psychotherapies through freeing it from the instinctual strivings and personal past without denouncing the importance of these. Instead, Yalom was pointing to something more primal in one's suffering and pathology—something ontological.

The ontological nature of existential psychotherapy is the primary challenge when adapting it to a short-term approach. How can one deal with what Yalom (1989) identified as *existence pain* in 12 to 20 sessions? Lest this be interpreted as being too harsh on the short-term existential approaches, let me clarify. It is not that the short-term approaches to existential therapy are superficial or anti-thetical to the core of existential practice, but rather they are different from existential psychotherapy. They remain a depth psychotherapy in the sense that they are rooted in a complex, holistic understanding of what it means to be human; however, they are more limited in scope.

Strasser and Strasser (1997) did, however, point out that there are some advantages of time-limited models. They maintain that the imposed time-frame helps to bring forth existential issues. When one knows therapy is to end and this is maintained in the forefront of one's consciousness, this changes the therapy. When therapists hold a frame with sensitivities to the existential condition, they can skillfully bring these issues into the discussion.

Therefore, there are advantages to the time-limited approach and, in certain situations, this may be a preferred method. Often, the therapist does not have the luxury to extend therapy over many months or even years due to client factors, economic conditions, time limitations, or other externally imposed realities. Therefore, it is a valid and important endeavor to seek out short-term adaptations.

David Elkins (2008) challenged the limitations of the various "short-term, linear approaches to psychotherapy" (p. 413), drawing upon reviews of the research, including important recent meta-analytic studies, that discredit the claims of the superiority of short-term models. Furthermore, he elucidated how the research, in fact, points to the likely superiority of longer-term approaches over time.

Many psychotherapists believe that the future of psychotherapy is the brief modalities and that the depth approaches will need to adapt or they will fade away. I disagree. There will always be a place for the brief psychotherapies, as well as a place for longer-term approaches. It is important for the depth therapies to be able to adapt in time-limited scenarios; however, longer-term therapy also has its place and will remain a demand in the marketplace.

The challenge of long-term therapy is, in part, economic. However, it is also cultural if using this word in the broadest sense. In the West, a primary challenge to longer-term therapy is what seems to be a decreasing valuing of mental health and self-awareness. As will be discussed in chapter 4, in China, as well as many other countries where the idea of psychotherapy is relatively new, there are different challenges inherent in getting people to invest in a longer-term therapy. These will be addressed in various ways throughout the book; however, at this point, I would maintain that this problem is a problem of creativity. The need for long-term and short-term depth psychotherapy approaches is there, but creativity is needed to help clients access it and learn about the value of it.

## Existential-Integrative Psychotherapy

The face of psychotherapy needs to be ever changing with the times, needs, and cultural contexts. Existential-integrative psychotherapy is particularly well suited to work with the needed adaptations (Nathan, 2008; Schneider, 2008b). Although outside of this section the use of the term *existential-integrative* will not be used much throughout this book; the word *integrative* often will be implied.

Integrative psychotherapies navigate between two extremes in the manner in which therapists relate to the theoretical foundations of therapy. First, there is the danger of *theoretical fundamentalism*. Many clinicians rigidly adhere to a particular theoretical orientation and the accompanying frame or structure. This negatively impacts the effectiveness of therapy, particularly when working with diverse groups. Although being rooted in a particular approach to therapy is beneficial, rigid adherence limits creativity, innovation, the utilization of good ideas from other approaches to psychotherapy, and cultural adaptation.

At the other extreme is eclecticism. Within the eclectic approaches, the common idea is to use what works. There are many problems with this idea. First, you have to ask, "To what ends does the therapy work?" These ends are necessarily influenced by one's theoretical frame; however, there is no universal intended outcome for therapy. Even if all therapists agreed upon an end—such as symptom reduction and improved quality of life—it is not likely they could agree upon what this means.

Second, eclecticism assumes that one can easily shift one's theoretical orientation to fit the needs of the client. It is not realistic for therapists to be competent, let alone an expert, in a number of varied orientations. Although some orientations and techniques are easy to learn, most depth psychotherapies, including existential-humanistic therapy, take years of training to establish competency. Being grounded in an approach to therapy that one believes in is more predictive of successful outcomes in therapy than the particular techniques used (Elkins, 2008a, 2009; Wampold & Imel, 2015).

Integrative denotes an approach in which the clinician has a foundation in a particular approach to psychotherapy and then integrates other approaches with this foundation. Although this sounds fairly straightforward, it can be more complicated than it initially seems. Many therapists integrate ideas that end up working against each other. An example may help illustrate this.

Existential therapists generally align with anxiety or utilize anxiety in the process of therapy. Therefore, an optimal level of anxiety is preferable to facilitate the therapy process. This can be challenging for integrating certain solution-focused strategies. If the anxiety is overly controlled, repressed, or alleviated, the therapist and client have lost one of their best guides in the therapy process. This does not mean that strategies to help modulate anxiety should always be avoided. Often it is necessary to help clients gain some competency in modulating their anxiety to enter into it and learn the lessons that await. Solution-focused strategies can be integrated into an existential-humanistic approach; however, they will be framed and used differently. [3] In a solution-focused paradigm, managing or controlling emotions is often the desired end while in existential-humanistic therapy it is utilized to help clients enter into their emotion as part of learning from and transforming emotions.

There are advantages to engaging with different therapeutic perspectives. Existential therapists should remain open to drawing on these diverse sources while retaining a critical and thoughtful approach to integration.

## Core Tenets of Existential-Humanistic Psychology

Craig et al. (2016), drawing on previous research, attempted five criteria that tend to be agreed upon across existential approaches:

> (a) that human beings are oriented to, and have a need for, meaning and purpose; (b) that humans being have a capacity for freedom and choice and function most effectively when they actualize this potential and take responsibility for their choices; (c) that human beings will inevitably face limitations and challenges in their lives and function most effectively when they face up to—rather than avoid or deny—them; (d) that the subjective, phenomenological flow of experiencing is a key aspect of being human and therefore a central focus for psychotherapeutic work; and (e) that human experiencing is fundamentally embedded in relationships with others and with the world. (p. 285)

Craig and colleagues acknowledged that these are not universally agreed upon by all who identify as existential therapists. Furthermore, even when there is agreement upon these as essential aspects of existential psychology, there remains variations pertaining to how these are understood and implemented within the different existential schools. In general, existential-humanistic therapists agree with these five criteria.

---

[3] Schneider's (2007) *Existential-Integrative Psychotherapy: Guideposts to the Core of Practice*, provides a number of examples of how different therapists have integrated existential therapy with other modalities, including cognitive-behavioral.

Bugental (as cited in Carlson, 2008) similarly noted that there is no one existential-humanistic therapy. The overviews of existential-humanistic therapy have often been labeled as *existential* instead of *existential-humanistic*, which has made them difficult to identify. In general, there are few comprehensive overviews of existential-humanistic therapy. Schneider and Krug's (2017) *Existential-Humanistic Therapy* is the most comprehensive overview to date.

Krug (in press) noted that existential-humanistic therapy is a relational and experiential approach to therapy that emphasizes the real encounter between therapist and client. Consistent with this foundation, existential-humanistic therapists work to assure that the client is understood first as a unique individual with their own lived experience that cannot be bound by theory. Therefore, in talking about the core tenets, it is important to recognized that these are not used as a prescribed or predetermined framework to interpret the client. Rather, existential-humanistic theory provides a lens that may help uncover aspects of human experience that may otherwise be missed. The theory is intended to open up possibilities instead of restricting ways the client can be understood.

## The Existential Givens

The existential givens maintain a core place in existential theory. The existential givens reflect core or universal aspects of the human condition that each individual must face. Death is the most evident of these themes. Few would claim that they will not have to face death, even if they believe they have attained some resolution, such as a belief in the afterlife. Each of the givens represents a challenge; however, there are varied interpretations of what this means. Yalom (1980) emphasized the starkness or insolvability of the challenge, while Greening (1992), who was critical that Yalom was too negative in his positioning of the givens, emphasized that the challenge comes with opportunity. For optimal psychological health and authentic living, it is imperative that individuals face these givens. The givens, however, often have a highly symbolic nature and, therefore, might not always be dealt with directly. Instead, they emerge symbolically. The existential lexicon and direct addressing of the givens infrequently occurs explicitly in psychotherapy; however, the themes are present. The art of existential psychotherapy resides in large measures in learning to talk about these givens of existence in the language of the client instead of the intellectual language of existential theory.

The claim for the universality of the givens is likely to raise concerns for some. However, proclaiming the existential givens are universal is not asserting that any particular belief about the givens is necessitated. The existential givens form universal challenges or questions, but also, they necessitate local or cultural answers (see also chapter 16). For example, any religion comprehensive enough to sustain over time must deal with the existential givens and, in its claims, provide answers or, sometimes, claims of ultimate truth pertaining to the givens.

The givens are often attributed to Yalom (1980); however, the idea of the givens can be seen in existential philosophy, as well as other authors' work that predates Yalom. The contribution of Yalom was primarily around the categorization and explication of the givens, which is what popularized them. This section draws upon Yalom's perspective as well as other categorizations of the givens. It is important to note that there are entire books devoted to each of the givens from an existential perspective; this is a condensed overview of the givens.

**Death, Finiteness, and Human Limitation**. Death can be seen as the ultimate given because, in many ways, it contextualizes each of the other givens. Each given is intimately connected to death. For example, death can be understood as challenging or focusing meaning. It is almost cliché today to ask the question of what one would do if one had only a small amount of time to live. Yet, this exercise could help bring into focus meaning and purpose. Death also can be seen as being necessary for meaning. Without death, without endings, meaning would not be the same.

The other side of the question, "What would you do if you only had a short time to live?" is, "What would you do if you knew you would live forever?" When I have asked this question when teaching, the most common response is that what is now meaningful would not seem as important or urgent. Often, at least one honest student will say, "I would probably start to take my family for granted." Occasionally, students remark that they would finally be able to live. This illustrates that for some, the fear of death is so pervasive and intense that it causes them to develop a fear of life. As Yalom (1980) suggested, once one embraces life they implicitly also embrace the reality that they are going to die; it is emotionally easier to remain unaware.

Becker (1973) suggested that death denial is at the core of the human dilemma. In considering Freud's theories, Becker stated that Freud was not so far off base; his basic structure largely was correct; however, he was wrong in placing sex at the center. Instead, Becker expressed the belief that the most basic repression today is not sex, but death. To truly live, one must face the reality of death and the reality that one is going to die. Becker also realized that death can become overwhelming. If constantly aware of death and one's fragility, one could become immobilized and unable to do anything. The denial of death, to some degree, is necessary. Although it is difficult to fully resolve the issue of death, it is necessary to face it through balancing death awareness with appropriate death denial.

Death might be best understood as symbolic of all forms of human limitation. This is why some thinkers, such as Bugental (1987, 1999) and Tillich (1952), preferred to focus on finiteness, which they used to indicate the limitedness of human nature. Human nature is full of limitations: limits of freedom, the longevity of life, influence upon others and one's environment, and limits on knowledge and understanding. For Tillich (1952, 1957a), who was a theologian and philosopher first, the ultimate sin or idolatry was to claim to know more than one can or does know. In the psychological realm, the parallel form of this is the defense of reification, which is making real or known that which is abstract or ambiguous.

In returning to Becker (1973), he argued that the root or basis of evil was the denial of death. Although there is debate among Becker scholars as to whether he intended death to be interpreted only literally or if he intended it to be interpreted symbolically, there is great power in this idea if interpreted symbolically. The root of all evil is the denial of one's finite nature or the denial of one's limitations. This point has been repeatedly illustrated by history; when individuals, groups, or countries lose sight of their own limitations, they often engage in great evil.

In existential thought, the motive of becoming comfortable with the unknowns has a moral implication. One must come to grips with the limitations inherent in one's nature to avoid doing harm to others. This is a difficult, but necessary truth. To resolve the issues of death and limitation, the therapist does not help the client overcome these issues but helps her or him to face this reality. In the end, the best way to prepare for a good death is by living a good life. Yet, paradoxically, it is often the fear of a bad death that keeps people from engaging life.

Yalom (1980) purported that most therapists do not recognize or engage death issues when they surface, which is likely largely due to the therapist not having faced his or her own death issues. This is a great tragedy and something that existential therapy can teach the broader psychological community. Although there are no clear answers to death and human limitation, the therapist can walk with clients as they face these terrifying issues. In doing so, clients might find their answers. In helping clients face death, the therapist helps the client to truly live. When the fear of death remains unconscious, or is too much in the forefront of consciousness, it can dominate one's entire existence.

**Freedom, Responsibility, and Destiny**. Freedom cannot be properly understood without also considering responsibility; one necessitates the other. It can be considered a fundamental form of pathology to attempt to have freedom without responsibility. This, then, is fundamental to psychotherapy. Yalom (1980) stated, "For the patient who will not accept such responsibility… no real therapy is possible" (p. 218). It is for this reason that many perceive freedom as a burden; it is a burden they try desperately to escape. True freedom is a curse as well as a blessing. Through freedom one becomes responsible for the good that flows from life choices but also for pain, suffering, and even tragedy that could also ensue.

In the United States, freedom is talked about frequently, but it is often talked about problematically from an existential perspective. Freedom becomes idealized with a fanciful belief that if they are free, they will be happy. This is not the reality of freedom. People in the United States also tend to confuse political freedom with a more existential, or personal, freedom. It seems ironic that many will fight hard for political freedom only to give up all of their personal freedoms. They abandon personal freedom to conformity, groupthink, and the tyranny of normalcy. Often, freedom is given up out of devotion to a political party or some other chosen affiliation.

Freedom cannot be understood apart from destiny, which May (1981) used to balance freedom. He pointed out that destiny is not mere determinism or fate; instead, there is an element of responsibility in destiny:

> The radical shift from determinism to destiny occurs when the subject is self-conscious about what is happening to him or her. The presence of consciousness creates the context in which the human being's responses to his or her destiny occur. (p. 88)

Destiny, then, entails an acceptance of one's determinism, to a degree, but also the ability to be aware and accept requisite responsibility in the face of it. Destiny prompts one toward accepting that freedom is always bound or limited, while concurrently accepting that one remains responsible for how each faces their lack of freedom and how they will act given these limitations. Victor Frankl (1959/1984), in talking about the limited freedoms during his experience in the German concentration camps, similarly stated, "...everything can be taken from man but one thing: the last of the human freedoms—to choose one's attitude in any given set of circumstances, to choose one's own way" (p. 86).

The limitations on one's freedoms do not negate freedom, as is sometimes presupposed. Tillich (1957b), similar to May, maintained that freedom and destiny are intertwined: "But freedom is the possibility of a total and centered act of the personality, an act in which all the drives and influences which constitute the destiny of man are brought into the centered unity of a decision" (pp. 42-43). Therefore, destiny is part of every decision, but so is freedom. One is never completely free, but also never completely determined. It is this element of freedom with which existential psychotherapy is most concerned.

To a degree, some existentialists believe one is as free as they become. A passive existence that forfeits one's agency can lead to destiny becoming fate, while awareness of one's limitations and asserting choice in the face of them allows one to live more freely. However, it must always be emphasized that how free one becomes is bound in limitations. Rank (1929/1978) noted that all those conditions that influence individuals have greater control when they remain outside of their awareness. Through increasing awareness of what influences them as individuals, they increase their freedom. Although one can never become completely free, one may become freer. Given the connection between freedom and responsibility, it could be maintained that the responsible life is one in which freedom is pursued and, with it, responsibility is taken.

For Jean-Paul Sartre (1943/1956), freedom was the centerpiece of existential thought. Sartre spoke of *bad faith* as the condition in which people are not acting in accordance with their freedom and values, or when they are living inauthentically. Thus, it could be said that one has a responsibility to act freely. Bakewell (2017) described Sartre and de Beauvior's view as follows:

> For Sartre, we show bad faith whenever we portray ourselves as passive creations of our race, class, job, history, nation, family, heredity, childhood influences, events, or even hidden drives in our subconscious which we claim are out of our control. It is not that such factors are unimportant: class and race, in particular, he acknowledged as powerful forces in

people's lives, and Simone de Beauvoir would soon add gender to that list. Nor did he mean that privileged groups have the right to pontificate to the poor and downtrodden about the need to 'take responsibility' for themselves. That would be a grotesque misreading of Sartre's point, since his sympathy in any encounter always lay with the more oppressed side. But for each of us—for me—to be in good faith means not making excuses for myself. (p. 156-157)

In this quote, the struggle between freedom, responsibility, and the forces that influence a person beyond their control (i.e., destiny) are evident. Some existentialists, largely from a misinterpretation of Sartre, have been presented as believing in an absolute freedom that is viewed as naïve. However, as Bakewell showed, this is not what Sartre intended.

There is a challenge, however, in understanding the relationship between freedom and destiny, including the implications for responsibility. Existential philosophers and psychotherapists vary in their interpretations of how these fit together and where to draw the line between them. Bakewell's (2017) biographical history of select existential philosophers highlights this debate regarding the place of freedom and what May would call destiny. Sartre, while acknowledging the limitations, still resisted them in many ways. Bakewell noted, "Everything in him longed to be free of bonds, of impediments and limitations and viscous clinging things" (p. 229). It may be that this internal longing for a more absolute freedom came through in his writing leading some to see existential thought as advocating a more radical, absolute freedom. De Beauvoir was more sympathetic toward recognizing the constraints on freedom, particularly as she approached her books, *The Ethics of Ambiguity* (1948/1976) and *The Second Sex* (1949/1989). Bakewell (2017) noted that Merleau-Ponty, too, was more comfortable focusing on the limitations of freedom. Merleau-Ponty and de Beauvoir bear greater similarity to May's (1981) more nuanced view of freedom and destiny.

Contemporary neuroscience and trauma research suggest that the more radical views of freedom might need to be tempered (see Levine 1997, 2015; van der Kolk, 2015). For instance, strong emotions could impact the brain through decreasing brain functioning in the other parts of the brain responsible for rational decision making, therefore, compromising an essential brain function needed for authentic free choice. For people who have been traumatized, they often are more easily triggered into these intense emotional states. Many other factors in one's personal history also might introduce some constraints or challenges to one's ability to exert freedom. The limitation, however, does not erase freedom, but rather complicates it. Freedom is not absolute, and also, it is indebted to courage, which often is necessary to actualize it.

Similarly, Riker (1997) discussed the role of the unconscious, which, as will be discussed later in the chapter, is a controversial concept in existential thought. In part, many existential thinkers are concerned that the idea of the unconscious could be used to undermine freedom and responsibility. Riker maintained that contemporary ethical systems have not been adequately updated to consider the implications of the unconscious. If people's behaviors and thoughts are influenced by the unconscious, it needs to be considered how this impacts responsibility. Similarly, if trauma compromises optimal brain functioning in a way that influences people to be more reactionary and less able to control aspects of their behavior, how does this impact responsibility?

The reality of the influence of the unconscious and trauma does not mean that people are, at times, not responsible for their behavior, nor does it require abandoning existential perspectives on freedom; rather, it suggests the relationships between freedom, responsibility, and agency are complex. Riker's (1997) position on the unconscious suggests that there is somewhat of a moral or ethical imperative for people to become more aware. Insights from contemporary neuroscience and trauma research indicate that it is important to take a compassionate view of the implications of trauma and take this into account when considering issues of responsibility.

May (1981) demonstrated greater reverence for destiny, or the limitations of freedom. This, in part, might have emerged from being a therapist. When sitting with clients who have been impacted by impoverished environments and trauma, one is continuously faced with the challenge of freedom. Freedom is not easy. While Sartre (1943/1956) recognized this as well, he did not demonstrate as nuanced an understanding as May did. When freedom is idealized and the constraints upon it are not fully appreciated, it can lead to shaming the client. At times, it might be better to focus on the potential for freedom rather than emphasizing freedom itself. Although through some lenses this could be a false distinction, recognizing the power of destiny allows one to approach freedom in a less shaming and more empowering manner.

In therapy, I consistently retain the goal of helping people actualize their freedom. However, in the process, it is important for clients to recognize the constraints on their freedom and how this impacts their responsibility. Paradoxically, I often find that when clients come to recognize how their past, including their trauma history, is impacting the present, they are better able to assert their freedom. Maintaining a framework that holds the clients' freedom as well as their limitations or destiny helps me to approach client's struggle with their own freedom in a nuanced and compassionate manner.

Freedom and responsibility also are connected to guilt. Rollo May (1958b) distinguished between normal, neurotic, and existential guilt. Normal guilt is a typical response to transgressions intentionally or unintentionally committed. Neurotic guilt is excessive guilt derived from taking on excessive responsibility or dwelling excessively in one's normal or existential guilt. Existential guilt is rooted in one's nature; it is a universal form of guilt that is not a product of violating personal or cultural norms, but rather emergent from one's self-awareness (Hoffman, 2018). There is also a constructive potential connected with existential guilt when it is faced.

May (1958b) connected existential guilt to three modes of being in the world: *Eigenwelt* (being-in-the-world), *Mitwelt* (one's social or cultural environment), and *Umwelt* (the physical world). Each of these modes connects to a type of existential guilt. Eigenwelt, for example, connects to guilt associated with not fully living up to one's potential. Mitwelt emerges from inevitable, often unintentional, harm caused to other people, such as participating in oppressive, racist, or sexist systems. Tillich (1957a) described this type of guilt:

> The citizens of a city are not guilty of the crimes committed in their city, but they are guilty as participants in the destiny of [humanity] as a whole and in the destiny of their particular city... They are guilty, not of committing the crimes of which their group is accused, but of contributing to the destiny in which these crimes happened. (p. 58)

May (1958b) identified Umwelt as the most "complex and comprehensive aspect" (p. 55) of existential guilt; however, Hoffman (2018) noted it is also the one least developed by May. According to Hoffman, environment or ecological responsibility could be a primary source of existential guilt.

Consistent with what will be discussed under the heading Embodiment and Emotion below, guilt, particularly existential guilt, is not a *negative emotion*. Rather, it is a normal experience rooted in one's nature. While it can be unpleasant, there remains a constructive, positive purpose to guilt. When this is identified, faced, and creatively used, guilt can lead to positive outcomes or positive changes.

**Relationship, Intimacy, and Encounter**. Human beings are relational creatures. Yet, relational needs are destined to be at least partially unfulfilled. One can never fully overcome loneliness or existential isolation. Bugental (1987, 1999) used the phrasing of *a-part-of* and *apart-from* to illustrate the paradoxical nature of relationships. This can be understood in two senses. First, we all have a desire to be a-part-of, or connected, and to be apart-from, or separate. Second, most people's reality is such that they are both connected, yet distinct. But being a-part-of and apart-from are essentially connected in human experience.

O'Donohue (1998) maintained that solitude is an essential part of relationship. In order to be fully present and able to relate on a deep level with others, some solitude, or time apart, is necessary. The amount of time varies from individual to individual, but the basic need remains. Solitude, for O'Donohue, has a reflective quality; it is not merely being alone. Solitude is a time when one works on one's relationship with oneself—the intrapersonal relationship—so one is able to genuinely and subjectively engage with others in one's interpersonal relationships.

When in connection with others, emphasis is placed upon the way one relates with the other person. It is not just being in relationship that is important, but the way one is in relationship. Many approaches to psychotherapy today, includeing many approaches to couples and group therapy, focus on communication skills, including efficient, effective communication. It is evident that being able to communicate effectively is important to a healthy relationship, but it is tragic if nothing more is sought, as good communication could suffice for working relationships, but it is unfulfilling as the ideal for an intimate relationship.

Existential perspectives tend to value relationships rooted in genuineness and authenticity, as in relationships that have a depth quality to them. These relationships require a certain amount of risk and vulnerability. One aspect of these relationships is the encounter that involves a way of relating in which both people are impacted and changed through the connection that is made. Vulnerability, risk, and a bi-directional relationship signify a considerable difference from what is focused on in some therapeutic modalities. From an existential perspective, however, it seems unrealistic to help clients improve their relationships and ability to make deep connections if one is unwilling to go there with them in therapy. Relationships are necessary and, as the common therapy adage goes, "it is the relationship that heals" (Yalom, 1980, p. 401).

For some, the relational dimension to connection could be focused toward something other than another human being. For example, some people meet their relational needs through connection with animals, nature, or a spiritual connection.

**Meaning**. Yalom (1980) began his discussion of meaning pointing to paradox: Human beings are innately meaning seeking creates; yet, there is no ultimate meaning to attain. Other existentialists, such as Frankl (1959/1984) and Tillich (1957a, 1957b), might have disagreed with Yalom's skepticism about the lack of evident meaning; however, there is general agreement that humans are never fully fulfilled in terms of meaning. Still, human beings are destined to search for meaning. As Becker (1973) stated, "Man cannot endure his own littleness unless he can translate it into meaningfulness on the largest possible level" (p. 196).

Meaning is not a simple concept; many distinctions can be made between different types of meaning (see Lincoln & Hoffman, 2018; Vos, 2018). A primary distinction Yalom (1980) made is between meaning discovery versus meaning making. Those who believe that ultimate meaning exists often spend their life trying to discover it or locate it with sufficient confidence. The most common of the meaning discoverers are those who identify as being religious, who believe that meaning is to be found in religion. Religious individuals are more prone to be suspicious of the idea of created meaning. For them, the only true meaning is that which is discovered in their religion. For the religious existentialists, though, this meaning can never be completely attained while in one's finite, human form. Because of this, meaning must be connected to faith, or a belief in what cannot be fully known (Tillich, 1957a).

Conversely, individuals aligning with the meaning creators position generally believe that there is no inherent meaning in the world; the only meaning that exists is that which one creates (Yalom, 1980). A radical perspective of this can be seen in a quote from Sartre: "All existing things are born for no reason, continue through weakness and die by accident... It is meaningless that we are born; it is meaningless that we die" (as cited in Yalom, 1980, p. 428). This extreme position is not agreed upon by all identifying with the existential perspective. Yet, there still is, and always will be, a great deal in life that is meaningless; this cannot be escaped.

A primary problem with meaning—whether created or discovered—is located in the question: "How does one know what is truly meaningful?" Yalom (1980) proposes that meaning is something that gives a person a sense of purpose and coherence. But this is not enough, for there are many ways a person could have a sense of purpose and meaning that are destructive and harmful. For example, terrorists often see their acts of killing and destruction as highly meaningful. Meaning must be held to a greater accountability. Becker (1973) proposed one solution:

> What is the ideal for mental health, then? A lived, compelling illusion that does not lie about life, death, and reality; one honest enough to follow its own commandments: I mean, not to kill, not to take the lives of others to justify itself. (p. 204)

This quote is perhaps the most compelling existential view of mental health and meaning. In breaking this down, it is possible to make a distinction between what is referred to as sustaining meaning other forms of meaning.

Breaking down the quote, Becker (1973) first pointed out that meaning is an illusion. From Becker's writings, it was never clear where he stood on religion. At times he seemed skeptical, almost antagonistic about religion and, at other times, he was more optimistic. What is evident is that Becker continually struggled with the religious questions all his life. In considering religion, Becker stated, "The best existential analysis of the human condition leads directly into the problems of God and faith" (p. 68). Religion, for Becker, whether true or not, was something that could not be escaped. Even if the essence of religion is true, Becker seemed to believe that it was still an illusion; religion was a matter of faith, not proof. This conception of illusion is essentially the same as May's (1991) conception of myth (see also chapter 16).

Next, Becker (1973) stated that meaning must be a lived, compelling illusion. By lived, it must be embodied; it must impact one's life and daily living. If an illusion is not lived, it has no meaning or purpose. In stating that the illusion is compelling, Becker indicated that one must truly believe in the myth, and it must provide a sense of coherence. In some instances, it is evident that people are adhering to illusions or beliefs systems as a protection or a defense but not out of genuine belief. These illusions are not sustaining. As Nietzsche (1894/1990) stated, "The most common lie is the lie one tells oneself" (p. 185). Similarly, Lu Xun (1925/1961), wrote, "True, we must dare look things in the face before we dare think, speak, act, or assume responsibility. If we dare not even look, what else are we good for?" (p. 198).

Becker (1973) then stated that the sustaining illusion "does not lie about life, death, and reality" (p. 204). This returns to a basic existential premise: Existential theory attempts to be honest about the human condition. Last, Becker stated that this illusion must "follow its own commandments" (p. 204). Again, it must be lived, and it must be lived honestly. Becker also pointed to the concept of evil. Implicit in this quote is that when one lives by a meaning system that is not embodied, compelling, and honest, then one often is drawn toward destructive acts, such as killing, to justify himself or herself. The person with sustaining meaning does not need to resort to such ends.

Meaning that is not sustaining now should be evident: It is not honest about the human condition; it is not lived; it is not compelling or truly believed, and one often must resort to extreme defenses to justify and protect it. Sustaining meaning, then, is not even necessarily true meaning, but it is a meaning that promotes healthy ends. As the postmodernists say, true meaning or ultimate meaning may not exist or may not exist in a form that one can access, but this does not render meaning meaningless (Hoffman & Kurzenberger, 2007). Rather, meaning remains a key criterion in psychological health even if the full comprehension of it is elusive.

Meaning changes over time, often as a result of both suffering and personal growth. Tom Greening (as cited in Hoffman & Vallejos, 2018) developed the concept of *existential shattering*, which refers to "sudden and unexpected dismantling, or shattering, of one's self-conception and worldview as a consequence of an event or process that the individual has experienced" (p. 1). Vallejos (2017) illustrated how this shattering experience also holds the potential for growth. In an experience of existential shattering, the meanings system or structures of an individual have been dismantled and are in need of reconstruction. This is not an easy process and, for many, being in therapy or experiencing some other type of support is an important aspect of establishing new meaning and actualizing the potential in the existential shattering.

Most meaning changes or transitions are not as dramatic as an existential shattering. Most occur gradually, often through a thoughtful, intentional process. However, meaning can also be seen as something that grips an individual and may develop outside of one's awareness. At times, part of the therapeutic process is helping clients to recognize the meaning systems that are driving their behavior and reconsider them. Despite the fluid, evolving nature of one's meaning in life, it remains a central aspect of one's existence.

**Embodiment and Emotion**. This given was not addressed by Yalom (1980), but it was central to Bugental (1987, 1999; Bugental & Sterling, 1995). In one sense, embodiment is the embodiment of the existential givens—the acknowledgement of these as lived realities. But embodiment, as understood here, goes beyond this; it refers to one's experience in the body, or, as Bugental and Sterling (1995) stated, it is the "constantly lived bodiliness of being" (p. 233). Yet, it is important to acknowledge that what constitutes embodiment is not always agreed upon within the existential literature. Emotions and how they are experienced in the body are an important aspect of embodiment as well, but embodiment cannot be reduced to being just about emotion.

From the beginning of existential thought, emotions were seen as something to be embraced and understood. Kierkegaard (1843/1985) wrote the first ever book on anxiety, *Fear and Trembling*. He saw anxiety, which is often considered the mother of all emotions, as something that was natural. Anxiety was not something to be feared, avoided, controlled, or repressed; it was something from which one could learn. Over 100 years later, May (1950/1970) wrote his doctoral dissertation on anxiety, published as the book *The Meaning of Anxiety*. May (1950/1970) drew on Kierkegaard to develop some of his central ideas in the development of an existential theory of emotions. Kierkegaard distinguished between what today is referred to as neurotic anxiety and normal anxiety (or existential anxiety). Neurotic anxiety is "a more constrictive and uncreative form of anxiety which results from an individual's failure to move ahead in situations of normal anxiety" (May, 1950/1970, p. 38). He contended that all anxiety, at its root, is normal anxiety. What makes anxiety normal or neurotic is not its presence, but the way the individual relates to the anxiety.

Nietzsche (1889/1990) discussed similar ideas with his basic premise that one should not fight that which is natural. In today's psychological language, Nietzsche proposed that one should not fight, deny, or repress emotions, which broadened Kierkegaard's ideas to include other emotions. As Peluso and Freund (2018) demonstrated, the avoidance or suppression of emotions is associated with poorer psychological outcomes (see also Schwartz & Kline, 1995). The normal and neurotic distinction could be applied to all emotions. However, he is not saying that one should just go with or act upon any urge. Instead, Nietzsche (1889/1990) was arguing that all that is natural needs to find expression. As will be discussed in the next section, this concept is related to the daimonic, creativity, and integration in existential thought. Returning to Kierkegaard and May, what is often needed is a creative expression of this emotion. Still, drawing from Becker (1973), one could say that what is needed is a creative expression of the emotion that does not lie about the basic reality of the emotion.

This conclusion is an existential position that lends itself to challenges cross-culturally. As Peluso and Freund (2018) noted, "With all emotions (primary or secondary), cultural issues will impact the trigger or theme, the display rules, and the attitudes about each emotion" (p. 462). Some cultures, including many Eastern cultures as well as many Northern European cultures, tend to be restrictive with emotions (Hoffman & Cleare-Hoffman, 2011; see also Sundararajan, 2015, for a thorough review and discussion of emotion in Chinese culture). This is where the creative element is essential. Existentially, it is often maintained that emotions need to find expression and that denying, controlling, and repressing them does not serve psychological health or well-being. However, how they are expressed will differ across cultures. For example, Eastern and Northern European cultures may seek out more subtle forms of emotional expression than what is typical in most places in the United States, African/African American cultures, and Southern European cultures.

Emotions are experienced in one's body; they convey important messages that can be used to increase self-awareness and inform one's choices. In essence, emotions can be understood as a way of knowing and potentially can be a form of wisdom. This does not mean one should blindly respond to everything in life based upon their emotions, but rather that they should take their emotions seriously and try to decipher the knowledge or wisdom that may found within them. Emotions often call one to search within and can lead to a better understanding of oneself.

**Awe: A Sixth Given?** At the First International Conference of Existential Psychology, Schneider (2010) proposed awe as a new existential given. Schneider (2004) described awe as being comprised of "mystery—incomprehensibility, and second of all, magnificence—bedazzlement. I am not simply speaking here of sentiment we experience when we gaze at stars...I am speaking of brute awareness that we exist at all" (p. xiii). While Schneider's existential development of the concept of awe has been influential (see Schneider 2004, 2009), it has not been embraced widely as a new existential given. It has, however, played an important role in a renewed and broadened interest in spirituality within existential-humanistic psychology.

## The Daimonic and the Nature of Being Human

Schneider (in press), in detailing the emergence of the existential-humanistic approach, noted that May and Bugental were both drawn to the humanistic approach; however, they shared a concern about the lack of attention to some of the darker or more challenging aspects of the human experience. This became a primary distinction between humanistic approaches, such as client-centered therapy, and existential-humanistic psychotherapy. For May (1969) and later Diamond (1996), the *daimonic* became a foundational concept in existential-humanistic therapy that illuminated these darker aspects of human existence. The daimonic addresses these challenging aspects of being human without relying upon reductionist approaches, such as diagnosis, or simplifying them through projection onto some external or metaphysical force.

According to May (1969), the daimonic is "any natural function which has the power to take over the whole person" (p. 65). He continued by clarifying that the daimonic itself is not good or evil:

> While the daimonic cannot be said to be evil in itself, it confronts us with the troublesome dilemma of whether it is to be used with awareness, a sense of responsibility and the significance of life, or blindly and rashly... When the daimōnic is repressed, it tends to erupt in some form. (p. 129)

Existential therapy is generally classified as a humanistic psychology; however, the daimonic is an essential divergence with most humanistic psychologies (Hoffman, Lopez, & Moats, 2013; Hoffman, Warner, Buck, & Fehl, 2011). While humanistic psychology focuses primarily on human potential, existential psychology maintains that it is also imperative that one recognize the potential for evil and human limitation, including one's own potential.

Psychology has often either relegated "evil" to psychopathology, as seen in much of mainstream psychology, or avoided engagement with this topic, as often seen in humanistic and positive psychology. In popular and religious culture, there is third tendency to identify many individuals or groups who engage in destructive acts as being essentially morally corrupt or evil (see Bernstein, 2005; Hoffman, et al., 2011). These approaches, however, reflect an over-simplification of the human condition.

According to Diamond (1996), the daimonic is essentially tied to what is labeled as evil in the world. In the definition of the daimonic discussed above, several themes can be highlighted. First, the daimonic is a natural tendency. It is not something foreign, external, or metaphysical; it is part of one's nature. Second, the daimonic is not inherently negative, although it retains potential to be used in a harmful manner. For example, drawing upon Diamond's focus on anger, it is natural for a person to experience anger. When anger is denied or repressed, it does not go away. When relegated to the latent, unconscious, and denied realms, its potential grows and begins to develop the strength to "take over the whole person" (May, 1969, p. 65) However, this same daimonic capacity can also be used positively or creatively. The creative use of anger, for example, has been the source of many social justice movements and great works of art (see Hoffman, Granger, Vallejos, & Moats, 2016).

According to Diamond (1996), self-awareness, integrity, and creativity are keys to dealing with the daimonic:

> Integrity is unity of the personality; it implies being brutally honest with ourselves about our intentionality. Since intentionality is inextricably bound up with the daimonic, this is never an easy, nor always pleasant pursuit. But being willing to admit our daimonic tendencies—to know them consciously and to wisely oversee them—brings with it the invaluable blessing of freedom, vigor, inner strength, and self-acceptance. (p. 233)

The beginning of utilizing the daimonic is awareness. From here, the individual must learn to accept this as an aspect of the self and creatively integrate it into one's self understanding (see Diamond, 1996; Hoffman, et al, 2013).

Becker (1973, 1975) placed denial of death, which could be interpreted as including the denial of all human limitation, as the root of evil. This runs parallel to the conception of the daimonic. It is only through self-awareness and self-honesty that one can contain evil in the world. As May (1982) stated, "I am not predicting doom. But I am stating that if we ignore evil, we will move closer to doom, and the growth and triumph of evil may well result" (p. 20). This could be applied at the group level as well. Groups that do not acknowledge their potential for evil increase the possibility of engaging in it.

**The Good Life**

> The point of both May and Nietzsche, and one of the major tenets of existential psychology, is the idea that what most of psychology calls "negative emotions" are in fact integral parts of being a human being and possessing the potential of both good and evil. Tragedy is part and parcel of human life. The attempt to deny this, whether it be carried out by utopian therapists who label nearly all of existence "pathological," or by psychiatrists who wish to obliterate such moods with mind-altering drugs, runs the risk of repressing the daimonic or Dionysian. (Hoeller, 1999, p. 120)

Perhaps, the greatest distinction between existential-humanistic psychology and most of the rest of the psychology is its view of *the good life*. Throughout much of the mental health field, it has become implicit that the good life is one that seeks pleasure and the avoidance of discomfort (see also Robbins, 2008; Slife, 2004).

Throughout this chapter and the book, variations of the existential good life will be discussed; this section will highlight a few common themes. First, it should be noted that in removing pleasure and happiness from the unquestioned pinnacle of mental health, existentialists are not intending to state there is anything wrong with happiness. Instead, as Frankl (1959/1984) was fond of illustrating that happiness is best understood as a *side effect* of a life well lived, but the more one pursues it directly the more elusive happiness becomes. Similarly, there is nothing wrong with helping clients find ways to decrease experiences that are uncomfortable or painful; however, at times, suffering is normal and even healthy. Existential-humanistic therapists work to collaboratively discern when it is preferred to work to alleviate suffering and when it is best to walk into the suffering together with faith that there is something better on the other side.

The existential-humanistic perspective on the good life is not, and should not be agreed upon by all adhering to this label; however, here are some central themes:

1) **The meaningful life**. Frankl (1959/1984) was the strongest advocate of this position; however, this is one perspective shared by most existentialists, including those who identify as existential-humanistic (see also Craig et al., 2016; Vos, 2018; Vos, Cooper, Hill, Neimeyer, Schneider, & Wong, 2017).
2) **The free life**. As May (1981) stated, "the purpose of [existential] psycho-therapy is to set people free" (p. 19).

3) **The aware life**. Existential-humanistic therapists tend to believe that there is an inherent goodness in self-awareness and self-honesty. This also serves to help one become free.

4) **The ethical or moral life**. Beginning with the existential philosophers, existential thought has been highly focused on morality. Ethics, from an existential-humanistic perspective, are not rooted in an ethical system, but rather in character. Furthermore, ethics should not be about conformity, or allegiance to a belief system, but should be personal, yet informed by and concerned with society. This is not relativism, but, rather, suggests a need for a degree of personal responsibility in all ethical determinations (see also Robbins, 2008, 2015).

5) **Life fully embraced, or the passionate life**. Individuals aligned with existential-humanistic therapy tend to believe, as Nietzsche (1894/1990) did, that one should embrace all aspects of life—the good and the difficult. Suffering should be faced directly, not avoided, and the varied emotions embraced. Passion is illustrated through one's character, living a life in which one embraces their emotions and their personal convictions.

6) **Transcendence**. May (1958) illustrates that transcendence is a central value of existential-humanistic psychology, but he is cautious regarding misunderstanding this term. Existential-humanistic psychology does not interpret transcendence in a metaphysical or other-worldly sense, but rather in the potential to see oneself as continually emerging, and to see oneself beyond the immediate context. Transcendence refers to the ability to see things fluidly and symbolically (as part of a meaning system) and in the context of a broader meaning system. This might or might not include specific spiritual beliefs.

7) **Intimate relationships and encounters**. Existential-humanistic therapists value relationships. Many are surprised when theorists, such as Yalom (1980), state that in the end, the good life is about love. But it is not just being in contact with others that is valued, but rather a particular way of *being relating* that includes genuineness and a depth of encounter. This is not a prescribed approach, but rather could vary significantly from culture to culture, and person to person.

8) **The compassionate life**. Although a bit more hidden in the literature and partially reflective of my personal bias, this theme emerges through Adler's (1929/1969) influence on May. Adler believed that a lack of social interest was a sign of pathology, and an end of successful therapy would be the increase in social interest. This, again, is a significant shift from the business of psychology as usual. The more hedonistically-based therapies

can promote a self-interest and selfishness that is quite the contrary to this end of therapy.[4]

It is imperative to point out that these are not values to impose upon clients. This is not what many clients are seeking from therapy, at least at first. Even if clients like the idea of the above formulated version of the good life, many begin therapy with more immediate goals of decreasing or managing intense suffering. Existential-humanistic therapy often needs to be adapted or adjusted to help clients meet a mixture of short-term goals, which may focus on intense suffering and a compromised level of functioning, and the long-term goals which may be more consistent with this picture of the good life. Maybe what is most significant of this view of the good life is the move beyond simplistic views of the good life as reduced to being about happiness and the lack of suffering.

### Core Tenets of Existential-Humanistic Psychotherapy

Aspects of this section of the chapter are the least existential of the book. As will be discussed, the ideas of techniques, and even structures are often viewed as antithetical to existential-humanistic therapy. As Minuchin and Fishman (1991) reflected:

> After this book [on therapy technique] is read, it should be given away, or put in a forgotten corner. The therapist should be a healer: a human being concerned with engaging other human beings therapeutically around areas and issues that cause them pain... The goal, in other words, is to transcend technique. Only a person who has mastered technique and then contrived to forget it can become an expert therapist. (p. 1)

Nietzsche, (1889/1990) had previously commented, "I mistrust all systematizers and avoid them" (p. 35). Nevertheless, in this section, I will attempt to *break down* and *categorize* processes that existential therapists often employ in therapy. In some ways, this approach does not fit with the spirit or essence of existential-humanistic therapy. However, there is also a value to it, particularly for the therapist struggling with how to envision this type of therapy.[5] For some therapists learning the existential-humanistic approach, and then to be thrust into the unstructured therapeutic relationship is too anxiety provoking. At times,

---

[4] As many therapists have experienced, it is a common end of therapy for clients to become more socially active in causes important to them, more compassionate to their friends and family, more concerned about what is going on in the world, and sometimes even consider becoming a therapist themselves. As one client near the end of therapy stated, "It's amazing how much my therapy has benefited my friends."

[5] May (1958b), in his introduction to existential therapy in the book *Existence*, similarly struggled when getting to the portion of technique, but also for similar reasons decided that it was necessary to include this section in order to give a practical illustration of existential therapy.

therapists need some structure and/or planned interventions that they can rely upon early in the process of becoming an existential-humanistic therapist before gradually transitioning to a process less reliant upon that structure.

I have often heard comments such as, "That existential psychology stuff is interesting, I just don't know what to do with it in therapy." This has led some, such as Yalom (1980), to maintain that existential psychotherapy cannot stand on its own. I disagree. To explain, it is necessary to dismiss the misnomer of theoretical purity. One can read Freud and see shades of behaviorism, cognitive therapy, humanistic therapy, and many other approaches. There is a potential for all therapies to be naturally integrative, at least to a degree.

This should not, however, lead to the equally naïve conclusion that all therapies are really the same with each merely incorporating a different vocabulary. Although a behaviorist could maintain that transference is nothing other than learned behavior, or mere classical conditioning, this does not make these concepts the same. Changing transference through a corrective emotional experience, too, could be explained by unlearning old patterns and relearning new ones. But there are many nuances of difference. When one only has a limited grasp of these concepts—or a very concrete understanding of them—it is easy to say that both explanations are the same. However, the more one understands these concepts the more evident it becomes that behaviorist principles only explain part of the transference reaction.

Similarly, common existential therapy processes can be broken down and isolated to talk about them; however, as soon as they are removed from the context and fluid process of therapy they are changed. From an existential perspective, it is essential that even when specific *techniques* are incorporated, they are never used in the same way twice. The Minuchin and Fishman (1991) quote at the beginning of this section illustrates this point. May similarly used to instruct his students and supervisees that it good to learn all you can about psychology and therapy, but then leave it at the door when going to see clients (Schneider, personal communication). The reason Minuchin and May encouraged leaving the specifics behind is not because of their lack of utility, but because techniques that are applied are not as effective as techniques that naturally emerge. This is the art of psychotherapy. Therapists are not technicians who apply techniques that *fix* the client; they are guides and fellow sojourners who walk with the client, at times illuminating insights, encouraging them to consider certain alternatives, and challenging them, but primarily engaging or encountering them.

Too much structure and planning stifles psychotherapy, despite any good intentions. When a therapist begins to plan interventions and apply techniques, she or he begins to objectify the client; they no longer are encountering her or him in the moment. This is not to say that clients do not, at times, benefit from the application of technique; it is evident that they do. Indeed, in regard to symptom reduction and other more objectively identified changes, the outcomes might be similar when therapy focuses on techniques. However, in life-changing therapy, as Bugental (1987) would call it, there is more to therapeutic change than symptom reduction.

One of the great errors in the mental health field is that therapists too often blindly settle into a utilitarian ethic that the ends justify the means. It is thought that if the client reaches the goals presented in the first session that therapy is a success; it matters not how one gets there. There are some exceptions to this. There are therapists who recognize the difference between alleviating depression through medication and through psychotherapy. However, therapists often fail to consider the difference between achieving goals through means that objectify the client and means that rely upon encountering the client as a valuable, subjective person. The method, or means, conveys a message and has an impact.

The implicit message given in therapy approaches rooted in techniques that objectify the client is that the person is more akin to a machine. If provided the right resources—coping mechanism, skills, and knowledge—they will function optimally. Second, there is an implicit reductionist mindset that therapy should fix a broken part of the client rather than address the client as a whole being. In the machine metaphor, therapy is more nearly akin to replacing the radiator on a car than helping the car. But a human being is very different than a car. A third implicit message given is that efficiency is valued over depth or substance.

Although this objectification model might sound distasteful to many who are drawn to reading this book, it could also be noted that this fits with much of the historic Western view of human beings. Furthermore, it is important to point out that this is what many clients want and expect from therapy. Yet, many clients also end therapy having achieved their goals, but still having a nagging feeling that something is amiss—that something has been left unresolved. Others abandon therapy altogether thinking that therapy is not for them.

Existential-humanistic therapy prefers to work with the person as a whole and to deal with what it means to be human, with an intention of balancing helping the person to function better with the higher aspirations of humanity such as intimate connections, meaning, and compassion. Therefore, existential therapy is a holistic, relational therapy at its core; it is a therapy that believes that the process of therapy, or the journey, is an essential part of the outcome. In other words, the ends do not justify the means, but the means are a part of the end.

Elkins (2009, 2016) is one of the important champions of the non-medical alternatives. As will be discussed in more detail later, Elkins provided important critiques of the empirically supported treatment movement and narrow approaches to Evidence Based Practice in Psychology. Building upon the work of influential researchers such as Bruce Wampold (Wampld & Imel, 2015) and Barry Duncan (Duncan, Miller, Wampold, & Hubble, 2010), Elkins (2009, 2016) has demonstrated both the empirical and theoretical support for humanistic and existential-humanistic therapy's nonmedical model as well as anyone.

**Process and Technique**

Existential therapy, as noted, has a reputation for being techniqueless, which has been one reason many have hesitated to identify with this approach. It is also a frustration for many who have attempted to teach the process of existential-humanistic psychotherapy. Teachers of this psychotherapy approach are fond of encouraging their students to "be in the moment," "let the client guide," and "follow the process." These ideas sound nice, even somewhat romantic; however, they can be ambiguous and anxiety-provoking for the new therapist. These are acceptable ideals for therapy; however, some students may need more guidance in the fundamentals of this process in order to grow into the ideals. In this section, I will attempt to break down existential psychotherapy into some of these funda-mentals, which may appear technique-like, if only to illuminate their application.

Some of the resistance to techniques is due to linguistic issues. Existential therapy stands firm against mechanized, linear, reductionist, and manualized approaches to therapy (see Elkins, 2008, 2009, 2016). Imposing a false structure on psychotherapy, although easing the therapist's anxiety and making research easier, is not beneficial to the overall therapy process. Therefore, existential-humanistic therapy seeks a less structured, more fluid approach.

Existential-humanistic therapists have viewed the language of technique with suspicion because it often typifies manualized and over-structured therapies. Instead of technique, existential therapists would prefer to talk about stances or processes occurring in therapy. However, this should not be seen as simply a mere linguistic distinction. By shifting from technique to stances or processes, the therapist moves into a different type of relationship with the client and a different form of therapy. The therapist is no longer applying something to the client (i.e., objectifying them), but rather engaging her or him in a particular manner.

In the rest of this section, I will engage in some of what I just strongly critiqued above: breaking down existential-humanistic psychotherapy processes and providing more structure to them. I will even introduce a few techniques, of sorts. However, this is done in the spirit of moving beyond the techniques. Stated differently, the hope is that the reader will read this section and then forget it. Once forgotten, the therapist will likely find these emerging naturally from the flow of the therapy process.

**Relationship and Presence**

> Actually, transcending the present is a form of escapism.
> ~Lu Xun, 1928/1961, p. 26

Existential-humanistic psychotherapy is rooted in the therapy relationship. This is most succinctly stated in the adage Yalom (1980) frequently repeated: "it is the relationship that heals" (p. 401). Throughout his writing, Yalom (1980, 2002, Yalom & Elkin, 1990) frequently used anecdotal evidence and informal research, as well as some references to more formal research, to illustrate that there often is a significant difference between what the therapist and the client think are the most important aspects of therapy. Therapists want to believe that it is their penetrating interpretations or artful use of technique that helps the client; however, clients generally point to empathy, the way their therapist shows she or he cares, and other aspects of the therapy relationship as being the most important ingredients.

**Presence**. Presence is one of the foundations for the psychotherapy relationship (Schneider & Krug, 2017). This should not be confused, however, with being fully present, which is a related concept popularized from humanistic psychology. Being fully present refers to a relational process in which a person is attending to the other while simultaneously *present* to their own subjective experiences and the experiences of the others person. Bugental (1987) defined presence as "a name for the quality of being in a situation or relationship in which one intends at a deep level to participate as fully as she is able" (p. 27). Being fully present may be an aspect of presence, but presence goes beyond this through being intentional about participating or engaging with the other. Presence, therefore, is connected with the emotional feel or quality experienced in relation to another person.

Presence has an intrapersonal as well as an interpersonal quality (Schneider & Krug, 2017). Cultivating therapeutic presence requires one to be attuned to their own intrapersonal experience in the moment as well as being attuned to the client and the interpersonal process. When this can be established, it serves as the ground for therapy. As Schneider and Krug noted, "There is a vivid distinction, in our view, between a therapist who approaches a client as a problem-solving 'doctor' and a healer who is available for inter- and intrapersonal connection" (p. 41). Presence allows for a deeply engaged real relationship.

Presence bears similarity to Rogers (1980) idea of *a way of being*. Essentially, Rogers argued that the craft of therapy was largely about developing a way of being that was healing, or growth facilitating. Most have experienced people who simply by being in their presence created the impulse to want to grow, heal, or be a better person. This is an aspect of presence.

May's (1988) description of Paul Tillich illustrates one aspect of presence. Tillich, after moving to the United States, drew large crowds to many of his lectures, even though his lectures were such that the listeners often could not understand them either because of his German accent, his struggles with English as a second language, or the abstractness of his ideas. However, there was a quality in his presence, how people tended to experience him, that drew people in to his lectures. May also noted that it seemed almost impossible to have a shallow conversation with Tillich; he drew people to the depths of experience.

There are limitations to presence, too. We all have aspects of presence that we do not like. For example, I recognize that many people, especially students, initially feel intimidated by me. This is not very therapeutic. I recognize that it comes, at least partially, from my introspective nature (intrapersonal presence combined with a reflective nature), my tendency to be drawn to abstract ideas and depth of thought, and also my physical presence (6-foot, 1-inch tall, fairly broad shouldered). Some of this way of being experienced is connected with factors beyond presence that I cannot change (physical stature), and other aspects are connected with things I like about myself (being reflective and drawn to abstract thought). Fortunately, most people, when sitting down with me one-to-one, as is often the case with therapy clients, they do not experience this, and most students report that this feeling fades especially after they get to know me, most often through additional conversations.

At times, presence can also be intimidating to clients. For example, in therapy, I tend to be highly attentive. Clients sometimes comment that, "I stare a lot," or note that my attentiveness feels uncomfortable. This is something that we discuss in session and, as a result, I temporarily modify aspects of my approach to being attentive. It is not necessary to change one's presence to become more therapeutic; however, it is important to recognize how others experience it.

Presence can increase the effectiveness of approaches, interventions, and techniques utilized by the therapist. Schneider and Krug (2017) noted, "presence holds and illuminates that which is palpably—immediately, affectively, kinesthetically, and profoundly—relevant within the client and between the client and therapist, and its cultivation is the ground, method, and goal of substantive [existential-humanistic] transformation" (p. 43).

Presence is not easy to develop, particularly when first beginning as a therapist. It is something that must be intentionally cultivated and developed over time. Doing one's own self-work, including possibly one's own therapy, can greatly enhance one's ability to utilize presence effectively. Engaging in mediation and centering activities also can help therapist develop this relational quality. While it is not easy to develop, it is a powerful therapeutic tool once established.

**Empathy and Genuineness**. When talking about the therapy relationship, Carl Rogers (1951, 1980) is regularly identified as a central figure. It has become cliché to say that *Rogerian therapy is a nice foundation for all therapies*. The second part of the sentence generally points to the limitations of this therapy approach by suggesting it is not a complete therapy. For many making this statement, one has to wonder if they have ever read Rogers's contributions. What is generally being referred to in his therapeutic triad of empathy, genuineness, and unconditional positive regard, which is often reduced to acting nice and caring about clients. Although I agree that there are limitations to Rogers's approach, there are more significant limitations to how Rogers work is often interpreted and presented.

Empathy and genuineness have received significant attention in the therapeutic literature, especially in literature related to empirically supported therapy relationships (see Elliott, Bohart, Watson, & Murphy, 2018; Kolden, Wang, Austin, Chang, & Klein, 2018; Norcross, 2002a, 2002b). Outcome literature, which will be discussed in more detail later, has consistently identified the quality of therapeutic relationships as one of the most influential contributors to therapy success after client factors (Elkins, 2008, 2009, 2016; Flückiger, Del Re, Wampold, &

Horvath, 2018; Lambert & Barley, 2002; Norcross & Lambert, 2018; Wampold & Imel, 2015). As an aspect of the therapy relationship, several therapist characteristics have been found to be important predictors of therapy success, including empathy (Bohart, Elliott, Greenberg, & Watson, 2002, Elliott et al., 2018), positive regard (Farber & Lane, 2002; Farber, Suzuki, & Lynch, 2018), and congruence (Klein, Kolden, Michels, & Chisholm-Stockard, 2002; Kolden et al., 2018).

The establishment of the therapy relationship as central to psychotherapy remains complex and the therapeutic triad remains largely misunderstood. For example, empathy is often poorly used by therapists. When supervising therapists, it is often evident that they are applying empathy as a technique instead of being empathetic.[6] Empathy as a technique is rarely effective and often leads to damage of the therapy relationship.

Similarly, many therapists misapply genuineness. A colleague, Mark Stocks (personal communication), was fond of saying, "You can't try to be genuine. As soon as you are trying you are no longer genuine." Genuineness and empathy are qualities of the therapist, not techniques. These are qualities that the therapist cultivates and allows to come forth, not something they try to do. In other words, it is more of a *letting go* process in which the therapist lowers his or her own barrier in order to connect with the client on a deeper level.

Contemporary psychoanalytic thinker Martha Stark (1999) provided important guidance on the application of genuineness (or authenticity) and empathy. According to Stark, when engaging in empathy one de-centers from their own subjective self in order to in order to take on the experience of the client. Conversely, genuineness is rooted in the therapist's subjective experience:

> (1) I am suggesting that empathy involves a kind of selflessness on the therapist's part, which she is able to achieve when she steps aside (decenters) from her own experience of self.
> (2) I am suggesting that authenticity involves the therapist's use of self... which she is able to do when she remains very much present—centered— within her own experience of self. (Stark, 1999, p. 46)

Although many therapists confuse empathy and authenticity, Stark illustrated that these are different therapeutic processes in that one is centered while the other requires a degree of de-centering. For therapists, it can be quite difficult to keep in touch with their own subjective (centered) experience of the client while also remaining in touch with their empathetic (de-centered) experience of the client.

---

[6] In teaching and supervision, I will often ask students and supervisees these questions: "Think of a time when someone was 'applying the technique' of empathy, or merely acting empathetic. How did it feel? What did you want to do in reaction to this?" Most respond by indicating they felt dismissed, hurt, or angry when empathy was used as a technique, but felt cared about and valued when they experienced embodied empathy. Yet, it is common for therapists in training to be taught to use empathy as a technique.

Furthermore, it often becomes difficult to distinguish between these two experiences. A common psychoanalytic illustration of a parallel process questions, "Whose unconscious is it?" The existential parallel could be, "Whose subjectivity is it?"

These relational illustrations demonstrate why it is difficult to become an existential or depth psychotherapist. When journeying beyond technique-based therapies, many nuances of relationship emerge. Without good self-awareness as well as the ability to identify and understand complex relational processes, the therapist can easily venture onto dangerous ground. This illustrates why the process of becoming a depth psychotherapist is generally longer and more focused on the person of the therapist.[7] It is this person that becomes the primary *tool* of therapy. Technique is replaced with the person of the therapist, with genuine encounter.

**Encounter**. This word encounter is preferred by many existential-humanistic therapists (May, 1983, 1999; Mendelowitz, 2008a). Encounter brings depth to the relationship and suggests a mutual impact. In many traditional therapies, impact is thought to be primarily in one direction (therapist impacting the client) and, when it is not, it is countertransference that needs to be kept under control and hidden by the therapist. Conversely, in existential-humanistic therapy, the impact is seen as something that is natural and healthy.

In supervision, I have encountered students who apologetically reported that they felt like crying when the client shared a powerful story. Many are shocked when they hear my response, "So why didn't you?" Of course, crying with a client is not always therapeutic. It is important to determine if this emotional response has mostly to do with the therapist's issues (i.e., countertransference) or rather emerges out of empathy and the genuine impact of being present when hearing the client's story. Many times, shedding a tear with a client can be the most effective intervention in the moment.

Olthuis (2001) told a beautiful story of crying with a client who responded by commenting that she did not know she was worth crying for! Clearly, this illustrates the power of encounter. Often, the greatest mistakes therapists make, especially neophyte therapists, is not what they do, but what they hold back. Unfortunately, by the time many therapists graduate they are so scared of making an ethical blunder that they do not allow themselves to care for or encounter their clients.

## Reflective Listening Beyond the Misconceptions
Reflective listening has been a cornerstone of client-centered therapy (Rogers, 1951, 1980) and is often used in existential psychotherapy. However, there is

---

[7] This also illustrates why it is important for therapists to have had their own depth therapy, whenever possible, and to undergo extensive supervision from a depth psychotherapist. Additionally, this points to the need of ongoing consultation across one's career. In fact, I believe that ongoing consultation is equally important to the continuing education required by most licensing boards.

tremendous confusion about what constitutes reflective listening. It often is thought that reflective listening is only reflecting the content the client just shared, and, perhaps, also reflecting the emotion. These are two aspects of reflective listening, but the mirror of reflective listening is much larger than this. Reflective listening can include reflecting the moment, reflecting the process, and reflecting the person in context.

Reflecting the moment includes reflecting the content and emotions; however, it can also include the non-verbal expressions. For example, Bugental (1987, 1999) would consistently reflect to clients their non-verbals, at times asking them to repeat them. He would also use his intuition to reflect many subtle changes that were ambiguous. For example, it was not uncommon to hear Bugental make statements such as "something changed there." He did not always know what that was, but he recognized a shift. In reflecting the shift, he and the client together could begin to understand the significance of the shift.

Reflecting the process broadens the reflections beyond the moment. Therapists could make reflections such as, "in the first few minutes of the session today, you have shifted between several different topics." This type of reflection can help the client identify the reason for such topic jumping. Sometimes there is an underlying theme of which the therapist, and often the client, are unaware. Other times, this may be the client's defense to avoid going into any topic in detail. The therapist can also reflect shifts in emotion, changes in the way the client is relating to the therapist, and other therapy processes.

Reflecting the person in context draws from a broader reflective pool. May (1958b) indicated that the root of individuals' problems often reflected their own inability to see themselves in context. As the therapist gets to know the client and becomes more aware of the broader context of his or her life situation, she or he can help the client build this context. This can serve several purposes. First, it can help the client become more empathetic with their life situation through understanding the various influences on and experience of their life. Second, it can highlight their potential. Through the broader reflections one could identify many influences on who or what one has become (i.e., their destiny, in May's terms), but also helps the person might come to understand one's potential for change (i.e., transcendence).

Each type of reflection serves to promote self-understanding, although each does so in different ways and to different degrees. Contrary to how reflective listening is often portrayed, it is a rather complex process that can be difficult for therapists to learn. Reflecting content in the moment is fairly easy for most therapists to master; however, it is more difficult to reflect the various layers of what is occurring in the moment. It requires the ability to attend to several lines of information at once. When reflecting the process and the person in context is added, there is a large amount of information which is being held by the therapist to reflect to the client. In order to master this broader aspect of reflective listening, therapists need to develop their therapeutic attention to keep many lines of information readily accessible. At this point, for some, reflective listening may have changed from being overly simplistic to a nearly impossible skill. However, with experience and intentionality about developing these skills, most therapists can develop them.

Bugental (1987) also demonstrated the art of how reflective listening is used relationally. In observing Bugental do therapy demonstrations, one can see how he used reflective listening to help clients develop a sense of curiosity. Through comments such as, "Did you notice that?" or "Something changed there," or, perhaps, "It seems something shifted there," Bugental invited clients to become curious. As clients experience this in therapy, they often develop their own curiosity and reflexivity. The art of this is that through the relational process the therapist helps the client develop the qualities of self-reflection and curiosity.

## Embracing Emotion and the Unknowns

Existential-humanistic therapists believe it is important to experience a broad array of emotions and learn to accept their limitations and the unknowns of life. In comprehensive reviews of the literature and meta-analyses, research has supported that experiencing moderate or higher levels of emotion in therapy was associated with better therapy outcomes (Peluso & Freund, 2018; Schwartz & Kline, 1995; Watson, Greenberg, & Lietaer, 2010). The challenge becomes how the therapist helps the client to accomplish this. Typically, this is a slow process that develops over time. Initially, the therapist often guides clients into these realms during therapy session; however, gradually clients expand these reflections and experiences into their life outside of therapy. In the next several paragraphs, I will attempt to break this down into specific processes and illustrations.

The starting point is inviting the client into these realms in therapy, beginning with helping the client identify her or his feelings in the moment and then just sit or be with them. Being with emotions is a complex act of consciousness that includes experiencing the emotions, and observing one's bodily sensations, impulses, cognitions, and other aspects of one's subjective experience. For example, the therapist could invite the client to sit with her or his anxiety, sadness, or anger. Or the therapist might ask the client to sit with her or his *unknowing*, which often leads into some emotions. Although this may seem overwhelming for the client to do on her or his own, the therapy setting and the therapist's presence provides some containment for the client. As one becomes more comfortable sitting with the emotion or the unknown, one will become able to reflect upon it.

For some clients, they might need additional resources to be able to stay with and reflect upon their emotions. For example, clients sometimes resist going into their emotions because they fear, "If I begin crying, I'll never stop" or "If I allow myself to experience my anger, I may hurt someone." In these instances, the therapist could help the client utilize coping resources to manage emotions. However, this is different from how these are typically used in solution-focused therapy. In many therapy approaches, the end goal is the teaching skills and developing resources is to enable the client to manage or control his or her emotions. In existential therapy, coping strategies are used to help clients go into their emotions more deeply and understand them.

The therapist's emotions often play an important role in helping clients become more comfortable with their emotions. Peluso and Freund (2018) found a positive correlation between the therapist's expression of emotion and positive therapy outcomes. While their research did not explain this relationship, this finding is not surprising from an existential-humanistic perspective. The therapist's expression of emotion is capable of modeling healthy expression of emotion, demonstrate that it is okay to experience emotion, show concern, and demonstrate that the therapy relationship is a real relationship.

As a client can stay with their emotions more comfortably, they enter a different phase of relating to her or his emotions and the unknown: one begins reflecting on them. The client has moved from avoiding emotions to trying to understand them. Curiosity, which was discussed in the previous section, can be important part of this process. As clients become curious about their emotions, it often changes the experience of the emotion. Instead of feeling overwhelming and chaotic, now emotion becomes a source of information or a clue to a puzzle. As clients are able to start bringing understanding and meaning to their emotions, they are better able to engage them.

Becker (1973) stated, "Man cannot endure his own littleness unless he can translate it into meaningfulness on the largest possible level" (p. 196). The feeling of littleness is often connected to one's finiteness, one's limitations, or one's inability to know. Other times, clients may feel small in light of the enormity of their emotions. When they begin to connect their emotions and limitations to meaning, they are able to begin venturing into them.

The meaning and value of vulnerability can also facilitate the client moving into her or his emotions. As an illustration, clients often associate their intense negative emotions as merely suffering not connected to anything good, beneficial, or meaningful. When a client journeys into this emotion in session, it can be quite powerful in that moment to highlight another aspect of this experience. For example, in a moment of deep emotion the therapist could comment, "I feel particularly connected to you right now." This often shocks the client, but if they are able to reflect upon it, they often will acknowledge that they, too, have a feeling of intimacy and connection with the therapist. This simple statement helps the client move to a paradoxical understanding of negative emotions: They can create pain and intimacy at the same time. In other words, suffering with another is not pure suffering; there is some good or positive in this experience.

This existential-humanistic approach to observing and becoming curious about emotions bears similarities to mindfulness (see Rockwell, 2019, chapter 12). Since the initial version of this book, mindfulness has emerged as one of the most influential trends in mental health. While the origins of mindfulness lie in Buddhism, the application of mindfulness in therapy is different than how mindfulness was originally used in its religious setting. Not all practitioners who utilize mindfulness connect it to its Buddhist roots, which adds to some confusion. Mindfulness in mental health today is a broader in approach and intentions. I have often lamented that it would have been better for the mindfulness craze in psycho-therapy and mental health to have used a different label to distinguish it from Buddhist mindfulness. Certainly, they are similar and there is much that can be gained from dialogue between Buddhist and psychological approaches to mind-fulness; however, there is a colonizing feel to the way mindfulness has been incorporated into the mental health world. Yet, the incorporation of mindfulness into psychotherapy is not likely to go away.

Similar to the existential-humanistic approach, mindfulness seeks to accept one's emotions rather than eradicate them (Rockwell, 2019). Observing one's self—including one's breathing, bodily sensations, emotions, and thoughts—is central to most approaches to mindfulness. Similar to Bugental's approach, mindfulness could encourage a curiosity about one's experience. As one observes and becomes curious, the way emotions are experienced changes. In ways, mindfulness, as understood in the contemporary mental health world, has been part of existential-humanistic therapy without the label long before it became popular to incorporate mindfulness into therapy. In this sense, it is necessary to incorporate mindfulness into existential-humanistic therapy. However, it could also be maintained that given the similarities, mindfulness is a natural approach to integrate into existential-humanistic therapy.

## Experiential Processes and "Techniques"

Despite the lack of agreement on how to understand or identify the experiential mode of psychotherapy, existential-humanistic therapists consistently agree that it remains important, if not essential. Schneider (1998) stated:

> The experiential mode is diversely interpreted by existential therapists. For example, Yalom (1980) appears to stress the immediate and affective elements of his therapeutic contacts, but he refers little to kinesthetic components. Bugental (1987) stresses kinesthetic elements of his encounters but places lesser emphasis on interpersonal implications of those elements. Tillich (1952) and Friedman (1995) accent the interpersonal dimension of therapeutic experiencing but convey little about the kinesthetic aspect, and so on. (p. 105)

In terms of the existential givens, the experiential mode is closely connected with the given of embodiment and emotions. This makes it a universal challenge, but it does not provide universal answers. Without tapping into the experiential mode, therapy is not holistic; it is incomplete. In my view, optimal experiential psycho-therapy would include (a) kinesthetic or embodied processes, (b) attention to the immediate (e.g., here-and-now), and (c) the interpersonal realms, although this could entail a shift of focus among these.

The primary approach to engaging in the experiential aspects of therapy is through attending to them as they naturally arise in psychotherapy. For example, when the therapist notices change in the client's nonverbal behaviors, she or he could make note of this by bringing it to the client's attention or asking the client to focus on sensations occurring in their body. When the therapist senses a change in the therapy relationship, she or he may comment on this change or ask the client about this. Existential-humanistic therapists might also engage in specific techniques or processes to facilitate the client's immersion in the experiential realm. For many existential-humanistic therapists, the *techniques* may be a last resort; however, others might utilize these more readily.

**The Kinesthetic Mode**. The kinesthetic mode has received increasing attention in the psychological literature over the past several years. The increased attention is largely due to the emergence of many approaches to integrating mindfulness into psychotherapy (Avstreih, 2008; Nimanheminda, 2008; Olson, Unger, Kaklauskas, & Swan, 2008; Rockwell, 2019). However, existential and Gestalt therapy (Bugental, 1987, 1999; Zinker, 1977) as well as somatic therapies (Levine, 1997) therapies have long utilized the kinesthetic mode. Serlin (2007a), an influential existential therapist who studied under Rollo May, advocated for *whole person healthcare*, drawing heavily on humanistic, existential-humanistic, and Gestalt psychology. The kinesthetic mode is also incorporated in dance and movement therapy (2007b; 2014) and animal assisted therapies, such as Lac's (2017) Human-Equine Relational Development (HERD) Approach.

As the world gets busier and many people spend less time in inactivity, it seems people are growing less and less aware of their bodies. This can be true even with fairly strong somatic sensations. Many therapists are surprised how much information can be gathered through simply asking clients to pay attention to what they are experiencing in their body. Unfortunately, increasing kinesthetic awareness is often not as easy as merely asking a client to focus on their body.

Clients often need assistance gaining bodily awareness due to having been largely unaware of their bodily sensations through much of their life. There are many models for helping people become more aware of their bodies. Bugental (1987, 1999) helped clients recognize and become curious when changes occurred, often without directly referencing the body. Mindfulness approaches (Rockwell, 2019; Rockwell & Valle, 2016) regularly incorporate a focus on bodily awareness. Schneider (1998) developed what he labeled *embodied meditation*, which combines some meditative, centering, and bodily awareness approaches (see also Schneider & Krug, 2017),

Drawing from various approaches, clients can be guided to improved bodily awareness. For example, clients can be asked to take a breath, close their eyes or focus on a spot on the floor, and do a body scan, which is simply having one pay attention to different parts of the body. The client may be guided with some simple questions or comments such as, "Notice if your hands feel warm or cold." and "Pay attention to how your legs feel on the chair and your feet on the floor." These simple comments help a client begin to attend to more subtle bodily sensations. Next, the client can be guided through a gradual relaxation process through breathing exercises. After obtaining some relaxation, even if minimal, ask the client if she or he can recognize a difference in how the body feels.

Therapists can also help clients identify bodily sensations in the moment, as was common in Bugental's approach (1987, 1999). For example, therapists can make observations about what they see in the client such as, "Did you notice how you are holding your shoulder up right now?" "Were you aware you just made fists with your hands?" "Wow, your whole body just seemed to sink when you said that." "That was a big sigh." Although simple, these observations can gradually help a client increase bodily awareness. Therapists do need to be careful not to overuse this lest a client become self-conscious.

As bodily awareness becomes more automatic, the therapist can encourage the client to engage these bodily sensations with curiosity. At first, this could be through questions such as, "What might that mean?" or comments, such as, "That change seems to signify something."

Another approach that encourages bodily awareness is Gendlin's (1982, 1996) focusing. As part of this, Gendlin developed the concept of a felt sense as what could be described as the most remote of the bodily sensations that could be classified as kinesthetic. Although a felt sense is not necessarily experienced at the level of a physical sensation, it is experienced in the body. According to Gendlin, it is a form of awareness that lies somewhere between the conscious and unconscious. Initially, it is usually experienced as something ambiguous; however, as bodily awareness increases, clients are able to improve their ability to identify it.

The felt sense is significantly more difficult to identify than the stronger bodily sensations. Additionally, it may take clients longer to begin identifying them. When working at this kinesthetic level, it is important to take time to prepare clients, which, in part, is letting them know that it may take some time to become efficient at identifying the felt sense.

One aspect of the kinesthetic mode is the emotional realm; however, many assume the kinesthetic realm is only about emotions. Emotions are largely socially constructed and people will use different terms for varied emotional and body states. In other words, individuals will label emotional states differently; there is not a universal agreement about what bodily experience signifies any particular emotion. Still, at times, various kinesthetic sensations may have meaning, yet not be associated with emotions for the client. It might be an urge, or the result of a repressed emotion, but not actually an emotion. At times, part of the job of the therapist is to bring language, including more nuanced labels, to different bodily states. Through applying language to emotional states, the client is able to develop an emotional language and ascribe meaning to the experience in a fuller manner.

Bringing awareness and meaning to the kinesthetic and emotional realms are part of *developmenting* insight, which will be discussed shortly. One aspect of the kinesthetic level is, to use the classic psychoanalytic language, making the unconscious conscious. As a parallel, it also can be helping the client make the preverbal become verbal or the sub-symbolic be understood as symbolic. Finally, tying to another therapeutic realm we will address shortly, this allows the client to integrate these various levels of experience into one's self-understanding and meaning system.

The translation to language entails several important aspects. When emotions or bodily sensations do not have language, they can feel more chaotic and out of control. Language can contain the experience. Furthermore, one could feel isolated or alone if they are unable to communicate their experience. Language allows for the experience to be shared with others, resulting in the individual feeling less alone and isolated.

**The Relational Mode.** The relational mode emphasizes that healing and growth occur in an interpersonal context. Stolorow (2007), from an existentially informed psychoanalytic perspective, suggests that all experience occurs in an interpersonal context. He focused on trauma to illustrate this point. According to Stolorow, trauma is more about the relational context in which the trauma occurs than the potentially traumatic event. Most individuals can identify this readily in their own life. Sometimes, small traumas will leave big impact because they occurred in an interpersonal context that ignored or did not allow the event to be processed; however, other *bigger* traumas might have relatively little impact because they occurred in a different interpersonal context.[8] As the creation of a problem arises out of an interpersonal context, so does the healing, growth, or adjustment. It is not just relationship, or mere contact with others, that promotes change; it is a particular type of relationship, which was discussed previously in detail.

Krug (2009) noted that while Bugental's approach to therapy and presence relied on the intrapersonal, Yalom represented an existential approach more rooted in the interpersonal or relational mode. Yalom was acutely attuned to the relational process, including the client's feeling and reactions to the therapist. The engagement with and exploration of the real relationship between therapist and client become an important part of the therapy process.

**The Immediate Mode.** The immediate mode is often discussed as the here-and-now and is often approached with consideration to the kinesthetic and relational modes. It involves attending to what is occurring in the moment. Many people live their lives so stuck in the past or obsessed about the future that they seldom or never experience *the now*. At times, the past or future focus serves as a defense against the present. Other times, there may be particular events from the past or fears of the future, which create a feeling of being stuck.

---

[8] When teaching I often ask students to identify one or two small events from their childhood that have had a long impact on them. I then ask them to identify a bigger trauma that has had little long-term impact, and to examine the interpersonal contexts of the events. Most of the time, people will identify there was not opportunities to talk about, process, or make meaning of the small traumas with big impact, but the larger traumas with little impact were sufficiently processed. Parents often facilitate this without bad intentions. The small events, because they seem minor, are assumed to be something that needs little attention; however, with the larger trauma, parents often help the child process and make sense of these events more attentively and fully.

Existential-humanistic therapy sees the present as inclusive of the past and the future as experienced in the present moment. Within this context, existential-humanistic therapy is always pointing toward the future, but not to the neglect of the present (May, 1999), a point that illustrates important differences from other approaches to therapy. Psychoanalytic therapy, with the exception of contemporary psychoanalysis, works on the past in the past. In other words, they focus on the past experience believing once it is resolved, then it will no longer have such an impact on the present. Conversely, the existential therapist is concerned more with how the past is impacting the person in the here-and-now. When the client is discussing the past, instead of inquiring about one's experience at the time of the past incident, the therapist is more prone to explore the client's current experience of the past.

Similarly, while many goal-directed therapies talk about the future, they focus largely on making plans and goals. Existential therapists, conversely, have greater concern with how the person's goals, dreams, fears, and worries impact the present moment. Again, this will lead to a different process of inquiry and exploration as opposed to when the focus is on future plans. Existential-humanistic therapists do, at times, also deal with the past as past experience and the future in terms of goals for the future, but the main focus is on the here-and-now.

This illustrates that the past and the future can be talked about in the *there-and-then* or the *here-and-now*. For some issues, such as past trauma, the existential-humanistic therapist will discuss the past event, but they will do so from a different stance; the stance of the here-and-now. Therefore, the essential element of the here-and-now is not about content, but about the stance the therapist takes in addressing the content. From this here-and-now stance, the person is always pointed toward the future, but in a holistic sense, not limited to merely planning for future goals and events.

**Experiential Techniques.** Many of the experiential processes in existential-humanistic therapy have been derived from its close relative: Gestalt therapy. Some of these, such as "micro-focusing on the observed behavior and emotions of the patient at each moment" (Yontef, 1998), have already been discussed in the previous sections. Although existentialists might de-emphasize the technique aspect when promoting this type of awareness, it is a common process in existential therapy. Forms of the empty chair technique are used across many therapy modalities. This approach can be used in many variations. Often, the client is encouraged to speak to someone in the empty chair with whom they have unresolved issues. However, it can also be used to encourage a client to talk to different aspects of oneself. One example of this variation is having clients talk to themselves when one was much younger.

Engle and Arkowitz (2008) developed a variation of the empty chair technique applying an existential perspective on resistance. Bugental (1987, 1999) viewed resistance in a more positive light than many traditional therapies. He advocated that resistance always serves a purpose that can be adaptive in certain contexts but may not be adaptive in therapy or at the present point of the individual's life. Existential approaches also recognize that resistance, to a degree, is a given. Clients are generally in the paradoxical condition of moving toward change while also resisting it; moving toward relationship while also moving away from it. The two conflicting motives or directions create ambivalence, or what Engle and Arkowitz referred to as resistant ambivalence.

Engle and Arkowitz (2008) sought to bring the different aspects of resistance into dialogue with each other. For example, it is common for clients to experience fears of intimacy because of the increased possibility of being hurt; however, they also desire greater intimacy and connection with others. The empty chair technique can be used to facilitate a dialogue between the aspects of the self. The client could begin sitting in one chair, taking the perspective of resistance, and then switch to the other chair, taking the perspective of seeking connection. This can help create insight and well as mobilize the client to make a decision.

Another experiential technique relevant to resistance is what Schneider (2008b, 2008c) discussed as vivifying and confronting resistance. This helps the client become aware of her or his resistances through one of a variety of techniques or processes. Vivifying refers to intensifying the experience of the resistance in order to bring it to the client's awareness. Confronting, on the other hand, is not necessarily experiential; however, the way it is typically employed in existential therapy is experiential. One way it becomes experiential is through its emergence in the moment, while the resistance is occurring, and through addressing the emotional aspects. In psychoanalytic therapy, for example, the confronting of resistance is often more through interpretation and cognitive means; in existential therapy the relational and emotional aspects are highlighted.

Another approach to getting clients into the experiential realm is through the incorporation of *stark statements*. Essentially, stark statements involve use of short comments that jar the client into awareness. This bears some similarity to interpretation, but with the primary difference being that these are more ambiguous, making the clients connect the dots, and, therefore, are intended to evoke emotions. They are not intended to anger or upset the client, but rather to jar something into her or his consideration thereby eliciting emotion. The intention of eliciting emotions is to facilitate an experiential processing of the content instead of merely a cognitive processing of it. Rarely does this approach work when the therapist uses it with the intention of angering or upsetting the client.

An example can help illustrate the difference. It is common for clients to feel protective of their spouse in therapy. Whenever the therapist says something mildly critical of the spouse, the client might respond discounting it, correcting it, justifying the spouse's behavior, or talking about the good aspects of the spouse. An interpretation would focus on explaining this to the client. For example, the therapist might state, "I notice any time I say something critical of your spouse you respond by defending [them]. It seems you are worried that if you acknowledge anything negative about your spouse, that then the security you feel in your relationship with your spouse is no longer there." This can be effective in increasing insight, but it is more likely to push the client into her or his thoughts or cognitions.

Using the same example, stark statements could take a client in a different direction. For example, consider the following possibilities: "Wow, you really need to defend your spouse from me," "You are really angry at your wife," "You are really angry at me for being critical of your spouse," or "You really need to protect your spouse from your disappointment with them." Another aspect of the stark statement is that they feel somewhat out of context. The above statements may not be jarring if stated following the interpretation or as part of the interpretation above. However, when the client is engaged in defending her or his spouse and the therapist makes one of these statements, it becomes jarring because it seems out of context.

There is an interpretive aspect of using stark statements. The difference from an interpretation is that the stark statements are intended to take the client into their emotional experience instead of thinking about what is occurring. When making interpretations, including those embedded in stark statements, it is important that the therapist has first established a relationship with the client where they are able to disagree with the therapist.

The therapist must always be aware that the use of stark statements can also create some anger toward the therapist. As a general rule, they should not be used near the end of a session. There must be time to work through emotions and breaches to the therapeutic alliance that might result. They also should not be used until the therapeutic alliance is strong enough that the therapist feels confident in being able to work through any breaches to the alliance that could occur. As with all experiential techniques, this should not be overly used, but can be quite effective at times.

Other experiential techniques that can help clients engage within the experiential realm include letter writing, use of the arts or creativity, role-playing, and visualization, among others (see Serlin, 2007, especially Volume 3). Schneider (2008b, 2008c) talks of many of these experiential techniques and processes as *invoking the actual*. They are used to highlight what is relevant in the moment. May (1979, 1981), however, warned against over-relying on what he referred to as "gimmicks." Experiential techniques can deepen therapy, especially when a client is stuck, but they can also derail therapy. A balanced or cautious use of experiential techniques as they emerge in the moment can help a client connect with her or his subjectivity; however, over-reliance on them, especially in a planned manner, objectifies the client. Additionally, these techniques should always be used in the context of an ongoing therapy relationship. It is essential that the relationship remain primary and the technique secondary.

## Normalizing and Paradoxical Intention

Humanistic psychology, including existential-humanistic psychology, has been a strong critic of the DSM (Bradford, 2010; Elkins, 2017). When the DSM-5 was preparing to come out, the Society for Humanistic Psychology played the lead role in organizing an open letter voicing concerns and building a coalition to look at alternatives to the DSM (Robbins, Kamens, & Elkins, 2017). Hoffman and Cleare-Hoffman (2017), in a survey of existential-humanistic therapists, found that 62.5% of existential-humanistic therapists prefer not to diagnosis, but will if in the best interest of the client; 6.25% of the respondents never diagnosis.

Existential-humanistic therapists tend to normalize what others pathologize. It is recognized that *symptoms*, at one time, were adaptive and, in many situations, have helped clients to survive difficult situations. They may also be natural to the given moment in which they occur. Furthermore, existential therapists have a different view of human nature and the good life. As discussed, the good life is not the hedonistic idea of increasing pleasure while decreasing suffering; instead, the good life contains a variety of experiences. Also, as discussed previously, pathology often is understood as arising from the resistance to normal or existential emotions. Therefore, consistent with Nietzsche's (1889/1990) premise, one ought not to fight what is natural, and a wide variety of emotions and experiences are accepted as normal. In a sense, pathology arises, to a degree, out of labeling something as pathological.

For example, when a client labels grieving as unhealthy, they resist doing it and often feel guilty for their grief. This is the root of a more complicated form of grief that is often much more painful than the original response to the loss. Therefore, an existential-humanistic therapist would normalize the grief and help the client to engage it. In doing so, the client is able to work through the normal grieving process. This does not leave the client without some feelings of sadness in most situations, but the negative feelings are no longer as distressing or overwhelming. As will be discussed in the integration and meaning section below, the client often will also come to experience the grief differently, recognizing that the grief is part of the intimate connections, pleasant memories, and other positive aspects of the relationship before the loss.

Frankl (1946/1988, 1959/1984) coined the term *paradoxical intention* for a technique that often provides a normalizing effect. When using paradoxical intention, the therapist will prescribe the symptom, which would mean to encourage the client to intentionally increase what they fear. This often serves to create a shift in the client in which they recognize the irrationality of what they were afraid of and also recognize that, to a degree, what they are afraid of is a normal reaction, even if experienced excessively at times.

Therapists might take a softer approach to this. For example, in working with clients with obsessive-compulsive disorder (OCD), I will often encourage the client to allow themselves to engage in the behavior. In one instance, a client was compulsively checking to see that all the doors were locked during a period of increased stress. At one point, she had been up much of the night checking the lock. The therapist explained to the client that this seemed to be a reaction to stress and she should allow herself to continue to do this. The next week the client returned reporting she never had to check the lock more than three times a day since the last session. The symptom never returned during the course of therapy.

Examples this dramatic are rare, and there are many instances in which this sort of suggestion would not be appropriate, such as compulsions that could have negative consequences if engaged in more frequently.

In similar situations, clients have shown periods of significant improvement in symptoms and deepened insight following encouragement to allow themselves to be depressed, spending time alone when that is what they feared, or sitting with their anxiety. One shift that often occurs with this technique is that the client is able to stop trying to cope with or control the problem, which often leads to gaining insight. When the energy is no longer being used in the resistance to the symptom, it is then freed for trying to understand it. As the root of the problem becomes identified, then therapy can focus on the base problem instead of the symptoms.

## Insight and the Unconscious/Subconscious

A consistent feature of all depth psychotherapies is their belief that increased insight is beneficial. However, the nature of insight and why it is seen as important varies. In some depth therapies, insight is seen as valuable primarily because it serves to alleviate the symptoms. At other times, it is valuable as an end to itself. Some existential-humanistic thinkers understand insight as important, but the conception of the unconscious as unnecessary (Groth, 2001; Mishalani, 2001; Spinelli, 2004, Wyschogrod, 1961). However, as May (1958b) illustrated, it is not necessary for existential psychology to dismiss the unconscious. May and other existentialists share concerns about the defining of the unconscious as a separate realm of consciousness (dualism) and that the unconscious controls a person, thus, freeing them from conscious responsibility.

Existentialists who value the unconscious suggest that it is not a separate consciousness, but another realm of a broader conception of consciousness (May, 1958b). In other words, the unconscious and conscious are all part of the same spectrum of consciousness. Additionally, existentialists believe that the unconscious must be understood as part of an individual's subjective experience (May, 1958b; Mishalani, 2001), leading some to prefer the use of the word subconscious instead of unconscious. They are concerned with the tendency to view and interpret the unconscious objectively and separate from the experience of the person to whom the unconscious belongs. For example, a dream should not be interpreted objectively in terms of universal symbols; instead, it must be interpreted and understood in the context of it as part of the individual's subjective experience.

From an existential perspective, insight helps to serve a primary goal of therapy: setting one free (May, 1981). As noted earlier, Rank (1929/1978), a forerunner of the existential therapies, advocated that everything that influences a person, such as the unconscious, environment, relationships, and instincts, have control over them to the degree they are unaware of them. Through bringing these influences into awareness, one begins to have more control over them.

May (1981), however, provided an important balance to this idea. Freedom can only be understood in the context of destiny, or those things which limit one's freedom. May emphasized that the constraints on freedom and influences on one's behavior are great. Yet, even if one's freedom is small in comparison to their destiny, it is still incredibly valuable. Elsewhere May (1979) conceptualized freedom as the "pause between stimulus and response" (p. 191).

A primary purpose of insight is to serve freedom, which often has positive impacts on mental health. But the goal of insight is to increase freedom or to enable living the good life, not happiness or the removal of painful emotions. However, insight could also have direct positive effects, including increased happiness. It has become popular to maintain that insight does not produce change. While insight might not always produce change, it is often necessary for it to occur. Insight sometimes has a jarring effect resulting in an immediate impact. Most people can identify a moment of insight, or a shift in awareness, where they were powerfully impacted emotionally and, after that moment, they could never be fully the same. Although this type of insight is rarer and is not the reason for seeking insight in existential therapy, it reveals the potential inherent in insight. These jarring insights are more common when one is engaged in psychotherapy or other forms of self-discovery.

## Moving In and Out of the Depths of Psychotherapy

Bugental (1987) clarified an important misconception about the depth realm of therapy. Many therapists think that *depth therapy* means that the therapist always pursues and tries to stay at the emotional and relational depth. This is not only difficult, but also counterproductive and could lead to the client abandoning therapy. Therapists should move in and out of the various depth realms (emotional depth, depth of insight, and depth of ideas). Holding clients at the depth realm is often similar to holding their head under water—eventually they need to come up for air. The longer the client is in therapy, the longer she or he will be able to stay at these depth realms before coming up for air; however, the eventual ascent remains necessary.

A primary reason that existential therapy is an experiential therapy is because of the belief that healing, growth, and change should be holistic. It involves the biological, behavioral, cognitive, emotional, and interpersonal realms. It entails the surface realms and the depth realms. To remain only at the depths renders therapy just as incomplete as when it remains only at the surface.

Part of the art of existential-humanistic therapy is gently guiding clients into and out of their emotion. This can be done through a variety of means, including directing clients to attend to either their emotions or to step back from their emotions. To guide clients into their emotions, therapists might use comments such as, "Stay with that," "Try to attend to that feeling; let it expand," and "Get in touch with that feeling if you can." To encourage clients to move away from the emotions, the therapist could say, "Take a breath there," "Let's step back from that for a moment," or "Let's come out of that and discuss what it was like."

The intentional use of comments and questions can also be effective in guiding clients in and out of their emotions. Questions have a tendency to encourage people to think or focus on their rational thought process. Statements are often more effective in helping clients stay with their emotions. The intentional use of statements and questions, then, can be used to help guide clients in and out of their emotions. For many therapists, the questions are easier than the statements. When working with this in supervision, I often encourage the supervisee to consider ways to turn their questions into a statement. For example, instead of asking, "What are you feeling?" a therapist might state, "It seems that brought something up in you." Practicing this in supervision or when reflecting upon sessions will help the therapist become more fluid at turning questions into statements. The better therapists are able to subtly guide clients in and out of their emotions, the more natural and effective this process will become.

## Integration and Meaning

The instillation of meaning is a primary component of most existential approaches to psychotherapy. The deepest forms of meaning can be experienced in various realms related to our biological, behavioral, cognitive, emotional, and interpersonal realms of experience; in other words, it is a holistic meaning.

While meaning holds transformative potential, not all forms of meaning are sustaining. Meaning provides the basis for transcendence, or the ability to see one's life in context and to recognize one's potentialities. Meaning helps one to go into suffering, difficult emotions, and the unknowns. As Nietzsche (1889/1990) stated, "If we possess our why of life we can put up with almost any how" (p. 33). Meaning also can bring joy and happiness to one's life—sometimes even in the midst of suffering.

Existential-humanistic therapists understand meaning largely in terms of symbols and myths (May, 1961, 1991), which are derived, in part, culturally and, in part, personally. According to May (1961), "Symbols are specific acts or figures, while myths develop and elaborate these symbols..." (p. 44). Individuals discover or create meaning in the context of a culture, but these do not determine personal meaning. Still, it would be a mistake to separate meaning, symbols, and myth from culture.

May (1958a; 1991) was concerned about the way that meaning is impacted by cultural transitions. Although he did not use the terminology of postmodernism until his final publication (Schneider & May, 1995), he seemed to be acutely attuned to the transition from modernism to postmodernism that was occurring. Part of this transition was the deconstruction of the modern myth, but there were not yet cogent postmodern myths to provide sustaining meaning. New meaning systems were, and continue to be needed.

For meaning to be sustaining, it must help the individual address the existential givens. As is discussed in chapter 16, sustaining myths address the universality of existential givens in a culturally specific manner. Thus, in sustaining cultural myths, there is always universality, and also a distinctive culturally-specific element. Individuals also have personal myths, which generally exist in dialogue with one's culture and cultural myths. The realms of personal and collective myths are the central focus of the third section of this book.

The attainment of meaning is one of the most central aspects of human existence, which is necessary to address in existential-humanistic therapy (Hoffman, Vallejos, Cleare-Hoffman, & Rubin, 2015). Additionally, myths have an integrative function. They help make sense of the varied aspects of their existence, weaving them into a meaning system, albeit inherently incomplete due to the individual's finite and limited nature. Similarly, myths of self can serve the integrative function in how individuals understand oneself (Hoffman, Steward, Warren, & Meek, 2014). In other words, personal myths can assist in bringing meaning to the daimonic, personal suffering, and one's future direction in life.

Wong (2012), who developed meaning-centered therapy derived partially from Frankl's Logotherapy, advocated for a dual-systems model of meaning. He was concerned that meaning, in the context of therapy, was primarily focused on meaning as a way to overcome suffering and problems. Instead, Wong advocated that meaning also plays in important role in human flourishing, growth, and well-being. While this may have been implicit in much of the existential scholarship on meaning, Wong's assertion is important for therapists to remain cognizant of the dual roles meaning can play.

Meaning, as Vos (2018) illustrated, is increasingly established in the field of psychology. In his book, Vos discussed the evidence-based foundations of meaning interventions in therapy. As he demonstrated, there is strong empirical support for value of meaning in therapy.

**Creativity and the Arts in Therapy**

A powerful way to address the element of meaning is through creativity and the arts (Dias & Hoffman, 2017; Hoffman, 2014; Serlin, 2007b). Many existential therapists integrate writing, poetry, dance, and drawing or painting into the therapy process. This serves both a cathartic purpose as well as insight-oriented and integrative purposes when utilized well. For example, the unconscious often finds expression in poetry or drawings that could be used in therapy or when the client brings them to therapy. These can be utilized in ways similar to dreams to facilitate insight into the unconscious.

The arts, through their integrative function, create meaning. For example, when a client turns painful emotions into a beautiful painting, one is able to directly and symbolically see some beauty in the pain. In other words, it serves a transcendent purpose through moving the painful experience into a broader context and allowing it to serve a different purpose. This is illustrated beautifully by Mendelowitz (2008a). In *Ethics and Lao-Tzu*, Mendelowitz utilized the story of one of his clients who was diagnosed with Dissociative Identity Disorder as a thread throughout the book. The client is an artist who painted her experience of Dissociative Identity Disorder. While the art did not cure her problems, it did help her to communicate her suffering and create meaning that helped her progress.

Art can also facilitate encounter or be used in a progressive nature (Hoffman, 2014). For example, the therapist could draw with the client in the therapy sessions, which might facilitate encounter and a shared creation of meaning. The therapist could also provide alternative visions of what is being expressed in the creative venture. When the client draws a picture illustrating the threats in their current environment, the therapist might illustrate a safe space in the drawing that the client did not recognize or suggest integrating this into the painting. Similarly, the therapist could have the client paint the same theme over the course of therapy in order to see how it changes. In this way, the art documents the progress of therapy while bringing meaning to the change.

Finally, arts can facilitate encounter in a different way. As the use of arts generally entails very deep and personal aspects of oneself, the sharing of art can facilitate a deep encounter between the therapist and client through vulnerability (Hoffman, 2014). The use of art holds the potential to guide therapy in an unanticipated direction, while unveiling deeper levels of meaning, as well as opening to vulnerability, interpersonal connection, and choice.

### Therapy Outcomes: Does Existential Therapy Work and Why

Little traditional outcome research has been conducted directly on existential psychotherapy (Craig et al., 2016). Existential therapists, along with other depth psychotherapists, have been critical of the idea of outcome studies (See Elkins 2008a, 2009, 2016; Hoffman et al. 2015; van Deurzen & Adams, 2011). Despite the limitations of outcome research, it is vital that all forms of psychotherapy engage in self-critique and examination respective to the effectiveness toward the intended goals or desired outcomes of psychotherapy. In this section, I will briefly discuss some of the philosophical problems that have contributed to existential therapists not conducting outcome studies along with an overview of the literature that provides support for the effectiveness of existential approaches.

#### Philosophical Limitations of Outcome Research [9]
The philosophical critiques of outcomes research from an existential perspective can be summarized as being epistemological, or relating to how we know what we know, and ontological, or related to the basic nature of being. Most outcome research is reductionistic, which deflates the ontology while utilizing an overly simplistic epistemology.

**Epistemological Limitations.** The epistemological limitations are fairly straightforward, but also tap into the deeper ontological problems. Most outcome studies focus on the reduction of symptoms, although a few may also look at increasing positive states. There are many problematic assumptions with most

---

[9] For more extensive and detailed critiques see Elkins (2007, 2008a, 2008b, 2016), Wampold and Imel (2015), Duncan, Miller, Wampold, and Hubble (1999), and Norcross (2002a, 2002b).

outcome measures. First, they are rooted in the idea of generalizability, focusing on shared aspects of human existence and states. For example, most depression measures focus on common traits of depression without taking into account that there are many forms of depression and that all forms of depression are experienced subjectively by the individual. Therefore, a sterile, depersonalized form of depression is what is measured.

Most outcome research is rooted in objective, quantitative research. One of the oddities about such research is that most people, when completing an objective questionnaire, are filled with questions and frustrations about the wording of many items. When individuals read these objective questions, they are interpreted differently as far as basic meaning, temporal elements, and intensity. For example, what is little distress for some may be interpreted as severe distress by others. Similarly, what is recent for some may seem more distant for others. Last, many with depression, trauma, and other distressing emotional states experience distortions in time that often make it difficult to remember specific time frames (Levine, 2015; van Der Kolk, 2015).

Furthermore, outcome research assumes a hedonistic bias that may not be appropriate for all individuals. This, as is evident, has ontological implications as well. However, from the epistemological perspective, many individuals seek therapy not simply to decrease discomfort while increasing pleasant feelings (i.e., the hedonistic bias); they often want to learn how to cope with or find meaning in their suffering. Many clients are looking not to rid themselves of suffering, but rather to *suffer well* or change their experience of the suffering. When they present with this concern, therapists often interpret this within the dominant paradigm as wanting to decrease suffering.

From an existential perspective, the initial phase of therapy can be conceptualized as helping the client identify what they want from therapy. However, as Elkins (2008) illustrated, it is problematic to assume that the reason for being in therapy will remain the same; indeed, an important aspect of good therapy is being able to track the client's ever-changing outcome desires and recognizing the fluid, emergent nature of wants and desires. When the entire direction of therapy is based upon what comes up in the first session, the very constraints of this focus relegate the therapy goals to assumptions and needs that the therapist projects upon the client. As Elkins stated:

> If clinicians cannot divine a client's problems in one or two initial sessions, then any treatment plan based on information gained in those sessions is clinically naïve at best and dangerous at worst. Clinicians who assume, because of institutional demands or their own clinical naïveté that the presenting problem is always the real problem may spend the ensuing therapy sessions dealing with the pseudo-problems and never getting to the client's real problems. (p. 416)

This penetrating analysis by Elkins provides the basis for an essential difference in the assumptions about clients' ability to know or divine their needs and desires in therapy.

Clients usually do not or are unable to clearly construct or identify a complete, realistic picture of their desired outcome of therapy in the initial meetings. This is not intended to question the intelligence, intentions, or potential of clients; instead, it is simply noting that most clients do not have the psychological background, life experiences, and frame of reference to be able to articulate such information. Often because of their rigid allegiance to a particular approach to therapy, therapists are not effective in assisting clients to identify and make these discoveries and determinations.

Many clients base their initial treatment goals largely on their preconceived ideas about psychotherapy. Often these ideas are inaccurate, such as the depictions of the therapy found in mass media portrayals. In the United States, what clients expect psychotherapy to be like is heavily influenced by popular figures such as Dr. Phil and from a skewed and inaccurate view of therapy as presented in the movies and on television. In other countries, therapy might not be as visible in the popular media; however, other cultural factors could influence therapy expectations (see chapters 3 and 4). Many clients begin therapy during times of crisis or desperation. Their initial therapy needs may be based largely upon symptom alleviation; however, many of the shorter-term approaches to therapy do not continue to watch for emergent concerns after the initial crisis is resolved. Bunting and Hayes (2008), along with Wolfe (2008), have nicely elucidated how cognitive-behavioral interventions can successfully treat initial presenting concerns, but the therapist can remain open to transitioning into more existentially rooted approaches. In doing so, a more holistic therapy experience is offered while avoiding the dangers identified by Elkins (2008).

This idea that clients' presenting problems are fluid and emergent indicates a need for a paradigmatic shift in psychotherapy that has broad implications for training. Given these factors, regardless of whether an existential approach is being utilized or not, the initial phase of therapy should focus on establishing rapport and helping clients identify what they want from therapy. This often takes anywhere from 3 to 12 or more sessions; the entire time often allotted to reaching the outcome in therapy from many perspectives.

Last, existential-humanistic therapy points toward the need for more qualitative and subjectively based approaches to outcome research. This is not to suggest that quantitative approaches are bad or should be discontinued; to the contrary, these remain important and, to a degree, it will be important for existential-humanistic therapy to consider engaging more in this type of research in the future. However, it must be recognized that there are always significant epistemological limitations in outcome research. Quantitative research must be balanced with qualitative. I close this section with a couple of examples.

First, clients dealing with chronic conditions, including chronic contextual conditions, may not have significant changes in some of their symptoms, including the intensity of their symptoms; however, they may experience a significant change in the way they experience and utilize these symptoms. For example, an individual who is subjected to chronic racism, sexism, or homophobia may continue to feel hurt and angry about their situation, but learn to experience it as less personally wounding, and utilize this hurt and anger to promote positive social change. For this individual, becoming too comfortable in their unjust situation would serve to enable an unjust system and decrease their motivation to be involved in advocating for social change (see Prilleltensky & Fox, 1997). Although *successful therapy* in the traditional sense of reducing discomfort and symptoms may help an individual feel better at some levels of experience, the person could also experience a loss of meaning as well as feel existential guilt for their passivity about the injustice.

Second, many people who have lost a person they love connect the sadness of the loss with the joyful and meaningful memories (Hoffman & Moats, 2015). They may not desire to give up the pain of the loss because it would symbolize the fading of the good aspects of the relationship. Many of these clients experience a transition in the way they experience their suffering that contains a degree of reduced *symptomology* while placing ongoing suffering in a meaningful context. In this new context, the suffering is transformed, or transcended, and the client is able to experience her or his suffering differently; one is able to experience one's suffering as part of the joy and meaning of the relationship. In many ways, existential-humanistic therapy helps people embrace the complexity of their subjective experiences and, in doing so, experience their *symptoms* differently.

**Ontological Limitations.** In the previous section, I began to transition into the ontological problems with outcome research. The problems are evident just in the following questions: How does one measure existence or ontology? How do you evaluate the ontological levels of depression and anxiety? How does one differentiate between normal, existential, and neurotic anxiety? In other words, there is a measurement problem.

May (1958a) stated that existential therapy is an ontological therapy because existential-humanistic therapy addresses the issue of what it means to be human. As already noted, what many therapies label as pathology existential-humanistic therapy conceptualizes as existence pain. In other words, existential-humanistic therapy often seeks to normalize what other therapy approaches seek to pathologize. I have already discussed Nietzsche's (1889/1990) premise that one should not fight human nature. In many or most situations, it is fighting what is natural that turns what is normal, or existential, into something that is neurotic, or pathological. In other words, it is the avoidance, denial, or repression of normal anxiety, normal guilt, and normal suffering that turns these into their more destructive symptoms. In existential-humanistic therapy, the transition to health is about learning to accept, integrate, and utilize these symptoms in the service of transforming how they are experienced instead of coping, reducing, or controlling them.

The challenge, then, is how one measures this type of change. How does one measure the transition from symptoms as problematic to symptoms as integrated and accepted? Undoubtedly, this will vary between individuals. For example, individuals who have transitioned from constant denial and resistance to anxiety and its root causes to embracing this anxiety will likely experience some reduction in their overall subjective experience of anxiety. However, their perceptions of their anxiety might become more disparate. Because they experience their anxiety differently, some could rate the same levels of anxiety lower on objective measures than they rated the same levels of anxiety previously. Existential-humanistic therapy, therefore, demands a paradigmatic shift in the way outcome therapy is conceived. This also demonstrates why different measures are necessary to evaluate different forms of therapy.

The greatest problem of outcome research is that it assumes everyone is seeking a similar outcome or way of being. This is implicit in the idea of generalizability and reliance upon objective outcome measures. In this way, outcome research can be understood as an oppressive type of conformity that imposes a universal, socially sanctioned view of mental health. While this is problematic in the Western psychology paradigm in which it was developed, it is even more problematic when applied to cross-cultural and international psychology. In these cross-cultural aspects, Western values implicit in diagnosis, outcomes measures, and therapy modalities are imposed upon individuals from a different culture with different values.

The religious and spiritual traditions provide important contradictions regarding this approach to ontology. All of the major world religions advocate that suffering is an essential part of being human (see Dias, 2017). Psychology, then, imposes a view of human nature upon people that may contradict their religious and spiritual beliefs. Western psychology has not adequately addressed the issue of how to distinguish between normal suffering and pathological suffering. Furthermore, it has not considered individual and cultural differences in values pertaining to suffering.

From my perspective, any psychology that advocates for a singular way of being as being psychologically healthy has an inherent value problem. The field of psychology has not adequately engaged in the self-reflective process advocated for by most psychotherapies. If it did, maybe Western psychology would begin to recognize its internal inconsistencies. Cross-cultural and international psychology hold great potential to help these problems become more evident.

**Support for Existential-Humanistic Therapy as an Evidence-Based Practice**
Despite the critique of outcome literature, it is quite clear that even within the limitations of conventional outcome research there is significant evidence for the

efficacy of existential-humanistic therapy.[10] Through a review of the literature, including the research, meta-analytic studies, and critical reviews of the research, there are four important conclusions relevant to existential therapy that can be made:

1) Psychotherapy tends to be effective regardless of the treatment modality (Bacher, 2008; Elkins, 2007, 2008a, 2008b, 2009, 2016; Wampold & Imel, 2016, 2005; Wampold, Mondin, Moody, Stich, Benson, & Ahn, 1997).

2) Common factors, generally identified primarily as client factors and relationships factors, account for the majority of psychotherapy effectiveness while specific ingredients account for little variance (Ahn & Wampold, 2001; Bacher, 2008; Cooper, 2008; Duncan, Miller, Wampold, & Hubble, 2010; Elkins, 2007, 2008a, 2008b, 2009, 2016; Elliott et al.., 2018; Flückiger et al, 2018; Gelso, Kivlighan, Jr., & Markin, 2018; Kolden, Wang, Austin, Chang, & Klein, 2018; Messer, & Wampold, 2000; Norcross & Lambert, 2018; Wampold, 2005, Wampold, 2010; Wampold & Imel, 2016).

3) With increasing consistency, it is being demonstrated that after client factors, the therapeutic relationship is the most important ingredient in successful psychotherapy (Farber & Lane, 2002; Fischer, 2008; Klein et al., 2002; Lambert & Barley, 2002; Norcross, 2002a, 2002b; Norcross & Lambert, 2018; Wampold, 2005; Wampold, 2010; Wampold & Imel, 2015; Wampold, Mondin, Moody, Stich, Benson, & Ahn, 1997).

4) Based upon the preceding evidence, existential-humanistic therapy has strong empirical support (Elkins, 2008a, 2016; Hoffman & Bowers, 2016; Hoffman et al., 2015; Hoffman, Dias, & Soholm, 2012; Nathan, 2008, Schneider 2008a, 2008b; Wampold, 2008) and provides an ideal foundation for integrative psychotherapy (Nathan, 2008; Schneider 2008a, 2008b, 2008c; Wampold, 2008).

The first of these conclusions is very well established, although still debated by some adhering to more rigid positivistic epistemologies. The second and third conclusions similarly are well-established. The fourth, however, is more controversial. Over the past 7-years, considering the evidence-based foundations of existential-humanistic practice has been a growing interest of mine (Hoffman & Bowers, 2016, Hoffman, Dias, & Soholm, 2012; Hoffman et al., 2015). After emerging myself in the literature, I am convinced that existential-humanistic therapy is on solid ground pertaining to its evidence-based foundations. However, I also recognize there are areas of weakness that need to be addressed.

---

[10] For a more in-depth review of the literature relevant to humanistic and existential psychology in general, see Craig et al., (2016), Coooper, Watson, and Holldampf (2013), Schneider (2008b), and Elkins (2008a, 2016). Additionally, Wampold and Imel (2015), Duncan, Miller, Wampold, and Hubble, 2010), and Norcross (2002b) provide comprehensive reviews of the literature relevant to the common factors of psychotherapy, which is highly relevant to existential-humanistic psychology.

There is still significant confusion about the meaning of "evidence-based practice." According to Wampold, Goodheart, and Levant (2007):

> Evidence is not an unambiguous term and is usually undefined, but the term exists in a context and has a particular meaning. Evidence is not data, nor is it truth. Evidence can be thought of as inferences that flow from data. (pp. 616-617)

Evidence-based practice was conceived and developed partially in response to the overly restrictive idea of the empirically supported treatments that had a strong inherent bias toward many short-term, linear, and manualized treatments (see American Psychological Association [APA] Presidential Task Force on Evidence-Based Practice, 2006; Elkins, 2009; 2016).

The APA Task Force on Evidence-Based Practice (2006) indicated that multiple types of research evidence were valid, including clinical observation (which includes case studies), qualitative research, systematic case studies, single-case experimental design, public health and ethnographic research, process-outcome studies, randomized controlled trials, and meta-analytic studies. They also advocated for the validity of clinical experience and expertise as a basis for evidence-based practice. Framed in a manner consistent with the establishment of basic competencies, this includes clinical experience and training; interpersonal expertise; the ability to utilize appropriate research; understanding of cultural, individual, and contextual differences; ongoing self-reflection; seeking additional resources when needed (e.g., consultation, supervision, supplementary or alternative services); and a cogent rationale for treatment approaches. Finally, the task force suggested that client characteristics, culture, and preferences should be considered. Thus, for a therapy to be considered evidence-based, it should be able to demonstrate (a) research support (broadly defined); (b) evidence based upon foundational competencies, clinical experience, expertise, and well-developed theory; and (c) consideration of individual differences and preferences, which includes cultural differences. As will be demonstrated, existential therapy clearly meets these three criteria.

In the seminal article on Evidence-Based Practice in Psychology (EBPP, the APA Presidential Task Force on Evidence-Based Practice (2006) avoided the labeling of specific therapy modalities as evidence-based practices. Instead, evidence-based practice is rooted more in the individual therapist than the therapeutic modality. *In essence, evidence-based practice is a competent therapist practicing in a manner that is informed by relevant research in consideration of individual and cultural differences.* This broad, inclusive definition better serves the field of professional psychology and mental health consumers. Sadly, many in the field of professional psychology have reverted to using EBPP as nearly synonymous with the ideas of the empirically supported treatments that focused on vetting therapies for particular disorders based largely on research relying upon a positivistic bias.

While many in humanistic and existential psychology bemoan the rise of EBPP, if there is a return to the original understanding of EBPP derived from the 2006 article by APA Presidential Task Force on Evidence-Based Practice, then there is nothing to fear in the rise of EBPP. The concern is about the evolving definition. Unfortunately, many in humanistic and existential psychology took the tactic of prematurely criticizing EBPP instead of engaging in the scholarly and professional dialogues to advocate for maintaining a broad, inclusive understanding of EBPP. As demonstrated below, this broad, including understanding of EBPP fits well with existential-humanistic psychology. Existential-humanistic therapy easily can be practiced consistent with this conception of EBPP. Indeed, existential-humanistic therapy is on solid ground. However, this conception of EBPP also helps existential-humanistic psychotherapy grow and advance.

**Research.** Research support, when defined broadly as suggested by the APA Presidential Task Force on Evidence-Based Practice, should come from multiple formats. The literature is replete with numerous published examples of case studies on existential-humanistic therapy (Bugental, 1976, 1990; Curtin, 2008; Greening, 2008; Hoffman, 2007, 2008a; Hoffman, Margiotta, Granger, Moriarty, 2008; Mendelowitz, 2008a; 2008b; Moats, 2008; Rice, 2008; Rubin, 2008; Serlin, 2008; Yalom, 1989; 1999, Yalom & Elkin, 1990). A limitation of these studies, which should be addressed in the future, is that many of them are not systematic case studies, some were combined characters (i.e., fictional characters inspired by real events woven into a single narrative for illustrative purposes). However, the aforementioned studies are drawn from actual existential-humanistic therapy cases that have had successful outcomes. Further, as is noted by Mendelowitz (2008a; 2008b), success must be defined contextually and is not necessarily synonymous with *a cure*. Rather, success, from an existential perspective, should be defined by the client and therapist in accordance with the client's values and desired outcome. With this caveat, existential therapy has research support for its efficacy in both the traditional understanding of symptom reduction and the existential perspective based upon the client's desired outcome and subjective experience. The following will focus primarily on the traditional understanding of successful outcome as symptom reduction.

Meta-analytic research provides support for existential-humanistic psychotherapy through the common factors, as these factors have typically been a part of existential-humanistic therapy (Elkins, 2007, 2008a, 2008b; Schneider, 2008b). The common factors are central to most, although not necessarily all, approaches to existential-humanistic therapy.

Although there has been limited traditionally-oriented research on existential-humanistic therapy, there is support in a few studies. One of the most interesting research projects, the Soteria Project, is a long-term study on the treatment of schizophrenia and schizophreniform disorder in a setting utilizing minimal psychotropic medication and focusing on an existentially and relationally based treatment model (Bola & Mosher, 2003; Mosher, 2001). The results of research on this model provided support for this treatment model through a 2-

year follow up. This is particularly note-worthy given that it is widely believed that schizophrenia is largely untreatable except with medications.

Additionally, there is significant empirical and neurological support for emotion-focused therapy (Elliott, Greenberg, & Lietaer, 2004; Greenberg, 2008; Greenberg & Johnson, 1988; Greenberg & Watson, 2005), which bears close similarity to aspects of existential-humanistic approaches to working with emo-tion in therapy. Both of these approaches emphasize the importance of the client experiencing emotion and not over-controlling it. As was already noted, there is significant support for relationally based therapies (Farber & Lane, 2002; Fischer, 2008; Flückiger et al., 2018; Gelso et al., 2018; Klein et al., 2002; Kolden et al., 2018; Lambert & Barley, 2002; Norcross, 2002a, 2002b; Norcross & Lambert, 2018; Wampold, 2005; Wampold & Imel, 2016; Wampold et al., 1997). As existential-humanistic therapy is relationally based, there is significant empirical support for this approach.

Hoffman et al. (2015) maintained that that an experiential way of working with emotion, relationship, and meaning are core elements of existential-humanistic therapy. Furthermore, they demonstrated that there is a strong empirical foundation for the existential-humanistic approach to working with each of these. While this article focuses on three aspects of the existential-humanistic approach, the same strategy also can be applied to other core aspects of existential-humanistic therapy. Implicit in Hoffman and colleagues' argument is a different approach to researching the effectiveness of therapy approaches. Often, in the positivistic outcome approach models, psychotherapy approaches need to be adapted to a manualized approach to be researched in order to assure that each research participant receives a similar type of therapy. This does not reflect how therapy often works in actual practice, particularly in approaches such as existential-humanistic therapy. Instead, Hoffman and colleagues argue that effectiveness can be demonstrated through researching the various components of the approach.

Schneider and Krug (2017), in their broad review of the research support, report that existential-humanistic therapy has support in elaborate and formalized qualitative research, case studies, and quantitative research. Despite the fact that there are areas which need further development from a traditional research perspective, the existence of varied types of research supporting the existential-humanistic approach is consistent. It is also diverse in that support emerges from traditional research as well as research that fits better epistemologically with existential-humanistic theory. Last, it is broad in that it has been shown to have research support in working with a broad range of disorders, including depresssion, anxiety, and the psychotic disorders, amongst others, and with individuals from diverse cultural backgrounds.

Perhaps, the most important support for the research basis of existential-humanistic therapy comes from the words of one of the leading researchers on the effectiveness of psychotherapy, Bruce Wampold (2008), in his review of Schneider's book *Existential-Integrative Psychotherapy*:

> I have argued that the principles of change in EI [Existential-Integrative Psychotherapy] are as scientific as those of any other psychological treatment (Wampold, 2007); I have no doubt that EI approaches would satisfy any criteria used to label other psychological treatments as scientific. (¶ 13)

Wampold's endorsement of the research basis of existential-integrative therapy, which is derivative of existential-humanistic therapy, addresses the most commonly cited weakness of this approach. It is particularly valuable given that Wampold is an outsider; he is not an existential-humanistic therapist.

Terror Management Theory (TMT) and other experimental existential psychology approaches have also provided empirical support for existential-humanistic therapy. Drawn from the work of Ernest Becker (1973), TMT has received considerable empirical support (Burke, Martens, & Faucher, 2010; see also Greenberg, Koole, & Pyszczynski, 2004). Along with its offshoots, TMT provides significant evidence of existential-humanistic psychology as a way for understanding the human condition and experience. Furthermore, TMT has increasingly been incorporated into existential-humanistic theory and practice (Schneider, 2013, 2017).

**Competency, Expertise, and Well-Developed Theory**. The primary thrust of the second domain is the development of basic competencies that are relevant across different theoretical orientations, such as assessment, diagnosis, treatment planning, and self-refection. While applicable and similar across therapy orientations, these competencies are informed by and interpreted through one's own theoretical orientation. For example, diagnosis does not need to be from the current Diagnostic and Statistical Manual of Mental Disorders (DSM) or International Classification of Diseases (ICD; Hoffman et al., 2015). There are other ways that therapists can collaborate with clients on problem identification and diagnosis. It is valuable for therapists to be competent in the mainstream approaches to diagnosis in their country or region, even if one does not plan to use diagnosis in their practice. However, caution should be used when applying any diagnostic system developed in one culture in a different culture. Diagnostic systems contain implicit values reflecting cultural norms. Using a diagnostic system in a culture other than the one in which it was developed represents an imposition of cultural values.

Until recently, existential-humanistic therapy was lacking in the development of an existential-humanistic approach to problem identification, diagnosis, and treatment planning (i.e., case conceptualization/case formulation). Without the development of an existential-humanistic approach, therapists were dependent upon using other approaches to case conceptualization. Recently, however, there have been attempts at developing an existential-humanistic approach. Krug and Schneider (2016) developed an approach to case conceptualization that utilized an integrative, narrative approach. This is flexible enough to incorporate more mainstream components, such as a DSM or ICD diagnosis; however, it is embedded in a broader narrative approach that that is more congruent with existential-humanistic theory.

Hoffman and Cleare-Hoffman (2017, 2018) also have been developing an existential-humanistic approach to case conceptualization and treatment planning. This approach originated with research asking existential-humanistic therapists to identify content and process elements of their approach to problem identification, case conceptualization, and treatment planning. From this, a form was developed to guide the process.[11] Similar to Krug and Schneider's approach, this utilizes a flexible approach that can incorporate DSM and ICD diagnosis as well as treatment goals that may be required in certain treatment settings or contexts along with goals that fit better with an existential-humanistic framework. Additionally, this approach to case conceptualization incorporates an option that allows for therapists to incorporate information demonstrating the evidence-based foundation of how they are working with the client. Within this approach, a number of the sections are optional. For example, this approach allows for inclusion of a DSM and/or ICD diagnosis if it is required or beneficial to the client but can be excluded if not needed. The therapist is encouraged to consider and discuss the advantages and risks of diagnosis with the client before incorporating it into the case conceptualization and therapy process.

Another aspect of competency that is having a "cogent rationale for clinical strategies" (APA Task Force on Evidence-Based Practice, 2006, p. 276), which should be informed about multiple forms of research. This also can include practice-based evidence in the form of well-developed theory drawing from clinical experience, research, and input from experts. Existential-humanistic psychology is well-established to inform this competency. The Task Force for the Development of Practice Recommendations for the Provision of Humanistic Psychosocial Services (1997, 2004) appointed by Division 32 (Society for Humanistic Psychology) of the American Psychological Association has developed clear guidelines and strategies for the various humanistic psychotherapies, including existential-humanistic. In reading through these guidelines, the existential-humanistic influence is clear.

Kirk Schneider and Orah Krug's (2017) *Existential-Humanistic Therapy* and an accompanying video published by the American Psychological Association in addition to another recent video of Kirk Schneider published by the American Psychological Association are recent examples of useful strategies and guidelines. In addition to the current book, several important books have been published on the process of existential-humanistic therapy including *Existential-Integrative Psychotherapy* (Schneider, 2008), *The Art of Psychotherapy* (Bugental, 1987) and *Psychotherapy Isn't What You Think* (Bugental, 1999), *Existential Psychotherapy* by

---

[11] This approach to case conceptualization and treatment planning continues to be developed and adapted, including plans to develop a manual. The forms and information on the continued development of this approach can be followed on Research Gate (www.researchgate.net; under Louis Hoffman) and www.existential-therapy.com.

Yalom (1980), *The Psychology of Existence* (Schneider & May, 1995), among others. Existential-humanistic therapy also has had a strong and regular presence in the *Journal of Humanistic Psychology* and *The Humanistic Psychologist.*

An increasing number of training opportunities in the United States are available in existential-humanistic psychotherapy. The International Institute for Humanistic Studies (IIHS) and the Existential-Humanistic Institute (EHI) provide regular opportunities for training including conferences, retreat style training, and consultation groups. The International Institute for Existential-Humanistic Psychology provides systematic training in Southeast Asia and is seeking to develop international online programs and supervision that complement the training programs by IIHS and EHI focusing on specific aspects of existential-humanistic practices, such as case conceptualization and treatment planning.

Other competencies include ongoing self-reflection, interpersonal expertise, and seeking out available resources. The first two of these, in particular, are longstanding foundations of existential-humanistic therapy. Seeking out additional resources, such as supervision, continuing education, and referrals, are important competencies regardless of theoretical orientation. The increasing training and supervision opportunities, such as those mentioned in the previous paragraph, further expand the ability of existential-humanistic therapist to seek out appropriate resources. Additionally, with secure video conferencing more available, opportunities for supervision and consultation with experts in existential-humanistic therapy are expanding.

**Individual Differences and Preferences**. Although not addressed by the APA Task Force on Evidence-Based Practice, this domain, in part, should be interpreted to indicate respecting the client's freedom to choose the type of therapy they desire and work toward goals that fit with their values. As discussed by Schneider (2008b, 2008c, 2008c), Nathan (2008), and Wampold (2008), existential-integrative therapy provides an ideal foundation to adapt psycho-therapy to the needs of the client. The anti-dogmatic core of existential-integrative approaches facilitate adaptation to the unique needs of the client, including the ability to integrate other psychotherapeutic approaches as needed. However, no therapy modality, no matter how flexible, is appropriate for all clients. Developing and maintaining the openness to recognize one's own limitations and the limitations of one's therapeutic approach is an essential competency for ethical practice.

Until recently, humanistic and existential-humanistic therapy approaches failed in actualizing their valuing of multiculturalism and diversity (Hoffman, 2016; Hoffman, Cleare-Hoffman, & Jackson, 2014). Recent trends in existential-humanistic psychology are changing this. Adaptations and illustrations have been developed for working with African American clients (Rice, 2008), Latino clients (Comas-Diaz, 2008), Chinese clients (Galvin, 2008), Native American clients (Alsup, 121), gay and lesbian clients (Monheit, 2008), female clients (Brown, 2008; Serlin, 2008), religious and spiritual diversity (Comas-Diaz, 2008; Hoffman 2007, 2008a, 2008b), elders (Bugental, 2008), and children (Curtin, 2008; Rubin,

2008). The original publication, as well as this revised edition and *Existential Psychology East-West* (Volume 2) have sought also to address some of these weaknesses. *Humanistic Approaches to Multiculturalism and Diversity: Perspectives on Existence and Difference* (Hoffman, Cleare-Hoffman, Granger, & St. John, in press) seeks to build upon the progress made thus far through examining the foundations of culturally sensitive humanistic and existential-humanistic therapy, including unique existential-humanistic contributions to multicultural psychology. Furthermore, existential therapy demonstrates its adaptability to the needs of clients through the integration with other approaches such as feminist therapy (Brown, 2008), cognitive-behavioral approaches (Bunting & Hayes, 2008; Wolfe, 2008), psychodynamic therapy (Dorman, 2008; Portnoy, 2008; Rubin, 2008; Stolorow, 2008), and positive psychology (Hoffman, Granger, & Mansilla, 2016).

**Concluding Thoughts on EBPP.** A case has been built for there being clear and strong evidence about the effectiveness of existential-humanistic psychotherapy demonstrated in the empirical and professional literature (see Hoffman et al., 2015). It is advocated that existential-humanistic therapy can readily be practiced consistent with the principles of evidence-based practice without compromising its core tenets. As Wampold (2008) explained, what this means for existential-humanistic approaches is still unclear, particularly regarding greater acceptance in the mainstream psychological community. Furthermore, as the application of existential-humanistic therapy in Eastern cultures is a primary concern of this volume, it important to consider a number of factors. Yang and Hoffman (2019) maintained that it is important to engage in cultural critique, cultural adaptation, and consideration for the incorporation of indigenous or local approaches prior to the application of a therapy modality in a culture other than the one in which it was developed. Additionally, it is evidence-based practice should be an ongoing process. In other words, consideration for new research, practice-based evidence, and theory development is an important component of response evidence-based practice. Cross-cultural dialogue pertaining to any particular therapy modalities are important—maybe essential—for informing this ongoing process. Cross-cultural dialogue can help identify hidden biases, assumptions, and limitations while informing continued development.

## Conclusion

One repays a teacher badly if one always remains nothing but a pupil.
~Nietzsche, 1892/1966, p. 78

But a people unable to reform will not be able to preserve its old culture either.
~Lu Xun, 1926/1961b, p. 138

Yang and Hoffman (2019) advocated that cultural critique, cultural adaptation, and incorporation of indigenous approaches was an important aspect of international psychology. This chapter primarily reflects existential-humanistic psychology as it was developed in Western culture with some consideration to cultural issues. As the chapter comes to a conclusion, it is important to return to these concepts. Readers of the chapter and the book are encouraged to engage in the cultural critique, cultural adaptation, and incorporation of indigenous approaches. This book is intended to be a start of a conversation to be continued in the flesh-and-blood world beyond these pages. Any psychology that takes multiculturalism seriously must be willing to reconsider and change even core aspects of its theory and approach (Hoffman, 2016).

The ongoing mission of existential-humanistic psychology should be to continuously develop and expand. Cross-cultural dialogue and exchange are powerful opportunities for personal and professional growth (Moats, Claypool, & Saxon, 2011). It is also a wonderful opportunity for the development of systems of thought, including existential-humanistic psychology and psychotherapy. Since the first edition of *Existential Psychology East-West* 10-years ago, cross-cultural exchange has played an important role in the development of existential-humanistic psychology. Hopefully, this updated edition will continue to encourage and inspire the ongoing development of existential-humanistic psychology through cultural exchange.

## References

Adler, A. (1969). *The science of living.* New York, NY: Anchor. (Originally published in 1929)

Ahn, H. & Wampold, B. E. (2001). Where oh where are the specific ingredients? A meta-analysis of component studies in counseling and psychotherapy. *Journal of Counseling Psychology, 48,* 251-257.

Alsup, R. (2008). Existentialism of personalism: A Native American perspective. In K. J. Schneider (Ed.), *Existential-integrative psychotherapy: Guideposts to the core of practice* (pp. 121-127). New York, NY: Routledge.

American Psychological Association Presidential Task Force on Evidence-Based Practice. (2006). Evidence-based practice in psychology. *American Psychologist, 61,* 271-285.

Avstreih, Z. (2008). The body in psychotherapy: Dancing with the paradox. In F. Kaklauskas, S. Nimanheminda, L. Hoffman, & M. Jack, (Eds.) *Brilliant sanity: Buddhist approaches to psychotherapy* (pp. 213-221). Colorado Springs, CO: University of the Rockies Press.

Bacher, A. (2008). Shaking the foundations. In D. N. Elkins (Chair), *A shaking of the foundations.* Symposium conducted at the Existential Humanistic Institutes Second Annual Conference, San Francisco, CA.

Bernstein, R. J. (2005). *The abuse of evil: The corruption of politics and religion since 9/11.* Malden, MA: Polity Press.

Becker, E. (1973). *The denial of death.* New York, NY: Free Press.

Becker, E. (1975). *Escape from evil.* New York, NY: Free Press.

Bakewell, S. (2017). *At the existentialist café: Freedom, being, and apricot cocktails with Jean-Paul Sartre, Simone de Beauvoir, Albert Camus, Martin Heidegger, Maurice Merleau-Ponty and others.* New York, NY: Other Press.

Bohart, A. C., Elliott, R., Greenberg, L. S., & Watson, J. C. (2002). Empathy. In J. C. Norcross (Ed.), *Psychotherapy relationships that work: Therapist contributions and responsiveness to patients* (pp. 89-108). New York, NY: Oxford University Press.

Bola, J. R. & Mosher, L. R. (2003). Treatment of acute psychosis without neuroleptics: Two-year outcomes from the Soteria project. *The Journal of Nervous and Mental Disease, 191,* 219-229.

Bradford, G. K. (2010). Fundamental flaws of the DSM: Re-envisioning diagnosis. *Journal of Humanistic Psychology, 50,* 335-350. doi: 10.1177/0022167809352007

Brown, L. S. (2008). Feminist therapy as a meaning-making practice: Where there is no power, where is the meaning? In K. J. Schneider (Ed.), *Existential-integrative psychotherapy: Guideposts to the core of practice* (pp. 130-140). New York, NY: Routledge.

Bugental, E. K. (2008). Swimming together in a sea of loss: A group process for elders In K. J. Schneider (Ed.), *Existential-integrative psychotherapy: Guideposts to the core of practice* (pp. 333-342). New York, NY: Routledge.

Bugental, J. F. T. (1976). *The search for existential identity.* San Francisco, CA: Jossey-Bass.

Bugental, J. F. T. (1987). *The art of the psychotherapist.* New York, NY: Norton.

Bugental, J. F. T. (1990). *Intimate journeys: Stories from life-changing therapy* (Rev. ed.). San Francisco, CA: Jossey-Bass

Bugental, J. F. T. (1999). *Psychotherapy isn't what you think: Bringing the psychotherapeutic engagement into the living moment.* Phoenix, AZ: Zeig, Tucker & Co.

Bugental, J. F. T. (2007). Preliminary sketches for a short-term existential-humanistic therapy. In K. Schneider (Ed.), *Existential-integrative psychotherapy: Guideposts to the core of practice* (pp. 165-168). New York, NY: Routledge.

Bugental, J. F. T., & Sterling, M. M. (1995). Existential-humanistic psychotherapy: New perspectives. In A. S. Gurman, & S. B. Messer (Eds.), *Essential psychotherapies: Theory and practice* (pp. 226-260). New York, NY: Guilford Press.

Bunting, K. & Hayes, S. C. (Ed.), Language and meaning: Acceptance and commitment therapy and the EI model. In K. J. Schneider (Ed.), *Existential-integrative psychotherapy: Guideposts to the core of practice* (pp. 217-234). New York, NY: Routledge.

Burke, B. L., Martens, A., & Faucher, E. H. (2010). Two decades of terror management theory: A meta-analysis of mortality salience research. *Personality and Social Psychology Review, 14,* 155-195. doi: 10.1177/1088868309352321

Carlson, J. (Director). (2008). *Existential-humanistic psychotherapy with James Bugental* [DVD]. Mill Valley, CA: Psychotherapy.net.

Comas-Diaz, L. (2008). Latino psychospirituality. In K. J. Schneider (Ed.), *Existential-integrative psychotherapy: Guideposts to the core of practice* (pp. 100-109). New York, NY: Routledge.

Cooper, M. (2016). *Existential therapies* (2nd ed.). Thousand Oaks, CA: Sage.

Cooper, M., Watson, J. C., & Hoffdampf, D. (2013). *Person-centered and experiential therapies work: A review of the research on counseling, psychotherapy, and related practices* (Reprint ed.). Ross-on-Wye, UK: PCCS Books.

Cooper, S. L. (2008). Review of the heart and soul of change: What works in therapy. In D. N. Elkins (Chair), *A shaking of the foundations.* Symposium conducted at the Existential Humanistic Institutes Second Annual Conference, San Francisco, CA.

Correia, E. A., Cooper, M., & Berdondini, L. (2015). Existential psychotherapy: An international survey of the key authors and texts influencing practice. *Journal of Contemporary Psychotherapy, 45*, 3-10.

Craig, M., Vos, J., Cooper, M, Correia, E. A. (2016). Existential psychotherapies. In D. J. Cain, K. Keenan, & S. Rubin (Eds.), *Humanistic psychotherapies: Handbook of research and practice* (pp. 283-317). Washington, DC: American Psychological Association.

Curtin, S. (2008). The inner sense of the child: The case of Joey. In K. J. Schneider (Ed.), *Existential-integrative psychotherapy: Guideposts to the core of practice* (pp. 321-331). New York, NY: Routledge.

de Beauvoir, S. (1976) *The ethics of ambiguity*. New York, NY: Kensington Publishing. (Original work published in 1948)

de Beauvoir, S. (1989). *The second sex* (H. M. Parshley, Trans.). New York, NY: Vintage Books. (Original work published in 1949)

Diamond, S. A. (1996). *Anger, madness, and the daimonic: The psychological genesis of violence, evil, and creativity*. New York, NY: State University of New York Press.

Dias, J. (2017). *Values of pain: How a culture of convenience shapes our spirituality*. Colorado Springs, CO: Superluminal Velocity Books.

Dias, J., & Hoffman, L. (2017). Introduction: Learning to savor the flavors of suffering. In J. Dias, & L. Hoffman (Eds.), *Connoisseurs of suffering: Poetry for the journey to meaning* (Poetry, Healing, and Growth Series; pp. vii-xvii). Colorado Springs, CO: University Professors Press.

Dorman, D. (2008). Dante's cure: Schizophrenia and the two-person journey. In K. J. Schneider (Ed.), *Existential-integrative psychotherapy: Guideposts to the core of practice* (pp. 236-245). New York, NY: Routledge.

Duncan, B. L., Miller, S. D., Wampold, B. E., & Hubble, M. A. (Eds.). (2010). *The heart and soul of change: Delivering what works in therapy*. Washington, DC: American Psychological Association.

Elkins, D. N. (2007). Empirically supported treatments: The deconstruction of a myth. *Journal of Humanistic Psychology, 47*, 474-500.

Elkins, D. N. (2008a). Short-term, linear approaches to psychotherapy: What we now know. *Journal of Humanistic Psychology, 48*, 413-431.

Elkins, D. N. (2008b). *A shaking of the foundations: Research findings on what actually helps the suffering client. In D. N. Elkins (Chair), A shaking of the foundations.* Symposium conducted at the Existential Humanistic Institutes Second Annual Conference, San Francisco, CA.

Elkins, D. N. (2009). *Humanistic psychology: A clinical manifesto*. Colorado Springs, CO: University of the Rockies Press.

Elkins, D. N. (2016). *The human elements of psychotherapy: A nonmedial model of emotional healing*. Washington, DC: American Psychological Association.

Elkins, D. N. (2017). The paradigm shift in psychotherapy: Implications for the DSM. *Journal of Humanistic Psychology, 57*, 667-674. doi: 10.1177/0022167817737415.

Elliot, R., Bohart, A. C., Watson, J. C., & Murphy, D. (2018). Therapy empathy and client outcome: An updated meta-analysis. *Psychotherapy, 55*, 399-410. doi: http://dx.doi.org/10.1037/pst0000175

Elliott, R., Greenberg, L., & Lietaer, G. (2004). Research on experiential psychotherapy. In M. Lambert (Ed.), *Bergin & Garfield's handbook of psychotherapy & behavior change* (pp. 493–539). New York, NY: Wiley.

Engle, D. & Arkowit, H. (2008). Viewing resistance as ambivalence: Integrative strategies for working with resistant ambivalence. *Journal of Humanistic Psychology, 48,* 389-412.

Farber, B. A. & Lane, J. S. (2002). Positive regard. In J. C. Norcross (Ed.), *Psychotherapy relationships that work: Therapist contributions and responsiveness to patients.* (pp. 175-194). New York, NY: Oxford University Press.

Farber, B. A., Suzuki, J. Y., & Lynch, D. A. (2018). Positive regard and psychotherapy outcome: A meta-analytic review. *Psychotherapy, 55,* 411-423. doi: http://dx.doi.org/10.1037/pst0000171

Fischer, D. (2008). A summary of John Norcross, Psychotherapy Relationships that Work: Tailoring the Relationship to the Individual Patient. In D. N. Elkins (Chair), *A shaking of the foundations.* Symposium conducted at the Existential Humanistic Institutes Second Annual Conference, San Francisco, CA.

Flynn, T. F. (2006). *Existentialism: A very short introduction.* New York, NY: Oxford University Press.

Frankl, V. E. (1984). *Man's search for meaning: An introduction to logotherapy* (3rd ed.). New York, NY: Simon & Schuster. (Original work published in 1959)

Frankl, V. E. (1988). *The will to meaning: Foundations and applications of logotherapy.* New York, NY: Meridian. (Original work published in 1946-1947).

Flückiger, C., Del Re, A. C., Wampold, & Horvath, A. O. (2018). The alliance in adult psychotherapy: A meta-analysis synthesis. *Psychotherapy, 55,* 316-340. doi: http://dx.doi.org/10.1037/pst0000172

Galvin, J. (2007). Brief encounters with Chinese clients: The case of Peter. In K. Schneider (Ed.), *Existential-integrative psychotherapy: Guideposts to the core of practice* (pp. 168-175). New York, NY: Routledge.

Gelso, C. J., Kivlighan, D. M., Jr., & Markin, R. D. (2018). The real relationship and its role in psychotherapy outcome: A meta-analysis. *Psychotherapy, 55,* 434-444. doi: http://dx.doi.org/10.1037/pst0000183

Gendlin, E. T. (1982). *Focusing.* New York, NY: Bantam.

Gendlin, E. T. (1996). *Focusing-oriented psychotherapy: A manual of the experiential method.* New York, NY: Guilford Press.

Greenberg, J. Koole, S. L. & Pyszczynski, T. (Eds.). (2004). *Handbook of experimental existential psychology.* New York, NY: Guilford.

Greenberg, L. S. (2008). Emotion and cognition in therapy: The transforming power of affect. *Canadian Psychology, 49,* 49-59.

Greenberg, L. S. & Johnson, S. (1988). *Emotionally focused therapy for couples.* New York, NY: Guilford Press.

Greenberg, L. S. & Watson, J. (2005). *Emotion-focused therapy of depression.* Washington, DC: American Psychological Association Press.

Greening, T. (2008). Reflections on the depressed and dying: The case of Carol. In K. J. Schneider (Ed.), *Existential-integrative psychotherapy: Guideposts to the core of practice* (pp. 342-345). New York, NY: Routledge.

Greening, T. (1992). Existential challenges and responses. *The Humanistic Psychologist, 20,* 111-115.

Groth, M. (2001). Existential psychotherapy today. *Review of Existential Psychology and Psychiatry, 25,* 7-27.

Hoeller, K. (1999). The tragedy of psychology: Rollo May's Daimōnic and Friedrich Nietzsche's Dionysian. *Review of Existential Psychology and Psychiatry, 14,* 111-125.

Hoffman, L. (2007). Existential perspectives on God image theory and practice. In G.
        Moriarty & L. Hoffman (Eds.), *The God image handbook for spiritual counseling
        and psychotherapy: Theory, research, and practice* (pp. 105-137). New York NY:
        Routledge

Hoffman, L. (2008a). An existential-integrative approach to working with religious and
        spiritual clients. In K. J. Schneider (Ed.), *Existential-integrative psychotherapy:
        Guideposts to the core of practice* (pp. 187-201). New York, NY: Routledge.

Hoffman, L. (2008b). An existential framework for Buddhism, world religions, and
        psychotherapy: Culture and diversity considerations. In F. Kaklauskas, S.
        Nimanheminda, L. Hoffman, & M. Jack, (Eds.) *Brilliant sanity: Buddhist
        approaches to psychotherapy* (pp. 19-38). Colorado Springs, CO: University of the
        Rockies Press.

Hoffman, L. (2014). The therapist's use of poetry in therapy: Deepening relationship and
        understanding through creativity. In M. Heery (Ed.), *Unearthing the moment:
        Mindful applications of existential-humanistic and transpersonal psychotherapy*
        (pp. 208-221). Petaluma, CA: Tonglen Press.

Hoffman, L. (2016). Multiculturalism and humanistic psychology: From neglect to
        epistemological and ontological diversity. *The Humanistic Psychologist, 44,* 56-
        71.

Hoffman, L. (2018). Existential guilt. In D. Leeming (Ed.), *The encyclopedia of psychology
        and religion* (3rd ed.). Advanced online publication. Berlin, Germany: Springer.
        https://doi.org/10.1007/978-3-642-27771-9_200194-1

Hoffman, L., & Bowers, V. (2016, March). *Existential-humanistic therapy and evidence-
        based practice in psychology: We are on solid ground.* Paper presented at the 9th
        Annual Society for Humanistic Psychology Conference. San Francisco, CA.

Hoffman, L., & Cleare-Hoffman, H. P. (2011). Existential therapy and emotions: Lessons
        from cross-cultural exchange. *The Humanistic Psychologist, 39,* 261-267.

Hoffman, L., & Cleare-Hoffman, H. P. (2017, August). *An existential-humanistic approach
        to case formulation and treatment planning.* Poster presented at the 125th Annual
        Convention of the American Psychological Association, Washington, DC.

Hoffman, L., & Cleare-Hoffman, H. P. (2018, August). Researching existential-humanistic
        case conceptualization and treatment planning. In L. Hoffman (Chair),
        *Existential-humanistic case conceptualization and treatment planning.*
        Symposium presented at the 126th Annual Convention of the American
        Psychological Association, San Francisco, CA.

Hoffman, L., Cleare-Hoffman, H. P., & Jackson, T. (2014). Humanistic psychology and
        multiculturalism: History, current status, and advancements. In K. J. Schneider, J.
        F. Pierson & J. F. T. Bugental (Eds.), *The handbook of humanistic psychology:
        Theory, research, and practice* (2nd edition; pp. 41-55). Thousand Oaks, CA: Sage.

Hoffman, L. Dias, J., & Soholm, H. C. (2012, August). *Existential-humanistic therapy as a
        model for evidence-based practice.* In S. Rubin (Chair), Evidence in support of
        existential-humanistic psychology: Revitalizing the 'third force.' Symposium
        presented at the 120th Annual Convention of the American Psychological
        Association, Orlando, FL.

Hoffman, L., Granger, N., Jr., & Mansilla, M. (2016). Multiculturalism and meaning in
        existential and positive psychology. In P. Russo-Netzer, S. E. Schulenberg, & A.
        Batthyany (Eds.). *Clinical perspectives on meaning: Positive and existential
        psychology* (pp. 111-130). New York, NY: Springer.

Hoffman, L., Granger, N. Jr., Vallejos, L., & Moats, M. (2016). An existential-humanistic perspective on Black Lives Matter and contemporary protest movements. *Journal of Humanistic Psychology, 56,* 595-611. doi: 10.1177/0022167816652273

Hoffman, L. & Kurzenberger, M. (2008). The miraculous in mental illness (Premodern, modern, and postmodern interpretations of the miraculous and mental illness from religious and psychological perspectives). In J. H. Ellens (Ed.), *Miracles: God, science, and psychology in the paranormal* (Vol. 3, pp. 65-93). Westport, CT: Praeger Books.

Hoffman, L., Lopez, A., & Moats, M. (2013). Humanistic psychology and self-acceptance. In M. Bernard (Ed.), *The strength of self-acceptance: Theory, research, and practice* (pp. 3-17). New York: NY: Springer.

Hoffman, L., Margiotta, D., Granger, N., Jr., & Moriarty, G. (2008, August). *Experiential processes in working with spiritual issues in therapy: An existential approach.* Paper presented at the Second Annual Humanistic Psychotherapies Conference, Boston, MA.

Hoffman, L., & Moats, M. (2015). Introduction. In L. Hoffman, & M. Moats (Eds.), *Capturing shadows: Poetic encounters along the path of grief and loss* (pp. 11-26). Colorado Springs, CO: University Professors Press.

Hoffman, L., Serlin, I. D., & Rubin, S. (in press). The history of existential-humanistic integrative psychology. In E. van Duerzen, K. J. Schneider, E. Craig, A. Langle, & D. Tatum (Eds.), *Wiley world handbook of existential therapy.* Hoboken, NJ: Wiley.

Hoffman, L., Stewart, S., Warren, D., & Meek, L. (2014). Toward a sustainable myth of self: An existential response to the postmodern condition. In K. J. Schneider, J. F. Pierson & J. F. T. Bugental (Eds.), *The handbook of humanistic psychology: Theory, research, and practice* (2nd edition; pp. 105-133). Thousand Oaks, CA: Sage.

Hoffman, L., & Vallejos, L. (2018). Existential shattering. In D. Leeming (Ed.), *The encyclopedia of psychology and religion* (3rd ed.). Advanced online publication. Berlin, Germany: Springer. https://doi.org/10.1007/978-3-642-27771-9_200193-1

Hoffman, L., Vallejos, L., Cleare-Hoffman, H. P., & Rubin, S. (2015). Emotion, relationship, and meaning as core existential practice: Evidence-based foundations. *Journal of Contemporary Psychotherapy, 45,* 11-20. doi: 10.1007/s10879-014-9277-9.

Hoffman, L., Warner, H. J., Gregory, C., & Fehl, S. (2011). Existential-integrative perspectives on the psychology of evil. In J. H. Ellens (Ed.), *Explaining evil* (Vol. 3: Approaches, responses, solutions; pp. 263-286). Santa Barbara, CA: Praeger.

Jaspers, K. (1971). *Philosophy of existence* (R. F. Grabau, Trans.). Philadelphia, PA: University of Pennsylvania Press.

Kierkegaard, S. (1985). *Fear and trembling* (A. Hannay, Trans.). New York, NY: Penguin Classics. (Originally published in 1843)

Klein, M. H., Kolden, G. G., Michels, J. L., & Chisholm-Stockard, S. (2002). Congruence. In J. C. Norcross (Ed.), *Psychotherapy relationships that work: Therapist contributions and responsiveness to patients* (pp. 195-215). New York, NY: Oxford University Press.

Kolden, G. G., Wang, C-C., Austin, S. B., Chang, Y., & Klein, M. H. (2018). Congruence/genuineness: A meta-analysis. *Psychotherapy, 55,* 424-433. doi: http://dx.doi.org/10.1037/pst0000162

Krug, O. T. (2009). James Bugental and Irvin Yalom: Two masters of existential therapy cultivate presence in the therapeutic encounter. *Journal of Humanistic Psychology, 49,* 329-354. doi: 10.1177/0022167809334001.

Krug, O. T. (in press). Existential-humanistic and existential-integrative therapy: Method and practice. In E. van Duerzen, K. J. Schneider, E. Craig, A. Langle, & D. Tatum (Eds.), *Wiley world handbook of existential therapy.* Hoboken, NJ: Wiley.

Krug, O., T. & Schneider, K. J. (2016). *Supervision essentials for existential-humanistic therapy.* Washington, DC: American Psychological Association.

Lac, V. (2017). *Equine-facilitated psychotherapy and learning: The Human-Equine Relational Development (HERD) approach.* London, UK: Elsevier.

Lambert, M. J. & Barley, D. E. (2002) Research on the therapeutic relationship and psychotherapy outcome. In J. C. Norcross (Ed.), *Psychotherapy relationships that work: Therapist contributions and responsiveness to patients* (pp. 17-32). New York, NY: Oxford University Press.

Levine, P. A. (1997). *Walking the tiger: Healing trauma.* Berkeley, CA: North Atlantic Books.

Levine, P. A. (2015). *Trauma and memory: Brain and body in a search for the living past.* Berkeley, CA: North Atlantic Books.

Lincoln, J., & Hoffman, L. (2018). Toward an integration of constructivism and existential therapy. *Journal of Constructivist Psychology.* Advance online publication. doi: 10.1080/10720537.2018.1461719

May, R. (1970). *The meaning of anxiety.* New York, NY: Norton. (Originally published in 1950)

May, R. (1958a). The origins and significance of the existential movement in psychology. In R. May, E. Angel, & H. F. Ellenberger (Eds.), *Existence* (pp. 3-36). Northvale, NJ: Jason Aronson.

May, R. (1958b). Contributions of existential psychotherapy. In R. May, E. Angel, & H. F. Ellenberger (Eds.), *Existence* (pp. 37-91). Northvale, NJ: Jason Aronson.

May, R. (1961). The meaning of the Oedipus myth. *Review of Existential Psychology and Psychiatry, 1,* 44-52.

May, R. (1969). *Love and will.* New York, NY: Delta.

May, R. (1979). *Psychology and the human dilemma.* New York, NY: Norton & Company.

May, R. (1981). *Freedom and destiny.* New York, NY: W. W. Norton & Company.

May, R. (1982). The problem of evil: An open letter to Carl Rogers. *Journal of Humanistic Psychology, 22,* 10-21.

May, R. (1983). *The discovery of being.* New York, NY: Norton & Company.

May, R. (1988). *Paulus: Tillich as spiritual teacher* (Rev. ed). Dallas, TX: Saybrook.

May, R. (1991). *The cry for myth.* New York, NY: Delta.

May, R. (1999). Existential psychotherapy. *Review of Existential Psychology and Psychotherapy, 14,* 3-9.

May, R., Angel, E., & Ellenberger, H. F. (Eds.). (1958). *Existence.* Northvale, NJ: Jason Aronson, Inc.

Mendelowitz, E. (2008a). *Ethics and Lao Tzu: Intimations of character.* Colorado Springs, CO: University of the Rockies Press.

Mendelowtiz, E. (2008b). Meditations on dissociation: Kristina and the enigmatic self. In K. J. Schneider (Ed.), *Existential-integrative psychotherapy: Guideposts to the core of practice* (pp. 245-266). New York, NY: Routledge.

Mendelowitz, E. & Schneider, K. J. (2007). Existential psychotherapy. In R. J. Corsini & D. Wedding (Eds.), *Current psychotherapies* (pp. 295-327). Brooks-Cole.

Messer, S. B. & Wampold, B. E. (2000). Let's face the facts: Common factors are more potent than specific therapy ingredients. *Clinical Psychology: Theory, Research, Practice, 9,* 21-25.

Minuchin, S. & Fishman, H. C. (1981). *Family therapy techniques.* Cambridge, MA: Harvard University Press.

Mishalani, J. (2001). On making conscious: An existential interpretation. *Review of Existential Psychology and Psychiatry, 26,* 27-38.

Moats, M. (2008). *An existential-humanistic case study using cinematherapy as a catalyst for growth.* Paper presented at the Second Annual Humanistic Psychotherapies Conference, Boston, MA.

Moats, M., Claypool, T. R., & Saxon, E. (2011). Therapist development through international dialogue: Students' perspectives on personal and professional life changing interactions in China. *The Humanistic Psychologist, 39,* 276-282.

Monheit, J. (2008). A lesbian and gay perspective: The case of Marcia. In K. J. Schneider (Ed.), *Existential-integrative psychotherapy: Guideposts to the core of practice* (pp. 140-146). New York, NY: Routledge.

Mosher, L. R. (2001). Treating madness without hospitals: Soteria and its successors. In K. J. Schneider, J. F. Pierson, & J. F. T. Bugental, & (Eds.), *Handbook of humanistic psychology* (pp. 389-410). Thousand Oaks, CA: Sage.

Nathan, P. (2008, November). *Contextual factors as a point of integration for diverse psychotherapies.* Paper presented at the Second Annual Existential Humanistic Institute Conference, San Francisco, CA.

Nietzsche, F. (1966). *Beyond good and evil: Prelude to a philosophy of the future* (W. Kaufmann, Trans.). New York, NY: Vintage. (Original work published in 1886)

Nietzsche, F. (1966). *Thus spoke Zarathustra: A book for all and none* (W. Kauffman, Trans.). New York, NY: Penguin. (Original work published in 1892)

Nietzsche, F. (1990). Twilight of the idols. In R. J. Hollingdale (Ed. & Trans.), *Twilight of the idols and the Anti-Christ* (pp. 31-122). New York, NY: Penguin Classics. (Original work published in 1889).

Nietzsche, F. (1990) The Anti-Christ. In R. J. Hollingdale (Ed. & Trans.), *Twilight of the idols and the Anti-Christ* (pp. 125-199). New York, NY: Penguin Classics. (Original work published in 1894)

Nimanheminda, S. (2008). Group as a mindfulness practice. In F. Kaklauskas, S. Nimanheminda, L. Hoffman, & M. Jack, (Eds.) *Brilliant sanity: Buddhist approaches to psychotherapy* (pp. 161-174). Colorado Springs, CO: University of the Rockies Press.

Norcross, J. C. (Ed.). (2002a). *Psychotherapy relationships that work: Therapist contributions and responsiveness to patients.* New York, NY: Oxford University Press.

Norcross, J. C. (2002b). Empirically supported relationships. In J. C. Norcross (Ed.), *Psychotherapy relationships that work: Therapist contributions and responsiveness to patients* (pp. 3-16). New York, NY: Oxford University Press.

Norcross, J. C. & Lambert, M. J. (2018). Psychotherapy relationship that work III. *Psychotherapy, 55,* 303-315. http://dx.doi.org/10.1037/pst0000193

O'Donohue, J. (1998). *Anam cara: A Celtic book of Wisdom.* New York, NY: Harper Collins.

Olson, E. A., Unger, H., Kaklauskas, F. J., & Swan, L. (2008). In F. Kaklauskas, S. Nimanheminda, L. Hoffman, & M. Jack, (Eds.) *Brilliant sanity: Buddhist approaches to psychotherapy* (pp. 309-334). Colorado Springs, CO: University of the Rockies Press.

Olthuis, J. H. (2001). *The beautiful risk: A new psychology of loving and being loved.* Grand Rapids, MI: Zondervan.

Peluso, P. R., & Freund, R. R. (2018). Therapist and client emotional expression and psychotherapy outcomes; A meta-analysis. *Psychotherapy, 55,* 461-472. doi: http://dx.doi.org/10.1037/pst0000165

Portnoy, D. (2008). Relatedness: Where existential and psychoanalytic approaches converge. In K. J. Schneider (Ed.), *Existential-integrative psychotherapy: Guideposts to the core of practice* (pp. 268-281). New York, NY: Routledge.

Prilleltensky, I., & Fox, D. (1997). Introducing critical psychology: Values, assumptions, and the status quo. In. D. R. Fox, & I. Prilleltensky (Eds.), *Cricial psychology: An introduction* (pp, 3-20). Thousand Oaks, CA: Sage.

Rank, O. (1978). *Truth and reality* (J. Taft, Trans.). New York, NY: Norton. (Originally published in 1929)

Rice, D. L. (2008). An African American perspective: The case of Darrin. In K. J. Schneider (Ed.), *Existential-integrative psychotherapy: Guideposts to the core of practice* (pp. 110-121). New York, NY: Routledge.

Riker, J. H. (1997). *Ethics and the discovery of the unconscious.* Albany, NY: State University of New York Press.

Robbins, B. D. (2008). What is the good life? Positive psychology and the renaissance of humanistic psychology. *The Humanistic Psychologist, 36,* 96-112. doi: 10.1080/08873260802110988

Robbins, B. D. (2015). The heart of humanistic psychology: Human dignity disclosed through a hermeneutic of love. *Journal of Humanistic Psychology, 56,* 223-237. doi: 10.1177/0022167815591408

Robbins, B. D. (2017). DSM-5 reform efforts by the Society for Humanistic Psychology. *Journal of Humanistic Psychology, 57,* 602-624. doi: 10.1177/0022167817698617

Rockwell, D. (2019). Mindfulness and courage: Livelong training in clinical Psychology: Implications and applications of a 3-year study. In L. Hoffman, M. Yang, M. Mansilla, J. Dias, M. Moats, & T. Claypool (Eds.), *Existential psychology east-west* (Vol. 2). Colorado Springs, CO: University Professors Press.

Rockwell, D., & Valle, R. (2016). Mindfulness as therapy: How Buddhist psychology contributes to enhancing therapist efficacy and client outcomes. In R. Valle (Ed.), *The changing faces of therapy: Evolving perspectives in clinical practice and assessment* (pp. 323-362). Alameda, CA: Argosy University.

Rogers, C. R. (1951). *Client-centered therapy.* New York, NY: Houghton Mifflin.

Rogers, C. R. (1980). *A way of being.* New York, NY: Houghton Mifflin.

Rogers, C. R. (1982). Notes on Rollo May. *Journal of Humanistic Psychology, 22,* 8-9.

Rubin, S. A. (2008, August). A return to depth. In K. J. Schneider (Chair), *Psychology, science, and the sea: A return to depth.* Symposium conducted at the 116th Annual Convention of the American Psychological Association Annual Convention, Boston, MA.

Sartre, J. P. (1956). *Being and nothing* (H. E. Barnes, Trans.). New York, NY: Washington Square Press. (Originally published in 1943)

Schneider, K. J. (1998). Existential processes. In L. S. Greenberg, J. C. Watson, & G. Lietaer (Eds.), *Handbook of experiential psychotherapy* (pp. 103-120). New York, NY: Guilford Press.

Schneider, K. J. (2004). *Rediscovery of awe: Splendor, mystery, and the fluid center of life.* St. Paul, MN: Paragon House.

Schneider, K. J. (Ed.). (2008a). *Existential-integrative psychotherapy: Guideposts to the core of practice.* New York, NY: Routledge.

Schneider, K. J. (2008b). From segregation to integration. In K. J. Schneider (Ed.), *Existential-integrative psychotherapy: Guideposts to the core of practice* (pp. 15-22). New York, NY: Routledge.

Schneider, K. J. (2008c). The theory of the existential-integrative (EI) approach. In K. J. Schneider (Ed.), *Existential-integrative psychotherapy: Guideposts to the core of practice* (pp. 35-48). New York, NY: Routledge.

Schneider, K. J. (2008d). Therapeutic implications of the theory. In K. J. Schneider (Ed.), *Existential-integrative psychotherapy: Guideposts to the core of practice* (pp. 49-87)). New York, NY: Routledge.

Schneider, K. J., (2009). *Awakening to awe: Personal stories of profound transformation.* New York, NY: Jason Aronson.

Schneider, K. J. (2010, April). *Awakening to an awe-based psychology.* Keynote presentation at the First International Conference on Existential Psychology, Nanjing, China.

Schneider, K. J. (2013). *The polarized mind: Why it's killing us and what we can do about it.* Colorado Springs, CO: University Professors Press.

Schneider, K. J. (2017). *The spirituality of awe: Challenges to the robotic revolution.* Cardiff, CA: Waterfront Press.

Schneider, K. J. (in press). Existential-humanistic and existential-integrative philosophy and theory. In E. van Duerzen, K. J. Schneider, E. Craig, A. Langle, & D. Tatum (Eds.), *Wiley world handbook of existential therapy.* Hoboken, NJ: Wiley.

Schneider, K. J. & Krug, O. T. (2017). *Existential-humanistic therapy* (2nd ed.). Washington, DC: American Psychological Association.

Schneider, K. J. & May, R. (1995). *The psychology of existence: An integrative, clinical perspective.* New York, NY: McGraw-Hill.

Schwartz, G. E., & Kline, J. P. (1995). Repression, emotional disclosure, and health: Theoretical, empirical, and clinical considerations. In J. W. Pennebaker (Ed.), *Emotion, disclosure, and health* (pp. 177-193). Washington, DC: American Psychological Association.

Serlin, I. A. (2007a). *Whole person healthcare* (Vol. 1-3). Westport, CT: Praeger.

Serlin, I. A. (2007b). Theory and practice of art therapies: Whole person integrative approaches to health care. In. I. A. Serlin (Ed.), *Whole person healthcare* (Vol. 3: Psychology, Spirituality, and Health; pp. 107-119). Westport, CT: Praeger.

Serlin, I. A. (2008). Women and the midlife crisis: The Anne Sexton complex. In K. J. Schneider (Ed.), *Existential-integrative psychotherapy: Guideposts to the core of practice* (pp. 146-163). New York, NY: Routledge.

Serlin, I. A. (2014). Kinesthetic imaging. In B. E. Thompson, & R. A. Neimeyer (Eds.), Grief and the expressive arts: Practices for creating meaning (pp. 116-119).

Slife, B. D. (2004). Theoretical challenges to therapy practice and research: The constraint of naturalism. In M. J. Lambert (Ed.), *Bergin and Garfield's handbook of psychotherapy and behavior change* (5th ed.; pp. 44-83). New York, NY: Wiley.

Spinelli, E. (1997). Tales of un-knowing: Eight stories of existential therapy. Washington Square, NY: New York University Press.

Spinelli, E. (2004). *The mirror and the hammer.* Thousand Oaks, CA: Sage.

Stark, M. (1999). *Modes of therapeutic action: Enhancement of knowledge, provision of experience, and engagement in relationship.* Northvale, NJ: Jason Aronson.

Stolorow, R. D. (2007). *Trauma and human existence: Autobiographical, psychoanalytic, and philosophical reflections.* New York, NY: The Analytic Press.

Stolorow, R. D. (2008). Autobiographical and theoretical reflections on the "ontological unconscious." In K. J. Schneider (Ed.), *Existential-integrative psychotherapy: Guideposts to the core of practice* (pp. 281-290). New York, NY: Routledge.

Strasser, F. & Strasser, A. (1997). *Existential time-limited therapy: The wheel of existence.* New York, NY: Wiley & Sons.

Sundararajan, L. (2015). *Understanding emotion in Chinese culture: Thinking through psychology* (International and cultural psychology series). New York, NY: Springer.

Task Force for the Development of Practice Recommendations for the Provision of Humanistic Psychosocial Services (1997). Guidelines for the provision of humanistic psychosocial services. *The Humanistic Psychologist, 25,* 65-107.

Task Force for the Development of Practice Recommendations for the Provision of Humanistic Psychosocial Services (2004). Recommended principles and practices for the provision of humanistic psychosocial services. Alternative to mandated practice and treatment guidelines. *The Humanistic Psychologist, 32,* 3-75).

Tillich, P. (1952). *The courage to be.* New Haven, CT: Yale University Press.

Tillich, P. (1957a). *The dynamics of faith.* New York, NY: Harper & Row.

Tillich, P. (1957b). *Systematic theology* (Vol. 2). Chicago, IL: University of Chicago Press.

Vallejos, L. (2017). *Shattered: How everything came together when it all fell apart.* Castroville, TX: Black Rose Writing.

van der Kolk, B. (2015). *The body keeps the score: Brain, mind, and body in the healing of trauma* (Reprint ed.). New York, NY: Penguin.

van Deurzen, E., & Adams, M. (2011). *Skills in existential counseling and psychotherapy.* Thousand Oaks, CA: Sage.

Vos, J. (2018). *Meaning in life: An evidence-based handbook for practitioners.* London, UK: Palgrave.

Vos, J., Cooper, M., Hill, C. E., Neimeyer, R. A., Schneider, K. J., & Wong, P. T. (2017). Five perspectives on the meaning of meaning in the context of clinical practices. *Journal of Constructivist Psychology.* Advance online publication. doi:10.1080/10720537.2017.1390511.

Wampold, B. E., & Imel, Z. E. (2015). *The great psychotherapy debate: Models, methods, findings* (2nd ed.). New York, NY: Routledge.

Wampold, B. E. (2005). Do therapies designated as ESTs for specific disorders produce outcomes superior to non-EST therapies? Not a scintilla of evidence to support ESTs as more effective than other treatments. In J. C. Norcross, L. E. Beutler, & R. F. Levant (Eds.), *Evidence-based practices in mental health: Debate and dialogue on the fundamental questions.* (pp. 299-308). Washington, DC: American Psychological Association.

Wampold, B. E. (2008, February 4). Existential-integrative psychotherapy: Coming of Age [Review of the book *Existential-integrative psychotherapy: Guideposts to the core of practice*]. *PsycCRITIQUES-Contemporary Psychology: APA Review of Books, 53* (No. 6).

Wampold, B. E. (2010). The research evidence for common factors models: A historically situated perspective. In B. L. Duncan, S. D. Miller, B. E., Wampold, & M. A. Hubble (Eds.), *The heart and soul of change: Delivering what works in therapy* (2nd ed.; pp. 49-81). Washington, DC: American Psychological Association.

Wampold, B. E., Goodheart, C. D., & Levant, R. F. (2007). Clarification and elaboration on evidence-based practice in psychology. *American Psychologist, 62,* 616-618.

Wampold, B. E., Mondin, G. W., Moody, M., Stich, F., Benson, K. & Ahn, H. (1997). A meta-analysis of outcome studies comparing bona fide psychotherapies: Empirically, "All must have prizes." *Psychological Bulletin, 122,* 203-214.

Wang, X. (2011). Zhi mian and existential therapy. *The Humanistic Psychologist, 39,* 240-246.

Wang, X. (2019). The symbol of the iron house: From survivalism to existentialism. In L. Hoffman, M. Yang, M. Mansilla, J. Dias, M. Moats, & T. Claypool (Eds.), *Existential psychology east-west* (Vol. 2). Colorado Springs, CO: University Professors Press.

Watson, J. C., Greenberg, L. S., & Lietaer, G. (2010). Relating process to outcome in person-centered and experiential psycho- therapies: The role of the relationship conditions and clients' experiencing. In M. Cooper, J. C. Watson, & D. Holldampf (Eds.), *Person-centered and experiential therapies work: A review of the research on counseling, psychotherapy and related practices practices* (pp. 132–163). Ross-on-Wye, UK: PCCS Books.

Wolfe, B. E. (2008). Existential issues in anxiety disorders and their treatment. In K. J. Schneider (Ed.), *Existential-integrative psychotherapy: Guideposts to the core of practice* (pp. 204-216). New York, NY: Routledge.

Wong, P. T. P. (2012). Toward a dual-systems model of what makes life worth living. In P. T. P. Wong (Ed.), *Meaning: Theories, research, and applications* (2nd ed.; Chapter 1; Kindle version). New York, NY: Tayor & Francis.

Wyschogrod, M. (1961). Sartre, freedom and the unconscious. *Review of Existential Psychology and Psychiatry, 1,* 179-186.

Xun, L. (1961). On looking facts in the face. In Y. Xianyi & G. Yang (Eds. & Trans.), *Lu Xun: Selected works* (Vol. 2; pp. 198-204). Beijing, China: Foreign Language Press. (Original work published in 1919)

Xun, L. (1961a). Stray thoughts. In Y. Xianyia & G. Yang, Ed. & Trans.), *Lu Xun: Selected works* (Vol. 2; pp. 158-160). Beijing, China: Foreign Language Press. (Original work published in 1925)

Xun, L. (1961b). Sudden notions. In Y. Xianyia & G. Yang, Ed. & Trans.), *Lu Xun: Selected works* (Vol. 2; pp.169-170). Beijing, China: Foreign Language Press. (Original work published in 1925)

Xun, L. (1961). *Literature and revolution.* In Y. Xianyi & G. Yang (Eds.), Lu Xun: Selected works (Vol. 3; pp. 25-28). Beijing, China. (Original work published in 1928)

Yalom, I. D. (1980). *Existential psychotherapy.* New York, NY: Basic Books.

Yalom, I. D. (1989). *Love's executioner.* New York, NY: HarperPerennial.

Yalom, I. D. (1993). *When Nietzsche wept: A novel of obsession.* New York, NY: Perennial.

Yalom, I. D. (1997). *Lying on the couch: A novel.* New York, NY: Perennial.

Yalom, I. D. (1999). *Momma and the meaning of life.* New York, NY: Perennial.

Yalom, I. D. (2002). *The gift of therapy.* New York, NY: HarperCollins.

Yalom, I. D. & Elkin, G. (1990). *Every day gets a little closer: A twice-told therapy.* New York, NY: Basic Books.

Yang, M., & Hoffman, L. (2019). *An existential-humanistic framework for international psychology.* In L. Hoffman, M. Yang, M. Mansilla, J. Dias, M. Moats, & T. Claypool (Eds). Existential psychology East-West (Vol. 2). Colorado Springs, CO: University Professors Press.

Yontef, G. (1998). Dialogic Gestalt therapy. In L. S. Greenberg, J. C. Watson, & G. Lietaer (Eds.), *Handbook of experiential psychotherapy* (pp. 82-102). New York, NY: Guilford Press.

Zinker, J. (1977). *Creative processes in gestalt therapy.* New York, NY: Random House.

# Chapter 2

## An Existential-Humanistic Psychotherapy Case Illustration

Louis Hoffman
Nathaniel Granger

This chapter provides an overview of existential-humanistic therapy with the intent of illustrating the theoretical concepts, therapeutic processes, and clinical techniques presented in chapter 1. To accomplish this, the following is a fictional client that has been developed and inspired by real therapeutic experiences of both authors. Any references to identifying information or actual experiences have been altered and fictionalized. To avoid confusion, we will refer to the therapist in the first person singular.

### Anastasia[1]

### History

**Presenting Problem**. Anastasia arrived for her first therapy session meticulously plain. It was soon evident that there was no mistake in her presentation. Anastasia could easily fit in where ever she went, but more importantly, she could just as easily fade into the background. Yet, when she desired, Anastasia could also stand out and make her presence known. These days, this did not happen often, as she preferred to remain hidden.

In the first session, Anastasia reported that she was coming to therapy to work through issues of grief. One year before the session, Anastasia's 2-year-old daughter, Sarah, died following an allergic reaction while at a babysitter's house. At the time, Anastasia was engaged to her daughter's father, Tim, who left Sarah with the babysitter's while he put in a few extra hours of work over the weekend. He had neglected to tell the babysitter about the allergy. Anastasia was grieving the loss of her daughter but also grieving because she believed that at 34 years old, she might not have another opportunity to have children.

**Family History**. Anastasia was the oldest of 3 children born to her parents who remained unhappily married. Her father was Chinese American, and her mother was Caucasian. Anastasia's father worked many hours and was rarely home. Anastasia perceived him as being dominated and controlled by her mother, who was a powerful figure in her life. Her mother did not work regularly, but kept

---

[1] Anastasia means resurrection, or one who will be reborn.

busy through involvement in the community. Anastasia's mother was also highly critical of her, as well as everyone else in her life. This led to Anastasia both fearing and admiring her mother.

As the oldest child, Anastasia was expected to fill the mother-role to her younger siblings while her mother stayed busy in her many activities. There were high expectations that came with this role. She was to keep her younger brother and sister in line, but never lose her temper. Because of the roles in which they all placed, Anastasia was never close with her siblings who often aligned against her. In general, Anastasia's family tended to avoid emotion, although her mother was, at times, prone to fits of rage. When this occurred, as Anastasia learned, it was not acceptable to respond with anger or rage. Instead, she learned to passively take in her mother's anger.

As an adult, Anastasia became closer to her father, who often provided financial support and verbal encouragement, although little emotional support. She avoided talking to her mother, and her talks with her father were often kept secret. Anastasia longed for a closer relationship with her parents, even though she was too scared to seek it out. She had vowed that someday she would have a better relationship with her own children.

**Personal History.** Describing her college years, Anastasia stated, "I rebelled against my parents in any way I could think of that would make them mad." She reported wanting to "punish them" for what they could not provide for her. She had a number of tumultuous relationships, romantic and otherwise, that often involved her initially idealizing the other person to some degree. She would quickly attach to the person, but when the emotions became too intense, she became scared and distanced herself.

One rebellion Anastasia reported was joining a small, extremist political group that also had some unusual religious ideas. She stayed involved with this group through college and several years after graduating, gradually becoming less involved while retaining the belief system. She joined not for the specifics of the group's beliefs, but for a mixture of the support the group offered and the reaction of her parents.

Through her 20s, Anastasia was in several long-term relationships, but never married. She described these as "safe and lifeless." She also struggled with alcohol occasionally through this period of her life, often drinking more heavily toward the end of the relationships. Two of her boyfriends ended the relationship because of her increasing struggles with alcohol.

After a couple years of sobriety and no significant dating relationships, Anastasia became depressed shortly after her 30th birthday. She began to drink more heavily and focused on "finding a husband, any husband." She met Tim, who, like many of her boyfriends, was stable but not very exciting. Anastasia described Tim as a "workaholic who tolerated my drinking and occasionally partied with me." When Anastasia became pregnant, Tim immediately proposed and she accepted; however, Tim wanted to "secure his finances" before they got married. After the birth of Sarah, they remained engaged but did not live together because

Tim's family strongly opposed living together outside of marriage due to their religious beliefs. This was one of the few times Tim stood up to Anastasia.

Anastasia and Tim's relationship began having problems before the death of their daughter. On the nights that he joined Anastasia in drinking, Tim became increasingly concerned about her flirting with other men and experimenting with methamphetamines. She reported she was doing this in order to try to make Tim jealous and get him to commit to a wedding date, even though she knew rationally this was not the best approach. Tim did, however, become more motivated to get their finances in order to get married, and he began spending more time at work. Sarah, meantime, was spending more time at various babysitters. Anastasia often complained that Tim did not thoroughly check out the babysitters before hiring them, but she was not willing to stop drinking and stay home with her daughter.

The night of Sarah's death, Anastasia was drunk and high. When she arrived at the hospital, she was checked into a detox unit after becoming unruly. Both Tim and Anastasia were devastated. As she sobered up, the guilt set in. Usually controlled and avoidant of emotions, she frequently went into rages against Tim blaming him for Sarah's death. Although they tried to work through the problems, they ended their relationship a little after a month later.

In the year following the ending her relationship with Tim, Anastasia had several short relationships with "increasingly poor choices." She continued to sporadically use methamphetamines "when the alcohol wasn't working." About 3 months before beginning therapy, Anastasia reported that she "went to church out of desperation." She reported a "conversion experience" that changed her life. She stopped drinking and was happy for the first time since Sarah's death. This lasted 3 months before she, "had a lapse in faith and was tempted into a relapse." Two times, she went out drinking, used methamphetamines, and "went home with a complete stranger." After the second of these incidents, she decided to resume therapy. She had tried therapy a couple of times before her religious conversion; however, she reported that she "never connected" and that her therapists "just wanted to tell me that it would get better with time and then tell me what to do."

## Therapy

**Early Phase**. The first session, Anastasia reported that she sought out a therapist with a specialty in grief work, knowing that, "I know I need to work on grief, but I'm pretty messed up in general." She also reported a pattern of increasingly unhealthy relationships with men and substance use as primary concerns. Her presentation was emotionally flat, even though she was quite open in disclosing a detached description of her life beginning with the period shortly before her daughter's death. After giving this overview she flatly stated, "I need therapy to work this time." Her words suggested a sense of urgency, but she displayed no hint of emotion. The lack of emotion was something that I noted and recognized as a potential barrier to therapy.

The first several sessions focused on building a therapeutic relationship and clarifying Anastasia's reason for coming to therapy. Although Anastasia appeared to have good insight into her reasons for coming to therapy, often, additional issues surfaced that she had a difficult time recognizing. Anastasia was able to recognize quickly that she had problematic relationship patterns that went beyond her romantic relationships, and she was open to the possibility that her desired outcome of therapy might change over time. I also encouraged Anastasia to begin by identifying and expressing her emotions, something she was quite resistant to doing at first.

Often, it will take between 6 or more sessions to solidify a therapeutic alliance. Even after this, the relationship continues to deepen, which allows new, more difficult issues to rise to the surface. A deepening of trust, related to interactions in these first sessions, usually signifies this shift from the early to middle phase of therapy. With Anastasia, several events helped the transition into the second phase of therapy.

First, as noted, Anastasia was resistant to experiencing her emotions. As this was explored in therapy, she made comments such as, "I'm afraid if I start crying I'll never stop." As it was evident that Anastasia would not be willing to go into her emotions until she had some confidence in her ability to modulate them, I began helping her to develop some emotional management skills. In comparison to many solution-focused approaches, an existential-humanistic approach emphasizes the danger in using coping skills or emotional management to over-control one's emotions. Therefore, with Anastasia, it was discussed with her that there were approaches to therapy that just focused on coping skills, but that this was not my approach (i.e., informed consent). Additionally, I explained that the coping skills, instead of controlling her emotions, could be used to help her gradually begin experiencing her emotions without becoming overwhelmed.

We began practicing relaxation techniques that incorporated mindfulness in sessions. As part of this, I included a focus on developing body awareness [kinesthetic mode]. Anastasia quickly began identifying body states or sensations present when she was attempting to control and repress her emotions. For example, she noticed that she kept a lot tension in her jaw and the back of her neck. I also observed some non-verbal behaviors during these times. For example, when trying to hold in emotions, she would often clench her jaw and push her thumb against her fingers. At first, Anastasia became somewhat self-conscious about these physical expressions; however, her recognition of my nonjudgmental, empathetic response helped to soften her discomfort into curiosity and awareness.

I also used many reflections, but avoided simple content reflections. Anastasia already focused her attention on the content and the cognitive levels as a defense against emotions. Therefore, while providing some content reflections, I focused more on reflecting the underlying subtle emotions. It was evident that Anastasia often was not aware of an emotion when it arose in her, but she would begin to notice her feelings more when I asked about them. At times, she was surprised I noticed emotions she thought she had hidden from me. At first, this would again cause Anastasia to become self-conscious and back away or hide. I reflected this back away as well.[2]

These process reflections were important. Anastasia often felt overwhelmed by the streams of awareness being brought to her attention. The switch to discussing the process allowed for a break from the more intense focusing on her emotions and kinesthetic levels. However, more importantly, it also allowed for opportunities to normalize her experience and make sure she was in control.[3] The process reflections, at least in this context, were more cognitive and allowed Anastasia to step back from the intensity of the emotions and return to the safe space of thinking. I would also ask questions, at times, to bring her out of the depths of her emotions. The questions drew her back to thinking and reflecting upon the emotions she had just experienced. During these times, I would also comment that her avoidance of emotion had served her well as a defense [aligning with the resistance]. We discussed how this way of protecting her had helped her survive some difficult experiences. Additionally, I encouraged her to use this as needed [similar to paradoxical intention], especially in her life outside of therapy. Gradually, Anastasia began to *experience* that she was able to have some control over her emotions through retreat to the cognitive levels of processing. I experientially helped Anastasia gain some confidence over her emotions relying largely on approaches she already employed, and only rarely would I draw on psychoeducation or the teaching of coping skills in our sessions. In part, these process comments were used to begin helping her form a relationship with her emotional life. This was essential as we moved into more difficult emotional issues. Nonetheless, she was gaining confidence in her ability to experience and manage her emotions.

Another process, which involved a shift in the content focus, helped deepen the therapy relationship and transition into a working phase of therapy. Despite frequently stating she wanted to work on grief issues, Anastasia regularly avoided this topic. An interesting parallel process seemed to emerge. In life, Anastasia often would use promiscuous sex, which she engaged in regularity during the first months of therapy, to distract her from her emotions. In therapy, she would often

---

[2] The reader may notice a couple of processes here. First, the type of reflection used was heavily influenced by various client factors. Second, multiple forms of reflection were utilized. An over-reliance on any one type of reflection can also become stagnant and may even feel patronizing to the client. Different reflective patterns encourage the client to become aware of different aspects of their experience, broadening their overall awareness. As Anastasia had difficulty identifying emotions and tended to focus on using cognitive understanding as a defense, I focused on reflections that would increase her kinesthetic awareness and emotions.

[3] This also reflects the process of moving in and out of depths, or processing the emotion. Anastasia was not used to being aware of her emotions and non-verbal communication styles. She quickly became overwhelmed with the emotional reflections, so I guided her back to the cognitive realms to allow her to "come up for air." Also, my attunement of times she needed a break was an important part of this pacing and conveyed respect for her process. The moving in and out of emotions was discussed explicitly with the client, not imposed upon her through me imposing an overly structured process upon her.

switch to the topic of sex when the emotions became too intense, which often occurred when discussing Sarah's death. This led to the following exchange:

> **A:** I was thinking of Tim again last night. He really was good in bed, and I miss that. I almost called him up, but didn't want to revisit that relationship. So instead I went to the bar and found some random guy to go home with.[4]
>
> **T:** You've been doing that a lot lately.
>
> **A:** Yeah, I know, it's not good. But, hey, I'm single and I just really like men.
>
> **T:** You've always "liked men," but you haven't always gone out looking to hook up with random men.
>
> **A:** I'm okay with it. I enjoy it and, as I said, I just really like men, and I like sex.
>
> **T:** It's not sex or men, you like the distraction that sex provides [stark statement].[5]
>
> **A:** (noticeably reacting, upset). What? (pause, I do not respond) What do you mean?
>
> **T:** It's not about the men, not about the sex. It's about you.
>
> **A:** Yeah, *I* want sex.
>
> **T:** It's more than that.
>
> **A:** Well, sure, it's better than the pain, but I enjoy the sex, too.
>
> **T:** I know. But I've noticed a pattern. Since you've begun here, when you are having a difficult week, and often after a difficult session, you go out looking for sex. In therapy, when we are talking about Sarah, you often shift to talking about your sexual relationships [reflection the person in context]. I'm not saying you don't enjoy men and sex, I am just saying sex comes up as a topic or something you seek out when you are in pain.[6]

---

[4] The dialogues included are generally abbreviated, which some times may give the appearance of appearing "too easy." Although there are limitations in presenting the dialogue in this matter, it provides demonstrations of general themes and examples of therapeutic responses that hopefully are helpful to the reader.

[5] Notice here that this statement was somewhat jarring. It didn't flow naturally in the conversation. Similar to an interpretation, it brought something uncomfortable quickly to her attention, but it did so without explanation. This pushed Anastasia to connect the meaning, but also quickly brought up emotions. It is important to be careful with statements, and they are best used after there is a solid therapeutic relationship established and the client has shown that they are able to disagree with the therapist when the therapist makes an inaccurate statement.

[6] This is a big mirror reflection in that it reflects several pieces of information and places them in context. This, again, is similar to an interpretation; however, it is left a bit less clear than most interpretations. There are intentionally some gaps that Anastasia will still need to connect for herself. Stated differently, some unknowns were intentionally left in place. Additionally, as previously noted, it is important that the client is able to disagree with the therapist before statements such as this are made, and it is important that the therapist is diligent in clarifying and adjusting anything that may not fit as the conversation continues.

Anastasia was upset by this conversation, but progress had been made, as she gained some awareness through this exchange, and she allowed herself to show a small degree of anger. When I asked about her feelings, she still denied that she was upset. A follow-up to this occurred in the next session that seemed to symbolize the transition into deeper therapeutic work.

> **T**: I wanted to start off with something today. Last week it really seemed like you were mad at me.
> **A**: No, I was a bit frustrated, but not mad.
> **T**: You looked mad. I'm a little unclear about the difference between being mad and being frustrated in your experience.
> **A**: (long pause). I guess it is that I wasn't very upset, it wasn't a big deal.
> **T**: It doesn't feel very safe to be angry at me.
> **A**: What do you mean? I wasn't angry. (slightly irritated)
> **T**: Okay, but would it be safe to be angry at me?
> **A**: I guess…. I just really don't get angry.
> **T**: It is okay to get angry—everyone does sometimes. I wonder if it is hard for you to express it.
> **A**: I guess, maybe.
> **T**: Maybe? Now that makes me angry. You're just blowing me off.
> **A**: (surprised). I didn't mean to make you angry. I just meant I'm not sure. I'm not comfortable with anger… I did have something I wanted to bring up today.
> **T**: Just wait, I think this is important.
> **A**: I just don't want to talk about anger. You said I was in charge of what we talk about.
> **T**: You are, and if you really want to move on, we will. But I imagine this would still be on your mind—on both of our minds. I don't think either of us will really be able to focus on something else if this is sitting there unresolved.
> **A**: Alright (with a look of disgust).
> **T**: See, there, you seem angry again.
> **A**; Yeah, maybe, because you're trying to piss me off.
> **T**: No, I'm not. I am trying to understand, and I may be wrong. I think it is necessary for us to be completely honest with each other.
> **A**: I never lied to you, what are you talking about?
> **T**: I didn't think you lied. It just seemed like you may not be telling me everything, maybe not telling yourself everything. It seemed you were not acknowledging your anger.
> **A**: It doesn't feel safe. This is supposed to be a safe place.
> **T**: It hope it is. But how can it truly be safe if you cannot be angry with me?
> **A**: (pause, Anastasia appeared to be considering this). I guess that makes sense. It's just that I was never allowed to get angry before. It was not okay in my family. If you got angry, then you were really going to get it.

**T**: And you're afraid I'm going to let you have it, too.

**A**: Or you'll get rid of me.

**T**: (leaning in) I'm not getting rid of you. In fact, I feel quite close to you right now.

**A**: (long pause) I do feel connected to you right now, too. I'm not sure what that means.

**T**: Maybe it means, in part, that this is something you needed to talk about in here. You can't get too close to someone when you're hiding something that needs to be talked about.

This was a key moment in therapy. Anastasia was able to recognize the paradox in that moment: in the midst of uncomfortable feelings of anger and sadness, she also felt connected, which felt good.[7] Through this exchange, Anastasia began to believe that I was not going anywhere. Even if both of us were mad, the relationship would go on.

A second aspect of this is important to note, too. I had role modeled my anger and expression of anger to Anastasia. As discussed in chapter 1, the therapist's emotions can also be connected to positive outcomes, and a real relationship entails a variety of emotions, including some that are not comfortable. It was not a dramatic expression of anger, but rather expressed directly and calmly. Some clients need to be able to raise their voice and express their anger more dramatically. For Anastasia, part of her resistance to anger was associating it with the more dramatic outbursts her mother occasionally had. As she learned that she could experience and express her emotions subtly, without the dramatic expressions of it, it began to feel safer. From an existential-humanistic perspective, it is important to be able to experience and express emotion, but it is not dictated how that should be done.[8]

Some will be surprised by the directness of this exchange, which may not appear consistent with the more phenomenological or client-centered approaches to existential and humanistic therapy, including some of those who would identify as existential-humanistic but are more rooted in the phenomenological side of the tradition. This exchange might not fit with all existential-humanistic therapists. The phenomenological and client-centered approaches focus more exclusively on exploring and describing the client's experience. In this exchange, influences of

---

[7] In our experience, examples such as this are very common, although they may not always be centered on the emotion of anger. Sadness, for example, is equally as common. The essence of this experience therapeutically is twofold. First, the client recognizes that the intense emotions will not drive off the therapist. Second, this helps change the experience of the emotion. The emotion is the same, but it is not experienced as painful. Through these encounters, clients also learn that it is okay to go into their emotions and explore their meaning.

[8] There are also important cultural variations in emotional expression. As will be discussed in Chapter 3, many Eastern cultures tend to be leery of intense emotional expression. With Anastasia, once she learned that the emotional expression did not need to be the dramatic style of her associations, it become much easier to acknowledge, experience, and express emotion.

existential-humanistic therapists such as Yalom are more evident. Yalom (1994) emphasized and illustrated that therapy is a real relationship. This allows for a broader incorporation of genuineness, including, at times, being more direct. While the foundation of the relationship could be more in exploration and description most of the time, there are often real encounters between two unique participants. Prior to exchanges such as the two illustrated above, there is significant time devoted to establishing a therapeutic relationship. In particular, it is critical to establish a basis for the client demonstrating that they can disagree with the therapist when a reflection or statement is not accurate and share feelings about what is happening in the here-and-now of therapy.

**Middle Phase.** As we transitioned into the next phase of therapy, Anastasia seemed to feel comfortable addressing a broader array of issues. Despite this, she still avoided talking about Sarah. Instead, she focused mostly on her relationship with men. It became apparent that Anastasia saw most men as weak, and she felt like she could control them with sex or manipulation. A pattern seemed to emerge, even in her short relationships in which she would use her sexuality to attract men and control them while in relationship with them, but then, she would get bored with the relationship. When seeking to get out of the relationship and then attempt to get back in the relationship until she became bored, she dressed up to draw attention to herself. Once she became bored, she started to try to look plain again. During this time, the following interchange occurred.

> **T:** Anastasia, I've noticed you've been dressing quite differently for therapy lately.
> **A:** How so? (It was evident that she knew and was playing coy.)
> **T:** Well, you've been dressed up more and wearing more make-up. I'm curious as to what that is about.
> **A:** I'm just feeling better, so I'm dressing up.
> **T:** That's a little different from what you are saying in sessions, though. It doesn't sound like you're feeling better. It seems there is something different.
> **A:** Like what?
> **T:** Well, I'm feeling a bit uncomfortable with your dress at times. [here-and-now therapist self-disclosure]
> **A:** How? Like you are attracted to me?
> **T:** That's not what I am getting at. We've talked about your pattern with men that you dress up to get their attention and to get control over them. I think it may be important for us to explore if that is what is happening here.[9]

---

[9] This illustrates a couple of challenges for many therapists. First, therapist self-disclosure was utilized. It focused on the here-and-now, not personal details again. Second, therapists are often overly hesitant in addressing issues of sexuality in therapy. In this instance, it was necessary to address sexuality straight on.

Erotic transferences in therapy happen more often than most therapists realize or are willing to admit to themselves. In this situation, it did not appear as if there was an erotic transference; however, Anastasia was using her sexuality as a defense. This pattern emerged after several emotionally difficult sessions. As Anastasia started to dress up for therapy, she also became more resistant. This pattern, again, is not uncommon when an erotic transference emerges as the client will then often try to present themselves in the best light.

My instinct was that this was a resistance pattern, not an erotic transference; however, the intent in the dialogue above was to encourage Anastasia's recognition and curiosity about the exchange. This dialogue opened the conversation in a way that could allow the erotic transference to emerge, if that was the case, or could deal with using sexuality as a resistance pattern. Through the exploration that followed this discussion, it became clear that it was a resistance pattern. As we discussed this over several weeks, the client was able to become aware that she felt overwhelmed by the intensity of the previous sessions, so she began to act out a pattern from her life in the therapy relationship. Yalom (1995) talked about therapy being a social microcosm. In other words, clients will gradually start acting in therapy like they do outside of therapy. He emphasizes this more in his work on group therapy; however, it often applies in individual therapy, as well. When patterns that are part of the client's challenges in life outside of therapy begin to emerge in therapy, this provides an important opportunity to work with it experientially. Thus, when I recognized that one of Anastasia common patterns in life was playing out in therapy, I saw it as an important opportunity. In this next brief excerpt, we discussed the relationship implications for this:

> **T:** Anastasia, when you were "dressing up for therapy," my experience was that I felt much more disconnected from you.
> **A:** (surprised) Most guys seem to like that.
> **T:** I would guess so, but I am more curious about your experience in here.[10]
> **A:** I guess I was more disconnected, too.
> **T:** You guess? Come on, you know that doesn't cut it in here. Look inward, what was your experience like?[11]

---

[10] Anastasia was getting much better at reflecting on the moment in therapy, but she often needed guidance or pointing back to this process, which I regularly provided. Over time, clients frequently develop a curiosity impulse and begin to make these reflections more naturally, even outside of therapy.

[11] I established pretty early on in therapy that "I don't know" and "I guess" are limiting in therapy, which is something I commonly do in therapy. When Anastasia used this as an answer, I regularly made a comment such as the one in the dialogue with a teasing voice tone. This tone made the confrontation easier to take, but also pointed her to looking inward to find her answer. Eventually, she would catch herself when she said, "I don't know" or "I guess" and settle in to reflecting for an answer in which she was more certain.

> **A:** Alright, alright. (pause). I really was disconnected. But I also felt powerful.
>
> **T:** Powerful?
>
> **A:** Yeah, I guess…. I mean, yeah, that seems right. I do that a lot with men. It is safer to be with them when I'm in control, when I have some power over them.
>
> **T:** But there is something missing, too.
>
> **A:** The intimacy is gone. It's not really a relationship anymore.

Anastasia was starting to see that many of her relationships did not meet her relational needs; they were just a distraction.

Not long after this issue was addressed, Anastasia reported feeling that she needed to "get back to church and get back to God." Over the next several weeks, she became more focused on talking about her church and religious issues. She discussed feeling guilty about her sexual promiscuity, but there never seemed to be any emotional connection when she talked about her guilt. Her nights out at the bar and looking for men decreased and then desisted. The desire to go out remained, but now she was talking about urges to go out partying as "the devil tempting" her. She spent more and more time at church growing increasingly active.

The impression I developed was that Anastasia had a genuine religious commitment and faith, but she was increasingly using religion as a protection, or a psychological defense, which emerged as a curiosity or a wondering, and it was important for me to make sure that my wanderings did not close me to understanding Anastasia's experience. It is often difficult to explore particular religious *beliefs* of the client without challenging their *faith* or *spirituality*. At the same time, it appeared Anastasia was not getting the deeper meaning benefits of being religious because it was being utilized in the role of a psychological defense. The challenge in working with this issue with Anastasia, as with many clients, is to help her retain the meaningful aspects of religion while encouraging her to gradually explore and recognize the potentially limiting or destructive aspects of her beliefs. It was particularly challenging to do this while respecting Anastasia's beliefs, even though I had concerns about them. It was important for me to remain aware of my reaction and assumptions to avoid imposing anything upon Anastasia. Still, I recognized that if her beliefs were being used as a psychological defense, they lacked the genuineness to provide sustaining meaning. By working through the defense aspects of the religious or spiritual beliefs, Anastasia would gradually be able to have a more authentic faith or spirituality that is sustaining and meaningful.

I had been encouraging Anastasia to explore her religious beliefs and how it was impacting her with some limited success. I began encouraging Anastasia to look at the grief issues that she had initially said she wanted to work on in therapy. Whenever Sarah came up, she responded by saying, "She's in a better place now.

God has freed me of that concern." During this period Anastasia came in with the following dream:

> **A:** I was at the beach on a retreat with friends. Sarah was there. It was a beautiful spot on the beach with high cliffs behind us. It was just a small beach area with a single road leading to it. We were having a celebration—partying. Sarah was playing down by the water. I was distracted by the others and lost track of Sarah. Next thing I knew, Sarah was swimming and getting caught in the waves, pulled out to sea. As I tried to get down there, Sarah was caught in the undertow and pulled under. I knew she was going to drown and there was nothing I could do about it. Then things changed. It was night and there was a fire on the beach. I was still trying to get to Sarah. It was no longer my partying friends with me; now it was my church friends. They were holding me back, telling me Sarah was okay and to come and join the singing. But I knew Sarah was not okay. I was mad, furious. I wanted them to help me find Sarah, but no one would listen. Then Tim was there. I made him get in this little air raft by himself and go out looking for Sarah. He was trying to navigate the boat among the rocks and being sucked out to sea. Then I woke up.

As she finished telling the dream, Anastasia was sobbing. She had never gone into emotion like this before—never allowed herself just to cry. After several minutes she said, "I don't know why I am crying so hard."

We began to process the dream. I encouraged Anastasia to think about what the dream could mean to her. She responded with the following:

> **A:** Some of it is obvious. I can't save Sarah. And I know I can't. But I don't understand the rest. Why did my friends change? Why wouldn't my church friends help me find Sarah?

The dream led into some powerful therapy work and it unveiled itself over the next several sessions. The dark, vastness of the sea seemed symbolic of the unconscious, the great unknown. This was something that Anastasia was terrified to face, something she did not want to know about herself, yet there was part of her that was being beckoned by the sea. She could not deny that. All along she had been seeking meaning from the depths, but terrified of where she needed to go to get there.

Through the dream, Anastasia recognized that her partying friends represented her own guilt hidden away in her unconscious. She began to acknowledge that she felt it was her fault that Sarah died, not Tim's. She said Tim was being responsible and working while she was out partying. Although she was able to recognize that Tim also made mistakes, she was facing her guilt and how it connected to the grief. She also began recognizing that she felt that she had treated Tim unfairly: "I often sent him on dangerous and unfair missions. Sarah was my excuse for doing so. I'm not sure I ever wanted him to succeed, but he would diligently go out among the rocks for me." She, too, began to understand the sea as symbolizing her great needs and all her unfinished business with the pain of her past that drove her to the lifestyle she was living when Sarah died.

In many ways, the most difficult symbolism that Anastasia faced in the dream was that of her church friends. Early on, she ardently maintained that her church friends were there to provide her comfort and were doing what they ought to do. She said that they were encouraging her to move on and be thankful for what God had given her, but she was resistant. I was suspicious of this interpretation, but I did not want to force my own opinion upon her. Yet, the emotion that she expressed when talking about how her church friends did not seem to line up with her positive portrayal of them in the dream. In one session, she began looking at this differently:

> **A:** I keep coming back to the one dream, to the church friends that were there with me. I can't get that part of the dream off my mind.
> **T:** And the rest of the dream, that is not as pressing anymore?
> **A:** No, I don't seem to think about that much anymore.
> **T:** Maybe there is something else in that part of the dream, something you haven't recognized yet.
> **A:** There must be; I can't let it go. I even had another dream last night. I was back at the beach. The church friends were there singing away, and I was so mad at them. Finally, I grabbed one of their guitars and threw it on the fire.
> **T:** Wow, it sounds like you were pretty mad at them.
> **A:** I was furious, but I don't know why. They weren't doing anything wrong.
> **T:** I wonder if you can just sit with that image from the dream for a minute. Go ahead and close your eyes, focus in on the image.... Notice how you feel.... Check in with the different parts of your body.... (I continued with some imagery work, just having her bring the image to mind combined with some body scans).
> **A:** (Crying). I'm so mad at them.
> **T:** Something about them is making you mad. Yet, you are crying.[12]
> **A:** (pause, still crying). I am so alone.
> **T:** (pause) Even with your friends there, you still feel alone.
> **A:** They are not really there; they are not there for me. They are only there for me if I can feel good.

---

[12] Several things can be noticed here. First, the temptation here would be to ask a question, yet I did not want to do this. When the therapist asks a question, this often draws the client into thinking—into their head; I wanted Anastasia to stay with the emotion. Statements and comments are much more effective in keeping a client with their emotions. Second, I pointed out the incongruence, which made Anastasia consider why she said she was mad but she was crying.

**T:** They won't go with you into your suffering, your pain.

**A:** No, that's a weakness to them. Christians aren't supposed to suffer. God, if another person tells me Sarah is in a better place I'm just going to punch them. I know she's in a better place, that's not the point.

**T:** The point is that you miss her.

**A:** I miss her! Dammit (sic), I miss her! No cliché is going to make that go away. I miss her! (crying)

**T:** You feel even more alone when they discount your feelings with their simple answers.

**A:** I can't stand it. I just want them to be there with me. I want someone to let me cry, let me be mad; to let me even be mad at God!

This encounter was a powerful experience for Anastasia. She was able to gain important insight as well as do some powerful experiential work going into her emotions. The next couple of sessions were also very intense as she continued to process her emotions around Sarah's death and her anger at her church, to which she hadn't gone back.

The day of the third session after this dialogue, Anastasia called a few minutes before the appointment to say that she was drunk and unable to drive herself to the appointment. She went to have lunch at a bar and had a couple of drinks that led to a couple of more drinks. She never went back to work. I made sure that she was not planning to drive home, as she was still at the bar, and confirmed the appointment for next week.

The next week Anastasia arrived a few minutes late for her appointment and appeared nervous:

**T:** You appear nervous today.

**A:** I'm worried about how you're going to react about me missing last week.

**T:** Let's start there. You worry that I had a negative reaction to what happened last week.

**A:** I'm guessing you were mad at me.

**T:** And imagined I would express may anger today.

**A:** I don't know, maybe I worried that you were going to let me have it, or you would be disappointed in me.

**T:** Anastasia, I was concerned about you last week. In particular, I wanted to make sure you had a ride to get home safely, without attempting to drive yourself.

**A:** You weren't mad?

**T:** It doesn't seem you really believe me.

**A:** Well, no, I mean, you had a right to be mad at me.

**T:** I supposed I did, but have I ever not been honest with you about how I was feeling or what I was thinking before?

**A:** There's always a first for everything.

**T:** Fair enough, but does it seem like I am mad at you or disappointed with you? Or did it seem that way on the phone last week?

**A:** No, it didn't. You just seemed concerned.

**T:** I was. I was very concerned. And I was concerned about you getting drunk could have been connected to the work we've been doing in here.

**A:** Really?

**T:** We've been doing some pretty intense work in here. Alcohol has been one of your escapes. I wondered if we were going too fast, pushing too hard.[13]

**A:** Yeah, but that's my responsibility.

**T:** You going out drinking, that is your responsibility. Us going too fast in here, that's *our* responsibility. And I think that *our* pushing hard in here impacted your choices out there. It was still *your* choice; I don't mean to let you off the hook for that. But many factors and forces influence our choices.

**A:** But I thought you said this is what we needed to be doing.

**T:** I do believe we've been on the right track of important things for you to work on. Maybe we need to just be more aware of the pace we are moving and how you feel about being able to manage it at the time.[14]

As the discussion continued, we addressed many patterns. I commented to Anastasia that although she had improved tremendously in tolerating her emotions, she still tended engage in certain old patterns to help her escape difficult emotions. At this point, it had been 6 months since our conversation about using sex to avoid talking about Sarah's death. I made the following reflection to Anastasia:

**T:** Anastasia, a while ago we discussed that you had been using sex—either as a topic of discussion or engaging in it—to avoid dealing with the difficult emotions around Sarah's death. We worked through that and you were focusing more on your emotions again. After engaging in your emotions for a while, you turned to religion. We discussed that you had been using religion, at the encouragement of your friends, to avoid dealing with the difficult aspects of your emotions, particularly around Sarah's death. You also identified that there seemed to be a part of you that felt it was neces-

---

[13] This illustrates a couple of points. First, it again illustrates the need to move in and out of the depths. Second, it demonstrates Bugental's (1987) idea of aligning with the resistance. I am demonstrating to Anastasia, through the dialogue, that various defenses have been used to help her survive. However, it is also communicating to her that we all have our limits. These may change over time, but at this point we were pushing Anastasia beyond what she could handle.

[14] This dialogue shows the shared responsibility of therapy, while also not taking away Anastasia's own freedom of choice and accompanying responsibility. It may not have been that we were going too fast, but that we were going to fast without attending to making sure Anastasia felt she had the resources to deal with the pace and the emotions that were emerging.

sary to deal with Sarah's death. Following the dream, we went back into your emotions rather intensely, again, for several weeks. Then, you called in drunk, seeming to numb out your emotions. Each time, in these avoidant patterns, I also have felt that you were pushing me away; I didn't feel as connected to you.[15]

In the next session, we picked up with this theme using a version of the two-chair technique. I asked Anastasia to identify the part of her that was resistant to going into her emotions to talk about Sarah. Then I had her imagine in the other chair was the part of her that recognized the need to deal with her emotions and Sarah's death. Anastasia spoke for about 5-minutes, expressing her feelings and fears. One theme that emerged was that she was afraid that if she fully grieved for Sarah then she'd really be gone—from her life and her memories.

As Anastasia moved to the other chair, speaking to the resistant part of herself, she expressed how unhappy she was with life. For the first time, she acknowledged that she did not really know what she was living for [meaninglessness]. She was not expressing any thoughts of suicide or wanting to die, but rather speaking to the depths of her feelings of emptiness about Sarah's death. After stating this, she stopped and looked at me saying:

**A:** You're not going to have me locked up now, are you?
**T:** No, I don't see any reason, as of now, to have you locked up.
**A:** I didn't mean to say that. I kind of got lost in talking to myself there, but when I said it I all of a sudden realized what I had said. I thought you therapist types generally lock people up for statements like that, don't you?
**T:** You therapist types?[16]
**A:** Sorry, but you know what I mean.
**T:** Yes, I know what you mean. Listen, I didn't hear you saying that you were going to kill yourself. I heard you saying you were in a lot of pain.

---

[15] This looks very much like an interpretation again, but my intent is different. I want to focus on reflecting the patterns. I am trying to help Anastasia see the various ways she tries to escape her emotions through defense patterns. I am also highlighting how it impacts our relationship. It is like reflecting with a large mirror once again—a mirror that reflects more than the present moment through reflection the present moment in the context of ongoing patterns. Through this broader reflection, Anastasia can begin to reflect upon her understanding and meaning of what transpired and how it is influencing the current moment.

[16] This shift in language is important, and I would return Anastasia to it later; however, it was not the critical issue at this point. The shift to refer to me as "you therapist types" is an objectifying language, something that had not occurred in a while in our therapy relationship. We later returned to this to better understand its meaning. Anastasia was able to identify that when she thought of me in these terms, as another of the "therapy types," that she was not relating to me as a person, but based on her past experiences (i.e., transference). I continued to point this out when I observed it, often saying, "Am I one of those therapy-types now?" Over time, she became more aware of when this was occurring and would bring it up directly on her own.

**A:** Yes, my life feels pretty empty right now. I miss Sarah and the meaning she brought to my life. I miss my church, even though I am still mad at them and don't want to go back. And I even miss Tim.

**T:** Those were sources of meaning in your life, things worth living for.

**A:** Yes, they were.[17]

This interaction was another critical point in therapy. First, I deepened Anastasia's trust. Previous therapists had quickly rushed to consider hospitalizing Anastasia when she made any statement that could have suggested the possibility of suicide. She stated that she has never really considered harming herself, but her previous therapists could never hear her when she stated she was not intending to harm herself.

Second, Anastasia was able to deepen her understanding of her resistance to dealing with Sarah. She had been in therapy for close to a year at this point. Anastasia had made significant progress over this time, including increasing her ability to tolerate and process emotions, decrease her reliance on sex, alcohol, and drugs to numb out her emotions, and she did not experience depression as frequently or as profoundly. Additionally, she had worked to develop a solid therapy alliance, and she had greater insight and awareness. However, two important issues were becoming increasing evident as necessary to face at this point of therapy. First, she was still avoiding grieving for Sarah. Second, Anastasia was starting to recognize that she had been avoiding developing any sustaining meaning or new relationships of any depth. She had developed many surface relationships, but none that were really meaningful to her.

Anastasia and I used this opportunity to review what she had accomplished in therapy and refocus the future direction of therapy. It was important that Anastasia recognize the gains she had made, particularly to help give her confidence to address these next phases of therapy. I encouraged Anastasia to reflect her perception of her progress and followed this sharing how I felt she had grown and changed. Next, we set course for these next two issues.

---

[17] Notice I never focused on the suicide issue. If by the end of the session I did not have adequate assurance that Anastasia was not going to harm herself, I would have evaluated this before ending the session. However, if I had evaluated for suicide at this moment, it would have breached her trust. Anastasia had already told me pretty bluntly that she was concerned that I would react by hospitalizing her. I wanted to make sure that if suicide is a concern in the future that she would feel safe to talk with me about it and know that I would not jump to conclusions. Instead, I was communicating trust to her and implicitly telling her that in the future I would work with her on these issues and not just immediately rush to hospitalizing her without considering other options. Furthermore, this showed that even though we had a very strong therapy alliance, she still had difficulty fully trusting me on certain issues. Therapists, fearing possible suicide, often immediately pursue suicide before understanding feelings such as this in context This often damages the therapeutic relationship in trust, and is acting upon the therapist's fears for the client's safety before attending to the clients current emotional needs.

Part of integrating and grieving the loss of a loved one is a returning to engagement in the world (Moats & Hoffman, 2015). Often this means deepening existing relationships or developing new, meaningful relationships. Anastasia had lost both Sarah and Tim, but she had not replaced them with any new relationships. Because of this, I would, at times, encourage Anastasia to talk about Sarah in her relationships outside of therapy. She gradually began to focus on the grieving process. As she did this outside of therapy, she started to develop some new relationships with sustaining meaning. The grieving was difficult and painful for Anastasia. In some sessions, I had her bring pictures of Sarah. She told me about the pictures, sometimes sharing stories about Sarah that she had not spoken of since her death. At times, we would place the picture in a chair and use the empty chair technique to facilitate the grieving. She apologized to Sarah several times for not being there more when she was alive and also for not being there the night of her death. She told Sarah what she missed about her and, gradually, she was also able to talk about and grieve the things she did not always like or appreciate about Sarah. It became a full grieving process. It is important to note, too, that in spending almost a year before focusing on the grieving, therapy was able to address the issues that prevented her from being able to grieve for Sarah earlier. These same patterns had made it difficult for Anastasia to work through many other difficult emotions, too. By focusing on the patterns and deeper issues instead of rushing to grieving, we were able to engage in a more through therapy process consistent with Bugental's (1987) idea of life-changing therapy.

Anastasia was beginning to develop more sustaining sources of meaning in her life through the grieving process; however, this was still an area of concern for me, and I brought this up to her. She would regularly mention religion as having been important to her at times in her life, but also that she no longer trusted religion much. She recognized that the political/religious group from her college days was about rebellion. She also recognized problems with the Christian church with which she later affiliated.

> **T:** You know, I am noticing that religion seems to be coming up more and more in sessions again.
> **A:** I know, that must mean I haven't worked through my anger at them yet, right?
> **T:** Now you know I'm not going to answer that for you.
> **A:** Yeah, but I guess that must be what it is.
> **T:** Well, let's look at it. Give it some real consideration, not one of the "I guess" answers.
> **A:** Okay (pause). It seems like I must be angry with them, but I really don't feel it. I mean, I've kind of just come to accept that it was their limitations.
> **T:** What I hear you talking about with religion are the people that failed you. Is that all there was to your involvement in religion?
> **A:** No, well, at least I didn't think so, but... well, maybe it was.

> **T:** Anastasia, you have to decide if a spiritual perspective is something you want to pursue or not. It seems you have been focusing a lot on the religious people that failed you, and not much on what the religion itself was all about.

Over the next several weeks, Anastasia began to re-examine her religious beliefs and what religion was all about for her. She elected not to return to her own church, but started to explore different avenues of spirituality, including different world religions. Eventually, she returned to a Christian church that was much more open to different perspectives as compared with her previous church. She became involved in the service aspects of the church, which she found deeply meaningful. She also started to develop new meaningful relationships at this church and began dating again. It was at this time that we began talking about ending therapy.

**Final Phase.** As we began talking about ending therapy, the topic of Tim came up regularly. Anastasia reported that she recognized that Tim was not the best person for her to marry, but that she deeply loved him. The ending process of therapy often brings up unresolved grief from the past, and it was evident that this was what was occurring with Tim. Anastasia focused so much on grieving for Sarah that she never realized she also needed to grieve the loss of Tim. After a couple of sessions, she called Tim and asked to get together. Tim, too, had struggled greatly since their separation. They were able to have a good talk and say a proper goodbye.

After this diversion, we resumed working toward the ending of therapy. I emphasized to Anastasia the importance of having closure with our relationship, especially given how difficult it had been for her to work through so many endings of relationships before. I encouraged Anastasia to write a summary of therapy, including what she felt she accomplished and what areas she still struggled with in life. Anastasia retuned the next session having written about the process of therapy and her accomplishments; however, she was resistant to acknowledging what she wanted to change or improve. In discussing this, Anastasia said that she did not want me to leave with the feeling that I had not completed the process with her. After assuring her that I knew none of us are ever a *finished product*, she was able to consider the issues that still lingered. She recognized that she still struggled with being open in relationships and felt guilty anytime she experienced anger. She also still deeply missed Sarah, especially on birthdays and holidays. However, Anastasia's statement in the last session helped me to know that she was ready to end therapy:

> **A:** I guess I know now that life is never complete and, after all, what fun would it be if it was. I am okay with still hurting and know that is part of what it is about. I'll think of you when I suffer from now on—not in a bad way—but in recognition that you helped me learn how to suffer and that

it's not such a bad thing. But I'll also be sure to think of you and be thankful sometimes when things are going well, too.... I'll miss you.

I let the *I guess* go this one time.

## Concluding Remarks

This case, as is hopefully evident, illustrates Anastasia's wrestling with the existential givens and her existential pain while also illustrating the psychotherapy process. A few concluding comments might help to frame this case. First, many people are often surprised by the conversational tone used by many existential-humanistic therapists. Many therapies utilize a special and seemingly mysterious way of communicating with their clients. Others rely upon an excessively technical language. Existential-humanistic therapists may use these at times, as well; however, part of the art of existential-humanistic psychotherapy is being able to be therapeutic in a way that is not so distant from the communication of everyday life. Even reflections, when not overused, appear more conversational. The dialogues chosen intentionally include various types of reflections along with here-and-now self-disclosure that involves intentional use of statements and questions, and experiential techniques. Last, the existential themes were evident in the dialogues, even though they were never discussed in the abstract language of the previous chapter.

Therapy, for Anastasia, extended over about 2-years. Existential-humanistic therapy is not always this long, and sometimes much can be accomplished in a few sessions. It was not always as intense as it may appear in the discussion above. As with any long-term therapy process, there were lulls and times where little progress seemed to be occurring. Generally, these did not last long. When they lasted more than several sessions, we discussed this together and were generally able to get therapy back on track. On a couple of these occasions, Anastasia responded with statements such as, "This is what I need right now." It is difficult for therapist not to be critical of the client or themselves when therapy progress is slow, but it is important not to force the therapist's expectations on the client in these situations. After the dialogue in which we addressed the pace of therapy, which was several months into the therapy process, Anastasia become very good at setting the pace and telling me when she needed to slow down.

As therapy concluded, I discussed with Anastasia that she could call me in the future if the need arose. It is not uncommon for clients to set up occasional *check-in sessions*, especially in the first couple of years after therapy. Therapy is an important part of an individual's life and the therapy relationship is often reflected upon well after therapy has ended. It is only natural that clients would want to check in from time-to-time and it is unfortunate that some therapy approaches pathologize such tendencies. As the lead character in Carol Gilligan's (2008) book, *Kyra,* tells her therapist, there is something unnatural about the conclusion of a successful therapy relationship entailing the therapist leaving and a permanent ending of the relationship. For Anastasia, it would be important for me to "still be real," in her words, so she would call from time-to-time with an update for several years. She did not want me to be one aspect of a memory of something she did, but rather an important person who accompanied her on a difficult part of her journey. Anastasia also continued a regular practice of sending a yearly birthday update, letting me know how her life was progressing. For my part, I looked forward to her birthdays. Anastasia would often conclude these updates echoing the sentiment of the final session, "Life is not perfect, but I no longer expect it to be that way."

## References

Bugental, J. F. T. (1987). *The art of the psychotherapist.* New York, NY: Norton.

Gilligan, C. (2008). *Kyra.* New York, NY: Random House.

Hoffman, L., & Moats, M. (2015). Introduction. In L. Hoffman & M. Moats (Eds.), *Capturing shadows: Poetic encounters on the path of grief and loss* (pp. 11-26). Colorado Springs, CO: University Professors Press.

Yalom, I. D. (1995*). Group psychotherapy* (4th ed.) New York, NY: Basic Books.

# Part 2

## East and West Perspectives
on Existential Psychology

# Chapter 3

## Existential-Humanistic Psychology Dialogues in China: Beginning the Conversation

Jennifer Christy Thrash
Francis Kaklauskas
Michael Dow
Elizabeth Saxon
Albert Chan
Louis Hoffman
Mark Yang

A primary purpose of this chapter as well as chapter 4 is to provide a history of the development of existential-humanistic therapy in Southeast Asia and set the stage for the rest of the book. Thus far, the book has provided an overview of existential-humanistic psychology as developed in the United States.[1] In this chapter, which is co-authored by United States and Chinese scholars, we begin to engage the East-West dialogue through the identification of many of the challenges and opportunities inherent in this dialogue. This chapter introduces many of these questions and challenges, but will not fully address them as they will become the premise of the subsequent chapters. The journey of this chapter, and this book, began in 2008 when a group of United States graduate psychology students and their professor journeyed to China to engage with Chinese psychologists about the theory and practice of existential psychology. The trip inspired countless dialogues and revelations regarding the similarities and differences between *East* and *West*, which often overturned expectations. We left with a deeper appreciation for not only how an existential-humanistic psychology might be relevant to China and other regions in Southeast Asia, but also for how a Chinese perspective offers fresh insights for existential-humanistic psychology, as it is practiced in the West. Indeed, since the original version of this chapter, the dialogues emerging from the cross-cultural exchanges that began as detailed

---

[1] As noted in chapter 1, existential psychology began in Europe and there continues to be several schools of existential therapy, as discussed by Cooper (2016). This book focuses mostly on existential-humanistic psychology, which developed in the United States and was strongly influenced by Rollo May and James F. T. Bugental. Some chapters, such as chapter 5, draw more broadly on other existential psychology traditions.

herein have started to influence existential-humanistic psychology in the United States.

## Background

During the past 30 years, China has emerged as an economic, political, and military global power. The Communist Party's reform policies of the 1980s marked the start of China's transformation from an impoverished, agriculturally-based society into an industrial powerhouse with a booming economy growing at a staggering rate of 10% per year over the past decade (The US-China Business Council, 2008). Along with the country's foray into global economic markets came the development of many Western institutions, ideas, and practices, including psychotherapy (Chang, Tong, Qija, & Zeng, 2005). The practice of psychotherapy in China is heavily influenced currently by Western approaches; however, differences between the cultures have led to the development of new hybridized forms of psychology that take into account Chinese cultural beliefs, philosophies, and help-seeking practices.

Chinese natives often demonstrate a preference for short-term, problem-focused psychotherapy that emphasizes symptom removal over personal growth (Chang et al., 2005; see also chapter 3 and 4). Psychotherapists are viewed as expert healers who can provide speedy results. Not surprisingly, behavioral therapy was identified as the most common mode of treatment in mainland China in a 1992 survey (Qian & Chen, 1998). Insight-oriented approaches such as existential and humanistic psychotherapy, with their emphasis on inner emotional life, were slower to gain influence (Chang et al., 2005); however, this appears to be changing. Traditional Chinese culture dictates strict emotive control because it is believed that excessive emotions, desire, and self-indulgence adversely affect the balance of yin and yang and may lead to physical illness (Veith, 1997).

Since the goals of most Western models of psychotherapy emphasize individuation, self-efficacy, and self-actualization, which are goals that may conflict with the Chinese view that the self must be in harmony with the collective—the question of whether Western psychological interventions are appropriate and effective with Chinese nationals is often queried (Hoffman, Stewart, Warren, & Meek, 2009; Mosig, 2006). In fact, the underutilization of mainstream mental health services by Chinese living in the United States is often attributed to disparities between Western models of treatment and traditional Chinese beliefs (Chang et al., 2005). However, demand for counseling services in China is growing at an exponential rate, far outpacing the ability of the country's small, but growing number of trained mental health professionals to provide services. As the need for mental health services expands, no single therapeutic approach is likely to adequately and appropriately meet the variety of demands.

While existential-humanistic psychology is relatively new to China, existential philosophy is not new. The most spectacular intellectual event in the reconstruction of Chinese consciousness during the 1980s was a great debate among academics on culture (Lin, 1993). The discussion included the study of Chinese premodern traditional culture and then spread to the comparative study of Chinese and Western cultures and the theories and methods of cultural analysis (Lin, 1994). A much more radical departure was identified as the *Sartre fever*, *Nietzsche fever*, and *Freud fever* that appeared in the early 1980s. Nietzsche's "transevaluation of all values" (Lin, 1994, p. 622), or rethinking of all values, seemed to have caught the imagination not only of the academic circles, but also of the thinking public. No longer content with understanding and changing the world, many began to search for larger sense of meaning and purpose. Wang Ruoshui, the standard bearer of Marxist humanism in post-Mao China, closed his famous article "In Defense of Humanism," by asserting the reemergence of humanity:

> A specter stalks the earth of China.
> "Who are you?"
> "I am Humanity" (as cited in Lin, 1994, p. 614).

Tradition-based scholars who are versed in Chinese philosophy or familiar with Chinese cultural heritage also recognize the exceedingly rich metaphysical thinking in Confucianism, Taoism, and Buddhism (Lin, 1994). The other strand is Western-based, drawing its inspiration from the existentialist trend on the one hand and Christianity on the other. The debate on culture breathed life into the Chinese soul with ideas and values derived from various cultures, ancient and modern, Eastern and Western.

The discussions of the feasibility of applying natural scientific methodology to the study of humanities constituted another intellectual event in the post-Mao era (Lin, 1993). Jin Guantao, the most influential initiator of the scientist trend, explained that in the past 20 years of his philosophical exploration, epistemology and methodology were only "the beginning of the reconstruction of the edifice of rational philosophy," the peak of which is "the value, the meaningfulness, the ultimate concern for human life" (Guantao, as cited in Lin, p. 178). Through self-assertion, self-exploration, and self-fulfillment (the humanist quest of the new intellectual discourse), a new soul was nurtured by a new culture emerging in China.

Lin, (1994) suggested that Chinese scholars and reformers of the Post-Mao era were influenced by Western thinkers from Kant and Hegel to Nietzsche and Heidegger. Psychology, after decades of being denounced as pseudoscience, suddenly became a serious subject of inquiry with theories of psychoanalysis, humanistic psychology, and developmental psychology drawing the greatest attention. Lin explained that representative works of Freud, Jung, Adler, Fromm, and others were translated and often cited to support new innovations in interpreting Marx.

Depth psychology emerged as the interest of reformers encompassed intuit-ition, inspiration, and creativity as they sought to explore a multilayered, multidimensional, and multifunctional process. Scholars explained inspiration as "the power of intuitive thinking, [which is] formed and developed when the subject uses his personal experience, feeling, and conceptual knowledge, forms, and methods in an integrative, holistic way" (Lin, 1993, p. 176).

Ancient Chinese philosophers and writers have also sought answers to many of the same existential questions posed by Kierkegaard and Nietzsche. For instance, Lao Tzu, author of the famous Taoist treatise the *Tao Te Ching* (Lao-Tzu, Trans, Mitchell, 1998), emphasized that evil is not a force to resist but rather a state of disharmony with the universal process. This freedom from moral cate-gories is similar to the existential notion that there is no absolute evil. Rather, human beings encompass both good and evil (see Bohart, Held, Mendelowitz, & Schneider, 2012; Hoffman, Warner, Gregory, & Fehl, 2011). Lao Tzu also talked frequently of paradoxes and the paradoxical nature of being human; a theme quite prevalent in existential psychology.

Despite the cultural challenges, there is a natural convergence between exis-tential psychology and traditional Chinese thought. When teaching existential psychology in the West, it is not uncommon for students to note how similar it sounds to Eastern thought. It may very well be that no Western psychotherapy theory has as much natural convergence with Eastern thought as existential psychology. However, there are areas of dissonance that come into view when attempting to apply existential ideas to Chinese culture, such as the differing values placed on emotional expression, the importance of individual insight versus familial or societal harmony, and the duration of psychotherapy needed to produce meaningful change.

### Beginning the Dialogue

Five representatives from the Colorado School of Professional Psychology of the University of the Rockies embarked on a trip to China in March, 2008. The goal of the trip was to engage in culturally-sensitive dialogues with Chinese graduate students, professors, and psychotherapists regarding existential-integrative psychology. Louis Hoffman, Francis Kaklauskas, Christy Thrash, Michael Dow, and Elizabeth Saxon were joined in Hong Kong by Mark Yang and Albert Chan in dialogue with the Chinese academic psychology community regarding existential-humanistic psychology and how such a psychology might be applied in the Chi-nese context. The forum for these dialogues included a series of workshops and guest lectures at Chinese colleges and universities in Hong Kong and Beijing. Informal avenues, such as site seeing, multi-course meals, and late-night card games also gave rise to passionate and informative discussions. The expectation was that the Chinese participants would examine models of existential-humanistic psychotherapy within their own cultural context and understanding of psychology while determining for themselves how well the model fit with their clinical settings and clientele.

## Existential Dialogues in Hong Kong

The first East-West dialogue took place on March 16th at the City College of Hong Kong between the Colorado School of Professional Psychology group and Mark Yang's class of masters-level psychology students. After introductions, Yang lectured briefly on the basics of existential-humanistic psychology. A case study was presented by a Hong Kong student and then utilized by the group to illustrate examples of the existential-humanistic approach and to launch discussions and an exchange of ideas between the two groups. The Hong Kong students described typical challenges they face in counseling clients who, due to cultural influences, which include being resistant to sharing emotions, feeling burdened to meet familial obligations, and feeling pressured to succeed financially. Although the Chinese psychology students were enthusiastic about the existential-humanistic approach, they believed that getting their clients to buy into this form of therapy would be difficult as the clients expect the psychotherapist to act as the *expert* and provide a quick, inexpensive fix to their mental health and interpersonal problems. Generally speaking, the existential-humanistic model of psychology does not embrace the *quick fix* approach.

Louis Hoffman and Mark Yang lectured on existential-humanistic psychology at three additional workshops held at the Hong Kong Institute of Christian Counselors from March 17th through March 20th. Francis Kaklauskas, Michael Dow, Christy Thrash, and Elizabeth Saxon gave brief presentations on related topics including mindfulness-based approaches to psychotherapy, Buddhist psychology, and Rollo May's theories regarding myth. Hong Kong students volunteered to provide case demonstrations and present role plays. Hong Kong psychotherapists had already considered many of the difficulties of this cross-cultural integration, from the applicability of William James's functionalism to contemporary Chinese culture to whether Freud, Adler, Jung, or Klein had the most accurate and applicable theory of personality.

Through dialogue, it was evident to all engaged in the discussions that while Hong Kong has been more influenced by the Western culture than other Chinese cities, traditional Chinese cultural beliefs run much deeper than the recent impact of Westernization. For generations, the Chinese have emphasized the importance of the collective identity, group and familial affiliation, filial piety, traditional gender and family roles, and not *losing face*. An applicable psychotherapy needs to recognize or incorporate these cultural subtexts without pathologizing them, as is often done from a Western perspective.

To a surprising extent, the case examples that Hong Kong students presented were similar to those with which Western psychologists are familiar, characterizeed by client complaints of financial stress, depression, relationship problems, and anxiety about career decisions. However, there were some striking differences; in the West, mental health care is generally socially acceptable while, among the Chinese, mental health issues continue to carry stigma and shame. A pressure to conform to societal norms appeared to occupy a more central place in concerns of the average person, including both clients and psychotherapists.

## Existential Dialogues in Beijing

The next stop for the Colorado School of Professional Psychology contingent was Beijing, where Louis Hoffman and Mark Yang lectured on existential psychology at a one-day workshop held at the China Youth Polytechnic Institute on March 21st. Louis Hoffman also demonstrated a role play with a Chinese student based on an actual case involving a hotline client experiencing suicidal and homicidal ideation. Group discussions between the Chinese students and the Western visitors followed. Topics included Maslow's hierarchy of needs, Victor Frankl's book *Man's Search for Meaning*, and the differences between existential guilt and neurotic guilt.

During the Beijing training, some of the challenges that arose included issues with translating the more abstract, Western conceptualizations of existential-humanistic psychology into language familiar to the Chinese. Quite often the nuance of ideas was lost in translation and, as a result, questions such as the one regarding the difference between existential and neurotic guilt were repeated. Additionally, the practical matter of translating Hoffman's role play with the Chinese student was slow, as it required two interpreters translating consecutively so that both Chinese-speaking and English-speaking audiences could understand the exchanges. These and other challenges, as well as congruencies and future opportunities, will be discussed in the following section.

## Challenges and Future Opportunities

There are obstacles to the realization of existential-humanistic psychology as a widely-used model of psychotherapy in China. Differences between Western and Eastern views of the self, specifically the importance that the Chinese place on the collective identity and their emphasis on group and familial affiliation, appear to contradict existential themes of individual introspection and choice. However, it is important to note that existential-humanistic psychology is not essentially connected to individualistic perspectives, as often perceived. Furthermore, there has been more attention given to the importance of collectivist perspectives in existential-humanistic psychology in the last 10-years (Hoffman, Cleare-Hoffman, & Jackson, 2014).

The widespread use of behavioral models of psychotherapy in China poses another challenge to introducing existential-humanistic psychology as a viable mode of treatment. Problems with translation create a formidable obstacle to those wishing to convey the tenets of existential-humanistic psychology to

Chinese-speaking audiences. Over the last 10-years, working with a more consistent group of translators has begun to address this limitation. Furthermore, cultural taboos against the open expression of emotion are also viewed by many as a problem in adopting a mode of psychotherapy that encourages emotional exploration and expression. This taboo against open expression of emotions does appear to be changing to some degree, and often the therapy context appears to grant an exception.

In addition to challenges and obstacles, there are also many opportunities and convergences. When the disparities between Eastern and Western views are investigated at a deeper level, congruencies start to emerge, and opportunities for Eastern and Western schools of thought to engage in constructive dialogue present themselves.

## Western and Eastern Views of Self

Historically, existential psychology focuses on an individualistic view of the self, which is conceived as engaging in various personal struggles between (a) freedom and responsibility, (b) expansion versus constriction, and (c) the maladaptive defenses developed to avoid confronting the anxiety of death (Schneider, 2008a; 2008b). The interdependent, family-based nature of the Chinese self, cultural norms against emotional exploration and self-absorption, as well as differing views on issues of authority and power, all appear, at least on the surface, to be incongruent with these basic tenets of existential-humanistic psychology. However, as noted, while the more extreme individualistic perspectives do exist in existential psychology, some perceptions of existential thought, which are rooted in excessive individualism, are inaccurate.

Chinese society was built on Confucian values, which acknowledged piety, obedience and respect as the primary virtues while maintaining a vast web of communications and economic relations on the basis of a shared sense of what could and could not be done (Malloch, 2006). The Chinese parents' perception of attributes of the ideal child are closely related to traditional values in Chinese culture and include good academic outcome, positive attitude toward studying, fulfillment of responsibility in studying, and high education attainment (Shek & Chan, 1999). The Chinese term *tinghua* means, "you should listen to your parent," and is sometimes understood as conforming to one's parents.

The concept of familial piety emerged repeatedly in the dialogues with Chinese psychotherapists. Contemporary Chinese often appear conflicted between respecting their long cultural and family histories and adopting the individualistic orientation towards life that predominates in Western societies. Individual growth, if too far afield, is often viewed as a threat that will disturb the harmony of the collective whole. These forces clash powerfully, and no simple answer for this dialectic is readily available for any unique individual or for the culture at large.

Conversely, these incongruencies offer a window of opportunity to explore how Eastern thought might sharpen and improve Western existential psychological theories. Rather than encouraging the Chinese to change their views of the world and the self, perhaps Western existential psychologists could strive to integrate more Eastern conceptions into their theories by giving more credence to the interrelatedness of human beings. In many ways, this is already inherent in the existential understanding of the paradoxes of self, but it has received only limited attention in the psychological literature (see Hoffman et al, 2009) and more often has been misrepresented in many portrayals of existential thought. This challenge is also addressed by Chan in Chapter 19.

**Emotional Expression**
Emotion, as we have noted, is another challenge for existential-humanistic psychology in Eastern settings. Again, this may not be as difficult to overcome as it may initially appear. Traditional Chinese poetry, for example, is often described as expressing emotions directly via visual imagery of the natural world (Sun, 1995). The speaker implies emotion powerfully through his or her selection of images and word choice and, one could argue, expresses it even more directly, but without using emotion-oriented words attributed to the self (Owen, 1980; Sun, 1995). One might consider that there are alternative, less individually centered forms of emotional expression that represent equally existentially honest confrontations with life than the Western style of more overt personal expression of *deep* emotion. Both Americans and Chinese, alike, benefit from examining the ways in which cultural influences have shaped their understanding of human behavior, thought processes, and emotions.

Many potential answers to the challenges also emerged through the dialogues. For example, the most difficult problem that seemed to emerge repeatedly was the avoidance of overt emotional expression in Chinese culture. Expression of emotion is considered risky as it threatens the peace of the collective. Over-emotionality is seen as the gateway to disharmony and conflict. Existential therapy, as a phenomenological and experiential therapy, values the experiencing and expressing of emotion. The example that emerged in one of the case discussions in Hong Kong was that the experiencing and expressing of emotion does not need to be *Hollywood emotion*. A person can quietly, calmly, and subtly experience deep levels of emotion and interact from this place without the more dramatic expressions of the emotional experience. The lesson learned was that emotional expression is no less necessary in China; however, it may look quite different than it typically does in the United States.

**Lost in Translation**
Problems with translation offer another challenge to the development of existential psychology in China. Direct translations of Western texts into Chinese are limited three concerns: language, the translator's understanding of the topics, and cultural biases (Chang et al., 1998). The same limitations exist when English-

speaking educators present complex, abstract concepts to Chinese-speaking audiences. Additionally, few existential psychological texts have actually been translated into Chinese, although this is changing, as will be discussed in the following chapter.

In Hong Kong, the dialogues were fast paced and fruitful, as most of the individuals in the audience were able to discuss the topics in English and even help with the translation of some difficult concepts. Many psychological words do not have an equivalent Cantonese translation, and it was typical to have discussions in which most of the words were spoken in Cantonese with terms such as *countertransference* and *meta-analysis* spoken in English. Some students used German, French, and Japanese words from original texts in addition to explaining the differences between the Cantonese and Mandarin understanding of psychological terms. This created an atmosphere that clearly illustrated how powerfully language impacts thought and culture.

In Beijing, our dialogues were slower as most communication had to be translated by multiple interpreters. As in Hong Kong, the audiences wanted their Western guests to provide examples of what psychotherapy looks like in North America. Role playing produced a fascinating slowing of the therapeutic process. A Chinese student speaking Mandarin presented a client. This communication was translated into English and then the English reply was translated back into Mandarin. Although one might imagine that such a process would become tedious, the opposite was, in fact, true. During the translation process, all involved had additional time to digest the content and feeling of each statement. The cultural norms and niceties of communication were stripped away. This produced more direct communication that quickly moved to the heart of the matter. With these particular challenges of language and translation come the opportunities for Chinese scholars to adapt concepts of existentialism to their own vernacular, essentially creating their own vocabulary in which to express existential concepts.

## The Prevalence of Brief Therapy

As mentioned previously, the pragmatic approach of behavioral therapy is much more common in China than insight-oriented therapies. According to Chang et al. (1998), mental health services are frequently provided in mainland China via general outpatient hospital clinics. These services generally consist of 10 to 20-minute drop-in appointments during which the patient receives a brief assessment, is given direct advice, psychoeducation, supportive listening, and prescription medication, if needed. An ongoing, therapeutic relationship is not commonly developed and follow-up appointments are not scheduled.

For example, because many Chinese people put considerable emphasis on academic achievement, therapists can design courses or programs that are educational in nature. Instructions using a cognitive-behavioral training approach within a psychosocial educational intervention might generate better outcomes within a traditional Chinese population than an emotion-focused intervention

(Chan & Palley, 2005). As the need is great and resources are minimal, such adaptations are necessary and appropriate. Until more psychological resources are made available, it may be beneficial for Chinese psychologists to develop similar educational and consulting adaptations with existential-humanistic sensitivities along with the more traditional existential therapy options. Some of this is being done through the International Institute for Existential-Humanistic Psychology (IIEHP; www.iiehp.org). For example, IIEHP is developing courses on poetry, healing, and growth to be offered in China that incorporate existential-humanistic perspectives.

It is becoming common for people to comment on the similarity between Eastern thought and existential psychology. Both share an appreciation of suffering, paradox, and introspection. The resemblance between writers such as Lao Tzu, Zhuangzhi, and many existential writers is also quite startling. They share a recognition that the deeper changes often occur slowly. However, many in China, despite the recognition of needing discipline and time for deeper change, see psychotherapy in a different context. It may be that existential-humanistic psychotherapy, even in the therapeutic applications, needs to be re-envisioned, at times, to meet certain cultural needs that mandate a more time-limited focus. Longer-term approaches could be conceptualized as connected to a different type of change that is slower, deeper, and akin to change as discussed by the Taoist philosophers. As noted in chapter 1, similar adaptations already exist.

Given the significant need for mental health services and the shortage of mental health professionals, it is only to be expected that market forces will create a demand for brief, pragmatic approaches that allow a larger volume of clients to be seen. However, this need not be seen as antithetical to the development of more open-ended approaches. In fact, the familiarity of brief therapy among Chinese is a potential stepping stone to introduce more ongoing, intensive models of psychotherapy such as existential-humanistic therapy.

While there are many psychological problems that can be addressed in a brief way, there are many others which only yield to a more in-depth approach. As awareness of the need for mental health services in China increases, especially in the wake of the devastating 2008 Sichuan earthquake, the Chinese are likely to be more willing to explore alternatives to short-term psychological interventions. Indeed, as more and more of the younger generation are becoming better educated and exposed to Western influences, there is more appreciation for a variety of therapy approaches, including emotionally-focused and insight-oriented therapy offered by existential-humanistic psychologists. Beyond pragmatism, the younger generation are more and more interested in self-exploration and exploring the ultimate concerns in their individual lives.

**The Importance of Choice**
Many Westerners who interact with Asian cultures mistakenly believe that the natives blindly embrace a collective identity, without thought or choice. In fact, there has been an ongoing debate in China regarding the nature of self and culture

for the past 4 decades. The first signs of the *revival of human nature* or the *humanist quest* appeared in the late 1960s (Lin, 1993).

When the era of reform and opening up begin in 1978, cultural change emerged as the central concern of the discourse regarding China's modernization (Lin, 1993). Two concepts preoccupied the participants: self and culture. The urge for self-realization merged with the quest for cultural identity, foreshadowing a long process of the rebirth of China's soul. The discussions yielded a decisive step toward the rediscovery of individuals in contemporary China by triggering a "thought emancipation movement" (p. 614) that spread the message of independent thinking across the entire country.

Similarly, possible resolutions to the collectivist challenge also emerged. It may be, too, that much of existential psychology has been over identified with individualism. Perhaps, deep in the Chinese collective psyche, there is a fear that self-awareness of emotion creates conflict with others and personal growth is too individualistic (see also Ch. 22). Existential philosophy and psychology, engaged at a deep level, emphasizes the limitation of individual striving and recognizes the power and importance of many levels of interrelationship.

Nonetheless, there remains an individualist slant to much of the Western existentialist thinking. The Chinese participants, however, did not consider this as big a challenge as the presenters anticipated. The lesson, which emerged, was that the Chinese recognized the value of individual choice, but valued the choice to prioritize the collective. Thus, choice and the recognition that one must own one's choices are shared by both cultures; the different cultures simply value different decisions.

## Future Directions

A number of the contributors to this book besides the authors of this chapter, including Myrtle Heery, Erik Craig, Kirk Schneider, Ilene Serlin, and Ed Mendelowitz have made trips to Eastern countries that have created excitement about the future of this dialogue. The First International Conference on Existential Psychology was held in China in 2010, and three subsequent conferences have followed. Chapter 4, as well, discusses many other developments that have occurred since the original publication of *Existential Psychology East-West* in 2009.

Due to the devastation left in the wake of the 2008 earthquake in Sichuan Province, China recently has been facing a mental health crisis of unimaginable proportions. The official death toll stands at 69,107 with an estimated 10,000 school children among the victims (Wong, 2008). Grieving parents who have lost their only offspring due to China's one-child per family law have been particularly traumatized. Brief therapy focused on symptom alleviation is not likely to bring relief to the thousands who have lost close family members and friends, not to mention their homes and livelihoods. Existential issues also have been brought to the forefront of Chinese mental health needs through this tragedy and no doubt will need continued exploration over time. Since the Sichuan earthquake, there has been an increased awareness in China of the need to train psychotherapists in trauma work. A number of existential-humanistic therapists from China, including Mark Yang and Xuefu Wang, have been active in developing and expanding training programs in existential-humanistic therapy that help meet these expanding needs. A number of Western psychologists, including Louis Hoffman, Erik Craig, Ilene Serlin, Richard Bargdill, Michael Moats, Jason Dias, Monica Mansilla, Stanley Krippner, and Todd DuBose have been active in collaborating on these trainings.

## References

Bohart, A. C., Held, B. S., Mendelowitz, E., & Schneider, K. J. (Eds.). (2012). *Humanity's dark side: Evil, destructive experience, and psychotherapy.* Washington, DC: American Psychological Association.

Chang, D.F., Tong, J., Qija, S, & Zeng, Q. (2005). Letting a hundred flowers bloom: Counseling and psychotherapy in the People's Republic of China. *Journal of Mental Health Counseling, 27* (2), pp. 104-114

Chan, C. L., & Palley, H. A. (2005). The use of traditional Chinese culture and values in social work health care related interventions in Hong Kong. *Health and Social Work, 30* (1), 76-78.

Cooper, M. (2016). *Existential therapies* (2nd ed.). Thousand Oaks, CA: Sage.

Hoffman, L., Cleare-Hoffman, H. P., & Jackson, T. (2014). Humanistic psychology and multiculturalism: History, current status, and advancements. In K. J. Schneider, J. F. Pierson & J. F. T. Bugental (Eds.), *The handbook of humanistic psychology: Theory, research, and practice* (2nd edition; pp. 41-55). Thousand Oaks, CA: Sage.

Hoffman, L., Stewart, S., Warren, D., & Meek., L. (2009). Toward a sustainable myth of self: An existential response to the postmodern condition. *Journal of Humanistic Psychology, 49*, 135-173.

Hoffman, L., Warner, H. J., Gregory, C., & Fehl, S. (2011). Existential-integrative perspectives on the psychology of evil. In J. H. Ellens (Ed.), *Explaining evil (Vol. 3: Approaches, responses, solutions*, pp. 263-286). Santa Barbara, CA: Praeger.

Holyoak, L. (2007). Obstacles to rural development in China: Local minorities, cadres, and ritual. *Urban Anthropology & Studies of Cultural Systems & World Economic Development, 36*(1-2), 73-88.

Lin, T. (1993). A search for China's soul. *Daedalus, 122*(2), 171-181.

Lin, T. (1994). Subjectivity: Marxism and "The Spiritual" in China since Mao. *Philosophy East & West, 44*(4), 613-638.

Malloch, T. R. (2006). *Spiritual enterprise.* New York, NY: Encounter Books.

Mosig, Y. D. (2006). Conceptions of the self in Western and Eastern psychology. *Journal of Theoretical and Philosophical Psychology, 26*, 39-50.

Qian, M. & Chen, Z. (1998). Behavior therapy in the People's Republic of China. In T. P. S. Oei (Ed.), *Behavior therapy and cognitive behavior therapy in Asia* (pp. 33 – 46). Glebe, New South Wales: Edumedia.

Schneider, K. J. (2008a). The theory of the existential-integrative (EI) approach. In K. J. Schneider (Ed.), *Existential-integrative psychotherapy: Guideposts to the core of practice* (pp. 35-48). New York, NY: Routledge.

Schneider, K. J. (2008b). Therapeutic implications of the theory. In K. J. Schneider (Ed.), *Existential-integrative psychotherapy: Guideposts to the core of practice* (pp. 49-87)). New York: Routledge.

Shek, D. T. L., & Chan, L. K. (1999). Hong Kong Chinese parents' perceptions of the ideal child. *Journal of Psychology, 133*(3), 291.

Sing-Kiat Ting, R. & Watson, T. (2007). Is suffering good? An explorative study on the religious persecution among Chinese pastors. *Journal of Psychology and Theology, 35*(3), 202-211.

Sun, C. C. (1995). *Pearls from the dragon's mouth: Evocation of scene and feeling in Chinese poetry*. Ann Arbor, MI: University of Michigan Press.

Veith, I. (1997). *Huang Ti nei ching su wen: The yellow emperor's classic of internal medicine*. Selangor Darul Ehsan, Malaysia: Pelanduck.

The US - China Business Council. (2008, January 31). *Forecast 2008: China's economy*. Retrieved from: http://uschina.org/ public/documents/2008/02/2008-china-economy.pdf

Wong, E. (2008, June 4). Chinese Stifle Grieving Parents' Protest of Shabby School Construction. *The New York Times*. Retrieved from: http://www.nytimes.com/2008/06/04/world/asia/04china.html?scp=2&sq=Chinese+Parents&st=nyt

# Chapter 4

## Further Development of Existential-Humanistic Dialogues in Southeast Asia

Anne Hsu, Rodger Broomé, Monica Mansilla, Evone Phoo, Jason Dias, Michael Moats, Louis Hoffman, and Mark Yang

This chapter is a collaborative effort to provide a synopsis of 10 years of dialogue on existential psychology, particularly existential-humanistic psychology, between the East and the West. This chapter builds off chapter 3, which discusses the early development of the dialogues prior to the First International Conference on Existential Psychology held in Nanjing, China, in 2010. We begin with an overview of the first several International Conferences on Existential Psychology, which first sowed the seeds for the emergent dialogues that have developed since this time. Over the years, what began to take shape is a developing international existential psychology training model as well as the spreading of existential-humanistic psychology beyond greater China. To better contextualize the challenges and opportunities ahead, a basic descriptive synthesis of the development of psychology along with the economical, spiritual, and mental health climate in various parts of Asia is provided. Future directions regarding culturally inclusive research and practices, and standardized training of international existential psychology are suggested.

### The International Conference on Existential Psychology

The First International Conference on Existential Psychology took place in 2010 in Nanjing, China. Xuefu Wang, Mark Yang, and Louis Hoffman served as the co-chairs of the conference, which was held at Nanjing Xiaozhuang University and drew a crowd of several hundred attendees. The first edition of *Existential Psychology East-West* was published prior to this conference with the intention of providing an initial foundation for dialogue. The first conference provided an opportunity for scholarly exchange, but also had the added benefit of creating opportunity for developing personal and professional relationships as well as collaborative research and scholarship. Westerners not only offered their perspectives of Western psychology, but also shared pictures and small gifts that represented their home states and subcultures. Easterners shared their perspectives of how they see psychology being utilized within the varied cultures within China, as well as presenting their history, cultural gifts, personal life stories, and delicious cuisine. Both the East and West participants were appreciative for the space given to one another to share themselves and of the very act of sharing ourselves with one another. It was a common statement that the most valuable exchanges came in the personal settings granted by the conference.

A number of publications emerged from the first conference, including a special section of *The Humanistic Psychologist* (Vol. 39, Section 3; Dias, Chan, Ungvarsky, Oraker, & Cleare-Hoffman, 2011; Hoffman & Cleare-Hoffman, 2011; Mendelowitz, 2011; Moats, Claypool, & Saxon, 2011; Schneider, 2011; Wang, 2011; Yang & Hoffman, 2011) and presentations at the American Psychological Association (Bargdill, Hoffman, Kuriansky, & Zelinski, 2011; Hoffman, Yang, Claypool, Serlin, Schneider, & Gordon, 2011). While many of the papers and presentations were based upon Western presentations in China, some were inclusive of Chinese perspectives and experiences emergent from the cross-cultural dialogues.

The First International Conference on Existential Psychology helped to spur interest in Chinese perspectives on existential psychology among scholars from the West. At the first conference, many leading voices in existential-humanistic psychology in the West, including Kirk Schneider, Ilene Serlin, Erik Craig, and Ed Mendelowitz, participated in the conference. The sharing of experiences from these and other Western scholars and students stimulated interest and curiosity pertaining to how the cross-cultural dialogues could help advance and energize existential psychology.

The flexibility of existential-humanistic psychology helped facilitate addressing cultural differences and honoring the respective cultures. Honoring differences and acknowledging similarities were important themes and continued to be central in the conferences that followed. The progression of the following conferences has evolved including more intentionality in creating dialogue and building from the lessons of the first conference.

The Second International Conference on Existential Psychology took place in 2012 and was held at Fudan University in Shanghai, China, building upon the effort and learning from previous conferences. There was an intentional effort to create more dialogue by having sessions that included presenters from both the East and West. The conference again drew a large crowd resulting in a sold-out conference.

In contrast with the First International Conference of Existential Psychology, with a number of keynote presentations featuring one speaker addressing a large audience with limited reciprocal interaction, the Second International Conference of Existential Psychology increased the number of break-out sessions between Western and Eastern speakers. The rooms were smaller than in previous iterations but also more intimate, with plenty of interaction between scholars and students. Although dialogue was always a primary goal, the lessons learned from earlier conferences enhanced the dialogue focus in subsequence conferences.

The Third International Conference on Existential Psychology was held at Guangzhou at the Guang Dong University of Foreign Studies in 2014. Eastern and Western presenters gave keynote addresses and breakout sessions, with only the preconference and post-conference workshops being weighed with more

Western presenters for local practitioners and students. This conference welcomed personal life stories of meaning, relationships, culture, and belonging through the keynote stage by presenters, such as Erik Craig from the West and Anne Hsu from the East. Graduate student and therapists' presentations were also encouraged by their mentors, who embodied humanistic and generativity ideals. The structural set up allowed for varied breadth and depth of dialogue to take place. Unique to this conference was incorporating the use of the hosting university's students to facilitate translations of slides, interpretation of presentations, and guiding Western presenters during their stay. Because of the frequency of interaction, the East-West dialogue that began prior to the arrival quickly strengthened upon meeting in person and continued directly between Western presenters and the local students.

In many ways, consistent with the previous conferences, this conference solidified Western presenters' relationships among one another with hopes and plans for future collaborations as well as continued dialogue with Eastern presenters and students. The natural development of friendship and colleagueship took place between meals and tending to travel and lodging needs with enduring interaction assisted by the use of social media. What resulted were relationships among and between presenters and local students through dialogues of meaning, relationships, culture, and belonging, which were the themes of this conference.

The Fourth International Conference on Existential Psychology was originally planned for Beijing; however, it was moved to the University of Hong Kong. This cosmopolitan hub of the world brought people together from various places in the world and various ethnicities and nationalities. This conference differed from the previous ones in that it was the most intimate in scale and was also the first conference that prominently featured African American scholar-practitioners with Theopia Jackson and Nathaniel Granger Jr. Jackson presenting on therapeutic praxis inspired by theories, concepts, and themes such as generational trauma, collectivity, colonization, and family systems. Granger presented on the experiences and dynamics of race relations in the United States through an existential-psychological lens, which provided deep insights for those attending. The intimate scale and sharing during the sessions of the conference was fruitful and moving. Cross-cultural connections again were made by conference participants both during the sessions and in-between sessions at breaks, meals, and social events.

Granger became a center figure in a discussion of race, privilege, and discrimination during a social gathering in the hotel lobby. The gathering involved women and men from various nationalities, ethnicities, socioeconomic classes, and races. Discussion involved debate about social categories and their meaningful consequences in different social contexts. Much of the discourse revolved around dimensions of human and social difference that constitute the root justification of *othering* one another as person(s) in order to self-identify in a particular way (Brons, 2015; de Beauvior, 2012; Hegel, 1977). The struggle was both emotional, yet demonstrative that international efforts to gather and discuss matters of difference are possible and do help us all to grow. While this small collection would never create a wave in the Global frame, these kinds of encounters send ripples across the waters of the individuals taking the experiences back to their own worlds.

## Developing a Certificate Training Model in Asia

In 2011, Mark Yang, Louis Hoffman, Jason Dias, Trent Claypool, and Michael Moats formed the Zhi Mian International Institute for Existential-Humanistic Psychology as a training organization located in the State of Colorado in the United States with intentions to support the development of training in China and Southeast Asia. The organization, which now goes by the abbreviated name of the International Institute for Existential-Humanistic Psychology (IIEHP; see www.iieghp.org), began developing collaborative relationships with institutions in the United States and China to establish systematic training in existential-humanistic psychology in China and Southeast Asia.

Mark Yang and Louis Hoffman, also the founders of the International Conference on Existential Psychology, began envisioning a systematic training program in China that would integrate Eastern and Western perspectives on existential psychology. The initial trainings, which began in 2014, relied more heavily on practitioners from the West. However, 5 years after offering the first certificate program, select students from the initial certificate program now teach in a complimentary fashion with instructors from the West in a new 2-year certificate program.

The initial certificate programs were year-long in duration consisting of two separate week-long modules each year. For students who were interested in advanced clinical training, both face-to-face supervision conducted in Chinese by Mark Yang and online supervision with translation was offered by practitioners from the West. The first year of the program focused on humanistic psychology as a foundation for the second year that focused on existential psychology. Yang and Hoffman were each responsible for teaching one of the on-the-ground, week-long modules each year. Given Yang and Hoffman's affiliation with Saybrook University, students and faculty from various programs at Saybrook joined in the opportunity to assist in the various training workshops throughout the years including the initial 2-year certificate.

While the therapy training is rooted in Western models of existential and humanistic therapy, the trainings have always sought to include cultural critique, cultural adaptation, and the incorporation of indigenous Chinese existential perspectives (see Yang & Hoffman, 2014, 2019). Thus, the focus of this certification is to bring the Western based philosophy of existential and humanistic psychology the East, while constantly considering its cultural validity and applicability in the East. The trainings aim to reinforce the awareness of the intuitive and relational stands in the humanistic and existential tradition, highlighting a non-prescriptive structure, which has been described as an art rather than a science (Bugental, 1999). This focus emphasizes therapists' ability to prioritize focusing on process over content, although not discounting the content.

The humanistic and the existential certificates in China have been conducted separately while highlighting the unique philosophical and psychological foundation of each theory. The uniqueness and convergences between humanistic and existential psychology are discussed, considering the differences between the two approaches, such as the fact that humanistic psychology sees being humans as foundationally good (Hoffman, 1988, Rogers, 1961, 1959), while existential psychology augments this perspective adding that within the foundational goodness of people also exists a latent potential for evil, better understood through the daimonic (May, 1969). Finally, these certificates place special attention on the differences between the application of humanistic and existential approaches within either individualistic or collectivist cultures. Moreover, the two certificates attempt to bring union between the knowledge of Western Psychology and the wisdom of Eastern philosophy.

## Expanding into Malaysia and Taipei

Malaysia's psychology practice has been heavily influenced by the climate of American psychology; therefore, the predominant psychotherapy and counseling approach in Malaysia has been Cognitive Behavioral Therapy. Some other psychotherapeutic approaches slowly on the rise are Family Therapy, Acceptance and Commitment Therapy, Choice Theory/Reality Therapy, Psychodynamic, and Expressive Arts Related Therapy. Generally, existential-humanistic psychology is an unfamiliar territory to many mental health practitioners in Malaysia. Hence, to organize any existential-humanistic related training or conference is a challenge due to its limited recognition. However, the thirst among the mental health practitioners to gain exposure to the existential-humanistic psychology is apparent, as evidenced by the positive responses to the existential-humanistic psychology related workshops and conferences held in the past 4 years.

When the Malaysia's First Existential-Humanistic Psychology Conference was held in June 2016, it attracted curious young minds, primarily undergraduates and new practitioners with little understanding of existential-humanistic psychology, but appreciative of the chance to learn more about the approach. Approximately 200 participants attended the conference. The majority of the speakers at the conference were from the United States, and presentations at the conference revolved around the theme of authenticity. The post-conference feedback was mostly positive. Many said that they have never attended a conference where the most fundamental questions in life were explored, and they felt a sense of enlightenment from the conference. There were also overwhelming requests for more conferences in the future. Therefore, a second conference was held in June of 2018 which revolved around the theme of grief and loss. This time around, there were more speakers and presenters originating from Malaysia, with nearly

300 attendees, which provided evidence of the growing appreciation for existential-humanistic psychology.

With the culture of psychotherapy practice in Malaysia being largely skill-based approaches, most trainings and conferences focus on content skills and applicability in scientific practice. In contrast, existential-humanistic therapy emphasizes the process and art of the therapeutic relationships. Thus, it is not surprising that few veteran therapists attended the conference. The obstacle in raising therapists' awareness of existential-humanistic therapy lies in the local attitude that topics such as meaning in life, death, and responsibility are spiritual and philosophical rather than practical, thus overlooking its place in psychology.

In June of 2018, the first existential and humanistic psychology conference was held in Taipei, Taiwan. This conference focused on grieving, loss, and post-traumatic growth. The attendees were largely comprised of international exchange students of various backgrounds including first responders. A small number of multidisciplinary scholars and practitioners from Asia, including individuals from Hong Kong, Japan, and Taipei, also participated. This response generated more conversations and curiosity and set the stage for future collaborations with broader inclusion of local psychologists and therapy practitioners.

## Bringing Existential Humanistic Training to the Middle East

Qatar and the United Arab Emirates are two affluent Middle Eastern countries that are undergoing rapid development. These countries are highly influenced by the practice of psychology from the cognitive behavioral and positive psychology perspectives. However, these two countries are also quite distinct in their approach to mental health. The United Arab Emirates has several counseling centers. Most of these centers are run by psychologists and psychotherapists influenced by cognitive behavior and positive psychology approaches. Conversely, Qatar does not have any mental health services solely based on psychology and/or psychotherapy. Qatar's mental health needs are managed through psychiatry and some psychologists practicing as part of multidisciplinary health teams in hospitals or health centers. In addition, these two countries do not have access to mental health training. Thus, only the more financially privileged practitioners have access to training, often through traveling to Europe or North America in order to stay current within their practices.

In 2015, the first humanistic-existential-integrative training was delivered in Qatar. This training brought the concepts of existential-humanistic theory into the practice of couple therapy while integrating four major couple therapy approaches, including Imago Relationship Therapy, Emotionally Focused Therapy for Couples, Gottman Couple Therapy, and Existential Systemic Therapy. This training was designed as a research study intending to investigate "The outcome of the development and delivery of an Existential-Humanistic-Integrative Couples-Therapy (EHICT) training" (Mansilla, 2016) while also considering the cross-cultural applicability of this Western theory into an

Eastern culture. As a result, this study found that "EHI couples-therapy training effectively contributed towards participants' experience of skillfulness and readiness to conduct couples-therapy in a culturally sensitive and culturally applicable approach" (Mansilla, 2016). The results of this study ignited national and international interest in existential-humanistic couple therapy training. This resulted in developing additional trainings in Qatar in 2017, the United Arab Emirates in 2018, and Pakistan in 2019. Currently, this approach is established as the Humanistic-Existential Approach to Relationship Therapy (HEART), designed to be to taught and practiced cross-culturally.

The Middle East is also the founding place of a second existential humanistic approach. Concurrent to the development of HEART, the Mindfulness-Based Existential-Humanistic approach (MBExist) was developed as a cross-cultural group therapy in the Middle East. This practice utilizes some of the concepts of Mindfulness Based Stress Reduction and Mindfulness Based Cognitive Therapy, integrated into a mindfulness approach to existential-humanistic group therapy. The development of MBExist began in 2011, and it is now practiced both in Qatar as an eight-week group therapy program, as well as a six-days full immersion retreat in Shri-lanka.

The introduction of existential-humanistic theory into the HEART and MBExist approaches in Qatar triggered the development of the first Counseling Centre in Qatar. In 2019, this center will open doors and offer counseling and psychotherapy services to the local and expatriate communities in this country. Furthermore, the HEART and MBExist based counseling center will operate exclusively under the humanistic-existential-integrative approach.

Due to the large community commitment and funding from Qatari nationals, it is expected that Qatar may become the leader in mental health initiatives and services in the Middle East with existential-humanistic therapy becoming a leading practice.

## Challenges and Opportunities

### Sociocultural and Economic Factors

From an economic standpoint, psychotherapy can be considered a luxury both in terms of studying professional psychology as well as utilizing the services in much of Southeast Asia. Table 4.1 shows that the average household income in Beijing (Wen, 2018), Hong Kong ("Quarterly Report on General Household Survey", 2018.), Taiwan ("Report on the Survey of Family Income", n.d.), and Malaysia (Department of Labor and Statistics Malaysia [DLSM], 2017). As most mental health services in these parts of Asia are not covered by insurances, national or otherwise, private practices are almost deemed a luxury. Private practices in certain areas like Malaysia, Taiwan, and China are regulated by health departments; in these cases, it comprises mostly group practices in quasi commercial areas. Hong Kong differs. With a longer history of expat communities and mixed

East-West practices, Hong Kong has a greater number of individual private practices in residential areas. In comparison, registered group practices in commercial districts tend to be the norm for private practice in other parts of Asia. When considering the cost of psychological services in light of average income and the lack of mental health insurance coverage, many households simply cannot afford psychotherapy.

Table 1

*Average Income Converted to USD and Cost of Psychotherapy in Parts of Asia*

| Localities | Average Income | Mental Health Insurance coverage | Fees and accessibility of services |
|---|---|---|---|
| Beijing | $571/Month per Urban Disposable Household Income in 2015 | N/A | $45-$290/hour in private practice. |
| Hong Kong | $3,103/ Median Month Income per person in 2016 | Only in selective private group insurance plans | $130-$230/ 50 min in private practice. (Gov provides less but up to 6 week) |
| Taiwan | $3,312/ Month Gross Income per Household in 2017 | National Medical Insurance covers part of psychological testing. Therapy is only covered in selective corporate EAP plans. | $50-$140/hour in private practice. (Government supported community center $10 per 30 min session) |
| Malaysia | $1,200/Median Monthly Income per household in 2016 | N/A | $40-$110 / hour in private practice. (Government hospital charges $7 for first visit; $1 for subsequent visits |

To illustrate, with the income of the average household in Hong Kong, for a family to support a family member for one hour per week therapy, the family will have to spend around 20-36% of its monthly household income. For Taiwan, the cost would be approximately 8-18%. As a result, rarely do the lay public engage in regular private therapy. Instead, those who could not afford the service but need it would turn to public therapy for substantially more affordable pricing; however, they may wait up to 4-8 weeks for one appointment. The need for the service and the accessibility and affordability poses one of the greatest challenges for psycho-therapy in Asia. This has been an ongoing challenge that has been brought to the attention of the various localities (Branigan, 2014; "Psychologists say Quacks are Posing", 2013).

On the other hand, there are non-therapy alternatives that people from these parts of Asia access for their emotional and personal development. Religion is the common thread for social support and ritualistic healing practices ("Hong Kong-the Facts", 2016; 卢云峰, 2014; DLSM, 2015; see Table 1). Of interest to existential-humanistic psychology is the overlap between many of the religions practiced in Asia and the philosophical teachings embedded in them, such as Taoism (See chapter 5 & 7 in this volume; Yang, 2017). Also, much of Southeast Asia has varying degrees of Confucius influence that encourages learning and prides members on being contributors to the system in which they hold membership. Conversely, be-ing a dependent or a client carries the connotation or stigma of being a burden. Thus, it is not surprising that short term coaching or positive psychology work-shops or training camps are growing in popularity as they are considered socially more acceptable and realistic as a human development practice as compared to the stigmatized psychotherapy that is associated with mental illnesses. Further, as individuals are more often viewed as members of their system, mental illnesses or psychological needs are considered a disharmony with the family. An ingrained common belief is likened to the Western saying to not "air one's dirty laundry in public." To reveal or discuss domestic struggles is to bring about shame to one's family or injury to the family's face (Hwang, 2012).

In sum, while psychotherapy may not be as widely accepted and accessible as it is in the West, it is a developing field to certain social economic groups. Cultur-ally, as the trend of recent generations go, there are cross-cultural influences and changes in the mindset over psychotherapy and individuality (Hwang, 2012).

### Legislation of Education, Training, Licensure, and Ethical Codes Relevant to Therapy Practice

Psychotherapy in Southeast Asia is a relatively young field compared to the West. As such, the requirements for education, training, certification, licensure, and legislation are mostly in the developing stages and subject to change, which is sometimes rapid. The particulars also vary widely from one place to another with many gray areas in practice. For instance, the national license exam was recently annulled in China and everyone is waiting to see what will take its place. The pre-vious exam was grossly insufficient with no clinical training requirements.

In Hong Kong, there is no statutory registration regulating the practice of psychology. There are, however, at least two professional associations, but mem-bership is fully voluntary. The Hong Kong Psychological Association has adopted a code of ethics; however, adherence to the code applies only to its members. As a result, the quality of psychotherapy that is available is neither standardized nor safeguarded. Related in culture, Taiwan and Malaysia are equivalent in that they both require a Master's degree in psychology (Seal, 2017; Wu, 2018). However, there is about a 15-year gap between Taiwan and Malaysia in terms of licensure and credentialing requirements. Taiwan has a credentialing examination, and licensure requirements and policies, following the psychologists act of 2011. The two major governing bodies for psychologists in Taiwan are the Taiwan Counseling Psychology Association and the Taiwan Association of Clinical Psychology. In Malaysia, counselors are governed by the Board of Counsellors Malaysia and need to be licensed in order to practice. Currently, there is no legislation that governs clinical psychologists and other mental health practitioners. Similar to Hong Kong's system, The Malaysian Society of Clinical Psychology (MSCP) serves as a professional association to oversee ethical practices of its members and promote advancement of clinical psychology in Malaysia. However, starting from 2019, the Allied Health Professions Act 2016 will enforce a registration process to ensure ethical practice for psychotherapists (Seal, 2018; Fong, 2018). It can be anticipated that there will be a credentialing/ licensure system in place in the near future. Table 1 provides an overview of the requirements in these different countries in Southeast Asia.

## Natural Disasters Impacting Psychological Services

Regardless of culture, disasters and traumatic events crush one's sense that the world is safe, life affirming, and just (Greening, 1997; Hoffman & Vallejos, 2018). Emergency responders recognize the need for mental health services in times of natural existential crises (Halpern & Tramontin, 2007). Since the implementation of Critical Incident Stress Management in the 1980s, mental health workers have come to extend their training to become educated too in Psychological First Aid and Incident Management Systems, which improves communities' chances of recovery. However, this preparation alone may not be equally adequate across cultures (see Ren, 2009). A number of natural disasters took place in Asia over the past couple of decades, such as the 1999 Earthquake in Taiwan and the 2008 Sichuan Earthquake in China, which provided a glimpse of how Asian psychological services function under crisis. Follow up studies have found that while Western psychology can benefit those recovering from emergencies, it is essential to adapt or incorporate Eastern psychology and philosophy when serving these indigenous posttraumatic populations.

An interesting paradox is that while human suffering is often the same, cultural competency is even more important when dealing with various cosmologies in the context of disasters. For instance, while Shen (2002) found short-term group play therapy to be effective for posttraumatic children, garnering support for Western psychotherapy, other researchers found areas of challenges. Yaw-Shen (2009) found bereavement and psychological healing to take a life-long course as much of the Taiwanese/Chinese population regard the deceased to continually hold a presence in the family lives. Chang (2005) also indicated that older generations from certain villages are uncomfortable with foreign psychotherapy, and prefer seeking psychological services from shamans through rituals. In these situations, it would be counterproductive if emergency psychological professionals are insensitive or ignorant of the indigenous practices. Chang (2005) emphasized the need to contextualize psychotherapy and agrees with Halpern and Tramontin's (2007) advice on building a trusted community network. This not only serves the post trauma survivors but also the mental health workers witnessing the aftermaths.

Table 2

*Alternatives to Psychotherapy and Dominant Religions in Parts of Asia*

| Localities | Non-Therapy Practices | Major Religions |
|---|---|---|
| China | Religion/ Psychotherapy training/ coaching workshops/ camps | Chinese Folk Religion (81.1%) Atheists (6.3%) Buddhism (6.2%) Christianity (2.3%) Salvationist religions (2.2%) Islam (1.7%) Other faiths (0.2%) |
| Hong Kong | Religion/ Coaching workshops/ camps/ Spiritual Camps | Chinese Folk Religion, Buddhism, Taoism or Atheism (82.8%) Protestantism (6.5%) Catholicism (5.1%) Islam (4.1%) Hinduism (1.3%) Sikhism (0.2%) |
| Taiwan | Religion/ Coaching workshops/ Spiritual Camps | Buddhists (35%) Taoists & Local religions (33%) Christians (3.9%) Non-religious (18.7%) Taoist or Confucian rooted religious movements (10%) |
| Malaysia | Religion/ Coaching workshops/ Spiritual Camps | Islam (61.3%) Buddhism (19.8%) Christianity (9.2%) Hinduism (6.3%) Confucianism, Taoism and Tribal/Folk/Other Traditional Chinese religions (1.3%) |

Table 3
*Legislation of Education, Training, Licensure of Psychotherapists in Parts of Southeast Asia.*

| Localities | Education | Training | Certification and Licensure | Ethic Codes and Governing Legislation |
|---|---|---|---|---|
| China | Bachelor's Degree | N/A | Awaiting New Certification/ Licensure Requirements | No governing body to enforce |
| Hong Kong | Master's Degree in psychology OR diploma in counselling with 6 years of counselling work experience | According to education programs | No Statutory Registration | No governing body to enforce |
| Taiwan | Master's degree in counselling or clinical psychology | 1-year full time Internship in recognized educational /medical settings | National Examine Board for Certification. Registration with Ministry of Health and professional associations | Violations result in legal consequenc es and loss of license |
| Malaysia | Master's Degree in Counselling or Clinical Psychology, or other Diploma Certification training | According to degree programs | N/A | Board of Counsellors Malaysia for licensing of counsellors and Allied Health Professions Act 2016 for psycho- therapists to be implement- ed in 2019 |

Zhengjia Ren (2009) spent several years working with people impacted by the earthquake that occurred in the Sichuan province of China on May 12, 2008. He reported that despite his training and supervision in medicine and psychiatry, he felt unprepared for what he experienced when beginning his work (Ren, 2009; see also Ren & Dias, 2019). As he reflected upon his experience, he identified many themes that connect with existential-humanistic psychology, including the primacy of the therapeutic relationship, the importance of dealing with issues of meaning, and the importance of community. Ren, along with colleagues, later investigated the personal transformation of the mental health relief workers involved in the recovery efforts after the earthquake (Ren, Gao, Yang, & Qu, 2018). The model developed from their research proposes a stage model of personal transformation that begins with existential shattering, progresses to existential learning, and then moves into what is termed existential integrity. This can be conceived of as a model of posttraumatic growth that was experienced by many of mental health relief workers and fits well with existential-humanistic therapy.

Tragedy and trauma often thrust people into facing the existential realities of life (Greening, 1997; Hoffman & Vallejos, 2018). While culture cannot protect people from trauma, it is essential that culture plays a role in how trauma is faced. The work of individuals such as Ren (2009; see also Ren et al., 2018) is inspiring on its own; however, it also points to the great need in China for mental health relief workers and the opportunity for existential-humanistic psychotherapy to help meet those needs.

## Future Directions

In the dawn of the 21st century, the global influence of American Capitalism has impacted the world economy and humanity. Technological advancement provides individuals with new connections across long distances and time zones allowing cross-cultural studies and dialogues to take place. But the technocracy that is growing overshadows the human populations that it was initially intended to liberate, such is the limitations of the East overprizing Western practices. For existential-humanistic therapists and psychologists, there are great possibilities and opportunities to grow and also influence the developing world through genuine relationships, dialogues of humility, and work that values humanity and its historical wisdom. However, it is important that this work is conducted in a manner that values and respects the contributions of the East and avoids the colonizing approaches common in the West.

Brown (2014) uncovered an unpublished manuscript written by Abraham Maslow indicating that the source material for his famous Hierarchy of Needs was adopted from the Blackfoot Tribe of Native Americans. Prior to this, Taylor (1999) described the influences of indigenous peoples from around the world coming to North America and doing psychotherapeutic work with people. The wisdom from their heritage blends reflections of nature and community connections. For instance, the familiar pyramid image of Maslow's Hierarchy of Needs was actually derived from the image of the conical teepees' reflection in lake surfaces. The reflection communicates a continuation of ancestry heritage; the conical shape of the teepee adds the cyclical nature of native wisdom. Maslow simplified the image by removing water reflections, the dimensions of teepees, and the idea that teepees were home to families and communities. The end result is an upright two-dimensional pyramid model used to describe an individual's stages of needs. In a related vein, Taoists reasoned many of their conclusions about life and the world through their contemplations in solitude, which focused on their experience of nature (Fung, 1997) and mirrors many of the conclusions on human conditions drawn by existentialists in Europe during the 19th and 20th Centuries. Research in mainstream psychology, however, has been based largely on logical-empiricism, which has led to a truncated view of humanity and the cosmos. Mainstream professional psychology continues to embrace empirically supported short-term linear models, which are often preferred by insurance companies (Elkins, 2009). Philosophical-leaning practices, including ancient philosophies from a variety of epistemological and cultural streams, struggle to be recognized (Husserl, 2012). An ironic example is the mindfulness revolution in psychology. Although mindfulness is rooted in Eastern philosophies of life, it has made its way into professional psychology by scientifically restructuring the practice in such a manner that traditional master practitioners would barely recognize it as mindfulness.

In sum, research has achieved much for and in the interests of the West, but many indigenous peoples have had their cultures and cosmologies misrepresented or undervalued by Western scholars (Hwang, 2012; Smith, 2012). Often, philosophies and ways of knowing have a different meaning conveyed when filtered through the language and thinking of foreign scholars. To complicate the matter, indigenous scholars sometimes underappreciate local cultural wisdom in the process of adopting Western teachings for global recognition. As existential-humanistic psychology continues to develop and evolve, it is imperative that it does so in consideration of the many varied cultural perspectives, such as those in Asia. These dialogues will help existential-humanistic psychology grow while advocating for approaches to practice that are culturally sensitive.

## Developing Systematic Training

Developing systematic training for any psychological approach outside of its culture of origin is complicated. The easy path is to replicate what is done in the culture of origin in the new cultural context; however, this leads to the imposition of values and colonization through psychological education and training. As systematic training in China continues to develop, it is important that Yang and Hoffman's (2004, 2009) triad of (a) cultural critique, (b) cultural adaptation, and (c) incorporation of indigenous approaches remain a foundation of the training.

While the early attempts at training have been offered primarily by scholar-practitioners from the West, it is important that this begins to shift to include more practitioners from the East. This will change the training and develop it in a manner that is more appropriate to be applied in Southeast Asia. No matter how much trainers from the West familiarize themselves with the Eastern cultures, there will remain limitations in the ability to fully adapt to the cultural conditions in the East. When the trainings incorporate a balance of perspectives from the East and West with all remaining open to learning from each other and committed to respecting the culture in which therapy in being conducted, there are many opportunities for new insights and developments.

Similar to how the International Conference on Existential Psychology progressed toward greater balance in presenters and more focused on dialogue, the systematic training has evolved in a similar manner. In 2018, a second iteration of the 2-year certificate training in existential-humanistic psychology was launched in China. This second certificate training is much more extensive and comprehensive compared to the first. In order to ensure quality, cohort sizes are limited to 36 students consisting of six small groups of six members each. Consistent with the original certificate program, the first year of the program will focus on humanistic psychology as a foundation while the second year will focus on existential psychology. Furthermore, instead of a certificate for each year, only one participation certificate will be offered for both years. The requirements have become stricter in line with the rapid development of the field in China. A more advanced Existential-Humanistic Psychotherapist's certificate will also be offered for those students who complete clinical supervision along with a written exam. Instead of periodic week-long intensive trainings, students now have weekly interactions with each other and the teaching materials. The new certificate program takes advantage of developments in online technology allowing students more access to foreign instructors and each other given that students are located throughout various regions in China. Consistent with the tenets of humanistic psychology, the program emphasizes relational and embodied forms of experiential learning through monthly small group discussions and a 4-day, on-the-ground workshop every 6 months. This is all made possible because the trainings now have become more indigenized with local instructors and small group leaders taking on the bulk of the teaching and mentorship. As discussed above, the local instructors consist of selected students from the original certificate program who have engaged in additional, continuous on-the-ground group training conducted by Mark Yang in China supplemented by online supervision and periodic on-the-ground experiential workshops given by Western practitioners.

In addition to the new certificate training program, a second 3-year systematic training is also being offered to the University Counseling Center therapists in Beijing. This training is still spear-headed by Western practitioners and, thus, involves only periodic on-the-ground intensive trainings every 6 months. However, different from the first certification program, the assistant trainers for this new program now consists of local instructors instead of students from Saybrook University. As much as possible, the training programs in Southeast Asia continues to integrate and create dialogue between the East and the West.

Moreover, four training centers affiliated with the International Institute for Existential Humanistic Psychology opened in Beijing, Chongging, Chengdu, and Suzhou. And in addition to China, Yang is training and developing additional local instructors from Hong Kong, Malaysia, and Singapore with an eye towards developing the next generation of existential-humanistic psychotherapists in these regions in the near future. Partnerships with universities and other organizations are continuing to be developed to help reach a broader range of students. These developments provide an important testament to future possibilities.

## Expanded International Presence

Correia, Cooper, and Berdondini (2014) noted that existential-humanistic psychology was largely contained within specific regions, with most of its training institutions and practitioners located in the United States. They also identified one training institution in China and one in Russia. This is beginning to change. In China, Correia and colleagues noted that the existential-humanistic approach was the most widely identified of the existential therapy approaches. The training centers in China have expanded since the time of the study. Furthermore, as discussed, the interest in Southeast Asia is expanding into Malaysia and Tapei, as well as some practitioners present in Singapore. Anne Hsu, Mark Yang, and Rodger Broomé have been integral to the expansion into Tapei; Evone Phoo and Mark Yang have been integral in the developments occurring in Malaysia. Anthony Nkyi, who trained in the United States and participated in the First International Conference on Existential Psychology in 2010, has begun developing existential psychology in Ghana. Nkyi draws from existential-humanistic and logotherapy foundations. He has also been involved with the World Congress of Existential Therapy, attending the first one in London, and he is scheduled to present on existential therapy in Africa at the 2019 World Congress of Existential Therapy in Buenos Aires. Additionally, Nkyi has several publications, including chapters in this book and *Existential Psychology East-West*, Volume 2 (see also Nkyi, 2014, 2015a, 2015b, 2015c). Monica Mansilla, as noted, also has been successful in helping to develop existential-humanistic psy-chology in several countries in the Middle East as well as doing work in Spain and New Zealand. Ilene Serlin, too, has been engaged in existential-humanistic inspired work in Israel, particularly through expressive arts therapy.

While Correia et al. (2014) are correct that existential-humanistic psychology historically has been contained in limited regions, this is changing. It is noteworthy that many of the people who have been heavily involved in international work in existential-humanistic psychology are early and middle career therapists deeply committed to the development and expansion of existential-humanistic therapy through international dialogues.

**Translated Scholarship**

Since the first edition of the current volume was published, there have been numerous English works that have been translated into Chinese, partially resulting from the conference and trainings discussed in this chapter. However, outside of the chapters' first edition of *Existential Psychology East-West*, Wang's (2011) article in *The Humanistic Psychologist* on "Zhi Mian and Existential Psychology," and Kan Chen's (2016) article in the *Journal of Humanistic Psychology* on "Wuhua Therapy," there has been limited Eastern scholarship translated into English. As the East-West dialogues on existential psychology continue, it is imperative that translations are more balanced to reflect a valuing of the different perspectives and contributions and to seek a more mutual dialogue.

**Ethical Considerations**

The ethics codes and standards for psychotherapy in the West gradually developed over many years as therapists came to understand the implications of this new profession more deeply. The ethics codes are not just a product of the field of psychotherapy, but they are a product of culture. In Southeast Asia, ethical standards and codes are still in development. While there is much that can be learned from the ethics codes of the West, applying these without consideration of cultural differences in Southeast Asia will result in harm. Ethical codes must be rooted in the culture in which they are practiced.

During some of the trainings that various authors of this chapter have been a part of in Southeast Asia, there have been times where we encountered reluctance to share what is actually being done out of fear that the Western scholars will rebuke the practices of therapists in Asia on ethical grounds. This fear emerged out of prior experiences of this occurring when prominent Western scholars have presented in Southeast Asia. These unfortunate occurrences hinder the development of dialogue and interfere with cultures developing ethics codes that reflect the culture in which therapy is being practiced.

## Conclusion

The journey to the second edition of this book began in 2007, when Mark Yang, Xuefu Wang, and Louis Hoffman met at a psychology of religion conference in China and discovered their convergent interests in existential psychology. Much has occurred since this time fostering the development of existential-humanistic psychology in China and the advancement of existential-humanistic psychology, internationally. In 2015, Emmy van Deurzen initiated the First World Congress of Existential Therapy, which was the largest and most important gathering of existential therapists in history. Many of the scholars and practitioners involved in the dialogues discussed in this chapter were part of the Congress, including several people serving on the Scientific Organizing Committee. However, the first congress was still comprised primarily of individuals from Europe, the United

States, and South America, with severely limited representation from Southeast Asia and Africa. While this was not intentional, and there were attempts to recruit from existential therapists globally, it did reflect a significant limitation, particularly when considering how population is distributed globally. In looking forward to the 2019 Second World Congress of Existential Therapy, it does appear that there will be greater representation from Southeast Asia.

This chapter reflects many of the advancements and challenges with the development of existential-humanistic therapy in Southeast Asia. While we are now over 10-years into this development, it is still early in the developmental process. We are confident that over the next 10 years there will be many more voices involved and progress made.

## References

Bargdill, R., Hoffman, L., Kuriansky, J. & Zelinski, S. (2011, August). *A global view of humanistic psychologies: International activities of division 32*. Poster presented at the 119th Annual Convention of the American Psychological Association, Washington, DC.

Branigan, T. (2014, September 3). It's good to talk: China opens up to psychotherapy. Retrieved from https://www.theguardian.com/world/2014/sep/03/china-psychiatrists-talking-therapy-counselling

Brons, L. (2015). Othering, an analysis. *Transience, 6*(1), 69-90.

Brown, S. S. (2014). *Transformation beyond greed: Native self-actualization*. Shiprock, NM: Sidney Stone Brown.

Bugental, J. (1999). *Psychotherapy isn't what you think: Bringing therapeutic engagement into the present moment*. Phoenix, AZ: Zeig & Tucker

Chang, I. I. (2005). Theatre as therapy, therapy as theatre transforming the memories and trauma of the 21 September 1999 earthquake in Taiwan. *Research in Drama Education, 10*(3), 285-301.

Correia, E. A., Cooper, M., & Berdondini, L. (2014). The worldwide distribution and characteristics of existential counsellors and psychotherapies. *Existential Analysis, 25*, 321-337.

De Beauvior, S. (2012). *The second sex* (C. Borde, & S. Malovany-Chevallie. Trans.). New York, NY: Vintage.

Department of Statistics Malaysia (2015, May 7). *Population distribution and basic demographic characteristic report 2010.* Retrieved from https://www.dosm.gov.my/v1/index.php?r=column/ctheme&menu_id=L0pheU 43NWJwRWVSZklWdzQ4TlhUUT09&bul_id=MDMxdHZjWTk1SjFzTzNkRXYzcVZ jdz09

Department of Statistics Malaysia (2017, October 9). *Report of household income and basic amenities survey 2016.* Retrieved from https://www.dosm.gov.my/v1/index.php?r=column/cthemeByCat&cat=120&b ul_id=RUZ5REwveU1ra1hGL21JWVlPRmU2Zz09&menu_id=amVoWU54UTl0a2 1NWmdhMjFMMWcyZz09

Dias, J., Chan, A, Ungvarsky, J., Oraker, J., & Cleare-Hoffman, H. P. (2011). Reflections on marriage and family therapy emergent from international dialogues in China. *The Humanistic Psychologist, 39*, 268-275. doi: 10.1080/08873267.2011.592434

Dias, J., & Ren, Z. (2019). On the Sichuan earthquake. In L. Hoffman, M. Yang, M. Mansilla, J. Dias, M. Moats, & T. Claypool (Eds.), *Existential psychology East-West* (Vol. 2; pp. ). Colorado Springs, CO: University Professors Press.

Elkins, D. N. (2009). *Humanistic psychology: A clinical manifesto. A critique of clinical psychology and the need for progressive alternatives.* Colorado Springs, CO: University of the Rockies Press.

Fong, L. F. (2018, September 8). 40,000 allied health professionals required to register with Health Ministry. Retrieved from https://www.thestar.com.my/news/nation/2018/09/05/40000-allied-health-professionals-required-to-register-with-health-ministry/

Fung, Y. L. (1997). *A short history of Chinese philosophy: A systematic account of Chinese thought from its origins to the present day.* New York, NY: Free Press.

Greening, T. (1997). Posttraumatic stress disorder: An existential-humanistic perspective. In S. Krippner & S. M. Powers (Eds.), *Broken images, broken selves: Dissociative narratives in clinical practice.* Washington, DC: Brunner/Mazel.

Halpern, J., & Tramontin, M. (2007). *Disaster mental health: Theory and practice.* Belmont, CA: Thomson Brooks/Cole.

Hegel, G. W. F. (1977). *Phenomenology of spirit* (A.V. Miller, Trans.). New York, NY: Oxford.

Hoffman, E. (1988). *The right to be human: A biography of Abraham Maslow.* Los Angeles, CAJeremy P. Tarcher, Inc.

Hoffman, L., & Cleare-Hoffman, H. P. (2011). Existential therapy and emotions. Lessons from cross-cultural exchange. *The Humanistic Psychologist, 39,* 261-267.

Hoffman, L., & Vallejos, L. (2018). Existential shattering. In D. Leeming (Ed.), *The encyclopedia of psychology and religion* (3rd ed.). Advanced online publication. Berlin, Germany: Springer. https://doi.org/10.1007/978-3-642-27771-9_200193-1

Hoffman, L., Yang, M., Claypool, T., Serlin, I., Schneider, K. J., & Gordon, S. (2010, August). *Reflections from the First International Conference on Existential Psychology.* Presented at the Society for Humanistic Psychology (Division 32 of the American Psychological Association) Hospitality Suite at the 118th Annual Convention of the American Psychological Association, San Diego, CA.

Hong Kong: *The facts- Religion and custom,* (May, 2016). Retrieved from www.hab.gov.hk

Hwang, K. K. (2012) *Foundations of Chinese psychology: Confucian social relations.* New York, NY: Springer.

Husserl, E. (2012). *Cartesian meditations: An introduction to phenomenology* (D. Cairns, Trans.). New York, NY: Klewer Academic

May, R. (1969). *Love and will.* New York, NY: W.W. Norton.

Mendelowitz, E. (2011). Transience and possibility: The legacy of Rollo May. *The Humanistic Psychologist, 39,* 253-260. doi: 10.1080/08873267.2011.594332

Moats, M., Claypool, T. R., & Saxon, E. (2011). Therapist development through international dialogues: Students' perspective on personal and professional life changing interactions in China. *The Humanistic Psychologist, 39,* 276-282. doi: 10.1080/08873267.2011.592439

Nkyi, A. (2014). Loneliness among senior high school students in Ghana. *British Journal of Psychology Research, 2*(1), 1-13.

Nkyi, A. (2015a). Existential psychotherapy: The historical development and current practice especially with reference to its usage in African communities. *International Journal of Psychology, 19*(3), 27-42.

Nkyi, A. (2015b). Relationship between alcohol use and purpose in life among senior high school students in Ghana. *Indian Journal of Health and Wellbeing, 6*(11), 1080-1083.

Nkyi, A. (2015c). Purpose in life among senior high school students in Ghana. *Journal of Global Research in Education and Social Science, 3*(4), 187-197.

Psychologists say Quacks are posing as Counsellors, (2013, February 3). Retrieved from http://www.scmp.com/news/hong-kong/article/1142193/psychologists-say-quacks-are-posing-counsellors

Quarterly Report on General Household Survey, (2018, August 31). Retrieved from https://www.censtatd.gov.hk/hkstat/sub/sp200.jsp?productCode=B1050001

Ren, Z. (2009). On being a volunteer at the Sichuan earthquake disaster area (translated version). *Hong Kong Journal of Psychiatry, 19,* 123-125.

Ren, Z., Gao, M., Yang, M., & Qu, W. (2018). Personal transformation process of mental health relief workers in Sichuan earthquake. *Journal of Religion and Health.* Advance online publication. https://doi-org.libproxy.uccs.edu/10.1007/s10943-018-0584-4

Report on the Survey of Family Income and Expenditure Per Household by Industry of Household Heads, (n.d.). Retrieved from https://eng.stat.gov.tw/ct.asp?xItem=3458&CtNode=1597&mp=5

Rogers, C. (1959). A theory of therapy, personality and interpersonal relationships as developed in the client-centered framework. In S. Koch (Ed.), *Psychology: A study of a science* (Vol. 3: Formulations of the Person and the Social Context; pp. 184-256) New York, NY: McGraw Hill.

Rogers, C. (1961). *On becoming a person: A therapist's view of psychotherapy.* London, England: Constable.

Rogers, C. (1980). *A way of being.* Boston, MA: Houghton Mifflin.

Schneider, K. J. (2011). Awakening to an awe-based psychology. *The Humanistic Psychologist, 39,* 247-252. doi: 10.1080/08873267.2011.592464

Seal, D. (2017, Feb 13). How to become a clinical psychologist in Malaysia. Retrieved from http://www.psychologist.com.my/carerrs/malaysiaClinPsychCourses.html

Shen, Y. (2002). Short-term group play therapy with Chinese earthquake victims: Effects on anxiety, depression and adjustment. *International Journal of Play Therapy, 11*(1), 43-63.

Smith, L.T. (2012). *Decolonizing methodologies: Research and indigenous peoples* (2nd ed.). London, UK: Zed.

Taylor, E. (1999). *Shadow culture: Psychology and spirituality in America.* Washington, DC: Counterpoint.

Wang, X. (2011). Zhi Mian and existential psychology. *The Humanistic Psychologist, 39,* 240-246. doi: 10.1080/08873267.2011.592465

Wen, Y. (2018, Jan 8). Income and living standards across China. Retrieved from https://www.stlouisfed.org/on-the-economy/2018/january/income-living-standards-china

Wu, H. (2018). *A study on entrepreneurship of psychologists in Taiwan: A case-based approach* (Master's thesis). Retrieved from https://hdl.handle.net/11296/2qz8c2.

Yang, M. (Ed.). (2017). *Existential psychology and the way of the Tao: Meditations on the writings of Zhuangzi.* New York, NY: Routledge.

Yang, M., & Hoffman, L. (2011). Introduction to the special section on the First International Conference on Existential Psychology. *The Humanistic Psychologist, 39,* 236-239. doi: 10.1080/08873267.2011.592467

Yang, M., & Hoffman, L. (2014, August). Training and practice in an international context. In C. N. Shealy (Chair), *International humanistic psychology: Implications and applications for research and practice.* Symposium presented at the 122nd Annual Convention of the American Psychological Association, Washington, DC.

Yang, M, & Hoffman, L. (2019). An existential-humanistic framework for international psychology. In L. Hoffman, M. Yang, M. Mansilla, J. Dias, M. Moats, & T. Claypool (Eds.), *Existential psychology East-West* (Vol. 2; pp. ). Colorado Springs, CO: University Professors Press.

Yaw-Sheng, L. (2009). The unclaimed traumatic experience: Bereavement and psychological healing regarding earthquake disasters in Taiwan (in Chinese). *Journal of Psychology in Chinese Societies, 10*(1), 1-17.

卢云峰(2014). 当代中国宗教状况报告—基于 CFPS（2012）调查数据. *World Religious Cultures, 2014*(1), 11-25.

# Chapter 5

## Tao, Dasein, and Psyche:
## Shared Grounds for Depth Psychotherapy[1]

### Erik Craig

Tao, Dasein, and Psyche: Such strange and disparate terms from such distant and yet resonant times and traditions. From ancient far Eastern philosophy, the venerable Tao disclosed the Way—the Way of Being itself—the Ground or Source of all that is, as well as the teaching that arises from this fundament. From modern and postmodern Western philosophy, the miraculous Dasein, reveals that being who seems, among all others, to be concerned with understanding being, including its own being, that kind of being we call human. Finally, from Greek mythology and, later, from that branch of Western scientific medicine called psychoanalysis, the sonorous Psyche announces the human being's soul, the life of the soul, that richly textured, sumptuously colored fabric of lived experience that imbues our very own existence with passion and meaning. While the Tao reminds us of all that is and of our humble participation in this wholeness, it is Dasein in which we dwell that opens us to this wholeness as inseparable oneness with it, and Psyche that endows this open dwelling with pathos, value, and wonder. And all this ultimately, a mystery and unspeakable.

This chapter dialogues the thought and practice of three traditions of psychotherapy: Tao psychotherapy, daseinsanalysis, and psychoanalysis, the first being from the East and the latter two from the West.[2] My hope is to uncover some shared grounds for understanding human existence and human suffering as well as our care for them in depth-oriented psychotherapy. Ultimately my question is this: What is it that makes depth-psychotherapy even possible in the first place?

---

[1] The original version of this chapter was written as an invited address for The Society for Humanistic Psychology at the American Psychological Association's 2006 Annual Convention in New Orleans, LA. Due to space constraints, some of the extended footnotes of the chapter had to be removed. For the full version of this paper including the extended footnotes, please contact the author.

[2] Today Western psychoanalytic and existential psychotherapies and Eastern psychotherapies can each count among their practitioners many distinctive approaches. I will be dialoging only one specific approach from each of these broader traditions: from psychoanalysis, Freud's classical humanistic psychoanalysis; from existential therapy, Medard Boss's daseinsanalysis, the first systematic approach to existential depth psychotherapy; and from the East, Korean psychiatrist, Rhee Dongshick's Tao psychotherapy that seeks the essential unity of Western depth psychotherapies with Eastern philosophical traditions such as Confucianism, Buddhism, Tao, and Zen.

My approach will be one of open, immediate inquiry, not authoritative, apodictic speech: I intend to ask, not tell.

I will begin with a brief explication of what I mean, as an existential psycho-therapist, by the term depth psychotherapy, and then go on to identify and discuss epistemological concerns regarding *otherness* and *ownness*. Next, I will briefly explicate the three ontological domains of being—Tao, Dasein, and Psyche—with which Tao psychotherapy, daseinsanalytic psychotherapy, and psychoanalytic psychotherapy are respectively concerned. Finally, I will address foundational depth psychotherapeutic premises and promises held in common by practitioners of psychoanalytic, daseinsanalytic, and Tao psychotherapies.

## What is Depth Psychotherapy?

Depth psychology (*Tiefenpsychologie*, German), is a term first used by Eugen Bleuler (1910) to designate, in everyday language, the approach to psychological treatment, called *Psychoanalyse* founded by Sigmund Freud. Contrary to the common erroneous belief that depth psychology refers to Jungian psychology exclusively, today, depth psychology is more widely and accurately used to refer to all those psychologies that developed out of Freud's psychoanalysis, including but not limited to classical psychoanalysis, analytical psychology, object relations, psychoanalytic ego psychology, psychoanalytic self-psychology, interpersonal psychiatry, psychodynamic psychology, intersubjective psychoanalysis, relational psychoanalysis, existential analysis, and so forth. Certainly, Eastern psychologies, with their grounding in ancient philosophical traditions, are also among today's most significant depth psychologies.

The foundational claim of all depth psychologies is that the totality of the human remains largely hidden to the eye and even to thought at all. In other words, depth psychologies all acknowledge the indisputable reality of ontological secrecy, not only in the human but in everything that is. Thus, depth psychology is simply that kind of psychology that takes seriously the unseen, the unthought, and, even, the unthinkable and unspeakable. Most simply put, depth psychology is "*a psychology of the invisible, a psychology of the secret, a psychology of concealment as such*" (Craig, 2007, p. 317). Depth *psychotherapies*, therefore, all have at least two purposes in common: first, to coax gently out of the darkness those secrets that contain the key to understanding the individual's suffering and, second, to liberate those possibilities for being that have been held hostage by that suffering.

Ironically, one could say that the essence of Western depth psychology and depth psychotherapy was actually disclosed in the East millennia before psychology as a field even existed at all. Recall this from the first chapter of the *Tao Te Ching*:

> Free from desire, you realize mystery.
> Caught in desire, you see only the manifestations.

Yet mystery and manifestations
Arise from the same source.
This source is called darkness.

Darkness within darkness.
The gateway to all understanding.
(S. Mitchell, Trans. 1988, Ch. 1)

### How is it with Otherness?

When engaging in a discourse within and between such radically different, culturally grounded, philosophical and healing traditions as those found in Eastern and Western psychologies, one can hardly avoid asking, "How can we aspire to understand the so-called other, or otherness as such?" In this case, for example, having grown up in a poor, little New England village, through and through an ordinary Westerner and a 20th century one at that, how can I hope to understand that which arose millennia ago, from opposite side of the Earth, within a culture and ethos, a people and time, so palpably other than my own? What can I say of what I am not? How can we meet and understand one another within the complexity of unity and diversity, the predicament, within our common humanity, of our otherness? How can we bridge these remote cultures of the East and West, which have given rise to such distinctive languages for being? How can we rise to the challenges inherent in comparative philosophy and practice? Ultimately, how can we realize and put to good account our own possibilities for human empathy.

It is this same question of whether we can truly grasp otherness that one evening nearly 80 years ago led to an impasse in a discussion among Martin Heidegger and colleagues. According to Petzet (1993) and Pöggeler (1987), Heidegger joined these colleagues for discussion after a 1930 lecture in Bremen, Germany. When the conversation floundered on the problem of human empathy, Heidegger asked the host for a copy of Martin Buber's translations of the *Parables of Chuang-tzu* and, that delivered, proceeded to read the following allegory:

Chuang Tzu and Hui Tzu
Were crossing Hao river
By the dam.

Chuang said:
"See how free
The fishes leap and dart:
That is their happiness."

Hui replied:
"Since you are not a fish

How do you know
What makes fishes happy?"

Chuang said:
"Since you are not I
How can you possibly know
That I do not know
What makes fishes happy?"

Hui argued:
If I, not being you,
Cannot know what you know
It follows that you
Not being a fish
Cannot know what they know.

Chuang said:
Wait a minute!
Let us get back
To the original question.
What you asked me was
*How do you know*
What makes fishes happy?'
From the terms of your question
You evidently know I know
What makes fishes happy.

I know the joy of fishes
In the river
Through my own joy, as I go walking
Along the same river.
[Merton, Trans., 2004, pp. 109-110]

With this allegory, Heidegger hoped to free up the discussion of how it is that human beings can grasp the otherness of others. As I understand it, the philosopher's primary gesture, was to suggest the possibility that we know otherness by being fully in our ownness, that when we mindfully participate in the immediacy of our own individual human existence, we also participate in our common humanity and, with this, in the event of Being itself. The key to the riddle is in the line "as I go walking along the same river." Only as you and I "walk along the river," that is, allow ourselves to be in the world freely and openly as we are, can we at all know what it is like for another to walk and to be as well? For Heidegger, to empathize with another meant, first of all, to be on our own way in the world. As the Zen saying goes, "The wondrous Tao consists in carrying water and chopping wood." Mindfully engaging in the immediate projects of our everyday lives, whether carrying water, chopping wood, cleaning the house, or driving to work, we experience the Tao and, through this, begin to know what it is like for others to do so as well. As Mitchell put it in his rendering of chapter 70 of the *Tao Te Ching* (trans.,1988): "If you want to know me, look inside your heart." Such advice comes close, doesn't it, to the recommendation in our field that those who practice psychotherapy and psychoanalysis begin with themselves?

Naturally, we should not let Chuang Tzu's fishes allegory lull us into smugly thinking that, within our common humanity, human difference and diversity are insignificant. There were still differences between Chuang Tzu and Hui Tzu, as there are between you and me, between those of us from the East and those of us from the West. Certainly, human love relations give ample testimony that empathy is no easy achievement, even among those who are closest to us. However, Heidegger's use of Chuang Tzu's allegory serves to remind us that the beginning of human empathy and human understanding is to be genuinely on our own way.

## How is it with Ownness?

The problem of otherness always presumes the problem of *ownness*. How we are as ourselves inevitably shapes how we are with others. Our own origins and circumstances, whether Eastern or Western, unavoidably structure and color our understanding of each other's traditions, as well as of each other as individuals. Whenever we seek to understand something, in this case Eastern and Western depth psychotherapy, we always bring our own fore knowledge, our own predispositions, our own pre-understanding to the table of our inquiry. For existential investigators it is important to recognize and declare our pre-understanding or orientation in advance.

### Explicating My Predisposition

It is with some apprehension that I write this paper in the first place. Not only do I fear of my own possibilities for misappropriation, especially in the form of what I call *Western academic colonialism*, but also, I am well aware of the even more fundamental circumstance that "The Tao that can be told is not the eternal Tao" (S. Mitchell, Trans., 1988, Ch. 1).

With respect to the first concern, Western misappropriation, it is important to at least declare my hermeneutic stance or *démarche*[3] as being guided, on the

---

[3] A phenomenological hermeneutic researcher understands that all knowledge or understanding is perspectival, that is, that one always has a predisposition to phenomena that unavoidably shapes one's understanding of them. Phenomenological researchers acknowledge and declare, at least to the extent possible or feasible, the nature and epistemological significance of their predisposition or foreknowledge. Naturally, the way researchers handle their predispositions depends largely on their own epistemological beliefs. Some phenomenologists, for example those following Husserl, believe

one hand, by the philosophically grounded hermeneutic phenomenology of Martin Heidegger's *Daseinsanalytik* and, on the other hand, by the everyday demands of an existential or daseinsanalytic psychotherapeutic practice. In the present situation, I justify the use of a daseinsanalytic approach on three grounds.

First, daseinsanalysis strives, above all and to the extent possible, not to impose predetermined concepts and theories on what is encountered but, rather, to proceed phenomenologically, that is, to allow *what* is to show itself precisely as that which it is and is on its way to being. In other words, a daseinsanalyst is forewarned by Hamlet's caution that there are more things in heaven and Earth than are dreamt of in our philosophy. One of Freud's (1892-94/1966) favorite stories of Charcot also comes to mind: when Freud commented that one of the French physician's observations contradicted prevailing theory, Charcot rebuked him with the words, "La théorie c'est bon; mais ça n'empêche pas d'exister" (Theory is good; but it doesn't prevent things from existing, p. 139). Daseinsanalysis takes such openness to what is very seriously and it is just this commitment to radical openness in scientific, philosophic, and therapeutic inquiry that allows me to dare to employ a daseinsanalytic *démarche* in approaching or allowing myself to be approached by the Tao.

Another ground upon which I justify using a daseinsanalytic perspective is that we now know that the founder of *Daseinsanalytik*, Martin Heidegger, had studied Taoist texts and, in spite of his secrecy about them, these studies unquestionably influenced his own thinking. Graham Parkes (1996) noted, Heidegger's contact with East Asian thought precedes even the writing of his magnum opus, *Being and Time* (1927/1962). Given that Heidegger's own thought was so significantly influenced by ancient wisdoms of the East, we ought not be surprised to find the profound thematic affinities that immediately strike us when reading his texts along with the *Tao Te Ching*.

---

that they can suspend or bracket out their presuppositions or, in the language of depth psychology, transferences and, thus, achieve a pure, descriptive, and even transcendental understanding of a given phenomenon. Other phenomenologists, for example those following Heidegger or Gadamer, believe that one can never escape the influence of one's personal, cultural, and linguistic perspectives, sometimes called one's thrownness. Such existential or hermeneutic phenomenologists are content with a fundamentally historical, contextualized, or relational understanding of phenomena; do not aspire to absolute, objective interpretations and, therefore, necessarily live with more uncertainty than the more pure, descriptive, or transcendental phenomenologists who find refuge in the certainty of objective, ahistorical, absolute meaning and truth. Daseinsanalysts, especially those who follow the spirit of the early Heidegger (1927/1962) of *Being and Time*, seek to be especially cognizant of their foreknowledge or predispositional relationship with phenomena, not with the vain aspiration of overcoming this predisposition but, rather, like the modern psychoanalysts use of transference and countertransference, with the hope of employing it in the service of minimizing concealment and maximizing disclosure of the phenomenon in question. In keeping with this spirit of Heideggerian, existential, or hermeneutic phenomenology, therefore, here I use the French word *démarche*, meaning "step" or "gait," to designate what more pure phenomenologists might call set, stance, or lens. The reason I prefer the word *démarche* is that it captures the sense of motion and "being on a path" of thinking that the other more commonly used English words do not.

The final ground upon which I justify using a daseinsanalytic perspective is my intent: namely, to listen for and dialogue basic affinities between the thinking of the East and the West, without prioritizing either or establishing any apodictic, metaphysical equations. My "reading" here is purely heuristic, serving to discover what it is that the East and West share in order to enrich and open up our experience and understanding of what we share, not only within ourselves as being human but also of our being, as psychotherapists, in relation with our clients.

## Explaining My Use of Language

Many students of Eastern thought have pointed out that Western thinkers are almost unnaturally attached to theory and verbal explanation, using it to establish their difference from others and authority over things and, thereby, unwittingly confining themselves to a self-made "conceptual prison" (Barrett,1956, p. xvi). Western daseinsanalysts like myself also use concepts. So, the question arises, "How might we understand language and our use of concepts such that they do not diminish but rather open up and liberate the phenomena with which we are concerned?" In other words, how might we use language lovingly?

In his little book entitled *Basic Concepts* (*Grundbegriffe*), Heidegger (1981 /1993) distinguished basic or *ground* concepts (Grundbegriffe) that bring the world before us from "mere concepts [that] are nothing concrete and lead nowhere" (p. 2). Heidegger saw such basic concepts as a way to *con-ceive*, to grasp, to hold that which "grounds everything and gives ground to everything" (p. 2) For Heidegger generally, an authentic language of experience is a way of giving Being a home, a way "to take into care beings as a whole" (p. 3). With such care in mind, Heidegger (1947/1977b) once called language the "house of Being" and wrote that "In its home man dwells. Those who create with words are the guardians of this home" (p. 193). If I understand him correctly, the philosopher was not suggesting that language itself was the real, the Tao, but, rather, that language is our way of hosting or shepherding the real. Heidegger might say that it is with language that Dasein "lets beings be the beings they are" (Heidegger, 1943/1977c p. 127f). Thus, for Heidegger, language is our way of disclosing being, of allowing being to be and to show itself, like providing a chair, a bed, or a room for a guest whom we have invited into our home. Is it not often the case that when the guest leaves our home, the thought of the chair, bed, or room still holds the one who was so hosted? So, it is with our words: they are not the beings themselves but they hold and host the beings, bringing them before us in the fullness of their being.

Here is an analogy from everyday life. I recall Medard Boss's obvious pleasure in showing me, on the ground floor of his home in Zollikon, Switzerland, the white arm chair where Heidegger would sit to read, meditate, or lecture. Boss always thought of that chair as the *Heidegger chair*, and it held the famous philosopher and friend, whether he was in it or not. It seemed to me that whenever Boss spoke of the chair or sat in it, he was with Heidegger, or, rather, Heidegger became present with him. I would suggest that, in a similar way, our words hold, host, serve, or care for Being.

Nevertheless, just as Boss would never mistake or be willing to exchange that arm chair for the actual presence of his friend Heidegger, nor would we mistake or be willing to exchange our concepts of beings for the beings themselves, our concept of Tao for Tao itself. Lying infinitely beyond the *concept of Being* is Being, itself. Lying infinitely beyond the idea of the Tao is the Tao itself. Here, the first lines of the *Tao Te Ching*:

> The tao that can be told
> Is not the eternal Tao,
> The name that can be named
> Is not the eternal Name.
> (S. Mitchell, Trans., 1988, Chapt. 1)

Those familiar with Eastern thought might be reminded, here, of the famous distinction between the finger pointing at the moon and the moon itself. This distinction is not intended to disparage fingers, names, or concepts. As limited as they may be, without fingers or words, with what could we host or care for the world? As Rhee Dongshick (2002), the founder of Tao psychotherapy, has suggested in the face of this conundrum, when you have really caught the experience, let go of the words, for only, "Then [as he explained it], you become friendly with the Tao" (p. 94). Rhee's view concurs with Heidegger's: Although concepts first show us the way to beings, they are not the beings themselves which lie, beyond all pointing and holding, in the breath and heartbeat of lived experience. As Heidegger (1977b/1947) put it, "If man is to find his way again into the nearness of Being, he must first learn to exist in the nameless" (p. 199).

With this preliminary disclosure of my own hermeneutic *démarche* at least begun, I can move on to the problems at hand. What are Tao, Dasein, and Psyche and what do they have to do with depth psychotherapy?

## Tao, Dasein, and Psyche:
## Ontological Grounds for Psychotherapy[4]

---

[4]Here we need to distinguish between two aspects of being, the ontic or ontical on the one hand and the ontologic or ontological on the other. The *ontic or ontical refers to the particular beings in the course of our everyday, mundane lives.* Ontic refers to the specific, individual beings that appear to us as we go about living our lives, to the particular beings that show themselves in our ordinary, prosaic existence. *The ontologic or ontological refers, not just to particular beings, but to their "being-ness," to what makes them the very kind of being they are, for example, the treeness of trees, the cowness of cows, the seaness of seas or the humanness of humans.* Ontologically speaking, our human beingness is that way of being in world in every moment of our lives that we have in common with all other human beings in every moment of their lives. The ontologic or ontological refers to what actually makes human beings human beings and not any other kind of being and, thus, to what necessarily obtains in every moment of every human being's life (See Craig, 2008a).

Each of the three particular approaches to depth psychology, namely, psychoanalysis, daseinsanalysis, and Tao psychotherapy are grounded in a concern for a particular ontological domain of being. I will touch briefly on each these realms, beginning with the most familiar and delimited, the Psyche of psychoanalysis; moving from there to the least well known, the Dasein of daseinsanalysis; and ending with the oldest and most all-encompassing, the Tao of Eastern Philosophy.

## Psychoanalysis: The Realm of Psyche
Even as a young man Freud (as cited in Mason, 1985) was hungry for a vocation, a calling, an object of devotion worthy of his intense intellectual fervor. A few years after opening his private practice he wrote his friend and confidant, Wilhelm Fliess, that "a man like me cannot live without a hobby horse, without a consuming passion, without...a tyrant. I have found one. In its service I know no limits. It is psychology, which has always been my distant beckoning goal" (p. 129). Thus, it happened that Sigmund Freud, the founder of depth psychology, gave his existence to understanding what he called the life of the soul (*Seelenleben*), describing his science of psychoanalysis as *Wissenschaft vom Seelenleben*, a science of the life of the soul (Freud, 1933/1940, p. 4). For Freud, the human psyche or soul (*Seele*) was an ambiguous and indefinable reality but also it was that which we hold most dear in our lives. Indeed, the master recommended psychoanalysis, not for its healing potential but, rather for "the truths it contains (*Wahrheitsgehalts*)... about that which comes most near to human beings, namely, their very own essence (*Wesen*)" (Freud, 1933/1940, translation mine, p. 169). There can be no doubt that what he intended to designate by this essence was nothing other than the human soul (*Seele*) or life of the soul (*Seelenleben*). Freud did not understand the soul as any substantive or transcendental entity, but rather, he saw it as a kind of historical, cultural, experiential essence, the very heart of an individual's existence as lived. That such a reality eludes precise definition is obvious. In fact, among the many dictionaries of psychoanalysis one will rarely, if ever, find the words psyche, soul, or life of the soul listed among its entries. The limits of language in such ontological domains have been known by philosophers and thinkers from every age and culture. One only has to recall the first lines of the *Tao Te Ching*, cited

---

Generally speaking, ontology refers to the philosophical discipline whose task is the study of being. Historically, the aim of ontology is to understand the kind of being (beingness) any particular being is. Phenomenological ontology begins with the everyday appearance of a *particular being* (ontic) in order to understanding its *beingness*, the fundamental structure or essence of *what makes the particular being the kind of being it is*: not just this particular tree, but tree*ness*;, not just this particular human being, but human*ness*. The task of disclosing the ontological characteristics of human beings, beings Martin Heidegger (1927/1962) that called Dasein, was the whole purpose of his magnum opus, *Being and Time*. This section addresses three different kinds of being (Tao, Dasein, and Psyche) that are not only central to each of the three representative approaches to psychotherapy but also to the existence of psychotherapy as such.

above: "The tao that can be told is not the eternal Tao" (S. Mitchell, Trans., 1988, Chapt. 1). Not surprisingly, Freud seems also to have felt that to define the soul is to miss it entirely (Freud, 1933/1964, p. 95), that, like the Tao, the soul that can be told is not the true soul. But what is this human quiddity, the soul or psyche? Although it has been suggested that what we mean by soul, existentially speaking, is "an individual's *very own situated gathering of lived experience*" (Craig, 2008b, p. 257), even this language fails to capture the flesh and blood essence of our experience whenever we call upon the soul. Could it be that, as a devoted disciple of the Unseen and mysterious, Freud was passionately obsessed with the life of the soul not in spite of but, rather, because of the impossibility of ever actually capturing its essence with words?

A thought: *Where Being and mystery lie, there language cannot go.*

## Daseinsanalysis: The Realm of Dasein

Just as Freud grounded his entire work and life in the realm of being we call psyche, or soul, existential analysts ground the whole of their scientific and clinical endeavor in human existence as a whole, that is, in that realm of being the philosopher Martin Heidegger designated with the everyday German term *Dasein*. For Heidegger, Dasein meant the existing human both individually and collectively. Dasein refers not just to our human personality or our inner or subjective psychic life, what Freud called *Seelenleben*, but rather to our whole existence. Dasein means, literally, a there (*da*)–being (*sein*), a being-there, under-scoring our human existence as a realm of world openness, an ever unfolding opening up right here, right now. For Heidegger and his psychological protégés, Ludwig Binswanger and Medard Boss, the respective founders of the approach to existential psychology and psychotherapy called daseinsanalysis, we do not exist *in-there*, inside our epidermis, but rather *out-there* in the world. Dasein, that is you and I, exist as being-in-the-world (*In-der-Welt-sein*). With this under-standing of human existence as Dasein, Heidegger also sought to overcome what Rollo May (1958) referred to as "the cleavage between subject and object which has bedeviled Western thought and science since shortly after the renaissance" (p. 11). Unfettered by such dualism, we no longer find ourselves existing as self-contained intra-subjective entities, in any way separate from our world and merely interacting with it but, rather, as encountering our world as a unity, as our very self (see Buber, 1910/1957, p. 37). For example, right now, as I am writing and you are reading, we constitute one another's very existing, we exist inextric-ably as being-with-one-another, indeed, *as-one-another-being-with-one-another*. For Heidegger, Boss, and Binswanger, to be Dasein is to be a whole realm of world openness, of world open-ing (See Craig, 2009). Here, Western daseinsanalysis and Eastern Taoist thought are impressively consonant; both perspectives understand that we exist together with one another and with world as a singular unity, as one, or, even better, as *one-ing*. In daseinsanalysis it is understood that we exist in, with, and for one another as a whole realm of relational possibilities. In Taoist thought, as the philosopher and allegorist Chuang Tzu (as cited in Giles, 1926) put it, "The universe and I come into being together; and I and everything therein, are ONE" (p. 23, capital in the original).

Another thought: *Where self lies, there also other: One.*

## Eastern Thought: The Realm of the Tao

Just as Freud grounded his work in the intra-subjective realm of being we call psyche, or soul, and existential analysts grounded their endeavors in human existence as a whole, that realm of being human we call Dasein, much of Eastern philosophy is grounded in an even wider domain, that all-encompassing realm called the Tao. Tracing the Tao to as early as the 5th or 6th Centuries B.C.E., today the term is generally understood to refer both to the Way of Being and to the virtue of being in accord with this Way of Being. The word Tao means literally means *the Way* and refers to the Way of all that is, the entire spatial-temporal horizon of all the beings that ever have been, that are now, and that will ever be. Therefore, the Tao refers to that which precedes and gives birth to beings as a whole. The realm of the Tao is the realm of the All, taken both as a whole and with respect to each and every particular being that comprises this Whole. Further, the Way is not some static condition but, rather, an immediately present, ever unfolding destining of Being itself. Thus, the entire cosmos, the entire universe of Being has its very own Way, its very own *Waying*, its very own coming-into-presence even right here-and-now. But more, each individual being manifests an individual Tao or Taoing. Thus, you and I each have our very own Tao, our very own Waying, our very own inimitable coming-into-presence, which has been and is now unfolding. So, the Tao refers not just to the comprehensive Way of all Being, but to the distinctive Way of each and every particular being, including each and every one of us here-and-now, as well as each and every one of those whom we serve in our practice of psychotherapy.

The Tao is often thought of as akin to certain Western understandings of *Nature* as primordial Being. For example, Ellen Chen (1989) spoke of the Tao as "an image (hsiang) of the unnamable Urgrund...the dark hidden Urgrund, the mother of all" (p. 63). As this ground of all being, the Tao is the way of Nature itself, which Hölderlin (1952) described as "older than the ages and above the gods of East and West" (p. 162, translation mine). As Le Guin (1997) put it, the Tao "was born before the gods" (p. 7) and signifies the immanently, unfurling destining of all that is. It is ineffable, mysterious, miraculous, unitive; both human and not human, particular and universal, concrete and unsubstantial, meaningful and meaningless, visible and invisible, real and unreal, something and, yet, nothing at all. In this ontological sense then, the Tao refers, in part, to what Heidegger called Beingness as-such (*Seyn*) as well as his understanding of *world* in both the ontic and ontological senses that he designated as "the totality of entities" (*Das All des Seienden*).

Still another thought: *Wherever anything is, wherever you are, there also is the Tao.*

**Tao, Dasein, and Psyche: Ineluctable Grounds for Depth Psychotherapy**
Now, you may be wondering what any of this has to do with the question, "What is it that makes such a process as psychotherapy possible in the first place?" Clearly, if any one of these three domains of being, Tao, Dasein, or Psyche did not exist, there would be no such thing as psychotherapy in the first place. That anything is at all, especially what we call the Tao or Beingness as such, is required for psychotherapy to be. Without Dasein, the kind of being we call human being, the one who has the capacity to be open to being, to perceive and understand being, without this Dasein, psychotherapy could not be. And finally, without psyche or Seele, without soul, that is, without individual and collective experience; without sentience or awareness; without memory, language, culture, and history psychotherapy would not only be unnecessary but nonsense and impossible. The Tao has given birth to the human, the human has given birth to the psyche; all three are necessary preconditions for the psychotherapy to even exist at all. So, ontologically speaking, Tao, Dasein, and Psyche all make any kind of psychotherapy possible in the first place. Remember, none of this has to be at all. It could just as well *not* be. Tao, Dasein, and Psyche are not the kinds of beings to be taken for granted.

As you may have already suspected from the above, whereas Freud's psychoanalysis provides the theoretical and technical foundation for almost all depth psychotherapies today, daseinsanalysis and Eastern thought bring to depth psychology a philosophical, ethical, and ontological foundation for that theory and practice. One's understanding these three, Tao, Dasein, and Psyche, is both necessary and essential for the theory and practice of depth psychotherapy, even if one's understanding remains pre-reflective or even largely unexplicated. In what follows, I will show how such a synthesis of certain basic premises and promises of depth psychotherapy from Eastern, existential, and psychoanalytic thought and practice can strengthen and enrich our understanding and conduct of the art and science of depth psychotherapy.

## The Shared Premises of Depth Psychotherapy

In the following section, I will briefly discuss four foundational premises for the theory and practice of depth psychotherapy shared by psychoanalysis, Tao psychotherapy, and daseinsanalysis.

### The Problem of Suffering
Lying at the very heart of all three traditions of thought and practice is the recognition of the inevitable and unavoidable reality of human suffering. Although as a physician Freud was specifically concerned with the severest forms of what he called *neurotic misery*, he also recognized most assuredly, that to be human was to suffer. His conviction about the ubiquity of human suffering, first implied in his early remark that the hope of psychoanalysis was in "transforming ...hysterical misery into ordinary unhappiness" (Breuer & Freud,1893-1895/1955, p. 305),

was spelled out quite explicitly in his later works, particularly in his companion works, *Future of an Illusion* (1961b/1927) and *Civilization and its Discontents* (1961a/1930), where he described human suffering as *fatefully inevitable* and threatening from three directions: our bodies "which are doomed to decay and dissolution…," "the external world which may rage against us with overwhelming and merciless forces of destruction" (p. 77) and, finally, our relations to other human beings, a suffering he acknowledged was "perhaps more painful to us than any other" (p. 77). Although Freud apparently read very little if any Eastern writings, he was as convinced of the ubiquity of human suffering as the Buddha whose very first of Four Noble Truths was the "Truth of Suffering" (*Duhkha*, Sanskrit). Indeed, for the Buddhist suffering is one of the three basic characteristics (*Trilakshana*) of existence. This understanding of suffering can also be found in the great Taoist allegorist, Chuang Tzu (as cited in Hinton, 1998), and seen in this passage:

> Once we happen into the form of this body, we cannot forget it. And so, it is that we wait out the end. Grappling and tangling with things, we rush headlong toward the end, and there's no stopping it. It's sad isn't it? We slave our lives away and never get anywhere, work ourselves ragged and never find our way home. How could it be anything but sorrow? People talk about never dying, but what good is that? This form we have soon becomes others and the mind vanishes with it. How could it be called anything but great sorrow? (p. 20)

As you can imagine, existential writers and philosophers from Dostoevsky to Hemingway and from Kierkegaard to Camus would find little to argue here. Just hear some of their titles: *Notes from the Underground, The Idiot, Crime and Punishment, Sickness unto Death, Fear and Trembling, The Concept of Dread, The Stranger, The Plague, No Exit, A Happy Death,* and *For Whom the Bell Tolls.* Perhaps, among these thinkers, none were terser than Ibsen (1867/1963) when he wrote, "Life is a terrible price to pay for birth" (p. 155). Whether our suffering is neurotic, as in the case of psychoanalysis, existential, as in the case of daseinsanalysis, or mental, as in the case of Taoism and Eastern philosophy, what is inescapable for all three forms of depth psychology is the brute living reality of human suffering, itself.

## The Possibility of Virtue

Another basic premise shared by our three representative depth psychotherapies is the possibility of some kind of human virtue. As I mentioned briefly earlier in this chapter, the second fundamental meaning of the Tao denotes the teaching and practicing of the Tao, that is, being in accord with the Tao. This second signifycation of Tao is found in the little Chinese word, Te, as in *Tao Te Ching.* Usually understood as virtue, Te refers specifically to the way we find or do not find our very own reconciliation with what is and is becoming, with the Tao. Daseins-analysis and psychoanalysis are also concerned with the possibility *the well lived life*, with virtue, broadly defined. In all three streams of thought, such virtue is not about how things are but, rather, how *we* are with how things are. Naturally, this virtue could appear in different linguistic costumes. For the Taoist, virtue is in accordance with the Tao, with what is; for the daseinsanalyst, virtue is openness and authenticity; for the psychoanalyst virtue is worthwhile, minimally conflicted love and work and the capacity to live both realistically and well with the disappointments and sacrifices required in exchange for the reasonable protections and comforts provided by civilized existence. Fully recognizing their many specific differences, one can still say that all three traditions extol the virtuous life as one that is in harmony with the real, the true. Although I do not recall James Bugental (1965), one of the founders of humanistic psychology, ever mentioning the Tao as such, he quite aptly articulated this second meaning of Tao, that is Te, the teaching and practicing of Tao, when he described the challenge of authenticity as follows: "A person is authentic in the degree to which his being in the world is in accord with the givenness of his own nature and of the world" (pp. 31-32).

Now, one rather inconvenient difficulty is that regardless of how desirable it might be, virtue is not a way of being that can be achieved without considerable personal effort and sacrifice. All that given us is existence and, with this, suffering. Virtue, however it is defined, is merely a possibility, and a possibility that comes, for all its benefits, at considerable expense including sacrifices in time and money; forsaken personal gratifications; the shouldering of inevitable sorrows and disappointments; the bearing of responsibility for one's own feelings, behaviors and attitudes; and a ready concern for others that at least matches our concern for ourselves. All this, not to mention the unfortunate circumstance that virtue is not always a particularly welcome attribute can make the pursuit of virtue plainly unappealing. Indeed, in our own lifetime, we have all known extraordinary human beings who have paid for their virtue with their lives.[5]

## The Primacy of Lived-Experience
A third area of confluence is in the basic way to overcome human suffering or achieve virtue. All three traditions agree that one can neither overcome suffering nor achieve virtue vicariously or even intellectually but must, in fact, engage these hopes through immersion in immediate, personal experience. Whether the path leads, as Freud put it, to *ordinary unhappiness*, or all the way to clarity of mind (Shūnyatā), enlightenment and the highest form of transcendent conscious-ness (*Nirvana*), there is no other way except going on one's own way. Thus, another

---

[5] As the reader may well have guessed, I am thinking here of such individuals as Mohatma Ghandi, John and Robert Kennedy, and Martin Luther King all of whom represented certain kinds of virtuous lives that were perceived as threatening to others. That said, I am not attempting to idealize these men as they, like all of us, were far from virtuous in every aspect of their lives, however the term is defined.

basic premise shared by these approaches to psychological life is that one must actually live them through to ever understand and appropriate their possi-bilities. As Chuang Tzu (1998) suggested, "traveling the Way makes it Way" (p. 23). One's destining is forged and found, ultimately, not in words or theories or trainings, but in living it through. As Heidegger (1927/1962) explained, speaking of the fundamental question of ontology, "One must seek a way...and this is the way one must go. Whether this is the only way or even the right one at all, can be decided only *after one has gone along it*" (p. 487, emphasis Heidegger's). The German poet, Friedrich von Schiller (1805/1972) wrote, speaking of the fate of the oppressive Swiss governor Gessler, "He has no choice but through this sunken way to come to Kussnacht...there is no other road" (p. 109) and, later, "all who travel make their destined way to their own tasks" (p. 111). For psychoanalysis, too, there is no escaping the onerous trials of personal experience, namely in the form of a personal analysis. Although Freud's (1912/1958) standard for analysts of "psychoanalytic purification" (p. 116) was more exacting than his standard for patients, namely, the transformation of "hysterical misery into ordinary unhap-piness" (Breuer & Freud, 1893-1895/1955, p. 305), the path through painful and uncanny personal experience was still unavoidable.

Psychoanalysis, daseinsanalysis, and Tao psychotherapy all agree that psy-chic liberation can only be achieved by passing conscientiously through the fires of one's own lived experience. The word conscientious is the critical one here for, although we must all obviously live through our life in one way or another, to do so conscientiously, that is, mindfully, with a heightened sense of awareness and personal responsibility, is another thing entirely. Given the ubiquity of suffering, who would want to have to endure this suffering conscientiously? If our human existence is inevitably one of profound sorrow and suffering, who would not wish for an escape, a way around, a way out? Given the demands of a virtuous existence, the effort and sacrifices it requires, regardless of the means that are chosen, who would not at least consider the possibility of giving up virtue for the fantasy of a pleasurable, uncomplicated, mindless existence?

## The Penchant for Flight
Thus, a fourth premise shared by all three representative approaches to depth psychology is that human beings have an understandable penchant to avoid that which is painful, unpleasant, or in some way threatening to their sense of them-selves or their functioning status quo even if this comes at the price of one's own authentic existence, one's own-most truth. For Freud (1905/1953c), this elusive-ness took the form of repression and a host of other tactical psychological defenses. Underlying all of these defenses was the human tendency to cling to fam-iliar forms of suffering rather that open up to what is new and true. As Freud put it "the patient clings to his disease and even fights against his own recovery" (p. 261). For Daseinsanalysts, the individual flees *in the face of itself*, in the face of being-in-the-world as such, by falling into absorption by what Heidegger called

the They-self (*Man-Selbtsein*), the everyday herd-like concern with whatever practical matters lie at hand. For Eastern thinkers, this flight from reality is achieved, not only by absorption in everyday concerns or what might be called the familiar appeal of the status quo, but also it could be attained by the stubborn attachments to desires and *false views* (see Rubin, 1996). For Rhee Dongshick, such "false views" often come in the form of what William Barrett (1956) called a "conceptual prison" (p. xvi), that is, abstract concepts that keep an individual away from his or her own living experience.

Regardless of how this flight from reality is construed, all three of these depth psychologies recognize the ubiquity of fleeing in the face of what is, whether that fleeing is in order to avoid the exacting rigors of the virtuous life or the unforgiving vicissitudes of human suffering. As one patient exclaimed to me recently, "I don't want to be human!" Another patient, chuckling almost proudly to himself, recently began his session by announcing a fantasy that had occurred to him earlier in the day. His image was of staging a one-man protest in front of my office. As the image had it, he was waving a placard reading on one side, "I don't want to be enlighten-ed" and on the other, "I just want what I want." His ridicule accepted; we went on to discuss his understandable ambivalence about the relatively moderate prom-ises of psychotherapy in relation to its immoderate demands. Somewhere along the way, hoping to assure him that his doubts placed him good company, I men-tioned the American author, Saul Bellow's remarked that although Socrates said, "The unexamined life is not worth living," and Aristotle countered, "The unlived life is not worth examining," sometimes, Bellow rejoined, "The examined life makes you wish you were dead." With this, the patient's proud, wry grin returned.

Considering these four shared premises as a whole naturally begs this question: If our suffering is so great, our virtue so demanding, our relation to the lived-experience of both so ambivalent, and our penchant for flight so ubiquitous, what could make depth psychotherapy at all possible in the first place? Who would want it? Certainly, the possibility of some relief from acute suffering is one factor, but are there also certain characteristics of depth psychotherapy that contribute to its hospitality as a project?

## The Promises of Psychotherapy

Following the medical customs of his day, when Freud first began his practice as a physician, he combined lengthy home visits with hypnosis, massage, and hydrotherapy with the hope of alleviating the various enigmatic sufferings to which his patients were prone. However, he soon realized the complication of such fashionable remedies, especially with respect to their untoward influence on his relationships with the individuals he promised to help. Gradually, with some quirky but impeccable feedback, especially from gifted female patients, along with the impressive yields of his own self-analysis, Freud developed psychoanalysis, the first systematic approach to modern depth psychotherapy. Although psycho-analysis has since grown into a whole chorus of depth psychological healing voices, they concur on a few basic therapeutic promises. Underlying depth psy-chotherapy's potential appeal and efficacy are these three essential features: its framework, its attitude, and its mode.

## The Framework of Depth Psychotherapy: A Sanctuary for Being
To my mind, with all their present-day cultural and historical limitations, Freud's (1904/1953a, 1905/1953c, 1912/1958a, 1915/1958b, 1913/1958c, 1912/1958-d, 1914/1958e) papers on technique are still among the most sound, well-written treatises on the fundamentals of depth psychotherapeutic practice. These tech-nical works include, among other things, time tested recommendations for establishing a sturdy, trustworthy framework within which the vicissitudes of an-alytic or psychotherapeutic relating could safely and freely proceed. Although in some ways contrived and artificial, the framework offers a reliable set of con-stants, a clearly defined environmental capacity for evoking, containing, and sustaining the radical, revolutionary, and often dangerous experiment conducted by the therapeutic partners involved. Agreements with respect to time, space, compensation, and the roles, rules, and responsibilities governing the behavior and attitude of each of the participants all contribute to building a structure or framework for the conduct of depth psychotherapy.

The term framework was first used by Marion Milner (1952) to describe the therapeutic pact, comparing it to the frame of a painting which sequesters its reality, preserving it from intrusion, and establishing for it a living refuge. Win-nicott (1957) first referred to this same therapeutic structure as the setting, by which he meant "the summation of all the details of management" (p. 297). Winnicott went on to call this unique setting the *facilitating environment* and *the holding environment* (Winnicott, 1958, 1965, 1986, 1989) likening the later to the infants "being held by a mother. [He emphasized that] "The mother holds a situ-ation" (Winnicott, 1975, pp. 262-263) allowing both mother and child to "*live an experience together*" (1975, p. 152, italics Winnicott's). This therapeutic setting or framework has also been called a *therapeutic cocoon*, an *analytic sphere* (Vider-man, 1974), a *safe place* (Havens, 1989), and a *sanctuary* (Craig, 2000). However, whatever it is called, it is clear that this framework requires two fundamental features: first, *a sound but appropriately flexible perimeter* that contains, protects, and accommodates its contents, and, second, *an open, free area, a pregnant emptiness* where what is contained and accommodated is given space to appear and develop according to its own nature.

That being requires emptiness has long been known. In the *Tao Te Ching* we read that "being and non-being create each other" (S. Mitchell, trans., 1988, Ch. 2) and that the Tao itself is "like an eternal void: filled with infinite possibilities" (Ch. 3). In daseinsanalysis, it is the encounter with emptiness that brings us face-to-face with Being as such, with the very circumstance that we are at all. Although Heidegger (1929/1977) was speaking philosophically, not psychologically, his ontological assertions, are remarkably apt for the ontic everyday situation of depth psychotherapy: "For human existence the nothing makes possible the open-edness of beings as such" (p. 106). In the same paper he added, "human existence can relate to beings only if it holds itself out into the nothing" (p. 111) and "From the nothing all beings as being come to be" (p. 110). Concurring with these psycho-analytic and daseinsanalytic perspectives are these from the East, presented here in side-by-side translations of the same passage from the *Tao Te Ching* on the pregnancy of the nothing, the empty:

| | |
|---|---|
| We throw Clay | Hollowed out, |
| to shape a pot, | clay makes a pot. |
| but the utility of the clay pot | Where the pots not |
| is a function of the nothingness inside it. | is where it's useful. |
| We bore out doors and windows | Cut doors and windows |
| To make a dwelling, | to make a room |
| But the utility of the dwelling | Where the room isn't |
| Is a function of the nothingness inside it. | There's room for you |
| (Ames & Hall, 2003, p. 91) | (Le Guin, 1997, p. 14) |

When read phenomenologically, Freud's recommendations for therapeutic practice constitute a psychical pact, a *"working alliance"* (Greenson, 1967) that establishes in the midst of everyday life a concrete opportunity or opening up to and for the patient's being and becoming in the midst of everyday life. Freud's depth psychotherapeutic framework is nothing less than a human refuge for the real. As Masud Khan (1974), the defrocked but still sage British psychoanalyst, put it, the essential yield of the framework or *holding* for patients is nothing less than their very own "experience of *being*" (p. 204, emphasis Khan's).

All three of our representative approaches to psychotherapy construe it as a deliberately structured situation that allows human beings to take their own being seriously, that wrests from the harried world of everyday existence an asylum within which the patient's own reality can show itself from itself in the very way in which it shows itself from itself.[6] One could fairly say that depth psychotherapy intentionally recreates in the ontic realm of everyday life, the ontological char-acteristic of Being Heidegger (1927/1962) called the Open or Clearing (*Lichtung*) and the Taoists call emptiness or nothing. Ontologically speaking, "the Opening means the beginning of Being, the unfurling of Being, the sheltering of Being, and the freeing of Being" (Craig, 2009). Ontically speaking, the opening of psycho-therapy evokes the beginning of the patient's being, the unfurling of the patient's being, the sheltering of the patient's being, and the freeing of the patient's being. In other words, again essentially speaking, psychotherapy is a kind of asylum or sanctuary (Craig, 2000) for the being and the becoming of the patient; the asylum

---

[6] Heidegger's (1927/1962) famous exposition of the essence of phenomenology was "to let that which shows itself from itself be seen from itself in the very way in which it shows itself from itself" (p. 58).

creates time, space, and human relationship, the singular purpose of which is to open the way for human individuals to appear precisely as they are and are on their way to being.

## The Attitude of Depth Psychotherapy: Letting Being Be
From this perspective, a major challenge is to keep therapeutic ambition from getting in the way of what is arising at the moment, to provide an open forum, imbued with the safety and freedom for the individual to be whoever or whatever he or she is at the moment. Indeed, this is the very foundation for Western psychoanalysis and all real depth psychotherapy. But, again, if suffering is so great, virtue so demanding, and the penchant for flight so ubiquitous, what could possibly entice individuals, even in the safest and coziest of sanctuaries, to undergo such an ordeal as depth psychotherapy in the first place?

**Psychoanalytic Letting Be**. Freud well understood that any intensive depth psychotherapy worth its salt was carried out in the grip of ambivalence, a wish to escape suffering that is at once sufficient reason for entering psycho-therapy and for avoiding it. The person does not exist who is not profoundly reluctant about genuine, thoroughgoing self-knowledge. As noted earlier, the examined life does not cheery advocates make. Having seen for himself the value of self-understanding, Freud was eager to discover a way to maximize self-disclo-sure and minimize resistance.

Freud became convinced that if patients could follow one simple behavior, called *Einfall*, it would lead to the revelation of everything required for a cure.[7] Einfall or free association, involved letting whatever appeared in one's stream of consciousness to do so without interference and then reporting these *associations* directly. Thus, Freud would say something like:

> Let's not bother ourselves here with our customary habits of social discourse and decorum. Just lie down, relax, and simply say, without exception, whatever passes through your mind. Oh, and, by the way, don't be concerned with me: I'll get out of your way and just listen to whatever you have to say, without any of the kinds of personal feelings and judgments you've come to expect from others.

With such reassurances setting the stage for the patient's practice of free association, Freud hoped to create as relaxed and open minded a situation as possible,

---

[7] Freud discusses his "Basic Rule," *Einfall*" translated free association a number of times throughout his collected works (see for example, 1900/1953b, pp. 100-106; 1904/1953, pp. 250-252; 1913/1958c, pp. 134-136; 1915-1916/1961, pp. 114 -115; 1916-1917/1963, pp. 287-289; 1923/1925, pp. 237-238; 1926/159, pp. 187-188;1940/1964, p. 140). However his first detailed discussion, found in chapter two of *The Interpretation of Dreams* (1900/1953, pp. 100-106) remains the most informative.

essentially one in which the individuals could completely indulge themselves in the observation of their own experience, however irrational, ridiculous, or inappropriate it might appear. Here was a situation free of judgment, ridicule, interference, or retaliation, the entire design of which was to provide an opportunity to share one's deepest secrets, one's most private memories and longings with another human being, assured of the other's genuine interest, empathy, and care. All this would take place in the interest of the patient's own self-discovery, understanding, and acceptance.

Fine idea! The catch was no one could do it. Thus, Freud began taking great pains to help patients overcome their reticence to proceed as advised. For example, he would encourage patients to let go "as you would in a conversation in which you were rambling on quite disconnectedly and at random" (Freud, 1904/1953a, p. 251). Or he might advise, "So say whatever comes to your mind. Act as though, for instance, you were a traveler sitting next to the window of a railway carriage and describing to someone inside the carriage the changing views which you see outside" (Freud, 1913/1958c, p. 135). Still no one could do it.

So, in addition to these more persuasive methods, Freud (1904/1953a) also tried an educative approach to his technique for "the widening of consciousness" (p. 250). For instance, in *The Interpretation of Dreams,* Freud (1900/1953b) distinguished between the everyday attitude of self-reflection and psychoanalytic attitude of self-observation with the former being influenced by the critical faculty and the later requiring its suspension. For such self-observation, he wrote one needs only to "increase... the attention paid to [one's] own psychical perceptions [and to eliminate] the criticism by which [one] normally sifts through thoughts that occur to [one]. Suspend disbelief [and] accept what shows itself" (1900/1953b, p. 101, brackets mine) were the gentle battle cries of the couch.

Thus, well over a century ago, Freud was essentially claiming that to be helped by depth psychotherapy, you must practice what we would describe today as a sophisticated form of mindfulness, a form of self-observation requiring that one be calmly interested in one's own unfettered stream of consciousness and accept the psychic reality of whatever occurs. However, Freud not only recommended this strikingly enlightened manner of being as the Fundamental Rule for patients, but also, he recommended essentially the same manner of being for the therapist. For instance, in his case study of Little Hans (1909/1955a) he described his own therapeutic *démarche* as follows: "We... suspend our judgment and give our impartial attention to everything that there is to observe" (p. 23). Freud's name for this "fundamental rule for analysts," was *Gleichschwebende Aufmerksamkeit* (1912/1958c, p. 111), translated roughly as *a similar evenly hovering attentiveness.*[8] So therapists, too, were advised to let themselves go, to be

---

[8] The German-English translations run somewhat as follows: Gleich = like or similar; schwebender = suspended, hovering, floating; Aufmerksamkeit = attentiveness or consideration. Although Strachey's English translation is "evenly-suspended attention," other common translations in

as open and free as possible in receiving whatever occurs in the moment. Again, as this is not a common everyday attitude, Freud offered a number of supportive instructions. For instance, he discouraged analysts from deliberately concentrating on anything in particular, instructing them, instead, to give "equal notice to everything" and to "simply listen, and not bother about... keeping anything in mind" (1912/ 1958c, p. 112). For Freud, this rule of "evenly hovering attention" (p. 111) for the therapist was, "intended to create for the doctor a counterpart to the 'fundamental rule of psychoanalysis' which is laid down for the patient:"

> Just a patient must relate everything that his self-observation can detect, and keep back all the logical and affective objections that seek him to make a selection from among them, so the doctor must put himself in a position to make use of everything he is told...without substituting a censorship of his own...To put it in a formula: he must turn his own unconscious like a receptive organ towards the transmitting organ of the patient. (1912/ 1958c, p. 115)

Now, in order to achieve this kind of a radically open, objective mind, Freud also added that the therapist "must himself fulfill one psychological condition to a high degree. He may not tolerate any resistances in himself" (1912/1958c, p. 115). For Freud, it was not sufficient for the therapist to be "an approximately normal person [but that he should undergo] psychoanalytic purification [and thus become fully cognizant of] those complexes of his own that would be apt to interfere with his grasp of what the patient tells him" (1912/1958c, p. 116). Other psychoanalytic practices shaping the therapeutic interaction, are neutrality and abstinence. Whereas being neutral means the therapist makes every effort to avoid leaping into the patient's experience to take sides, offer opinions, or prize one idea, thought, feeling, or form of communication over any other; Being abstinent means not seizing the therapeutic situation to gratify either the patient's or the therapists wishes but, rather, making every effort to allow what comes with those wishes to show itself in order that it can be more deeply understood. Given these basic Western depth psychotherapeutic attitudes, one could fairly say that the psychoanalyst's stance is not so different from what in the East is called the empty mind (*Shūnyatā*). Indeed, with this talk of the "widening of consciousness" (1904/1953a, p. 250), of radical openness and permissiveness toward what is, of neutrality and abstinence, Freud was not only sounding like an existentialist but also like a Zen Buddhist master worthy of his own robes![9]

---

psychoanalytic literature include "evenly hovering attention" or "free-floating attention," the latter attempting to emphasize the similarity with "free association" (*Einfall*).

[9] I do not want to suggest that free association and evenly hovering attention are the precise equivalents of meditative mindfulness nor that Freud had the same kind of wisdom one finds in the masters

**Taoist Letting Be**. Freud's recommendations regarding the two fundamental rules of depth psychotherapy were essentially an invitation for the patient and therapist alike to let what is, be, to allow whatever is beginning to show itself to come into its own being.[10] But how does such thinking actually stand with the Tao? Remember, Tao is the Way, the immediate and ever unfolding path of all that is, Being's becoming. Ancient is this Way, older than memory, older than recorded history, older than the oldest thing of which we know.[11] According to the Tao, not only does all that is have a certain energy or impulse to be, but also, everything that is has a certain essential Way of being. In other words, every being has its own Way of being that is tirelessly unfurling itself in time. It is this very Way that the psychoanalysts and depth psychotherapists are pledged to attune themselves to, to let be, and to serve. In Taoist thought there is a name for this *being in accord with being*. It is called *wu wei* and has been the East's preeminent spiritual practice for millennia.

Exactly what is *wu wei*? The Chinese *wu* means "without" in the sense of "free of" or, more literally, "empty of" and *wei* means "to do," "to act," "to make," or "to work." Taken together, then, the term *wu wei* means literally to be "free of acting or doing," "empty of working or producing." Alan Watts (2000) preferred to think of *wu wei* as "not forcing" and John C. H. Wu (1989) translated the term as "Non-Ado" (p. 7) as in not making a fuss about. Thus, *wu wei* means "not tampering with," "grabbing," or "grasping after" (see J. C. H. Wu, 1989, p. 59). A basic distinction in the practice of *wu wei* is between *doing* and *being*, with *wu wei* emphasizing the possibility of simply being what one is and letting other beings be what they are, rather than striving *to make* oneself or others or things into something else, some wished for something else, or some desired something else. Wu's translation of *wu wei* as not tampering or meddling with being means not interfering with the natural order of things, the Tao. For example, we find such aphorisms in the *Tao Te Ching* as "Practice non-doing and everything will fall in place" (S. Mitchell, 1988, Chapt. 3) and" When the beautiful strives to be beautiful it is repulsive... when the good strives to be good, it is no good... this is why sages abide in the business of non-action" (Ivanhoe, 2002, p. 2). We also find these words: "The Way does nothing, yet nothing is left undone" (Ivanhoe, 2002, p. 37).

---

of the East. My point is mainly that the existence of such striking similarities deserves our attention and understanding.

[10] Years later, the British analyst Wilfred Bion (1967/1970) pithily summarized the primary requirement of evenly hovering attention as the "disciplined denial of memory and desire" (p. 41).

[11] The concept of the Tao is in this context akin to certain Western understandings of Nature as primordial Being. For example, Ellen Chen (1989) speaks of the Tao as "an image (hsiang) of the unnamable Urgrund," "the dark hidden Urgrund, the mother of all" (p.63). As this ground of all being, the Tao is the way of Nature itself, which Hölderlin (1952) describes as "older than the ages and above the gods of East and West" (p. 162, translation mine). As Le Guin (1997) puts it the Tao "was born before the gods" (p. 7).

Recalling the essential attitude required of free association, evenly hovering attention, neutrality, and abstinence, you find something very close to that non-interfering, non-manipulating presence that in the East is called simply, *wu wei*.

**Daseinsanalytic Letting Be**. Although Martin Heidegger's (1927/1962) task was ontological and not at all concerned with the practice of psychotherapy, he, too, spoke of the possibility *of letting being be*. For example, in *Being and Time*, Heidegger described the task of phenomenology itself as *"to let (lassen)* that which shows itself be seen from itself in the very way in which it shows itself from itself" (p. 58, emphasis mine).[12] Later, in *"On the Essence of Truth"* (1943/1977c), he wrote, "the essence of truth is freedom," (p. 125) and then defined freedom as *"letting beings be"* (*Seinlassen vom Seindem*, p. 127, emphasis mine), or, from another translation of the same work (Heidegger, 1943/1949a), as letting "whatever is at the moment be what it is" (*Lässt das jeweilige siende das Seinde sein, das es ist*, p. 333). Finally, in 1949, Heidegger used the term *Gelassenheit*, which literally means "the-gathering-of-letting-be-ness"[13] that Heidegger interpreted as a *"releasement toward things"* (1959/1966, p. 54, emphasis Heidegger's). For him such a releasement-toward-Being involved something quite like the practice of *wu wei*, in that it required a willing renunciation of willing (p. 59), a "letting-oneself-into-nearness" with beings or, in Eastern thought, a coming close to the Tao.

As Medard Boss (1958/1963, 1979/1971) tirelessly pointed out, of particular concern for the practice of psychotherapy is Heidegger's (1927/1962, pp. 157-159) distinction between the two different ways in which we care for human beings, namely, intervening care (*einspringende Fürsorge*) and anticipatory care (*vorauspringende Fürsorge*). Very briefly, intervening care is that kind of care by which we leap into patients' lives to take responsibility for them when we determine that they are incapable of doing so for themselves. Such intervening care can take the form of anything from giving advice to recommending medication, interventions for addiction, or hospitalization. On the other hand, anticipatory care is, as Boss (1988) pointed out ever since first reading the above cited passages in Heidegger, very close to the kind of care that Freud had designated for psychoanalytic or depth psychotherapy. When practicing anticipatory care, the therapist does everything possible to respect the patient's own integrity and capability and, instead of leaping in with recommendations and strategies, *leaps ahead,* or *out of the way* of the patient just in order to create an opening for a patient's existence, with all its limitations and possibilities, first, to show itself as

---

[12] The German word here, lassen, which literally means to leave something in a certain state, that is, to let is be as it is, becomes what might be called a "way-word" or "play-word" for Heidegger's thought over the next several decades. In this paragraph I only briefly mention a very few of the many different ways Heidegger follows the possible meanings and implications of the verb throughout his philosophical journey.

[13] See Heidegger's *Essay Concerning Technology* (1954/1977) for his translation of *Ge* in various German compound words as "gathering." For instance, *Gebirg* is a gathering of mountains, a mountain range. Thus, Ge-lassen-heit is, literally, the "gathering of- letting be -ness."

it is and, second, to develop in accordance with its own circumstances and freedom. As a psychotherapeutic manner of being, anticipatory care aspires *to let* patients be in and as their truth, to let them be precisely who they are and who they are on their way to being. Thus, anticipatory care invokes an opening up and coming close to what is, a *releasement* to the very existing of the individual as such. Boss, drawing on Heidegger, often spoke of Dasein's ontological vocation as "a shepherd of being." For Boss (1988), it was this ontological understanding of the relation of Dasein to Being that gave us the philosophical ground for what it is that makes such an endeavor as psychotherapy even possible in the first place.

Perikles Kastrinidis (1990), a Swiss psychiatrist and Daseinsanalyst, tried to clarify what such shepherding or *Gelassenheit* (the-gathering-of-letting-be-ness) might mean in the context of human relationships. Although his main concern was everyday love relationships, his thoughts regarding the development of serenity or the development of letting-be-ness (*Gelassenwerden*) is evocative for psycho-therapeutic relationships as well. Kastrinidis described three constituents of *Gelassenwerden*: *zulassen*, *loslassen*, and *sich einlassen*. I will consider each of these with respect to the conduct of psychotherapy.

Following Heidegger, for Kastrinidis (1990) *zulassen* means *to let near*, that is, to allow whatever it is that begins to show itself to continue to approach us, to come near to us, whether it be perceptions, dreams, fantasies, thoughts, feelings, or whatever. Such letting near refers not only to so called *mental things* but also to actual persons. For example, in psychotherapy, this means that patient and therapist alike allow each other to get close to one another, to come into each other's existence, to provide a home for the other in one's very own existence. The next constituent of *Gelassenwerden* is *loslassen*, which means *to let go*. In psycho-therapy this means, at least in part, letting go of old wishes, expectations, concepts, or prejudices. Whereas *zulassen* permits old, historically shaped ways of loving and being (i.e., transferential phenomena) to show themselves in the first place, *loslassen* allows patent and therapist alike to let go of those same old, rigid, or conflicted ways of being. For example, patients must let go of their idea of the therapist as the new, perfect, or omniscient parent, partner, or friend. Likewise, therapists must let go of their fantasies for the patient's life and allow each patient to follow his or her own-most way in life. On this, by the way, Freud (1919/1955a) was eloquent:

> We refused most emphatically to turn a patient who puts himself into our hands in search of help into our private property, to decide his fate for him, to force our own ideals upon him, and with the pride of a creator to form him in our image and see that it is good....*The patient should be educated to liberate and fulfill his own nature, not to resemble ourselves.* (p. 164-165, emphasis mine)

Naturally, one of the most poignant implications of *loslassen* is that at some point both patient and therapist must let go of the other, once and for all, without clinging or resentment, bitterness or guilt, thus releasing each to live their own-most future. Such letting go is a central way of being in the East. Rhee Dongshick (1995), frequently paraphrased Lao Tzu's words: "the Tao is gained by daily loss. Loss upon loss until it comes to wu-wei" (p. 165). Kastrinidis's (1990) under-standing of *Loslassen*, is thus very much in keeping with the wisdom of the Tao: to let things be means, in part, to let things go. The third constituent of *Gellas-senwerden* is *sich einlassen*, which means *to let oneself near*, that is, to let oneself get close to what shows itself. In psychotherapy, this suggests that both therapist and patient alike dare *to let themselves* come close to whatever it is that shows itself, to have the courage to let oneself come close to whatever appears.

The above reflections reveal a remarkable consonance among these three approaches to depth psychotherapy with respect to the basic attitude of *letting be* that makes the depth psychotherapy possible at all.

## The Mode of Depth Psychotherapy: Human Relationship
However crucial the framework of sanctuary and the attitude of letting be may be, these still do not touch the single most essential feature that makes depth psycho-therapy possible at all and that one single most important factor is a human relationship. No one entering depth psychotherapy would want to bear its de-mands if it were not for the possibility of a genuine human relationship with a genuine, trustworthy companion.

Freud (as cited in Breuer & Freud, 1893-1895/1955) understood the impor-tance of this indispensable aspect of psychotherapy even in his earliest years as a physician, when he wrote to his fiancée that he had come to realize that one cures patients more with one's own personality than with any kind of technique. In his earliest writing on psychoanalytic psychotherapy he spoke of the importance of the *personal relation* between the therapist and the patient which he called "*a sine qua non* to a solution of the problem" p. 266). In addition to the time and effort expended on behalf of the patient, for Freud, the therapist was also expected to bring such human qualities as patience, respect, sympathy, and friendliness (pp. 282-283). Thus, very early on, Freud readily acknowledged the irreplaceable value of "the special solicitude inherent in the treatment" (p. 302), and the *af-fective factor* of the *personal influence* of the therapist which one "can seldom do without" (p. 283). Although Freud (1915/1959) soon began to intellectually reify this human relation with a reductionistic and deterministic conceptualization of the therapeutic relationship as mere transference, he also wrote that "one has no right to dispute the 'genuine' nature of the love which makes its appearance in the course of analytic treatment" (p. 388). Further, in more private contexts he ac-knowledged the importance of personal human emotions, especially love, in the therapeutic situation. For instance, in a December 6, 1906 letter to Jung, Freud (as cited in McGuire, 1974) wrote of psychoanalysis, "Essentially, one might say, the cure is affected by love" (p. 12-13). Although, at the time, Freud was speaking of the curative effect of the patient's love for the therapist, he also understood that therapists, too, found themselves loving the person with whom they shared so many intimate hours. In a 1913 letter to Binswanger, Freud (as cited in Fichtner, 2003) addressed the problem of what a therapist should "give to the patient" (p. 112), especially with respect to love. Although cautioning that a therapist should beware of *giving* out of his or her own countertransference needs, he also said that "to give someone too little because one loves him too much is unfair to the patient and a technical error" (p. 112).

Subsequent to Freud's death, in the absence of such a powerful adjudicator of psychoanalytic thought and practice, depth psychotherapy as a whole became increasingly flexible and relational. For example, 15 years after her father's death, Anna Freud (1954) expressed the importance of personal human relatedness in therapeutic situation even more forcefully. She wrote:

> so far as the patient has a healthy part of his personality, his real relation-
> ship to the analyst is never wholly submerged....With due respect for the
> necessary strictest handling and interpretation of the transference, I feel
> still that we should leave room somewhere for the realization that analyst
> and patient are also two real people, of equal adult status, in a real
> personal relationship to each other. (pp. 618-619)

Today, at least in America, many psychoanalysts openly acknowledge the importance of the real, authentic human relationship that develops in intensive depth psychotherapy, and they even write about the significance of both the patient's love for the therapist and the analyst's love for the patient in the process of healing.

Daseinsanalysts, from Ludwig Binswanger (1963) and Medard Boss (1957/1963, 1971/1979) to Paul Stern (1972), all emphasize the realness of the relationship that emerges in the context of depth psychological exploration. None would deny that of all the factors contributing to the patient's long-term development and well-being, the genuine relationship stands without equal. The founder of daseinsanalytic psychotherapy, Medard Boss (1971/1979), said so explicitly: success in psychotherapy, he wrote, "depend[s] primarily on the physician's ability to allow this being-together to ripen in a way that [is] fruitful to the patient" (p. 259, brackets mine).

Tao psychotherapists also emphasize the importance of the human relationship in depth psychotherapy. For Rhee Dongshick (1995, 2002a) the therapist's genuine empathy and compassion are crucial for the patient's sense of well-being while undergoing depth psychotherapy. Empathy comes from the Greek words *em* and *pathos*. The word pathos means suffering and is also akin to sorrow or mourning. The word *em* means with. So, to be empathic is to be with the suffering, sorrow, or mourning of the other. Compassion comes from the combination of the Latin *pati*, which means suffering, and com, which means with. Thus, like empathy, compassion is to suffer with. However, compassion, even etymologically, contains a hint of adding something else that was not quite present with empathy, namely, not only *feeling with* but also *feeling for.* Whereas empathy brings the therapist into a profound relationship with the patient in his or her moment of suffering; compassion adds to this a sense of concern for that suffering, a sorrow for that suffering, a desire for the other to be somehow relieved of that suffering when the time is right. This understanding of compassion of adding to empathy's *feeling with*, the hint of also *feeling for*, is certainly in keeping with the Buddhist notion of compassion (*Karunā*) which speaks of the heart being moved on behalf of a person who is suffering. Thus, for Rhee, psychotherapy is essentially a cure brought about by a genuine human relationship.

How could it be otherwise? Depth psychotherapy is no vision quest. For all its potential benefits, it is a journey that can be full of terror, suffering, and uncertainty. For in depth psychotherapy, the icons and illusions upon which individuals have relied for so long can disintegrate before their very eyes and soon lie crumbled in the sand like the great stone visage of Shelley's Ozymandias. As if this were not enough, individuals often find old friends and relatives haunting one's dreams, not as the saints or saviors once imagined, but as ghosts, ghouls, or goblins, prostitutes or gangsters, intent on seduction, oppression, or simply the taste of our own blood. To make matters even more unpalatable, individuals often discover equally mangy aspects of themselves lurking in dark, long overlooked corners of desire. Why would anyone undertake a journey of such unflinching truthfulness alone?

Relationship – rich, full, honest, empathic, gentle being together – is surely, of all the above factors, the most consequential promise of depth psychotherapy. Insight, structure, technique, and knowledge, though utterly necessary, all pale in significance to the power of human being-with-one-another as the indispensable factor making depth psychotherapy possible at all.

## Summary

I have tried to touch on just a few very foundational matters regarding the nature and practice of psychotherapy, especially those matters on which there are important confluences among these three specific approaches to depth psychotherapy: classical psychoanalysis, daseinsanalysis, and Tao psychotherapy. I began with a brief explication of the term depth psychotherapy and then went on to identify and discuss certain epistemological concerns grounded in the problems of otherness and ownness, concerns particularly relevant to understanding traditions arising from contexts so unlike one's own. Throughout the remainder of the paper I attempted to address the question "What is it that makes depth psychotherapy even possible in the first place?" Beginning with the implications of the ontological domains of Tao, Dasein, and Psyche, I went on to disclose and discuss four basic premises of depth psychotherapy: the problem of suffering, the possibility of virtue, the primacy of lived–experience, and the penchant for flight. I then concluded with a consideration of three promises of depth psychotherapy, namely, its framework as a sanctuary for being, its attitude of letting be, and its mode of genuine human relationship. Naturally, this is just a beginning exploration of such themes and correspondences and I hope this paper will stimulate further reflection and investigation on the part of other psychotherapists regarding what is essentially human or what is the being-centered essence of depth psychotherapy.

As members of our own modern technological, results-driven culture, not to mention our now compulsively evidence-based profession, we have become increasingly pressured to focus on doing at the expense of being and, with this, increasingly forgetful of the very foundations of human existence in our practice of psychotherapy. Psychoanalysis, daseinsanalysis, and Tao psychotherapy, though in varying ways and to varying degrees, all point to the importance of being, the importance of being open to being, the importance of being in accord with being. As Medard Boss (1988) once reminded us, "as human beings we are never alone in this calling to respond to Being. We are always together with other human beings...and therefore never isolated in this humble but dignified vocation" (p. 61). Hopefully, with this encouraging attitude, we can learn ways to more effectively resist the dehumanizing aspects of our profession and work together to develop forms of psychotherapy that honor what is deepest and truest in our gentle profession.

## References

Ames, R. T. & Hall, D.L. (2003). *A philosophical translation of the Dao De Jing: Making this life significant.* New York, NY: Ballentine Books.

Atwood, G. E. & Stolorow, R. D. (1984). *Structures of subjectivity: Explorations in psychoanalytic phenomenology.* Hillsdale, NJ: The Analytic Press.

Barrett, W. (1956). Introduction: Zen for the West. In W. Barrett (Ed.), *Zen Buddhism: Selected writings of D. T. Suzuki.*, (pp. vii-xx). New York, NY: Doubleday Anchor Books.

Binswanger, L. (1963). *Being-in-the-world* (J. Needleman, Ed. & Trans.). New York, NY: Basic Books. (Original works published 1930- 1957)

Bion, W.R. (1967). Notes on memory and desire. *Psychoanalytic Forum, 2,* 271-280.

Bion, W. R. (1970). *Attention and interpretation: A scientific approach to insight in psycho-analysis and groups.* New York: Basic Books.

Bleuler, E. (1910). Die Psychanalyse Freuds: Verteidigung und kritische Bemerkungen. Jahrbuch fur Psychoanalytische und Psychopathologische Forschungen, II Band (II Hälfte), 623-730.

Boss, M. (1963). *Psychoanalysis and daseinsanalysis* (L.B. Lefebre, Trans.) New York, NY: Basic Books. (Original work published 1957)

Boss, M. (1979). *Existential foundations of medicine and psychology* (S. Conway & A. Cleaves, Trans.). New York, NY: Aronson. (Original work published 1971)

Boss, M. (1988). Recent considerations in daseinsanalysis. *The Humanistic Psychologist, 16* (1), 58-74.

Breuer, J. & Freud, S. (1955). Studies on Hysteria. In J. Strachey (Ed. and Trans.). *The standard edition of the complete psychological works of Sigmund Freud* (Volume 2). London, UK: Hogarth Press. (Original works published 1893-1895)

Buber, M. (1957) *Pointing the way.* New York, NY: Harper & Brothers. (Original work published 1910)

Bugental, J. F. T. (1965). *The search for authenticity.* New York, NY: Holt, Rinehart, and Winston.

Chen, E. M. (Trans.). (1989). The *Tao Te Ching: A new translation with commentary.* St. Paul, MN: Paragon House. (Original work attributed to Lao Tzu)

Craig, E. (1988a). An encounter with Medard Boss. *The Humanistic Psychologist, 16,* 24-55.

Craig, E. (Ed.). (1988b). Psychotherapy for freedom: The daseinsanalytic way in psychology and psychoanalysis. *The Humanistic Psychologist, 16.*

Craig, E. (2000). Sanctuary and presence: An existential view of the therapist's contribution. *The Humanistic Psychologist, 28* (1-3), 267-274.

Craig, E. (2007). Hermeneutic inquiry in depth psychology: A practical and philosophical reflection. *The Humanistic Psychologist, 35,* 307-321.

Craig, E. (2008a). A brief overview of existential depth psychotherapy. *The Humanistic Psychologist, 36,* 211-226.

Craig, E. (2008b). The human and the hidden: Existential wonderings about depth, soul, and the unconscious. *The Humanistic Psychologist, 36,* 227-282.

Craig, E. (2009). The opening of being and Dasein. *Review of Existential Psychology and Psychiatry.*

Feng, G-F. & English, J. (Trans.). (1972). *Tao Te Ching.* New York, NY: Random House. (Original work attributed to Lao Tzu)

Fichtner, G. (Ed.) (2003). *The Sigmund Freud-Ludwig Binswanger Correspondence, 1908-1938* (A.J. Pomerans, Trans.). London, UK: Open Gate Press.

Freud, A. (1954). The widening scope of indications for psychoanalysis. *Journal of the American Psychoanalytic Association, 2,* 607-620.

Freud, S. (1953a). Freud's psycho-analytic procedure. In J. Strachey (Ed. & Trans.), *The standard edition of the complete psychological works of Sigmund Freud* (Volume 7, pp. 247-254). London, United Kingdom: Hogarth Press. (Original work published1904)

Freud, S. (1953b). The interpretation of dreams. In J. Strachey (Ed. & Trans.), *The standard edition of the complete psychological works of Sigmund Freud* (Volumes 4 & 5, pp. 1-627). London, United Kingdom: Hogarth Press. (Original work published 1900)

Freud, S. (1953c). On psychotherapy. In J. Strachey (Ed. & Trans.). *The standard edition of the complete psychological works of Sigmund Freud* (Volume 7, pp. 255-268). London, United Kingdom: Hogarth Press. (Original work published1905)

Freud, S. (1955). Lines of advance in psychoanalytic therapy. In J. Strachey (Ed. & Trans.), *The standard edition of the complete psychological works of Sigmund Freud* (Volume 17, pp. 157-168). London, United Kingdom: Hogarth Press. (Original work published 1919)

Freud, S. (1957). On the history of the psycho-analytic movement. In J. Strachey (Ed. & Trans.), *The standard edition of the complete psychological works of Sigmund Freud* (Volume 14, pp. 1-66). London, United Kingdom: Hogarth Press. (Original work published 1914)

Freud, S. (1958a). The dynamics of transference. In J. Strachey (Ed. & Trans.). *The standard edition of the complete psychological works of Sigmund Freud* (Vol. 12, pp. 97-108). London, United Kingdom: Hogarth Press. (Original work published 1912)

Freud, S. (1958b). Observations on transference-love (Further recommendations on the technique of psychoanalysis III). In J. Strachey (Ed. & Trans.). *The standard edition of the complete psychological works of Sigmund Freud* (Vol. 12, pp. 157-171). London: Hogarth Press. (Original work published 1915)

Freud, S. (1958c). On beginning the treatment: (Further recommendations on the technique of psychoanalysis I). In J. Strachey (Ed. & Trans.). *The standard edition of the complete psychological works of Sigmund Freud* (Vol. 12, pp. 121-144). London, United Kingdom: Hogarth Press. (Original work published 1913)

Freud, S. (1958d). Recommendations to physicians practicing psycho-analysis. In J. Strachey (Ed. & Trans.), *The standard edition of the complete psychological works of Sigmund Freud* (Vol. 12, pp. 109-120). London, United Kingdom: Hogarth Press. (Original work published 1912)

Freud, S. (1958e). Remembering, repeating and working through (Further recommendations on the technique of psychoanalysis II). In J. Strachey (Ed. & Trans.), *The standard edition of the complete psychological works of Sigmund Freud* (Vol. 12, pp. 145-156). London, United Kingdom: Hogarth Press. (Original work published 1914)

Freud, S. (1959). Further recommendations on the technique of psycho-analysis: Observations on transference-love. In J. Riviere (Trans.), *Sigmund Freud collected papers* (Vol. 2, 377-391). New York, NY: Basic Books. (Original work published 1915).

Freud, S. (1961a). Civilization and its discontents. In J. Strachey (Ed. & Trans.). *The standard edition of the complete psychological works of Sigmund Freud* (Vol. 21, pp. 57-145). London, United Kingdom: Hogarth Press. (Original work published 1930)

Freud, S. (1961b). The future of an illusion. In J. Strachey (Ed. & Trans.). *The standard edition of the complete psychological works of Sigmund Freud* (Vol. 21, pp. 1-56). London, United Kingdom: Hogarth Press. (Original work published 1927)

Freud, S. (1961c). Introductory lectures on psychoanalysis. In J. Strachey (Ed. & Trans.), *The standard edition of the complete psychological works of Sigmund Freud* (Vol. 15&16). London, United Kingdom: Hogarth Press. (Original work published 1916-1917)

Freud, S. (1964). New introductory lectures on psycho-analysis. In J. Strachey (Ed. & Trans.). *The standard edition of the complete psychological works of Sigmund Freud* (Vol. 18, pp. 1-182). London, United Kingdom: Hogarth Press. (Original work published 1933)

Freud, S. (1966). Preface and footnotes to the translation of Charcot's Tuesday Lectures. In J. Strachey (Ed. & Trans.). *The standard edition of the complete psychological works of Sigmund Freud* (Vol. 1, pp. 129-143). London, United Kingdom: Hogarth Press. (Original work published 1892-1894)

Greenson, R. (1967). *The technique and practice of psychoanalysis* (Vol.1). New York, NY: International Universities Press.

Hartmann, E. (1991). *Boundaries of the mind: A new psychology of personality.* New York, NY: Basic Books.

Havens, L. (1989). *A safe place: Laying the groundwork of psychotherapy.* Cambridge, MA: Harvard University Press.

Heidegger, M. (1949a). On the essence of truth (R. F. C. Hull & A. Crick, Trans.) In W. Brock (Ed.), *Existence and being* (pp. 317-351). London, United Kingdom: Vision Press, L.T.D. (Original work published 1943)

Heidegger, M. (1949b). What is metaphysics? (R. F. C. Hull & A. Crick, Trans.) In W. Brock (Ed.), Existence and being (pp. 353-392). London, United Kingdom: Vision Press, L.T.D. (Original work published 1929)

Heidegger, M. (1962). *Being and time* (J. McQuarrie & E. Robinson, Trans.). New York, NY: Harper and Row. (Original work published in 1927)

Heidegger, M. (1963). Preface (Letter to Father W. J. Richardson). In W.J. Richardson (Ed.), *Heidegger: Through phenomenology to thought* (pp. viii-xxiii). The Hague: Martinus Nijhoff.

Heidegger, M. (1966). *Discourse on thinking* (J. M. Anderson & E. H. Freund, Trans.). New York, NY: Harper & Row. (Original work published 1959)

Heidegger, M. (1971). *On the way to language* (P. D. Hertz, Trans.). New York, NY: Harper & Row. (Original work published 1959)

Heidegger, M. (1977a). *Basic writings* (D.F. Krell, Ed.). New York, NY: Harper and Row. (Original works published from 1927-1976)

Heidegger, M. (1977b). Letter on humanism (J. Sallis, Trans.). In D. F. Krell (Ed.), *Basic writings* (pp. 189-242). New York, NY: Harper & Row. (Original work published 1947)

Heidegger, M. (1977c). On the essence of truth (J. Sallis, Trans.). In D. F. Krell (Ed.), *Basic writings* (pp. 113-141). New York, NY: Harper & Row. (Original work published 1943)

Heidegger, M. (1977d). *The question concerning technology and other essays* (W. Lovitt, Trans.) New York, NY: Harper & Row. (Original work published 1954)

Heidegger, M. (1977e). *What is metaphysics?* (D. F. Krell, Trans.). In D. F. Krell (Ed.), Basic writings (pp. 91-112). New York, NY: Harper & Row. (Original work published 1929)

Heidegger, M. (1993). *Basic concepts* (G. E. Aylesworth, Trans.). Bloomington, IN: Indiana University Press. (Original work published 1981)

Heidegger, M. (1999). *Contributions to philosophy (from enowning)* (Parvis, E. & Maly, K., Trans.). Bloomington, IN: Indiana University Press. (Original work published in 1989)

Hinton, D. (Trans.). (1998). *Chuang Tzu: The inner chapters.* New York, NY: Counterpoint.

Hölderlin, F. (1952). *Hölderlin poems* (M. Hamburger, Trans.). New York, NY: Pantheon Books.

Ibsen, H. (1963). *Peer Gynt* (M. Meyer, Trans.). New York, NY: Anchor Books. (Original work published 1867)

Ivanhoe, P. J. (Trans.). (2002). *The Daodejing of Laozi.* New York, NY: Seven Bridges Press.

Kastrinidis, P. (1990). *Wenn Liebe krank macht (When love creates illness).* Zurich: Kreuz Verlag.

Kastrinidis, P. (2004, March). *Between human illusion and inhuman reality: A daseinsanalytic contribution to the understanding of masochism.* Paper presented at a symposium on daseinsanalysis, the 22nd Annual Symposium of the Simon Silverman Phenomenology Center of Duquesne University, Pittsburgh, PA.

Khan, M. M. R. (1974). *The privacy of the self: Papers on psychoanalytic theory and technique.* New York, NY: International Universities Press.

Lau, D. C. (Trans.). (1963). *Tao Te Ching.* London, UK: Penguin Books. (Original Work attributed to Lao Tzu)

Le Guin, U. K. (Trans.). (1997). *Tao Te Ching: A book about the way and the power of the way.* Boston, MA: Shambala. (Original work attributed to Lao Tzu)

Masson, J.M. (Ed. & Trans.). (1985). *The complete letters of Sigmund Freud and Wilhelm Fliess: 1887-1904.* Cambridge, MA: Harvard University Press.

May, R. (1958). Contributions of existential psychotherapy. In R. May, E. Angel, & H. F. Ellenberger (Eds.) *Existence: A new dimension in psychiatry and psychology* (pp. 37-91). New York, NY: Basic Books.

Merton, T. (2004). The way of Chuang Tzu. Boston, MA: Shambala.

McGuire, W. (Ed.). (1974). *The Freud/Jung letters: The correspondence between Sigmund Freud and C. G. Jung* (R. Manhein & R. F. C. Hull, Trans.). Princeton, NJ: Princeton University Press.

Milner, M. (1952). Aspects of symbolism in the comprehension of the non-self. *International Journal of Psycho-Analysis, 33*, 181-195.

Mitchell, S. (Trans.). (1988). Tao Te Ching: A New English Version. New York, NY: Harper Collins. (Original work attributed to Lao Tzu)

Mitchell, S. A. (1988). Relational concepts in psychoanalysis: An integration. Cambridge, MA: Harvard University Press.

Parkes, G. (1996). Translator's preface. In R. May, Heidegger's hidden sources: East Asian influences on his work (pp. vii – xiii). London, United Kingdom: Routledge.

Petzet, O. (1993). *Encounters and dialogues with Martin Heidegger, 1929-1976* P. Emad & K. Maly, Trans.). Chicago, IL: University of Chicago Press.

Pöggeler, O. (1987). West-East Dialogue: Heidegger and Lao-tzu. In G. Parkes (Ed.), *Heidegger and Asian thought* (pp. 47-78). Honolulu, HI: University of Hawaii Press.

Rhee, D. (1995). *The Tao and Western psychotherapy.* In Psychotherapy East and West: Integration of psychotherapies (Revised edition of the proceedings of the 16th International Congress of Psychotherapy; pp. 162-168). Seoul, Korea: Korean Academy of Psychotherapists.

Rhee, D. (2002a). *The Tao and empathy: East Asian interpretation.* In World Congress Proceedings, pp. 75-87. Seoul, Korea: Korean Academy of Psychotherapists.

Rhee, D. (2002b). The Tao, psychoanalysis and existential thought. In World Congress Proceedings, pp. 89-95. Seoul, Korea: Korean Academy of Psychotherapists. (Original work published 1990)

Rubin, J. B. (1996). *Psychotherapy and Buddhism: Toward and integration.* New York, NY: Plenum Press.

Sartre, J. P. (1956). *Being and nothingness: An essay on phenomenological psychology* (H. E. Barnes, Trans.) New York, NY: Philosophical Library. (Original work published 1943)

Stern, P.J. (1972). *In praise of madness: Realness therapy – the self reclaimed.* New York, NY: W.W. Norton.

Stolorow, R. D. & Atwood, G. E. (1992). *Contexts of being: The intersubjective foundation of psychological life.* Hillsdale, NJ: The Analytic Press.

Suzuki, D. T., Fromm, E. & De Martino, R. (Eds.). (1960). *Zen Buddhism & psychoanalysis.* New York, NY: Grove Press.

Tzu, C. (2004). *The way of Chuang Tzu* (T. Merton, Trans.). Boston, MA: Shambala. (Original work by Chuang Tzu)

Viderman, S. (1974). Interpretation in the analytic space. *International Review of Psycho-analysis, 1,* 467-480.

Von Schiller, F. (1972). *Wilhelm Tell* (W. F. Mainland, Trans.). Chicago, IL: University of Chicago Press. (Original work published 1805)

Watts, A. (1960). *Psychotherapy East and West.* New York, NY: Pantheon Books.

Watts, A. (2000). *What is Tao?* Novato CA: New World Library.

Winnicott, D.W. (1957). Mother and child: A primer of first relationships. New York, NY: Basic Books.

Winnicott, D. W. (1958). T*hrough pediatrics to psycho-analysis.* New York, NY: Basic Books.

Winnicott, D. W. (1965). *The maturational processes and the facilitating environment: Studies in the theory of emotional development.* New York, NY: International Universities Press.

Winnicott, D. W. (1986). *Holding and interpretation: Fragment of an analysis.* New York, NY: Grove Press.

Winnicott, D. W. (1989). *Psycho-analytic explorations.* Cambridge, MA: Harvard University Press.

Wu, J. C. H. (Trans.). (1989). *Tao Te Ching.* Boston, MA: Shambala. (Original work attributed to Lao Tzu)

# Chapter 6

## Spiritual Warrior in Search of Meaning:
## An Existential View of Lu Xun
## Through His Life Incidents and Analogies

### Xuefu Wang

With the emergence of Modern Chinese Literature and the upsurge of the New Cultural Movement in China, Lu Xun emerged as the most brilliant writer and acute observer of the Chinese psyche during the early 20th century. He directed his critical gaze at what he considered the cultural backwardness and psychological cowardice of the Chinese people throughout history up to the time when he was writing. His penetrating perception and exposure of the shadowy realm of the Chinese Psyche is evident throughout his novels and essays.

### Grandfather's Case

Lu Xun was born to a scholar/official family in Shaoxin, in Southeastern China. When he was 13 years old, his grandfather, a retired official, was convicted of fraud and spent a number of years in jail. This led to the family's decline. Lu Xun's (1981a) early years were deeply affected by this sudden change, as he commented later, "He who plummets from the heights may gain perspective to discern human snobbishness to the core" (p. 415).

### Father's Illness and Death

Another incident that profoundly influenced Lu Xun was his father's chronic disease and eventual death. From the age of 14 to 16, Lu Xun was a frequent visitor to the pawnshops and drugstores in Shaoxin. He used to pawn his family belongings and "take the money given to me with contempt" (Lu Xun, 1922/2000). He went to all possible places to purchase unusual drugs and adjuvant prescribed by quack doctors of Chinese medicine. This included items such as aloe roots dug up in the winter, sugar-cane exposed to frost for 3 years, original mating pairs of crickets, and essentially non-existent *fecund ardisia* plant usually characterized by its barrenness.[1] However, his father's illness went from bad to worse until he finally died at the age of 37. This experience engraved in Lu Xun's (1922/2000) mind a skeptical view toward Chinese medicine: "I gradually came to the conclusion that those physicians were charlatans, either unintended or deliberate" (p. 5). Such skepticism deeply affected his later examination of the long feudal history of China.

## Seeking a New Path

From his childhood to the age of 18, Lu Xun studied classical Chinese at the Three Flavor Study (三味书屋), which led to official examinations. After the death of his father, Lu Xun's family's financial situation worsened, so he decided to leave his hometown to study Western knowledge and technology, which was a more affordable program. As Lu Xun recalled, "Anyone who studied 'foreign subjects' was a social outcast regarded as someone who could find no way out and was forced to sell his soul to foreign devils" (Lu Xun, 1922/2000, p. 5). To the contrary, Lu Xun's acting out of his own convictions "struck out on news paths, opening himself to novel places, while searching for a new breed of people with different characteristics – a new personality" (Lu Xun, 1981a, p. 415).

Lu Xun went to Nanjing to study physics, arithmetic, geography, history, drawing, and physical training at the Jiangnan Naval Academy (江南水师学堂). He also gained some knowledge regarding physiology. It was during this period that Lu Xun opened his mind and began to assimilate the influence of foreign cultures. By this time, many books on science, philosophy, and literature of the West had been translated into Chinese. Lu Xun read Western literature through Lin Shu's translation of foreign novels (林译小说). He also recalled how he was engrossed in reading the works of famous figures in science and philosophy of the West, such as Huxley, Socrates, Plato, Tolstoy, and Nietzsche. After years of traditional education of classical Chinese, Lu Xun's worldview was, for the first time, broadened by the new thoughts from the West.

## Slides at Sendai Medical College

Lu Xun's (1999) thinking on national salvation originated from the most profound recesses of his soul. In 1902, Lu Xun went to Sendai Medical College in Japan to study Western medicine. His intention was to save his fellow countrymen who, like his father, suffered from inadequate treatment. He continued to read widely in philosophy and literature while studying medicine. At the same time, he began to ponder the Chinese character: "What is the ideal human character? What is most lacking in the Chinese character? What is the root cause of the problem?"

---

[1] The essence of all these quack remedies is that they are rare to the point of absurdity. The idea was, the more absurd, the more healing power was ascribed to these charlatans.

(Shou-chang Xu, 1999, pp. 226, 443, 487). An incident that occurred during this period of study at Sendai Medical College prompted Lu Xun to give up medicine for literature. In the preface to *Call to Arms*, Lu Xun (1922/2000) recalled, "If the lecture ended early, the instructor might show slides of natural scenery or news to fill up the time. Since this was during the Russo-Japanese War, there were many war slides" (Lu Xun, 1922/2000, p. 35). One day, during a class interval, Lu Xun saw his fellow Chinese compatriots on the slides. One of them was bound in the middle and the rest were standing around him. They were all strong and capable but appeared completely apathetic. According to the commentary, Lu Xun stated:

> the one with his hands bound was a spy accused of working for the Russians, who was to be beheaded by the Japanese military as a warning to others, while the Chinese people beside him had come to enjoy the spectacle. (p. 7)

The disparity between his people's physical sturdiness and spiritual apathy caused Lu Xun much sadness. He became convinced that medical science was not as important as he originally assumed. Thus, Lu Xun decided to give up the study of medicine in order to pursue literature because he believed that literature had the ability to transform the minds, spirit, and character of the Chinese people.

### The Boundless Desert and Huge Poisonous Snake

Lu Xun's enthusiasm was initially channeled into starting a magazine named *New Life* (新生). He put his all into this endeavor but, due to lack of support, the enterprise eventually failed. Lu Xun then dedicated his time and energy to the translation of foreign literature. In collaboration with his brother Zhou Zhuoren, he published two volumes but sold only 21 copies of Volume 1 and 20 copies of Volume 2. Lu Xun returned to China in 1909 but the political situation caused him to be more disappointed. He became lonely and sighed:

> If a man's proposals were met with approval, this should encourage him to advance; if they were met with opposition, they should make him fight back; but the real tragedy was for him to lift up his voice among the living and be met with no response, neither approval nor opposition, just as if he were stranded in a boundless desert completely at a loss. That was when I became conscious of loneliness. (Lu Xun, 1922/2000, p. 8-11)

Lu Xun continued, "And this sense of loneliness grew from day to day, entwining itself about my soul like a huge poisonous snake." Here, the huge poisonous snake and related other themes, such as poison, inner darkness, and ghosts, were analogies symbolizing hopelessness or meaninglessness.

Lu Xun's (1922/2000) greatness lies in the fact that he was able to respond to the tragedy of his time. He confronted the contradictions of his ego, undertaking an extremely painful self-critique in the form of vigilant self-observation and profound and trenchant self-analysis in which he was conscious of his own inner darkness and poison, which he sometimes referred to as ghosts dwelling in the recess of his mind. However, in his writings, Lu Xun conscientiously kept such darkness to himself lest he poison his young readers. His wife likened him to a cow eating grass but producing milk, rather than a snake eating grass while producing poison. Ultimately, upon consuming the metaphoric grass of various other thinkers, Lu Xun realized that he could not avoid assimilating what he considered some of the poisonous ingredients such as the nihilism of Zhuang Zi, the ancient Chinese philosopher and the pessimism of Schopenhauer and various Buddhist teaching. Paradoxically, Lu Xun also admired the higher realm of wisdom to be found in these same poisonous ingredients.

Lu Xun (1922/2000) was often in conflict in battles between his strong desire for meaning and his skeptical attitude towards life, which resulted in his occasional retreats into nothingness and despair. Yet in the depth of his heart he maintained a fire, which refused to be extinguished and easily rekindled whenever new possibilities of life came knocking at his door. Lu Xun was not a superficial optimist who chose to live by ignoring the negative aspects of life. On the contrary, he endeavored to seek meaning through staring directly at reality in the face (直面). His suspicious, discerning eye uncovered all kinds of duplicity in the feudal society, exposing it to its rotten roots. He often fluctuated between hope and despair, but his despair could never keep him from seeking hope. The serpent might have entwined his soul for a time, but he would not be strangled to death.

## The Iron House

Lu Xun's loneliness stemmed from his experience of calling out but receiving no response. He reflected that he was not the type of hero who could rally multitudes with one call. Lu Xun's disappointment with his fellow country-men led him to sink into a disheartened silence for nearly 10 years (1909-1918) during which time he lived essentially a secluded life at the Shaoxin Hostel in Peking, now Beijing. Instead of standing out to be a hero, he withdrew into the hordes of commoners. In order to deaden his senses to reality, he secluded and retreated to the past by copying ancient tablet inscriptions. This was the period in which Lu Xun was entangled and poisoned by the serpent of helplessness from within his own heart. He assumed that he could do nothing except allow his life to slip quietly away.

Then came the day when there was a knock at the door. A friend, Qian Xuantong, came to visit. His friend sat down face-to-face with Lu Xun and questioned his work on copying the inscriptions:

"What's the use of copying these?"

"There isn't any use," was Lu Xun's reply.

"What's the point, then, of copying them?"

"There isn't any point," again answered Lu Xun ("No use" and "No point" indicate *No meaning*).

After appreciating Lu Xun's current state, Qian Xuantong began to persuade him to write something for *New Youth*, a leading magazine of the New Cultural Movement. It was a light of hope brought into the darkness of Lu Xun's life that would ignite something within him to let him feel there was meaning.

Being fully aware of his mission as a writer, Lu Xun expressed his thoughts through an image of an *iron house*, showing an attitude of hesitation:

> Imagine an iron house having not a single window and virtually indestructible, with all its inmates asleep and about to die of suffocation. Dying in their sleep, they won't feel the pain of death. Now if you raise a shout, and awaken a few of the light sleepers, making these unfortunate few suffer the agony of irrevocable death, do you really think you are doing them a good turn?
>
> But if a few wake up, you can't say that there is no hope of destroying the iron house. (Lu Xun, 1922/2000, p. 12-15)

Symbolically, the iron house was the China in which people had long fallen asleep. Lu Xun was the man standing in front of the iron house. Hesitating for some time, he finally determined to shout and bang on the outside of the house. Lu Xun had reason to hesitate. The people inside might die if they were not awakened. However, if they awoke and found no way out, they would die a painful death. Lu Xun also had reason to take action by calling them to awaken. There was hope, however slight, that they would be able to break the iron house and free themselves. It was appropriate for Lu Xun to sound the warning for he himself shook off the snake that coiled around his mind prior to uttering his shout. An examination of Lu Xun's past experience of his father's illness would also reveal a similar desire to bring about salvation and the related hesitation before uttering the shout. Interestingly, in the Chinese culture, filial duty would have the eldest son of the family repeatedly calling out to the father upon his deathbed. Lu Xun, being the eldest son, called numerous times for his father to "wake up" intending to hold him back from dying to the living world. However, Lu Xun's father was so annoyed that he asked Lu Xun to stop calling. This might explain some of the unconscious motivation behind Xun's reluctance for calling out to his fellow countrymen. Nevertheless, over and over again, we hear Lu Xun's calls outside the gate of the iron house of China. Lu Xun never stopped calling for the rest of his life.

## A Madman's Diary

*A Madman's Diary* (狂人日记) (1918) was Lu Xun's first short story published in *New Youth*. It is considered to be one of the first and most influential modern works written in vernacular Chinese, marking the beginning of modern Chinese literature. *A Madman's Diary* is Lu Xun's first "shout" (呐喊) in front of the iron house, attempting to reveal the oppression of feudal values upon the Chinese people. The imagery of cannibalism is applied to describe and symbolize the ways in which feudalized Confucian values were eating away at the individual. *A Madman's Diary* is a masterpiece out of Lu Xun's conscious literary creation in response to the calling of the ongoing May 4 New Culture Movement.

The main character of the story, namely, madman, suffers from paranoid delusions. His behavior is consistent with the diagnosis. However, this is not merely a medical case of schizophrenia; it has deeper implications. Symbolically, the madman is the one who sees through the hypocritical veil of the tyrannical tradition. He made an extensive study of Chinese history as outlined in the Four Books and Five Classics (四书五经), all of which were filled with statements of virtue and morality. But in a sleepless night he read them over and over again and saw the words "Eat People!" written between the lines of the texts. He, therefore, realized that the whole history of China was but a cannibalistic history. Seeing the people in his village as potential cannibals, he is gripped by the fear that everyone, including his brother, his venerable doctor and his neighbors are plotting to eat him. The narrator (the author of the diary in the story) allegorically integrates two roles: one is a mental patient who sees a perverse, confused world through his delusional mental lens with which even the genuine concern of his brother and the considerate treatment of a veteran doctor are regarded as disguised threats; the other role is an acute thinker who discerns the covered-up truths of a feudal society, that is, the callousness of *cannibalism* under the gloss of virtue and morality. At last the madman, with the help of his brother and the doctor, are *restored to health* and go on to fill a vacant official position. This, again, is symbolic of what has been called a "warrior of the spiritual realm" (精神界之战士), or the loner in the crowd after a strenuous fight with feudal traditions became finally suppressed or compromised by the power of darkness, often represented by the ignorant masses or "subjects of the tyrant" (暴君的臣民), as termed by Lu Xun.

In one of his essays, namely, *Subjects of the Tyrant* (1919), Lu Xun revealed, in extreme form, the indignation of the subjects of the tyrant:

> A tyrant's subject will, in the main, be much more violent and vicious than the tyrant. The tyrant's tyranny frequently cannot satisfy the wishes of the subjects under his rule. Instead of China, let us take an example from overseas. When the prosecutor wanted to release Jesus, the crowd demanded that he be crucified. The tyrant's subjects have a simple wish, that tyranny takes its toll on someone else. This they watch happily. Cruelty is their pleasure, the suffering of others their enjoyment and

comfort. These subjects' own talents lie in their lucky escape, to safety, from which they again choose the sacrifice of others, satiating their thirst for blood, but no one understands. The one who is tortured to death is groaning in pain, saying 'aiya,' while others around him are enjoying his painful groans by showing much happiness. (Lu Xun, 1981a, p. 366)

This is what prompts Jesus to say on the cross, "Father, forgive them, for they know not what they do."

Persecution of the hero by the subjects of the tyrant is a common theme in Lu Xun's literary creation. The persecution often takes the form of framing the madman. This is not uncommon in reality. Lu Xun's teacher, Zhang Taiyan, a radical thinker of modern China, was called *Zhang Fengzi* (Madman Zhang) at his time. In some of Lu Xun's novels, there are characters who are revolutionaries and anti-tradition activists. These include Xia Yu in *Medicine* (1919, in Lu Xun 1981a), who is despised as 'mad' by the people in the teahouse; and the fool in the *Lamp that Was Kept Alight* (1925, in Lu Xun, 1981b), who claims to burn down the temple, extinguishing the lamp, symbolizing the spiritual oppression of the feudal tradition. Also. in *Revenge II* (1924, in Lu Xun 1981b), Lu Xun wrote a new version of the crucifixion of Jesus, one that is contrary to the Biblical account in which Jesus pleads for the forgiveness of the persecuting crowds. In this new account, Jesus, tortured and mocked (as a madman who claimed himself to be a King) by the evil crowd, shouted forth accusations, curses, and threats of revenge upon the crowd and their posterity. However, in *A Madman's Diary* (1918), Lu Xun, through the lips of the madman, raised perhaps the most significant question regarding the cannibalistic history of China. As accounted in the novel, when the madman brought up cannibalism (symbolizing the cruelty of feudalism) from cover-up of feudal hypocrisy, his brother's (representing feudal moralist) facial expression grow ghastly pale by saying "That's the way it's always been.... Does that make it right?" (Lu Xun, 1922/2000, p. 41) was the reply of the madman, which means, "you cannot justify cannibalism because it has been the case all along?" (p. 41). This question directly points at the passivity of our national character.

## The Dark House

The goal of Lu Xun's literary creation is based on the premise that to establish a nation one must first establish its people and that in order to establish the people one must first enlighten them. In regard to enlightenment, Lu Xun chose to expose the rotten roots of the Chinese national character, such as servility, passivity, compromising attitude, and fear of change.

The dark house is another metaphor Lu Xun (1981a) created to expose the deep-rooted concessionary/compromising attitude in the Chinese psyche:

The disposition of the Chinese is an irredeemable compromise, ready to take a middle course with everything. Supposed that you are in a house that is too dark. If you suggest opening up a window, all others will not allow such a change. Yet if you make a strong enough proposition of removing the roof so as to let the light in, all the rest will then approach to make the concession by agreeing to your former suggestion of opening a window. So, without a strong enough proposition people will not bother to budge even a moderate step for reform. (pp. 13-14)

Lu Xun's observation is that in order to achieve any kind of significant change with such a conforming/concessionary/compromising society, one needs to *shoot for the moon* in hopes of simply rising above one's peers. If one's proposition is of sufficient strength, perhaps the masses will grant you a small percentage that for which you originally asked.

In Lu Xun's (year) critical analysis, the compromising character is the result of self-yielding constriction under the deprivation of feudal tyranny. With limited space to live, people have to constrict themselves, almost without limits, in order to gain a margin for survival in this abnormal social environment. By way of unending concessions, they sink to the level of slavery, readily paying any price for security. From this perspective, or by this standard, Lu Xun divided the history of China, despite its many dynasties, into but two ages—one in which the people could live securely as slaves and the other that people could not even gain themselves a secure life of slavery. This degradation of living status under the endless feudal oppression left a deep-rooted sense of insecurity in Chinese psyche and passivity in Chinese character. In this setting people become terrified of any change that might affect their minimum security. That is why in China, even in present times, any kind of reform will be met with strong opposition of all kinds and only result in the sacrifice of the reformer himself or herself.

Lu Xun's analogies of the iron house, the madman, and the dark house are reminiscent of Nels F. S. Fere's (1953) old barn parable. The parable described an old barn that was very wide with no windows and a low ceiling. The lighting within the barn was very dim as the lamps of the Law were smoky and easily extinguished. The people were busy keeping these lamps lit. The people sighed, waiting for a new and brighter Light to appear. But century after century would pass while people went to their graves disappointed. Then one day a prophet with a bright countenance arrived telling the people of the bright sunshine outside— all they needed to do was to step outside and see for themselves. The prophet said, "I come from the Light. I know the Light. I am the Light. Trust me. Follow me into the Light" (p. 12). Many heard and marveled. But there was much fear. The prophet kept imploring the people to leave the dark barn and step into the Light but they became angry and hated him.

Similar to Lu Xun's allegories, this parable indicates that people living in the old barn have become habitually accustomed to the darkness. They might harbor a secret desire for light, but they are also possessed by a stronger fear of the light.

They are afraid of stepping out to see real light. They could even deny the existence of the light outside. Finally, as the parable of the old barn points out, they eventually killed the prophet of Light.

Contrary to Lu Xun's admonition regarding "zhi-mian" (直面), literal-ly translated to mean *direct facing*, people tend to employ innumerable defense mechanisms to escape the realities of life. They do not know who they are or what they are doing. Their behavior is motivated by an unconscious sense of insecurity. They avoid calls for change because they are afraid of activating a sensor that would bring them trouble. In order to maintain security, they keep everything in order by adhering to the status quo. Anyone who proposes change will be regarded as a potential threat and trouble-maker. If they cannot coax others to conform, they will plot to get rid of those who cause them fear.

In May 2008, Mark Yang and I led a workshop on existential psychology at Zhi-Mian Institute for Psychotherapy in Nanjing. Yang introduced the following story found in the opening of the chapter on meaninglessness in Irvin Yalom's (1980) book *Existential Psychotherapy*:

> Imagine a happy group of morons who are engaged in work. They are carrying bricks in an open field. As soon as they have stacked all the bricks at one end of the field, they proceed to transport them to the opposite end. This continues without stop and every day of every year they are busy doing the same thing. One day one of the morons stops long enough to ask himself what he is doing. He wonders what purpose there is in carrying the bricks. And from that instant, on he is not quite as content with his occupation as he had been before.
>
> I am that moron who wonders why he is carrying the bricks. (p. 419)

As Yalom informed us, this was a suicide note left behind by a despairing soul who killed himself because he saw no meaning in life.

I could ask, how would Lu Xun understand this story? I imagined that Lu Xun would suggest that this moron has discerned the meaninglessness of traditional society and decided to depart and seek meaning elsewhere. The moron may have even tried to raise similar questions to the other morons. In the beginning, the other morons would likely not respond. But gradually pressure is applied to the one questioning moron to conform. If the questioning moron continues his line of inquiry, the other morons might even plot to get rid of him. Perhaps it is this pressure that drives the questioning moron to end his life. This has been the case repeated many times in Chinese history.

### The Wounded Wolf

Qu Qiubai (1953), one of Lu Xun's friends, likened Lu Xun to a legendary figure of Remus in Roman mythology. According to this myth, Numitor was the king of Alba

Longa but was dethroned by his brother Amulius (Romulus & Reomus, 2008). Out of fear that Numitor's daughter, Rhea Silvia, would produce children who would one day overthrow him as king, Amulius forced Rhea to become a Vestal Virgin, a priestess sworn to abstinence. But Mars, god of war, was smitten by her and secretly, while she slept, bore two sons. They were twin boys of remarkable size and beauty, later named Romulus and Remus. Amulius was enraged and ordered that Rhea be buried alive and the twins thrown into the Tiber River. The servant could not bear to carry out the order, but instead placed the twins in a basket and laid the basket on the banks of the Tiber River. The river, in flood season, rose and gently carried the basket and the twins downstream. Romulus and Remus were kept safe by the river god Tiberinus, who brought them up onto the Palatine Hill. There they were nursed by a wolf. Later, Romulus became the founder of Rome while Remus was killed over a dispute about which one of the two brothers had the support of the local deities to rule the new city and give it his name.

Similarly, Lu Xun was born into an official-scholar gentry but was symbolically nursed by the milk of wild animals, the revolutionary figures of both China and abroad. Under their nurturance, he grew up to be a rebellious son of the feudal patriarchal clan society. Instead of paying allegiance to the gentry class of the feudal society, he became a revolutionary leading thinker who spread forth his thoughts to many commoners. Lu Xun suffered numerous injuries in his battle against the "old stronghold" of feudalism, but he concealed his wounds and kept on fighting. He likened himself to a wounded wolf, limping deep into the woods. Sad and lonely, he lay down to lick his wound and later emerged from the woods again, only to fight. From his own feudal gentry, he is viewed as a rebellious wolf. But in the eyes of the Chinese people he represents a fighting spirit for the transformation of China. He fought continuously until the time of his death in 1936 and was eulogized as *the soul of the nation* (民族魂) at his funeral.

While studying abroad, Lu Xun began laying the foundation of his axiom: In order to establish a nation, one must first establish her people (立国必先立人). He searched all over China and abroad for a spiritual model that could be an antidote to the weakened Chinese personality. He exclaimed, "If we search all over China today, where will we find such a warrior spirit? Will anyone speak out in sincerity; anyone to call our people to goodness, beauty, strength and vigor? Where are the compassionate voices to save our people from desolation?" (Lu Xun, 1981a, p. 100). Then he found the rebellious *Mara Poets* in foreign, alien lands. Mara means the devil or Satan, representing the European Romantic thinkers who are the positive (originally perceived as negative) forces which moved society forward, but nicknamed by the ignorant society as Mara poets. Lu Xun began to admire figures such as, Nietzsche, Schopenhauer, Kierkegaard, Shelley, Byron, to name only a few. Lu Xun's early writings, including, *On the Power of the Mara Poetry* (1907, in Lu Xun, 1981a), *On Extremities of Cultures* (1907, in Lu Xun, 1981a), and others, can be understood as a chronology of Western heroes of the spiritual/moral/intellectual[2] realm. It was Lu Xun's fervent hope that visionaries such as these would emerge in China and "speak with powerful voices, breaking bonds of loneliness, bringing new life to his compatriots, and helping to advance China's prominence in the eyes of the world" (Wang, 1989, p. 97).

At his birthday gathering, Lu Xun was presented with a couplet of praise from his friend Liu Bannong (刘半农): "托尼学说，魏晋文章," which recognized Lu Xun's integration of the teaching of Tolstoy and Nietzsche with the literary heritage from ancient China. This accomplishment is especially enlightening given that the divergent teachings of Tolstoy and Nietzsche, not to mention the culture divergence between Russia, Europe, and China. Lu Xun, especially during his youth, advocated Tolstoy's humanitarian values derived from Christianity. As perceived by Cao Juren (2006), one of the Lu Xun's biographers, Lu Xun's protestations against war and advocacy for international communication and exchange are influenced by Tolstoy's writings. At the same time, he admired Nietzsche's individualism and the writing style of *Thus Spoke Zarathustra* 1892/1954). We find traces of Nietzsche's philosophy and writing style in Lu Xun's *Wild Grass* (1927/1981b), a collection of prose, especially pieces like *Preface to Wild Grass*, *The Passer-By*, and *Such A Fighter*. This collection of prose or short essays, possibly the most existential literary work by Lu Xun, touched on the topics of hope and despair, darkness and light, meaning and sense of void or nothingness, choice, fighting with hypocrites, and living and dying. In fact, Lu Xun, for a period of time, was regarded as *China's Nietzsche*. The two figures shared many similarities. Both Nietzsche and Lu Xun launched vigorous, wholesale attacks on their respective cultural traditions. Nietzsche (1892/ 1954) declared *God is dead*, which shocked the entire Western Christian world. Lu Xun (1981b), on the other side of the world, exposed unrelentingly how Confucian morality was eating its people. Ironically, however, both figures were more deeply connected to the essence of their own cultures than most of their fellow country-men. Upon deeper examination, we find Nietzsche's spiritual attachment to Jesus echoing Lu Xun's personality similarities with Confucius. Both figures were criticizing the degenerated parts of their own culture. Both sought to enlighten and inspire people to transcend from lower realms of awareness and to seek freedom from their bondage to the culture and environment. In his treatment of the national character, Lu Xun, exactly like Nietzsche, enumerated all the drawbacks in order to draw attention to a cure. In one of Lu Xun's (1981a) letters to Qian Xuantong, we find this passage:

> Jesus said if you see a cart about to overturn, put out a hand to hold it up. Nietzsche said if you see a cart about to overturn, give it a push. I naturally

---

[2] The Chinese word is difficult to translate here. It encompasses both the spiritual/moral and the intellectual realm. In the East, Lu Xun is understood more as a "spiritual" warrior. In the West, Lu Xun can be better appreciated as an "intellectual" warrior or gian akin to that of Nietzsche.

agree with Jesus, but I also think that if a person is not willing to receive your support, then there's no reason to force it on him. Do what they say and be done with it. If later the cart hasn't overturned, all well and good. If it does overturn in the end, then go and give practical help in raising it. My elder brother, it takes less energy to raise a cart than to support it from falling; and in the latter case, the results are less evident. To raise the cart after it falls is much more beneficial than to give a supporting hand when it's on the verge of falling. (p. 36)

In this passage we find evidence of Lu Xun's preference to integrate both the teachings of Jesus and Nietzsche. Lu Xun was practical and unrelenting while holding up and raising the great and difficult task of reforming the national character. But other times, similar to Nietzsche, he would be deliberately provocative in his words and behaviors so as to *give a push*, but harbor a private intention *to raise the cart*. Lu Xun was deeply concerned about his country and his people and was persistent and sincere in raising his concerns. But often times, he kept his fervent compassion behind an austere exterior. Lu Xun desperately sought to awaken the deep slumbering spirit of his people across the vast land of China. Yet, with profound sorrow, Lu Xun portrayed group after group of apathetic and cruel souls in his fiction, displaying an attitude of "Grief Over Their Misfortune [and] Indignant Toward Their Servility" (哀其不幸，怒其不争).[3]

## The Locked Gate of Darkness

In *A Madman's Diary*, Lu Xun (1918) depicts a world of callousness in which people eat people, from history to the present times. However, Lu Xun's peers remarked to him that this novel was too dark. Some asked, "Must the world be so dark?" to which Lu Xun finally added the phrase "save the children" to the novel as the ending sentence, upon whom he placed the hope of the Chinese society, because, as he stated, "Perhaps there are still children who haven't eaten men?" (p. 53).

In his satirical essays, as well as in his life, Lu Xun was relentless in pointing his critical pen, or more exactly, the top of his writing brush at many of his enemies. But he always showed leniency towards the young, even if they offended him. He likened himself to a cow, ready to serve the young. He pinned his hope for change in China upon the young. In one of his early articles, *How Should We Be Fathers Today?* Lu Xun (1981) employed the metaphor of "the gate of darkness" by writing "We, as fathers, should 'shoulder' the sinking gate of darkness and guide our children out to a vast land full of brightness, to live happy lives as normal, upright human beings." This metaphor originated from a parable of a dungeon in the evil underworld. Every day a giant monster captured children from

---

[3] A term most often used in association with Lu Xun's attitude toward Chinese, but it is a resource that cannot be found.

the human world and locked them in the dungeon. A hero ventured into the underworld to attempt to save the children. The dungeon is in complete darkness and the locked gate is heavy and impregnable. The gate is only lifted briefly every day when the monster leaves the dungeon to snatch more children. This becomes the only chance for the hero to enter and rescue the children. The hero takes the initiative one day and guides the children out while the gate is open. However, while the gate begins to drop, the hero sees that some of the children have yet to escape. Thus, the hero props up the sinking gate with his shoulder in order for the rest of the children to escape. This results in the hero's death in the end as he is crushed by the gate of darkness.

This is Lu Xun: a hero that chose to fight and even "sink with the darkness." In his contemporary periods of gloom, Lu Xun explored his own path and sometimes found nowhere to turn. Instead of crying and turning back at the end of the road, as the case with Ruan Ji (阮籍), one of his favorite ancient poets, Lu Xun chose to remain and ponder his fate, before eventually resuming his exploration. Throughout his life, Lu Xun never stopped exploring lonely paths in his quest to discover and create new meaning. His quest is not just for himself, but for China as a nation, and even for all humanity.

The parable of *shouldering the locked gate of the dungeon* expresses the full sense of existential psychology in terms of choosing suffering for meaning. This reminds me of Victor Frankl (1963), who was thrown into the concentration camp by the monstrous forces of evil. There he had to face a reality that his life was devoid of everything except for cold, hunger, and all kinds of brutal torture and humiliation. In his famous book *Man's Search for Meaning*, Frankl questioned his existence when everything was deprived. What does it mean for me to exist when living in such a state? What is there still left for me to live for? These were questions that launched his school of logotherapy. "The main tenets of logotherapy were justified by the acid test of the concentration camp" (as cited in Hall, 1968, p. 63). Frankl had to find answers for himself, for his inmates who despaired, and for all of us who cannot escape the suffering in our lives. Frankl witnessed that the basic motivation in humanity is what he called the *will to meaning*, rather than *will to pleasure* (as Freud assumed) or *will to power* (as Adler assumed). It is this will to meaning that motivates human beings to seek meaning in their life and to fulfill it in various ways. According to Frankl, there are three ways to make life meaningful: love, work, and suffering.

Similar to Frankl's experience, from the existential point of view, we find that Lu Xun's life is essentially also a process of the will to meaning realizing itself. First, he obtained the highest value of creativity through his literary creation, which turned out to be a spiritual contribution to his nation. Second, he practiced genuine love for his fellow countrymen, through which he gained what Frankl (1963) termed *the value of experience*. Finally, through the experience of his personal suffering and the suffering of the Chinese people, Lu Xun realized *the value of attitude* by finding our own ways of shouldering the gate of darkness so people may pursue a better, more meaningful life. His pain found its meaning. We can always hear his sincere voice calling his people of the iron house to wake up and seek meaning in a seemingly meaningless environment.

Lu Xun's (1981c) existential attitude is fully revealed in his term of *zhi mian*, which, as mentioned earlier means *directly facing* reality. He championed the zhi mian warrior, as one who "dares to face life as it is, no matter how gloomy it might be" (真的猛士，敢于直面惨淡的人生; p. 271). Lu Xun lived out Nietzsche's axioms "He who has a why to live for can bear with almost any how" (as cited in Frankl, 1963, p. 12) and "That which does not kill me, makes me stronger" (as cited in Frankl, 1963, p. 103). These remarks found meaning for Frankl as well. Both Lu Xun and Frankl, in my opinion, are meaning-making heroes. They fully agree with Nietzsche in believing that, for human beings, ultimately, there is no other choice except the choice of living as heroes.

## References

Ferre, N. F. S. (1953). *The sun and the umbrella*. New York, NY: Harper & Brothers.

Frankl, V. E. (1963). *Man's search for meaning: An introduction to logotherapy*. New York, NY: Washington Square Press.

Hall, M. (1968, Feb.). Conversation with V. E. Frankl. *Psychology Today, 1,* 56-63.

Juren, C. (2006). *Critical biography of Lu Xun*. Shanghai, China: Fudan University Press.

Lu Xun (1981a). *Complete works of Lu Xun* (Vol. 1). Beijing, China: People's Literature Publishing House.

Lu Xun (1982b). *Complete works of Lu Xun* (Vol. 2). Beijing, China: People's Literature Publishing House.

Lu Xun (1982c). *Complete works of Lu Xun* (Vol. 3). Beijing, China: People's Literature Publishing House.

Lu Xun (2000). *Call to arms* (Y. Xianyi & G. Yang, Trans.). Beijing, China: Foreign Languages Press. (Original work published in 1922)

Nietzsche, F. (1954). *Thus Spoke Zarathustra: A book for none and all* (W. Kaufmann, Trans.). New York, NY: Penguin. (Original work published 1892)

Qiubai, Q. (1953). *Preface*. In *Seclected essays of Lu Xun. Collected works of Qu Qiubai* (Vol. 2). Beijing, China: People's Literature Publishing House.

Romulus and Reomus (2008, October). In *Wikipedia, the free encyclopedia*. Retrieved from http://en.wikipedia.org/wiki/Romulus_and_remus

Shouchang, X. (1999). *Impressions on Lu Xun, my deceased friend,* The reminiscences of Lu Xun. Beijing, China: Beijing Publishing House.

Wang, X. (1989, June 10). Xiayu and Jesus: A comparison (J. Wickeri, Trans). Nanjing Theological Review, 97-100.

Yalom, I. D. (1980). *Existential psychotherapy*. New York, NY: Basic Books.

# Chapter 7

## Existentialism, Taoism, and Buddhism:
## Two Views

Kirk J. Schneider
Benjamin Tong

In this chapter, we focus on two contemplative styles—the existential style, which emphasizes the *mystery* of being; and the Taoist-Buddhist style, which accentuates the *harmony* of being. We then go on to consider how these respective emphases play out in a variety of life-contexts—individuality, development, society, and nature.

When one tackles a subject of this magnitude, it is necessary to be explicitly frank about our objectives. While this chapter addresses several key issues in the debate/dialogue about the relation among existentialism, Taoism, and Buddhism, it is but a very brief musing on a time-honored inquiry. For this reason, we have confined ourselves to general descriptions about the respective worldviews, rather than finely calibrated formulations. For those readers desiring an elaboration on these descriptions, see Aronson (2004); Barnes (1967); Barrett (1958); Batchelor (1990); Bradford (2008); Epstein (1995); Friedman (1991); Galvin (2008); Hoffman, Stewart, Warren, & Meek (2009); Jordan (1985); Mendelowitz (2008); Rubin (1996); Schneider (1999, 2002, 2004); Tong (1992, 1999, 2003, 2009); Walsh (2002); Watts (1961); and Welwood (2000).

In the passages to follow, we present two views on existential, Taoist, and Buddhist forms of contemplation (In Dr. Tong's section, Confucianism is also considered). From the outset, we wish to make clear that although these perspectives differ slightly in approach, they each share a common root—the elucidation of being. In this chapter, we hope to tease out the nuances of this common root and to dispel the stereotypes about the approaches, which highlight either extreme differences or rigid similarities.

In the spirit of the many fruitful exchanges on this subject between the authors, we decided to divide this chapter into three basic parts. In the first part, we feature a reflection by Kirk Schneider, drawing on his background in existential-spiritual psychology, and in the second portion, we present a commentary by Benjamin Tong, drawing on his background in Taoist studies and existential philosophy. In the final portion, the authors discuss and summarize their views.

## Agnosticism, Awe, and the Existential-Spiritual Lineage
## Kirk Schneider

Below I consider "existential spirituality" or what I have more recently termed "awe-based awakening" (Schneider, 2004, 2009), as a context for our Taoist-Buddhist dialogue. The basis for this examination is the existential-spiritual tradition, which, over and above the atheist existential heritage, embraces the humility and wonder, thrill and anxiety, or in short, *awe* of life (Friedman, 1991; Schneider, 2004). By awe of life, I mean neither absolute godlessness nor certain theism, but the invigorating *space* between (Buber, 1970; Friedman, 1991; Heschel, 1951; Tillich, 1957). I am reminded, here, of a parable that I am fond of invoking when asked about the difference between atheistic and agnostic forms of existentialism: "Whereas the agnostic-existentialist stands before the cosmos and throws up his hands in amazement (a la Martin Buber and Abraham Heschel), the atheist-existentialist stands before the cosmos and just simply throws up!" (a la Jean Paul Sartre). To be sure, the dividing line between an atheist and agnostic-existentialist is elusive. However, there is more than a grain of truth to the stereotypes of the atheist-existentialist as a curmudgeonly loner in contrast to the agnostic-existentialist as a *tragically optimistic* communalist (Frankl, 1984; Friedman, 1991).

At the same time, the agnostic and atheist-existentialist lineages converge on several key points: the sense of puzzlement, or even absurdity concerning the ultimate questions of life, the stress on responsibility, or ability to respond to this problematic plight, and the accent on choice. On the other hand, the agnostic-existentialist tends not to share the atheist's cynicism. Questions of the divine nature of being are held in abeyance for the agnostic-existentialist, and the enigmatic qualities of life, while anxiety provoking, are also viewed as occasions for fascination, even revelry. Among the agnostic and theologically-oriented existentialists pertinent to this chapter are Blaise Pascal, Soren Kierkegaard, William James, Emanual Levinas, Paul Tillich, Martin Buber, Gabriel Marcel, Abraham Heschel, Ernest Becker, Rollo May, and even, at points, Friedrich Nietzsche, Martin Heidegger and Albert Camus.

In the foregoing, I will draw mainly from the agnostic-theistic existential heritage in my comparison/contrast with Taoist-Buddhist traditions. Again, these comparisons are introductory, but may spark deeper considerations.

### Mystery and Harmony in Dialogue
The core basis of agnostic existentialism is mystery. We know not from whence we came nor whither we are going. Or as Gabriel Marcel (1967) put it, in effect: life is not a problem to be solved but a mystery to be contemplated. At the same time, agnostic-existentialists tend to view mystery as more than simply "unverifiable data," as the tough-minded scientist might look at it, but as the wellspring of a profound paradox. Taking their cue from Rudolf Otto's (1923) classic study of the origins of religiosity, these existentialists define the mystery of being in terms of two entwined yet separable dimensions: The dimension of *mysterium tremen-*

*dum* or dread, and the dimension of fascination or wonder. Add these together and you have an *awe-based* philosophy of life (Heschel, 1951; Schneider, 1993, 2004, 2009; Tillich, 1952, 1957).

While Taoism and Buddhism also affirm life's mystery (see Tong, this chapter), they take different approaches to that mystery. Buddhism for example, tends to view mystery or the unknown as *matter of fact* qualities of life. Life, for Buddhism is *impermanence* and impermanence is ultimately uncontainable. However, the Buddhist attitude toward impermanence is one of equanimity or harmonious accommodation. There is much less of the angst or daunting quality associated with the uncontained, as is common in the existential position; there is also less of the impassioned and fascinating element. From the Buddhist point of view, there is no need to be either daunted or enthralled by mystery, but simply to accept it.

Acceptance or *suchness* from the Taoist and Buddhist points of view are key sensibilities toward life. They lead to the ability to *relax* into and trust life rather than contend with it. Although existentialists also foster trust and acceptance of life *as is* they also seem more susceptible to being affected (or moved) by the *as is*, or to experience it in some kind of tension. As previously intimated, whereas Taoists and Buddhists stress the correspondence of all things; existentialists emphasize the dialogical tension of being separate-yet-related (Tillich, 1957). What this means practically is that there is a comparatively greater emphasis in existentialism on struggle, passion, and poignancy in the face of the unknown. There is also a commensurately greater stress on the tragic dimension of life within the existential purview. From this standpoint, tragedy is viewed as an integral part of living *well*—richly, fully—not just living. Or to put it another way, suffering is more than merely an inevitable part of life, as stressed by Buddhism, but it is, at the same time, *key* to a life fully lived. This is a life marked by depth, intensity, and the impetus for reform.

Below I address this perspective in the light of a variety of life-contexts, beginning with individuality. Momentarily, Dr. Tong will address the same life-contexts.

**Individuality**. Existentialists view individuality as a dialogical *process* rather than as a discrete or static category (Bugental, 1987). As noted earlier, individuals are viewed by existentialists as neither separate, self-isolated monads nor open, unbounded deities, but as *fluid-yet-centered*, separate-but-related mortals (Becker, 1973; Schneider, 2004; Tillich, 1957). For existentialists, there is no absolute dividing line between self and not self, being and nonbeing, or even primitive (*prepersonal*) and enlightened (*transpersonal*). But there is no necessary all-encompassing connection among these polarities, either. To this degree, existentialists are skeptical of all attempts to bifurcate the human being, including, at points, the Buddhistic notion of nirvana, which implies a kind of absolute purity of consciousness juxtaposed to attached and suffering consciousness (Schneider, 1987; Smith, 1986). On the other hand, this does not mean that existentialists, as I have defined them, believe in a discrete, bounded self. To the contrary, the parameters of self are ambiguous for existentialists, and the potential for expansion indefinite. However, is not the same as *all-pervading* or *pure* and it is ever subject to challenge. To this extent, the deconstruction of the self is both encouraged and yet questioned at appropriate points in existential circles, just as the mysterium tremendum of creation is both marveled at and yet gasped before, as well. The question as to where these junctures reside and who or what is best to address them is an ongoing, whole-bodied challenge.

For existentialists, a key component of this challenge is presence. The more we can be present to ourselves, the more we can open to and be responsive about the world; and this responsiveness (vs. reactivity) increases our latitude for *choice* (Buber, 1970; Heidegger, 1962; May, 1981).

**Growth and development**. As Dr. Tong noted in the section below, growth and development are integral to both existentialist and Taoist-Buddhist belief systems. Here again, the question is one of approach. Whereas existentialists place a comparative stress on *active* transformation (e.g., grappling, encountering, clarifying, doing), Taoist-Buddhists place an emphasis on pliant, being-oriented forms of maturation. Among these are experiences of beauty in simplicity (e.g., Japanese flower arrangement), humility (e.g., deference to others), and basic life acceptance.

**Passion**. The question of passion for existentialists is more subtly the question of *engagement*. Where is the line between engagement and fixation, effort and attachment to outcome? Is there a place for savoring (temporary) attachments, immersing in them with one's whole bodily being? And to what extent? On the other hand, when does savoring, lingering become fixating and, therefore, devitalizing? At what point do therapy clients, for example, need to let go of their internal battles, and at what point should they dwell in them, and steep in their complexities? At what point do I give up wrestling with this essay and simply allow it to *write itself*? Will it write itself—gratifyingly—If I do not tussle with it or stay up nights over it? Correlatively, what is the place for sentiment, intensity, and depth? How much can I revel in my son's romp through the ocean waves, or the graceful slope of my wife's neck before they become obsessions? I always appreciated the Taoist notion of *effortless effort*, or what I call *effortful nonattachment*. This is the notion of full and deep engagement of a given inclination, but without the fixation on outcome. This notion strikes me as deeply existential, but also ideal. Maybe the best we can do is approach it, investigate it, and marvel at the perplexities.

**Relationship to Society and Nature**. As with most things, existentialists have an ambivalent relationship to society and nature. They are both potentially freeing and entrapping. Although I do not subscribe to the Sartrean notion that "hell is other people" (p. 45). I also do not buy into *group think*. The dialogical imperative of existentialism intimates that our relations to the social milieu can be either deeply fulfilling or imprisoning, depending on how we interact with it and negotiate its demands. Tillich (1967) described the approach of *listening love* to address the moral dilemmas of our society. Listening love "is a listening to and looking at the concrete situation in all its concreteness, which includes the deepest motives of the other..." (p.109). He suggested, "The more seriously one has considered all the factors in a moral decision...[the individual as well as social, past influences as well as long term possibilities]...the more one can be certain that there is a power of acceptance in the depth of life" (p. 111) and in our own lives, I might add, for the decision we risk (p. 111). Listening love, in other words, gives us a *whole-bodied*, experiential way to engage with others and the world. It fosters neither robotic attachment nor nihilistic detachment, but a comprehensive and practical response (Schneider, 2013). Buddhism says something similar about finding the middle way, and Taoism about attention to what we are not, in addition to what we are.

**True Knowledge**. For existentialism, as with Taoism and Buddhism, there is no absolute when it comes to either society or nature, the best we can do is be maximally present, and appreciate the poignancy of our predicament; we are neither worms nor angels, but we can thrive nonetheless.

### Taoism and Existentialism/Existential Psychology: Brief Comparative Notes
### Benjamin Tong

In juxtaposing Taoism with existentialism and existential psychology, a starting point needs to be the acknowledgement that Taoism is an inseparable part of a syncretic *whole* of longstanding in East Asian cultures – namely, Buddhism, Taoism, and Confucianism. While there are clear distinctions among all three, the differences among these "wisdom traditions" have frequently been viewed as largely matters of emphasis. A brief consideration of their commonalities will be able to provide an appropriate backdrop against which to contrast Taoism with existentialism and existential psychology.

For one thing, this *whole* has the singular, common focus of *transformation*. The point of human existence to the Buddhists is the achievement of nirvana. In everyday language, nirvana simply refers to *The Great Escape*: That is to say, transcending the Earthly realm of perpetual suffering and never having to return except by choice. This psychospiritual evolution involves virtually countless lifetimes of difficult karmic work and uncertain struggle.

With its more Earth-bound, relational preoccupations, Confucianism envisions the mature individual—indeed, the mature civilization as well—as one in which only a single type of conflict is permitted. In concrete, everyday terms, this simply (and movingly) refers to "Who's going to pick up the check?" at a restaurant. The transformed human being is poised to be kinder than the next person. The popular bumper sticker imperative to *Commit Acts of Random Kindness* resonates to this interpersonal imperative. Akin to this state, another hallmark of the mature or properly transformed individual is the ability to know what questions one should worry about in life.

For Taoist people, the central aim in a world, which is essentially without *meaning* is the achievement of *wu wei*. In the contemporary language of Star Wars movies, this is a state in which the individual is "at one with the (Universal Life) Force" Also referred to as the Spirit of Nature, wu wei is characterized by both yin and yang forces being in balance. Put another way, action, or being-ness in the moment, is an integral fusion of maximum involvement as well as maximum aban-donment. Focused, concerted effort is tempered with non-attachment to outcome.

For example, the followingis an illustrative example from Nature: A wolverine and her cubs who are cornered by a hungry bear and have very little hope of surviving. Either as a result of instinctual knowing or observational learning, she *knows* that their only chance is for her to lunge up in the air at the bear's exposed throat the moment the huge animal charges in for the kill. She does just that: She jumps straight at the huge animal's throat, fully aware that contact with even a casual swipe by the bear's paw would break every bone in her tiny body. She knows she might die while attacking but is not attached to the outcome. All that matters is getting her sharp teeth into the bear's exposed throat. In the existential moment, in the here-and-now, there is maximum involvement (yang) and maximum abandon (yin).

> Two other themes are equally pervasive in these three traditions: *mystery* and *harmony*. The "ways of the Force" are as much of a mystery to those in the Judeo-Christian tradition as they are to adherents of the syncretic wisdom tradition of Buddhism, Taoism, and Confucianism. It is a mystery, for example, as to why the almighty, omnipotent God or the Force would allow for the possibility of evil people mastering and abusing the Power of the Universe. As millions have come to know, it is a phenomenon of awesome dimensions—both fascinating and terrifying. (Conniff, 1994)

I am reminded of the story about the night the God of Jewish internees in a Nazi death camp was put on trial for failing his people. Following the verdict of "guilty as charged," and right before a sentence was to be pronounced, someone in the court room shouted, "Wait, it is 8 o'clock, we must stop! It is time for evening prayer."

In his famous novel, *Walden Two*, B. F. Skinner (1948) envisioned the ideal society to be a harmonious one in which conflict of any sort does not exist. With a nod in the direction of ego psychology, we might say that this would be the ego's *sphere of conflict-free-ness* writ large. By way of contrast, *harmony* in the tripartite Eastern traditions is understood to emerge not from the *elimination* of conflicts but, rather, from the *management* of conflictual tensions. The classical Chinese metaphor for life is war. The achievement of, or the return to, the state of wu wei enables one to engage in the management of perpetual conflict or war in this arena of perpetual suffering—without going mad.

Let us now turn to a few thumbnail comparisons between Taoism and exis-tentialism and existential psychology. In particular, we will consider seven themes: the nature of being, non-being, individuality, growth and development, passion, one's relationship to society and Nature, and the essence of true knowledge.

**The Nature of Being.** Both traditions appeal to a reality underlying or standing behind subjectivity and objectivity. They differ, however, with respect to the means for achieving rapport with that *Tao* or *Ground of all being* (see Tillich, 1952). Martin Buber (1970) and Erich Fromm (1956) would emphasize the role of relationships: In authentic relationships that "work," the experience of the Other—the *Thou* in the I and Thou, paves the way for the Tao. In feeling both united and separate at the same time, there is an experiential approximation of being that is *one with all that is.* Taoists, like Zen practitioners, have stressed the role of such disciplines as meditation, archery, healing and the martial arts in achieving increasingly close rapport with the Universal Life Force (Liu, 1979).

**Non-Being.** Existentialists like Tillich speak of the perpetual "threat of non-being" as an experience that Westerners (with the possible exception of R. D. Laing (1967/1983) anticipate with dread (see also Cushman, 1990). Taoists, and other Eastern persons identified as being esoteric, refer to non-being as an experience to be actively pursued. Non-being, in fact, is the essential source and origin of all being (all things that exist). Zen people sometimes use the synonym, *no-mindedness*, while at least one contemporary Taoist scholar, Chang Chung Yuan (1975), spoke of *no-identity as true identity.*

**Individuality.** Existentialism and existential psychology are concerned that the individual stand out, as separate from other beings. This is Nietzsche-inspired *separate peace* that must somehow be won over and over again (see Nietzsche, 1883/1961). Taoists are preoc-cupied with the same thing but they also stress, paradoxically, with Sartre, the im-portance of achieving a deep and thorough identification with all of Creation. Bad faith, to Sartre (1957), is failure to acknowledge that "in choosing myself, I choose [for] man" (p. 18).

**Growth and Development.** Both traditions insist the human person comes into a fullness of self by immersing him/her self into the arena of worldly life. Both place a high premium on assuming total responsibility for oneself and one's ac-tions, all the while living in a spirit of risk, adventure and freedom. For Sartre (1956), the choice of life *projects* is critical, as one is shaped entirely as a result of commitment to choices. Frankl (1984) would say that discovery of one's very own special *meaning,* through creative endeavor, is *the* project, while Taoists stress the attitude of "non-attachment" in living out that meaning.

**Passion.** Existentialists frequently seek to acquaint mortals with their capa-city for passion, particularly in a contemporary world wherein so many are *dead but not buried* as a result of lack of passion. Theater plays like "Equus" imply that the attachments in many a Westerner's life lack passion – i.e., because they are lifeless, inauthentic, alienated, which cuts the person off from the rest of life.

Taoists, on the other hand, seek to liberate themselves from *enslavement* to passion of any sort. All living beings are born, they live for a while, and then they die. Other than for a few basic givens, we homo sapiens really do not understand much else. In the interim between entry and exit in this Earthly dimension, those human beings who would be serious about living naturally should endeavor to exist in much the same manner as plants and animals: simple, discrete, and without baggage. Health or wellness resides in not getting hung up on the necessary meaning or outcome of any event or behavior. Alan Watts (1994) reminded us of this path of *suchness* and simplicity in a marvelous story of old:

> Once a upon a time there was a Chinese farmer whose horse ran away, and all the neighbors came around to commiserate that evening. "So sorry to hear your horse ran away. This is most unfortunate." The farmer said, "Maybe." The next day the horse came back bringing seven wild horses with it, and everybody came back in the evening and said "Oh, isn't that lucky. What a great turn of events. You now have eight horses!" And he said "Maybe." The next day his son tried to break one of these horses and ride it but he was thrown, and broke his leg, and they all said, "Oh dear, that's too bad," and he said, "Maybe." The following day the conscription offices came around to conscript people into the army and they rejected his son because he had a broken leg. Again, all the people came around and said, "Isn't that great!" And he said, "Maybe." (p.157).

**Relationship to Society and Nature**. "The most difficult thing in life is to see it as it really is" (Personal Communication, late professor at the California School of Professional Psychology, Murray Bilmes, 1974). According to existentialism and existential psychology, humankind must face this essential condition of *thrownness* (Heiddeger's "dasein"), and own up to what it actually is—complete with its brutal contradictions, radical contingency, and dehumanization (Blair, 1997). This is an uncompromising honesty that necessarily involves the response of despair. One comes to feel empty, homeless, adrift and lost.

Taoists agree with the analysis. Paradoxically, they also contend that life is also not real: Our social and material *reality* is but an extremely minute part of a much larger and eternal Reality, without beginning or end. Earthly life is tantamount to Buddhism's "Wheel of Life and Death," to which an individual soul continually returns" to work through karmic business until it is finished. In light of this perspective, the response need not be despair; it just is not any big deal to come into human existence again and again. The feeling should be a kind of (cultivated) *no feeling*. One should live as simply as possible, with a minimum of passionate attachments, and then die when the time comes.

**True knowledge**. Both traditions agree that we know what is really *true* only by being in its *grasp*. We do not *know* truth as much as we are_seized by it. (e.g. Kierkegaard's notion of *truth only as it is produced in action*). Truth is always much more than logical judgments or that to which only the mind can attend. There are definite (finite) limits to ordinary human knowing.

## Summary and Conclusion

In this chapter, we have examined several shared tenets of existentialism, Taoism, and Buddhism. Far from being exhaustive, this is a thumbnail overview. Among the themes highlighted are the shared inquiry into being, the shared concern with living—both individually and collectively—in the face of this condition, and the shared problem of truth. We have shown that although the respective worldviews converge on these points, they also exhibit nuances of difference. For example, while existentialists emphasize the mystery, and thereby (dynamic) tension of self-cosmic relations, Taoists and Buddhists stress the correspondence, and thereby, (restorative) harmony of self-cosmic relations. Further, whereas existentialists stress the intensity, meaning, and passion of a life well lived, Taoists and Buddhists accent the acceptance, nonattachment, and unfoldment of a life continually in flux.

In closing, it is our sincere hope that we have stimulated a fresh dialogue about existentialism, Taoism, and Buddhism. Undoubtedly, we have raised more questions than we have answered, but if these questions prove fruitful, if they inspire others to enlarge their horizons, then we will have more than fulfilled our task.

## References

Aronson, H. B. 2004. *Buddhist practice on Western ground: Reconciling Eastern ideals and Western psychology.* Boston, MA: Shambhala.

Barnes, H. (1967). *An existentialist ethics.* New York, NY: Knopf.

Batchelor, S. (1990). *The faith to doubt: Glimpses of Buddhist uncertainty.* Berkeley, CA: Parallex Press.

Becker, E. (1973). *Denial of death.* New York, NY: Free Press.

Blair, M. (1997). *Heidegger and Aquinas on the self as substance.* In R. T. Caipalo (Ed.), *Postmodernism and Christian philosophy* (pp. 39-46). American Maritain Association.

Bradford, G. K. (2007). The play of unconditioned presence in existential-integrative psychotherapy. *Journal of Transpersonal Psychology, 39,* 23-47.

Buber, M. (1970). *I and thou.* (W. Kaufmann, Trans.). New York, NY: Charles Scribners & Sons.

Chang, Chung-Yuan (1975). *Tao: A new way of thinking.* New York, NY: Harper and Row.

Bugental, J. F. T. (1987). *The art of the psychotherapist.* New York, NY: Norton.

Conniff, R. (1994, March). Healthy terror (essay). *Atlantic Monthly.*

Cushman, P. (1990). Why the self is empty: Toward a historically situated psychology. *American Psychologist, 45*(5), 599-611.

Epstein, M. (1995). *Thoughts without a thinker: Psychotherapy from a Buddhist perspective.* New York, NY: Basic Books.

Frankl, V. (1984). *Man's search for meaning.* (I. Lasch, Tr.). New York, NY: Simon & Schuster.

Friedman, M. (1991). *The worlds of existentialism: A critical reader.* Atlantic Highlands, NJ: Humanities Press.

Fromm, E. (1956). *The art of loving.* New York, NY: Harper & Row.

Galvin, J. (2008). Brief encounters with Chinese clients: The case of Peter. In K. Schneider (Ed.), *Existential-Integrative psychotherapy: Guideposts to the core of practice.* (pp. 168-175). New York, NY: Routledge.

Heidegger, M. (1962). *Being and time.* (J. Macquarrie & E. Robinson, Trans.). New York, NY: Harper & Row.

Heschel, A. (1951). *Man is not alone: A philosophy of religion.* New York, NY: Farrar, Straus, and Giroux.

Hoffman, L., Stewart, S., Warren, D., & Meek., L. (2009). Toward a sustainable myth of self: An existential response to the postmodern condition. *Journal of Humanistic Psychology, 49,* 135-173.

Jordan, J. R. (1985). Paradox and polarity: The Tao of family therapy. *Family Process 24,* 165-174.

Laing, R.D. (1983). *The politics of experience.* NY: Pantheon. (Original version published in 1967)

Liu, Da. (1979). *The Tao and Chinese culture.* New York, NY: Schocken Books.

Marcel, G. (1967). *The philosophy of existentialism.* New York, NY: Citadel.

Mendelowitz, E. (2008). *Ethics and Lao Tzu: Intimations of character.* Colorado Springs, CO: University of the Rockies Press.

Nietzsche, F. (1961). *Thus spoke Zarathustra: A book for everyone and no one.* New York, NY: Penguin Classics. (Original work published in 1883)

Otto, R. (1923). *The idea of the holy.* London: Oxford University Press.

Rubin, J. B. (1996). *Psychotherapy and Buddhism: Toward an integration.* New Your, NY: Plenum Press.

Sartre, J. P. (1956). *Being and nothingness.* (H. Barnes, Trans.). New York, NY: Philosophical Library.

Sartre, J. P. (1957). *Existentialism and human emotions.* New York, NY: Philosophical Library.

Sartre, J. P. (1989). *No exit and three other plays.* New York, NY: Vintage. (Original work published in 1946)

Schneider, K. J. (1987). The deified self: A centaur response to Wilber and the transpersonal movement. *Journal of Humanistic Psychology, 27,* (196-216).

Schneider, K. J. (1999). *The paradoxical self: Toward an understanding of our contradictory nature.* Amherst, New York, NY: Humanity Books.

Schneider, K. J. (2002). A reply to Roger Walsh. In K. Schneider, J. Bugental, & F. Pierson (Eds.), *The handbook of humanistic psychology: Leading edges in theory, research, and practice.* (pp., 621-624). Thousand Oaks, CA: Sage.

Schneider, K. J. (2004). *Rediscovery of awe: Splendor, mystery, and the fluid center of life.* St. Paul, MN: Paragon House.

Schneider, K. J. (2009). *Awakening to awe: Personal stories of profound transformation.* Lanham, MD: Jason Aronson.

Schneider, K. J. (2013). *The polarized mind: Why it's killing us and what we can do about it.* Colorado Springs, CO: University Professors Press.

Skinner, B. F. (1948). *Walden Two.* New York, NY: Macmillan.

Smith, H. (1986). *The religions of man.* New York, NY: Perennial Library.

Tillich, P. (1952). *The courage to be.* New Haven, CT: Yale University Press.

Tillich, P. (1957). *Dynamics of faith.* New York, NY: Harper Torchbooks.

Tillich, P. (1967). *My search for absolutes.* New York, NY: Simon & Schuster.

Tong, B. R (1992) The Tao of Chaos. *The Social Dynamicist, 3*(4), 9-10.

Tong, B. R (1999, Fall). Taoism: Concerned about wellness and then again not. *The Empty Vessel: A Journal of Contemporary Taoism 6*(1), 32-40.

Tong, B. R. (2003). Taoist mind-body resources for psychospiritual health and healing. In S. G. Mijares (Ed.), *Modern psychology and ancient wisdom: Psychological healing practices from the world's religious traditions.* Binghamton, New York, NY: Haworth Press.

Tong, B. R. (in preparation). The Breath of the Tao and the Tao of Breathing. S. J. Mijares (Ed.), *The revelation of the breath: A tribute to Its wisdom, power and beauty* (working title).

Walsh, R. (2002). Authenticity, conventionality, and angst: Existential and transpersonal perspectives. In K. Schneider, J. Bugental, & F. Pierson (Eds.), *The handbook of humanistic psychology: Leading edges in theory, research, and practice.* (pp. 609-619). Thousand Oaks, CA: Sage.

Watts, A. (1961). *Psychotherapy East and West.* New York, NY: Pantheon.

Watts, A. (1994). *Talking Zen: Written and spoken by Alan Watts* (M. Watts, Ed.). New York, NY: Weatherhill.

Welwood, J. (2000). *Toward a psychology of awakening: Buddhism, psychotherapy, and the path of personal and spiritual transformation.* Boston, MA: Shambhala.

# Chapter 8

## Existential Themes in the Parables of Jesus

### Mark Yang

This chapter explores the relationship between Christianity and existential psychology by presenting a few of Jesus's parables. Given that we will be presenting various myths from the East and the West in the following chapters, it is only appropriate that we understand Jesus's teachings through his parables; for parables like myths are embodiments of great truths that challenge us to think and wrestle with its symbolism and meaning; they represents *Truths*, even if not literal truths. The first and main parable that I will present is the Parables of the Ten Virgins found in the New Testament book of Matthew 25:1-13. It was a rather cryptic parable to me when I first read it. I was confused and could not believe that such a parable was told by Jesus and included in the Bible. However, my study of existential psychology helped to enlighten me to the wisdom in the moral of that parable. Similarly, existential themes helped me to have a deeper understanding of the parable that follows immediate after: The Parable of the Talents (Matthew 25: 14-30). Contrary to popular misconception, it is my passionate belief that existential psychology and philosophy share many more commonalities than differences with Christian teachings. My hope is that upon reading the existential themes presented in this chapter and book, you too will come to a deeper understanding of the wisdom to be found in the parables told by Jesus.

### Parable of the Ten Virgins

Then the kingdom of heaven will be like ten virgins who took their lamps and went to meet the bridegroom. Five of them were foolish, and five were wise. For when the foolish took their lamps, they took no oil with them, but the wise took flasks of oil with their lamps. As the bridegroom was delayed, they all became drowsy and slept. But at midnight there was a cry, 'Here is the bridegroom! Come out to meet him.' Then all those virgins rose and trimmed their lamps. And the foolish said to the wise, 'Give us some of your oil, for our lamps are going out.' But the wise answered, saying, 'Since there will not be enough for us and for you, go rather to the dealers and buy for yourselves.' And while they were going to buy, the bridegroom came, and those who were ready went in with him to the marriage feast, and the door was shut. Afterward the other virgins came also, saying, 'Lord, lord, open to us.' But he answered, 'Truly, I say to you, I do not know you.' Watch, therefore, for you know neither the day nor the hour. (Matthew 25: 1-13)

This is indeed one of the more cryptic parables told by Jesus. Usually the reader cannot understand why Jesus would tell a story in which the wise virgins will not share their oil with the foolish virgins. After all, is not generosity and sharing some of the basic foundational teachings of Christianity and other religions? Furthermore, this parable is talking about the end times when the return of the bridegroom can be compared to Jesus's Second Coming in which he will return to take the *believers* back with him to heaven. So, a lot is at stake here. We are talking about heaven, entering into the Kingdom of God! Thus, it is even more strange when this is compared to the Great Commission (Matthew 28:16-20, Mark 16:14-18, Luke 24:44-49, Acts 1:4-8, and John 20:19-23) in Christianity in which the Christians are called to "make disciples of all nations . . ." (Matthew 28:19) Thus, one would think that Jesus would have rebuked the wise virgins for not sharing their oil instead of calling them wise. How can these *selfish* virgins be wise when they told the foolish virgins that "since there will not be enough for us and for you, go rather to the dealers and buy for yourselves" (Matthew 25:9). Where is the wisdom in being selfish? However, upon the Bridegroom's return, he took with him to the marriage feast (heaven) those wise virgins who were *ready* while the foolish virgins went to buy their own oil. The frightening thing is, when the foolish virgins returned and asked to be let into the marriage feast, Jesus said "Truly, I say to you, I do not know you. Watch, therefore, for you do not know neither the day nor hour" (Matthew 25: 12).

I am not sure what your reaction to this parable was, but I would classify this as a *terrible* story, full of terror. But what helps to assuage this terror is an understanding of the existential themes throughout the parable. First of all, the key to understanding this parable hinges upon understanding the symbolism of the oil. The oil symbolizes *preparation*. The wise virgins were prepared and ready in anticipation of the bridegroom's return. They were alert (Mark 13:32-33). If the oil symbolizes preparation, the next question then is, "how do we become prepared?" In the language of the parable, "how or when do we buy the oil for ourselves?" I propose that being prepared and purchasing the oil for ourselves has everything to do with facing the four existential givens as proposed by Irvin Yalom (1980) in his classic textbook, *Existential Psychotherapy: Death, Freedom, Isolation, and Meaninglessness*. This chapter will endeavor to address the relationship between preparedness and these four all important existential givens.

Most Christians will immediately understand that this parable has to do with death and the end times. I believe that this understanding is not just intellectual, but also visceral as this is not a pleasant parable to read. My own reaction is to run away from this parable. Who would want to read about selfish people who refrain from sharing, only to be rewarded with eternal life; while the poor souls who were unprepared, perhaps simply lethargic, are punished by being kept out of the ultimate party and told by God, "I do not know you."? Most of the time, I prefer to avoid such unpleasantness, just as I prefer to deny the reality of death. Yet, Saint Augustine reminded us that "It is only in the face of death that a man's self is born" (as cited in Montaigne, 1965, p. 63). Seneca (as cited in Montaigne, 1965) said likewise, "No man enjoys the true taste of life but he who is willing and ready    to quit it" (p. 61). Cicero (as cited in Montaigne, 1965) suggested that "to philosophize is to prepare for death" (p. 56). And finally, Irvin Yalom (2008) told us "though the physicality of death destroys us, the idea of death saves us" (p. 7).

In regard to the first existential given, the importance of facing our own death or limits, it all begins with awareness or mindfulness. In the parable, both the wise and foolish virgins became drowsy and slept. The symbolism of drowsiness is powerful here. It is not just simply lethargy. Drowsiness can be understood as the lack of awareness, or the unwillingness to thinking more deeply, which is a certain kind of *forgetfulness of being* as proposed by Martin Heidegger (1962). In contrast, in this parable as in other parables, Jesus's followers are often warned to be watchful, to be alert. A majority of the time, these warnings occur in the context of Jesus's death and Second Coming: "Therefore keep watch, because you do not know on what day your Lord will come" (Matthew: 24:42).

> It's like a man going away: He leaves his house and puts his servants in charge, each with his assigned task, and tells the one at the door to keep watch. Therefore, keep watch because you do not know when the owner of the house will come back—whether in the evening, or at midnight, or when the rooster crows, or at dawn. If he comes suddenly, do not let him find you sleeping. (Mark 13:34-36)

Existentially, this alertness can be understood as mindfulness, what the Greeks referred to as the Ontological mode of existence where one remains not only mindful of the fragility of being (death), but mindful too of one's responsibility for one's own being. According to Heidegger (1962), this mindfulness entails being authentic and responsible for one's choices; where one embraces one's possibilities and limits; one faces absolute freedom and nothingness and is anxious in the face of them (note, not the absence of anxiety). More on the theme of freedom and nothingness will follow later in the chapter.

Of what are we to be aware? First, the awareness begins with an attitude, that includes the belief that life and death are simultaneous and interdependent. The fact that life and death are interdependent is well known. Most people know that in order to die well, one has to live well. In the words of Irvin Yalom (1980) "behind every fear of death is a life unlived" (p. 207) or "death anxiety is inversely proportional to life satisfaction" (p. 207). On the other hand, most people do not understand life and death to be simultaneous. Most people understand that death follows life; they are consecutive. Indeed, the pronouncement of death, also known as the Final Medical Act, is required to be performed by a physician. The barrier between life and death needs to be exact. Not so in the view of existential psychology. The act of baptism in Christianity symbolizes death followed by re-birth. Life and death were very much simultaneous in the life of Jesus as he warned constantly about the departure of himself as the Son of Man. The Trium-phal Entry of Jesus (Matthew 21-22, Mark 11-12, Luke 19-20, John 12) also was very much about Jesus's awareness of his limited time on Earth. Even the dual nature of Jesus being *both* human and divine is about the simultaneous existence of both mortality and immortality, life and death. The fact that Jesus's ministry and time on Earth was very much limited added to the urgency and vitality of his min-istry.

However, this awareness of the omnipresence of death is painful and anxiety producing. Indeed, one's confrontation with death is a terrible experience. It has been compared to *Staring at the Sun*, the title of Irvin Yalom's (2008) latest book on "Overcoming the Terror of Death" (e.g., the book's subtitle). One must not stare directly at the sun, this is utter foolishness. Instead, one confronts death obliquely, similar to how one is to experience the literal presence of God. Therefore, because the direct confrontation with death is so filled with anxiety, human beings have actively erected numerous defenses against this awareness. Such defenses are replete throughout the stories in the Bible. I have presented but two of these parables. The drowsiness on the part of the virgins, the beloved disciples of Jesus, and by extension to other followers, results not from passive laziness/lethargy or the lack of obedience but active denial. How else would one explain Jesus's exas-peration as he time-and-again warned the disciples of his imminent departure with statements such as "the Son of Man will suffer..." (Mark 8:31, Mark 9:12, Luke 9:22, Luke 24:7) and "the Son of Man will come at an unexpected hour..." (Matthew 24:44, Luke 12:40). One wonders how the disciples can be so thick-headed and ignorant. Yudhishtara (as cited in Branfman, n.d.) understood this when he said "of all the world's wonders, which is the most wonderful? That no man, though he sees others dying all around him, believes that he himself will die." Laziness has its limits and such ignorance can best be explained by an understanding of the active denial (versus passive laziness) that is required to avoid the unpleasant in-evitable.

Instead of defending against death, existential psychology teaches that the best solution regarding the fear of death is to live life fully. In the words of Zorba, the Greek, live life in such a way so as to "leave death nothing but a burned-out castle" (as cited in Yalom, 2008, p. 50). Nietzsche implored us to "Consummate your life and Die at the right time" (as cited in Yalom, 2008, p. 50). Sartre (1981), in his autobiography, "I was going quietly to my end... certain that the last burst of my heart would be inscribed on the last page of my work and that death would be taking only a dead man" (p. 198). This is the principle behind the Parable of the Rich fool found in Luke 12:16–21, where Jesus warned about the foolishness of storing material things up when death comes calling. Instead, Jesus urged people to be rich towards God (v. 21) and store up our treasures in heaven (Matthew 6:19-21). This storing up of treasures in heaven is the essence behind the principle of rippling.

Rippling is perhaps the singular idea that brings the most comfort in countering a person's death anxiety and distress at the transience of life. Rippling refers to the fact that each of us creates—often without our conscious intent or knowledge—concentric circles of influence that may affect others for years, even for generations. The idea that we can leave something behind of ourselves, even beyond our knowing, offers a potent answer to those who claim that meaninglessness inevitably flows from one's finiteness and transiency. (Yalom, 2008, p. 83)

Rippling is also behind the idea of stewardship. In the parable immediately following the parable of the Ten Virgins, Jesus told the Parable of the Talents (Matthew 25: 14-28). The moral of the parable is that we are all given talents according to our abilities. What is asked of individuals is that they put their talents to work such that our talents will multiply. The number and characteristic of the talents, and how we are to trade with them is individually defined. However, what is expected of Jesus's followers is that the talents will be used and this is where rippling applies. Christians are to steward their talents to allow its effects to multiply and ripple across generations. This is the work of the preparation that will assuage the fear of death and gain eternal life.

## Parable of the Talents

Again, it will be like a man going on a journey, who called his servants and entrusted his property to them. To one he gave five talents of money, to another two talents, and to another one talent, each according to his ability. Then he went on his journey. The man who had received the five talents went at once and put his money to work and gained five more. So also, the one with the two talents gained two more. But the man who had received the one talent went off, dug a hole in the ground and hid his master's money. After a long time, the master of those servants returned and settled accounts with them. The man who had received the five talents brought the other five. 'Master,' he said, 'you entrusted me with five talents. See, I have gained five more.' His master replied, 'Well done, good and faithful servant! You have been faithful with a few things; I will put you in charge of many things. Come and share your master's happiness!' The man with the two talents also came. 'Master,' he said, 'you entrusted me with two talents; see, I have gained two more.' His master replied, 'Well done, good and faithful servant! You have been faithful with a few things; I will put you in charge of many things. Come and share your master's happiness!' Then the man who had received the one talent came. 'Master,' he said, 'I knew that you are a hard man, harvesting where you have not sown and gathering where you have not scattered seed. So, I was afraid and went out and hid your talent in the ground. See, here is what belongs to you.' His master replied, 'You wicked, lazy servant! So, you knew that I harvest where I have not sown and gather where I have not scattered seed? Well then, you should have put my money on deposit with the bankers, so that when I returned I would have received it back with interest.' 'Take the talent from him and give it to the one who has the ten talents. For everyone who has will be given more, and he will have an abundance. Whoever does not have, even what he has will be taken from him. And throw that worthless servant outside, into the darkness, where there will be weeping and gnashing of teeth.' (Matthew 25: 14-30)

The Parable of the Talents also embodies the themes of freedom, responsibility, and destiny. In the parable, each of the servants was free and responsible to choose what to do with their talents. The same freedom applied to the wise and foolish virgins from the previous parable. The wise servants from the Parable of the Talents were cognizant of their responsibilities and chose to trade with their talents. The foolish servant, fearing the master, chose to run away from his responsibility and destiny, dug a hole in the ground and hid his talent. As the result of his choice, even what he had was taken away from him and he was thrown into the darkness where there was gnashing of teeth (v. 30). Again, this seemed to be a terrible story, full of terror! How then do we make sense of the fear of the foolish servant and such strong reaction on the part of the master?

This is where an existential understanding of the concept of freedom can shed some light. Eric Fromm (1941) famous work *Escape from Freedom* informs us that we all are condemned to freedom. This is a very paradoxical understanding regarding the concept of freedom. Generally, freedom is something to be desired and people will lay their lives down for freedom, not to escape from it. Furthermore, condemnation is the antonym for freedom and yet Fromm stated that we are condemned to freedom such that we want to escape from it. How do we understand this paradox?

According to Fromm, freedom is unavoidably tied to responsibility and destiny. Responsibility is equated with authorship. Jean-Paul Sartre (1956) wrote that to be responsible is to be "the uncontested author of an event or a thing" (p. 633). To be aware of responsibility is to be aware of creating one's own self, destiny, life predicament, feelings, and, if such be the case, one's own suffering. Sartre, like Fromm, believed that human beings are *doomed* to freedom. Again, this is a paradox (Doomed versus Free)! One is entirely responsible for one's life, not only for one's actions but also for one's failure to act. In the parables, the foolish servants failed to act, and the foolish virgins acted too late (failed to act in time), both with terrible consequences! Such responsibility is immense. Both to constitute (to be responsible for) oneself and one's world and to be aware of one's responsibility is a deeply frightening insight. Like the awareness of death, freedom is fraught with anxiety! James Truslow Adams (as cited in May, 1981) observed that "Eternal anxiety is the lot of the free man" (p. 185). Rollo May (1981) stated that "Freedom and anxiety are two sides of the same coin—there is never one without the other" (p.

190). And finally, Dostoevsky in his legend of the Grand Inquisitor in the *Brothers Karamazov* (1880/1990) said, "Man is tormented by no greater anxiety than to find someone quickly to whom he can hand over the gift of freedom with which the ill-fated creature is born" (p. 32).

Such anxiety is an unavoidable experience of freedom. Rollo May (1981) talked about the *anxious prophet* as one who experiences the anxiety that comes with his freedom to see into the future, to see beyond the usual limits in which other people see. May stated,

> One way to distinguish between the authentic prophet or saint from the fanatic or charlatan is this: the authentic prophet feels anxiety about his role and the charlatan does not. Like the prophets in the Old Testament, the authentic ones do not want to be prophets; they do their best to decline the role. They would escape if they could because of the dizziness and dread such great freedom entails. Jonah even fled from Nineveh and had to be brought back by a whale to give his prophecies. (p. 193)

Indeed, we see Jesus struggling with his freedom, choice, responsibility, and destiny in the Garden of Gethsemane (Matthew 26: 36-45) when he prayed three times for the cup to be taken away from him. Jesus's prayer revealed his struggle with his destiny, "if it is possible, may this cup be taken from me" and with his freedom of choice, "Yet not as I will, but as you will" (v. 39). Even though Jesus's prayer was for the Father's will to be done, he still had to choose whether to obey God's will and the anxiety related that choice. The anxiety was distressing to the point to which Jesus uttered "my soul is overwhelmed with sorrow to the point of death" (v. 38).

Jesus's confrontation with freedom and destiny was evident throughout the entirety of his life, not only near the end. Jesus's ministry began with the three temptations from the devil (Matthew 4:1-11) in which alternative choices were offered to Jesus's destiny. In each case, Jesus made the *decision* to seek his own destiny, aligned with that of the Father, and follow the written word. Decisions are difficult because they require renunciation, relinquishment, exclusion, and limitation, all associated with death. For every Yes, there must be a No, or a multitude of No's. The old priest in John Gardner's (1971) novel *Grendel* wisely told us that "Things fade; alternatives exclude.... The ultimate evil is that Time is perpetual perishing and being involves elimination" (p. 115). As one therapist commented to an indecisive patient, "Decisions are very expensive; they cost you everything else." The temptations of Jesus make these points abundantly clear. The temptations were all about renunciation. Jesus's himself talked about renunciation when he lovingly told a rich young man "to go and sell everything he had and give to the poor, and you will have treasure in heaven. Then come and follow me" (Mark 10:21). How difficult was/is (this) choice? Jesus later taught his disciples "that it is easier for the camel to go through the eye of the needle than for a rich man to enter the kingdom of God" (Mark 10:25). The decision was painful because it involved death.

As the quote above from the novel, *Grendel,* teaches us, death is associated with the painfulness of decisions. Things fading with time perpetually perishing is about death. The root of the word decide, *cidium,* means slay, *the act of killing* as in homicide, suicide, pesticide, The rich young man knew of the wisdom of Jesus's words and went away sad (v. 22). The young man experienced the existential pain of renunciation, and knew that the decision involved death. Many think the rich young ruler was sad because the choice with which he was faced involved the renunciation of his material wealth, but such an understanding does not go far nor deeply enough. The choice was also painful because it involves the death of his former life. Decisions are painful because they limit possibilities. Indeed Martin Heidegger (1962) defined death as the "impossibility of further possibility" (p. 93). The decision with which Jesus and the rich young man were faced involved renunciation, death, and eternal life.

Furthermore, the difficulty of deciding is that decisions are continuous. Often, we think of monumental decisions. But decision making is often more of a gradual subtle process. Gaining awareness, therapists often help clients to appreciate that therapeutic change often does not consist of a single willful choice, but a gradual series of decisions each leading to the next. Although Jesus's ministry is bracketed by the monumental decisions above, we also read of Jesus making continuous choices to head towards Jerusalem and his destiny. Jesus choosing his destiny involved him explaining over and over again how the:

> Son of Man will be betrayed to the chief priests and teachers of the law. They will condemn him to death and will hand him over to the Gentiles, who will mock him and spit on him, flog him and kill him. Three days later he will rise. (Mark 10:33-34)

In the words of Bronislaw Malinowsky (as cited in May, 1981), Jesus was making the choice to accept the *chains which suited him*:

> Metaphorically, freedom in its essence is the acceptance of the chains which suit you and for which you are suited, and of the harness in which you pull towards an end chosen and valued by yourself, and not imposed. It is not, and never can be, the absence of restrictions, obligations or law and of duty. (p. 83)

Or in the poetic words of Lord Byron (as cited in May 1981, p. 204):

> My very chains and I grew friends,
> So much a long communion tends
> To make us what we are; - even I
> Regain'd my freedom with a sigh.

Jesus, in choosing his destiny, understood who he was and is, the Messiah, and the implications of him accepting his identity and his responsibilities. This is in contrast to the disciples who continually ignored Jesus's explanations and warnings about who he was and his destiny. How can one explain such ignorance? One is tempted to view the disciples as simple fisherman who simply could not grasp the reality of what Jesus was saying to them. Perhaps this is a passive kind of ignorance and lack of sophistication or intelligence. I do not think so. It makes more sense to understand the disciple's ignorance as an active form of defense; a defense against Jesus's destiny and their own destinies, the defense against death. How else might we account for such repeated ignorance of Jesus's clear warnings. It is not that the disciples did not understand Jesus's warnings. At some level, they understood too well Jesus's warning and were struggling to accept their destinies as Jesus was marching toward his. Knowing in hindsight how most of the disciples were martyred, it is entirely understandable how one would repeatedly choose ignorance for such existential courage is not easily found.

This constitutes Jesus's suffering for his beloved disciples were forever unaware of the reality of Jesus's destiny. We read of Jesus's exasperation as he beseeched the disciples over and over again, "How long will I be with you?" This is evidence of Jesus's loneliness; Jesus's suffering in the form of existential isolation. Although Jesus was surrounded by his disciples throughout the years of his ministry, we surmise that he was not suffering from inter-personal isolation or loneliness. In fact, Jesus often sought the sanctuary of solitude in order to pray and perhaps commune with himself. Indeed, Jesus was a model of balance between intrapersonal and interpersonal connectedness. He represented the ideal balance between being in relationship with others and maintaining time for solitude." As written above, Jesus began his ministry in isolation in the desert. Such solitude can be understood from the framework of Jesus nurturing his relationship with himself and with God, making sure that he was not intra-personally isolated. However, despite being interpersonally and intra-personally connected, there is no escaping the suffering that Jesus faced in the form of Existential Isolation.

In addition to the constant disconnectedness between Jesus and his disciples in regards to Jesus's true destiny, perhaps the greatest instance of Jesus struggling with existential isolation was again his experience in the Garden of Gethsemane (Matthew 26:36-46). In the Garden, although Jesus had continually been headed towards Jerusalem and his death, he had to confront the fundamental decision once and for all whether to face up to his destiny. And again, this decision was continuous for Jesus, as he, both literally and symbolically, had to face up to this decision to take the bitter cup of suffering three times that early morning in Gethsemane. Such fundamental decisions confront each of us with existential isolation, which refers to an unbridgeable gulf between oneself and any other being (Yalom, 1980). And death and dying is perhaps the loneliest of human experience. No one can die with another or for another. Martin Heidegger (1962) stated that "though one can go to his death for another, such 'dying-for' can never signify that the other has had his death taken away in even the slightest degree. No one can take the other's death away from him" (p. 284).

Like death and freedom, a decision is a lonely act, and it is *our* act; no one can decide for us. No one could decide for Jesus. The decision was so painful that Jesus begged the Father on three occasions for "the cup to be taken away from him" (vs. 39, 42 & 44). Jesus also shared with Peter, James, and John that "his soul is overwhelmed to the point of death." And in the midst of this pain, Jesus asked his most beloved disciples to "stay and keep watch with him" (vs. 38). Although Jesus took Peter, James, and John to be with him, he was fundamentally alone. No relationship can eliminate existential isolation. Each of us is alone in existence.

Yet, aloneness can be shared in such a way that love compensates for the pain of isolation. "A great relationship," says Martin Buber (1965), "breaches the barriers of a lofty solitude, subdues its strict law, and throws a bridge from self-being to self-being across the abyss of dread of the universe" (p. 175). But the disciples fell asleep at the Garden of Gethsemane and were not able to provide Jesus with the companionship he was seeking. Perhaps this is symbolic of that unbridgeable gap. Such was the depth of Jesus's isolation and sorrow. It is again interesting that the disciples, like the virgins in the parables, were also asleep. For it is difficult and painful to maintain awareness and alertness in the midst of such great suffering. Ah, for the relief and escape provided for by sleep to the depressed. Nevertheless, the courage to remain alert and aware is exactly what is required of companions, whether one be therapists or friend.

The episode in the Garden of Gethsemane is perhaps the penultimate event in Jesus's life and ministry. For Christians the world over, the importance of Jesus's decision for sacrifice and to follow the will of God unto death (with faith for resurrection) cannot be underestimated. As written above, Jesus could not escape the fact that his decision at the Garden of Gethsemane was his alone. His ministry and his life necessitated that he face this all-important decision and face it alone. It was the essence of his decision, for to *exist* means to stand-out. Often times, Jesus is characterized as fully integrated with the Father and the Holy Spirit in the Trinity. To the extent that this integration is not understood as three separate beings, such integration can be described as a form of fusion. However, it is my understanding that the meaning of Jesus being fully human (along with being fully divine, thus a mysterious paradox) meant that he had to depart and separate from the Father, taking on human likeness. Jesus's decision at the Garden of Gethsemane is perhaps the clearest illustration that there were two wills, Jesus's will and the Father's will for Jesus asked that "not as I will, but as you will" (Matthew 26: 39). So, in many ways, Jesus's descent to be *with* us, meant that he had to separate, perhaps even individuate apart from the Father. This is the meaning of Jesus's existence—to stand out. The significance of Jesus's isolated decision, indeed the meaning of Jesus's redemption for the human race, required that he descend from heaven and make that isolated decision to pay the ultimate price. I do not think the decision, and the meaning and power of Jesus's decision to take on the sins of the world, would have had much significance if Jesus did not make a separate decision from the Father. For without struggle and suffering and, thus, faith, the decision and sacrifice would have been meaningless. In other words, if Jesus was fused with the Father so as to obviate the need to face this existential crisis, then the decision would have been meaningless; I argue that the meaning and redemptive power behind his decision and sacrifice would have been meaningless as well. In short, there are some who believe that the decision for Jesus to obey was *easy* because Jesus's will was so in-line (fused) with the Father. But I would view this as a form of fusion defense similar to the disciple's lack of understanding regarding the meaning of Jesus's decision to choose his destiny.

This theme of fusion-isolation, attachment-separation is a major existential developmental task. To relinquish a state of interpersonal fusion means to encounter existential isolation with all its anxiety and dread. But not to separate means not to grow up. The price for individuation is isolation. As Irvin Yalom (1980) taught us:

> Existential isolation and interpersonal isolation are intricately interwoven. Emergence from interpersonal fusion thrusts the individual into existential isolation. A dissatisfying state of fusion–existence or too early or too tentative emergence leaves the individual unprepared to face the isolation inherent in autonomous existence. The fear of existential isolation is the driving force behind many interpersonal relationships and is, as we shall see, a major dynamic behind the phenomenon of transference. (p. 362)

James Bugental (1965) in his discussion of the problem of relatedness, plays on the word, *apart* (p. 309). The human being's basic interpersonal task is to be at once *a-part-of* and *a-part-from*. Interpersonal and existential isolation are way stations for each other. One must first separate oneself from the other in order to encounter isolation; one must be alone to experience aloneness. But, it is the facing of aloneness that ultimately allows one to engage another deeply and meaningfully.

Bugental's discussion regarding a-part-of and a-part-from is an excellent understanding of Jesus being both fully human (a-part-of) and fully divine (a-part-from). In the end, Jesus is perhaps our greatest model of how to engage our developmental task of attachment-separation. He emerged from the unity of being in *perfect* relationship with the Father and individuated from the Father, acknowledged and resolutely confronted his isolation in human existence, and, as the result, he was able to return to the unity with the Father while delivering salvation for the human race as the ultimate sacrifice of love.

Another way to understand Jesus's destiny was that his destiny was very much his purpose and meaning in life. Existential psychology places great emphasis upon the importance of one's meaning in life. Jung (1966) held the belief that meaninglessness was equivalent to illness. He wrote:

> Absence of meaning in life plays a crucial role in the etiology of neurosis. A neurosis must be understood ultimately as a suffering of a soul which has not discovered it's meaning... about 1/3 of my cases are not suffering from any clinical definable neurosis but from the senselessness and aimlessness of their lives. (p. 83)

Similarly, Victor Frankl (1959) stated that 20% of the neuroses he encountered in clinical practice derive from a lack of meaning. Frankl believed that the lack of meaning is the paramount existential stress. To him, existential neurosis is synonymous with a crisis in meaninglessness. Conversely, according to Frankl, there is nothing in the world that would so effectively help one to survive even the worst conditions, as having the knowledge that there is a meaning in one's life. There is much wisdom in the words of Nietzsche (as cited in Frankl, 1959): "He who has a *why* to live for can bear almost any *how*" (p. 59). In Frankl's Nazi concentration camp experience, he could see that those who knew that there was a task waiting for them to fulfill were most apt to survive. Nicholas Hobbs (1962) agreed:

> Contemporary culture often produces a kind of neuroses different from that described by Freud. Contemporary neuroses are characterized not so much by repression and conversion... not by lack of insight but lack of a sense of purpose, of meaning in life. (p. 742–748)

Jesus's life was imbued with meaning. It is this meaning and purpose which helped him to endure the suffering that he endured for much of his ministry. Nietzche's words from above are illuminating for it was because Jesus's knew *why* he was in life that allowed him to know *how* to live his life and put up with the suffering he endured.

Meaning in life can be very simply categorized into two different categories: Religious and secular. What I hope to show here is that although these are distinct categories, the similarities between them are far more important than their differences. Secular understandings of meaning in life, or more appropriately meaninglessness in life, are embodied by the nihilistic philosophies of Camus (1955) and Sartre (1956). Camus used the world "absurd" to refer to the human being's basic position in the world–the predicament of a transcendent, meaning-seeking being who must live in a world that has no meaning. Camus referred to this as the absurd human condition. This is the essence of nihilism. Camus' solution for facing up to this absurdity is what he called "heroic nihilism." He heartened individuals to contemplate this basic absurdity and construct a new life meaning by cherishing what he called *our nights of despair*, by facing the very essence of meaninglessness and arriving at a position of *heroic nihilism*. This would be Camus's understanding of Jesus's night of despair as Jesus fully faced up to his destiny and the meaning or possible meaninglessness of his life. It was only through this confrontation that Jesus was able to become fully who He wanted to be or was meant to be. Thomas Hardy (as cited in May, Angel & Ellengerger, 1958) would agree, as he said that "if a way to the Better there be, it exacts a full look at the Worst" (p. 3). Similarly, a human being, Camus believed, can mature only by living with dignity in the face of absurdity. The world's indifference can be transcended by rebellion, a prideful rebellion against one's condition. So, the values of heroic nihilism consist of courage, prideful rebellion, fraternal solidarity, love, and secular saintliness.

Sartre (1956) had a very similar understanding of the importance of being heroic in the face of this absurdity. Although Sartre's sense of freedom was uncompromisingly defined by meaninglessness, his solution, as embodied by the fictional characters in his book, is very similar to that of Camus. The characters in Sartre's books find meaning not by looking into *faith* in the religious sense, but by embracing commitment, action, and above all engagement, and these commitments and engagements are not characterized by self-fulfillment but service to others. Frankl (1959) agreed wholeheartedly when he described the "self-transcendence" of human existence. He continued:

> I wish to stress that the true meaning of life is to be discovered in the world rather than within man or his own psyche, as though it were a closed system... It denotes the fact that being human always points, and is directed, to something, or someone, other than oneself – be it a meaning to fulfill or another human being to encounter. The more one forgets himself – by giving himself to a cause to serve or another person to love – the more human he is and the more he actualizes himself. What is called self-actualization is not an attainable aim at all, for the simple reason that the more one would strive for it, the more he would miss it. In other words, self-actualization is possible only as a side-effect of self-transcendence" (p. 133).

Metaphorically, Frankl (1959) reminded us that a boomerang returns to the hunter who threw it only if it misses its target; in the same way, human beings return to self-preoccupation only if they have missed the meaning that life has for them. Finally, in the words of Arthur Ashe (n.d.), the great American tennis champion, "From what we get, we can make a living; what we give, however, makes a life" (n.p.). What we get is destiny. What we give is freedom and responsibility.

In the end, what is important for both Camus (1955) and Sartre (1956) is that human beings recognize that one must invent one's own meaning (rather than discover God's or nature's meaning) and then commit oneself fully to fulfill that meaning. However, we classify that meaning, whether it is secular or religious, whether it arises out of meaninglessness or a dedication to a higher cause, as in the case of Christianity, it is worthwhile to observe that there are very important common elements that consists of courage, commitment, engagement, fraternal solidarity, love, and secular/religious saintliness. Although the lack of under-standing between Christians and existentialists would likely place the basic philosophies of Camus, Sartre, and Jesus at opposite ends of the spectrum, in the end they all share some very important commonalities.

Camus (1955) and Sartre's (1956) called for individuals to be committed and engaged is embodied by the Parable of the Talents described above. The moral of the parable is engagement. The wrath of the master was reserved for the servant who buried his talent. The servant was labeled wicked and lazy for *burying* and refusing to trade with his talent. The servant refused to commit and engage. Instead of committing, he withdrew from the world. His fear was symbolized by his act of burial. It is interesting to note here that this servant's view of the master, perhaps his view of the world, was one characterized by harshness, unfairness and unpredictability (Matthew 25: 24 & 26), similar to Camus's sense of absurdity. Yet, unlike the other two servants who traded and committed to action their given talents, this servant gave in to fear, and lacked the courage to engage and commit. Camus and Sartre would point out that this servant lacked courage, resoluteness, and even rebelliousness, and gave up in the face of absurdity. It is also interesting to point out that the *reward* for the other two servants were even greater talents, commitments, and actions, and the "sharing of the master's happiness" (Matthew 25: 21 & 23). Perhaps this is illustrative of Frankl's (1959) wisdom in re-minding us that meaning, success, love, and happiness *ensue*, they cannot be *pursued*. The servants in the parable were entrusted with their master's property. I imagine that they had to act upon some form of faith in order to make the de-cision to trade with their talents. It is also worth noting that both the two servants who traded with their talents were decisive and went at once to put their talents to work (Matthew 25: 16-17). It can be said that they embraced their freedom, responsibility and destiny. But it was not certain that their reward and their happiness were sure to follow. For some reason, most likely out of faith, they chose to engage and trade; or perhaps it was simply out of the joy or meaning to be found in trading. Never-theless, the meaning of their actions was to be found later. Meaning begets meaning; commitments and engagement beget more commitments and engagement, which results in happiness.

Another understanding of the lack of commitment from the *lazy* servant of the above parable is through the existential concept of authenticity. The parable begins with the master giving to each servant talents according to their individual abilities. To one servant he gave five talents and two talents to the other. Note that the master did not give equal numbers of talent to each servant. He gave according to ability, and he was rewarded in the end according to ability. The master recog-nized individuality, which has to do with authenticity. Existential philosophers and psychologists place great importance upon the concept of authenticity, which involves being congruent and being true to oneself. Nietzsche (as cited in Yalom, 1992) challenged us to become ourselves and to consummate our lives!". Similar-ly, Paul Tillich (1952), the Existential Theologian, wrote, "Man is asked to make of himself what he is supposed to become, to fulfill his destiny" (p. 52). Otto Rank (1945) also said, "We feel ourselves guilty on account of the unused life, the un-lived life in us" (as cited in Yalom, 1980, p. 278). Finally, the Hasidic rabbi, Susya, (as cited in Friedman, 1965) shortly before his death said, "When I go to heaven they will not ask me, 'Why were you not Moses?' Instead they will ask 'Why were you not Susya?' Why did you not become what only you could become" (p. xix)? Jesus had his destiny to fulfill. The different servants in the parable had their des-tinies to fulfill, and we all have our own destinies to fulfill. Frankl (1959) reminded us over and over:

> Life's tasks form man's destiny, which is different and unique for each individual. No man and no destiny can be compared with any other man or any other destiny... When a man finds that it is his destiny to suffer, he will have to accept his suffering as his task; his single and unique task. He will have to acknowledge the fact that even in suffering he is unique and alone in the universe. No one can relieve him of his suffering or suffer in his place. His unique opportunity lies in the way in which he bears his burden. (p. 98–99)

As Christians, individuals are called to be *like* Jesus, not to *be* Jesus.

Each of the two servants in the parable accepted their different talents and traded with them. The third servant was identified as being *lazy* and chose to bury his talent. A simple understanding of laziness has to do with physical laziness. But if he was so lazy, why did he even bother to dig a hole to hide his talent. His laziness had much more to do with fear, the fear of the master, and perhaps the fear of fulfilling his potential. The fourth cardinal sin in the Christian tradition is the sin of *accidie* which is defined as: sloth, torpor, acedia: apathy, boredom. As an aside, it is interesting to point out that boredom and apathy leads to lethargy and drowsiness which has been discussed above. A number of existential thinkers from Buber, Fromm, Allport, Rogers, Jung, Maslow, and Horney, have come to interpret accidie not in the simple terms of slothfulness but the sin of failing to live up to one's potential. Thus, the sin of the servants and virgins were not sins-of-commission of having committed some criminal act, but the sins of omission, the regret of self-condemnation, of failing to act. Such regret is certainly thematically central to both the Parable of the Virgins followed by the Parable of the Talents.

Finally, the solution to defeating death in the Christian sense is to believe in Jesus and gain salvation. What does it mean to believe in Jesus and receive salva-tion? Both of these Parables above told by Jesus warns us that death is inevitable and that we must be prepared, which involves not burying but actively trading our talent. Such preparation and trading in the existential sense involves Rippling. In the words of Irvin Yalom (2008):

Of all the ideas that have emerged from my years of practice to counter a person's death anxiety and distress at the transience of life, I have found the idea of ripping to be singularly powerful. . . . Rippling does not necessarily mean leaving behind your image or your name. . . . Attempts to preserve personal identity are always futile. Transiency is forever. Rippling as I use it, refers instead to leaving behind something from your life experience; some trait; some piece of wisdom, guidance, virtue, comfort that passes on to others, known or unknown (p. 83–84).

For existentialists, rippling is the solution that defeats death. Jesus's life is the ultimate example of rippling in Christianity. The effects and consequences of Jesus's death and sacrifice have not just rippled on at a *nano* level but powerfully across generations and generations of time. His legacy, what he left behind, is the ultimate in self-transcendence and self-actualization according to the definitions above. It must have been his sense of purpose that helped him to cope with his suffering, his isolation, humiliation, and the multiple rejections he faced. Again, Nietzsche's (as cited in Frankl, 1993), words ring powerfully true here. "He who has a 'why' can bear with almost any 'how'" (p. 59) And as Christians, we are called to believe in Jesus, to follow him, and to be like him. This means that each of us must *work out* our own salvations as Jesus worked out his own. As the parables of Jesus and the existential philosophers and theologians have reminded us over the ages, this has everything to do with how we deal with the unavoidable existential givens of life: Death, Freedom, Isolation, and Meaninglessness. We have been given our talents and the bridegroom will come for us all. How will we choose to trade those talents in preparation for his eventual arrival?

## References

Ashe, A. (n.d.) *Quotes*. Retrieved December 7, 2008 from http://www. cmgww.com/sports/ashe/about/quotes1.htm

Branfman, F. (2008, Dec. 7). *The Salon interview, Irvin Yalom: A matter of life and death.* Retrieved from http://www.salon.com/weekly/yalom960805.html

Buber, M. (1965). *Between man and man.* New York, NY: Macmillan.

Bugental, J. F. T. (1965). *The search for authenticity.* New York, NY: Holt, Rinehart & Winston.

Camus, A. (1955). *The myth of Sisyphus and other essays.* New York, NY: Alfred A. Knopf.

Dostoevsky, I. (1990). *Brothers Karamazov* (R. Peaver & L. Volokhonsky, Trans). New York, NY: Farrar, Straus, and Giroux. (Original work published 1880)

Frankl, V. (1959). *Man's search for meaning.* New York, NY: Pocket Books.

Friedman, M. (1965). Introduction. In M. Buber (author), *Between man and man.* New York, NY: Macmillan.

Fromm, E. (1941). *Escape from freedom.* New York, NY: Holt, Rinehart & Winston.

Gardner, J. (1971). *Grendel.* New York, NY: Ballentine Books.

Heidegger, M. (1962). *Being and time.* New York, NY: Harper & Row.

Hobbs, N. (1962). Principles of international psychotherapy. *American Psychologist, 17,* 742–748.

Jung, C. G. (1966). *Collected works: The practice of psychotherapy,* (Vol. XVI). New York, NY: Patheon Bollingen Series.

Kazantzakis, N. (1952). *Zorba the Greek.* New York, NY: Simon & Schuster. (Originally published in 1946).

May, R. (1958). The origins and significance of the existential movement in psychology. In R. May, E. Angel, & H. F. Ellenberger (Eds.), *Existence* (pp. 3-36). Northvale, NJ: Jason Aronson.

May, R. (1981). *Freedom and destiny.* New York, NY: Norton.

Montaigne, M. E. (1965). *The complete essays of Montaigne* (Ed. & Trans., D. Frame). Stanford, CA: Stanford University Press.

Rank, O. (1945). *Will therapy and truth and reality.* New York, NY: Alfred A. Knopf.

Sartre, J. P. (1956). *Being and nothingness* (H. Barnes, Trans.). New York, NY: Philosophical Library

Sartre, J. P. (1981). *The words.* New York, NY: Vintage Books. (Originally published in 1964).

Tillich, P. (1952). *The courage to be.* New Haven, CT: Yale University Press.

Yalom, I. D. (1980). *Existential psychotherapy.* New York, NY: Basic Books.

Yalom, I. D. (1992). *When Nietzsche wept.* New York, NY: Basic Books.

Yalom, I. D. (2008). *Staring at the sun: Overcoming the terror of death.* San Francisco, CA: Jossey-Bass.

# Chapter 9

## The Heart of Jungian Analysis
## and Existential Psychology

Heyong Shen

My first formal class of Jungian Psychology took place at the Institute of Transpersonal Psychology (ITP) in Palo Alto, California. Several important Jungians, such as June Singer and Thomas Kirsch were teachers there. I conducted a seminar on "Psychology of the Heart and the Heart of Psychology" at the ITP, and presented my work to integrate Analytical Psychology (i.e., Jungian) and Chinese Culture. The significance of Jungian psychology to me, my work, and the practice of Jungian analysis has been integrated with Chinese culture and further influenced by transpersonal and existential thought.

There are three important points in Jungian analysis: (a) the experience of the Self, (b) active imagination, and (c) the individuation process. Each of these will be illustrated through stories about Jung in what follows. After his separation with Freud, Jung (1963) went through a period of personal difficulty, which proved highly formative on the development of his thought. He described this time in his autobiography *Memories, Dreams, Reflections:*

> After parting ways with Freud, a period of inner uncertainly began for me. It would be no exaggeration to call it a state of disorientation. I felt totally suspended in mid-air, for I had not yet found my own footing. (Jung, 1963, p. 170)

Later in the chapter "Confrontation with the Unconscious," it is important for the reader to keep in mind an old Chinese proverb which says, "the real learner learns from the heart, not from the master." In this chapter, Jung conveyed how he stood his ground to face the unconscious by himself, which represents a transition in Jung's thinking, which emerged from working through these trials. He experienced many dreams and images later realizing, "dreams like this, and actual experiences of the unconscious, taught me that such contents are not dead, outmoded forms, but belong to our living being" (p. 173). He identified that below the threshold of consciousness, everything is seething with life. This is the most important point for Jungian psychology and represents a transition in the understanding of the unconscious in the depth psychologies

In *Memories, Dreams, Reflections*, using the image of Philemon, who was Jung's (as cited in Rosen, 1997) inner Chinese Taoist teacher, Jung made further exploration, "there are things in the psyche which I do not produce, but which produce themselves and have their own life" (Jung, 1963, p. 183). Here we touch a key point of Jungian psychology, the autonomy of the psyche; the psyche produces things which have a life of their own. For Sigmund Freud, the heart of psychoanalysis is the Oedipus myth. For Jung, the Oedipus complex is very important, *but most important is the fact that the psyche itself is producing myth.* This understanding is the key for the Jungian concept *Active Imagination.* Jung first formally expressed this idea in the book he wrote in conjunction with Richard Wilhelm: *The Secret of the Golden Flower* (Wilhelm & Jung, 1929/1931). He wrote commentary on the Chinese Taoist inner alchemy. Jung said in the book:

> What then did these people do in order to achieve the progress that freed them? As far as I could see they did nothing (*wu wei*), but let things happen, for, as Master Lu Tzu teaches in our text, the Light circulates according to its own law, if one does not give up one's accustomed calling. The art of letting things happen, action in non-action, letting go of oneself, as taught by Master Esckehart, became a key to me with which I was able to open the door to the 'Way'. The key is this: we must be able to let things happen in the psyche. (p. 90)

Allowing things to happen in the psyche is important for active imagination as well as for healing, for personal growth, and for the individuation process.

For Jung, the goal of the individuation process is the synthesis of the self. As Daryl Sharp (1991) described in *Jung Lexicon: A Primer of Terms and Concepts*, the process of individuation leads to the realization of the self as a psychic reality greater than the ego. Thus, individuation is essentially different from the process of simply becoming conscious.

Jung expressed his early experiences encountered with Wilhelm through the cooperated work of *The Secret of the Golden Flower:*

> Some years later (in 1927) I obtained confirmation of my ideas about the center and the self by way of a dream. I represented its essence in a mandala which I called Window on Eternity. The picture is reproduced in The Secret of the Golden Flower. A year later I painted a second picture, like wise a mandala, with a golden castle in the center. When it was finished, I asked myself, Why is this so Chinese?
>
>     It was a strange coincidence that shortly afterward I received a letter from Richard Wilhelm enclosing the manuscript of a Taoist-alchemical treatise entitled The Secret of the Golden Flower, with a request that I write a commentary on it. I devoured the manuscript at once, for the text gave me undreamed-of confirmation of my ideas about the mandala and the circumambulation of the center. That was the first event which broke through my isolation. I became aware of an affinity; I could establish ties with something and someone. (Jung, 1963, p. 197)

The experiences of the Self, along with the way of Active Imagination and the reality of the psyche, helped Jung journey through the process of his individuation. Jung presented such summery in the *Secret of the Golden Flower*:

> Its effect is astonishing in that it almost always brings about a solution of psychic complications, and thereby frees the inner personality from emotional and imaginary entanglements, creating thus a unity of being, which is universally felt as a release. (Wilhelm & Jung, 1975, p. 105)

## Psychology of the Heart

There is a strong inner relationship between Jungian psychology and Chinese culture. Jung learned the Chinese language, studied *I Ching* and Daoist inner alchemy, and Chinese philosophy in general. I utilize the Psychology of the Heart, to present the system of Chinese cultural psychology, which involves the integration of Jungian psychology and Chinese culture. To understand the Psychology of the heart, we need to start with the following story from Jung.

In 1924, Jung travelled to America, where he visited the Taos Pueblos in New Mexico. He befriended the chief of the Taos Pueblo Indians, Mountain Lake. The two of them had a conversation, and Jung asked Mountain Lake why he thought the European white people were all mad. Mountain Lake replied: "Because they say that they think with their heads." Jung said, "Why of course," and asked him in surprise, "What do you think with?" Mountain Lake said, "We think here" and pointed at his heart (Jung, 1963, p. 251). Jung, in *Memories, Dreams, Reflections*, said that he fell into a long meditation:

> This Indian had struck our vulnerable spot, unveiled a truth to which we are blind. I felt rising within me like a shapeless mist something unknown and yet deeply familiar. Something else that Mountain Lake said to me stuck in my mind. It seems to me so intimately connected with the peculiar atmosphere of our interview. (Jung, 1963, p. 248)

Jung believed that American Indians were native Chinese who had travelled to the Americas through the Bering Strait thousands of years ago.

Let us compare this to the Chinese way of *thinking*, which involves thinking with head and heart together. I call this the *thinking-heart.*

This Chinese character, above, has two parts: the upper part is the top of the head (the fontanel); and the lower section, like a support and container, is the heart. According to the dictionary, Shuo-Wen-Jie-Zi of the Han dynasty, the explanation of *Si* (i.e., thinking) is: "for thinking, following the heart and head, from the fontanel to the heart, consistent, non-stop connecting and communicating." What is most important in the image is that head and heart are combined together. This is the key point of Jung's transcendental function as well as the real meaning of the doctrine of thinking in the Chinese tradition. Furthermore, in the Chinese character of Si, the relationship between the fontanel and the heart conveys the symbolic meaning of communication between the human heart and heaven. The image of the fontanel in Chinese is described by the esoteric alchemist as "heaven top" (the head is usually compared to heaven in the symbolic system of *I-Ching*). So, in the image of the Si (the thinking-heart): *Tian-Ren-He-Yi,* represents the Unity of Heaven and Man combined together to create the ideal state.

The meaning of the heart in Chinese can be briefly described in three dimensions. First, in the physiological sense, the ancient Chinese believed that the heart is the root and nature of life, and at the same time, the heart is the changing of mind and spirit. Second, in the psychological sense, the heart represents thinking, emotion, will, love, and hate. The Chinese perceived the heart as the totality or synthesis of all psychological phenomena and processes. Third, in the metaphysical sense, the ancient Chinese used the heart to express the heaven mind, heaven heart, and the heart of Tao. The Heart of Tao is the most important image in the book of *I Ching*. As Confucius said in the Great Commentary: "the sage wash the heart with *I Ching*. In Chinese Confucian tradition, benevolence, righteousness, propriety, and knowledge (the four pillars of Confucianism), they are all rooted in the heart" (Fu Huisheng, 2008, p. 396-397).

The heart is also the most important issue of Taoist tradition. Zhuang Zi (Chuang Tzu, about 369-286 BC) once said, the highest essence of truth is used for examining the heart. Guan Yi Zi (Yin-his, about 545-460 BC) took the heart, things, and the Tao as the three basic elements, but the three can become a unified one, and the most important thing is to use the heart to get the unified one. That is just what the Taoist Guan Zi expressed, cultivate your heart first, and then the Tao will come to you naturally.

The Chinese Chan Buddhism was called the Heart Sect. Hui Neng, the real founder of Chinese Chan Buddhism, once said to his teacher Hong Ren,

> Who would have thought that the Essence of Heart is intrinsically pure! Who would have thought that the Essence of Heart is intrinsically free from becoming or annihilation! Who would have thought that the Essence of Heart is intrinsically self-sufficient! Who would have thought that the Essence of Heart is intrinsically free from change! Who would have thought that all things are the manifestation of the Essence of Heart? (Huang Maolin, 1996, pp. 20-21)

This understanding and wisdom is the foundation for the psychology of the heart.

### Existence, Expressive, and Embodiment

In both Jungian analysis and the Psychology of the heart, the purpose of psychotherapy involves healing, the individuation process, wholeness, and pursuing the meaning of life. Feelings of meaninglessness lead to psychological diseases. These diseases can be overcome by creating one's own values and by finding the meaning of life.

For the Chinese, finding the meaning of the heart is to find the meaning of life. For example, while working in Sichuan recently after the 512 earthquake, the psychological support that was provided can be expressed in the two Chinese characters: *Ci-Bei* (grace, compassion, mercy), which I translate as *loving-grief* Let us look at the following images of the two Chinese characters "Ci Bei":

They are both based on the heart, the lower part of the two characters is the image of the heart. The image of the first character, is nurturing the heart, and the second, is the lost heart. According to the psychology of grief and trauma, when we experience too much stress and trauma, disassociation and split occurs. The second character of Ci Bei (Bei) has an image of disassociation, the heart is lost, is not your heart anymore (*fei*, the upper part of Bei, in Chinese means lost and not), and the heart is flying away like a broken kite. When someone has lost his or her heart, grief and trauma will take over. The image of the first character of Ci (grace and love) conveys the meaning of associating, and nurturing, and heart-growing. Healing occurs through associating the disassociated pieces of psyche, nurturing the heart, and understanding the meaning of life, through Ci-Bei (i.e., through love and grace).

We named our psychological-aid, work-station, which is in the Sichuan area, as the "Garden of the Heart and Soul." The main methods we are using is Jungian analysis, Jungian Sandplay, and the psychology of the heart. Dora Kalff (2004), who developed the Jungian Sandplay, had learned Chinese when she was young. In her book *Sandplay: A Psychotherapeutic Approach to the Psyche*, she used Chinese philosophy as the most important foundation of sandplay therapy. She started with Zhou Dunyi`s I-Ching model and ended with Hexagram 29 of the I-Ching: "Only the heart can penetrate the difficulties and find the meaning of the situation." To me, the Jungian sandplay manifests the Chinese saying: "Receive from the heart, and respond with the hands" (p. 140). Combining active

imagination and sandplay therapy, we can use the Chinese way of embodied imagination through the body knowledge embodiment process, to body-heart enlightenment.

The practice of both the psychology of the heart and Jungian analysis in China involves healing and transformation. There is an old Chinese saying: "a sick heart (psychological disease) needs heart-medicine for treatment." It needs creating peace in one's heart, as well as psychological education (i.e., enlightening the heart for the individuation process) and transformation. The most important principle for such a practice is from the *I-Ching*, especially from the 31st Hexagram: "Wholehearted influence" (touching by the heart and responding from the heart):

> Heaven and Earth exert their influences, and ensure the transformation and production of all things. The sages influence the heart of men, and the result is harmony and peace all under the sky. If we look at (the method and issues) of those (wholehearted) influences, the true character of heaven and Earth and of all things can be seen. (*I-Ching*, 31, The Great Commentaries).

So, psychology of the heart, combined with Jungian analysis, is the key point to understanding our work at the Sichuan earthquake area; it essentially involved heart-thinking and thinking-heart.

There are three important steps in our work that involve a Jungian-style psychological intervention. First, we start with association and building the safe, contained, empathetic, free, and protected relationship. Then, we utilized symbols, images, Jungian Sandplay, expressive and embodied work to deal with grief and trauma issues. Finally, we work to find the lost heart, to find the opportunity within the crises, to find the value of existence, to find the meaning of everyday life, and ultimately, to experience the meaning of transformation.

**References**

Fu Huisheng (Trans.). (2008). *The Zhou book of changes (I Ching)*. Chuangsha, China: Hunan People's Publishign House.

Huang Maolin (Trans.). (1996). *The sutra of Hui Neng*. Chang Sha, China: Hunan Publication.

Jung, C. G. (1963). *Memories, dreams, reflections*. New York, NY: Pantheon.

Kalff, D. M. (2004). *Sandplay: A psychotherapeutic approach to the psyche*. Cloverdale, CA: Temenos Press.

Rosen, D. (1997). *The Tao of Jung: The way of integrity*. New York, NY: Penguin.

Sharp, D. (1991). *Jung lexicon: A primer of terms and concepts*. Toronto, Canada: Inner City Books.

Wilhelm, R. & Jung, C. G. (1931). *The secret of the golden flower: A Chinese book of life* (C. F. Baynes, Trans.). New York, NY: Causeway Books. (Original work published in 1929)

# Chapter 10

## Global Authenticity

### Myrtle Heery

> I know what you want. You want a story that won't surprise you. That will
> confirm what you already know. That won't make you see higher or further
> or differently. You want a flat story. An im-mobile story. You want dry,
> yeastless factuality.
>
> ~ *Life of Pi*, Yann Martel

Dry factuality does not have the capacity to make meaning out of life; however,
surprise does have that capacity. My experience of teaching globally has certainly
been full of many dry facts and activities, such as gathering visas, organizing papers, purchasing airline tickets, and so on. These dry facts formed a container
where surprises created in me what I have come to call *global authenticity*.

Over the past 12 years, I have taught students of psychology and psychotherapists in Canada, China, England, Switzerland, Holland, Mexico, Russia, and the
United States. I have introduced the basics and application of existential-humanistic psychotherapy to students of psychology in classes, seminars, and workshops.
Some of my students have extensive knowledge of psychotherapy and others are
beginners. These years of global teaching have formed a colorful tapestry of rich
and diverse stories from students and their clients, as well as from my own experiences. The threads I have used to weave this tapestry are the givens of the human
condition, which are central to existential-humanistic psychotherapy.

### Four Givens

Different theorists in the existential school (Yalom, 1980) and the existential-
humanistic school (Bugental, 1965) expound on the givens of the human condition. I will review with you four givens that Bugental and I (2005) presented in a
chapter titled *Listening to the Listener*, focusing on therapy with the therapist
using the existential-humanistic model.

### 1. Embodiedness
Everyone has a body, a vehicle through which to experience life. This is the given
of *embodiedness* (Heery & Bugental, 2005). From moment to moment, we experience dualities such as hunger and satiation, pleasure and pain, robustness and illness, and high or low energy. Over time, our bodies grow, mature, and age, contin-

ually reminding us that life is change. Our bodies also remind us that each of our lives is unique even as our bodies are unique.

Some people spend much time caring for and enhancing their bodies. This can become an obsession; a desperate act to pretend there is physical permanence in the face of inexorable physical change. Psychological distress often arises when one denies or confronts the impermanence of the body. No one is immune to this, no matter the country in which you live.

## 2. Finitude

As each *now-moment* slips away into the next moment, we continually experience the given of *finitude*, the limitedness of life (Heery & Bugental, 2005). We face loss with situations beyond our control and because of continual change. Yet, we seek certainty in a variety of ways: by training to become a therapist, passing exams as a student, or buying fine furniture for our office. We try to avoid unwanted contingencies, but there are always circumstances beyond our control.

The one finitude that lurks beyond our control is our death. The awareness of death is the ultimate experience of finitude. We seldom know when, where, or how we will die; however, we do know that we will die. Listening to concerns of death is a reminder of one's own death (Heery, 2001). The simultaneous certainty and uncertainty of death impacts us powerfully. Each of us is impacted differently in the way we live our lives. Some of us seek certainty by saving money while others risk money by gambling or investing in the stock market.

We can view all of this—risking as well as seeking security—as attempts to deal with the ultimate finitude of death. Everyone lives accompanied by the shadow of death, regardless of social status or culture or whether we are American, Chinese, European, Mexican, or Russian.

## 3. Choicefulness

Life presents us with choices on every front, from what to eat for breakfast to what to do with the rest of our lives. This is the given of *choicefulness* (Heery & Bugental, 2005). It is paradoxically and inextricably interwoven with our experience of finitude: The choices available to us may not be endless; nonetheless, even declining to choose is making a choice.

Traveling to different countries and teaching psychotherapy is a choice. Picking up this book and reading this chapter is a choice and to stop or continue reading this chapter is a choice. We have the capacity of choice no matter what we face; there is always a choice. Inherent in our choosing is our responsibility for acting or not acting. No matter where you live or under what circumstance you find yourself, no matter how limited the circumstance may be, there is always the element of choice; even with limited circumstances, which give us limited choices, choice is still present.

## 4. Being a part of and apart from

Being *a part of* and *apart from* is another given of the human condition that existential-humanistic psychotherapy recognizes (Heery & Bugental, 2005). Just as life continually presents us with choices, so we continually face the experience of feeling *a part of* some situations and *apart from* others. This given involves a paradox: We can no more feel connected with everyone and everything around us than we can feel disconnected from them. We connect with humanity all the time, yet we are each uniquely apart from it at the same time.

Teaching in different countries can be enriched by being a part of different students' and therapists' journeys in learning. When I complete a training and wave good-bye to my colleagues at the airport, I turn to myself. I am surrounded by other travelers, but I sit alone. I look out the airplane window remembering all the shared moments of honesty, vulnerability, and courage. I may or may not ever see these individuals again. There is a sharp aloneness to these moments, which I recognize. I, along with everyone else, arrived in this world alone and, ultimately, will leave alone. Life is with others, yet each of us is ultimately alone. This paradox of being *a part of* and *apart from* follows each of us no matter where we live.

### Authenticity Remembered

As I look over my shoulder at my international teaching experiences, I see faces, stories, tears, laughter, and so much more all weaving the givens of the human condition. I feel humbled by the depth of each individual's story, by their ability to reach deep inside themselves, in front me and other students who were primarily strangers to them, to make meaning of their lives.

I remember a tall well-dressed Russian woman attending my training in Russia. The suit she wore every day was the same, and it was always in perfect order. I noticed her physical appearance each day and wondered about her. I remember her certainty and her quiet manner. I trusted she would speak in time, which she did, and there was the surprise.

On the second day of the training, I began speaking to the given of finitude and how each of us carry the fact of our death. She raised her hand and said with certainty that she had cancer and might be dead in a few months. She continued to share that she was making the best of each moment which included looking her best and being as honest as possible in all relationships. She actually felt grateful to her cancer for her present depth of appreciation in living each moment.

I shared through my translator how deeply moved I was by her honesty and courage. Since I do not speak Russian, I relied on my intuitive sense to connect with her and the participants at this vulnerable moment. I was sensitive to the depth of her sharing, looking closely in her eyes and gently moving my eyes to each participant. The caring from participants was palpable in the room. Some eyes were moistened, and all were obviously moved. I invited the participants to share their feelings with her if they felt moved to do so. One of the participants who knew her and her health crisis spoke with great depth of appreciation. First, she thanked the woman for her honesty with the group about her health. Then with great emotion she shared how important she was to her in deciding to stop complaining about her own life and appreciating it. By watching her friend face her cancer with dignity, she had gained a new life. Others followed with sharing their own stories that were moving, and the group drew closer.

The experience of sharing a life-threatening illness with a group is powerful no matter what country or circumstance. In this teaching situation the students immediately experienced the connection of sharing the possibility of an individual death. In teaching there is *talk about* a subject and a *lived experience* of a teaching.

This experience was many years ago, and I do not know if this participant lived or died. I do know that her vulnerability brought the group into an immediate depth of authenticity, which I had seen in many other groups in many other locations. The fact of her likely soon-approaching death and what she chose in facing her end was a huge piece of global authenticity. The consideration of her impending death brought each of us into the reality of death. Even now 8 years later, I can still see her in my mind and hold this experience close to my being. The courage to share her confrontation with her own death with me, whom she did not know, and with others who were mostly strangers to her, has been engraved on my heart.

My memories of authenticity were captured in other surprises. Preparation for all my international teaching has been arranged primarily on email. The fabric of trust and responsibility is woven through this electronic medium. On my first trip to Russia, I had not met some of my organizers, so, when I arrived in the airport and was greeted by no one, I realized I did not know what they looked like. They did know what I looked like from a video I had sent, but still, there was no one there greeting me.

My fear began to rise, as I looked through the sea of unknown faces. Then a striking blonde woman emerged from the crowd. She looked at me and said in clear English, "Seminar, seminar?"

"Oh yes, yes, seminar," I gleefully responded.

I restrained myself from embracing my apparent rescuer and we politely shook hands. In broken English, she introduced me to a gentleman I took to be the professor who had been emailing me.

We laughed about our email. Then, they asked where the other person was. I explained with the help of my fingers that there was only one, never two people. We proceeded to the sidewalk with my luggage. I was then informed that the seminar started that night. This was not what we had arranged, but I let this communication pass as the language barrier seemed insurmountable in my tired state. They said they would take me to my hotel. As the door to the car opened, I communicated as clearly as possible that in the last email, we had confirmed my staying with the professor and his family. They assured me this was absolutely not true. I stepped back from the car. The woman then said in very clear English, "Football seminar!"

I responded, "Psychology seminar!"

They rushed back toward the terminal. I stood on the sidewalk with my luggage and looked at the distant terminal, with no clue about my next step. I could not help but laugh, as I thought of missing my son's football game that day. And yes, if I had come for the football seminar, I might actually get some fame and money. My journey was definitely not one for the ego. At this point, I would need some heavy reliance on my soul.

It was certainly an existential moment. What were my choices? I decided to return to the terminal and wait by my arrival gate. As I pulled my bag, I looked into the terminal. For the first time, I had the very sharp awareness that the area I was walking into was filled primarily with men. There were very few women. The voice of fear came up. What am I doing here? Then a wave of courage and determination, which I knew I could depend on to support me, overcame the fear. I had come to know this part of myself in many other circumstances in my life. I knew I would be fine. I could meet this situation with quiet resolution.

Within minutes after I got to the gate, another blonde woman arrived, and said to me, "Seminar?"

This time I responded, "Psychology seminar?"

She smiled and immediately hugged me. I felt a physical relief for both of us, as we stood for a few seconds longer in our shared hug. In excellent English she said, "Myrtle, welcome to Russia. I am so sorry we are late. There was a terrible traffic problem."

The story of my arrival would be told and retold in Russia and America. It would be a central thread in my adventure. In so many ways, all of the human emotions that needed to come up for me did so during this airport experience. My fears, doubts, mistrusts, excitement, humor, and hopes were all present. My ability to make choices, to take responsibility, and to recognize the limits of my situation were all present. The knowns and unknowns were present. My capacity to transcend the boundaries of the present moment was supported by a deep reverence and trust for life. (Heery, 2001).

There were so many more experiences that brought surprise in connection with other human beings. I remember running with a Chinese student in Beijing to catch an underground train and her shouting, "Professor is late, please." And so many people moving aside to let me get in the train first so I could quickly get to the university. The respect for me as a professor still brings tears to my eyes, as I recall this experience of global authenticity.

## Global Authenticity in the Psychotherapy Room

I invite you now into the lives of two American psychotherapy clients. Their stories might surprise you as through their stories you might begin to see yourself no matter the country where you live or in what language you are reading the story. You will begin to see the face of global authenticity, sometimes harsh and sometimes soft.

At 47, Ron entered therapy. His wife was exasperated at the renewed drain on the family income, which was comfortable but had never permitted the little extras she thought their ages and position should have warranted. Ron heard her out, promised to try to keep the cost of therapy down, and committed to trying to earn a little extra to pay for those extras and then dismissed the matter. In therapy, Ron insisted he could afford no more than one visit a week and formed a strong bond, yet, he kept a distance between us. We worked together well in some ways, but therapy with Ron was a frustrating experience for me. He was pleasant and appreciative; he spent the time in sessions confirming what he knew and avoiding the unknown. There were no surprises. This case was challenging. The questioning of what stops us and what moves us is part of our great quest for authenticity in living. This fact of living gets put to the fire in an authentic psychotherapeutic relationship

At 45, Vicki entered therapy with me. Her husband had very little tolerance for her seeking therapy, stressing that they could not afford therapy. Vicki heard him out and made a plan to pay for the therapy herself. In therapy, Vicki insisted that she could not afford more than one visit a week and the therapy began under these restricted conditions.

Vicki was eager to work, yet she stayed at a distance. At first this seemed to be due to the time restriction on our sessions, but I suspected the distancing was the actual work: I wondered why Vicki was keeping distance from living her life fully? To bridge this distance, we worked in many ways to get through her resistance to deeper life-changing processes, but nothing seemed to help. Vicki was very compliant in many ways and her compliance frequently put her in a rather passive role during the therapy hour. This was a clear mirror of how she lived her life outside of the therapy hour. I could choose to describe how we attempted to work through her passivity, but that would not surprise you. Instead I would like to turn your attention to the larger story that helped her see deeper and differently.

Very similar to Ron, Vicki was a *good client*, following what she thought to be the rules of therapy, which meant coming faithfully once a week, reporting her life story for that week, and paying for her therapy on time. Both clients filled their therapy rooms with boredom, mirroring the life they lived outside the therapy room. I thought more than once of suggesting that Vicki stop coming, but I did *not*. This *not* with both clients is what I want to share with you

As clients, Ron and Vicki had some similarities in lifestyle. Both were married with children. Their lives were good by many standards: They owned their own homes, had successful jobs, and steady marriages, accompanied by all the material things that are supposed to make people happy. Both were unsatisfied and reported being at odds with their outer lives and wanted to change how they were living. Before entering therapy, they had individually decided to break away from their ordinary lives and take a week's vacation alone. To break away from their respective lives even for a week—especially alone—was enormous but they each surmounted the hurdles to it.

Their individual experiences of being alone for a week opened their eyes to a world that they had previously known only as a fantasy, but now was a reality. Their perspective days began and ended as they chose, with no expectations, obligations, or responsibilities to or from others. Now, Ron and Vicki do not know each other. There were similarities and differences with these two individuals that drew a deeper search. This deeper search brought them each into therapy. In my listening to their respective recounting of their one-week vacation, I consistently found a quality of timelessness that filled each of their days on this vacation, which both reported had renewed and awakened them.

They each had experienced their lives from inside, not out, which is a primary step in the journey toward authenticity (Bugental, 1965). There is a story of Native Americans in Oklahoma who had lived in hovels for many years and then became suddenly very wealthy from oil rights. They hastened to buy radios, washing machines, and other gadgets of affluence with which they stocked their homes. But they had no electricity!

The deeper implication here is that the present global collection of material objects can only be created and tolerated by people who are in large part dead to focusing on their inner potential. In that statement, I include us all, certainly myself as much as anyone. We each intend to start living authentically one day but when? There is an inner terror that is happening across the globe, the terror of not living our given life.

I have said that Ron and Vicki came to some awareness that they were *dead*; each felt like a non-being. The reasonable question was why do they not change? Since they knew how dead they felt and obviously wanted to be more alive, what stopped them? What stops each of us?

No matter where you are physically living, there is a fear of authentic living in each one of us.

> For fear, real fear, such as shakes you to your foundation, such as you feel when you are brought face to face with your mortal end, nestles in your memory like a gangrene: it seeks to rot everything, even the words with which to speak of it. So, you must fight hard to express it. You must fight hard to shine the light of words upon it. (Martel, 2001, pp. 160-161)

In Ron's and Vicki's search for an authentic life, they each found on their individual retreats a quality of timelessness that filled their days with a sense of renewed life. They both felt awakened, and yet, when they returned to their ordinary lives they felt stuck again and again. They were unable to take the risks in the moment to be authentic. Their retreats had given each a glimpse of the possibility of authenticity, but how could they realize that authenticity in their daily lives of work and family? They were awakened to their human potential out of context, yet, both fell back asleep when they returned to their ordinary lives. Both individuals faced fear concerning the limitations of being human.

As I see it, Ron and Vicki faced an existential crisis. Each given of the human condition was in operation: being finite, being able to choose and be responsible, and somehow being related to others even as they experienced the concurrent gulf of separateness that divided them from others. Each of these conditions gave rise to the fear and anxiety. To the extent that they let themselves meet this anxiety head-on and incorporate it with courage into their very being—to that extent—Ron and Vicki would be able to experience being authentic.

> "Vicki, how is it serving you right now, in this moment, to not look at other choices you have concerning your work?"
>
> "Oh, I appreciate your thoughtfulness about possible other work for me, but gee, I think it might be best if I just settle back into my work and stop all this complaining."
>
> "Vicki, that is your choice to settle back. The question remains, how do the choices you are making serve you? It is your life we are speaking to in this moment."

This vignette shows us how Vicki's resistance moved her away from the deeper search for an authentic life. The story shows how the therapist's job is to *hold to the possibility of the authentic* for Vicki by questioning the moment, "How does your choice serve you in this moment?" Hopefully, Vicki will not stand apart from her life but rather experience *how* standing apart interferes with her living. It is her life. Her family relations, her work, her recreation—quite literally all that she does—are expressions of her search for or flight from authenticity. Every choice is present in the moment in psychotherapy, and the therapist's job is to mirror and question those choices in the moment, in the room. We are not asking about her work nor about her family of origin, we are asking *how the choices she is making in this moment are serving her.* I continue to take small steps with Vicki, noting the resistance patterns that interfere with the searching process in the here-and-now. In time, Vicki will come to experience the interference of limiting her choices in the present and begin to choose for herself a life in the actual moment (Bugental, 1999).

I experience being a part of Vicki's dilemma. I encounter Vicki. This does not mean a kind of exhibitionism or display of myself. It does mean a willingness to *be there* with her, to confront her directly as shown above, to take responsibility for my own thinking, judgments, feelings, and to be authentic in my own person with Vicki. My model of authenticity has a curative effect my client. Our work is real. Vicki's ways of relating to herself and her world are continually challenged through our relationship until she begins to open to other possible choices in her daily life, not just on a week's vacation. Through *a challenging relationship of psychotherapy* Vicki began her small steps toward an authenticity that feels as real to me as it is to her.

We all know too well these choices of Ron and Vicki. It is not unusual for people with very busy lives to take a week's vacation on their own and to find when they return they are starved for more in the life they have chosen. These dilemmas are pervasive in all we say and do. We cannot stand apart from the issues of inauthentic being, for indeed our lives are caught up in just such matters. Ron, Vicki, and Myrtle have a common plight of authenticity. When I return from each international teaching, I face bringing my expanded awareness into my daily life. It is a challenge I face each time I teach internationally. Will I return and if I do, where will I be inside and outside?

This commonality is essential to the therapeutic alliance, where the therapist recognizes how he or she, too, struggles with similar issues. This recognition is often renewed in consultation with other therapists. During these consultations I openly discuss my deep concerns and uncertainties that continually renew my journey full of all its foibles. I must dare to walk my talk. The walk of authenticity is a courageous walk, which is filled with of paradoxes. As I share these thoughts with you today, I hold the very real possibility that my life will end one day and that my mentor, James F. T. Bugental, PhD, age 92, has just died. His death was not a surprise, yet I miss his physical presence. I celebrate his courageous, authentic life with each of you now as I share the awesome potential of living with the search for authenticity, globally as well as individually.

In order for any individual to make this leap into authentic being, he or she must be willing to hold uncertainty. This is the paradox of authenticity: We want authenticity but we also want certainty. Embracing authenticity is a great act of faith, an act of embracing uncertainty. Just as we do not know when we will die, we hold the fact that one day we each will die.

> We are floating in a medium of vast extent, always drifting uncertainly, blown to and fro; whenever we think we have a fixed point to which we can cling and make fast, it shifts and leaves us behind; if we follow it, it eludes our grasp, slips away, and flees eternally before us. Nothing stands still for us. This is our natural state and yet the state most contrary to our inclinations. We burn with desire to find a firm footing, an ultimate, lasting base on which to build a tower rising up to infinity, but our whole foundation cracks and the earth opens... (Pascal, 1662/1966, p. 63)

For all clients, as well as for myself, we face this authentic paradox every moment. We each live on a very thin thread. The conditions of being human are not unique to the client but rather are held as a mutual reality in the therapeutic alliance. The therapeutic relationship holds the power to heal the individual through this present-tense, authentic relationship. I recognize the finiteness of this relationship and, paradoxically, the continued healing of this relationship in other relationships beyond my knowing.

Holding the unknown is what we each face in becoming globally authentic, and the surprises emerge from the unknown and become known, part of the tapestry of our lives that are so interconnected.

## Response and Responsibility

My international teaching and my therapy work with Ron and Vicki so clearly reminded me of my own search for authenticity. Their search renewed my own search of authenticity, which is always a work in progress. Vicki and Ron renewed their lives in their own unique ways, making creative decisions about their daily lives by learning to listen to their truth and follow that truth more and more. Understanding the imperfection of this listening is part of their individual authenticity.

One of the forms of genuine authenticity in the therapist is his or her acceptance of the fact that the therapist has but limited knowledge of the client. Since the therapist gets to know their clients so much more thoroughly than others, there is an illusion that the therapist knows the client fully. Therapists never know all about their clients, only those aspects the client is willing to reveal. These may be terribly important aspects and certainly significant to know, but the full knowledge of the person is not known.

What we experience as an essential quality of authenticity is humility, of allowing ourselves to not know and be humbled by the not knowing for others and ourselves. Certainly, this has been very true in my international teaching.

Along with the humility of uncertainty there is the solidity of responsibility. We each have a life to live and to pick up our lives with full responsibility is an authentic life. I wish to invite you to explore your responsibility as an authentic therapist or person.

What are the "rights, responsibilities and privileges" associated with being a psychotherapist? I believe that the rights and privileges of being a psychotherapist in private practice, research, or teaching bring a responsibility to make good use of the knowledge and skills we have each acquired.

What does *good use* mean in the world of 2019? Our good use is joined by a long line of distinguished professors, researchers, and clinicians who have made excellent use of their knowledge and pursued their goals with passion for many decades. We are grateful for this foundation. Our profession of psychology is gifted with the extraordinary ability to understand human beings and to communicate that understanding to others. We often make judgments without the comfort of stable rules and categories, and navigate uncertainty without a map and without guarantees. Yet, we proceed with our passion for our work, moving forward through the unknown to the known and back again.

If you are a traditional psychotherapist reading this chapter, I invite each of you to look closely at the choices available to you, to think outside of the box as you reflect on the good use of your knowledge of people and your knowledge of communication in today's world. I invite each of you to take off your glasses and see beyond the therapy room, the classroom, or your research, to envision the intention of your work reaching out of the room of one-on-one psychotherapy or even from the classroom to the community in which you live and work, to the state in which you live, the nation of which you are citizen. and the world in which we all live.

We each have a choice about how to respond to challenges. My invitation to you is the same we ask of our clients: look closely at how you usually hold and react to your world and embrace new ways of being over and over in each challenge you face. Each time a challenge comes, begin opening to the choices and their consequences. This process of facing challenges by holding choices mindful of the paradoxes of freedom and human limitation is the fundamental work of becoming authentic.

On an international, national, and local levels we are now experiencing a major crisis in our response to terrorism and economic crisis. This present us-versus-them response of pointing at the bad guy works to continue war and catastrophe. The question is whether we can use this crisis to develop new choices that reflect wisdom, or whether our choices polarize the world. What does psychology have to offer in this continual crisis of who and what is the bad guy?

And what if we chose to not use the language of the good guy and bad guy? This is a question we often search deeply and naturally in our profession. If, as a profession, we are so adept at this searching process, how can this search inform our larger community? Is this a responsibility of our profession? If so, how can you participate? What I am proposing is *global authenticity* of the twenty-first century. Who we thought we were and who we can become as a profession are being challenged and require authentic responses.

I know many clinicians who have responded by picking up a mantle of responsibility reflecting their individual passions; working with hospice, proposing alternative global economic plans, addressing the aging crises, and more.

Clinicians are trained to listen to the good guy/bad guy conversation with their clients. My wife or husband, my ex-, my boss or my co-worker, my child or aging parent can easily fill an hour of being the bad guy. Listening to this story's endless variations with a trained ear, eye, and heart, you may interrupt at a moment that brings the client face-to-face with the ever-present option of authenticity. We invite an inner search, a deeper awareness of the story, going to the inner pain behind and underneath the concerns, giving rise to care, hope, and commitment for something more. We hold hope for change, with certainty that the individual can own the darkest part of his or her painful story and be transformed in the telling, to use that story as a creative resource for wholeness, not separation from self and others. This is the work of becoming authentic.

In exploring the self, we need to look at the client's relationship not only with the therapist but also the world in which the client lives. We must address integrating gains as a goal every bit as important as making gains. The client finishes psychotherapy and returns to what and to whom? We need to be vigilant in communicating responsibly in and to our clients, their families and society in which the clients live. For us to be an authentic human means not only being attentive to the care of self but also to the self in relation to the world in which the client lives, to embody concern about our world and caring toward others. Authenticity is not limited to the therapy hour or the classroom; it is a deeply human process of bringing forth all we are made of, inwardly and outwardly, into the world in which we live.

I have had the great honor of teaching many helping professionals, including psychologists, teachers, and hospice workers across this beautiful globe. In all the places I have traveled, I have always enjoyed a large piece of humble pie, eating it frequently as the unknown stands both quietly and loudly beside the known.

In each country I have taught, my heart has been deeply touched by stories filled with joys and sorrows. I am consistently moved by the sincerity of each person I have taught and how each person continually teaches me. We are searching together for all the possibilities of each moment. These authentic searchers represent an emerging global family which goes beyond race, nation, color, or gender, and unites us in our condition of being human. Out of all these searches, I have developed trainings for helping professionals with the signature name, *Unearthing the Moment*. This large family, which continues to grow, is a mirror of *global authenticity*.

Let us each find our common ground as helping professionals, as people serving each other for the full potential latent within ourselves. Let us celebrate this grand and glorious experiment of human potential with all of its paradoxes. To do so, we must honor and work diligently for the things that unite us rather than focus on what separates us.

Successful responsibility is the ability to respond to life within your own world, where you live. This is the work of becoming an authentic human being first, and then an authentic nation and world.

It is in this deep concern for living authentically that as psychologists and psychotherapists we have moved into the world with all that we have been trained. In our forming the International Institute for Humanistic Studies, I have found this has increased our ability to respond, to be responsible, and to actualize our global authenticity in the world. I support people in expressing their uniqueness and help them to listen to themselves, others, and the world with courage, hope, compassion, resilience, and tolerance. This invitation to live global authenticity is not limited to psychotherapists and their clients, but to people in many professions: ministers, doctors, teachers, and politicians, as well as to everyone seeking wholeness and peace.

I believe that changes in individuals lead to changes in small groups of people, which contribute to major shifts in a society. I trust psychotherapy to enhance individual changes and open people to the journey of authenticity. From this perspective of personal and social interconnectedness, therapy is not only a tool for psychological help and change, but is also instrumental in bringing about social transformations that enhance authentic cultures. I am aware of our professional potential as well as our responsibility to participate in promoting a society that embodies humanistic values.

I am inviting each one to the experience of being *magnanimous*, to be open to the unknown, to share in the moment with all of who you are. We are each doing work that benefits the whole (Potter, 2004). The authenticity of psychology is to step outside the walls of academia and the consultation room, to put our knowledge and skills to good use within ourselves and in the marketplace by building bridges of communication among a large variety of professions. The invitation is open-ended—to advocate, question, listen, and inspire. This is the work of becoming authentic individuals, authentic cultures, and an authentic world.

## References

Bugental, J. F. T. (1965). *The search for authenticity,* New York, NY: Holt, Rinehart, and Winston.

Bugental, J. F. T. (1999). *Psychotherapy isn't what you think.* Phoenix, AZ: Zeig Tucker & Co.

Heery, M. (2001). Inside the soul of Russian and American psychotherapy trainings. *Journal of Humanistic Psychology, 42*(2), 89-101.

Heery, M. & Bugental, J. F. T. (1999). Unearthing the moment. *Self and Society, 27*(3), 26-27.

Heery, M. & Bugental, J. F. T. (2005). Listening to the listener: An existential-humanistic approach to psychotherapy with psychotherapists. In J. D. Geller, J. C . Norcross, & D. E. Orlinsky (Eds.), *The psychotherapist's own psychotherapy* (pp. 282-296). New York, NY: Oxford University Press.

Martel, Y. (2001). *Life of Pi.* Orlando, FL: Harvest.

Pascal, B. (1966). *Pensees* (A. J. Krailsheimer, Trans.). New York, NY: Penguin. (Original work published in 1662)

Potter, R. N. (2004). *Authentic spirituality.* St. Paul, MN: Llewellyn.

Yalom, I. (1980). *Existential psychotherapy.* New York, NY: Basic Books.

# Chapter 11

## Zhaungzi's View of Freedom[1]

### Zhaohui Bao

During the Warring Period, about the same time as Aristotle was alive in the West, a philosopher in China (368–286 BC) named Zhaungzi (1994) proposed ways of attaining a sense of freedom during a period of time ravaged by war. In his writings, Zhaungzi did not use the word *freedom*; instead he used the word *wandering* to represent his idea of the basic existence of life. Statistically, the word, wandering, appeared over 100 times in the book of *Zhaungzi*. He titled his first chapter "Carefree Wandering" to lend emphasis to the concept of wandering. The concept was further developed twice more in this chapter. In fact, wandering was the main theme in six out of the seven chapters of the book. In the chapter titled "On the Equality of Things," Zhaungzi emphasized "wandering beyond the limits of this mundane world." The chapter "Essentials and Nurturing Life" describes the state where there is "plenty of room for the blade to wander." In "The Human World," he promoted "simply riding along with things as you let your mind wander. Entrust yourself to inevitability thereby nourishing what is central." The chapter "Symbols of Integrity Fulfilled" emphasized "wandering among grace and harmony," and finally "The Great Ancestral Teacher" and "Responses for Emperors and Kings" described the possibility of someone achieving the state of "wandering between heaven and Earth" and "wandering between existence and non-existence." Zhaungzi promoted the state of *wandering* as a way of life in the pursuit of freedom and peace of mind.

### Zhaungzi's Reasons for Choosing Freedom

According to Zhaungzi (1994), the reason why people fail to wander was because of too little room in their hearts. They did not achieve the state where their hearts had enough space for wandering; the reason being that their hearts were tied and bundled up, having submitted themselves to worldly perspectives and popular thinking. However, many people became exhausted from chasing after worldly standards. They were not willing to allow their hearts to settle. Such worldly people chased after their own shadows for a living without awareness that they are actually afraid of their own shadows. They became disgusted with their own living and sought to escape their current uneasiness. They searched endlessly in

---

[1] Pages numbers are not included for translated quotes.

the external world for a place to settle. They ran ahead fast, followed by their shadows, which they were unable to shed, so they ran even faster. In the end they would run out of breath and die. They were unable to see that happiness and freedom were in fact within themselves. In his chapter "An Old Fisherman," Zhaungzi stated:

> There was a man, who, afraid of his shadow and disliking his own foot-prints, tried in vain to run away from them. But the more he ran, the more footprints were created. And the faster he ran, the closer his shadows followed. He thought he was going too slow, so he kept running faster and faster without stopping, until dying of exhaustion. The man failed to realize that, by staying still, he could have expunged his footprints. Such was the extent of his foolishness.

People in the world chase after worldly things. We do not even know if these popular things fit us or not. We forget who we are and what we experience in the midst of following the things that are popular. Zhaungzi (1994) offered the following parable. In his chapter "Autumn Floods," he stated:

> Haven't you heard of the young lad from Shou ling who tried to learn to walk the way people do in Hantan? Yet, before he was able to acquire this new skill, he had forgotten how he used to walk. So, all he could do was to crawl home on all fours.

"Symbols of Integrity Fulfilled," another parable by Zhaungzi, also recorded a story of a man called Cheng Tse Tsan who went to learn the Tao from Hunbowuren so that he could increase his understanding of essence of the mental/spiritual world. But Cheng chose to be influenced by popular thought. He was proud of his physical health and bragged about his status as a high government official. He despised his contemporary Sin Tao Yia who had no status and was physically disabled. Cheng admonished Sin for being rude to him because he did not pay his respects to Cheng. But Sin stated to Cheng that Cheng should not use physical appearance and status to measure Sin's worth. If Cheng has truly learned and embraced the way of the Tao, he would not be judging Sin's worth based upon physical appearances. Cheng felt ashamed after hearing this.

Those who follow worldly thoughts and ideas are like "someone who knows nothing about the cause of being" (Zhaungzi, 1994). They are lost in the "worldly standards of right and wrong and do good out of obligation." They are living a life with no self-reflection. They have lost themselves to the material world and are not able to live a free and pleasant life.

People are slaves to their own desires. They are unsettled because they are trapped by their desires of their physical needs and lured by the desires of their eyes. This sense of being unsettled is triggered by worldly desires. According to Chi Wu Lun, a philosophical perspective titled "The Equality of Things" explained:

> Once people have received their complete physical form, they remain conscious of it while awaiting extinction. In their strife and friction with other things, they gallop forward in their course unable to stop. (as cited in Zhaungzi, 1994)

As a result, "their contacts turn into conflicts, each day involving them in mental strife." Zhaungzi deplored such a way of living. He asked, "Isn't this sad? We toil our entire lives without seeing any results. We deplete ourselves with weari-some labor not knowing what it all adds up to. Isn't this lamentable?" In its place, Zhaungzi in his chapter "The Great Ancestral Teacher," advocated, "I detach myself from my body and my desires, dim my intelligence, depart from my form, leave knowledge behind, to become identical with the Transformational Thor-oughhfare."

People surrender themselves to the social standards and ideas of others. They lose their authenticity. In the story, "The death of Wonton," the emperor of the Southern Sea, Lickety, a place that represented social effectiveness and suc-cess in the world, joined with the emperor of the Northern Sea, called Split, in their desire to reward the supreme emperor (Wonton) for his goodness. They decided to transform 'Wonton' according to popular opinions and social standards. They believed that human beings are unique because they have a total of seven orifices: ears, nostrils, mouth, and more. So, they tried to dig openings one-a-day for a total of seven days. Wonton died. In understanding this parable, the American scholar Girardot (1983) suggested:

> What is implied is that a civilized condition does not necessarily bring about the fulfillment of human nature. Indeed, from the Taoist point of view it amounts to the fall of man from the godlike condition of the paradise time. (p. 94)

The emptiness before civilization was similar to our time in heaven, symbolizing the authentic state of human existence. Humankind's false heroes, Lickety and Split, made the mistake of relying too much on the value of human civilization, which they relied upon to replace the most pure, spontaneous, inner values of humankind. This resulted in the loss of sacredness for humankind.

The worldly perspectives and popular ideas require us to be useful through contributing ourselves according to societal standards. These standards may result from fame, profit, money, power, status, nationality, or race. They turn us into slaves of others or society; slaves to schools of thoughts; slaves of prag-matism; slaves to enterprises or structures. Zhaungzi (1994) espoused that no-thing was useful. He believed that existence in and of itself was sufficient; that the meaning of one's existence did not depend on one's usefulness to society. In his chapter "The Human World," through the stories about what he called *the rubber tree and forgotten wood*, Zhaungzi revealed the secret of the useless rubber tree and its meaningful existence. In the fourth story of this chapter there was a carpenter named Si. He was on his way to Nation Chi and passed by the trunk of a big tree. This tree was so big that it could offer shade to thousands of cattle. Si told his apprentice:

> This tree is not useful. If you use it to make it into a boat, the boat will sink. If you made it into a coffin, the coffin will wear out. If you made utensils out of it, the utensil will break. If you use it to make windows, the windows will shatter. If you use it as a pillar, the pillar will soon be consumed by termites.

Then one day the rubber tree explained the importance of its uselessness to Si in a dream. The carpenter at last sadly expressed that if he were to follow the rationale of the world in understanding the rubber tree to be useless, then they and his apprentice will be unlikely to find out the secret and value of this tree.

The next story is about a wise man called Nam Pau Tze. He traveled to the Shang qiu city in He nan Province (是河南省商丘市). He understood the secret and value of the useless tree. At Shang qiu city, all the trees were very big; big enough to shelter thousands of horses. However, these trees could not be made into pillars; could not be made into coffin; their leaves had no taste; and there was no scent to them. But according to Nam Pau Tze, these qualities are what made these trees unique. He viewed human life the same way–of high value. If one does not surrender to the standards of the world, namely that one's worth is tied to one's usefulness to the world, then like both of the trees mentioned above, one can avoid being taken away by the world. They grow in their own ways, not under the influence of any other. The other tress such as pear, orange, and pomelo tress rely on the standard of the world. They become useful when ripe. But, then, their fruits are picked and their branches get chopped off and destroyed. Zhaungzi (1994) offered to people the choice of growth and freedom. He selected these trees as symbols to remind us of the way we should grow. He reminded us to stay away from being possessed or encumbered by worldly concepts and popular ideas. Zhaungzi espoused the usefulness of uselessness. Life itself and integrity is far more important than investing oneself to attain a particular goal or function.

Zhaungzi (1994) chose a life of freedom, but not life according to the required life style as defined by others. He made the important decision to withdraw from this noisy/busy world and followed his inner heart. Originally, Zhaungzi had the opportunity to become useful in the eyes of others. During Zhuangzi's time, intellectuals were respected by the authorities. The Nation Chi had set up the Jixia Academic Center (稷下学宫) to nurture the best talents of the nation. Many of the brightest minds were invited to the center to apply their talents in service to the nation. There, they had freedom, and intellectuals, such as Mencius and Chung Lin—with a similar personality as Zhaungzi—had their own liberty. They did not have to worship high officials on bended knees, and they could all work at the academic center. Zhaungzi could have chosen the same path if he so desired. Similarly, a good friend of Zhaungzi name Wai Tsu worked at the royal house in the nation Leong. Zhaungzi had the same opportunity to work as a high commissioner for Nation Chu. But Zhaungzi explained his belief about these choices in his chapter "Autumn Floods" that the commissioners in Nation Chu were like the dead tortoises from 3,000 years ago: "the king stores them (the tortoise bones) in his ancestral temple inside a hamper wrapped with cloth…. Do you think these tortoises would rather be dead and have their bones preserved as objects of veneration?" To the contrary, Zhaungzi desired freedom and a life filled with vitality. He chose be a living tortoise, *rolling around in the mud and muck*, rather than receive the venerations accorded to tortoises that are long dead. So Zhaungzi withdrew from the noisy/busy world and chose a life of poverty without fame.[2] His lived in a poor house, married, and had a child. He made grass shoes for a living and had to humble himself when he was hungry to borrow grain from the marquis, the overseer of a River. Although he was occasionally rejected, overall, he lived a pleasant life: he went fishing and had fun with fishes; he listened to the wind; he pursued a life without burden.

Zhaungzi (1994) gave us a model on how to actualize our human nature. We first need to learn how to retreat from this noisy/busy world and not be tied up. In order to cultivate that inner peace, it begins with finding external places of solitude. Only in such places of peace and quiet are we able to transform the external solitude into inner tranquility. In retreating from his noisy/busy world, Zhaungzi modeled for all of us how to experience quiet times in our own environment. We need to learn to do nothing, even if it causes us pain. Sometimes we need to just sit, allow ourselves to become a slow person, and learn to let go of what we have; let go of things such as the present-day orientation towards success, hard work, and achievement. While under such contemporary influences we cannot avoid our feelings of guilt and we are, thus, tied up by our work and fast pace of life.

Retreating from the world will allow us to detach from the value and influences of the world. Furthermore, it will prevent us from imposing our views upon others. In this way, we not only set ourselves free, we are also able to set others free. Zhaungzi's (1994) books have a number philosophical parables to remind us that human beings have created numerous unanticipated consequences. Despite our best intentions, bad things still result. For example, in the parable he called, *The Marquis Birds,* in the chapter "The Human World," Zhaungzi wrote of the Marquis of Lu who welcomed birds in his ancestral temple. He prepared a party with food, wine, and music to welcome the birds. However, the eyes of the birds were glazed over with sadness as they were unwilling to eat so much as a single sliver of fish, nor drink a single drop of wine. Three days later, all the birds died.

---

[2] In Zhaungzi's time, especially compared to the pervasive influence of the Confucius and Mohist schools of thought, Zhaungzi was without fame and influence, he had only one student whose name was LinQie recorded in "Zhaungzi."

The Marquis Lu made the mistake of nourishing the birds with his own nourishment. He did not nourish the birds as birds. In the same book, Zhaungzi wrote a similar parable of a person who was extremely fond of horses, so much so that he bought an expensive container to collect the horse's wastes. Consequently, horseflies gathered and began to annoy and torment the horse. The owner then frightened the horse while slapping the flies away. Consequently, the frightened horse broke the expensive container and inadvertently treaded on the owner. Both the marquis and the horse lover were filled with good intensions, but painful unanticipated consequences resulted nevertheless.

Zhaungzi's (1994) extreme poverty and self-imposed limitations motivated him towards his pursuits. The Japanese scholar Fukunaga Mitsuji (1969) suggested:

> Zhaungzi was able to contemplate his freedom because of a history of living under such extreme poverty and facing the realities that come from such extreme limitation without freedom. Zhaungzi's situation differed from monks who lived in monasteries while mediating on freedom and ordinary people who lived in a stable society while contemplating their freedom. According to Friedrich Hegel, freedom was impossible while living under the ugly reality of ancient Chinese tyranny. Therefore, people struggled for freedom. This is what Zhaungzi referred to as the freedom within non-freedom and he viewed this as a vital character of freedom. (p. 5)

Fukunaga's views were only partially accurate in regards to Zhaungzi. He failed to account for Zhaungzi's will and choice. While it was true that Zhaungzi lived in a society without freedom, thus, motivating him to reflect and write about freedom, Zhuangzi did not submit himself under the popular concepts of that worldly rule. He chose a life of poverty with freedom. He desired a life of freedom and, therefore, made his decision to retreat from the world. Zhaungzi's views towards freedom did not result from extreme poverty; instead, they resulted from his will to choose poverty and lead a simple life.

After Zhaungzi (1994) attained inner peace and freedom, he traveled the world with this peace of mind and sense of freedom. Regardless of where he went or what he did, he chose to co-exist with the noise and stress from the external world.

## The Origin of Zhaungzi's Freedom and Problems

According to Zhaungzi (1994), human freedom originated with the genesis of the world: "Heaven and Earth were born together with me and the myriad of things are one with me." When our hearts are joined with the world, we can find the way to the origin of all matters, which then leads us back to dwell in the Tao. Within the Tao matters exist in authenticity. In the chapter "On the Equality of Things,"

Zhaungzi emphasized the uniqueness of existence: "All things are possessed by that which we say is so; all things are possessed by that which we affirm. There is nothing that is not so; there is nothing that is not affirmable." All things exist with affirmation and admiration. Zhaungzi also emphasized that Tao is everywhere. Tao is among the low and the high with the same value "And is indifferent to baseness and honor...." In other words, in Tao all things do not require an external factor to determine the value of self. The self is valuable because of its pure existence, like "the voice of the pipes of earth [and] the voice of the pipes of man" with their original pure form of existence. They reach "the voices of the pipes of heaven."

The Tao is the way. It is a way to perceive things. Only those who perceive the Tao can let go of their stubborn attachments to material values. "Only the perceptive understand that all things join in Unity. For this reason, they do not use things for themselves but lodge in commonality" (Zhaungzi, 1994). To those who are able to perceive the Tao, they are willing to let go of their own perspectives and believe in observing things around them. The goal of their observation is to let the things be as they are, like the beauty and strength of the *osmanthus* flower shining through between its bloom and wither. For those who are unable to perceive things, they are stuck because of their stubbornness regarding their perceptions, unwilling to let go, like the conflict between the Confucius and Mohist schools of thought during the period of war.[3]

In the chapter "On the Equality of Things," Zhaungzi (1994) revealed that, all things have the same origin, all things are integrated. Life and death is simply a transition from one stage to another, all belonging to one large cosmic world. "Life and death are predestined. Their constant alternation, like that of day and night, is determined by heaven." To individuals, life and death are temporal, ordinary; just like the night, it comes and goes. Although human beings only live and die once, it does not impact humanity at large. Therefore, individual men and women are like travelers of the world, passengers in transition. When the time comes, individuals will return to the yellow earth. "That which we borrow to maintain our lives is merely dust. Life and death alternate like day and night." "Ultimate Joy" recorded that when Zhaungzi lost his wife, not only he did not cry, he even "sang with the drum." He used the same principle of cosmic integration to respond to his wife's transition from life to death.

---

[3] The conflict between the Confucius and Mohist schools of thought revolves around status. Confucius advocated a form of filial piety and society love, based on clearly defined status and hierarchy, whereas Mohists advocated an egalitarian social structure within the family and society. Similarly, Confucius advocated for extravagant burial ceremonies where as Mohists preferred burial ceremonies that are characterized by practicality and simplicity.

I reflected on her beginning and realized that, originally, she was unborn. Not only was she unborn, originally, she had no form. Not only did she have no form, originally, she had no vital breath. Intermingling with nebulousness and blurriness, a transformation occurred and there was vital breath; the vital breath was transformed and there was form; the form was transformed and there was birth; now there has been another transformation and she is dead. This is like the progression of the four seasons–from spring to autumn, from winter to summer.

Zhaungzi used the principle of cosmic oneness to give order to a confused and uncertain world. Human beings, thus, can let go of suffering and settle in this cosmic order.

However, Zhaungzi (1994) also knew that, sometimes, it can be difficult to give order to destiny, not even the Tao can do so. To him, people lived in mystery. This can be very difficult to understand. These mysteries and uncertainties are beyond human comprehension. Sometimes, destiny is determined by the Tao. Zhaungzi understood that one can only learn to accept helplessness when confronted with higher guidance, particularly facing life and death. In "The Great Ancestral Teacher," Zhaungzi mentioned a man who was physically deformed because of disease. When this man confronted the meaningless of his unreasonable illness, he was only left with sarcasm as a form of acceptance.

Besides the mystery of Tao, which is beyond anyone's comprehension, the brutal political suppression and killing during the war period also enhanced the sense of uncertainty and powerlessness. Zhaungzi (1994) lived in a dark era, during which there were numerous wars among nations. Various emperors were fighting for their sovereignties. The emperor of Yee, Wei, and Chung all devalued the lives of the peasants. Even the contemporary of Zhaungzi, Mencius, in his book titled, *Mencius,* also commented and endorsed that "All the authorities was like to kill and Peasants were the abused." He thought this was the worse period of time. Zhaungzi wrote a number of parables describing such kinds of brutal acts in this dark age.

When facing the gigantic wheel of destiny, Zhaungzi (1994) adopted the attitude of acceptance. He admitted that human beings were powerless and without control in the face of uncertainty and the higher power. He focused on the passive nature and dark side of the mystery of human destiny. It is regrettable that Zhaungzi did not discover the other side of human destiny. It is through disasters, suffering, and adversity that individuals are able to strengthen their beliefs and find unexpected courage. In fact, Zhaungzi himself modeled for us how to face our own suffering and adversity with great faith and courage. He paid a handsome price while preserving his belief in living a life which valued freedom. The price paid was his perseverance in living a life that was not driven by the values of the world. He chose to retreat from the noisy/busy world and live a modest life. He could have gone further. The reason why he retreated from the world was because he wanted to preserve his own freedom as well as protect himself from being harmed by the world. Yet Zhuangzi's pessimism was also evidence of his lack of courage for he did not persist in maintaining his determination and courage in pursuit of freedom. In other words, he protected himself by giving in too easily to pessimism and failed to pay enough attention to the potential of human faith and courage. He overlooked the potential manifestations of faith and courage in human sufferings, adversity, and disasters. Because of his pessimism, Zhuangzi was unable to uphold his moral courage when confronted by his own destiny and social conscience. He was not as consistent as Confucius, who devoted himself to promoting moral conscience to various nations, even though he was unsure how to accomplish his task. This was what was missing with Zhaungzi, which are the same things that are missing within the Chinese culture at large.

In the end, through Zhaungzi (2004), we are able to find out where to locate freedom; freedom comes from being aligned with the Tao. Through aligning with the Tao, Zhaungzi was able to find the ways of freedom as well as the meaning and value that are attached to it. However, his view of freedom did not inspire the great faith or courage that can be gained through suffering. Because of his understanding of the order of Tao, Zhuangzi anticipated and accepted death as an attitude of living. Actually, this can diminish the wish for living as well as the value of living. Zhaungzi held a conscious and desperate attitude towards living. Zhaungzi did not mention love and never talked about hope. In fact, love and hope have tremendous power to activate faith and courage. In the end, Zhaungzi did not further reflect on how we can preserve freedom, relate to it, and apply it in society. Zhaungzi's sense of freedom remained individualistic because he failed to inspire society to a greater sense of collective freedom.

## References

Mitsuji, F. (1969). *Chuang-tzu: Ancient Chinese existentialism* [福光永司：《庄子：古代中国的存在主义], Chen Guanxue [陈冠学译], Taibei [台北]：Sanmin Publishing House [三民书局].

Girardot, N. J. (1983). *Myth and meaning in early Taoism.* Berkeley, CA & Los Angeles, CA: University of California Press.

Guo Qingfan 郭庆藩. (1961). *The complete works of Chuang Tzu* [《庄子集释》]. Wang Xiaoyu [王孝鱼]. Beijing: Zhonghua Publishing House [点校，北京：中华书局].

Zhaungzi. (1994). *Wandering on the way: Early Taoist tales and parables of Chuang Tzu.* (V. H. Mair, Trans., from the original book Zhaungzi in Chinese.) Hawaii, HI: University of Hawaii Press.

# Chapter 12

## A Contemplative Approach to Existential Psychotherapy: Mindfulness as Existential Praxis

### Michael Dow

In recent years, psychotherapy approaches, which incorporate or are inspired by the Buddhist practice of mindfulness (Germer, Siegel, & Fulton, 2005; Hayes, Follette, & Linehan, 2004), are proliferating rapidly. What is perhaps less appreciated is that mindfulness, properly understood, is at heart an existential practice, which is to say as much about death as it is about life, and less about *getting better* than it is about *living fully*. Mindfulness confronts one experientially, as opposed to abstractly, with not only the alarming automaticity of one's habitual mental patterns, but the pain and the inability of grasping the nature of existence itself, as revealed in each successive moment of awareness.

This chapter argues that mindfulness and existential psychotherapy make for complementary if also contradictory partners. Mindfulness provides a praxis with which to experience one's existence with immediacy and without filters; existential therapy provides an interpersonal context in which to understand it. Both orient the individual towards a relationship to experience characterized by *being* as opposed to *having* (Batchelor, 1983). But, there will always be a necessary tension between these two approaches drawn from East and West, between daring to articulate the self and letting go of the self altogether; between *just noticing* without interpreting, and *consciously seeking* reparative, interpretive self-narratives. We might conceive of a mindfulness-oriented existential therapy, which integrates both, which is oriented towards developing both existential meaning and experiential immediacy and helps patients to live with both aware-ness and authenticity.

Yalom (1980) defined existential psychology as involving attempts to help patients confront the four ultimate concerns of life: death, freedom, existential isolation and meaninglessness. Although such a therapy sounds far from cheery, the idea here is that if existential concerns can be faced directly without suppressing them from awareness, untold reservoirs of energy will be released that allow one to live more freely and joyously. De Wit (2008) and others have argued that most of our suffering is neurotic, which is to say most of our suffering is created unconsciously and defensively as an attempt to ward off the pain of existence. On top of the pain of existence we heap the suffering of resisting that pain: wishing, hoping and otherwise pretending that life could be without limitation, pain, and disappointment. There are other possibilities, however. It is probably axiomatic that nothing inspires one to live life fully more than accepting the reality of death, which more often than not comes sooner than we think.

Buddhism, from which mindfulness is principally drawn, takes the analysis to another level. It is not so much that the self's vitality is hampered by suppressing awareness of death and associated existential angst, but the very notion of self, and especially the centrality of that notion to our awareness, is itself seen as symptomatic of a reflexive contraction away from reality. At every moment, we are turning away from the "great, blooming, buzzing confusion" (James, 1890/1950, p. 488) and withdrawing into the artifice of *self*. Mindfulness, and Buddhism in general, practiced with an existential frame of mind (Batchelor, 1983, 1998), provides a practice as opposed to an intellectual exercise for both clients and therapists to reverse that resistance and experience the reality of moment to moment awareness directly.

## Mindfulness

Mindfulness is a translation of the Pali word, *sati,* which comes from the Sanskrit *smrti*, both of which originally meant something akin to *memory*. The Buddhist use of the word came to mean something closer to the quality of mind, which facilitates memory, both in terms of retaining new memories and recalling old ones (Sujato, 2005). A popular contemporary translation of mindfulness, which reflects this original meaning of memory, while also giving a flavor for the Buddhist usage, is Chogyam Trungpa's (1995) "recollecting the present" (p. 66). In traditional Buddhism, mindfulness is conceived as the ability to stay with the object of attention without, as usually happens, getting lost in self-referential associations and abstractions that miss the naked moment of perception (Wallace, 2006). It is both already there as part of the perceptual process and something that one must cultivate over time. In Buddhism, the cultivation of mindfulness is done in the context of a simultaneous cultivation of ethics and wisdom/compassion, known collectively as *The Three Trainings*, and in more detailed fashion as *The Noble Eightfold Path* (Rahula, 1974). It can be seen as a remedy for and a direct contrast to Heidegger's (1998/1946) "forgetfulness of being," (p. 250) in which we retreat from the authentic questioning of our existence into the ready-made answers of various ideologies. Practiced with correct understanding—without a desire for anything in particular to happen—mindfulness moves one in the direc-tion of authentic being-alone and authentic being-with others (Batchelor, 1983), as opposed to our more typical mode of *having*, the consumer-driven orientation of getting and spending, which can never be fully satiated.

In the context of psychotherapy, clinicians applying mindfulness have emphasized the importance of a component of acceptance or nonjudgment (Germer, 2005; Kabat-Zinn, 2005), also termed *maitri* or compassion (Wegela, 1997). This emphasis has been important to counter the self-aggressive tendencies that *pure mindfulness,* at times, can elicit (Germer, 2005; Linehan, 1993). Germer helpfully defined so-called *therapeutic mindfulness,* as consisting of three components: awareness, a present moment focus, and an attitude of acceptance. To simplify, mindfulness gets us out of our heads and into our senses. While mindfulness is a conscious de-coupling from the endless activity of storytelling arising in our minds, a therapy alive to existential concerns picks up those threads, and from them, helps clients weave and enact a subjective narrative of meaning. Both are important for a vibrant and vivid life: to disconnect from our default mode and rest in *self-as–context* rather than *self-as-content* (Hayes, Strosahl, & Wilson, 1999), and to wrest a deeply felt intersubjective narrative that sustains and propels us further into the chaos of what comes next.

## Dialectical Tension Between Mindfulness and Existential Therapy

Unsurprisingly, these two modes of understanding the self—mindfulness and existential therapy—are at odds. But both modes when held together often provide a generative dialectical tension. Mindfulness arose, at least initially, within a collectivist worldview with little focus on a well-differentiated individual self; existentialism arose, at least initially, within an individualistic worldview, with little focus on letting go of self-oriented awareness (see Hoffman, 2008, for more discussion of this issue). The whole point of mindfulness meditation is, in a sense, to drop the search for meaning, which, in itself, can be seen as a strategy to avoid suffering. The search for meaning is seen as part of the illusion of ego, which creates a false separation between one's self and one's life:

> Existential philosophers have largely missed this point. Their effort—to live authentically by finding individual meaning in a chaotic universe— presupposes that we are separate from the world we experience. To live authentically, we have to stop trying to avoid suffering and death by look- ing for meaning. We have to enter into the mystery of life itself. (McLeod, 2001, p. x)

And yet, patients come to therapy because they no longer know how to tell a story about their lives that works for them. Their narrative, their meaning-making machinery, has ceased to function smoothly or, perhaps, never has. Patients often come to talk and be heard and—through that process of talking and being heard— to learn new ways of doing both. Therapy, after all, is made of words. Although patients always both want and resist change, the change needed, one might say, is an orienting framework—call it a sense of meaning, positive introjects, secure attachment, a coherent self-narrative, schemas—that allows them to settle and feel more deeply into the intensity of their lives. The therapist helps to construct such a framework with the patient, again, by using words, at the right time, and infused with the right feelings. Paradoxically, for the patient, this likely involves both tolerating a wider range of feelings without understanding them and putting that non-understanding into words.

As an interesting aside, it can be argued, as mentioned before, that there is a revolution going on in the behavioral sciences occasioned by mindfulness-based therapies and that, at heart, it is an existential one. A symptom-reduction focus is fast losing its appeal as the limitations of such are being shown by empirical studies (Baer, 2003; Segal, Williams, & Teasdale, 2001). The focus in academic research psychology is shifting away from cognitive-mediated change and towards strategies which direct one to experience difficult thoughts and feelings with acceptance. Acceptance and Commitment therapy, for instance, a new mindfulness-based behavioral therapy with a growing evidence base, in consonance with existential approaches, is explicitly geared towards accepting rather than reducing anxiety (Bunting & Hayes, 2007; Hayes, Strosahl, & Wilson, 1999). Clients are encouraged to clarify and commit to their values and to move towards them regardless of anxiety. Because of their mindfulness focus, Dialectical Behavior Therapy (DBT; Linehan, 1993) and Mindfulness-Based Cognitive Therapy for Depression (MBCT; Segal, Williams, & Teasdale, 2003) are, likewise, more concerned with developing an openness to experience than with explicitly or only, reducing symptoms.

Psychodynamic therapy informed by Buddhist meditation similarly tends to eschew interpretations in favor of both direct and indirect emotional communication, and principally trains therapists to remain open to the range of feelings and associations, which are exchanged in the therapeutic encounter with a client (Kaklauskas, Nimmanheminda, Hoffman, & Jack, 2008).

## Parallels between Existential Philosophy and Traditional Buddhism

Though there are very important differences between traditional Buddhism and Western existential psychology, notably their understanding of the self (see above, and also, Hoffman, 2008), there are some interesting parallels regarding the nature of existence being avoided. In traditional Theravadin Buddhism, the goal of developing mindfulness is to stabilize the mind so that one can then examine awareness with precision and develop insight or *prajna* into the nature of existence. Particularly the insight sought is regarding what are known as *the three marks of existence*: suffering (*dukkha*, Pali), impermanence (*anicca*, Pali), and no-self (*anatman*, Pali) (Rahula, 1974). A deep insight into the three marks leads to liberation from attachment or clinging to experience, otherwise known as enlightenment. Although these themes are generally not specifically emphasized in Buddhist-inspired psychotherapies (as of yet), there may be a parallel in this traditional Buddhist formulation with the four existential themes as outlined by Yalom (1980).

In Buddhism the primary insight is into the non-existence of not only a separate permanent self (*anatman*), but the non-existence of any separate, permanent thing altogether. It is because of the lack of self or the lack of a separate essence inhering in any phenomena that the second mark of existence, impermanence (*anicca*), is true. Things arise and pass away in interdependence on one another, and do not stay because there is nothing to stay. It is even more complex than that, because no separate things are said to exist that arise or pass away in the first place. Suffering (*dukkha*), the third mark of existence, arises because we grasp onto phenomena that do not exist—in the way we think—due to our ignorance or rejection of these first two marks. Freedom or liberation comes from a deep non-conceptual realization of these three marks (Rahula, 1974).

In Yalom's (2000) summary of existential thought, there are also three marks of existence: death or human limitation, existential isolation, and meaninglessness. We can similarly only move towards freedom by accepting the fundamental limitations of existence and abandoning our fantasies of perfect oneness, such as limitless achievement, painless existence. Only by accepting limitation and death can we reclaim passion for life; only by acknowledging our existential isolation can we become truly intimate, and only by taking responsibility for authoring meaning that does not come pre-ordered can we move towards freedom.

Interestingly, there is a lot of overlap between the marks of existence as seen from East and West, with one notable exception. Although suffering and impermanence are not exact equivalents of death and isolation, one can easily imagine both Buddhist and existential thinkers agreeing on these. However, while Buddhist thought has little to no emphasis on the need for the individual to craft meaning—deriving as it does from a collectivist culture—existential thought tends to miss the aspect of *no-self* (Batchelor, 1983). From a Buddhist perspective, existentialism might tend towards a nihilistic depression: suffering and impermanence are acknowledged by a very real and very separate self. From an existential perspective, Buddhism might tend towards passivity: one confronts death and isolation, but lacks the courage to boldly create (or discover) meaning from an inherently meaningless world. As Sartre (1957/1987) argued, "Man is nothing else but what he makes of himself. Such is the first principle of existentialism" (p. 15).

Buddhism and existential theory, then, suggest different but, perhaps, complementary avenues for facing existential reality. Buddhism suggests the practice of mindfulness, which allows one to experiences that are more than just thoughts, more than just feelings, and more than just sensations or anything else that passes through awareness, because, logically, if each of us is aware of something, then, we cannot be that thing of which we are aware. Mindfulness gradually, and at times suddenly, allows us to see through the illusion of a self that is separate in any fundamental way from the world and, thus, to discover compassion and spontaneous non-self-oriented action to help others.

Existential therapy suggests a different path towards facing existence. Existentialism encourages us to boldly craft meaning and direction from our lives, in spite or even because of the uncertainty and ambiguity inherent in being alive. It is up to us to be who we are and to create tradition anew from an engagement with the concrete givens of experience. As James Joyce (1916/1993) wrote in true existentialist fashion, "Welcome, O life! I go to encounter for the millionth time the reality of experience and to forge in the smithy of my soul, the uncreated consceince of my race" (p. 379)

## Case Example[1]

At this point, it might be helpful to discuss a clinical example to see how these different but complementary approaches might be integrated. Mary was a talented writer and poet whose career had stalled due to years of struggling with alcohol addiction. When she presented for treatment she was newly sober, but struggling with powerful, shame-fueled urges to drink again, which often were accompanied by fragmented images of abuse she had suffered in childhood. Initially, we worked on using these urges as an opportunity to briefly practice mindfulness. Although she could only tolerate doing so for a few minutes at a time, she would practice shifting her focus away from the images to just noticing the sensations in her body without attaching a story line to them. In introducing this exercise, both during and between sessions, I also stressed the concept of being kind and gentle with herself (*maitri*). We devised mindlessness exercises to turn down the volume on her distress, such as gripping an ice cube, going for a walk, swinging her arms, or watching television. Knowing she would be able to effectively turn down the distress later, helped her to tolerate mindfully by *leaning into* the difficult feelings associated with the memories/cravings.

During these mindfulness exercises, Mary learned to let go of the story line around the craving/traumatic memory and just to experience the craving as pure sensation. Her ability to shift into feeling her cravings rather than acting on them, was made possible, I think, only by the practice of *maitri*. Additionally, it was helpful that she knew that immediately after *mindfully feeling* the craving, she could do something distracting to effectively take her mind off of her distress. She had a number of distressing relapses, where she would *disappear* for months at a time and return to treatment with intense crippling shame. Eventually, she became able to sustain a longer period of sobriety. She experienced that the more she practiced her mindfulness/mindlessness exercises, the more she was able to have her feelings and thoughts about using without feeling compelled to act on them.

While working with Mary, I found my countertransference was powerful. I identified with her quite a bit, having aspired to be a writer myself in my early 20s. I found myself thinking, at times, that "we're just alike." Mary never objected to any intervention, and would sometimes go to great lengths to emphasize my rightness on some point. Any relapse she blamed wholly on herself. But while I found myself looking forward to our sessions, which were always intellectually and emotionally lively, this sense of "sameness" was also somehow frightening. I won-

---

[1] The following is a composite of different clients with identifying information changed to protect confidentiality.

dered if such fear was an *exchange*[2] with how Mary might be feeling. She seemed vigilant to erase any potential space of difference. Was she afraid of being separate from me, or that she would be rejected or not tolerated if she expressed any aggressive or separateness energy? Somatically, I would tend to feel very relaxed and then quite suddenly my stomach would get tense as Mary shifted the topic suddenly from an area I had not suspected was sensitive.

Mary had another lengthy relapse, but this time continued to come in for sessions. As her situation worsened, I started to feel complicit. I had a strong sense of being violated myself during one session in which Mary gleefully recounted her drinking and driving. She agreed to enter a 30-day alcohol treatment center, but I realized that there were some difficult feelings of violation and aggression which needed to be dealt with in treatment.

When again Mary returned to outpatient treatment, she was better able to tolerate distress and craving through her continued engagement of mindfulness exercises. But whereas mindfulness had been helpful and key thus far, in many ways Mary's therapy was only beginning. When the struggle with alcohol slowly slipped into the background, although still a bright, attractive woman, she realized she was almost 40, without a family, friends, or career. Existential anxiety about death, isolation, and meaninglessness began to overwhelm her. Mindfulness had, in a sense, allowed her to stabilize enough to be able to confront these existential issues more directly.

In addition to talking about these concerns directly, sensing that my exchange of sameness was key, I began to use the relationship more. Inviting conflict and disagreement with me, interestingly, was not successful, indicating to me that she needed more time being somewhat fused or identified with me (see Spotnitz's.1979 "narcissistic defense"). Instead, I emphasized joining with her, and found small but subtle ways to suggest that differences between us were not necessary, unless she wanted them. At times, I asked her a question, such as, "What makes you think we need to be different?" I was attempting to support the resistance to separateness, so that when she felt ready to express difference, it would be her choice and not mine.

Interestingly, the less I resisted the feeling of sameness with Mary, the more she began to disagree with me in small ways. I made a point of being very encouraging and curious about these small disagreements, while also careful not to collapse the space of difference between us. In the process, she gradually became more open to addressing her sense of loss over the last 10 years and her fear of a future alone and without meaning. A sense of imminent death began to haunt her and she vacillated between feeling that it was too late to do anything with her life and taking small, tentative steps towards future possibilities. Rather than denying

---

[2] In psychotherapy *Exchange* refers to "the direct experience of someone else" (Wegela, 1996, p. 127) unmediated by cognition, which is made possible by the fact, according to Buddhism, that the self does not exist in a separate, solid permanent way.

this sense of death, or encouraging her sense of imminence about it, we talked about what she would like to be able to look back on in her life when it was her time to die.

Although, at times, these fears were overwhelming for her, Mary slowly was able to define a life trajectory for herself. Appropriately, contrary to my desires for her, it had nothing to do with writing. As she came to terms with the depth of her suffering and loss over the previous 10 years, she felt a yearning to help others and decided to pursue a career in nursing. Her involvement in Alcoholics Anonymous (AA) led her to reconsider her Christian faith and she joined a local church while continuing to use her mindfulness exercises. Her use of mindfulness started to evolve away from a distress tolerance technique and more towards a sort of brief but restorative contemplative prayer. A few years into her sobriety, she was accepted into nursing school in another state and terminated treatment.

## Discussion

There are a number of ways that mindfulness and an existential orientation might inform the course of a psychotherapeutic treatment. We might see mindfulness as serving either a stabilizing or alternatively a deepening adjunct to an existentially oriented psychotherapy. In Mary's case, mindfulness was essential at the outset as a technique to help her stabilize her mind and life enough before existential and relational issues could be addressed. In other cases, mindfulness, either taught to the client directly or used relationally (Surrey, 2005), could come into play later in the treatment and function more as a deepening factor. Many patients have problems, which are more due to repressed anxiety than a surfeit of it. Mindfulness can come into play in such cases as a way to contact the dimension of being more directly, and in the process, to bring repressed existential anxiety to the surface.

In any case, mindfulness is best applied individually, depending on the presenting issues of the client. Often mindfulness can be incorporated into treatment without using the word, but by suggesting appropriate exercises that have some configuration of Germer's (2005) three components of noticing, present moment direct experience, and acceptance. Additionally, the most useful and immediate application of mindfulness to existential therapy is as a practice for the therapist. The ability of the therapist to be present with experience in the therapy room without conceptual filter (greatly assisted by mindfulness practice) allows one to be open to the always-present but fragile dimension of exchange, wherein what therapist and patient experience is simultaneous and non-conceptual. Allowing and using these moments of exchange, which from a Buddhist perspective are often happening outside of awareness, can help patients to contact repressed or unacknowledged aspects of their existential experience.

## Conclusion

Both mindfulness and existential therapy suggest that the domain of being is more fundamental and more inherently open and undefined than the realm of doing or having, with which we usually identify. Both suggest that we are more than what we think, and that this *more than* has little to do with thinking. But due to their different cultural backgrounds, mindfulness and existential therapy propose differing conceptions of the self. Mindfulness helps us to see through the fiction of the self; existential therapy challenges us to re-author that fiction ourselves.

How these two philosophies or theories or techniques might work together clinically is various and dependent on the needs of the presenting patient. The suggestion here is not prescriptive, but merely that a treatment that holds both perspectives in mind is most likely to benefit individuals because it acknowledges and engages the full depth and breadth of human experience. Mindfulness and existential therapy in different ways help patients to accept the necessary realities of existence and to live fully in the midst of those realities.

## References

Baer, R. (2003). Mindfulness training as a clinical intervention: A conceptual and empirical review. *Clinical Psychology: Science and Practice, 10*, 125-143.

Batchelor, S. (1983). *Alone with others: An existential approach to Buddhism.* New York, NY: Grove Press.

Batchelor, S. (1998). *Buddhism without beliefs: A contemporary guide to awakening.* New York, NY: Riverhead Books.

Bunting, K., & Hayes, S. C. (2007). Language and meaning: Acceptance and commitment therapy and the EI model. In K. Schneider (Ed.), *Existential-Integrative psychotherapy: Guideposts to the core of practice* (pp.217-234). New York, NY: Routledge.

de Wit, H. F. (2008). Working with existential and neurotic suffering. In F. Kaklauskas, S. Nimmanheminda, L. Hoffman, & M. Jack (Eds.), *Brilliant sanity: Buddhism and psychotherapy* (pp. 3-17). Colorado Springs, CO: University of the Rockies Press.

Germer, C. K. (2005). Mindfulness: What is it? What does it matter? In C. K. Germer, R. D. Siegel, & P. R. Fulton (Eds.), *Mindfulness and psychotherapy* (pp. 3-27). New York, NY: Guilford.

Hayes, S. C., Strosahl, K. D., & Wilson, K. G. (1999). *Acceptance and commitment therapy: An experiential approach to behavior change.* New York, NY: Guilford.

Hayes, S. C., Follette, V. M., & Linehan, M. M. (2004). *Mindfulness and acceptance: Expanding the cognitive behavioral tradition.* New York, NY: Guilford.

Heidegger, M. (1998). Letter on "Humanism." In W. McNeill (Ed. & Trans.), *Pathmarks* (pp. 239-277). Cambridge, United Kingdom: Cambridge University Press. (Original work published 1946)

Hoffman, L. (2008). An existential framework for Buddhism, world religions, and psychotherapy: Culture and diversity considerations. In F. Kaklauskas, S. Nimmanheminda, L. Hoffman, & M. Jack (Eds.), *Brilliant sanity: Buddhism and psychotherapy* (pp. 19-38). Colorado Springs, CO: University of the Rockies Press.

James, W. (1950). *The principles of psychology* (Vol. 1). New York, NY: Dover. (Original work published 1890)

Joyce, J. (1993). *A portrait of the artist as a young man.* New York, NY: Penguin. (Original work published 1916)

Kabat-Zinn, J. (2005). *Full catastrophe living: Using the wisdom of your body and mind to face stress, pain, and illness.* New York, NY: Random House.

Kaklauskas, F., Nimmanheminda, S., Hoffman, L., & Jack, M. (Eds.). (2008). *Brilliant sanity: Buddhism and psychotherapy.* Colorado Springs, CO: University of the Rockies Press.

Linehan, M. (1993). *Cognitive-behavioral treatment of borderline personality disorder.* New York, NY: Guilford.

McLeod, K. (2001). *Wake up to your life: Discovering the Buddhist path of attention.* New York, NY: HarperCollins.

Rahula, W. (1974). *What the Buddha taught* (Rev. ed.). New York, NY: Grove Press.

Sartre, J. (1987). *Existentialism and human emotions.* New York, NY: Citadel Press. (Original work published 1957)

Segal, Z. V., Williams, J. M., & Teasdale, J. T. (2001). *Mindfulness-based cognitive therapy for depression: A new approach to preventing relapse.* New York, NY: Guilford.

Spotnitz, H. (1979). Narcissistic countertransference. *Contemporary Psychoanalysis, 15,* 545-559.

Sujato, A. (2005). A history of mindfulness: How insight worsted tranquility in the satipatthana sutta. Retrieved from http://www.dhammaweb.net/dhammabook/view.php?id=95

Surrey, J. (2005). Relational psychotherapy, relational mindfulness. In C. K. Germer, R. D. Siegel, & P. R. Fulton (Eds.), *Mindfulness and psychotherapy* (pp. 91-112). New York, NY: Guilford.

Trungpa, C. (1995). *The path is the goal.* Boston, MA: Shambhala.

Wallace, B. A. (2006). *The attention revolution: Unlocking the powers of the focused mind.* Boston, MA: Wisdom Publications.

Wegela, K. (1996). *How to be a help instead of a nuisance: Practical approaches to giving support, service & encouragement to others.* Boston: Shambhala.

Yalom, I. D. (1980). *Existential psychotherapy.* New York, NY: Basic Books.

Yalom, I. D. (2000). *Love's executioner: & other tales of psychotherapy.* New York, NY: Harper.

# Chapter 13

## In and Out of the Distress:
## A Survival Philosophy of Shi Tie-Sheng

Wensheng Wang
Translated by Joseph Siu

Shi Tie-Sheng (2001a, b, c, d; 2002, 2008) is regarded as an outstanding writer who is worthy to be studied by modern psychologists. The characters in his writings provide us with great insight into the psychology of human nature, both the benign and the pathological. At the same time his literary writings contain a number of existential philosophical themes, which deepen our understanding of the nature of meaning in existential psychotherapy.

Shi, (2001c) was physically disabled and remarked that he chose writing as his career because it "kept him from taking his own life" (p. 19). Shi identified strongly with his characters who were often physically disabled, many afflicted with handicaps such as cancer or blindness. In 1972, Shi himself suffered from a tumor in his spinal cord, which caused the lower half of his body to be paralyzed at age 21. Shi's paralysis caused him a great deal of distress and impelled him to question his very existence. He felt completely hopeless and suddenly confronted with his helplessness. He had to come to terms with the fact that:

> He would never be able to stand up again. He had to give up the opportunity to receive a college education. He lived like in invalid without the ability to obtain a decent job in society. Sadly, everyone applauded his perseverance, but none would offer their daughters in marriage. (Shi, 2001b, p. 152)

During his hospitalization, Shi shared his pain with and befriended a number of his fellow patients. There was a 7-year-old boy from a remote village who became paralyzed for life after falling out of a car during play. The boy struggled mightily with accepting his painful reality. He was forever regretful. There was also a flourishing young man who had to give up a recent romantic relationship and his dream of studying abroad because of a medical mishap. These ordeals changed their lives forever. They reminded Shi of Heidegger's (1927) concept of people being abandoned onto the world, left to tremble at their encounters with an awesome transcending power.

Trembling best describes Shi's (2001b) inner state when was faced with this overwhelming force. It describes Shi's attitude as he began his journey into his spirit/soul. Because of this attitude, Shi's soul searching was distinguished from others in that he seldom raised the questions, "Why Me? or Why this suffering?" Instead of looking for reasons, Shi searched for the *meaning* of his suffering. Shi's reflections did not arise out of his Chinese tradition with words of wisdom such as, "Out of the Depth of Misfortune Comes Bliss" (否極泰來) or "Blessing is the flip side of Misfortune" (禍兮福之所倚). Instead, Shi's comprehension derived from his understanding of the book of Job in the Bible. This is evident from the fact that several quotations from the Biblical character of Job can be found in Shi's writings including *A Patient's Notes* (病隙碎笔) and his novel *My Ding Yi Journey (*我的丁一之旅).

The Book of Job in the Bible provides a narration of the mystery of suffering. Suffering is a difficult theological topic. In reading the Book of Job, Shi noticed two important themes that provided a mental map helping him to cope with suffering. The first theme was the sovereignty of God. Shi's character, Ding Yi, ponders, "What or who is causing me to suffer from my sin? For what purpose?" Shi recaped the story from the Bible, which "occurred long before Ding Yi's time wherein God asked Job 'Where were you when I created the Universe?'" (Shi, 2008). The second theme which helped Shi to cope with suffering was Job's faith:

> Job had a genuine faith towards God. Job's faith was not built on promises of blessings, instead it was tested with unceasing tribulations.... God's revelation of His almighty creation to Job allowed Job to gain perspective and submit to the mighty reality that suffering is an integral part of world and cannot be taken away. (Shi, 2002, p. 5)

Shi acknowledged with awe and respect that any causation of sufferings ought to be in the mystery of God. In addition, Shi also realized that Job's faith and his life were purified by his trials, which is the real meaning of suffering! This revelation subsequently led Shi to accept his persecutions as that from which he could discover the true meaning of his own suffering.

Although *Original Sin, Predestination (*原罪·宿命), one of Shi's (2001d) novels, was initially regarded as a fatalistic analysis in suffering, its tenets are quite different from fatalism. The narrator began his tale from the end of the story to explain how his tragedy was predestined. He ruminated:

> Because I was late for that one second, or if only I could have waited one more second, or in other words, because I departed one second too soon or if only I could have departed even one second earlier, then I could have avoided a lifetime of being paralyzed. (Shi, 2001d, p. 158)

The ultimate meaning of the story boiled down to a puzzle within the author's mind "Why did the ordeal happen?" (Shi, 2001d, p. 163). "The past merely vanished into thin air (烟消雲散). And the cold, inhumane callous world turned its back on you, leaving you utterly alone" (Shi, 2001d, p. 161). It can also be seen that the life of the fine young man, who had accomplished so much in regard to his plans to study abroad, was turned upside down in the wink of an eye, from prosperity to adversity in a second! Whose fault is it? Blame it on the distraction of the loud and passive fart from the dog, which provided the momentary distraction that caused the tragic and life-changing delay. It concerned none and was no one's fault. Such things happen sensibly. Nonetheless, tragedy occurs. Could it be true that their destiny was altered by the fart! Who could control a fart of a dog? Fatalists would explain this in terms of predestination. They might view that man is merely a pawn in human destiny. One's significance has nothing to do with whatever occurs. To this, Shi sighed asking:

> Why? Why? Why? Why the fart?"
> Why ask why?
> God said, Let there be fart. There was fart. And God saw that it was good. That's the way things are. There were evenings and there were mornings. All this happened in the days following the seventh day of creation. (Shi, 2001d, p. 170)

Shi's insights regarding the meaning of suffering made him a writer distinct from the fatalists. In many of his writings, Shi made sustaining arguments for the necessity of suffering. An individual's life is like a play on the stage, a spectacle unto the world. There are many roles to be acted out in the play. Without exception, both the fortunate and the misfortunate have their roles. Accordingly, Shi discovered the mission of his life. That is, to endeavor to fulfill his role and the suffering that has been commissioned by God. This rendered his life worthy and gave meaning to his existence. His commitment to his role not only enabled him to flee from self-blame, despair, and hopelessness, it also increased his self-esteem. As one of the many roles designated by Sovereignty, the disabled helps those who are normal, without physical handicap, to count their blessings. Thus, the disabled are accorded their full dignity and are deserving of respect by the world.

To those who ask, "Why should I suffer all of this?", Shi (2008) would repeatedly refer to the fortuity regarding God's random arrangement. This has nothing to do with justice. In this regard, Shi's concept of suffering is seemingly more pessimistic than the Christian view of suffering. In the Gospel of John in the New Testament, Jesus' disciples asked him, "Rabbi, who sinned, this man or his parents, that he was born blind?" Jesus replied, "Neither this man nor his parents sinned, but this happened so that the work of God might be displayed in his life" (John 9:1-3). Beyond this biblical view in the Gospel of John is the core belief of the incarnation of Christ, who died on the cross for the sin of all people. The Divine Himself in Christianity had to carry his own cross and take up the bitterness and tribulation for all who suffered.

Even so, in regard to affliction, Shi (2001c) did not clearly define the relationship between suffering and grace. He asked, "Where can we find salvation for all of our ill fates?" Shi sometimes expressed his pessimistic view regarding men:

> Men will perish, the Earth will be destroyed, the universe is approaching a deathly silence. Then, what is the value and meaning of all our wisdom and wit, striving and toil, luck and success? Where are we going to and heading towards? What is our goal? Where is our joy and happiness? Where is the way of our redemption? Are we headed towards an impasse and finding nowhere to go? Truly, we are in a hopeless situation. (p. 101)

Ignoring the relationship between grace and suffering, Shi emphasizes the need for individual works of self-transcendence and the importance of the *process* of overcoming one's own troubles. In the midst of suffering, the process becomes alive wherein individuals can surpass themselves, eventually with suffering attaining happiness.

Popular belief states that a noble objective is a prerequisite for a meaningful life. However, Shi (1985) did not hold such an ontological perspective. To him, the existence of the world itself does not require an objective. The only signif-cance of the end objective is to justify the ongoing process. In other words, the ends justify the means, or the end gives meaning to the means. The goal is in fact nonexistent. It is entirely presupposed to give meaning to the process. Regardless whether the goal was presupposed or the process created, both are in fact created by human beings. Hence, Shi placed his redemptive hope clearly onto individuals, themselves, instead of following the example of Job who looked upon God for hope.

In regard to the redemptive hope to be found within individuals, Shi (1985) emphasized the wisdom of survivorship. In his book, *Ming Ruo Qin Xian* (命若琴弦) (Life resembling a zither-liked, plucked instrument), a prescription in the form of a blank piece of paper passed down through succeeding generations of the blind represented the wisdom of survivorship. It was a perfect goal prescribed for all those who desperately wanted to see. The goal of sight was prescribed in the rules, which stated that the cure for blindness to be found on that piece of paper could only be granted after a thousand of strings of the *qin* (琴) were broken through play. As a result, performing *qin* in public was no longer just a means to earn a living, given that the act had been given a higher meaning. It became the motivation and full incentive for blind old men playing their *qin* over the next 70 years. The story revealed that an old blind man had finally achieved the target in breaking a thousand strings of his *qin*. Wryly, he realized that what he really received was merely a blank paper which contained no words. Despite his despair at discovering that the piece of paper was actually blank, signifying that in actuality there was no *cure* for blindness, nevertheless, the old blind man chose to follow the example of his old master and gave this same blank piece of paper to his young apprentice advising him just as his old master had prescribed. Fully cognizant of the ruse, the old blind man knew that the pull and hope of the distant promise of cure could become the driving force in the life of the young blind apprentice. The old blind man, after a lifetime of earning the prescription, chose to engage in the same *duplicity* in helping the apprentice to live his life. Rather than exposing the apprentice to the despair of the reality of life, which might have led to further desperation, the old man, in turn, allowed his young apprentice to live happily in a white lie as hope allows one to enter into the process of life.

*Ming Ruo Qin Xian* (命若琴弦) speaks of Shi 's (2001c) understanding of the existence of humankind, suggesting that the establishment of a life goal is an essential strategy for survival. Shi did not attempt to make sense of the life goal in terms of eternal meaning, nor did he presume that people were born to a purpose. Nonetheless, Shi did show empathy for the concept of nihilism. In other words, Shi believed that "All goals are vanity. Life has only one reality. The meaning of this reality can only be found in achieving a higher level of awareness in regards to one's spirit and soul" (p. 40). In his discussion of the goal of life, Shi's view was, somewhat, contradictory. On one hand, he emphasized that individuals can only be spurred through by holding firm to an objective; on the other hand, he alluded to the idea that the goal is more or less a vanity. How then can one determine if the empty goal is real or not? Shi (2001c) offered an allegory:

> We woke up in our primitive dream and were faced with an unfathomable loneliness. However, life becomes colored and enlivened when we tell ourselves lively myths. These myths protect us from our primitive loneliness. In their pilgrimage, people galloped towards the charming myth, which promised to bring them ultimate and genuine gaiety and felicity in life. (Shi, 2001c, p. 41)

Shi's objective in life can be found in this adorable tale. He held that individuals have to discover their life meaning in the walk and circumstances of their daily experiences, very much like the old blind man. Even though his life goal involved deception, the happiness experienced each time he broke the string was real. These hopeful and joyous experiences sustained him and gave his life meaning. However, the old blind man's dream was smashed when the secret was disclosed. In a moment, he lost the drive, as well as the meaning to his life, until one day he discovered that his young apprentice needed his help and consequently, the blind man regained his meaning and purpose. He was once again able to stand on his own. Guiding his young apprentice out of distress became his sole mission. In this respect, we can understand the suffering of the young blind apprentice as meaningful. It was the existential value of the young disciple.

*Ming Ruo Qin Xian* (命若琴弦) was Shi's (2001c) search for a way out for humankind's distress. Regardless of whether the purpose originated with the self, or others, individuals who can dedicate themselves to a mission will always find hope in the midst of hopelessness. It is in their love of offering meaning to others that allows people in distress to see their accountability and commitment. As Friedrich Nietzsche (as cited in Frankl, 1993), the German existential philosopher said, "He who has a *why* to live for can bear almost any *how*" (p. 59). This life philosophy fits well with Logotherapy developed by the existential psychiatrist, Viktor E. Frankl, who said, "the utmost importance is not what we hope for in life but what life hopes for us" (p. 59).

In Shi's (2001b) point of view:

> a person in despair has two options if he or she wants to escape the temptation of death. The first option is turn him or herself into an idiot. Or, the person can come to an understanding of how the process is always after the goal. (p. 155)

Of course, Shi recommended the latter approach:

> God arranges many hurdles and hardships in the process of life, so that human beings may experience joyfulness and pleasure. ...If someone could not taste and experience such blessings and joy, life becomes a ridiculous, laborious assignment filled with bitterness. (pp. 157-158)

This is Shi's existential philosophy. He believed that the existence of suffering and death is predestined. People do not have the liberty of fleeing from tribulations; however, they do have the freedom of choosing how they will face their difficulties. This internal frame of mind so often determines the outcome of various situations.

Upon the discovery of his paralysis, Shi (2001b) revealed his desire to end his life through suicide in his writing of the *Four Pieces of Dialogues* (對話四則). When asked why he did not commit the suicide, Shi borrowed the words of Charlie Chaplin's saying, "Why hurry? Sooner or later man will die." This excuse prevented Shi from killing himself and turned him into an outstanding writer. His novel *Poison* (毒藥) is a story of dying in order to live. The narrator in the story deliberately wanted to end his life and obtained two poison pills that could kill without pain. Paradoxically, the narrator did not die but continued living his live filled with blessings. This was because of the comfort provided by the two poison pills. Whenever the narrator encountered difficulties, he would take out the two poison pills for a glimpse. They reminded him that death is always waiting at his doorstep. Paradoxically, this inspired the narrator to do all that he could do to live. Shi henceforth remarked that "though death is despairing, Chaplin's statement nonetheless transformed it into hope" (p. 155). With the existence of this hope, people are empowered to continue living:

Shi (2001b) interpreted Chaplin's lines in the following way:

> One begins first by assuming an attitude of acceptance for when you are near the end of your life, rest assured that death will naturally reach out

to rescue you. Second, being fully aware of the certainty of death, why not give life your best try? You might even have some fun with it. Your life is already tough enough. As death is so reliable and certain for a dying man, what does one have to fear? What is there to lose? (p. 155)

Ordinary people are used to the *reduction method* of viewing their lives. That is, they calculate what will be left over after summing up their troubles. Particularly for those who are devastated, they will consider that there is too little of their lives left on which they could count. On the other hand, Shi shared Chaplin's wisdom, which encourages people to embrace the *adding-up* method for living. The baseline is that we are standing at the edge of death and indeed we are in possession of nothing. Having this perspective, we will learn to begin to add up all the possibilities in our lives. This summation of life not only sheds light on the hope for living, it also provides courage for people in despair to stand up for their lives once again.

Shi's (2001c) philosophy of survivorship addresses the necessity for love. "The magnificent and unified cosmic message is fragmented and shaped into flesh which requires love to help complete and integrate our fragmentation" (p. 261). Shi was also a man of affection, surrounded by people who loved and cared about him. Recalling the days of his hospitalization at the age of 21, Shi (2001a) realized that "his friendships kept him alive" (p. 39). In his book, *The Year When I Was 21* (我二十一歲那年), Shi (2010) recounted many of his lovely classmates and applauded the nurses and physicians who quietly offered him care and support during his recovery. Further evidence of Shi's affectionate nature can be found in *My Faraway Qing Ping Wan* (2001, 我遙遠的清平灣), which reflected Shi's rural sense of innocence and purity and *The Silk Tree* (2011, 合歡樹) and *I and the Earth Temple* (2011, 我與地), which portrayed Shi's affections toward his mother. Indeed, the maternal love Shi received was a main reason for his survival.

Shi always felt grateful and lucky for having a satisfying, loving relationship. In his letter to a friend Li Jian Ming (李健鳴), Shi wrote about his own love story:

> Somewhere in the past, Yi-Tong (一同) and I sat together alone in silent companionship, comforting each other, submitting to fate (聽天由命). This silent companionship allowed Shi to feel the breadth and width of love. Shi compared the gap between sex and love to the chasm between the finite and the infinite. This is why the experience of suffering is deeper and wider than the experience of attraction. Attraction cannot prove love whereas suffering can. (Shi, 2001c, 254-255)

According to Shi's (2002) life experience, disability and love are "the two fundamental sacred codes divinely inscribed into humanity" (p. 65). Shi likened the two codes to the concepts of original sin and redemption:

> Love belongs to the spirit. She is a dream and hope for human perfection
> and fulfillment. It is boundless and it renders the possibility in the break-
> through of our limitations and constraints. It also compensates for man's
> imperfections and disability. (p. 65)

Hence, love has the power of redemption. No wonder Shi expounded so much in
his writings regarding the rights for the disabled to love. People have often been
suspicious of the ability for the disabled to love. From this, Shi was able to discern
a deeper form of discrimination against the disabled. However, Shi's emphasis
upon the alienable rights for the disabled to love came not out of his own disability
nor people's deep prejudices against the disabled. Instead, Shi's motivation for
championing for the rights of the disabled arose out of a deeper metaphysical
conviction regarding the humanity of the disabled. Shi was most concerned with
the relationship between disability and love. He was not limiting himself to just
physical disabilities but included all those who were impaired and bound by external bondage and imperfections. People are isolated and desolated because of
their limitations as well as their disabilities, and a love relationship could be
viewed as a call for reconciliation, wherein our other half is found to possess a
similar soul yearning in loneliness. Shi, thus, professed that when it comes to
loving relationships, people's hearts are in heaven even if their bodies are mired
in the abyss. Shi realized this to be the fulfillment of love in religion. The possibility and hope of human redemption is to be grounded in the possibility of the
disabled to love.

In summary, the aforementioned acceptance of suffering, the analysis of
meaning for individuals in despair, the prescribed goal of life, the life process
creation as well as the redemptive power of love, are all characterized in Shi 's
philosophy of life. They also form a structure to his idea of survivorship. In
reading and reflecting upon these ideas, we see Shi's wisdom in life and the
effectiveness of his life meaning analysis for overcoming people's distress. The
intellectual insights formulated in Shi's survivor philosophy incorporate values
from both Western Christian culture and Chinese traditional philosophy.
Although Shi rarely elicited the latter, from his emphasis on the survivor wisdom,
his pursuit of happiness and his praise for the efforts for the individual, we can
understand that his propositions have their roots in the Chinese traditional
culture. With these attributes in place, Shi's writings can be recognized as useful
learning materials in development of an indigenous Chinese psychotherapy.

### References

Frankl, V. E. (1993). *Man's search for meaning*. Beijing, China: Translation & Publishing
    Corporation.
Heidegger, M. (1927). *Being and time*. (J. Stambaugh, Trans.) New York, NY: State
    University of New York Press.
Shi, T. (2001a). *Acacia*. Jinan, Shangdong, China: Literature Publishing House.
Shi, T. (2001b). *Dialogue practice*. Changchun, Shidai, China: Literature Publishing House.

Shi, T. (2001c). *Writing as destiny*. Jinan, Shangdong, China: Literature Publishing House.
Shi, T. (2001d). *Zhong Sheng*. Taiyuan China: Beiyue Literature Publishing House.
Shi, T. (2002). *A patient's notes*. Xian, Shan'xi, China: Shan'xi Normal University Press.
Shi, T. (2008). *My Ding Yi journey*. Beijing, China: People's Literature Publishing House.

# Chapter 14

## Dream Idioms:
## Using Chengyu, Idioms, and Proverbs to Interpret Dreams

### Richard Bargdill

Dreams have been useful in terms of helping people determine how to behave and what to look out for, as well as understanding what is going on in their lives that they could be overlooking. The principles of existential dream analysis were formulated by Medard Boss (1958, 1979) and Erik Craig (1987, 1990). Both Boss and Craig drew attention to dreams as real experiences that offer a chance to reflect on the situations they present. Thus, dreams are learning opportunities. Western people developed the saying that "Well, it's just a dream," as if dreams should be ignored. The West's negligence of dreams was confronted by Freud (1901), Jung (1960), and Boss (1958, 1979). From an existential perspective, dreams can show one's current emotional state, such as nightmares revealing anxieties and flying dreams revealing freedom. Dreams sometimes might reveal the future, and repetitive dreams can indicate one is stuck. The outstanding dream images can have powerful symbolic quality for the dreamer rather than being universal dream symbols, as Freud (1900/1998) proclaimed.

Boss (1958) suggested that it is important to look at the dreams themselves. This is a helpful and simple approach to interpreting dreams. This entails a phenomenological way of looking at the elements in the dreams. The goal is to describe in ordinary language what happened in the dream or describe what the confusing characters or things, in fact, are. Dreams have a linguistic quality to them; therefore speaking or writing down the dream often reveals clues to what the dream is trying to communicate. A small barking dog in a dream might be reflecting the saying that a "dog's bark is worse than its bite," which could reveal some current problem in one's life appears larger than it actually is.

Contemporary existential psychologists have concentrated on the attitude the therapist adopts toward a client's dream (Dias, 2016). Existential therapists offer the clients the chance to explore a dream. They listen closely with presence to the dream description, inquire about the client's understanding of the dream's meaning, highlight emotional nuances and significant dream actions, and reiterate powerful phrases that the client might utter about the dream without realizing the significance (Dias, 2016; Underwood & Bargdill, 2016).

I often recommend that people start a dream journal. It is best to place the journal next to one's bed before going to sleep and ask to be visited by a dream. This can be said out loud or just in one's head: "My dreams are important to me. I want to remember my dreams." When a dream comes forth, write down a few words to capture the main elements of the dream, and then, go back to sleep. Maybe, in the dream, the dreamer is out at sea on a boat and comes across a whale—then writing "Boat" and "Whale" is usually enough to remember the dream upon waking. If this does not do the trick, then try writing down a sentence. One might purchase a "light pen" that has a tiny flashlight at the end; it is helpful for making notes in the dark to avoid turning on the light, which may fully awaken a person making it more difficult to return to sleep. Writing down a dream, in a way, honors the dream and invites more to appear.

Dreams work behind the scenes. They are processing feelings and ideas pertaining to what happened during the day and mixing that in with one's memories. At night, dreams help formulate or process psychological material. Thus, often dreams are powerful communications from one's unconscious (Bargdill, 2014). People have discovered important insights that they were working on in dreams. For example, the famous Benzene ring was discovered at night in a dream (Van De Castle, 1995). The man who came up with the final formula of how the Benzene ring works had a dream where a snake was biting its tail, then he woke up and realized that that's how the carbon atoms were organized: in a hexagon. There are some famous stories about dreams that have really changed the world for the good. One time a man who was searching for oil in the desert found the place to drill in his dream—then in waking life he saw the same feature: a lone tree. There they found the largest oil reserve in the country (Van De Castle, 1995).

How does one understand these messages in dreams? I believe that many dreams contain idioms, which are linguistic turns of phrases. There are idioms in every language that become common sayings that are heard over and over. For example, one English idiom states: "a penny saved is a penny earned." If this idiom appeared in a dream, it might be that the dreamer finds a piece of gold, picks it up, and places it in a bag. She stores the bag in her room and when she needs the gold she goes and finds that instead of one piece there is a whole bag of gold. Psychologically, this might be telling a person to stay with one's strengths, instead of trying to add new skills—to keep advancing what one is already adept at doing. This way, one might become more masterful rather than trying to add another technique with beginner skills.

In Mandarin, there are a number of idioms that take the form of four-character collections called "Chengyu" (Rohsenow, 2002). They tell an entire story in a shorthand form. A noteworthy one is about Mengzi's (or *Mencius'*) mother, who moved three times. It is the story of how Mencius' mother was a single mother raising him alone. She found him socializing with the children of business owners or the children of young soldiers. Mengzi was playing shop or playing war with them. Concerned about this, Mengzi's mother moved a couple of times. Finally, she moved him to where the neighbors were educators so that when he was out playing, he would play like he was the teacher. She thought, "Oh, this is good." This story speaks to motherhood and surrounding yourself and your children with the people that you find admirable.

If I had a dream where I first was in my childhood house, then I was in a college dorm room, and then the dream ended with me in my current home with my spouse—the dream might have a Mengzi quality to it. It could be asked if this dream is really about me, either needing to move my child to be surrounded with the right people or asking if I am with the right people. What I am suggesting is that dreams are primarily understood by transcribing them into language (Bachino, 2009). Upon having a dream, one approach is to ask oneself if there are any idioms that have the same elements in them. In a dream workshop I facilitated, a Mandarin speaker told of a dream where there were dogs and chickens. It turns out there is a Chengyu in her region that has these two elements. The purpose of the proverb/idiom is to say that these two animals do not mix well. The dreamer reported that she and her boyfriend were currently having problems with their two families getting along.

At night while having a dream, sometimes there is a movie quality to it. While watching it, there is talking occurring. However, in the morning once awake and remembering the dream, it important to realize that dreams are largely visual and as one tries to figure out what the dream means, it may be necessary to put the images into language. Writing them out or speaking them out is where one often finds the clues to the dream's meaning. The dreamer can gain access to the meaning of the dream by listening to how one describes the dream and at the same time comparing the action of the dream with the events that have recently occurred in one's life. Sometimes it is important to consider that words can have multiple meanings, which indicates that what the dream is saying might have a secondary property rather than what appears to be the primary message. Once again, confusing dreams often indicate that the dream has a message that needs to be deciphered. For example, I had a dream that I *missed* a class that I was attending as a student. In waking life, I am very punctual and I never missed class because I also enjoyed school. I could not figure out the message of the dream that I missed or was absent and late for class. The dream made much more sense when I used a secondary definition of missed, meaning there was something I longed for. I missed being in school!

My understanding is that in Pin Yin version of Mandarin that the same word can have three different versions based on the pronunciations that are either neutral, sharp, or fluctuating (-, /, or ~). A dreamer who might remain confused about the meaning of the dream might have to consider other pronunciations of the same word in addition to potential idioms and double meanings that words might have. Frequently, it is advocated that a good interpretation for the dream has been achieved when there is an *Aha moment.* Usually, this means the dreamer says, "I think I know what this dream is about!" Often, this is what is sought in dream interpretation, as it suggests that an important meaning has been found.

I have a few are samples of dreams that I will use to illustrate a few final points:

- A woman dreams that she is sleeping and suddenly a big old sewer rat climbs up the footboard of her bed and is under the sheets.
- A man dreams that he is driving when he comes to a hill and starts to pick up speed. He tries to apply the brakes and they do not work. He sees that at the bottom of the hill there is a certain crash.
- A young man dreams that he is hiking up a huge mountain and the summit is near. Suddenly the path narrows, and he can look over the cliff; he sees it is a long way down. He fears falling and, in the dream, he slips.

It is important to note that all the dreamers are English speakers. If the dreamer would be a Mandarin speaker, this would change the interpretation. The reason is there are different associations to certain words in particular languages. For example, the word *rat* in English would almost unanimously be considered to have negative meanings to it. Rat suggests someone who is thief, a cheater, a manipulator or one who betrays another, or it represents filth or disease, to mention only a few. However, there are a few positive attributes that one would have to consider if they were a Mandarin speaker. There was a *year of the rat*, and at least some of the positive attributes of the rat are ambitious, intelligent, persuasive, sociable, charming, god like, charismatic, shrewd, industrious, meticulous, tenacious, and artistic.

In the first dream, the dreamer asked me what I thought her dream meant. I asked her one question that appeared to help her ascertain a primary meaning of the dream. I said, "Tell me about your boyfriend!" Her eyes widened and she said, "Ah ha, I understand the dream." The dream was about a rat who crawled in bed with her. Rat can be translated as *cheater*. In this dream, the dreamer was being told that she did not trust her boyfriend to be faithful. When he was in bed with her, she felt like she was in bed with a "dirty old rat!"

The second dream reflects a common theme. People are often confused by such dreams largely because they want to interpret it literally: They believe that the dream is saying that there is something wrong with their automobile. In English, the idiom that seems most relevant is, "You are going downhill fast," which means that due to your own behavior you are experiencing a number of unfortunate events and do not seem able to stop yourself. There appears to be a fatal crash ahead of you if you do not change your behavior. In other words, the dream is saying, "You are out of control and your behavior is destructive."

The final dream reflects a theme that people often have as they close in on a long-anticipated goal. It is a dream theme that students frequently have in the last year at the university. Upon nearing a summit of a mountain, they suddenly look down and see how high they are, and then fall off the path often walking toward their death. The dream speaks to fearing the end of a successful long journey. The idiom in English that might best describe this dream as: "Being scared of your own success." The dreamer might feel that the success they are about to achieve is suddenly not warranted. They are concerned that they cannot live up to the expectation of being a college graduate or whatever title they are about to receive.

In a sense, the dreamer feels like a fraud and has to come to terms with the fact that they deserve the achievement for which they are about to be acknowledged.

One way to understand dreams is to look into the wisdom history of one's own language and try to see if there might be an idiom that helps explain what the dream is trying to say. Any single dream interpreter—Freud, Jung, Boss, or my own ideas—will not work for all of the dreams. But if different approaches can help the dreamer find a valuable meaning, then these approaches are beneficial. This has two benefits. First, it gives the dreamer a hint at what a dream might be communicating. Second, it engenders interest in one's own language and where these particular idioms came from, what they initially meant, and how that meaning has changed. If dream idiom is found, the most important step is to ask how that idiom relates to one's life today. What is the dream trying to say?

In conclusion, a dream often contains a message to the dreamer. The message frequently can be discovered in the form of a linguistic idiom. An idiom is a common saying in the dreamer's native language. The dream action will loosely portray this idiom either through the plot of the dream or in a symbol that has some personal significance to the dreamer. The dreamer can discover this idiom by describing or writing down the dream and simultaneously paying attention to the common idioms that might emerge in the description. The dreamer then would try to determine if the idiom pertains to the events in one's life that are currently taking place. The dreamer often will have an intuitive *Aha* experience when they find the meaning of the dream.

## References

Bachino, M. (2009). *Two tongues for a dream: A hermeneutic study*. (Doctoral dissertation). Available from ProQuest Dissertations & Theses Global database (UMI No. 304882129)

Bargdill, R.W. (2014). *An artist's thought book: Intriguing thoughts about the artistic process*. Colorado Springs, CO: University Professors Press.

Boss, M. (1958). *The analysis of dreams*. New York, NY: Philosophical Library.

Boss, M. (1979). *I dreamt last night....* New York, NY: Gardener Press.

Craig, P.E. (1990). An existential approach to dream work. In S. Krippner (Ed.), *Dreamtime and dreamwork* (pp.69-77). Los Angeles, CA: Jeremy P. Tarcher.

Craig, P. E. (1987) The realness of dreams. In R. A. Russo (Ed.), *Dreams are wiser than men* (pp.35-57). Berkeley, CA: North Atlantic Books.

Dias, J. (2016). Existential psychotherapy and dreamwork. In J. Lewis & S. Krippner (Eds.), *Working with dreams and PTSD nightmares: 14 approaches for psychotherapists and counselors* (pp. 39-49). Santa Barbara, CA: Praeger.

Freud, S. (1998). *The interpretation of dreams*. New York, NY. Avon. (Original work published in 1900).

Jung, C. G. (1960) General aspects of dream psychology (R. F. C. Hull, Trans.) In G. Adler & R. F. C. Hull, Eds.), *The collected works of C. G. Jung* (Vol. 8, pp. 237-289). Princeton, NJ: Princeton University Press. (Original work published in 1969).

Rohsenow, J. S. (2002). *ABC dictionary of Chinese proverbs*. Honolulu, HI: University of Hawai'i Press.

Underwood, J. & Bargdill, R. W. (2016). Consciousness. In R. Bargdill & R. Broomé (Eds.), *Humanistic contributions to psychology 101: Growth, choice and responsibility* (pp. 54-59). Colorado Springs, CO: University Professors Press.

Van De Castle, R. L. (1995). *Our dreaming mind*. New York, NY: Ballantine Books.

# Chapter 15

## The African Usage of Existential Psychotherapy

**Anthony K. Nkyi**

Everything can be taken from a man but one last thing: the last of the human freedoms—to choose one's own attitude in any given set of circumstances, to choose one's own way.

~ Victor Frankl, 1985, p. 86

It has been a journey learning to live Victor Frankl's (1985) philosophy of existentialism. Frankl's quote resonated with me when I started reflecting on the Ghanaian Akan maxims "life is what you make it" and "the clan is merely a multitude." These two proverbs point to the principle of personal responsibility and the value of self-reliance, respectively (Gyekye, 1996). In line with the existential psychotherapy, it helps me to help people take personal responsibility and change their attitude while, at the same time, I learn to change mine. A central theme of existential psychotherapy is taking personal responsibility, as a result of the freedom to choose.

My experience with existential therapy began in the United States of America while studying for my doctorate in clinical psychology. A few months in China gave me the opportunity to build upon my knowledge and practice of existential psychotherapy in the West to prepare me to advance existential psychotherapy in Ghana. My interest grew from what I learned about existential therapy from my mentor, Louis Hoffman.

After immersion in the field of existential psychology, I appreciated the immense contribution it has had on my practice as a clinician working in Ghana. Indeed, my understanding and experience of existential psychology helped me recognize how it could be adapted and applied in different cultures, especially in Africa. Although existential psychotherapy might fit African culture or could require adaptation before it can be applied in a culturally-sensitive manner (see Yang & Hoffman, 2019), I am fully convinced of the psychotherapeutic value of the existential givens, which are universal conditions that all people must face that require culturally and personally specific answers (see chapter 16).

## Existential Psychology through an African/Ghanaian Lens

There appears to be a paradox related to the existential concepts and techniques in African usage (Nkyi, 2015b). While in one breath, Africans declare human existence to be the community responsibility and freedom of choice is placed on the community, on another breath, the place of freedom, choice, and responsibility for the individual in an African community is also emphasized. This paradox reflects the confrontation between the historical African values and the influence of Western modernity. Regardless, this paradox has something to offer the advancement of existential psychotherapy, which often has reflected an individualistic bias that may not fit with all cultures.

Existential psychotherapy in Africa cannot be understood without a discussion of the African worldview or, in Ghana, without the Ghanaian worldview. The assertion that the African worldview and Western thought/worldview exist and are different is supported by several studies (Gyekye, 1995). Van der Walt (1997) indicated that African thought exists and differs from Western thought in that Western thought generally ignores the spiritual dimension of phenomena and focuses on the visible, measurable, physical reality. In contrast, the African worldview is based on African cultural beliefs, practices, and values (Asante, 1987) and African culture (Barker, 1999). African culture refers to the customs, beliefs, values, ideology, and religious behaviour of the group, knowledge habits, skills, arts, and way of life of African people (Graham & Al-Krenawi, 2003) Mekada (1999) indicated that the African worldview embraces the understanding of the interconnectedness of all things; the spiritual nature of human beings; collective individual identity; the collective/inclusive nature of family structure; the oneness of mind, body, and spirit; and the value of interpersonal relationships. Despite the cultural diversity arising from ethnic pluralism in Africa, Gyekye, (1995) indicated that there are also common threads of underlying affinity running through the beliefs, customs, value systems, socio-political institutions, and practices of the various African societies. In discussing the African worldview, one must not forget to talk about the religious beliefs of the African people.

According to Gyekye (1996), religion has a central place in the life of the vast majority of African people, who hold the believe that God is ever present and a part of their consciousness. Invariably the African worldview does interpret the world as being comprised of polarities; it does not separate what is considered religious and non-religious, the sacred from secular, the spiritual from the material in their life and thoughts, as is present in the Western. The African worldview experiences everything as connected. Thus, in Africa, detaching oneself from the religion of the community is to lose one's meaning in life (Gyekye, 1996). To detach or separate the religious or spiritual component, as is often done in the West, would require a reworking of the beliefs—both implicit and explicit—regarding the nature of persons in the African worldview.

The existential characteristics in an African Ghanaian Community (Akan) is based on the belief of how we, the Akans in Ghana, see the human person. To the

Akan people, a person consists of a body (*nipadua*) made from the blood of the mother (*mogya*); an individual spirit, the *sunsum* derives from the father at conception, which is the main bearer of one's personality; and a third entity, the soul (*okra*) from God (Appiah, 2004; Sarpong, 1974). The *okra* is a sort of life force that departs from the body only at the person's last breath and is often said to be sent to a person at their birth, as the bearer of one's *nkrabea*, or destiny, from God (*Nyame*). The *sunsum*, unlike the *okra*, may leave the body during life (Appiah, 2004; Sarpong, 1974).

The personhood bestows on the individual issues concerning his existence. These include issues of meaning and meaninglessness, freedom and responsibility in the face of destiny (see May, 1981), communal duties and obligations, issues of possibilities and creativity, of being a being-unto-death, as well as many other issues related to one's existential condition. Thus, according to Gyekye (1996), the Akan maxim confirms an individual's personal responsibility to make meaning in life: "Life is what you make it." The Akan maxim appears to resemble the existentialist principle in the philosophy of Jean-Paul Satre (1948), "Man is nothing else but what he makes of himself" (p. 28).

Indeed, Sartre's (1948) version of existentialism encapsulates this point in his contention that we are what we make ourselves; that is, each person's identity is an evolving process rooted in the actions and meanings that make up existence. Although both the Akan maxim and existentialist principles point to individual responsibility for one's situation in life, the Akan maxim is more theistic (Gyekye, 1996, see also Nkyi, 2015b), thus, the sort of attitudes that an African sees as meaningful, and how he goes about achieving them, includes having to confront these issues to enable one's ability to find a sense of meaning in life.

I previously articulated the place of freedom, choice, and responsibility for the individual in an African community, including the essential place of destiny. (Nkyi, 2015b). The word *destiny* used in this paper is meant to explain in the context of the Akan understanding of it. Destiny here means the message given to the individual by God to come in this world that determines the manner in which the individual was to live. The word destiny has come to mean *fate*, involving what one is sent into the world to be. Gyekye (1996), suggested the philosophical question that one could ask is, "If the person is destined, can he be held responsible for his or her actions?" Although an African person is given their life and destiny by the Creator (Supreme Being), the individual has the freedom to work out the details of his destiny within the context of a closely-knit community that provides the necessary help for such a task (Gyekye, 1996). One is, therefore, tempted to conclude that the individual is held responsible for his actions, though not for the ultimate direction his life may take.

Thus, belief in the freedom and the capacity for human people in Africa is to make choices based on their uniqueness as individuals and their connection to a collective (Nkyi, 2015b). How then is existential psychotherapy applicable to African usage? Based on the worldviews, the cultural practices, and the proverbs in the Akan culture, I argue that as I indicated previously (Nkyi, 2015b) that the use of existential tenets appears to be paradoxical because, on one hand, personal responsibility, freedom and choice are rested on the community, and, on the other hand, freedom, responsibility, and choice are rested on the individual (Nkyi, 2015b). However, the principles of existential psychotherapy are quite amenable to African usage even though existential psychology in its usage in Africa appears to rest on the assumption that freedom, choice, and responsibility are inhibited by their culture (Nkyi, 2015b). Thus, the application in Africa requires some degree of adaptation to be applied in a culturally sensitive manner. This adaptation, though, could also be valuable when existential psychology is applied with many individuals in the West.

The view that human beings are born with the innate tendencies to grow, develop, and make a meaningful life, both in this world and the after-world, is in line with the African use of existential therapy. Nkyi (2015b) outlined some basic assumptions for the application of existential therapy in the Africa setting:

1.  Both communal and individualistic values of Africans are able to co-exist. That means the interactions between the individual and the community are both important in dealing with existential issues. This will reduce the position of *bad faith* among individuals and bring authenticity to the individual (see Sartre, 1948), to be true to ourselves, in the sense of being true to the fact that we are self-creating processes including the spiritual challenges;

2.  That each African must confront their life, even within the community, and to work within the community to make life meaningful;

3.  That meaning in life as an African is achieved by expanding one's abilities and experiencing these fully;

4.  That human existence is characterized by a radical sense of freedom that means that each individual African has to take responsibility for his or her choices and actions as well as the consequences to which those choices lead;

5.  That each African possesses the freedom to make decisions and is prepared to accept responsibility for their life circumstances;

6.  That spirituality is not egocentric, but in part communal, meaning that a person's spiritual needs are met within their community. It is within the community that the African is able to have a sense of belongingness and a connection with others.

7.  That the individual African would be much better understood within the social context in which he or she operates.

8.  In therapists/helpers' and clients' relationships, growth occurs primarily in bringing meaning to the client's life and that helpers need to direct and advise clients to make their own choices.

9.  That human existence is characterized by a sense of radical freedom that means that each individual African has to take responsibility for his or her

choices and actions and the consequences. Freedom to choose implies one being self-aware of who one is.

10. That the African worldview and socio-cultural context is necessarily help-ful to understand the African's experiences and conditions and recognize the particular financial and economic burdens in working with African clients (Nkyi, 2015a). For example, some clients see a therapist as a provider and helper who should be offering financial help to the client. Indeed, sometimes clients come to counselling with many different needs that include material and financial concerns that they expect the therapist to provide for them.

## What Do Africans Experience in the Midst of Existential Suffering: A Meaning in Life?

The African culture values collectivism, and primary consideration is given to what is good for the group. In such cultures, an emphasis on individual choice, personal responsibility, and autonomy is sometimes emphasized. For individuals in poorer countries, where many are often exposed to poverty, famine, underemployment, poor housing, poor health, and poor quality of education, the individual might fail to learn and accept their conditions of life. Furthermore, some of these individuals will attribute their life situation more toward external factors and, therefore, will not accept the responsibility for their personal re-sponses. Success and failures are, therefore, not due to their own efforts, but due to the society and group. While individuals can believe they are masters of their own fate, and their actions do affect the outcomes, they also believe that their achievement depends solely on the actions of the group. This sometimes could lead to many Africans adopting a position of *bad faith*—that is, of seeking to deny that freedom by giving many excuses in order to take refuge in external causes: "The circumstances forced me to behave in that way" or indeed internal causes: "I can't make it, I have no power, it's my nature." Existential therapy's emphasis on individual responsibility and freedom can, therefore, be misunderstood.

Existential psychology can be recognized as helping people recognize and assert their personal freedom even in situations where this might be limited by one's context, social condition, and other factors that one is thrown into and unable to control. This may not resolve the social challenges imposed upon a person, but it may help them to recognize the freedom they do have, which may further help them begin to address how they respond to what is beyond their control and even feel more empowered to challenge and possibly change the social context in which they are placed.

## References

Asante, M. (1987). *The Afrocentric Idea.* Philadelphia, PA: Temple University Press.

Appiah, K. A. (2004). *"Akan and Euro-American Concepts of the Person"* In: Lee M. Brown (Ed), *African Philosophy: New and Traditional Perspectives*, Oxford, England: Oxford University Press.

Barker, R. L. (1999). *The Social Work Dictionary.* Washington, DC: NASW Press.

Frankl, V. (1985). *Man's search for meaning.* New York, NY: Simon & Schuster.

Gyekye, K. (1995). *African Philosophical Thought: The Akan conceptual scheme.* Philadelphia, PA: Temple University Press.

Gyekye, K. (1996*). African cultural values: An introduction.* Accra, Ghana: Sankofa Publishing.

May, R. (1981). *Freedom and destiny.* New York, NY: Norton.

Mekada, J. G. (1999). The African-centered worldview: toward a paradigm for social work. *Journal of Black Studies, 30*(2): 53-59

Nkyi, K. A. (2015a). Development and Implementation of a psychoeducational group for Ghanaian adolescents experiencing parental divorce. *The Journal for Specialists in Group Work, doi: 10.1080/01933922.2015.1017069. Published online: 24 Mar 2015.*

Nkyi, K. A. (2015b). Existential psychotherapy: The historical development and current practice: Especially with reference to its usage in African communities. *International Journal of Psychotherapy, 19*, 3, 27-42.

Sarpong, P. (1974). *Ghana in retrospect: Some aspects of Ghanaian culture.* Accra, Ghana: Ghana Publishing.

Sartre, J-P. (1948). *Existentialism and humanism.* London, England: Eyre Methuen.

van der Walt, B. J. (1997). *Afrocentric or Eurocentric? Our task in a multicultural South Africa.* Potchefstroom, South Africa: Potchefstroom University.

Yang, M., & Hoffman, L. (2019). An existential-humanistic framework for international psychology. In L. Hoffman, M. Yang, M. Mansilla, J. Dias, M. Moats, & T. Claypool (Eds.), *Existential psychology East-West* (Vol. 2). Colorado Springs, CO: University Professors Press.

# Part 3

## Existential-Humanistic Perspectives on Culture and Myths

# Chapter 16

## Gordo's Ghost: An Introduction to Existential-Humanistic Perspectives on Myth

### Louis Hoffman

There can be no stronger proof of the impoverishment of our contemporary culture than the popular—though profoundly mistaken—definition of
myth as falsehood.

~ Rollo May, 1991, p. 2

Our greatest challenge today... is to couple conviction with doubt. By conviction, I mean some pragmatically developed faith, trust, or centeredness;
and by doubt, I mean openness to the ongoing changeability, mystery, and
fallibility of the conviction.

~ Kirk Schneider, 1999, p. 7

What is the ideal for mental health, then? A lived, compelling illusion [or
myth] that does not lie about life, death, and reality; one honest enough to
follow its own commandments: I mean, not to kill, not to take the lives of
others to justify itself.

Ernest Becker, 1973, p. 204

Just as nothing human can be found outside of culture, so too, the meaning
of everything human can be found only within one's culture.

~ Wade W. Nobles, 2006, p. 224

Myth is at the core of Rollo May's (1961, 1991, 1999a, 1999b) conception of meaning, which is a central tenet of existential-humanistic psychology (Hoffman, Vallejos, Cleare-Hoffman, & Rubin, 2015), and existential thought, in general (Vos,
2018; Vos, Cooper, Neimeyer, Scheider, & Wong, 2017). This can be seen dating
back to Nietzsche (1889/1999) as reflected in his famous statement, "If we
possess a *why* of life we can put up with almost any *how*" (p. 33). This same
sentiment was later reflected in Becker's (1973) statement, "Man cannot endure
his own littleness unless he can translate its meaningfulness on the largest
possible level" (p. 196).

Meaning provides a stabilizing and centering effect in a world that often is
dizzying and disorienting. From an existential-humanistic perspective, meaning
can be an important coping mechanism, but it is also so much more; meaning is a

basic human need. Meaning, too, is a central motivating factor that stands behind many behaviors, both constructive and problematic. In one stance, meaning drives people to the most humanistic of ideals; it inspires one to seek great personal change, to serve the greater social good, and to have compassion for the less fortunate. Without sustaining meaning, the inner experience of emptiness and meaninglessness can drive individuals to destructive pursuits of power, pleasure, and dangerous degrees distraction. As Wong (2012) pointed out, meaning serves a dual role: It helps one face, cope with, and transform suffering, and it also helps one attain psychological well-being.

As May (1991) stated:

> I speak of the *Cry* for myths because I believe there is an urgency in the need for myth in our day. Many of the problems of our society, including cults and drug addiction, can be traced to the lack of myths which will give us as individuals the inner security we need in order to live adequately in our day. (p. 9)

The lack of myth reflects a lack of meaning; a life without myth sets the foundation for many types of pathology, from the personal to the social.

The concept of *myth* can be confusing, particularly as it is used differently in existential-humanistic thought as compared with the common contemporary use of this word. A myth is a collection of related symbols, which create a worldview or meaning system; it serves as a reference for the way one sees the world and an interpreter of their experiences in the world.

The confusion around myth as a meaning system is reflected in the quote by May (1991) at the opening of this chapter. Today, myth is often misunderstood as something that is false or deceptive. Instead, May illustrated that myth refers to a meaning system in which the content cannot be *proven* true. It is not that myths are false; rather they are a matter of faith or belief. But even the idea of faith, whether interpreted in a religious sense or not, has been distorted over time. Faith, which also was traditionally understood as believing in something that cannot be proven, is frequently interpreted as factual knowledge today. Yet, the idea of the *certainty of faith is*, in reality, *contra*-faith.

Myth can be understood as more powerful than knowledge or facts; it provides a deeper and more holistic sense of meaning and security (Hoffman & Fehl, 2008; Hoffman & McGuire, 2008). Knowledge is concrete; it a partial aspect of one's experience focused on cognitions. But faith is holistic; it is a matter of belief (cognitions) and emotion. Faith, as Tillich (1957) stated, necessitates a degree of doubt. Doubt, in return, brings with it an element of potentially constructive anxiety. As discussed in chapter 1, anxiety becomes pathological when we resist or deny it. Anxiety, therefore, is a basic emotion that can help one thrive. When the reaction to anxiety is to rid oneself of it through convincing oneself of the certainty of what, in actuality, is not certain, then it becomes destructive. But anxiety and doubt can bring vitality to one's beliefs; it motives a person to continue in their pursuit of meaning and/or spirituality.

Myth is a healthier meaning system than knowledge because it has a degree of openness, doubt, and humility. In other words, myth can hold together the paradox of conviction and mystery (see Schneider, 1999); it allows one to have passion without certainty, truth without oppression, and faith without arrogance. Schneider (2004, 2009) referred to this openness to mystery as *awe*. Drawing on this language, the difference between the dry lifelessness of concrete facts is much less inspiring than the anxiety filled conceptions of mystery and awe. For Schneider, embracing awe can be an important aspect of facing many of the challenges of contemporary society, including polarization (Schneider, 2013) and the contemporary influence of technology and robotics (Schneider, 2017).

Religion provides a good illustration of this application of myth. Applying May's (1991) conception to religion, it could be stated that all world religions are myths. This is not stating that these religions are false; it is merely acknowledging that they cannot be proven true. Stated differently, *religion is a matter of faith, not knowledge*. Historically, this is not such a threat to religion as some could interpret it today. In the early premodern period, religion was a matter of faith; however, as seen in retrospect, where premodernism progressed and then gradually was replaced by modernism, the ideas of faith and belief were replaced with of the same content that is now understood as knowledge or facts (Hoffman & Kurzenberger, 2008). In other words, history turned mythos (i.e., myth) into logos (i.e., knowledge) and, thereby, changed the very nature of religion and faith.

Whether religious or not, it is difficult to deny the powerful, healing, and transforming qualities that religion and spirituality have in many people's lives. But one should not be naive about religion; it can serve destructive purposes as easily as constructive ones. When religion has gone astray, it has been at the root of many harmful judgments, hate crimes, and even wars. Religion has killed just as it has saved. When understood as a myth, religion is something that is powerfully constructive; however, when religion is turned into a rigid, definitive belief system, it often does more harm than good. This is the essence of this understanding of how religion and faith have changed provides the foundation for the distinction between the religion and spirituality in the contemporary usage of these terms. Historically, they were not separated. Over time, they were separated, in a sense, to *save religion through spirituality* (see Hoffman & Fehl, 2008; Hoffman, Hoffman, Hoffman, & Cleare-Hoffman, 2010).

May's (1991) recapturing of this classical Greek understanding of myth can be seen as a call to return to faith, although not necessarily a religious faith. Similar critiques could also be made of science, which, at one point, was understood as progressive and continually reformulating its ideas and hypotheses. There was no end to science because science was continually re-envisioning itself and reinterpreting the *facts* it discovered in the world. This is evident in the way Einstein spoke of science, which was to be awe-based, as opposed to the way science is often portrayed today in very stale characterizations.

Science, like religion, can be constructive or destructive. It is interesting that science is often used today to delimit and restrict the pursuit of knowledge. Rigid protocols, similar to religious laws, are applied to how knowledge should be pursued and the label of being *unscientific* is often intended as a very damning judgment. Science, which Freud (1927/1961) argued would replace religion, has too often instead become a religion. In psychology, this can be seen in how new and alternative approaches to science are often shunned and discouraged in the name of science (i.e., positivistic, narrowly defined understandings of science). The empirically supported treatments as well as the narrower understandings of evidence-based practice in psychology are good illustrations of this (see Hoffman & Thelen, 2018; Hoffman et al., 2015).

### Surprised by Myth: The Impact of Art

Many existentialists, as discussed in the first chapter, believe in the constructive power of the unconscious, or the *wisdom of the unconscious*. Instead of something to be feared, individuals can learn to use their unconscious productively. This is particularly true in the realm of myth. For instance, myths can be useful in helping to understand why stories, movies, or other forms of art impact us as they do.

Myths often emerge out of an individual or collective struggle in which the myth serves to provide meaning or a framework for understanding what is being experienced. Often, these needs or struggles are connected to the existential givens (see chapter 1). Sustaining myths are those which help bring meaning to the givens of existence. This, in part, explains why certain pieces of literature and art have sustaining meaning over time; they have provided meaning in the face of the existential givens. May (1991), in *The Cry for Myth*, provided examples of many myths of Western culture that have survived the test of time. The mythical nature present in some of these is evident, such as Dante's *Divine Comedy*, Goethe's *Faust*, and Fitzgerald's *The Great Gatsby*, all of which were great pieces of literature. Other myths are more allegorical and abstract, such as the myths of the frontier in United States history, the devil, and individualism. These stories and collective ideas have been able to provide sustaining meaning for many individuals. Their ongoing popularity reflects that these have been effective meaning systems in the face of the starkness of the givens. For example, the myth of the devil has been a way of dealing with issues of freedom and responsibility around the issue of evil; individualism has been a popular way of dealing with the reality of existential isolation; and Dante's *Divine Comedy* has touched on the value of painful or chal-lenging aspects of self-awareness.

This aspect of myth elucidates why people often have powerful emotional reactions to art, literature, and movies without knowing why. On the unconscious level, the person is recognizing the meaning level of the myth, particularly as it relates to the existential givens. For example, in chapter 20, Calvert and colleagues have discussed the movie *American Beauty*. Many individuals, however, would struggle at identifying what made this such an engaging movie. Its popularity was not based on action, comedy, or high drama; instead, the draw of movie was more subtle: *American Beauty* illustrated themes that many Americans struggle with when facing the givens of existence. At the same time, it may not seem as relevant to those not familiar with American culture; it is a uniquely American response to the givens.

This power of myth can be particularly useful in therapy. In recent years, several books have been written on the use of cinema therapy, or integrating the use of movies in psychotherapy (Hesley & Hesley, 2001; Solomon, 1995; Wedding, Boyd, & Niemiec, 2005). Although the approach of these books is different from an existential-humanistic approach to cinema therapy, they represent the power and influence that this form of art possesses. From an existential approach, cinema therapy and other forms of art therapy are used to promote exploration, engagement, and encounter. For example, a therapist may encourage a client to identify art, literature, or aspects of a movie that have impacted them and use these points to explore the meaning it holds for the individual. The therapist could even be more specific by asking the client to identify art or movies that impacted them or the therapist may *prescribe* a movie, instructing the client to pay attention to what stirs emotion in them. The therapist might also use movies, art, or literature to illustrate themes that emerge naturally in therapy. In essence, movies can be used to help the person explore and engage in various existential themes.

Myth also has relevance for poetry. Along with several colleagues, I recently began a series of poetry books on healing and growth that are informed by existential-humanistic psychology (Dias & Hoffman, 2017; Granger & Hoffman, 2017; Hoffman, & Fehl, 2016; Hoffman & Granger, 2015; Hoffman & Moats, 2015; Hoffman, Moats, & Greening, 2016). The series began as one book, *Stay Awhile: Poetic Narratives on Multiculturalism and Diversity*. Nathaniel Granger and I often present together on issues relevant to multiculturalism and diversity, and we began discussing our shared tendency to use poetry in our presentations on these topics. We noticed that while many conversations of about diversity often became entrenched intellectual debates where participants were no longer hearing each other, poetry often was able to break through these barriers to support the emergence of empathy and deeper listening. In part, the effectiveness of poetry is rooted in the ability to shift the focus from cognitive debate to heart-centered listening to the stories and experience of other people. The mythic element of poetry often allows for people to listen differently and, at times, relate across their differences.

The arts are not just entertainment. Art embodies a different way of being, and a different way of seeing and understanding the world. It represents a more holistic way of knowing with the potential to understand other people and the world more deeply than possible through the intellect alone. Through these qualities, art holds the potential to help people transform their emotions and who they are as a person.

## Universality and Particularity in Myths

A central tenet of this chapter, and this final section of the book, is that *myths represent the universality of the existential givens and the particularity of cultural responses to those givens*. This is principally true of the more sustaining myths. In the rest of this section, various myths are explored in the context of their meaning systems. For example, Cowan has illustrated how several novels provide powerful therapeutic effect for him in his struggles with aloneness and existential isolation. As May (E. Mendelowitz, personal communication) indicated, often the most powerful and innovative work being done on understanding human nature comes from literature and art departments at universities, not the psychology departments. The novels Cowan presented in the chapter that follows are direct in their engagement with the existential givens and were able to assist him in finding meaning in his experience. These novels, in particular, address a Western approach to dealing with the existential given of isolation.

In the East, many myths center on themes such as harmony, intercomnectedness, and choices that value the collective. Westerners will notice that the answers to existential givens are quite different than those represented in Western myths. For example, the frontier myth of the United States represents a conquering and control of nature. In the Eastern myths, what is emphasized is the idea of harmony with nature, similar to many Native American perspectives. Freedom and power are often used in the West to exert power over or mastery over; conversely, in the East, the motivation often is to use one's freedom to choose to be part of the larger whole, or to be in harmony with nature and one's culture. In the East and West, these values can be seen in the different political structures, family constellations, and values regarding material possessions. Many Eastern perspectives emphasize choices that reflect the collective first and individual second, which is the opposite of what is seen in Western myths.

In chapter 25, Cleare-Hoffman uses the Bahamian myth of Junkanoo to illustrate a response to the existential given of freedom and responsibility in a way that is neither Eastern nor Western. Junkanoo originated as an expression and celebration of freedom while still under the oppression of slavery. The Bahamians celebrated the little freedom they had, while Westerners too often take for granted or give up their abundance of freedoms. This illustrates the paradox that a genuine appreciation of freedom is often held more firmly when one's freedom is restricted or taken away. This is different than the Western ideas of freedom that often idealizes certain forms of freedom while neglecting and giving up personal freedoms at the same time.

Although myths can be personal or collective, they always emerge from a particular culture and point in history. Myths that provide particularly poignant responses to the existential givens, such as those represented in the major world religions, have a greater ability to sustain over time. Myths often are adapted, as May (1991) illustrated in the various versions of *Faust*, or they could be reinterpreted, as often seen in the sacred scriptures of the world religions. However, myths must stay relevant to maintain their sustainability for individuals.

Some myths are able to transcend culture, at least to a degree, while others are culturally limited. Hoffman, Stewart, Warren, and Meek (2014) addressed this in their discussion of *myths of self.* They illustrated that the ideals of the self are different in the East and the West. For example, Eastern cultures tend to value the collective over the individual and some perspectives, such Buddhism, value the idea of *no self.* In the West, the self is central to the Western psyche and often is aggrandized. This has powerful implications for mental health, and it must be considered anytime a Western psychology with particular assumptions about the self is applied in an Eastern context (see also Mosig, 2006; Yang & Hoffman, 2019).

Western psychology has been built around the idea of the centrality of the self and self-esteem. This might not be appropriate or could require significant modification when working with people from the East who often perceive this concept as unhealthy attachment to the self or the individual. According to Hoffman et al. (2014), the implications of this is that what is psychological healthy for people from Western cultures might not be psychologically healthy for people in Eastern cultures (see also Mosig, 2006). A danger exists in exporting Western psychology with its implicit values without considering whether it is appropriate to export it to other cultures. Similarly, it is dangerous for Eastern countries to uncritically import a Western psychology. This danger exists with existential-humanistic psychology, too. Hopefully, it is evident throughout this book that the approach of the editors and contributors is to be sensitive to this issue. Existential-humanistic psychotherapy should not be practiced the same in the East as it is in the West. Furthermore, until there has been a thorough cultural critique and the accompanying adaptations made, it might not be advisable to practice existential-humanistic therapy in the East (see Yang & Hoffman, 2019).

## Learning to See Through Myths

Existential-humanistic psychology emphasizes the importance of engagement with philosophy, literature, and the arts as part of the training process and ongoing professional development of the therapist. This seems odd to many; however, it remains essential to the process of becoming an existential-humanistic therapist. I would go as far as claiming that no existential-humanistic psychotherapy training is complete without direct engagement with the arts.

This engagement is evident throughout Rollo May's writings. In May's final book, *The Psychology of Existence* (1995) written with Kirk Schneider, the reader is introduced to the major philosophical and literary figures that have contributed to an existential-humanistic understanding of the human condition. Such themes are also seen in books such as Schneider's (1993) *Horror and the Holy: Wisdom*

*Teachings of the Monster Tale*. But the question remains as to why philosophy, literature, and the arts are so important to existential-humanistic psychology.

Existential-humanistic psychology is a holistic approach. One limitation of Western psychology today is its myopic focus on understanding human beings as a distinct biological entity with firm boundaries between itself and the world. Also, drawing from its roots in the physiology of Wundt and the internalized personality theories of early psychoanalysts, contemporary psychology continues to subtly and not so subtlety envision the individual as if in isolation. Western psychology can learn a great deal from the Eastern perspectives, as well as many other cultural views, which emphasize the interconnected aspects of being human. Although there are some signs that many in the West are beginning to consider these non-Western ideas, the entire basis of its psychological system has been built upon the foundation of Western thought. It may be that a dramatic re-envisioning of Western psychology is necessary to move away from these limitations.

When one knows only a single approach to the human condition, such as the biological, it deceptively appears easy to understand the essence of the human condition. When one explores what it means to be human through multiple perspectives, it becomes evident that human nature is incredibly complex. This is radically evident in many approaches to *pop psychology* as well as many scholarly approaches to psychology in which the individual has been deeply rooted in a singular subfield or specialty in psychology and viewed through a narrow lens that allows for simplistic answers to problems humans experience. Routinely, I find, that it is much more difficult to learn from even the most brilliant of scholars if they are not rooted in the breadth of interdisciplinary study; their assumptions are too narrow, too obvious, and too naïve. One should always be suspicious of anyone who thinks they have solved the human condition or can fully explain anything as complex as human nature. I would guess anyone who has made such claims has never read with any degree of seriousness or reflection the writings of Camus, Kafka, or Dostoevsky!

This is illustrated in a story told by Bohart (2017) in the Forward to Tom Greenings book, *Words Against the Void: Poems by an Existential Psychologist*. Bohart told a story of sharing Greenings poems with a colleague who takes a rigid scientific approach to psychology. The colleague responded with mockery and questioning why a psychologist would waste time with poetry when they could be engaging in the productive activity of research. In response, Bohart explained, "For me, I would prefer a world where some insights are best conveyed through poetry, and where some experiences can only be captured in words and not numbers, although I am not opposed to numbers" (p. vi). This openness to learn from both numbers and art is a broader, more holistic way of learning. I have no doubt that someone who can learn from scientific research as well as poetry, literature, music, and other forms of art is much more prepared to sit across from the rich complexities and nuances of a human being with some understanding of what it means for that person to exist. Existence can never be reduced to numbers or biology without the loss of its soul, which is the essence of what makes one human.

Philosophy, literature, and the arts help individuals improve their *psycho-logical vision*; they help see the human within the human condition. As alluded to earlier, one sees only those aspects of being human that they are prepared to see. In part, this is about their own emotional health; sometimes one does not see what they are not emotionally ready or able to see. However, people cannot see those aspects of the human condition that are outside of their referential frame. For example, when working with students learning to identify the themes connected to the existential givens in therapy, they often struggle the most in identifying death issues. This, at times, is because of their countertransference about death issues. However, most of the time, this occurs because they have never learned to identify or see death issues. Although reading a book such as Becker's (1973) *The Denial of Death* might help the student in identifying death issues, the more effective tool often is the literary one. Reading Kafka's (1946/1999) *The Trial* or Camus's (1957/1988) *The Stranger* could be a more powerful tool in helping students to understand the human condition, including the death issues—both symbolic and literal.

For several years, I led a monthly existential reading group through the Depth Psychotherapy Institute. Initially, we focused on reading the classics of existential-humanistic psychology while mixing in a few books on existential philosophy. However, at one point, we switched to rotating between a theory book, a novel, and a movie. It was amazing how the depth of the dialogue was enriched. I am certain the participants, including myself, gained a much deeper appreciation for the human condition as we have broadened the scope of our exploration to include fiction and movies. Theory is brought alive through art and creativity.

I firmly believe that therapists can *see* their clients better when they are engaged in music, poetry, literature, and other forms of art. In my mind, the training of an existential-humanistic therapist is never complete until they have engaged in this aspect of their training; nothing can substitute for the arts. In the next section, I have attempted to illustrate this through the use of a classic folk song that deals rather directly with the idea of vision and the ability to see the other person beyond the surface levels.

### Gordo's Ghost: Therapy and Vision

Gordon Lightfoot's (Gordo's) song, "If You Could Read My Mind" is a beautiful illustration of myth. Although the song is about a failed romantic relationship, in many ways the song parallels the story of psychotherapy. The song begins with the woeful strumming of the guitar, then Gordo's voice breaks in, full of soft emotion and heartbreak. The song begins in a story of isolation. Although the couple is still together, Gordo is painfully alone and feels trapped. At the end of the first stanza, Gordo sings of himself as if he were a ghost chained up in a dungeon, setting the stage for the song's powerful lyrics, "And I will never be set free/As long as I'm a ghost that you can't see." These lines speak powerfully to the existential condition of isolation, but also to psychotherapy.

A primary reason many clients enter psychotherapy is because they feel no one sees them. Friends, family, and often even their therapists have been unable or unwilling to truly see them, or to look beyond the mask. The most painful experience of loneliness is often the one experienced in the presence of those who are supposed to love you. Yet, this is a common form of loneliness.

It takes courage to allow oneself to be seen. Many clients choose to hide behind masks and heavy garments to protect themselves from being seen. In therapy settings, I have often encountered clients who reported feeling vulnerable with the receipt of my gaze, and they often have commented that they believe I can "see right through them." This is not uncommon for therapists. Clients often project special powers upon the therapists, believing that the therapist can see right through their defenses. Although many therapists are quite adept at picking up subtle cues and insights about the client, they hold no special powers and often are wrong in what they believe they see. Clients can all too easily hide away if the therapist is not able to create an environment where the client can become comfortable in their vulnerability.

But it is not hiding that makes Gordo's ghost so elusive; it is the lack of vision of his partner. Just as much as it takes courage to allow oneself to be seen, it also takes courage to see. Too often people do not want to see what is there; they do not want to see the pain, the suffering, and the scars. This is true even of therapists. One person tells the other, "It's okay," "It will pass with time," or "It is for the best." All these seemingly well-intended statements give the message that it is not okay for the other to see the person who feels invisible in their suffering; they tell the ghost to continue to hide away. Or they may stick with detached cognitive analysis or dialogues rooted in theories and psychobabble; anything to avoid engaging in the pain and suffering inherent in existence.

Gordo goes on to tell the next stage of the story, which returns to an earlier time when he was idealized as the hero, just like in the "drugstore novel." But the hero does not save the day "When you reach the part where the heartaches come/The hero would be me/But heroes often fail." The drop in Gordo's voice when singing "heroes often fail" can be felt, as well as heard; it embodies the cliché of the heart dropping. In all relationships, for them to reach the point of genuineness, one must see beyond the idealized hero. In therapy, this is illustrated time and again. Many couples who enter therapy have reached the place where the heroic transferences begin to fade. As Robert Murney (personal communication) was fond of saying, "We all marry our idealized mate and then, sometime after the ceremony, we meet the one we married." This is a painful time for most couples and many do not survive. They may begin again searching for the hero that will never fail, but at some point, they are forced to realize that what they need is not another hero; what they need is a fellow sojourner, who is just as imperfect as they are themselves.[1] Everyone fails. But only when one accepts their partner as human can they experience a genuine relationship. There is no true intimacy when relating to the idealized other, this only occurs with the much more human one behind the mask and behind the projections.

The same is often true in psychotherapy. Clients project idealized images upon the therapist, such as super-human powers of intuition, knowledge, advice, and compassion. For some therapists, this feels good. Many therapists spend their days hiding behind these idealized images, basking in the deception that their clients, who love and idealize them, are the ones who truly understand them. But this is not therapeutic for the client and not healthy for the therapist. For therapy to succeed, clients need to be in therapy with a real person. It is the therapist's job to break through the idealizations and create a genuine relationship with the person who also happens to be their client. When this does not occur, the next lines Gordo's song are haunting, "And you won't read that book again/Because the endings just too hard to take." For individuals stuck in the cycle of idealizations and fallen heroes, they eventually back away from relationships of depth. They continue to interact with others, and may even be quite social and popular, but they no longer allow themselves to be vulnerable enough for true intimacy.

The paradoxical nature of relationships is such that the more deeply one loves, the more deeply they can be hurt. Intimacy requires vulnerability, but so many choose to hide behind false intimacies in hope that they will never be hurt too deeply. This shallow existence has few rewards other than the surface smiles that hide the empty feelings behind them. They are alone behind the ever-present tragic smile.

In my own life, I can remember boldly thinking that I could endure any loss and suffer through it relatively unscathed. In part, this was due to having developed a rather existential approach to suffering early in life. When I experienced pain or loss, I boldly journeyed into it and found that the pain was never so bad when I faced it directly. But it was also due to routinely choosing *safe* relationships in which I was never pushed to be vulnerable. In the later part of this phase of my life, I encountered two friends who invited me to be more present, and gently called out my hiding. This prepared me for my next lesson. It was later, after I married my wife, that I first became terrified of a loss. Although I had been bold in my vulnerabilities and brash in my love in many relationships, it had never been to the same depths before. For the first time, I recognized that there was a potential for loss in my life of which the mere prospect was terrifying. The depth of my wife's love and her courage to truly see me showed me a potential deeper than I

---

[1] It has often been stated that a therapist cannot take a client beyond where they have been themselves. I disagree. Although there are certain advantages to having already been down that road, in reality, each client will be further along in some aspects of the journey than the therapist. What is essential, in my view, is that the therapist, too, is on the journey. The adage I would suggest as a replacement is that *we cannot guide a client on a journey we are not willing to go on ourselves.*

could imagine before. Yet, at the same time, the beauty she has brought to my life would make every tear, no matter how unbearable, worth what I would have to face. Our relationship is far from perfect, but we have learned the beautiful art of being broken together.

Not all relationships reach the depth of intimacy that one has in their closest relationships. Therapists do not love their therapy clients in the same way they love their spouse or children. Yet, hopefully, therapists love their clients enough to truly see them, and to offer them a genuine relationship where the therapist is not hiding behind heroic projections. As Rollo May (1958) stated, "One must have at least a readiness to love the other person, broadly speaking, if one is able to understand him" (p. 39). The genuineness and breaking of idealization discussed here is not intended to suggest the therapist must disclose their scars and wounds to their clients. Rather, it is about being vulnerable in the moment, about allowing oneself to be fully present with their clients as fallible, imperfect human beings.

Yalom (2002) discussed three types of self-disclosure: "(1) the mechanisms of therapy; (2) here-and-now feelings; and (3) the therapist's personal life" (p. 83). From an existential-humanistic approach, it is important to engage in the first two types of self-disclosure. Therapy should not be mysterious, which means therapists should be willing to disclose about their approach and assumptions about how therapy works. Therapists should also be willing to engage in here-and-now disclosures, which pertain to the therapist's reactions to the client in the course of therapy. Here-and-now disclosures can be in important part of therapeutic warmth and positive regard, which are important factors that predict positive therapy outcomes (Farber, Suzuki, & Lynch, 2018). The third type of disclosure—the therapist personal history and life—is something that requires more discretion. While this type of disclosure might be beneficial at times, it can also be counterproductive at other times.

As Gordo's story progresses, the relationship becomes entangled in patterns that are not so easily broken. Gordo laments about acting and feeling in ways that he cannot understand, and in ways he thought was not possible. The patterns have been set in the relationship and now they are difficult to break; they have become part of the couple's destiny. This pervasive pattern itself is a given; all relationships develop patterns that are hard to break, and they are more difficult to break when the patterns are not understood. Gordo recognizes the feelings and behaviors, but he does not understand them. These become additional chains on Gordo's ghost, keeping him bound in the dungeon, below the surface of conscious awareness.

As the song ends, there are no signs of hope in sight. Gordo is alone and unseen; accompanied, it seems, only by the experience of profound loneliness. There is a despondent feeling as if he feels the pattern is bound to reappear. But this, too, is life. For many, they begin to accept patterns as if that is all there is and no longer seek new ways and new understanding. It is not clear if Gordo's ghost even wants to leave the dungeon; maybe he is content with this pattern his life.

Maybe the security of the cold, damp dungeon is easier than being exposed by the light.[2]

For a more hopeful ending, it is necessary to go beyond the story of Gordo's ghost. There is a degree to which everyone is Gordo's ghost; no one can be fully seen by others no matter how vulnerable they are and how hard the other person tries to see them. But there is hope. The therapist's job, in part, is to *see* their clients, even at those times when they would rather look away. It is through a mutual fierce vision that clients discover choice and meaning.

From an existential-humanistic perspective, therapy does not really begin at any depth level until the therapist begins to see the client as they truly are. Again, this is not to deny the inherent impossibility of ever completely seeing others, but rather it is focusing therapy on the importance of their ability to see clients. As discussed earlier, it is often myths such as Gordo's ghost that help develop a therapeutic vision that better enables the therapist to see their clients.

## Conclusion

Gordo's ghost is a story about the interface of existential isolation and interpersonal isolation, but it is also a story about existential or ontological vision. One can never be completely seen and one can never completely see another person. This, in part, is why existential isolation can never be fully overcome. But one can be more seen and one can learn to see others more completely. As therapists, therapeutic vision is essential not because it gives any special knowledge or interpretive powers, but because it is necessary to encounter clients on a deeper level and allow them to encounter themselves and their world more fully, honestly, and meaningfully.

## References

Becker, E. (1973). *The denial of death*. New York, NY: Free Press.

Bohart, A. (2017). Forward. In T. Greening (Author), *Words against the void: Poems by an existential psychologist* (pp. iii-vi). Colorado Springs, CO: University Professors Press.

Camus, A. (1988). *The stranger*. New York, NY: Random House. (Original work published in 1957)

Dias, J., & Hoffman, L. (Eds.). (2017). *Connoisseurs of suffering: Poetry for the journey to meaning* (Poetry, Healing, and Growth Series). Colorado Springs, CO: University Professors Press.

Farber, B. A., Suzuki, J. Y., & Lynch, D. A. (2018). Positive regard and psychotherapy outcome: A meta-analytic review. *Psychotherapy, 55*, 411-423. doi: http://dx.doi.org/10.1037/pst0000171

---

[2] It could be noted that the dungeon could also be interpreted as Gordo's unconscious. In this interpretation, Gordo is not able to see himself and is bound by his own lack of awareness.

Freud, S. (1961). *The future of an illusion* (J. Strachey trans.). New York, NY: Norton & Company. (Original work published in 1927)

Freud, S. (1961). Dostoevsky and parricide. In J. Stratchey (Ed. & Trans.), *The standard edition* (Vol. 21). New York: Norton. (Original work published in 1928)

Granger, N., Jr., & Hoffman, L. (Eds.). (2017). *Silent screams: Poetic journeys through addiction and recovery* (Poetry, Healing, and Growth Series). Colorado Springs, CO: University Professors Press.

Hesley, J. W. & Hesley, J. G. (2001). *Rent two films and let's talk in the morning: Using popular movies in psychotherapy* (2nd ed.). New York, NY: Wiley.

Hoffman, L. & Fehl, S. (2008). *Spiritualizing the unknown.* In J. H. Ellens (Ed.), Miracles: God, science, and psychology in the paranormal (Vol. 3, pp. 194-209). Westport, CT: Praeger Books.

Hoffman, L., & Fehl, S. (Eds.). (2016). *Journey of the wounded soul: Poetic companions for spiritual struggles* (Poetry, Healing, and Growth Series). Colorado Springs, CO: University Professors Press.

Hoffman, L., & Granger, N. Jr. (Eds.). (2015). *Stay awhile: Poetic narratives about multiculturalism and diversity* (Poetry, Healing, and Growth Series). Colorado Springs, CO: University Professors Press.

Hoffman, L., Hoffman, J. L., Hoffman, J. L. S., & Cleare-Hoffman, H. P. (2010). Culture, religion, and spirituality: How spirituality saved religion. In J. H. Ellens (Ed.), *The healing power of spirituality: How faith helps humans thrive* (Vol. 2: Religion; pp. 191-206). Westport, CT: Praeger.

Hoffman, L. & Kurzenberger, M. (2008). The miraculous in mental illness. In J. H. Ellens (Ed.), *Miracles: God, science, and psychology in the paranormal* (Vol. 3, pp. 65-93). Westport, CT: Praeger Books.

Hoffman, L. & McGuire, K. (2008). Are miracles essential or peripheral to faith traditions? In J. H. Ellens (Ed.), *Miracles: God, science, and psychology in the paranormal* (Vol. 1, pp. 221-240). Westport, CT: Praeger Books.

Hoffman, L., & Moats, M. (Eds.). (2015). *Capturing shadows: Poetic encounters along the path of grief and loss* (Poetry, Healing, and Growth Series). Colorado Springs, CO: University Professors Press.

Hoffman, L., Moats, M., & Greening, T. (Eds.). (2016). *Our last walk: Using poetry for grieving and remembering our pets.* Colorado Springs, CO: University Professors Press.

Hoffman, L., Stewart, S., Warren, D., & Meek, L. (2014). Toward a sustainable myth of self: An existential response to the postmodern condition. In K. J. Schneider, J. F. Pierson & J. F. T. Bugental (Eds.), *The handbook of humanistic psychology: Theory, research, and practice* (2nd edition; pp. 105-133). Thousand Oaks, CA: Sage.

Hoffman, L., & Thelen, M. (2018). Interfaith dialogue. In D. Leeming (Ed.), *The encyclopedia of psychology and religion* (3rd ed.). Advanced online publication. Berlin, Germany: Springer. doi: https://doi.org/10.1007/978-3-642-27771-9_809-2

Hoffman, L., Vallejos, L., Cleare-Hoffman, H. P., & Rubin, S. (2015). Emotion, relationship, and meaning as core existential practice: Evidence-based foundations. *Journal of Contemporary Psychotherapy, 45,* 11-20. doi: 10.1007/s10879-014-9277-9.

Kafka, F. (1999). *The trial.* New York, NY: Schocken Books. (Original work published 1946)

May, R. (1958). Contributions of existential therapy. In. R. May, E. Angel, & H. F. Ellenberger (Eds.), *Existence* (pp. 37-91). Northvale, NJ: Jason Aronson.

May, R. (1961). The meaning of the Oedipus myth. *Review of Existential Psychology and Psychiatry, 1,* 44-52.

May, R. (1991). *The cry for myth.* New York, NY: Delta.

May, R. (1999a). Oedipus and self-knowledge. *Review of Existential Psychology and Psychiatry, 24,* 10-16.

May, R. (1999b). The healing power of symbols and myths. *Review of Existential Psychology and Psychiatry, 24,* 17-24.

Mendelowitz, E. (2008). *Ethics and Lao Tzu: Intimations of character.* Colorado Springs, CO: University of the Rockies Press.

Mosig, Y. D. (2006). Conceptions of the self in Eastern and Western psychology. *Journal of Theoretical and Philosophical Psychology, 26,* 39-50.

Nietzsche, F. (1990). Twilight of the idols. In R. J. Hollingdale (Ed. & Trans.), *Twilight of the idols and the Anti-Christ* (pp. 31-122). New York, NY: Penguin Classics. (Original work published in 1889).

Nobles, W. W. (2006). *Seeking the Sakhu: Foundational writings for an African psychology.* Chicago, IL: Third World Press.

Schneider, K. J. (1993). *Horror and the holy: Wisdom teachings of the monster tale.* Peru, IL: Open Court.

Schneider, K. J. (1999). *The paradoxical self: Toward an understanding of our contradictory nature* (2nd ed.). Amherst, NY: Humanity Books.

Schneider, K. J. (2004) *Rediscovery of awe: Splendor, mystery and the fluid center of life.* St. Paul, MN: Paragon House.

Schneider, K. J., (2009). *Awakening to awe: Personal stories of profound transformation.* New York, NY: Jason Aronson.

Schneider, K. J. (2013). *The polarized mind: Why it's killing us and what we can do about it.* Colorado Springs, CO: University Professors Press.

Schneider, K. J. (2017). *The spirituality of awe: Challenges to the robotic revolution.* Cardiff, CA: Waterfront Press.

Schneider, K. J. & May, R. (1995). *The psychology of existence: An integrative, clinical perspective.* New York, NY: McGraw-Hill.

Solomon, G. (1995). *The motion picture prescription: Watch this movie and call me in the morning: 200 movies to help you heal life's problems.* Santa Rosa, CA: Aslan Publishing.

Tillich, P. (1957). *The dynamics of faith.* New York, NY: Harper & Row.

Vos, J. (2018). *Meaning in life: An evidence-based handbook for practitioners.* London, United Kingdom: Palgrave.

Vos, J., Cooper, M., Hill, C. E., Neimeyer, R. A., Schneider, K. J., &Wong, P. T. (2017). Five perspectives on the meaning of meaning in the context of clinical practices. *Journal of Constructivist Psychology.* Advance online publication. doi:10.1080/10720537.2017.1390511.

Wedding, D., Boyd, M. A., & Niemiec, R. M. (2005). *Movies and mental illness* (2nd ed.). Cambridge, MA: Hogrefe and Huber.

Wong, P. T. P. (2012). Toward a dual-systems model of what makes life worth living. In P. T. P. Wong (Ed.), *Meaning: Theories, research, and applications* (2nd ed.; Chapter 1; Kindle version). New York, NY: Tayor & Francis.

Yalom, I. D. (2002). *The gift of therapy: An open letter to a new generation of therapists and their patients.* New York, NY: HarperCollins.

Yang, M., & Hoffman, L. (2019). *An existential-humanistic framework for international psychology.* In L. Hoffman, M. Yang, M. Mansilla, J. Dias, M. Moats, & T. Claypool (Eds). Existential psychology East-West (Vol. 2). Colorado Springs, CO: University Professors Press.

# Chapter 17

## The Kemet—Egyptian Myth of Osiris and Isis: The Eternal Drama of Creation, Generativity, Destruction, Death, Rebirth, and Resurrection of the Human Spirit

Alan G. Vaughan

The events which transpired 5,000 years ago, five years ago, or five minutes ago, have determined what will happen five minutes from now; five years from now or 5,000 years from now. All history is a current event.

~ John Henrik Clarke, in Browder, 1992

Myth lives vividly in our symptoms and fantasies and in our conceptual systems.

~ James Hillman, 1979, p. 23

More than death the Egyptians feared missing their chance to resurrect into eternal life

~ Thom Cavalli, 2010, p. 26

Much meaning can be found in the Kemet-Egyptian myth of Osiris and Isis. This creation myth speaks to the origin of consciousness, creation, life, death, resurrection, rebirth, and spirituality, especially as it is connected to the emergence of the historiography of the African Diaspora. The myth is about the archetype or universal nature of the divine family and its centrality to the organization of societies and cultures that comprise the human family and civilization past, present, and future. In addition to the origin of consciousness, it speaks to the genealogy of the gods as creators of the ecosystem, as creators and reflections of the human family, the life cycle, and psychodynamics of how we live, how we die, and how we mirror the divine in daily rituals and rites. It speaks of the constructive and destructive aspects of nature replicated in human nature and how humans cause tragedy and transform trauma resulting from tragedy into manageable human experience. It instructs us on how to heal our ailing souls.

## Origin of the Myth of Osiris and Isis in Kemet

The land to the north and east on the continent of Africa known today as Egypt was historically called Kemet, meaning *the Black land* or the *Land of the Blacks*. The term Egypt *Aigyptiakos* resulted from occupation of ancient Kemet by the Greeks (Ashby, 2003; Browder, 1992; Cavalli, 2010; Cushford, 1993). The terms Kemet or Kemet-Egypt are used here to denote the accurate historiography of the region. Kemet remained in power for 3,000 years before conquest by a succession of foreign powers: Romans, Greeks, and Persians (Cavalli, p. 26).

The Myth of Osiris and Isis was written around 2300 B.C., and was first mentioned in the Pyramid text dating back two millennia before the Bible. Much of what is known about Kemet is based on the early work of Greek historians Plutarch (AD 46–AD 120) and Herodotus (488 BC–425 BC) rather than on original Kemet-Egyptian papyri and pyramid texts (Cavalli, 2010, p 8). Several contemporary scholars have written on the numinous country of Kemet-Egypt where the Nile River flows upward to the north into the Mediterranean Sea from the south. Upper Kemet was located in the south, now the Sudan, and lower Egypt was located in the north (Ashby, 2004, 2006; Browder, 1992; Budge, 1973; Hornung, 1986). Part of the magic and mytho-poetic consciousness of the country is reflected in an extraordinary orientation to geography, cosmology, mythology, and the ecosystem that spawned modern civilization. "For Egyptians there were three levels of organization: the people, pharaoh and the gods. The people served the pharaoh and the pharaoh was the intermediary to the world above and below" (Cavalli, 2010, p. 26):

> The Egyptians, like the modern Africans, believed that the government of this world was, practically speaking, in the hands of a considerable number of gods and spirits, and that, in order to have success and happiness here and hereafter, it was necessary to obtain their good will and help. The performance of the duties and ceremonies connected with the proper worship of ancestral spirits was performed by a member of each family, who in dynastic times was called the 'servant of the KA,' and the direction of the worship due to the local god was committed to the care of the 'servant of god.' (Budge, 1973, p.169)

Early Christians understood Osiris to be the pre-figuration of Christ and similarly identified Isis with Mary the mother of Christ. Cavalli (2010) explained that Jung, Budge, and Mojsov showed direct parallels between major themes in Christianity presaged in Kemet-Egyptian rites that include: the Trinity, the Resurrection, and the Sacraments. Jung, too, visited Egypt, Cairo, while traveling in Africa (p. 14). Jung along with other researchers went further to show patterns that relate Western religious rituals to their Kemet-Egyptian antecedents, (p. 51).

## Personal Reflections

The myth of Osiris and Isis was first introduced to me as a candidate in psychoanalytic training for certification to become a Jungian analyst at the C. G. Jung Institute in New York. In the course of studying comparative Kemet-Egyptian, Greek, and Hindu mythologies, I came to understand the trans cultural and transpersonal nature of Jung's concept of archetypes as core structures in the metaphysical architecture of human psyche and the process of amplification; that is, tracking common existential human phenomena, symbols, narratives, and psychodynamics across cultures, mindful of nuanced differences.

The discovery came while reading Volume 11 of the Collected Works of C.G. Jung, *Psychology and Religion West and East*. As a recovering unconscious Catholic, I was drawn to two of his essays, "A Psychological Approach to the Dogma of the Trinity" and "Transformation Symbolism in the Mass." In the introduction to this first essay, Jung wrote about the pre-Christian parallels and antecedents to Christian mythology of the Christ specifically from mythologies of Kemet-Egypt, Babylonia, and Greece; he wrote about prominent existential themes of symbols, symbolism and meaning, purpose and transformation and wrote about creation and the cycle of life. This life cycle includes ontogeny, birth, love, suffering, sacrifice, death, mourning, loss, spirituality, resurrection, and rebirth of the human spirit as it separates from the body of matter (Jung, 1969, p. 107-193). Though unknown to me at the time, some early Christians understood Osiris to be the prefiguration of Christ and similarly identified Isis with the mother of Christ, born to Mary, through the *Immaculate Conception*. The content of the myth helped clarify the void of the unexplained dogma and ambiguity around these doctrines in the Catholic Church. The narrative of the myth of Osiris and Isis illuminated consciousness of the antecedent beliefs, rites, and rituals from Kemet. The conception and birth of Horus to his parents were indeed magical, mystical, and inventive in the face of modern science, if not *Immaculate*. Scholars from the African Diaspora, Sebai Muata Ashby (2003, 2004, 2006) and Walker (2006) among others, also knew and wrote about this truth not revealed in canons of the Catholic Church and Christian mythology. It was coming to understand the ancient Kemet-Egyptian myth of Osiris and Isis and their divine progeny, Horus, as precursor to Christian mythology of the Christ that captured my full attention and awakened my mytho-poetic imagination. As I delved into these essays, I also became deeply engaged, contemporaneously and subsequently, with travel and study of African Diaspora historiography, psychology, and culture and my own path toward individuation as an African American.

A visit to Kemet for a seminal birthday with a study tour organized by the Association for the Study of Classical African Civilization proved to be a numinous experience, traveling back to ancient times on the gift of Nun (divine water) the mystic Nile river; turquoise, beautiful cerulean blue and current so peaceful at day break; welcoming the Sun-god, Amen Ra each morning. The shimmering silver sheath of light at dusk invited Ra to descend into the ethereal darkness of the underworld ruled by the god Osiris. There were lectures by scholars from the African Diaspora and visits to the ancient cities, temples, museums, and great pyramids: Cairo, el Amarana, Abydos, Dendera, Edfu Aswan; Abu Simbel, the Temple of Ramses II, the Temple of Heru or Horus, Temples of Luxor, Karnak, Deir el Bahari, Dendera; the Sphinx Heru em Akhet; and the Valley of the Kings. The Aswan and Cairo Museums offered treasure troves of historiography and visual narrative, richly informative and rewarding. Sailing up the Nile was magical, a liminal space in time, remarkably tranquil and reflecting a new peace found within. I recognized from the experience that as a human being I was not exempt from the universal experience of the life cycle and eternal dramas articulated in the narrative of the myth of Osiris and Isis, as lived human phenomena. Kemet-Egyptian mythology touched my soul, opening wider and deeper the portal to the African unconscious that has supported me in my professional life and during a period of personal psychological difficulty. Later, seeing the contemporary work of the German abstract painter Anselm Keifer, who was also influenced by this particular Kemet-Egyptian myth, in the San Francisco Museum of Modern Art, further underscored its psychological importance to me (1985-1987; Auping, 2007).

The myth offers prescriptive properties of consciousness, and illuminates the psychology of ritual and universal elements and rites that heal ailing spirits through humanization, that is, transforming trauma of tragedy from the realm of the mythic into human proportions, more easily understood and metabolized by human psyche. This myth would appear later as an archetypal guide to the recognition and interpretation of counter transference and transference phenomena during the psychoanalysis of a patient. The patient had to come to terms with pathos emanating from gods Anubis and Thanatos as complex lived trauma in a major depression and ambivalent feelings toward his deceased father in human fratricide. The universal nature of the myth presaged the difficult period in my own life caused by the natural death of my father. While Jung's essays were instructive, I will narrow the discussion to a summary of the Myth of Osiris and Isis, the Existential themes presented therein, and psychological and cultural analysis of the myth in relation to Existential themes.

## The Myth of Osiris and Isis

The following is a paraphrasing of the myth of Isis and Osiris retold by Jules Cushford (1993):

> The Waters of Life were the beginning and they were everywhere. Nun was the name of the Waters. From the Waters all things came!
>
> Atum, "the One", lay motionless resting in the Waters and longed for the world to come into being. From this longing, a son, Shu, and a daughter, Tefnut, were born. Shu was Air and Tefnut was Moisture. For some time, they lay in the loving embrace of their father Atum and their mother Atum,

"the One." They then vanished, lost to the depths of the dark waters. The Eye of Atum separated from Atum and over many ages searched in the darkness for them. Upon their return, Atum kissed them and gave them new names: Shu became Life and Tefnut became Order, (p. 13).

Atum then rose from the waters as the First Hill and shone from the waters, the First Light. Atum became Atum-Ra: Ra was the visible face of Atum the Sun. Atum was the invisible whole.

In union Shu and Tefnut gave birth to a son Geb and a daughter Nut. Geb was Earth and Nut was Sky. Sky held Earth so tightly in embrace that there was no space between them. So Shu raised up Sky, his daughter Nut, into an arch so high that only her fingers and tips of her toes touched Earth, Geb, his son.

At dusk each day Nut swallowed the Sun through her mouth and the outside world became dark. The Stars came forth from Nut and moved across her body, sparkling in the night. At dawn each day Nut gave birth to the Sun, as a mother gives birth to her child.

Nut and Geb bore four children, two sons, Osiris and his younger brother Seth; and two daughters, Isis and her younger sister Nephthys.

Geb gave to Osiris, his first-born son, treasures of the Earth: rich soil, waving corn, clustering vines, seeds, flowers, and fruit. Osiris loved the Black Nile, an elixir, the river winding through the land called Kemet, orginally "Land of the Blacks," and later referred to as Egypt by the Greeks, flowing over its banks making the fields fertile and the crops grow strong and tall. At times, Osiris took the form of a bull.

Nut gifted Isis, her first born daughter, rain and dew and all wet and moist places on Earth. Without Isis neither seed could sprout nor plant grow. Isis was present when the moon was full of light, when the dawn came, and when the Dog Star, Sothis, rose on the eastern horizon just before the Nile overflowed. Her breath was the breath of life and her milk nourished all the creatures on Earth. At times, she took the forms of a cow, a star or a tree (p. 14).

Geb's second son, Seth, had hair as red as the desert, where the Sun burned all day, scorching the ground so nothing could grow. Seth sent harsh storm winds that blew hot dry desert sands across green fields of the Nile Valley. He loved the sea salt that scattered the Nile waters and the darkness that swallowed up the Sun each night. At times, Seth took the forms of a crocodile, a hippopotamus or an ass (p.15).

Nephthys, inhabited the darkness as her older sister Isis inhabited the light. Nephthys loved the waning and dark moon just as Isis loved the new and full moon. The morning star was the star of Isis and the evening star, that of Nephthys.

The sisters were so close they were like the opposite sides of one person, with different names: Isis was the visible one and Nephthys was the invisible one (p. 16).

Reaching maturity Isis married Osiris and Nephthys married Seth. One day, Atum wept tears of joy and from the tears came all people of the world.

As the son of the Earth (Geb) and Sky (Shu), Osiris cultivated civilization and within people, the arts of civilization. He showed them how to cultivate the land, gather fruit from trees, plough the fields and to plant wheat and barley that could be made into bread. He gave them laws to bring order to their lives and inspired them to honor the source of life, and the principles of justice (MAAT) in the universe. He traveled the entire world, bringing civilization to all nations, charming them with music and song. In his absence, Isis ruled peacefully watching over the land.

When Osiris returned home, everyone was happy except his brother Seth who rebelled against order and justice, disturbing the peace. His heart was heavy with desire to take the place of his older brother Osiris and his thoughts followed. He contrived a plot to do so with 72 conspirators. Steadfastly, he measured the body of Osiris and made a magnificent chest with bright colors around it and sized to the exact dimensions of Osiris. In a banquet hall, they held a party with everyone having a good time drinking, eating, and laughing. At the height of the festivities Seth had the chest brought into the room and said "Whoever shall lie down in this chest and fit it exactly, that person shall have it for himself. This I promise." All of the guests tried in turn but none would fit. Lastly, Osiris lay down in the chest designed to fit him perfectly. The conspirators rushed to the chest, slammed the lid closed and hammered in long nails and sealed it with lead. They then threw the chest containing Osiris into the Nile and the river swept the chest into the sea (p. 17).

Isis was heart-broken and, as such, cut off a braid from her hair and dressed herself in mourning clothes. She then set out to search for her husband Osiris. Children had seen the casket float past them while playing by the sea. They so informed Isis who now knew where to look. She discovered that the waves had gently laid the casket down on the shore of Byblos in Phoenicia. A Tamarisk tree had grown up around it, enclosing the casket in its trunk, until it was completely hidden. The Tamarisk tree was so beautiful that the king of Byblos had it cut down and made into a pillar at his palace (pp. 18-19).

Isis found her way to Byblos and in disguise sat down beside a spring from which the servants of the queen gathered water. Isis smiled at them and began to braid their hair, breathing sweetness over them. The fragrance attracted the queen, who wanted to know the source. She was so informed by the servants, sent for Isis and begged Isis to nurse her infant boy.

Isis agreed to nurse the baby. She gave the infant her finger to suckle instead of her breast. At night she placed the boy in a fire to burn away all that was mortal in him. While he was sleeping in the fire, she would turn herself into a swallow and fly around the pillar, mourning in songs. One night the queen looked in on them and saw her son lying in the flames. She screamed. In the aftermath, Isis was forced to reveal her true identity to an astonished palace. Isis requested the pillar containing the casket be cut down and given to her. She stripped away the bark to find the casket inside. She immediately fell upon it and wept. She commanded that the casket be lifted onto a boat and set sail for home. Out of sight, she opened the casket and saw her dearest husband and love, Osiris, lying as though asleep. She kissed him. Suddenly, she transformed into a kite—a huge bird with great strong wings. Beating her wings, she created a strong wind that infused the Breath of Life back into Osiris. She then conceived her son Horus, from and with Osiris (p. 19).

Home again, she concealed the casket among the tall reeds of the Delta marshes and went away secretly to give birth to Horus. However, by light of a full moon, one night while hunting wild boar, Seth saw and recognized the casket. He ripped off the lid and in an unimaginable rage he dismembered the poor body of Osiris into fourteen pieces and scattered them all over Kemet-Egypt.

Isis soon discovered what had happened and paddled through the swamps in a small boat looking for pieces of Osiris to put together again, to make him whole. The empathic crocodiles did not tip the boat over, as they were accustomed to doing with others. Once on land, Isis was aided by her sister Nephthys and her nephew Anubis who was like a jackal with a very good nose for finding things.

After much searching across Kemet she found all parts of Osiris with the exception of his phallus that had been swallowed by a fish. Isis made a model of the missing part then reassembled all the pieces of the body of Osiris until he appeared as he had been before. With the aid of Anubis, she performed a special ritual over him and he came back to life. Osiris went on to rule the Underworld as he had once ruled the Earth. Each night Ra, the Sun comes to wake Osiris just at the time when everyone else has fallen asleep.

## Existential Themes

The archetypal, transpersonal, and Trans-cultural character of the myth is constellated in complexes (feeling toned emotional responses with positive and negative polarities) around the universal human experience of many existential themes identified here, a few of which are discussed below. Universal themes include: Origins of consciousness, creation narratives in comparative mythologies across cultures; the divine family and divinity within family; family life, systems, and psychodynamics among human adults and trans-generational relations with their children. They also include the phylogeny of the life cycle and emotions both positive and negative common in the human family life, mirrored in the divine family of gods and goddesses. These are: love, perseverance, ingenuity, creativity, resourcefulness, magic, mystery, generativity, and relatedness to the others and the ecosystem. The theory of opposites, dialectics and counter point are depicted and can be seen in negative emotions of jealousy, envy, rage, hatred and acts of deception, cunning, destruction and death by fratricide, and brother killing brother. The psychology of ritual embedded and hidden in dogma, healing properties in ritual and rites of grief, mourning and loss generativity and rebirth are prominent themes in the myth. Spirituality, religiosity, and Eros as life force resurrecting the human spirit from descent into despair are also important existential themes. The best way to draw these existential themes, emotions, and psychodynamics of human experience into coherence of an integrated existential matrix is to reflect on them symbolically in the narrative of the myth of Osiris and Isis itself, closing with some personal reflections and pointing to clinical applications.

## Analysis and Discussion

There is a symbolic and dynamic relationship between behaviors found in the families of gods and their genealogies across cultures as they speak to creation that presages and reflects creation in humanity. The gods and their origins mirror psychological projections of the human psyche onto these unknown entities and the collective unconscious. The religious function of psyche makes these projections sacred, encoding them in dogma and performed in rituals and rites even when purpose and intent are not fully known or knowable. Most humans have a psychological need for a sense of origin and place in historiography and time, to feel secure and to mitigate existential fear and anxiety of the grand unknown or collective unconscious. Trans-generational beliefs in gods, myths, and organized religions help humans deal with this grand unknown and help us learn how to be ideally more human. The correspondence in psyche and behaviors of humans is more often unconscious than conscious.

In this myth, Nun has jurisdiction and provenance over the divinity of water and its sacredness as a necessity for all life. Atum nesting and longing in relation to Nun can be thought of as the nascent birth of consciousness awakening from the primeval waters of the collective unconscious. In this awakening, *One* and one's self is recognized within and in relation to the physical environment and ecosystem of which one is a part. The psychic state of stillness, being in repose and recognition of longing for connection to the eco-system and relationships to others, is seen and felt. This is fundamental consciousness becoming conscious of the self. Nun is the primordial water that covers 75% or more of the Earth's surface in oceans, rivers, and lakes. She constitutes 98% of the human body, in fluids replenished daily, and is the source of intrauterine waters in which new life gestates and from which it is born.

Creation is the act of bringing the new into being, new matter or new arrangements of existing matter and/or perceptions of matter and new consciousness. The acts of creation could be magical or mysterious even in the face of efforts of modern science and technology to deconstruct mystery and magic replacing them with epistemology, methodology, observable fact, and reliably reproduced results. Science, research, and design are systematic efforts of humans to gain mastery over nature in service of the survival and evolution of the human species despite the destructive shadow elements of an under regulated capitalism and its driver, the quest for excess. The origin and creation of the divine family and the divinity of family presage the flourishing of civilization that evolved in Kemet over 5000 years ago, if not earlier. John Henrik Clark (as cited in Browder, 1992) suggested, "The events which transpired 5,000 years ago; five years ago, or five minutes ago, have determined what will happen five minutes from now; five years from now or 5,000 years from now. All history is a current event." (p. 1). The late James Hillman in his theory of archetypal psychology asserted that we all live in myth even today.

This myth speaks to the compensatory and complimentary harmonies and oppositional tensions that exist between the elements of Nature and in human nature; her radiant sun-drenched days and cool moon-star lit nights in contrast to her wind-storm, freezing, destructive moods. In the genealogy of myth, the dialectic of opposites is apparent and profiled in the inheritances of the divine family members: in Atum's Consciousness, "the One" primordial father and mother gestating in the amnion of Nun as Primal Water. As parents Shu and Tefnut inherit provenance of Life and Order, Shu-Life and Tefnut–Order. Their children are Geb as Earth and Nut as Sky. The grandchildren are brothers Osiris and Seth and sisters Isis and Nephyths, who inherited refinements of existence intuiting evolution, along with positive and negative emotions, motivations, and behaviors underscored in the theory of opposites and opposites existing in nature and human nature.

Atum is the symbol of the *One*, of wholeness from which all things were born and developed with the mid-wifery of Nun, Water.  The astrophysicist Neil de Grasse Tyson (as cited in Levenson, (2004) noted the *Big Bang* in contemporary Western mytho-science as the origin of civilization four billion years ago and candidly refers to humans as Star people whose origins in theory are star-dust residue derived from the Big Bang. Within the discipline of astrophysics, he constructed a 20th century creation myth about the origin of civilization not devoid of the kind of magic and mystery seen in the Kemet-Egyptian myth of Osiris and Isis. The many cultures that comprise the one global culture have creation stories, mythologies emanating from the psychological and existential need for a sense of origin, place, time, and historiography in the world cultural narrative. These creation mythologies coexist and are embedded in organized religion, evolutionary biology, and genetics. The eye of Atum is a manifestation of consciousness seeking itself and searching for relatedness to and within the vast deep, dark unconscious, the ecosystem and humanity seen but yet to be born. By extension today, we have optic cables lining the ocean floors of Nun and satellites populating the heavens of

Nut. We have potential for greater consciousness of world culture, the planetary ecosystem and ourselves.

Shu speaks to life and the evolutionary-biological life cycle common to all living species, while Tefnut is the principle of its phylogenetic-order, an order required to manage the increasing chaos of life through the ages. She represents the order of nature, internal order, civil order and global order. Nun is the primal water of the oceans, rivers, lakes and amniotic fluid that nurtures interuterine life, the daily lives of humans and of the Earth. Geb is geophysical earth, layers of celestial elements held together by gravity and an archeology of objects across time. Nut is the sky, the heavens and all of its contents: Galaxies, planets, moons, and stars discovered and yet to be discovered. She is hostess to Amen Ra, the Sun-God.

Osiris, Seth, Isis, and Nephthys are the next generation of divine beings. They are sibling pairs that embody the dialectic of opposites, harmonies, complementarity, and compensation in vivid contrast to tensions of their negative polarities in the shadow of opposites as the force of opposition. Together they personify humanity and evolution and also highlight destructive elements of human nature found in negative emotions and in the behavior of Seth.

Osiris, the good son, the first-born son to parents Geb and Nut, appears to be favored by his father. He is the cultivator of civilization, the art of agriculture and industry, working toward a just and sustainable world. As the son of the Earth and Sky, Osiris cultivated civilization of the Earth and within people the arts and sciences of civilization. As the Bull, he carries earthy and strong potent relations to the Earth and fecundity. Resurrected from death and made whole again through the agency of Isis, in his divinity he goes forth to rule the underworld as he had once cultivated civilization on Earth.

Seth with his red hair, as the lover of the dry, hot arid dessert and the fury of dessert storms, embodies the opposite of the good son. He is a personification of the sibling who draws attention from negative behavior. He is the trickster who competes for attention through negative emotions and destructive patterns of behavior. As a psychopath, he rebels against order and justice. "His heart was heavy with desire to take the place of his older brother Osiris and his thoughts followed." Beyond sibling rivalry, under the pathological influences of envy, jealousy, anger, hatred in the arms of deception, cunning, and gang conspiracy, Seth commits fratricide; more commonly encountered in the Biblical tale of Cain and Abel, where Cain kills his brother and favored son Abel. These are the negative, un-redemptive energies, emotions, and patterns of behavior that result in the high homicide rates in contemporary American society, be they urban homicides, fratricides or wars between men and nations. They are agents of death.

Isis is the heroine of the myth with much to teach humanity from her constitution, mature character, and journey through the valley of death and rebirth. She is the morning dew, the nurturer of human souls, and the human spirit. She embodies beauty, filial love, majesty, magic, mystery, and perseverance in face of adversity and tragedy. She is transformation and the embodiment of generativity, spirituality, and divinity. She teaches us about the psychology of ritual specific to the funerary rites in dying and death. She teaches us how to heal an un-tethered soul lost to despair and how to heal deep despair in major depression by transforming the tragedy and trauma of death by fratricide/homicide into human sadness and loss through funerary rites and rituals of grief, mourning, and the mystery and magic of resurrection and spiritual rebirth. She is supported by her sister Nephthys, with whom she has a very close relationship, and nephew Anubis, the Kemet-Egyptian god of death. Nephthys is the mother of Anubis and both help Isis find and resurrect Osiris.

### Humanization in Psychological Transformation: Journey through the Underworld of Grief and Mourning; Mystery, Magic and Dogma of the Immaculate Conception

In the myth, Kemet-Egyptian visual art and representations, Isis transforms into a huge bird with great and strong spanned wings that she beats to create strong winds that infuse the breath of life back into a decimated Osiris. She brings him back to life and conceives with him their son Horus through an Immaculate Conception. Osiris is later killed twice by an irate, envious Seth who eventually comes before the god of Justice, Thoth, avenged by Horus. Isis brings Osiris to life a second time reassembling fourteen pieces of his dismembered body and fashions a missing phallus from a fish. She resurrects Osiris who then takes leave to rule the Underworld as he once ruled the earth through the agency of his Earth-father Geb. Here the holy trinity is Father–Earth-Geb, Son-Osiris as Civilization, with the Kite and Anubis as *Nature*, and the *Holy Ghost* that emerges into consciousness from the ancient myth. In perpetuity Ra the Sun-God comes to the Underworld each night to wake Osiris just at the time everyone else has fallen asleep.

The Trinitarian relationship between Geb, Osiris, and Horus (father-son-holy ghost) or that between Osiris, Isis, and Horus prefigure the Christian doctrine of the Holy Trinity and the Immaculate Conception. In the strong beating of spanned wings new breath, fuels the rebirth of Osiris. Also embedded in the myth is more about the story of the Holy Ghost and of the role of the feminine in Christian doctrine, mythology, and religion.

### Conclusion

Working clinically in the psychoanalytic treatment of patients who have experienced trauma, major depression, and despair from the tragic death of loved ones, this Kemet–Egyptian myth of Osiris and Isis from the African Diaspora is an instructive guide as to where and when meaning can be made of the archetypal, transpersonal, and Trans-cultural perspectives on the clinical narrative. Existentially and clinically, the myth provides a prescriptive path toward and through the journey of the Underworld of darkness and despair into the light of a new day, rebirth, and reconnection to Eros, to spirituality and resurrection of the human spirit. Darkened spirit is reborn, awakened with the coming of Amen Ra who brings light and life to each new day, generative light that illuminates consciousness, warms and heals our souls. Sun light gives life and sustains the ecosystems and planet Earth. The people of Kemet and Native Americans knew this truth and worshiped at sunrise each day. It is through the mature emotional agency, emotional literacy, and constitution of Isis that this happens in the myth and in clinical work with patients suffering trauma and major depression.

## References

Asante. M. (1992). *Kemet, Afrocentricity and knowledge.* Trenton, NJ: African World Press.

Ashby, M. (2004). *Egyptian mysteries: Shetaut Neter* (Vol. I). Miami, FL: Cruzian Mystic Books.

Ashby, M. (2006). *Egyptian mysteries encyclopedic dictionary of ancient Egyptian gods and goddess.* Miami, FL: Cruzian Mystic Books.

Auping, M. (2007). *Anselm Keifer, heaven and Earth.* Fort Worth, TX: Modern Art Museum of Fort Worth and Prestel.

Browder, A. (1992). *Nile valley contributions to civilization.* Washington, DC: Institute of Karmic Guidance.

Budge, W. (1973). *Osiris and the Egyptian resurrection* (Vol.II). New York, NY: Dover.

Bynum, E. (1999). *The African unconscious, roots of ancient mysticism and modern psychology.* New York, NY: Teacher's College Press.

Cavalli, T. (2010). *Embodying Osiris the secrets of alchemical transformation.* Wheaton Il.: Quest Books Theosophical Publishing House.

Cushford, J. (1994). The myth of Isis and Osiris. Boston, MA: ShambhalaHillman, J. (1979). The dream and the underworld. New York, NY: Harper and Row

Hornung, E. (1986). The discovery of the unconscious in Ancient Egypt. In J. Hillman (Ed.), *Spring: An annual of archetypal psychology and Jungian thought* (pp. 16-28). Dallas, TX: Spring

Ellis. N. (1988). *Awakening Osiris, a new translation of the Egyptian Book of the Dead.* Grand Rapids, MO: Phanes Press

Jung, C. G. (1969). *The collected work of C. G. Jung* (Vol. 11, Psychology and religion West and East). In H. Read, M. Fordham, G. Adler, & W. McGuire (Eds., 2nd ed.). Bollingen Series XX: Princeton University Press.

Levenson, T., Producer (2004). *Origins, fourteen billion years of cosmic evolution* [DVD]. Available from Nova DVDs, Online:shop.wgbh.org; hosted by Neil DeGrassee Tyson.

Walker, R. (2006). *When we ruled.* London, United Kingdom.: Every Generation Media Limited.

Wilkinson, R. (2003). *The complete gods and goddesses of ancient Egypt.* London, England: Thames and Hudson, Ltd

# Chapter 18

## On Existential Aloneness: The Earthly Pilgrimage

Emory G. Cowan, Jr.

Who indeed knows the secret of the earthly pilgrimage? Who knows for what we live, and struggle, and die? Who knows what keeps us living and struggling, while all things break about us? But this, the purpose of our lives, the end of our struggle, is beyond all human wisdom. Oh God, my God, do not Thou forsake me. (Paton, 1948, p. 94)

### The Beginning of Memory

My earliest memories are of reading the daily comic strips in the newspaper. They are warm reminiscences of being with my family and of lying on the living room rug reading what we then called "the funny papers" in the daily newspaper. The comics not only provided me with reading skills, they provided motivation to learn and discover the world. Folded into those pages were humor, irony, mystery, intrigue, and adventure, and as I began to come to consciousness about the world, I was already playing with those concepts and constructs and perhaps understanding relationships with people better than I might otherwise have. I must confess that reading the comic pages is still part of my daily ritual; they are the first thing I look for in the newspaper.

That experience of learning to read was an integral part of the formation of myself. Reading became my escape into the world. As a lonely teenager on a farm, encyclopedias were my window to the world, and tales of intrigue and adventure were a way of exploring faraway places and cultures that I could never imagine seeing or experiencing. I am aware that my memory formation was more than real time, life experiences; it was the sum of all experiences of thought, and the adventure and imagination that came from thought. No one else had the same thoughts or interpreted their experiences as I did mine. And in a strange way, by stimulating thought, reading raised my consciousness to the fact that I was ultimately alone on my journey of life.

### Understanding Ultimate Aloneness

I recently read a well written blog on *Existential Loneliness*; however, from my perspective, the author confused loneliness and aloneness as so many writers do.

Loneliness is a transient condition in life, marked by a longing to be connected with other humans. Yalom (1989) described it as, "The lonely *I* dissolving into the *we*." "It's the common denominator of every form of bliss—romantic, sexual, political, religious, mystical. Everyone wants and welcomes this blissful merger" (p. 43). Loneliness is experienced by all people from time to time, but it is not a constant state as is our ultimate aloneness.

If you want to understand your own experience of ultimate aloneness, you will be hard pressed to find a definition or an explanation of the experience. There is little in the literature that addresses the problem of existential aloneness. Moustakas's (1961) book *Loneliness* approached the issue by distinguishing between existential loneliness as being a part of human experience, and "...loneliness anxiety as self-alienation and self-rejection" (p. 24). Moustakas stated that loneliness anxiety is "...not loneliness at all but a vague and disturbing anxiety." (p. 24), and he described Existential Loneliness as:

> an intrinsic and organic reality of human life in which there is both pain and triumphant creation emerging out of long periods of desolation. In existential loneliness man is fully aware of himself as an isolated and solitary individual while in loneliness anxiety man is separated from himself as a feeling and knowing person. (Moustakas, 1961, p. 24)

Nevertheless, there seems to be a difference between Moustakas's (1961) explanation and the problem of aloneness as a condition of being human. He made an attempt to address aloneness by stating that "Every man is alone. Ultimately, each person exists in isolation. He faces himself in silence, wending his way in individual pathways, seeking companionship, reaching out to others" (p. 54). That being said, Moustakas resumed his exploration of loneliness without pursuing the real nature of aloneness.

For me, existential aloneness means that regardless of how close we become to another person, there is always a distance. We can touch, be close, and soothe the wounds of loneliness, but there is always a barrier to that full connection with another person. Only in Roddenberry's (1966) science fiction fantasy world creation, *Star Trek*, does Commander Spock have the ability to perform the Vulcan Mind Meld and be totally connected to the sum of the thoughts, feelings, rationalizations, as well as the sum of the memory of another person. Even then Roddenberry's Spock finds the experience of knowing the memory of another, with all its emotions, overwhelmingly painful and exhausting.

Frustrated in my attempt to find a clear understanding of the problem of existential aloneness, I turned to literature. Although I have read most of my life, I did not understand the hidden existential themes in the great works of literature until I reached my early 30s. Bultmann, Barth, Buber, and Tillich were my guides in my first career as a pastor and chaplain. Freud, Jung, Rogers, Whitaker, May, Frankl, Yalom, Bruner, Kozol and Conant, were my guides in my second and third careers as a psychotherapist and as an educator. Each contributed to my understanding and formation of my *self* and my awareness of my ultimate aloneness. Nevertheless, it was in the great works of fiction that I began to see stories similar to mine and understand more of my own journey of ultimate aloneness.

## Three Works of Fiction

In my early 30s, I took an informal course that explored the themes of some great pieces of fictional literature. Among them, three stand out because of the existential themes intrinsic to the life journey of the protagonists. These three works have informed me more about my life, and my ultimate journey of aloneness, than anything else. They have helped me make meaning from the fragments and pieces of my memory.

The first was Eric Maria Remarque's (1929) *All Quiet on the Western Front*, which I believe is the definitive expression of human experience in combat. It is Remarque's own memory of the horrors of World War I; he was a soldier in the German Army, and he was wounded five times as told through the experience of his character Paul Baümer. At the urging of his schoolmaster, Baümer, only 18 years of age, enlisted in the German Army along with six of his schoolmates. He and his comrades had dreams of glory and aspirations of serving the Fatherland. Yet at 20, the promises of glory, heroism, and pride had faded. Baümer loses all of his friends, his youth, his innocence, his hopes and ambition, and finds himself in despair, alone and facing his own death. In the midst of the terror of memory that he is living through, Baümer reflected on his aloneness:

> My strength is exhausted as always after an attack, and it is so hard for me to be alone with my thoughts. They are not properly my thoughts; they are memories which in my weakness haunt me and strangely move me. (Remarque, 1929, p.119)

Reading the story evoked terror laden combat memories of my own. Once again, I tasted the stench of death; I experienced my feelings of fear, hopelessness, and despair. Like Baümer, my memories include the closeness of friends, acts of unbelievable courage, times of joy, and moments of terror. There are also the smells of blood and feces, cries of pain, and the sounds of gunfire and explosions. But unlike Remarque's Baümer, my memories have to do with jungles, rice paddies, thatched hut villages, alluvial plains, and rubber tree plantations. There are noises, sights, and smells that can trigger for me what I call a Past-Now-Time experience. Although these are 38-year old memories, they are closer in time for me than the events of last week. I have never liked the term "flashback" because it implies going back to something and remembering the time as a vivid experience. A Past-Now-Time experience is memory coming into the now in such a powerful presence that it is being lived again, and not relived as some would surmise.

When I returned from Vietnam in 1971, my second tour in Southeast Asia, I did not realize how profoundly depressed, hopeless, guilty, joyless, and weighted with ontological anxiety I was. Although I struggled for years to outrun depresssion, surprisingly it was not in years of therapy but in reading Remarque's work that I discovered the meaning of my depression; my fear of living. It was in the futility of Baümer's dreams that I came to accept my experience of ultimate aloneness:

> I am very quiet. Let the months and years come, they can take nothing from me, they can take nothing more. I am so alone, and so without hope that I can confront them without fear. The life that has borne me through these years is still in my hands and my eyes. Whether I have subdued it, I know not. But so long as it is there it will seek its own way out, heedless of the will that is within me. (Remarque, 1929, p. 295)

The second important discovery for me was Albert Camus' (1956) *The Fall*. Camus provided another insight into my journey of aloneness. His protagonist, Jean-Baptiste Clamence, once a successful Parisian attorney, now holds court as a judge-penitent in the Mexico City Bar in the red-light district of Amsterdam. Through Camus, we hear one side of Clamence's dialogue with a stranger as he confesses and justifies his narcissism and life of debauchery. As an allegory of the Biblical story of the fall from grace in the Garden of Eden, Clamence attributes his professional demise to his failure to try to rescue a woman whom he believed had committed suicide by jumping into the river Seine. Her cries torture him. He hears voices laughing at him and is confronted with his own hypocrisy. The tyranny of his memory haunts him, propels him to reject his successful life, leave his friends, and flee Paris. He becomes a prisoner of the Germans in North Africa where his fellow prisoners elect him as a pope. In this role, he decides who among them gets the scarce water and food; who shall live and who shall die.

Although he is a person who prefers the heights of ships' decks and mountain peaks, Clamence ends up in Amsterdam, a city below sea level that consists of concentric canals reminiscent of Dante's view of Hell. There, as the judge-penitent, he confronts strangers with their hypocrisy. There he lamented:

> Then please tell me what happened to you one night on the quays of the Seine and how you managed never to risk your life. You yourself utter the words that for years have never ceased echoing through my nights and that I shall at last say through your mouth: 'O young woman, throw yourself into the water once again so that I may a second time have the chance of saving both of us!' (p. 147)

People of conscience, no matter how fragile the artifact is, question their life, their motives, and their perception of themselves. They delve into their memory to explore and explain their behavior, their courage or lack thereof, their inactivity, and their relationships. The echoes in my own mind of regretful things said, or not said; things done, or not done, are very few, but they are significant to me.

Therefore, while they can gnaw at my conscience, no one else could ever possibly understand them. The actions of a person's past are evidence of ultimate aloneness for they are, despite explication, explanation and justification, known only to the one with the memory of them. They are etched in the individual's memory and no other person has full access to what is in memory.

It is the third work, however, that speaks most profoundly to me and my journey in life. In 1948, Alan Paton published what would become a classic of 20th century literature; *Cry, the Beloved Country*. Set in his homeland of South Africa, the story centers around the life of a Black (Zulu) Anglican pastor, Stephen Kumalo, a deeply pious servant of his congregation, whose beloved son Absalom has left his homeland to journey to the great bustling city of Johannesburg. Notified by a fellow priest that his youngest sister, Gertrude, is ill, Father Kumalo takes what meager savings he and his wife have accumulated and makes the long journey by train to find his sister and her child. His trip, however, becomes an opportunity to connect with his brother, John, and search for his son, Absalom. Nevertheless, the journey comes to a heart wrenching culmination when he discovers that Absalom has been accused of murdering a prominent White man. Kumalo watches helplessly as Absalom is tried, convicted and sentenced to death.

In addition, with all that has happened to him, Kumalo experiences a great betrayal by his own brother, John, a successful labor leader. John saves his own son from murder charges, and he lets his nephew Absalom (Kumalo's son) carry the guilty verdict alone.

Paton also tells the story of James Jarvis, the White land owner whose only son was murdered by Absalom. After his son's death, Jarvis comes to understand his own son's progressive position toward relations with the native population, his son's views on the origins of crime, and the extensive impact of the destruction of tribal and family life. Jarvis and Kumalo touch each other because of their mutual loss. Filled with hurt and pain, they are ultimately kind, helpful, and respectful of one another. But each of them is still alone with the loss of his son. Each still lives with the memory of his little boy. For example, in the home of his murdered adult son, Jarvis walks down the stairway:

> He took off his hat and looked down at the dark stain on the floor. Unasked, unwanted, the picture of the small boy came into his mind, the small boy at High Place, the small boy with the wooden guns. Unseeing, he walked along the passage and out of the door through which death had come so suddenly. (Paton, 1948, p. 180)

Kumalo, facing the hanging of his son for that same murder, climbs to a mountain top near his home the night before the hanging is to take place in the far-off city of Pretoria. The mountain top is a place to which Kumalo has gone on several occasions to pray: the first time was when Absalom was a small boy close to death, and once when he was tempted to commit adultery:

It was an angle in the rock, sheltered from the winds, with a place for a man to sit on, his legs at ease over the ed ge. The first of these occasions he remembered clearly, perhaps because it was the first, perhaps because he had come to pray for the child that no prayer could save anymore. The child could not write then, but here were three letters from him now, and in all of them he said, If I could come back to Ndottsheni [his village] I should not leave it any more. And in a day or two he would receive the last letter he would ever write. His heart went out in a great compassion for the boy that must die. (Paton, 1948, p. 308)

Sitting alone Kumalo prepares for the sunrise. But he does more than grieve his loss of his son. He confesses his own sin, an act of recalling memory, and then he gives thanks for the many people who have loved him, provided for him, welcomed him, and supported him in his travail. He remembers his journey.

Paton's (1948) work was a cry against the emerging call for Apartheid in the late 1940s. His hope was that the veterans of World War II would have nothing to do with it. It was written out of his deep sense of the struggle that was changing tribal life, families, and the church for both Blacks and Whites. His love for the people and the land, and his hope for South Africa are clearly evident in this work. Nonetheless, amid the backdrop of the growing call of Whites for Apartheid, the story's existential theme of aloneness is amplified to an almost painful crescendo.

This story touched me because I grew up in the Southern United States in the era of racial segregation when the prevailing view was that White people were superior to Black people and that separation of the races was the rule. I remember very clearly, even the date of December 13, 1948, coming to consciousness about the issue of segregation in the South, and I knew something was wrong with this way of thinking and living. That night, while Christmas shopping with my family in the Atlanta's Sears Roebuck department store; a White male sales clerk grabbed me by the scruff of the neck as I started to get a drink from the water cooler. "What's the matter with you boy? Can't you read that sign? That there is a colored drinking fountain." At almost 8 years old, I had the awareness that I was alone in my feelings; I became acutely aware of the great injustice to Black people.

I went to college and seminary during the 1950s and 1960s, but I never heard of Apartheid, *Cry the Beloved Country,* or the history of the Union of South Africa for that matter. Nevertheless, like Kumalo, I did know what it was like to be ultimately alone. First as an associate pastor and later as the pastor of an inner-city Atlanta church during the Civil Rights struggle of the mid-1960s, I was ridiculed in the press, and scorned by some parishioners when I tried to establish a dialog between the races in our religious community. Although Apartheid in South Africa and racial segregation in the U.S. had different antecedents and roots, the effect was the same. They both divided communities, destroyed families and lives, and fostered hatred and mistrust.

## It Is Aloneness Not Loneliness

Like the protagonists of these stories, I have experienced times of hurt, despair and isolation. There are times when I too feared that God had indeed forsaken me. In addition, like the protagonists, I have also experienced the great pain of betrayal by close friends and loved ones. May I say that it is my belief that a person can only be betrayed by a close trusted friend or loved one. Betrayal is a violation of the profound trust we place in one so close that we think we know that person intimately. That is why it hurts so much when it happens. However, when a person known to you to have a characterological problem wrongs you, that is not betrayal, it is only behavior that you should have expected.

Nevertheless, it should be clear that in this essay I am not talking about personal experiences of loneliness. Although I have experienced periods of profound loneliness in my life, as I believe all people have, for the most part, I am seldom lonely. My life has been filled with joy by the love of a wonderful, selfless, caring woman; my wife of 32 years. I have been renewed by the innocent laughter and goodness of my grandchildren and their parents. I have been strengthened by wonderful, close, supportive friends whose love has empowered and lifted me in times when I could have easily given way to despair. Indeed, like Kumalo, Baümer, and even Clamence, I am surrounded by good loving and faithful people. And, like Father Kumalo, I give thanks for them.

## Memory Creates Our Aloneness

For over 50 years as a pastor, soldier, psychotherapist, and educator I have learned from the stories of people that we are each ultimately alone in our life's journey. I have also discovered in these and other works of fiction that my journey, indeed your journey, is unique. Like a fingerprint, a retinal scan, or the unique growth of dendrites from new learning, no one else will ever have your memory or be able to replicate it. Yet, we are all desperate to know and be known by another. Therefore, like small lifeboats on the turbulent ocean, we might touch for a time, but ultimately our journey is one of aloneness.

In reflecting on the journey of existential aloneness, I have concluded the red thread woven in each of the stories cited above, and indeed in each of our stories, is that of the uniqueness of our individual memory. Baümer, Clamence, and Kumalo, like you and I, have unique memories. It is the simple, unique, infallible memory of the events of their individual journeys, and ours, which produce existential aloneness. Because my memory is unique to my interpretation of my experience, and because it is infallible, that is it is not subject to review and alignment with the reality of others, I am ultimately alone with it. No one else has had my journey or your journey of experience. Others may have shared the same touch points of experience, as Baümer's friends did with him in the trenches, as Clamence's fellow prisoners did with him in the concentration camp, or Kumalo's fellow priests did in Johannesburg rectory. But, they could not ascribe the same meaning that Baümer, Clamence, or Kumalo did to the same experience.

For example, Clamence, in his reverie, laments that he did not act to prevent a suicide. In this lament he not only ascribes meaning to the woman's behavior, as a suicide, he places a moral judgment on his own behavior, and both occur as a result of his memory of the event. He feels guilt for failing to act, for being afraid, for being hesitant. Kumalo and Jarvis' reverie is for the youth and innocence of their sons; Baümer's memory is of the closeness he felt toward his dead friend when they stole a goose and spent the night cooking and then eating it. Each character ascribes meaning to the sights, the sounds, and the total experience recorded in their individual memory. Thus memory, although a distorted recording of reality, is infused with phenomenological experiences of sights, sounds, smells, touch and tastes. In addition, memory is interpreted by our intrinsic value judgments: It was good, it was bad, I am good, I am bad.

## Memory is the Key

I wish Descartes had said, I *remember,* therefore I am. Perhaps, that is what he meant to say. Nevertheless, it is our memory, and of course our thoughts about that memory, that signifies our existence. Although memory can be corrupted by a cardio vascular accident, the deterioration of our aging process, or even by interference from outside sources as was discovered in the *brain washing* experiments during the Korean War, or more recently in the false-memory conundrum of the 1990's, it is still the memory and not necessarily the reality of the individual experience that is important.

Therefore, to make a quantum leap, it seems to me that it is not the fear of death per se, or the fleeting thought that at some point we will not *be* that evokes ontological anxiety. On the contrary, it is the fear of not being able to remember beyond life that does so. We fear the loss of the one faculty that makes us an *I am.* The existential question that seems to be the central struggle of all great religions of the world is, Do I remember me beyond death? Will I continue to be an *I am*? Or will I cease to be an *I am* and be absorbed or adsorbed into nothingness. Most religious traditions and rituals, in general, are centered on remembering. We celebrate by remembering our ancestors, the acts of our deities, the promises that beyond death we will not just be remembered, we will indeed have memory.

Yet, as humans, we also struggle with the tyranny of memory, the terror of memory, and the hurt of memory as it affects our lives. All three are reasons we go to therapy or do therapy with others. We seek to calm the tyranny, make the terror less disruptive, and heal the hurts of memory. In a way, we make new memories from the dreams and reflections about our memory, and we call that making meaning from our experiences. For me, memory is the only truly individual activity we possess, and understood in this way, I am not averse to calling a suicide the murder of memory.

Over the past 40 years, cognitive psychology and neuropsychology have contributed to our growing, but as of yet incomplete, understanding of what memory actually is. In my neuropsychology courses I learned that memory, simply put, is our ability to store and recall sequences of experience as they are fixed chemically to neuronal communication, first in the frontal lobes, and then in the other lobes where sensory information, visual, auditory, gustatory, smell, and tactile experiences, and the accompanying emotions of the event, fear, hurt, frustration, joy are also affixed. Finally, as an intrinsic part of the memory, we include an overlay of our value judgments about the event and our behavior. What is then essentially brief or short-term memory, depending on its importance to us, can move to long-term storage. Other physical structures of the brain such as the amygdala and hippocampus assists the process of moving memory from short-term to long-term storage by changing neural connections, creating new pathways, and spreading memory throughout the brain. I leave all of that to my more scientifically minded colleagues who are exploring this three-pound universe called the human brain, and the ethereal mind that is the keeper of the memory.

## Summary

Existential aloneness is a constant of human existence. It is not dependent on loneliness or the lack thereof, our proximity to a loved one, or even to those who might betray or revile us. It is simply our human condition, spawned and maintained by our memory, which is the only legacy of our life's journey. What I have proposed in this essay is that the factor that makes us uniquely human is our ability to reflect on our journey and realize that we are ultimately alone. It is memory that is the vehicle by which we do this reflection. Alas, ultimate aloneness is our existential condition. Because of the uniqueness of our memory, of our journey, no one else can ever fully know us, which leaves us ultimately alone. To be sure others, including therapists, can categorize, diagnose, and reduce us to interpretation, but they can only know what we reveal to them from our memory. Even then, they cannot possibly understand our individual experience in full. Perhaps that frustration is what leads many therapists to simply employ their tool bag techniques to change behaviors in people rather than journey with them in the effort to make meaning from the experience of memory.

Nevertheless, the most important factor in this essay might well be my conclusion that anxiety about physical death is not the ultimate anxiety we as humans experience. In our existential condition of ultimate aloneness, it is our fear about loss of memory, of ceasing to be an *I am* that is the basis of real ontological anxiety.

## References

Camus, A. (1956). *The fall.* (J. O'Brien, Trans.). New York, NY: Vantage Books.
Moustakas, C. (1961). *Loneliness.* New York, NY: Prentice-Hall.
Paton, A. (1948). *Cry, the beloved country.* New York, NY: Scribner.
Remarque, E. (1929), *All quiet on the Western front* (A. W. Wheen, Trans.). New York, NY: Ballantine.
Roddenberry, G. (Producer). (1966). Star Trek [Television series]. Los Angeles, CA: NBC.

Yalom, I. (1989). *Loves executioner: And other tales of psychotherapy.* New York, NY: Perennial.

# Chapter 19

## In Harmony with the Sky (天, Tian, Universe): Implications for Existential Psychology[1]

### Albert Chan

Although the word psychology had not been introduced in Asia until recently, I have always thought that Chinese psychology has developed over the thousands of years of Chinese culture. It integrates science and the laws of nature, agriculture and industry, philosophy and poetry, and history and politics. This psychology favors the collective and social aspects of humans, their relationship with each other, and their harmony with the ever present symbolic and mythic principles of sky nature (天, *Tian*, universe) (He 2007; Wang, 2008). In Chinese psychology, personal phenomenological and ontological experiences of the individual have been neglected or compromised.

In this respect it is very different from many modern Western clinical theories, which are based in a scientific mythology based in the separateness and discreteness of each individual. Since Descartes' (1637, see also Watson, 2018) famous statement, "*Cognito ergo sum*, I think therefore I am." Western psychology has been focusing on individual consciousness and individualistic expressions of emotion, thoughts, and behaviors. These experiences are reduced, defined, measured, and analyzed, but rarely realigned with the whole person or the larger society context. This minimized psychology has helped to try to capture the label of a scientific discipline, but shuns addressing the larger questions of existence and how does one live a meaningful life.

On the other hand, Chinese psychology has more directly sought a more holistic, experiential, and embodied understanding the psyche (Bond, 1986; 1993; Wang 2008). However, this approach to existence has been deeply, and to a large degree, subconsciously, subjected to the ideas of Confucianism, and more specifically Confucianism's view of collectivism. In this chapter I am going to analyze the Chinese ideas and myths of the importance of humans being in harmony with the sky nature (天, Tian, universe) and its implications for the existential perspective of psychology. I believe that this foundational idea of finding harmony within the sky nature, has influenced the Chinese development of their collective psycho-social and political psyche, and in turn has had an immense impact on Chinese

[1] I want to acknowledge Francis J. Kaklauskas for his generous feedback and editorial assistance in completing this chapter.

cultural context, individuals' social relationships, and individuals' relationship with themselves. Collective and social harmony surely develops under such a context, but at the cost to the personal individuation of each member of society.

## Returning Home

I was born in Hong Kong, but most of my adult life, I lived in the Western communities of England, the United States, and Canada. Two years before this writing, I returned to live in Hong Kong. On the surface my return was for new opportunities to teach and lecture; however, in my heart, I have discovered hidden meanings. Living in Hong Kong makes me feel like I am already home, but sometimes I feel like I need to return to Canada where I founded my individual *self*. Perhaps, in the depth of my Chinese psyche I am yearning to be completed with a collective order, a collective sense of psyche, which Jung (1965) emphasized, but my individual self keeps questioning the validity of my yearning.

Recently I have been supervising a group of students in Shenzhen. We meet in a hotel named *Harmony*. The Chinese name is *Tien, Die, Yen* hotel, whose direct translation is, "Heaven, Earth, and Man." When I travel in China, I have seen similar names in different provinces and cities throughout the country. It makes me wonder if we, as Chinese, are yearning to be at peace with the universe, or in a more holistic sense, I wonder if we are reminding ourselves that we are part of the universe. My curiosity set me venturing into meanings in Chinese mythology.

## Sky

Sky (天, Tian, universe) bears the synonym of nature (He, 2007; Wang, 2008). It is the dominant force regulating the cosmic order. Besides being the home of the god and goddesses, Sky encapsulates moral commands, from on high, one might say. The ancient agricultural Chinese culture developed and co-existed with the sky. The importance of coexisting with and being in harmony with the sky nature, the sky cosmic orders, and the sky moral commands is embedded in the Chinese collective culture. Sky nature has been ingrained in each Chinese life for thousands of years. I believe this sky nature belief system provides insight into the Chinese personality, and is vital to understand and consider when working with Chinese clients in psychotherapy.

### In Sichuan

After the earthquake in Sichuan, on May 12, 2008, I went up to Chendu, where the disastrous response center was located. Many Tibetans, which are members of one of the minority peoples of China, live in Sichuan. In my travel there, I had the fortune of having a dinner with a Tibetan family. The family organized a traditional BBQ lamb dinner for travelers, and over the generous and delicious meal, I was told about the *Sky Burial*.

My hosts explained to me that Tibetans live at very high altitude; the average elevation is 4,900 meters (16,000 ft). It is the highest region on Earth and is commonly referred to as the *Roof of the World*. Tibetans rely on herding sheep and cows on the plateau grasslands. They believe their life is dictated by nature, the mountains, the sky, and the rivers. Tibetans believe that humans have two lives; a physical life and a spiritual life. The spiritual life is everlasting and death is the beginning passage. When someone is dying the passage from the physical life to the spiritual life breaks open. A close family member or a friend will gently talk to the dying person that his or her physical life is coming to the end. The dying person will be reminded to let go of the Earthy physical body and enter to the spiritual world, to mingle with the sky and the true nature of all existence.

A sky burial scaffold is built halfway up the mountain away from chilly winds, and from there, the spirit will ascend to heaven to join the gods and goddesses. The burial ritual is performed by a Tibetan Buddhist priest in three stages. First, the corpse with a cloth covering the head is put on the scaffold naked and facing downwards towards the Earth. Then smoke is raised to attract eagles to snatch the outer flesh. After this initial clearing of the flesh, the priest then uses a surgical knife to separate all the bones, organs, and tendons to allow the eagles full access to the body. Finally, the priest removes the cloth covering the face and head. It is believed that the faster the physical body is decimated, the sooner the spiritual body will start the homeward journey to heaven.

Sky Burial sounds mysterious but also horrific. I was told about this ritual just after dusk, and I felt the presence of the spirit world, of which they were talking, all around me. Tibetans believe humans are created by the nature of all things and that our spirits return back to this nature. Death and the destruction of the body allow us to achieve harmony with nature and the natural order of things. The inevitable cycle of life and death provides the ground for deep meaning in our limited time in human form (Ga, Cai, & Ge, 2000). Although this is a Buddhist ritual, it echoes the Taoist understanding of our search to be united with sky, heaven, nature (He 2007; Ho, 1995; Wang, 2008).

This cross-cultural and cross-religious Chinese belief of being reunited with nature has developed from Chinese philosophy (He 2007; Ho, 1995; Wang, 2008). It is believed that humans, as finite beings, need to rely on the unlimited sky to be complete and to become in harmony with nature. These ideas are found in all the major religions of China: Confucianism, Taoism, and Buddhism. Although there are differences between each understanding; however, I want to draw focus to the similarities.

These ideas could be simply explained in that sky nature dictates the fate of humans and at the same time grants blessings on us. We are dependent upon and are part of the sky nature. A human life is finite, but the sky is infinite. These concepts emerged during the period when China was primarily an agricultural society. Nature provided the resources for survival, while at the same time nature constricted the communities with impervious destructive forces such as drought, fire, and disease. Sichuan had just experienced recent economic growth that was lost in the aftermath of the deadly earthquake.

Infinite sky nature sets boundaries on humans, but we are not helpless. Humans have an endless reservoir of spirit that allows us to adapt and adjusts to changes and to coexist within these contradicting tensions. The sky nature does not necessary stand in opposition to the human existence, but co-exists with us. The sky nature is the passage between the infinite and the finite (He, 2007; Ho, 1995; Wang, 2008).

**In Harmony with Sky**
The concept of humans seeking to be in harmony with the sky nature has existed since ancient China. We have had to find a way to exist despite, and in co-existence with, the contradicting tensions between the infinite sky nature and human limitedness. The Chinese farmer has always given blessing to the infinite sky nature as it provides all the necessary resources for life: soil, rain, crops, and livestock. Simultaneously, the farmer is also at the mercy of the unpredictable and unwelcome aspects of sky nature: drought, sickness, earthquakes, and death.

While I was traveling from Hong Kong to Macau to teach at Macau Inter-University Institute, I met a coarse-looking man with tattoos down both of his arms. I had been talking with my dean about a student and had not realized that this man had been listening to our conversation. He came up to us and asked my profession. I told him I was a lecturer at a university and family therapist, and he took this as an invitation or opportunity to educate me about sky nature. He was like a modern sage that I met not on the ancient Silk Road, but on a state of the art hovercraft. He explained he retired as a fisherman 9 years before because the sea gave less fish than ever before. He said he was not so brash and foolish as to compete with the sky nature.

He described his experience of fishing. He would go to sea with his crew for a week at a time. He would travel into the ocean, where there was only the sea and sky as far as he could see in all directions. He awoke each day at dawn, and worked until dusk when he would be rocked to sleep by great waves. He said that although he made a living, he understood that he risked his life each trip. He felt tremendous humility in the power and vastness of the sea, but his greatest respect went to the sky. He said no human could complete with nature. Many of his friends had lost their life to the sea as sky nature did not give mercy to them. He believed that his life and his livelihood depended on the blessing and mercy of the sky. He praised the sea goddess for her generosity, but feared the sky immensely.

He explained that each time at sea, he would struggle and maneuver with and within sky nature to maximize his catch. He wanted to make his words clear so I understood that he was not only talking personally, but mythically. "This is not only the fate of the fisherman, but this is all of life." The immense contradicting tensions are shown in the lines of fear and gratitude in his face. On each journey, he was hopeful and hopeless, assertive and subservient. I finally understood what the spiritual traditions of China had been trying to teach me: One must find a union with oneself and sky nature. This is the essence of harmony.

Chinese culture and collectivism has been built upon this foundation. Perhaps, only through the notions of harmony and being in collective can humans survive. Striving for this harmony is a pragmatic journey, as it supports the individual but also the timeless Chinese collectivist values and institutions of family structure, social order, and survival. This shaped our shared and complicity agreed-upon ethics and morality.

## Grand Dad Sky

The following sky myth illustrates how earnestly the Chinese desire harmony. The story was told to me by a student I supervised. In his village, they have an annual festival for the *Grand Dad Sky*. It is the most important festival of his village; all households have to participate. All have to contribute food that gets redistributed after the celebration. The priest leads the worship and has the obligation to be fair in the redistribution of food, as *Grand Dad Sky* is fair. During the ceremony, the priest invites the gods and goddesses from heaven to give blessings to the village.

The annual festival recognizes the infinite of the sky nature. A myth that humanizes the gods and goddesses accompanies the celebration. The community is destined to receive both blessings and curses from the gods and goddesses. Therefore, by offering food, the community tries to bribe them to provide only blessing. The resolution comes as they meet in the middle. If the community agrees to be submissive to their orders and be harmonized with the sky nature, the gods and goddesses will be less wrathful.

### Chinese Collective Foundation

I believe that the phenomena I have described above form a significant part of the foundation for the prevailing cultural collectivism, belief systems, and myths of the contemporary Chinese civilization (Wang, 2008). The co-existing tensions and blessings between human beings and the nature sky (天, Tian, universe) are endless. To be in harmony with nature without disturbing the blessings and good faith from the sky (天, Tian, universe) nature is the destiny of human beings. This belief is core in Confucianism and Taoism: the union of humanity and the sky (天, Tian, universe) nature is the essence of harmony. These concepts continue to influence Chinese civilization and culture. Therefore, Chinese existence is based on harmony with the collective context and in relating to nature. The Chinese psychological sense of collective security has developed on the platform of harmony within collectivism (Gou, 2008; He 2007; Wang, 2008). Chinese security has emphasized its collective roots and skirted the Western individualism that has been exported globally by way of global mercantile structures and mass media. We recognize, however, that many Western ideas have already permeated the social organization of the East and that there will be a continued mutual interpenetration of ideas resulting from increasing contact through commerce, tourism, and the media.

## The Self and the Collective

In my heart and through my contemplations, I believe individualism is a given. But in the Chinese cultural collective context, individualist concepts have to be endorsed and legitimized by the rulers of the social order and in turn legitimized by the sky (天, Tian, universe) nature. This legitimizing of hierarchy is analogous to that achieved by ancient Chinese emperors. The worship of the sky (天, Tian, universe) in China was started with the Emperor of Huang (Huang Di) (He 2007; Ho, 1995; Wang, 2008). He built the worship altar not only to use it for worshipping the sky (天, Tian, universe), but also to ask heaven to legitimize his ruling legacy. Confucius stated that worshipping heaven signified emperors receiving the blessing and heavenly orders to rule their kingdom. This ritual signified the emperors of ancient China gaining the passage to rule. Those who received the blessings would rule and those who lost the blessings would lose their kingdom in chaos and die. Chinese culture, thus, embraced harmony, which enabled everyone to live cooperatively.

Ancient Chinese history records that emperors sent their daughters to marry the neighboring princes in order to establish a harmonized relationship between territories. If this harmony was not established, Chinese rulers were obligated to prevent chaos by any means at their disposal. The Great Wall was built under the command of many Chinese rulers between the 600 BC and the 16th century. The goal was to protect the northern borders of the Chinese Empire and to ensure harmony. We could say that these emperors merely did not want to be attacked, but psychologically, it bears the symbolic meaning of guarding the harmony. From my perspective, the Chinese emperors feared the disharmony, chaos, and consequences of war.

## Confucianism: Preservation of Order and Harmony

Most Chinese hold a psychologically-based fear of chaos and conflicts. They endorse a collective psyche and consequently a strict social order rooted back to the rise of Confucianism. During that chaotic time in ancient China, centuries before the birth of Christ, order set the boundaries that preserved individuals and the collective. Their fear is evident throughout history in seeking peace and harmony. Confucius wanted to have a social order in which everyone would be in harmony. The values of Confucianism, like the Great Wall, have preserved Chinese social and political systems, as well as family structures over millennia. Confucius constructed five relationships to which he wanted the Chinese to strictly adhere. These are relationships between: ruler and subject, father and son, husband and wife, elder brother and younger brother, and friend and friend (Bond & Hwang, 1986). With strict obedience to these five social orders, the harmony of the collective society will be preserved.

Filial piety, the father-son relationship, is considered the most important among the five Confucian relationships. Historically, a central Chinese value is the strict family structure that requires devotion and obligations of children to their parents. It is parallel to the strict devotion and loyalty to the emperor from officials (Bond, 1986; Bond & Hwang, 1986; Gou, 2008). Confucian filial piety provides an example of culturally defined intergenerational relationships with absolute obedience. Although some of its component ideas (obedience, for example) are shared by other cultures, filial piety surpasses all other ethical prescriptions in its historical continuity, the proportion of humanity under its governance, and the full, encompassing and imperative nature of its precepts. The attributes of intergenerational relationships governed by filial piety are structural, enduring, and invariable across situations within Chinese culture. They may be generalized to apply to authority relationships beyond the family, and they are, thus, potent determinants of not only intergenerational, but also superior-subordinate interactions.

I remember when I was a child; my father was, in a typical way, the outsider to the family. He worked, and we had a very distant relationship that appeared harmonious but had unseen tensions. He wrote on a board in our home that "when a family is harmonious everything is perfect and when a family is problematic there will be unceasing conflicts." In my father's eyes, *harmony* among family member was not just central guiding principle, it was the essence of his existence. His beliefs were deeply reinforced in the collective perspective that the security of the collective is rooted in harmony within the family. At this current stage of my life, having been a father myself, I understand and am deeply moved by this paternal essence. At the same time, I am conflicted by the attitudes I absorbed in my journey of adulthood in individualist communities of the West. Sometimes, I am puzzled by several notions: Do we become secure by first being self-differentiated and later are enabled to be united and connected with others in a more intimate union? Or do we find our integrity by playing the strict, assigned role and through acceptance of it come to appreciate the collective security of being? Or can both collective and individualistic natures of human beings co-exist in the paradox of human nature and, thus, be cherished by human existence? When these two "natures" are in conflict, it seems that the contraction within self could broaden to conflicts in other intimate relationships, which could eventually result in conflicts between groups and even nations. Nonetheless, from the family systems perspective, emotional conflicts and projections within the cross generational and nuclear Chinese family will generate the sense of a deep need for harmony as well as a fear of chaos and conflicts (Bowen, 1994). Hence, I believe my father desired harmony and feared conflicts.

During my studies in the West, I came to adopt Bowen's ideas of self-differentiation, which includes a view of the individual self as being both intrapsychic and interpersonal, that is both individualistic and collective. It is the ability to reflect on an individual's wish and feeling but not respond automatically to emotion. Perhaps the debate of individualistic and collective culture is only a rhetoric expression; the consciousness of a human's self, embraces both individual and collective meanings. Leading existential psychologists, Ed Menedelowitz (2008) and Kirk Schneider (2008), grounded the examination of the nature of self in ideas similar to Martin Buber (1970) and a contemporary Buber scholar, Maurice Fried-man (1999), who expressed an implicit recognition of these dual aspects of human nature. For a mature individual, one needs the blessing found in the paradox of individual independence and collective interdependence.

## Emotion in a Chinese Mind

For the Chinese people, showing emotions is risky business. Emotions are danger-ous because they demonstrate individual desire and chaos; both of which are often threats to relational and collective harmony. Consequently, Emotions need to be suppressed, denied, ignored, and jettisoned from the self-experience. From a traditional Chinese medicine perspective, emotions are evidence of internal imbalance. Therefore, emotions are signs of illness (Bond, 1993; Kleinman, 1986). Strong feelings are dangerous because they may be contagious.

When compared to the West, emotions are less valued and relevant in the Asian psyche (Potter, 1988). The expression of emotions has no social value, nor do they move the individual or the collective towards any possible constructive outcome. For example, unlike Westerners who engage with the emotional expressions of others, the Chinese believe that the open expression of feelings should be met with only indifference. My early training in emotional constriction served me poorly when I moved to the West, but the openness I worked hard to attain has often been met with concern and confusion when I returned to Asia. When I urge students to embody and passionately engage with the psychological concepts they are learning, they look at me as if I am speaking a foreign language and not our native Cantonese.

In the West, I learned to communicate in a more transparent, assertive, and candid manner. It was not an easy task. It was filled with false starts, awkward moments, and profound self-doubt and conflict. Not only did I have to fight against my internalized cultural bias, but I believe my temperament has always been introverted and shy. However, I learned that only through sharing my opinions that my knowledge and wisdom was expanded and enriched. Only by sharing myself did I move towards the true intimacy I longed for. When I returned to Hong Kong with my new skills, I experienced a cultural shock. Chinese colleagues and students desired hierarchy and harmony within the education context, not the interactive and fiery discourse I learned to admire in my Western education.

At first, I could not understand why students remained silent when I asked for their opinions and experiences, but after one class a brave and insightful student shyly approached me. She said that although the students appreciated my invitations they dare not disturb the classroom by interrupting the teacher to ask a question. They had never experienced a pedagogy in which their opinions were valued. This experience helped to reacquainted me with the power of filial piety and its psychological consequences. Within a collective learning context, a student never draws attention away from the teacher's expertise. Students may have questions, doubts, and even feelings, but these have to remain secret, as individual learning is subordinate to the social order. In Chinese culture, feedback and complaints must only be given by those higher in the collective social order. Therefore, despite my repeated invitations, I rarely received the honest feedback from students that would improve my teaching. It is a closed system that does not engage in process and consequently limits progress.

Professors are seen as the knowledge and wisdom experts; therefore, among students, acceptance and patience without contesting is the most respectful and harmonious attitude. It nullifies the possibility that the harmony within the learning environment will be disturbed. This sheds new insight into my understanding of the Chinese personality. The Chinese character reveres harmony and subverts itself to the societal and cosmic hierarchy. The Chinese have blindly accepted an oversimplified understanding of the Taoist beliefs that to be harmonized with the natural order is the supreme way of being.

### Avoidance of Conflicts

According to Tao, to avoid unnecessary controversy and to be in harmony with one's world is the goal of life (Gou, 2008; Ho, 1995). It is also a pragmatic way of life. The Tao is quintessentially Chinese allowing its adherents to attain harmony with the universe, the social orders, and with nature. If we seek harmony, we can alleviate and avoid suffering. A negative definition is adopted because, as in physical illness versus health, people more readily agree on what psychological suffering is than they do on happiness. Moreover, just as physical well-being is achieved in medicine through the prevention and cure of illnesses, so we shall attempt to achieve psychological well-being by the avoidance and alleviation of suffering. One is not just a metaphor of the other. From an evolutionary point of view, physical and psychological well-being go hand-in-hand. What is good for the body usually makes us feel good emotionally, and vice versa. The so-called pragmatic philosophies of Taoism and Buddhism as understood in China reinforce this belief.

All these stories deeply reflect the ancient Chinese belief that an individual becomes mature as his or her life harmonizes with heaven. These same ideas continue to be elaborated by modern Chinese philosophies (Gou, 2008; He 2007; Ho, 1995; Wang, 2008) The understanding these beliefs suggest is when people become mature, their minds will have integrated with the cosmic orders. Once they achieve this maturity, they breathe with the cosmic rhythms. I have found that my context has profoundly influenced my beliefs; as I settle more into my new life in China, I discover a deeper appreciation of these beliefs.

## Existential Givens in Chinese Psychology of Harmony

Recently, a couple sought my services to assist with their eldest son. He had not eaten for 5 days and had not spoken to them for over a month. I will call this family the Voiceless Family. There were four members in the family: the father is Chinese, the mother is Filipino, their eldest son (the identified patient), G, is 32 years old, and his brother is two years younger. The parents met in Canada and have been married over 33 years. Mr. and Mrs. Voiceless worried that their son's condition had worsened, over time. In Hong Kong, where they now live, crisis workers are not readily available. Since I had worked as a crisis therapist at a hospital in Toronto for several years, they were able to locate me in Hong Kong.

G studied in primary and secondary schools in Hong Kong. He then went abroad to attend college before returning home. After school, G had worked as a computer technician until he was laid off in 2007. Since then G had stayed at home with his parents. It was apparent that his mental health was declining. Mr. Voiceless was afraid that their sons would lose their facility with the Chinese language and forget their cultural roots, so the parents wanted them to return to Hong Kong.

G first returned from Canada when he was 3 years old. Both Voiceless parents went to work and put him and his brother under the care of his grandmother and aunts. Such familial support is common in China and indeed is virtually mandatory. The extended family was initially disturbed that G did not have the mastery of Cantonese that was typical of other 3-year-olds in their community. He was told that he was dumb because his language skills did not meet the family's expectations. Moreover, he looked different since his mother was Filipino. As G matured, he became markedly quiet and reserved. In his adolescence, he would try to defend the insults cast upon him by stating that he was introverted and shy like his father. Throughout his development, G rarely raised his voice to assert his ideas and tried to avoid of conflicts with his family and peers. Apparently, Mr. Voiceless was the biggest avoider.

My initial phone conversation was with G and his mother. G said that he did not really know his father. Mrs. Voiceless quickly discounted G's experience and stated that their boys love both their parents. G quickly asserted back that he did not know the love his mother was talking about. The mother then attacked her soon again by retelling an earlier consultation with psychiatrist in which G was labeled as capable of rationality, but incapable of having feelings. I did not engage in the dynamics over the phone and simply arranged a time for me to visit family in their home.

As I traveled to meet the family, I was not sure what to expect. I had the recollection of being struck by a paranoid youth 25 years earlier when I had just begun my career. As I entered the home, Mr. and Mrs. Voiceless looked worried and pointed me to G's room. When I entered the small room, G was sitting on the floor. He neither rose to greet me, nor did he look at me. He was quite slim and his sad and suspicious eyes stared out at the wall from under his greasy hair. My instincts told me to sit on the floor near the door and not force communication. In our silence, we heard voices of the family talking about him.

After a few minutes, I introduced myself again and explained that I had been invited by his parents to assist him and his family. He now had the choice to either engage with me or to ask me to leave. His first statement was, "Nobody listens; I have nothing to say." While I felt like I should get up and leave, I continued to sit with him silently. He soon began to talk directly and deeply with me. He stated that he was physically abused by his grandmother and aunts, and that he was teased and bullied by schoolmates because he looked different. He said that the best way for him to keep peace was to be silent. He only liked to go out late at night when there was no one on the street. He put his head down which seemed to symbolize that he was finished talking with me for now.

I returned to the living room and was met by Mr. Voiceless who quickly told me that G, like himself, does not like conflicts, keeping the peace was seen as vital to his family's survival. Mr. Voiceless went on to explain that his brothers and sisters have land in the New Territory that is very valuable and that it is essential that his wife and sons do not create trouble in his extended family. Mr. Voiceless explained that his brothers and sisters can be abusive and make his family the objects of their jokes. Mr. Voiceless tried to minimize contact with his extended family for this reason, but G protested that he did not want to see any of these relatives, not even once a year on the Chinese New Year. Mr. Voiceless admitted that there is conflict among his siblings about the land, but he accepted the way his family was. He denied that he was afraid of asserting his opinions with his family, but stated that he chose to make peace and avoid conflict. He accepted the collective family decisions even though he was not convinced that they were fair. He asked me if I understood that the collective co-existence prevails over any *individual*'s desire. I asked whether he had internal conflicts between his own needs and his family's collective decisions. He then smiled in a way that did not mask his underlying bitterness.

Mrs. Voiceless came and joined us. She stated that her husband never talks to her about his family, the land, or the conflicts that trouble his own family. She quickly became emotional. She said that she loves her husband and sons and feels that she did the best she could as a wife and mother, but felt her job was done as her sons had become adults. She desired to move forward into the next stage of her life with or without her family, although she worried that if she left, her sons would not be able to withstand the collective emotional ridicule from her husband's family. She has grown resentful of her husband's silence. In consequence, she also learned to be voiceless and, therefore, her sons are the same. Now each of her sons had turned into *hiding youths*, a new contemporary term to describe youth with emotional problems whose refuge is the isolation of their room where they spend their days playing computer games.

According to Mrs. Voiceless, her husband had been living a life without direction or meaning. He refused to change or grow. She gave the example that he ordered dim sum every time the family went out for lunch because that is the family tradition, even though neither he nor his family actually enjoyed this traditional meal. He lives and breathes, but has not done anything since he returned to Hong Kong. He just ate, slept and gambled to pass time. She was the one tackling life pressures and conflicts. Unfortunately, he *quietly* demanded that his wife and sons live as he has lived. If they did not comply, he verbally attacked them, accusing them of being angry people and then he would withdraw again.

In discussing the harmony with the sky (天, Tian, universe), I have often wondered how much China's way of collectivism stifles individuals' authentic self as proposed by existential psychotherapy. In my sessions with the Voiceless family, we explored these themes. I asked them if love could only be expressed through obedience; if life could be harmonious when life is only half lived, fulfilling prescribed roles; if harmony could only be achieved by sacrificing one's self and one's family?

Rollo May (1981), regarded freedom as "man's capacity to take a hand in his own development. It is our capacity to mold ourselves" (p. 7). In Mr. Voiceless's situation, he blindly followed his destiny without question and without allowing himself or his sons to grow. Tragedy happened not only to him but also to the next generation.

Any values that a person develops will be based upon his or her experience of autonomy and the sense of personal power and possibilities. G was not able to express himself. His voice and experience were not being heard and consequently he chose to shut down. I suspect that freedom is enhanced when one's expression is recognized regardless whether it is accepted or rejected.

G's first statement to me was, "Nobody listens; I have nothing to say." May (1981) suggested that freedom is life's creative goal and coercive destiny is the opposite because it "leads to decay" (p. 19). Therefore, freedom gives meaning to destiny. As there is no freedom or meanings in G's life, he chose to avoid life, to become a breathing corpse.

In terms of love. G had not felt loved. According to Eric Fromm's (1956/2000) *Art of Loving*, G had not felt the experience of an exchange of respect or the cherishing of self and other's ideas, desires, thoughts, life-goals, and performance. I asked Mr. Voiceless if he ever wanted his father to tell him about his internal emotional life. Mr. Voiceless quietly admitted his wishes. I simply asked Mr. Voiceless if he could do this for his sons. Over time, Mr. Voiceless and G began to speak more honestly and openly with each other. Although Mr. Voiceless did not change his stance of trying to maintain peace and harmony with his extended family, he was able to let the rest of his family make their own choices of not visiting with this side of the family.

Mr. Voiceless also began to identify and question the conflicting family roles he adhered to. I asked if he wanted to be the well-behaved younger brother of his family or would he prefer to be his sons' father. Did he want to lose his wife because she did not comply to the ideas of obedience that are not part of her culture, or was he willing to feel the anxiety of doing something new, uncharted, alive, and even passionate? Mrs. Voiceless also found more of her voice. She clearly stated that she is no longer would participate in a life of obedience and silence, and that she would like him to join her in the time they had left. While his father struggled with changing the strict societal roles, G surprising bloomed. The idea of creating his own destiny was not dissimilar to his journey in the computer games he used to use for escape, but G wanted to try this in his own life. He left the family home, returned to work in software engineering, and when I last meet with him, he was embracing the Filipino and Western elements of himself, and found some balance with his Chinese aspects that had held him and his family as prisoners.

## Chinese Psychological Freedom

I have encountered many clients that have difficulties making decisions due to limited resources and difficult social situations. They usually feel trapped and believe that they do not have free will to choose their destination in life. On the other hand, some clients with more impulsive or narcissistic qualities have abused their free will and ended up in overwhelming destitution. I suppose the virtue of freedom depends on how much we can handle it; a little child does not have the maturity of judgment to handle momentous issues and a non-benevolent dictator will abuse freedom. We see this not only in individuals, but also in a collective form. Various empires in history have abused freedom, imposing their will on other countries, which resulted in devastating consequences for all involved.

I appreciate the mistrust between East and West that has developed in the past few centuries. The transparency, openness, and idealism, at least in principle if not always in practice, of individualistic societies purport to equip the democratic social and political system with the means to promote equality for all. In an individualistic society, communities need to have idealistic forces to make individuals accountable to one another. However, in major portions of the Chinese population, it is the strict social orders, roles, and implicit moral codes that mitigate against malfeasance and disturbing collective harmony. The concept of individual growth is generally foreign to these populations. The self-actualization and growth of individuals are based on the well-being of the community rather than on the transcendence of the individual.

In China, the minority of people who promote creativity, freedom, and individualism do not find acceptance and, in some cases, are exiled to prisons or other countries. The lives and work of two of China's greatest poets Li Bai (*李白*, *the god dismissed from heaven*) and Du Fu (杜甫, *the poet of history*) provide poignant examples. However, when we seek universal harmony and obedience primarily, we compromise the necessities of individual differences, personal freedom, and creativity. Thus, traditional Chinese arts are sometimes regarded as only crafts. Although beautiful in their classic style and technical mastery, they lack the creativity and originality that has become increasing important among present-day Chinese artists. Contemporary film maker, Ang Lee (李安), however, is an excellent example of how many of China's current cultural visionaries integrate traditional and modern sensibilities, individualism and collectivism, and Eastern and Western influences in their art.

Chinese individualized transcendence reflects a union with the sky (天, Tian, universe) nature as a collective union. This notion, deeply rooted in the Chinese collective psyche, has inhibited the Chinese people from speaking up boldly and being assertive. This generated internal tensions between wanting a collective harmony and pursuing one's personal wishes. However, even today many Chinese prefer the collective ideal and grow indifferent within themselves and with the larger society. This internal chaos and disharmony within the self can often leak out onto the collective society that they are trying to protect.

May (1981) similarly challenged the one-dimensional aspect of traditional American psychology, which had been deeply rooted for decades in biological, experimental, and behavioral theories used in academia and research institutes. To some degree, psychology, at its best, will always challenge the cultural norms, even if in other places being a prime example of them. May's notion of freedom and destiny not only wakes up the soul of human existence in psychological terms, but also, it includes the moral and philosophical and spiritual quest that exists in current psychology.

I was recently supervising a team of young social workers in Shenzhen. Social work is a new profession endorsed by the central government in Beijing, and Shenzhen is a testing region for this profession. I have appreciated that the government wishes to bring in this new discipline for the harmony and well-being of the community. I have found that many young social workers are disappointed with the limited vision of their emerging role in China. Like many Western social workers and therapists, they complain that most of their time and energy gets used up in primarily administrative tasks rather in the engagement with individuals, families, and communities. What has complicated this matter is that these young social workers are suspiciously received by the existing government services. Under my encouragement, they have become more courageous in asking for appropriate social work assignments. To my surprise, the reviews have been very positive across individual, family, community, and governmental rating questionnaires. These young visionaries and hard-working social workers are forging important new ground in China. They have found the balance of helping individuals and the collective in a harmonious manner. They are viewed as both culturally cooperative and agents of change and growth.

## Conclusion

I have discussed the strengths and limitations of collective harmony in China. The strict moral and social codes of Confucianism need to be examined in light of our modern era. I believe the cross-cultural dialogue between East and West has had a positive effect in both societies. This interchange has helped to highlight the timeless wisdom in the various views of both traditions, while also exposing the myopic vision inherent in each of them. From my experience of *being in* and *in between* both cultures and traditions, I believe that individualism and collectivism are continuous variables. No person or community can be characterized as being entirely one or the other. At its best, the collective society allows families and communities to share life experiences, care, love, cooperation, responsibility, and meaning more closely with one another. At its worse, collectivism can suffocate creativity, freedom, and individual and collective growth. The sense of harmony needs to be achieved not only through strict social codes, but also through the processes of interpersonal engagement, discussions, mutuality, intellectual and emotional fearlessness, and appreciation and acceptance of our individual differences.

As for the individualistic perspective, I believe life starts with the blessings of collective unions, deep attachments, social supports, mentoring, and love. A person who is self-differentiated needs to connect not only to his or her personal wilderness but also to the larger collective. Freedom, courage, commitment, humanity, compassion, integrity, and love are all necessary for the general well-being of oneself and one's community. As Alfred Adler (1929/1969) taught, interest and involvement in the full life of one's community is characteristic of the healthy person. A good life is predicated on this spiritual-psychological dimension. We need to embrace and seek to understand the individual and collective tensions within ourselves, within our cultures, and within our global community. If we are accountable to ourselves and each other, this is the good life, individuated and connected, mature, realistic, and psychologically healthy and alive.

## References

Adler, A. (1969). *The science of living.* New York, NY: Anchor Books. (Originally published in 1929).

Bond, M.H. (Ed.). (1986). *The psychology of Chinese people.* Hong Kong: Oxford University Press.

Bond, M.H. (1993). Emotions and their expression in Chinese Culture. *Journal of Nonverbal Behavior, 17*(4), 245-62.

Buber, M. (1970). I and thou (W. Kaufmann, trans.). New York, NY: Carles Scribner & Sons.

Bowen, M. (1994). *Family therapy in clinical practice.* Lanham, MD: Jacob Aronson

Freidman, M. (1999). *The affirming flame: A poetics of meaning.* Amherst, NY: Prometheus.

Fromm, E. (2000). *The art of loving.* New York, NY: Harper Perennial. (Original work published 1956)

Ga, Z. Cai. D., & Ge, S. B, (2000). *Sky burial, Tibetan funeral culture.* LanZhou: Ga Su Cultural Press.

Gou, S. (2008). *The way of heaven and holy word, A comparative studies between Zhuang Zi and Bible.* Beijing, China: Religious and Culture Press.

He, X. L. (2007). *Nature worship in China.* Nan Jing, China: Jiang Su People Press.

Ho, D.Y.F. (1995). Selfhood and identity in Confucianism, Taoism, Buddhism, and Hinduism: Contrast with the West. *Journal for the Theory of Social Behaviour, 25,* 115-138.

Jung, C. G. (1965). *Memories, dreams, reflections.* New York, NY: Vintage Books.

Kleinman, A. (1980). *Patients and healers in the context of culture.* Berkeley, CA: University of California Press.

Potter, S.H. (1988). The cultural construction of emotion in rural Chinese social life. *Ethos, 16*, 181-208.

May, R. (1981). *Freedom and destiny*. New York, NY: Norton.

Mendelowitz, E. (2008). *Ethics and Lao Tzu: Intimations of character*. Colorado Springs, CO: University of the Rockies Press.

Schneider, K. J. (2008). From segregation to integration. In K. J. Schneider (Ed.), *Existential-integrative psychotherapy: Guideposts to the core of practice* (pp. 15-22). New York, NY: Routledge.

Wang, S. N. (2008). *Confucius: On being human*. Beijing, China: Chiang On Press.

Wang, L. L. (1999). *Interpersonal harmony and conflict in Chinese culture*. Taipei, Taiwan: Guerin Guan.

Watson, R. A., Rene Descartes: French mathematician and philosopher in Encyclopedia Britannica. Retrieved from https://www.britannica.com/biography/Rene-Descartes#re478309

# Chapter 20

## The Myth of Obedience:
## An Existential Analysis of *American Beauty*

Cathy Calvert
Kate Calhoon
Steve Fehl
Christine Gregory

A recent search on Amazon.com (2008) identified close to 162,000 titles dealing with the concept of obedience. In this first decade of the 21st century, the nature and meaning of obedience has become a hotly debated issue in Western society whether it is politics, spirituality, family relations, or cultural diversity. In this chapter, obedience will be discussed in light of Rollo May's concepts of freedom and responsibility utilizing images and characters from the 1999 Academy Award winning film, *American Beauty*.

### Myth

In his 1991 book *The Cry for Myth*, Rollo May explored the power and evolution of myth in human existence, in particular as it relates to American culture. Contrary to today's common use of the term *myth* as meaning a falsehood or popular fictitious belief, May described myths as important shared stories of a society and a way of making sense of our lives. May believed that myths give individuals a template for building their own values. In addition, myths provide relief from anxiety and guilt by helping the individual explain the how and why of what he or she thinks and does. Myths can be empowering, as well as limiting, depending on how they are used by individuals and the culture at large. For May, how an individual understands the concept of freedom and responsibility determines the way in which obedience is exercised and demonstrated. Because the terms freedom, responsibility, and obedience are used in such a variety of ways in current Western society, we will be using these three terms in the following manner.

### Freedom
Freedom, at its core, is the capacity to accept, bear, and live with anxiety. This freedom is anchored in the centered self that consciously chooses to be responsible for the interactions one has with the culture or society. Freedom and responsibility always imply each other and are inseparable. Freedom is experienced in choosing to accept our limitations and the choices we have made in the past, engaging in critical thought, and allowing ourselves the space to feel all that life

has to offer; pain and joy, sorrow and ecstasy, as well as engaging in the possibilities of the unknown that lay before us (May, 1979).

## Responsibility

To be responsible is to take ownership for one's own choices and their consequences, including the person an individual chooses to become. In addition, to be responsible is to consciously engage the world, of which one is a part; as well as to look past one's immediate needs, wants, or desires and, instead, think in long-term consequences. This conscious engagement accepts that there are limits to how one interacts with the culture or society (May, 1979).

## Obedience

Obedience, for our purposes, is understood as the active participation and/or conscious choices one makes with his or her thoughts, words, and actions in relationship to an individual's culture or society. In order for obedience to be exercised willfully and meaningfully, the person must have the choice concerning whether he or she will comply. When an individual is free, he or she is able to reflect on the system of beliefs before him or her, weigh out the options, as well as the possible consequences. Once the person has gone through this process, he or she can take action based on his or her own personal beliefs and values. Making such a conscious choice, knowing the possible outcomes of the choice, is exercising obedience with freedom and responsibility.

## Obedience and Western Culture

Existential ideals about obedience as an experience of choice and empowerment are often lost in the more common usage of the term *obedience* to denote submission or compliance to the commands or standards of another entity, individual, or authority. Furthermore, Western culture sends confusing, even conflicting, messages about the value and benefits of obedience. On one hand, the culture celebrates "fierce individualism" (May, 1991, p. 109) with its inevitable side effects of narcissism, isolation, and an insatiable quest for success. At the same time, however, Western measures of success are remarkably universal and narrow in scope, including such entities as money, titles, and SAT scores. In the end, hordes of *rugged individuals* find themselves racing like lemmings off the cliff of uniformity.

In Western culture, how one speaks, works, plays, eats, presents oneself, and engages the world can be judged against a sometimes-rigid set of acceptable standards. "Don't be rude." "Don't rock the boat." "Don't overdo it." "Don't question authority." "Go with the flow." "Do the right thing." "Be all you can be." "Never let them see you sweat." Our culture applauds the obedient child, the tireless worker, and the toned musculature and discipline of athletes. The rugged individual is affectionately embraced only when he or she does not challenge the majority too much or create discomfort with dramatic new ways of being. To understand obedience in Western society, it is important to look at the societal expectations, or dogmas, that are constricting and ultimately killing the spirit of freedom and responsibility for individuals.

## American Beauty and the Myth of Obedience

The film *American Beauty* chronicles one year in the life of an upper middle-class suburban family, their neighbors, and a few adolescent friends. The storyline centers on Lester and Carolyn Burnham who find themselves 20 years into a marriage that has lost its vitality as they have lost their own sense of freedom, choice, and self. In different ways, the film's characters demonstrate blind obedience, disconnection, awakening, and a struggle with the dawning awareness of individual freedom and its inevitable joys and pitfalls.

Each of the film's characters has something important to contribute to our understanding of the myth of obedience. The main character, Lester Burnham, refers to himself as a loser; he describes his life as "closely resembling Hell," with a loveless marriage to a woman he views as a "bloodless, money grubbing, freak," a daughter from whom he is completely disconnected, and a job he views as meaningless and insignificant. Lester appears bitter and resentful about the state of his life, a feeling, which up until relatively recently, he has repressed. He *bought into* the American Dream which stated that if one follows the norms for Western society, happiness is the end result. Lester is not happy. As Lester is on the verge of losing his meaningless job, his bitterness and resentment turn to anger and his perception of himself begins to change.

In the meantime, the mother character in *American Beauty*, Carolyn, holds her choices of obedience in high regard and wishes to be recognized in society for her success as the *perfect* wife, mother, and businessperson. However, Carolyn, like many others who choose this path of acceptance, is willing to be obedient, believing that her approach will provide the desired freedom. What is demonstrated throughout the movie is Carolyn's struggle to accept and live with the anxiety, which comes from not being true to oneself or following the myth of obedience. While she engages in the world, she is not willing or able to show her vulnerability to create meaningful relationships.

The Burnham's' new neighbors consist of a rigid ex-military father, a sedated and dissociated mother, and their pot-smoking, free thinking, loner son Ricky. The Western concept of obedience is evidenced in a scene from the film with the Colonel and his son:

> COLONEL:   You can't just go around doing whatever you feel like, you can't—There are rules in life... You need structure, you need discipline.
>
> RICKY:   Discipline. Yes, sir, thank you for trying to teach me. Don't give up on me, Dad.

The Colonel speaks for much of Western society today. For many, obedience means following a dogma, a set of rules and regulations established by an external authority. If one disagrees, or worse yet, disobeys these rules he or she is branded as defiant, rebellious, unpatriotic, or other negative conclusions. When individuals act disobediently, there frequently is swift judgment exercised, whether that is a court of law or a group of vigilantes taking discipline into their own hands.

Just prior to this dialogue in the film, the Colonel has burst into Ricky's room and punched his son in the face. What had Ricky done to deserve such strong discipline? Ricky had gone into a curio cabinet holding items the Colonel had collected during his military service to retrieve a piece of china from the third Reich that Ricky wanted to show his girlfriend. In this father-son relationship, obedience is strictly understood as an unquestioned allegiance to specific rules and beliefs the father has established. Ricky demonstrates his understanding of the Colonel's dogma by the way he responds to the Colonel. Ricky has learned there is no sense in trying to argue the point or even defend his perspective; rather Ricky simply capitulates to his father's outburst in order to protect his physical well-being.

However, obedience in its truest form is rooted in an individual's freedom to choose and then taking responsibility for the choice he or she makes. Only when an individual has the option to follow or not follow a set of guidelines or regulations is obedience truly and meaningfully exercised. When a person is coerced either by authority or by peer pressure to obey, obedience is reduced to acting out of fear and self-preservation. As is demonstrated in an encounter between the Colonel and Ricky later in the film, it is not until Ricky is willing to take responsibility for his choices that he is able to confront the Colonel and his disdain for the Colonel's values and beliefs.

While, on the surface, this Western perception of obedience appears to provide a sense of well-being and stability, a release from anxiety—it is strictly superficial with shallow roots. Ultimately, when an individual encounters the struggles and paradoxes of life, this superficial sense of security gives way and robs the individual of both well-being and stability. When the person adopts a dogmatic understanding of obedience, he or she creates a set of barriers that close off the ability to identify options and explore possibilities. All maneuverability is lost and the individual becomes a prisoner in a prison cell he or she has created. The basis of this closed perspective of obedience is fear, a fear of losing connection with an *ultimate truth*. In order to maintain this connection, the individual believes he or she must establish and adhere to a set of hard and fast rules or beliefs.

## Isolation

Obedience may offer the promise of acceptance and *fitting in* with prevailing expectations and standards; however, ironically, obedience often results in disconnection with self and others if an individual prioritizes doing the *right* thing over doing the thing that is most meaningful and true to oneself. Early in the movie, Lester's robotic existence leaves him disconnected from everyone, and Carolyn's social nature is a thin disguise for the isolation she experiences in her tireless pursuit of projecting an image of success at all times. She confuses her success with joy. She cannot experience an authentic moment or connection because she is distracted by her own persona and its maintenance.

Carolyn Burnham's fear of being perceived as anything less than perfect in the eyes of societal standards has created a lack of trust of others, and she believes she must rely on herself to make a place in this world. She allows no one to truly help her, and she is afraid of others' needs. She tells her daughter in one scene, "You cannot count on anyone except yourself!" Those words describe Carolyn's perception of the world and how to survive. While she is actively pursuing this societal obedience, she is unable to engage in meaningful relationships. This inability creates mistrust and reinforces, for Carolyn, the concept that she must do it on her own, which then becomes a vicious cycle.

It initially appears that Carolyn's obedience provides comfort and stability for her, but her obedience has no depth. Without the depth of true freedom and responsibility, she cannot reach deep enough within herself to allow others to be a part of her life. The barriers created by Carolyn's desire to be a part of society, through the choices made with her responsibility, freedom, and obedience has led this character to her ultimate fear: loneliness.

While an individual may assume if he or she follows societal expectations and dogma he or she will gain relationships and be a part of the group, the reality is that following the societal rules creates little space for the development of significant relationships. Conformity strips a person of his or her unique self, as well as the uniqueness of the person to whom he or she is trying to attach.

The hope for many in Western society, who follow rules or beliefs dictated by society, is that their efforts will provide success and acceptance into a group. The desire to not be isolated and alone can be a tremendous impetus to keep one following the rules. This doctrine suggests that successful living will lie within the rules and expectations of society and not within the ideals of each person's conscience. Carolyn lived and breathed this belief; she actively participated in Western society's worldview. Her expectation, which is similar for many, is to follow the rules of an upper middle-class working mother in order to create the perfect home, family, career, success, and beauty, with confidence. Without those perfections, she is nothing, and if she is nothing, then she will not belong and will be alone.

## Sedation

The isolation one experiences in the quest for obedience is both a cause and byproduct of a loss of self and feeling of sedation. The person who practices blind obedience sleeps through significant decisions about life. Sedation may be relaxing in terms of avoiding the anxiety of choice and responsibility; however, this sedation of self, robs the individual of the energy, awe, and emotions of life. Many characters in the film, *American Beauty,* are sedated into a lifestyle that lacks feeling or self-expression.

Returning to the character of Lester Burnham, we find this middle-aged, married father realizing his efforts to obey his wife, boss, and society's demands of his upper middle-class existence have transformed into a slow death over the previous 20 years of his life. His choice of blind obedience leaves him feeling dead inside until he finally awakens to true choice, responsibility, and the opportunity that awaits him every moment of the day. Lester speaks to this phenomenon as demonstrated in the following quotes from different moments in the movie,

> LESTER:    It's the weirdest thing. I feel like I've been in a coma for about 20 years and I'm just now waking up.

> LESTER:    I've lost something. I'm not exactly sure what it is, but I know I didn't always feel this... sedated. But you know what; it's never too late to get it back.

> LESTER:    It's a great thing when you realize you still have the ability to surprise yourself. It makes you wonder what else you can do that you forgot about.

Lester is not the only character in *American Beauty* who struggles with obedience to the point of sedation. Although his wife, Carolyn, in all of her perky phoniness appears quite different from Lester's dead eyes and monotone voice, she, too, is a prisoner of conformity. Perfect clothing, flawless gardens, and an image of success do little to assuage her anxiety and leave her struggling to maintain a rigid and unreal facade that alienates her from her husband, daughter, and herself. Carolyn relinquishes the power of choice in favor of the power of perfection and conformity. Her intense and ever-busy disposition might seem anything but sedate; however, she chooses to indulge in diminutive original thought, emotion, or action. Instead, Carolyn allows the autopilot of obedience to dictate everything from her choice of relationships to her color coordinated garden clogs. Like Lester, Carolyn rediscovers the world of choice through a forbidden sexual opportunity, but lacks Lester's carefree attitude toward its consequences.

## Letting Go of Society's Myth of Obedience

Lester recognizes he has been lulled into submission by consumerism; acquiring things had replaced meaningful interaction with himself as well as others. At one point in the film, Lester is trying to connect with his wife in a deeper way than she is use to when his wife shuts him down because he is about to spill beer on the sofa. Lester tells his wife "this is just stuff; it's not your life." The more Lester abandons his fear of losing (things, societal standing, image) the freer he is to accept responsibility for what he has created for himself and to make changes that reflect his deepest desires. Lester was willing to follow his desires into the unknown. Often, the individual can only know what his or her true desires are if he or she allows him or herself to experience them, or at least acknowledge that he or she has these desires. For example, Lester honestly believes that he wants to be sexually intimate with his daughter's adolescent friend. However, as he allows himself to walk down this road, he discovers that sexual intimacy with an adolescent is not at all what he truly desires.

Only when Lester seizes his freedom of choice and rejects blind obedience does he finally begin to connect in an authentic way with others and himself. His dramatic transformation is not welcomed by his wife or daughter, but he seeks comrades in unlikely new places like the fast food drive through manager and the teenage drug dealer next door. These new acquaintances do not hold Lester to any traditional standard. In some ways, he becomes obedient only to his *id* after 20 years of service to his *superego*.

Lester's awakening is triggered by his lustful fixation with his daughter Jane's adolescent schoolmate, Angela. This catalyst itself flies in the face of obedience to politically correct values about lust and underage girls, and yet it taps a more primal, even mythological, male attraction to youth and beauty. A near complete rejection of his obedient past and a newfound embrace of choice and its consequences follow Lester's awakening. Lester quits his job, confronts his wife, buys his dream car, smokes pot, and works out in order to *look good naked* for his fantasy dream girl. Lester decides that the myth of obedience is a raw deal and not one he chooses to make a part of the next chapter of his life.

As Lester "snaps" in his boss's office, he appears to be experiencing a healthy anger that Rollo May (1981) referred to as "an anger that pulls the diverse parts of the self tighter, that integrates the self, keeps the whole self alive and present, energizes us, sharpens our vision, and stimulates us to think more clearly" (p. 42). Even though Lester expresses himself in ways, which might be viewed as unhealthy by mainstream Western society (blackmailing his employer, smoking marijuana, and lusting after his daughter's adolescent friend), he begins to accept responsibility for himself and the decisions he has made in his life and commences to live as a free man. As he lets go of the expectations, which society has placed on him (conforming to a narrow role as an upper middle-class, Caucasian, married, middle-aged male), he immediately experiences an increase in his self-worth. Lester views himself as no more or no less than anyone else. He states that he is "just an ordinary man with nothing to lose." Here he rejects the Western myth, which implies the individual must compare who he or she is and what he or she does with everyone else in society, to see how he or she measures up.

Lester is awakening to the fact that he is okay just because of who he is not because of his accomplishments; he is realizing that self-worth has very little to do with one's success. He illustrates this by leaving his well-paying job to work at a fast food restaurant, signifying he is aware of exactly where he is in life and has rejected the myth of entitlement that states one must have something that is *better*. He has actively chosen to engage with his internal self, and has accepted a job with the least responsibility required in order to devote his time to what is meaningful to him. This shift from focusing on the outward self to the inward self is quite significant. Lester starts to be fully present in what he is doing.

The film leads us to believe that Lester Burnham would not have traded his new freedom to engage with himself for anything; even death. Lester Burnham found what he was looking for: acceptance and engagement with himself.

However, as May (1991) suggested, the demise of myth can be disorienting and devastating when it leaves society without reference, values, structure, and responsibility. Lester seeks freedom without limits and pays the ultimate price. At the movie's end, a misunderstanding leads to Lester's murder, suggesting that reckless abandonment of obedience confuses others and can be downright dangerous. Nonetheless, for the year preceding his death, Lester had finally exercised his choice and freedom and showed a newfound or rediscovered range of experience, including joy, rage, lust, disappointment, wonder, and power. It may be no wonder that Lester dies smiling. In death, Lester appears content.

The individual's willingness to live out what is meaningful to him or her takes a great deal of courage, and is in direct opposition to blind obedience where one lives for an illusion of something someone else states as the norm. So here again, we, as human beings and individuals, need to allow ourselves the experience, not just limit ourselves to what others dictate we should or should not do.

## Gratitude

The film, *American Beauty*, informs and illuminates the almost lost myth (in the positive sense) that brings knowledge of the importance of things that are not seen. This film asks the question, "Will we let go of things and the American Dream (a negative myth in this culture) to embrace those things that cannot be named?"

In the end, all eight main characters (Lester, Carolyn, Jane, Angela, Ricky, Ricky's father and mother, and Buddy) are impacted, in varying degrees, by the awakening that occurs in Lester's life. One can only speculate about what influence Lester's awakening and then sudden death will have on Carolyn. Within the context of the developing relationship with Ricky, Jane, Lester's daughter, begins to embrace her authentic self in ways that free her from the Western myth of beauty. She begins to accept her perceived flaws and admits to herself, Ricky, and Angela, that she would rather be a freak than to continue to try to fit into Angela's external and shallow world of normal. Ricky is very familiar with pain and suffering, and seems to have embraced pain in a way that allows him to open to that which is beautiful, but unseen. Meaning is created in Jane and Ricky's relationship as Ricky truly *sees* Jane and the pain she is in, and he is able to appreciate that quality in her as something which adds, not subtracts, from who she is. Ricky finds her quite beautiful. It is as if pain is a gift, which refines and informs one about the hidden beauty within the individual; it sharpens one's awareness of him or herself and allows him or her to see beauty in the mundane. Perhaps, as a human being, one does not have the ability to truly see beauty without embracing suffering and pain.

Lester Burnham's life illustrates a significant shift in consciousness; where once there was only fear that left him completely constricted, he moved into the realm of expanse, which allows him to become open to the authentic. As Lester is no longer resisting and moves into expansiveness, he now walks in the consciousness of the absolute. In the end, Lester Burnham saw the beauty in all—not by adhering to a narrow and rigid predetermined script of what is beautiful, but as it is; no more, no less. He was thankful for all aspects of his life. At the end of the movie Lester appreciates the stars at Boy Scout camp, the yellow leaves of a maple tree, his grandmother's hands, the first time he saw his cousin Tony's new Firebird, as well as his daughter Janie and his wife Carolyn.

In death, Lester states that it is "hard to stay mad when there is so much beauty in the world," and that sometimes he feels like he is seeing it all at once, and his heart fills up like a balloon about to burst, then he remembers to relax and stops trying to hold on to it; then it flows through him like rain. He recognizes the life behind things, just as Ricky did. Lester concludes by saying he, "can't feel anything but gratitude for every little moment of my stupid little life." Lester Burnham is the real American Beauty.

## Conclusion

As with many individuals, there are events that change everything and what one believes to be the path of obedience can be shaken. The myth of obedience lies in its promise that doing the *right thing* will give us comfort and confidence, maintain order, reduce anxiety, and garner admiration. It may deliver on some of these outcomes, but it is not guaranteed and not without costs. Furthermore, obedience comes in many shades of grey, not simply black and white. Nevertheless, black and white has the allure and illusion of certainty, as well as the avoidance of anxiety of the unknown and choice. Therefore, we seek the comfort of the myth of obedience and all of its gifts until we are shaken into the awareness that sometimes the costs are too high, we have gone too far, or we are just plain missing a fuller life of unknown beauty and experience. Such is the case in *American Beauty*.

## References

Amazon.com. Retrieved August 12, 2008 from http://www.amazon.com/s/ref=nb_ss_b?url=search-alias%3Dstripbooks&field-keywords=Obedience

Cohen, B. & Jinks, D. (Producers), & Mendes, S. (Director). (1999). *American Beauty.* DreamWorks.

May, R. (1981). *Freedom and destiny.* New York, NY: Norton & Company.

May, R. (1979). *Psychology and the human dilemma.* New York, NY: Norton & Company.

May, R. (1991). *The cry for myth.* New York, NY: Norton & Company.

# Chapter 21

## Funerary Rituals in China, Confucianism, and the Existential Issues of Death and Meaning

Bohan Zhang

In this chapter, I discuss the existential issues of death and meaning in Chinese culture and, more specifically, through a Confucian point of view. First, I introduce funerary rituals in China based on my experience and knowledge. Then I explore the discussion of death and meaning in Confucianism and how it informs the existence of people in Chinese culture.

### Funerary Rituals in China

Although the history of funerary rituals in China dates back much longer, a written set of standards can be traced back to *Li Ji* (礼记, The Book of Rites)—one of the "Five Canons" of Confucianism—compiled more than two thousand years ago. It appeared that a uniformed structure emerged later by the Ming and Qing dynasty, after Zhu Xi further simplified the standards and made them widespread (Watson, 1990). However, the ritual norms across China, albeit having more or less the same structure, present many variations due to factors such as ethnicity, religion, subculture, geographic region, and government policy. The interpretations and underlying meanings of some rituals vary for the same reason. The introduction I provide is based on the rituals of Han (the majority ethnicity in China) families in Xuzhou, the city where I spent my early childhood. Also, the rituals mostly apply to the death of elder people by natural causes. Rituals for deaths of children, or deaths by accident or suicide, for example, are not included, as the procedures are often different.

### Pre-burial Rituals
The first step is bathing the body of the deceased and dressing the body in *shou-yi* (寿衣, grave clothes, lit. *clothes of longevity*). It could be the favorite outfit of the deceased while alive, or prepared (made or purchased) by the family in advance. Then the body is transported from the hospital, as is most common, or home of the deceased to a funeral parlor, which is often arranged by the funeral parlor or a funeral agency hired by the family. When the hearse is on the way, pieces of joss paper, which is a type of spirit money, are thrown out of the window as offerings to the other world, with the message, "please look after the newcomer" being

conveyed. Upon arrival at the funeral parlor, the body is stored and grooming service is provided. The process of *bao-sang* (报丧, notification of death) to relatives and close friends of the family also starts at this time. Although phone calls are more accepted, now, in-person notification is still preferred.

When the family comes back from the funeral parlor, often, with the assistance of the hired funeral agency, they will set up a *ling-peng* (灵棚, spirit shed) where rituals will be performed and a place will be provided for people visiting and paying condolence. The spirit shed stands for 3 days, as it is understood in Chinese culture that the spirit of the deceased is reluctant to leave the family behind and will linger close to home for 3 days before setting off to the other world. After the spirit shed is set up, the family prepares an enlarged photo of the deceased, *gong-pin* (贡品, tributes), and *wan-lian* (挽联, elegiac couplets). In the spirit shed, an altar is set up, on which the photo and tributes are placed. A small stool sits in front of the altar with a *chang-ming-deng* (长明灯, lit. *ever-shining lamp*) placed on it. The oil lamp is believed to light up the way for the spirit, and serves a symbolic meaning in accordance with the Chinese saying, "a person dies the way a lamp goes out." In front of the stool, a clay pot is placed on the ground, in which visitors burn spirit money, serving as *pan-chan* (盘缠, travel expense) for the spirit to spend on the way. *Hua-quan* (花圈, wreaths) are placed inside the spirit shed provided by closest family and outside the shed from other relatives and friends. Also, *xiao-fu* (孝服, mourning dress, lit. *clothes of filial piety*) are worn by the family and relatives of the deceased, and can only be taken off when burial is completed. The mourning dress is worn differently by the children of the deceased, with added features, to indicate their relationship with the deceased. In addition, *shou-ling* (守灵, guarding the spirit) is performed for 3 nights, where the children of the deceased stay awake and keep adding oil to the lamp to ensure it does not go out, hence the name *ever-shining*.

## Burial Rituals

On the day of burial, the spirit shed is removed, and the family, relatives, and friends go to the funeral parlor. At the funeral parlor, the body of the deceased is transported to the *farewell hall*, which is the venue for ceremony of the family's choice. The farewell ceremony is led by a professional from the funeral parlor. First, people stand in silent tribute while funeral music is being played. Then the eulogy speech is given, usually by one of the family members or the head of the work unit of the deceased. Attendees, other than family, then walk around and pay their last respect to the body of the deceased that rests in a coffin on an elevated platform at the center of the hall, and they pay condolence to the family who are standing in line at one side of the hall. The family will then do the same. After the ceremony, the body is transported to the crematoria, which is often a part of the funeral parlor, and the family waits for the ashes in a waiting room. The ashes will be handed to the family in a cotton bag, and then placed in a wooden urn, which was prepared by the family. Another ceremony is then performed for people to bid farewell to the ashes of the deceased, during which time the clay pot that was placed in the spirit shed, with the ashes of all spirit money burned stored inside, is smashed onto the ground and broken into pieces. It is believed that by doing so, the clay pot could be taken by the spirit to the other world and serve as a container to receive spirit money sent by the family, and the family will be blessed with safety and peacefulness.

The ashes of the deceased are then taken to the cemetery for burial. Upon arrival at the cemetery, the burial ceremony is performed. First, a tomb-sweep is done, and tributes are placed in front of the tomb. The urn is then put into the grave chamber, together with a selection of the favorite objects of the deceased, such as books or glasses. Orientation of the urn matters too—the front of it often faces south for good *feng-shui* or the direction of the birthplace of the deceased for the spirit to return home. After the urn is situated, *gai-guan* (盖棺, covering the grave) is performed, where the marble cover of the grave chamber is placed at the top and sealed with cement. Another ritual then follows, in which relatives take off their mourning dress and tear apart the stitches, after which the dress returns to its original form of a piece of cloth, and then the children of the deceased do the same except after placing flowers on the marble cover, performing *kowtow*, and burning spirit money. This indicates that the formal send-off of the spirit is completed and, thus, the burial ceremony is concluded.

## Post-burial Rituals

These rituals include tomb-sweeping and respect-paying activities. They may be performed on various occasions, and again variations can be seen across China. The five most broadly shared are: (a) the anniversary of the death, (b) Qing-Ming Festival (15 days after Spring Equinox), (c) Ghost Festival (July 15 on the Lunar calendar), (d) Han-Yi (寒衣, winter clothes) Festival (October 1 on the Lunar calendar), and (e) Spring Festival (Lunar New Year). Around these times, the family goes to the cemetery and brings flower, tributes, and spirit money. They first sweep and clean the perimeter of the tomb, and then put out the flowers and tributes. Kowtow and bowing are, then, performed, followed by the burning of spirit money. The family also talks to the spirit of the deceased while performing these rituals, often sending regards and keeping the deceased up to date with major family events, such as if one of the family members graduated from college, or one is getting married, or relocating. Widely shared in Chinese culture is the belief that the connection between the two worlds is created or activated through fire (e.g. *shao-zhi* [烧纸], lit. *paper-burning*, done by the living) and dream (e.g. *tuo-meng* [托梦], lit. *dream-rendering*, done by the deceased), amongst other means. These beliefs and rituals play a pivotal role in the maintenance of family structure and values as well as in the preservation of bonds and reciprocity between the living and the dead.

## Confucianism and the Existential Issues of Death and Meaning

The issues of death and meaning in China, as with all existential issues, are best studied and understood when taking all of the various factors that has influenced Chinese culture—the three major forces being Confucianism, Buddhism, and Taoism—into consideration. I choose to focus on Confucianism as it is arguably the most influential amongst the three, and because I see it as relating to funerary rituals the most. Therefore, this section only presents my personal view of these issues from a certain angle and with limited scope. My hope is that it will provide a glimpse into the Chinese way of life, and garner interest in exploring additional aspects of Chinese culture and philosophy. I will also briefly introduce some non-Confucian concepts, as they are foundational in understanding funerary rituals as well as the aforementioned existential issues in the Chinese context.

First, it is believed in China that there is a correspondence and balance between *yin* (阴) and *yang* (阳), which is mostly a Taoist concept, such as the night and the day, the Earth and the sky, the moon and the sun. This is also true for the realm we inhabit (*yin-jian* [阴间], *the shade world* and *yang-jian* [阳间], *the light world*), as well as our existence of spirit and flesh. Therefore, death is understood less as a termination, although this notion is also present, and more as a journey to *the other side* and a transformation in the form of existence. This orientation informs funerary customs, and its influence can be observed across the ritual sequence. Second, the Chinese understanding of afterlife is closely connected with the Buddhist notions of *karma* (业报, the principle of cause [i.e. present actions] and effect [i.e. future prospects]), *samsara* (轮回, the repeated cycle of birth-death-rebirth), and *nirvana* (涅槃, the liberation from samsara through accumulation of good karma). The transformational aspect of death is, therefore, further strengthened and enriched by this understanding.

In Confucianism, the concepts of *li* (礼, propriety), *xiao* (孝, filial piety), and *ren* (仁, benevolence) are the most relevant to funerary rituals. Propriety refers to "ritualized norms of proper conduct regulating all aspects of human interactions" (Hsu, O'Connor, & Lee, 2009, p. 158) that guide one's behavior in the family, community, and society. Filial piety refers to respecting and taking good care of elders in the family, especially parents. Benevolence refers to treating others with good intention, compassion, empathy, and humaneness. One thing to notice is that these concepts are not mutually exclusive, but have overlaps and different emphases, as well as informing and complementing each other.

Confucius (孔夫子, lit. *Master Kong*), the founder of Confucianism, did not go to great length directly discussing the issue of death in his teachings. He did, however, offer ideas regarding the position one should take when thinking about and dealing with death. When the disciple Zigong asked about whether a dead person still have sensations, Confucius replied:

> I wish to say that a dead person has sensations, but I worry about people putting effort into preparing a grand funeral for the deceased instead of

treating them well while they were still alive. I wish to say that a dead person does not have sensations, but I worry about people not giving the deceased a proper burial. Whether or not a person has sensations after death, you will need to gradually reach your own understanding; and when you do, it will not be too late. (Liu, 1987, pp. 474-475)

It may seem as if Confucius was more concerned with propriety than talking about *the ultimate concern* of death, but there is more to it—he was urging people to live in the present moment of life instead of getting carried away by the uncertainty, anxiety, and illusions of death.

In *Existential Psychotherapy*, Yalom (1980) stated that the psychological life-death boundary is less clear-cut than the biological one, and "life and death merge into one another... [with death being]... not simply the last moment of life" (p. 30). In the same vein, Sartre (2012) wrote, "One is still one is going to cease to be and already one is going to become. One lives one's death. One dies one's life" (p. 2). Human beings are simultaneously living and dying every minute of their lives. Focusing on the present moment is not necessarily an attempt, whether conscious or unconscious, to deny or avoid the idea of death, but rather *choosing* to stay in the here-and-now while acknowledging the presence and weight of death. In chapter 1, Hoffman explained how death, and the anxiety it produces, is motivating just as much as it is paralyzing, "... the best way to prepare for a good death is by living a good life ... paradoxically, it is often the fear of a bad death that keeps people from engaging life" (p. 11). Therefore, how one decides to respond to death as an existential given becomes a vital factor in living a fulfilled life. It requires one to be mindful, courageous, and resolute; it demands one to execute one's freedom and assume responsibility for one's actions.

In returning to Confucius (2006), his position on life/death is more explicitly expressed through a passage in *Analects*, where he responded to the disciple Jilu's inquiry about serving spirits: "Yet able to serve the living, how could one serve spirits?" (p. 157). Jilu went on to ask about death, and again he replied: "Yet to know what life is, how could one understand death?" (p. 157). This passage also brings out another important point Confucius made—comprehending death through life. Ivanhoe (1990) wrote, "... to understand death and its significance for us is to understand what it will deprive us of... [which is] life and all the various things that make life worth living" (p. 142). Indeed, one cannot know what death entails until the value of life is realized. Such value is, of course, subject to interpretations and defined—some may use the word *created* while others may use *discovered*—through each person's unique meaning-making process.

What, to Confucius (2006), makes life worth living? What meaning does he make out of life? Some clues can be found in a passage where he said: "If I were to find *Dao* (道, *The Way*) in the morning, I will die content at night" (p. 44). This could be viewed as a general direction or guidance provided in Confucianism, but the problem is that the concept of Dao is rather grand and vague and, thus, difficult—if not impossible—to define. Before explaining Dao in greater detail, the concept of *jun-zi* (君子) needs to be introduced, as the two are closely related. Commonly translated into *gentleman* in English version of Confucian books, the term jun-zi has a much richer and deeper meaning. It embodies the good virtues in Confucianism and is the ultimate goal of self-cultivation (Hsu, O'Connor, & Lee, 2009). The many mentions of jun-zi in *Analects* each adds a facet to the well-rounded definition of this concept. For instance, the jun-zi should be someone who "assists in people's good deeds but not evil ones" (Confucius, 2006, p. 179), "unites people but not partisan" (p. 18), "acts in harmony with others but not blindly conforming" (p. 199), and "is poised but not arrogant" (p. 200).

Take a closer look and it is evident that the *self*-cultivation is largely oriented in relations. By saying this I do not mean that the actions of jun-zi originate from the interpersonal domain; it is instead driven by virtues, but the relational aspect is heavily emphasized. Also, the jun-zi should strive to "cultivate the self in order to give ease to all people" (Confucius, 2006, p. 227), so the relations are not limited to direct connections, such as those with family and friends, and the goal of self-cultivation extend beyond the individual and takes into consideration one's responsibility to the community, society, and entire human race. One of the teachings in *Analects* that directly connects the concepts of jun-zi and Dao, suggest, "The jun-zi works to achieve a solid root; when it is established, Dao will manifest" (p. 2). One may think of the *root* as self-identity (i.e., *who we are*) and Dao as the mode of existence (i.e., *how we interact with the world*). For jun-zi, then, Dao is the understanding, embodiment, and practicing of good virtues.

In Confucianism, benevolence is at the core of all virtues. It is also at the heart of Dao—in fact, many refer Dao as *ren-dao* (仁道, *the way of benevolence*). The most succinct and unmistakable definition of benevolence can be found in both *Analects* and *Mencius*, which is "愛人" and translates into "loving [all] human beings" (Confucius, 2006, p. 182; Mencius, 2012, p. 185). An interesting fact is that the Chinese character "仁" (benevolence) is comprised of two separate ones: "人" (human) and "二" (two), indicating that the concept deals with how people should treat one another. Therefore, like jun-zi, the concept of Dao also has a relational feature. The same characteristic can be found across Confucian thoughts and teachings. Throughout history, the notions of relationship and relationality have informed the Chinese way of being. With its emphasis on togetherness, mutuality, and the importance of family and community, Confucianism has been profoundly influential in the foundation and development of China's collectivistic culture.

## Some Further Thoughts

Bugental (as cited in Rowan, 2015) proposed that human beings are at the same time *a part of* and *apart from* others. These are concurrently existing conditions, but one may be more dominant than the other in a given situation. In a similar way, culture can be viewed as a combination of coexisting-but-opposing propensities, and therefore, just as one cannot be entirely and exclusively a part of or apart from others, there is not an absolute collectivistic or individualistic culture—only different emphases and priorities. In chapter 10, Heery added to Bugental's idea of *separate-but-related-ness* by stating that people are at once connected with and disconnected from their environment. This brings out a corresponding concept—the existential given of *isolation*. There will always be a part of the self that is not reached by the connection with others, and one cannot ever be fully recognized and understood. Yalom (1980) described it as "an unbridgeable gulf between oneself and any other being" (p. 355). This awareness is often made more evident when the presence of death is apparent, and the anxiety produced by both existential givens—isolation and death—cannot be eliminated, but can be alleviated and made tolerable through relationship and love (Yalom, 1980).

Tillich (2014), when writing about death anxiety, stated that it intensifies "with the increase of individualization" (pp. 40-41), and is lessened in collectivistic cultures by "the courage to be as a part" (p. 85). Consider funerary rituals in China: the public notification of death is an essential step as death is more than a personal matter—it changes the dynamic in the household and family as well as the social network of the neighborhood and community. What it implies is that the existence of individuals needs to be understood with the collective taken into consideration. In Chinese culture, the relational aspect is crucial in the identity formation of an individual; in other words, a large part of the sense of self is established within and through relationships. The same can be said for the way in which life meaning is constructed. It is not uncommon to notice people describing the self with terms indicating their relations and roles in social contexts, and hear words of concern regarding severed relationships rather than personal demise from someone in the dying bed. When death is pulled into the relational—where the aforesaid courage resides—the pain it inflicts is shared and collectively endured.

It was previously mentioned that one's existence is simultaneously being a part of and apart from others—the former can be seen as more dominant in Chinese culture, which is opposite to that of individualistic cultures. One could argue that because of this difference, intrapersonal isolation would be more prevalent than interpersonal isolation in collectivistic cultures, with the opposite applying to their individualistic counterpart. This conclusion might be partially true; however, it is drawn from the assumption that there is a clear dichotomy between the two tendencies and that *self* has a consistent definition—which is not always the case (see Hoffman, Stewart, Warren, & Meek, 2014). The self is partly cultural, which means that it takes on some characteristics of the culture with which it identifies. The Chinese self can be said to be more relational for this reason. It was pointed out in the last section that the post-burial rituals in China reflects the endeavor by the living to preserve the relationship with the deceased. I would add that it is also the means through which people in Chinese culture preserve an integral part of the self.

The unprecedented speed of modernization and globalization in the past century has presented challenges to both collectivistic and individualistic cultures. Each culture could face different challenges and respond in their own ways, but the loss of cultural heritage, myths, and identity appears to be an issue of common concern. Hoffman and colleagues (2014) stated that "culture provides a lens through which experience, behavior, and the self are interpreted" (p. 144). Indeed, culture gives people a particular sense of belonging and meaning, and it helps people situate the self in a world that lacks clear orientation and direction. In *The Cry for Myth*, May (1991) indicated that "myths are narrative patterns that give significance to our existence...[and it is through myths people]...make sense in a senseless world" (p. 15). When a culture "becomes less coherent or weakened" (Hoffman et al., 2014, p. 144), as the result of a loss of myths in itself and/or an excess of inputs from other cultures, its interpretive and evaluative function is diminished, and for individuals in such culture, the affirmation of the cultural self as a fundamental part of existence is threatened. This is not to say that cultures should exclude elements from other cultures, as doing so will endanger its vitality, growth, and even survival, but when a culture's myths are sustained, it is able to engage in better interaction and exchange with others without a part of itself getting distorted or lost. Myths to a culture are like identity to an individual—and the two are inseparable.

The loss of myths in cultures is often reflected in the identity confusion of their people. Modern China is no exception. The Chinese way of living and dying has changed more in the past five decades than it did in the previous five centuries. Amidst this period of drastic change is the disorientation of Chinese souls. When spirituality is labeled as superstition and materialism promoted as the principal ideology, China is at risk of losing its cultural heritage and putting its people in a society that lacks a system or structure of value, faith, and meaning. China's problem is both unique and universal. I have encountered many people who expressed that they feel a lack of humanness and warmth in our world today, and that numbers and facts are taking up the space, which previously was filled with wonder. The fluidity and flexibility of life is forced to give way to practicality and efficiency. Also lost is the subjectivity of truths and the fullness of human beings. In chapter 16 of this volume, Hoffman stated that as meaning is central to mental health and myth is central to meaning, the danger of the loss of myth is a lack of sustaining meaning, and that "the inner experience of emptiness and meaninglessness can drive individuals to destructive pursuits of power, pleasure, and dangerous degrees distraction" (p. 274). Everyone can think of examples of such futile pursuits, and many have come to realize what is at stake. The question that needs to be asked is: What can be done to revitalize myths and restore connection with them?

## References

Confucius. (2006). *Lun yu* [Analects]. Beijing, China: Zhonghua Publishing House.
Hoffman, L., Stewart, S., Warren, D., & Meek, L. (2009). Toward a sustainable myth of self. *Journal of Humanistic Psychology, 49*(2), 135-173. doi: 10.1177/0022167808324880

Hsu, C., O'Connor, M., & Lee, S. (2009). Understandings of death and dying for people of Chinese origin. *Death Studies, 33*(2), 153–174. doi: 10.1080/07481180802440431

Ivanhoe, P. J. (2011). Death and dying in the Analects. In A. Olberding & P. J. Ivanhoe (Eds.), *Mortality in traditional Chinese thought* (pp. 137-152). Albany, NY: State University of New York Press.

Liu, X. (1987). *Shuo yuan* [Garden of stories]. Beijing, China: Zhonghua Publishing House.

May, R. (1991). *The cry for myth*. New York, NY: W. W. Norton & Company.

Mencius. (2012). *Meng zi* [Mencius]. Beijing, China: Zhonghua Publishing House.

Rowan, J. (2015). Existential analysis and humanistic psychotherapy. In K. J. Schneider, J. F. Pierson, & J. F. T. Bugental (Eds.), *The handbook of humanistic psychology: Theory, research, and practice* (2nd ed.) (pp. 549-561). Thousand Oaks, CA: SAGE.

Sartre, J. (2012). *Saint Genet, actor and martyr* (B. Frechtman, Trans.). Minneapolis, MN: University of Minnesota Press.

Tillich, P. (2014). *The courage to be*. New Haven, CT: Yale University Press.

Watson, J. L. (1990). The structure of Chinese funerary rites: Elementary forms, ritual sequence, and the primacy of performance. In J. L. Watson & E. S. Rawski (Eds.), *Death ritual in late imperial and modern China* (pp. 3-19). Berkeley, CA: University of California Press.

Yalom, I. D. (1980). *Existential psychotherapy*. New York, NY: Basic Books.

# Chapter 22

## *Brokeback Mountain:*
## A Gay and Universal Love Story[1]

### Ilene Serlin

A young, gay client left my office, and I reflected on her urgent questions. She was intent on explaining to me the difference between enjoying being submissive in sex and enjoying the dominance or cruelty of her partner. One of her main issues, she said, is that she cannot have an orgasm or feel passion with this partner, who is stable and loves her greatly, but only with someone who is emotionally cruel or unavailable. My client was turning 30 years old and wanted to settle down. She had been with the same partner for 3 years and was desperate at her inability to feel passion. Although I appreciate the importance of these subtle distinctions of sexual identity, equality, and love, I am also aware of the many gaps in my own understanding and of the stereotypes that I, as a heterosexual psychotherapist, hold.

Looking at *Brokeback Mountain* as a lesson in sexual identity and relationship issues is only one of the ways it would be useful for psychologists to discuss this film with clients and one another. We should be as informed as possible about the nuances of all kinds of love and be aware of our own biases and perspectives. But are the concerns in this film only about gay love? I believe that the issues raised by this film are compelling and universal themes of passion, authenticity, loneliness, and partnership. These are the very human questions that show up in all great dramas: Can any romantic love that is fueled by challenges, secrecy, and idyllic settings live in the real world? Does domestic routine always kill passion? Is romantic love inevitably tragic?

### Setting

*Brokeback Mountain* is an exquisite story about two cowboys who fall in love. It is based on a short story written by Wyoming resident E. Annie Proulx, who won the Pulitzer prize for *The Shipping News*. First published in *The New Yorker* in 1997, it also appeared in the book *Close Range: Wyoming Stories*. The screenplay was adapted by Larry McMurtry and Diana Ossana, and the film was brilliantly

[1] This chapter was originally published as a book review for *PsycCRITIQUES: APA Review of Books*, March 15, 2006, Volume 51, Issue 11. Reprinted with permission.

directed by Ang Lee, director of *Crouching Tiger, Hidden Dragon* and *Sense and Sensibility*. The score was created by Gustavo Santaolla (*Motorcycle Diaries*) and contains excerpts from Merle Haggard, Willie Nelson, and Rufus Wainwright. Poetic visual images of the Western landscape iconography were created by Rodrigo Prieto. The film was produced by James Shamus, is rated R, and runs for 134 min.

The story is about two young men in 1963 who are hired to work for a rancher in Signal, Wyoming. The inarticulate and solitary Ennis Del Mar, played by Heath Ledger, and Jack Twist (Jake Gyllenhaal) both come from families of emotional cruelty, and one stormy night they find refuge in their tent and each others' arms. Although Ennis immediately says, "You know I ain't queer," and Jack says, "Me neither," their passion continues to smolder. After the summer, Ennis returns home to marry his childhood sweetheart (Michelle Williams, Ledger's real-life partner), and Jack goes to Texas and marries a rich boss's daughter (Anne Hathaway). Over the next 20 years, they continue to meet periodically for "fishing trips" on their idyllic *mountain*, while their respective marriages deteriorate. Scenes of silent male camaraderie taking place in wide open spaces are juxtaposed against images of the banality of domestic family life.

### *Brokeback Mountain*: Why Is It Relevant?

I went to see the film on the evening after I met with my client, and the 10:00 p.m. showing was sold out in San Francisco. Although *Brokeback Mountain* has sold out houses in liberal New York and Los Angeles, it is not just a gay or liberal film. It won seven Golden Globe nominations and was screened at the Venice International Film Festival, and more advance tickets for *Brokeback Mountain* were sold in a metroplex in Plano, Texas, than for the blockbuster film King Kong. Other movies with gay characters this year, such as *Capote and Rent,* had urban or campy settings, but Brokeback Mountain takes place in America's heartland. It is impossible to dismiss the film as a plot designed by latte-sipping liberals or Chelsea faux cowboys. Set in the same year as Martin Luther King, Jr.'s march on Washington and the publication of Betty Friedan's book *The Feminine Mystique*, the film shows the heartening progress we have made on civil rights since 1963. Even though the film was released around the time that the president "cynically flogged a legally superfluous (and unpassable) constitutional amendment banning same-sex marriage for the sole purpose of whipping up the basest hostilities of his electoral base" (Rich, 2005, p. 13), polls are nevertheless showing that a large majority of Americans support equal rights for gay couples if the relationship is not called marriage.

### Brokeback Mountain: Psychological Issues

The film's postmodern layering of perspectives and issues about identity, alienation, and the need for connection (Gergen, 1991) is revealed by a look at the fascinating array of review titles. Some examples include "Masculinity and Its Discontents in Marlboro County" (Dargis, 2005), "Two Gay Cowboys Hit a Home Run" (Rich, 2005), "Cowboys, Just Like in the Movies" (Trebay, 2005), and "Love Story with One Difference" (2005). Robert Roten (2005), from the *Laramie Movie Scope*, called it a "modern story about 'star-crossed lovers,'" a modern "Romeo and Jack." Rob Nelson called it "Midnight Cowboys, Lonesome Doves," and Roger Ebert said it was "as observant as work by Bergman" (*Brokeback Mountain*, n.d.).

Reviewers and writers have quite different ideas about what the film is about. Proulx, the author of the short story on which the film is based, has said that it is "about two confused young men 'beguiled by the cowboy myth'" (Dargis, 2005, p. 13). The irony is that the protagonists are not actually cowboys but technically shepherds. Dargis noted that *Brokeback Mountain* is a film about identity ("On Brokeback, the two men are neither straight nor gay, much less queer; they are lovers, which probably accounts for the category confusion that has greeted the film"; p. 13), and Rich (2005) made the same point tongue in cheek, calling it "a heavily promoted American movie depicting two men having sex" (p. 13). Epidemiologists attempting to categorize sexually transmitted diseases have the same problem with mixed identities, having no categories for men who have sex with other men but do not identify as gay. Being gay in American poses special questions and challenges about identity formation (Cass, 1979; Coleman, 1982; Isay, 1996).

*Brokeback Mountain* is also a film about the challenging societal factors that impinge on gay relationships. The film has been called a "landmark in the troubled history of America's relationship to homosexuality" (Rich, 2005, p. 13); Proulx's story, *Brokeback Mountain*, was written 6 years before Stonewall became a new frontier for gay rights, and gay student, Matthew Shepard, was murdered near Laramie, Wyoming, on October 6, 1998, the year after the story was published. Shepherd was pistol whipped by two men he met at a bar, tied to a split rail fence with his own shoelaces, and left to die in the cold. Consensual sex between two men was still a crime in some American states until 2002, when the Supreme Court reversed the sodomy laws; therefore, critic Trebay (2005) called the film a documentary that shows the violence so often part of gay men's experience. Other reviewers have pointed out that the problem in the film is not caused by the wife and family of the men but by their bullying bosses and shaming fathers-the patriarchy itself.

Noteworthy for clinicians are also the terrible alienation, depression, and loneliness that come with being gay in America (Herek, 1989). The name of one of the two protagonists, Ennis, brilliantly played by Ledger, means *island*, and we see him as unable to fully connect with either Jack, his wife, or his children. Jack, the other protagonist, played seductively by Gyllenhaal, is also lonely in his cold family, his wealthy and insensitive wife and in-laws. Both men live a secretive double life, and neither is able to commit authentically to either life. One rancher from Wyoming who was interviewed in a review (Trebay, 2005, p. 1) spoke of his great loneliness and said that he had considered suicide.

Another theme of *Brokeback Mountain* is purely a visual element-the power of nonverbal communication. From the grunting and wrestling between the two men and their use of silence, pauses, and body language, we feel their bond (Birdwhistell, 1970). They use understatement to make their points, as when Jack summarizes the whole story of the relationship as, "That ol' Brokeback got us good." The camera work echoes the poetic use of imagery, lingering on distant mountaintops and clear streams. The imagery even gets campy, as when the smoldering looks and shots of men's butts in tight jeans have the audience snickering. In psychotherapy, the nonverbal level is often minimized by our verbal, goal-directed, male therapeutic model. Because nonverbal and visual imagery are so directly connected to dreams and the unconscious, it would be helpful for therapists to be aware of this aspect of the therapeutic process.

Another layer of the film is archetypal. The image of the Western frontier is mythic in the American imagination, and the film shows the power of the imagination over reality. For example, the era of the cowboy actually existed for a relatively short time in American history—from the end of the large-scale cattle drives after the Civil War to the advent of the use of rail to move cattle. By the time movies were created, this era was over. The myth of wide open spaces lives on in the collective unconscious and symbolizes freedom to be oneself, away from the stifling conformity of domesticity and technology. Part of this myth shows the conflict between nature and culture in the human psyche. Other Western films that show this conflict and also have sexual overtones include John Wayne and Monty Cliff in *Red River*, Gary Cooper and Lloyd Bridges in *High Noon*, and Rock Hudson and James Dean in *Giant*. Outsiders have always been drawn to this freedom, as shown in the John Wayne genre. Even artists who perpetuated the myth, such as Aaron Copland, who wrote *Billy the Kid* and *Rodeo*, were outsiders; Copland was a Jewish boy from Brooklyn who was a Communist sympathizer and more comfortable in Paris than the West (J. Weisgall, personal communication, December 26, 2005). Agnes de Mille, the choreographer of *Oklahoma*, was the ugly duckling and outsider of the famous Hollywood de Mille family, and Oklahoma was one of the first American musicals that captured the hearts and minds of the American public. In the political arena, Ronald Reagan and Arnold Schwartzenegger (Serlin, 2003) posed before pictures of Teddy Roosevelt, evoking the myth of the rugged individualistic cowboy. However, the myth of freedom is an ideal and not real; for example, cowboy Rock Hudson spent his life living in the closet. The myth of the wild West shows the tension between the real and the ideal.

As Carl Jung (1958), Rollo May (1975, 1991), and others have shown, the influence of mythic images is as significant as the reality of human thoughts, feelings, and behavior. Mythic images can be used in psychotherapy as a template to see one's own personal mythology (Feinstein & Krippner, 1988) and also images of male partnership (Beebe, 1993). In the case of my psychotherapy client, for example, her mythology was partly about her need for freedom, commitment and flight, and doomed love. Myths capture the paradoxical complexity of human nature, whereas much modern psychology emphasizes a one-dimensional approach to diagnosis or treatment. For example, the trend toward manualized methods that help clients replace negative thoughts with positive ones, or those that emphasize happiness while leaving out tragedy, miss the drama of human life. Instead of fixing symptoms, a mythic approach to psychology aims to help people deal with the real complexity between individuation and adjustment to reality, freedom and fate, and multiple selves and identities. From a mythic perspective, as Shakespeare wrote in *As You Like It*, "all the world's a stage," and we play many roles.

Finally, a mythic perspective allows us to see that, like great art, life comes in genres. Is *Brokeback Mountain* a tragedy? Both heroes leave the community and go off to the island or paradise to find themselves a theme often found in Shakespeare. Yet can they individuate, or are societal factors such as homophobia and intolerance too strong? Greek tragedies portray the tension between freedom and fate. Is *Brokeback Mountain* in the genre of forbidden love?

Because everything else in the cowboys' life changed, but their love lasted all their life, I see this film as showing the enduring power of love. The director set out to sympathetically portray the challenges of two men in love and the human need to live an authentic life. To this end, he succeeds magnificently. The acting by Ledger may win him an Academy Award nomination, and the score and cinematography support the action seamlessly.[2] In short, *Brokeback Mountain* introduces many complex psychological issues that would be valuable for psychologists to see and understand.

## References

Beebe, J. (1993). Towards an image of male partnership. In R. Hopcke (Ed.), *Same-sex love and the path to wholeness.* Boston, MA: Shambhala.

Birdwhistell, R. (1970). *Kinesis and context: Essays in body motion communication.* Philadelphia, PA: University of Pennsylvania Press.

*Brokeback mountain (2005).* (n.d.). Retrieved January 30, 2005, from http://www.rottentomatoes.com/m/brokeback_mountain/?beg=75&int=28&page=4

Cass, V. C. (1979). Homosexual identity formation: A theoretical model. *Journal of Homosexuality, 4*(3), 219-235.

Coleman, E. (1982). Developmental stages of the coming out process. *Journal of Homosexuality, 7*(2), 31?43.

Costigan, M. (Producer) & Lee, A. (Director). (2005). *Brokeback mountain* [Motion picture]. United States: Universal Studios.

Dargis, M. (2005, December 18). Masculinity and its discontents in Marlboro country. *New York Times,* p. 13.

Feinstein, D., & Krippner, S. (1988). *Personal mythology.* Los Angeles, CA: Tarcher.

Gergen, K. (1991). *The saturated self.* New York, NY: Basic Books.

---

[2] This chapter was written prior ot the 2005 Academy Awards.

Herek, G. M. (1989). Hate crimes against lesbians and gay men: Issues for research and policy. *American Psychologist, 44,* 948-955.

Isay, R. (1996). *Becoming gay: A journey to self-acceptance.* New York, NY: Pantheon Books.

Jung, C. G. (1958). *Psyche and symbol* (V. de Laszlo, Ed.). New York, NY: Doubleday.

*Love Story with one difference.* (2005, December 23). Palm Beach Post.

May, R. (1975). *The courage to create.* New York, NY: Bantam Books.

May, R. (1991). *The cry for myth.* New York, NY: Norton.

Rich, F. (2005, December 18). Two gay cowboys hit a home run. *New York Times,* p. 13.

Roten, R. (2005, October 9). *Brokeback Mountain*: A song of doomed love for cowboys. *Laramie Movie Scope.*

Serlin, I. (2003, October 10). Image vs. reality: Daddy will take care of you. *San Francisco Chronicle.*

Trebay, G. (2005, December 18). Cowboys, just like in the movies. *New York Times,* Section 9, pp. 1, 6.

# Chapter 23

## Building the Great Wall of China:
## Postmodern Reverie and the Breakdown of Meanings[1]

### Ed Mendelowitz

### I

In the midst of his short story "Building the Great Wall of China," Franz Kafka (1971) related the following parable:

> The Emperor, so it runs, has sent a message to you, the humble subject, the insignificant shadow cowering in the remotest distance before the imperial sun; the Emperor from his death bed has sent a message to you alone. He has commanded the messenger to kneel down by the bed, and has whispered the message to him; so much store did he lay on it that he ordered the messenger to whisper it back into his ear again. Then by a nod of the head he has confirmed that it is right. Yes, before the assembled spectators of his death—all the obstructing walls have been broken down, and on the spacious and loftily mounting open staircases stand in a ring the great princes of the Empire—before all these he has delivered his message. The messenger immediately sets out on his journey; a powerful, an indefatigable man; now pushing with his right arm, now with his left, he cleaves a way for himself through the throng; if he encounters resistance he points to his breast, where the symbol of the sun glitters; the way is made easier for him than it would be for any other man. But the multitudes are so vast; their numbers have no end. If he could reach the open fields how fast he would fly, and soon doubtless you would hear the welcome hammering of his fists on your door. But instead how vainly does he wear out his strength; still he is only making his way through the chambers of the innermost palace; never will he get to the end of them; and if he succeeded in that nothing would be gained; he must next fight his way down the stair; and if he succeeded in that nothing would be gained; the courts would still have to be crossed; and after the courts the second outer palace; and once more stairs and courts; and once more another palace; and so on for thousands of years; and if at last he should

---

[1] This essay has been "built" out of fragments, much like Kafka's Great Wall of China itself.

burst through the outermost gate—but never, never can that happen—
the imperial capital would lie before him, the center of the world, cram-
med to bursting with its own sediment. Nobody could fight his way
through here even with a message from a dead man. But you sit at your
window when evening falls and dream it to yourself. (p. 244)

This parable, sometimes found standing on its own as "An Imperial Message,"
is a fragment that reflects perfectly the essence of the larger piece in which it is
set. It is a quintessentially Kafkan meditation, its modernist message, paradoxically, is the loss of revelation in a world cut off from sustaining meanings and
forms. Kafka has been called, in this regard, "the exemplary modernist" (Alter,
1991, p. vii), a "post-traditional Jew" (Alter, 1991, p. viii)—a scribe who waits
interminably for a message from on high while knowing full well that it will never
arrive. "We are, [as I, myself, wrote in *Ethics and Lao-Tzu* (2008).] "survivors in an
endlessly expanding universe of ever-diminishing returns" (, p. xiii). Messages of
definitiveness are now, irretrievably both behind and beyond us. How on Earth is
the bereft human specimen going to make it from here?

Ejected from Eden or, in Chinese terms, a Golden Age of harmony, peace and
prosperity, nothing proceeds as it should. Like the actual Great Wall of China
(whose construction began in the 6th century BCE), Kafka's Wall is built with the
goal of fortification in mind, protection against fearsome "peoples of the north"
(Kafka, 2007, p. 113). Is this not what is always at stake: our frantic quest for
safekeeping during the course of our fitful Earthly sojourn, shelter from the
omnipresent metaphorical storm, our insatiable desire to have precisely what we
cannot? In Kafka's telling of the tale, the grand design begins resolutely enough,
the northernmost point of the Wall being joined at its apex with sections from the
southeast and the southwest. From this starting point, however, the building of
the Great Wall proceeds, not systematically, but rather according to a system of
*partial construction*, gangs of 20 workers apiece sent off into the vast expanse of
China to erect random 500-yard sections while an adjoining gang then constructs
a section of equal length to meet it. In this manner, original order is compromised
and finally lost:

But then, after the juncture was accomplished, the construction was not
continued at the end of these thousand yards, as you might expect;
instead, the groups of workers were sent into quite different regions to
continue work on the Wall. In this way, of course, numerous large gaps
came about, and these were only gradually and slowly filled in, many only
after the Wall had already been announced as completed. Indeed, it is said
that there are gaps that have not been filled in at all; according to some
people these are much larger than the completed sections, although this
assertion may be only one of the many legends that have grown up around
the Wall and which, given the length of the Wall, is not something one

person can verify, at least with his own eyes and by his own standards. (Kafka, 2007, p. 113)

Grandiose schemes devolving into intractable confusion. The unreliability of stories and words. More gaps (or is it only another legend?) than wall. Do these images not evocatively depict an essential aspect of the state of things as we know it? Certainly, muses the Chinese narrator of our tale, it would have been more advantageous to "build continuously" or, at least, "continuously within the two main sections" rather than this strange method of "partial construction" (Kafka, 2007, p. 113). Such piecemeal proceedings can never afford adequate protection from enemies without and the gathering storm. And, yet, return to a "fixed place" (May, 1991, p. 53) of substance is a thing fanatically sought even as chances for attainment become increasingly remote. "I have been forty years wandering from Canaan," Kafka (1949/1988, p. 213) opined in his diary. This is our acutely modernist/postmodernist predicament. It is also what makes Kafka indispensable and palpably present.

Exile and the impossibility of return. The breakdown of meanings and forms. Our disconnection from Original Sources, the succor of traditional wisdom assumedly afforded in more coherent times. With Kafka, we are a long, long way from the world of the master builders with their blueprints and graphs, their raceways to expedient arrival, their voluble pronouncements seeming almost to command adjustment if not utter happiness in the midst of retreating voices and signs from beyond. "It is indeed a kind of Wandering in the Wilderness in reverse," muses Kafka, (1949/1988, p. 213), of our post-paradisiacal, post-Canaan/canonical world. Those looming capitalizations ("Wondering" and "Wilderness"), a kind of gnostic shorthand disclosing an urgency concerning what is at stake. "Not "castration," suggested Rollo May (1991, p. 81), "but *ostracism*." Enter a brave new world from which God has departed, leaving in her or his absence manifold truncations in which nothing completely adds up. Kafka, explorer of a vast new space of a world on the lam and the mortified mind, sheds light on dark truths that science itself does not adequately broach. Unlike the academics, Kafka was reverential, even penitent—like some latter-day and literary Darwin—before the gravity of his ordeal. While realizing that the past may never have been exactly what we remember, Kafka nonetheless embraced this desolate landscape with a countenance of awe and dread. "Kafka," sighed the Italian critic Pietro Citati (1991), "the man who has taught us to coexist with the death of the gods." (p. 171)

## II

Scarcely known in his own time, Kafka's name has (like the legends of China) spread far and wide, his star rising posthumously to astronomical heights even as Freud's has notably declined. Kafka seems to me to be the truer conquistador of modern-day consciousness, whereas Freud and his disciples—their sizable accomplishments notwithstanding—find touchstones significantly in shibboleths of the past. (*"This is how eager we are,"* reflects the narrator of our tale, *"to wipe out the present."*) In his survey of a world in which scripture is lost and meaning no longer coheres, Kafka lays bare our own lives in much the same way, as Auden keenly observed, that Dante and Shakespeare had those of their own epochs and place. With Kafka, we gaze dumbfounded at a world from which God has departed, "the single divine Truth decomposed into myriad relative truths parceled out by men" (Kundera, 1986, p. 6). What we are left with, to quote a prescient William James (1961), is a "string of facts…provisional and revisable things" (p. 335).

The French literary critics Deleuze and Guattari (1986) were wrong to project into Kafka an embrace of "socialism" or "anarchism" to be found in their own theoretical writing and minds. Still, they were right when they noted that Kafka "laughs with a profound joy" (p. 41). "I can also laugh," (Wagner, 2007, p. 303) Kafka once wrote to his fiancée Felice; "have no doubt about this." Walter Benjamin (Alter, 1991, p. 21), too, posits, counter-intuitively, that the key to Kafka's work may reside in deciphering *"the comic aspects of Jewish theology."* "And from one end to the other," Deleuze and Guattari (1986) noted, Kafka is "a political author, prophet of the future world" (p. 41). A political author, yes, in his unflinching gaze into the manifold conundrums of authority and meaning, spirit and self on a planet without compass that has seen better days. By no means, however, a proponent of newly minted systems to replace the "various, perhaps contradictory, statements [concerning] the obscurity of ancient times" (Kafka, 1954/1999, p. 9). We have only to think of this 21st century that has so fitfully commenced and our own tenuous ties to worlds inside and without when considering our narrator's reflections on Chinese emperors real and imagined and the lingering desire of the lowly individual to commune with what is deemed high:

> Just so, as hopelessly and hopefully, our people view the emperor. They do not know which emperor is reigning, and there is even doubt about the name of the dynasty . . . In our villages, long-dead emperors are set up on thrones, and one who lives on only in song has recently issued a decree that the priest reads aloud in front of the alter. Battles from our most ancient history are just now being fought, and with glowing cheeks your neighbor bursts into your house with the news. (Kafka, 2007, pp. 120-121)

With Kafka, we approach the numinous "limits of understanding" (Benjamin, 1968, p. 124). Even matters of leadership (where thoughts of current emperors merge beguilingly with memories of the dead ones) and transmission of knowledge, pressing as they are in an age of radical complexity, may be simultaneously matters of levity and even awe—touchstones not only for vagary but, ultimately, for reverie as well. Intimations of the spiritual are in Kafka everywhere implied, yet, remarkable for their insubstantiality and lack of fulfillment:

> In the leadership office—where it was located and who occupied it, no
> one I have ever asked knows or knew—in this office there surely revolv-
> ed all human thoughts and desires and, in countercircles, all human goals
> and fulfillments; but through the window the reflection of divine worlds
> fell on the hands of the leaders as they drew their plans. (Kafka, 2007, pp.
> 116-117)

Founding fathers, mothers, and architects, their plans gently illumined by the
gods. "Camouflaged within the social order," observed Roberto Calasso (2005, p.
23), "the cosmic order continues to exist and operate. After all, it has dealt not only
with stars and spheres but also with powers and archons" (p. 23). It is precisely
the manner in which divinity is intimated (merging seamlessly, albeit incon-
clusively, with authority) yet never disclosed that holds us eerily spellbound, as
though we were witnessing in Kafka a mythology perfectly reflective of our own
frenetic experience and nebulous time. "Anyone intent on concluding . . . that we
have no emperor at all," our narrator (Kafka, 2007, p. 122) coyly informs us,
"would not be far from the truth" (p. 22) The mysteries of Time, the mysteries of
Space, the mysteries of God and Authority as hearsay replaces scripture and
human beings now pose as gods.

### III

And, so, connections are lost not only temporally but, also, hierarchically with
incorporeal leaders replacing deities of old. Kafka's world was typified throughout
by the loss of what the German sociologist Arnold Gehlen (in Wagner, 2007) called
a "grand key attitude" (p. 308). As such, it constitutes a hallmark expression of the
"general uncertainty" (Kafka, 2007, p. 120) of our own experience and time:

> And while it is mainly the fault of the regime, which in the most ancient
> empire on earth has always been unable, perhaps through neglect of this
> concern in favor of other matters, to develop the institution of empire
> with such clarity that it would exercise its influence immediately and
> incessantly as far as the realm's most distant frontiers. On the other hand,
> this attitude also exhibits a weakness of imagination or conviction among
> the people, who are unable to embrace the empire obediently, in all its
> liveliness and presence, raising it from its submersion in Peking, and yet
> the subjects wish nothing more than just for once to feel this connection
> and drown in it. (p. 123)

No direction home commingling with a subjectively experienced imperative of
right of return. A "hierarchically structured purposelessness" (Bauer, 1999, ¶ 6)
and, consequently, the "search for a fixed spot in an otherwise chaotic" (May,
1991, p. 53) world. Yet, also, this notion that the problem may reside, ultimately,

in our own "weakness of imagination." It is a point to which we will return in due time.

## IV

The German-Jewish literary critic Walter Benjamin (1969), contemplating a painting he had purchased by the Swiss modern artist Paul Klee entitled *Angelus Novus,* once wrote down these words:

> A Klee painting named "Angelus Novus" shows an angel looking as though he is about to move away from something he is fixedly contemplating. His eyes are staring, his mouth is open, his wings are spread. This is how one pictures the angel of history. His face is turned toward the past. Where we perceive a chain of events, he sees one single catastrophe which keeps piling wreckage upon wreckage and hurls it in front of his feet. The angel would like to stay, awaken the dead, and make whole what has been smashed. But a storm is blowing from Paradise; it has got caught in his wings with such violence that the angel can no longer close them. This storm irresistibly propels him into the future to which his back is turned, while the pile of debris before him grows skyward. This storm is what we call progress. (pp. 257-258)

Throughout his abbreviated life, Benjamin carried on a passionate epistolary dialogue with Gershom Scholem, scholar of Jewish mysticism, centering (it should hardly surprise us!) often on Kafka. His insights into the modernist seer and postmodern psyche remain astonishingly brilliant to this day. Both men shared an evolving perception of Kafka as the artist who had, above all others, "mapped out the spiritual territory of the modern condition" (Alter, 1991, p. 14). Benjamin sensed in Klee's painting the essence of what the Jewish genius had spent his life pondering: the longing for paradise/revelation/Canaan and the gathering storm we mistake for progress. Benjamin used the painting as a mandala of sorts, an object for focus and reverie. After his suicide (when attempting to flee the Nazi occupation of France—the sinister face of totalitarianism and the obliging bureaucratic/clerical mind is everywhere lurking in Kafka—he was turned back at the Spanish border), the painting joined his friend Scholem in Jerusalem where it remained until Scholem's own death many years later. Robert Alter (1991) beautifully tells the whole story in a slim and relevant book entitled *Necessary Angels: Tradition and Modernity in Kafka, Benjamin, and Scholem.*

Diaspora, a dispersion into Wilderness or Desert; the spiritually/ metaphorically wandering Jew. "Losing one place without gaining another," reflects Zadie Smith (2008, p. 17) in her recent essay on Kafka. In Kafka's story, too, as in the Tower of Babel, there is a vision of harmony never finally attained: "unity! unity! breast on breast, a round dance of the people, blood no longer confined in the meager circulatory system of the body but rolling on sweetly and yet returning to its source through the infinity of China" (Kafka, 2007, p. 115). Indeed, among the many legends that sprout up around the Great Wall is one that claims that it is itself to become the foundation for a new Tower of Babel. Once again, the hubris of mortals who, in their irrepressible childishness, haven't yet realized their bankruptcy and the impossibility of agendas. "Human nature, giddy at heart, a thing of flying dust, cannot endure being fettered; if it fetters itself, it will soon go mad, begin to rattle its chains, and tear to pieces wall, chain, and itself, scattering them to the winds" (Kafka, 2007, p. 116). And, so, the desire not only for unthinking loyalty to the Emperor but also, by extension, the Universal Project, even though collective life remains unredeemed. "Not system," cautions Scholem (in Alter, 1991, p. 86), "but *commentary.*" It is an essentially Hebraic (and also modernist) point of view.

V

Now, surely, there must be some kind of message here for modern-day China as well. The rest of the world stands rapt before the burgeoning nation reborn now with newfound resources and intoxicating powers, its teeming populace and its great expanse. As I write these words, the sprawling city of Beijing, the rest of the planet in its thrall, prepares for its forthcoming Olympics. On the cover of this morning's Sunday edition of the New York Times, I peruse, coincidently, another meditation upon Chinese architecture and design. In "The Changing Face of Beijing, A Look at the New China," Nicolai Ouroussoff (2008) wrote with awe and irony about arrival at what is now the largest airport on Earth:

> If Westerners feel dazed and confused upon exiting the plane at the new international airport terminal here, it's understandable. It's not just the grandeur of the space. It's the inescapable feeling that you're passing through a portal to another world, one whose fierce embrace of change has left Western nations in the dust. (p. 1)

Dazed and confused. It is, of course, the contemporary state explored unflaggingly by Kafka. And with Kafka, too, one feels oneself passing, inexorably, through a portal to another world.

Reflecting China's "embrace of the modernist creed," Ouroussoff (2008) noted, also, the majestic new airport's "real precedent" in Albert Speer's (Hitler's chief architect) Tempelhof Airport in Berlin, a monument conceived by the Third Reich as the "gateway to a new Europe." "Both," wrote Ouroussoff, "are part of a vision of a mobile society, one that extends back through Grand Central Terminal to the great train halls of Paris" (p. 1). With this harking back to traditions both grand and disarming, we are, here, in today's American newspaper, very close to the spirit of Kafka:

Guided by twinkling lights embedded in the terminal's ceiling, arriving visitors glide up ramped floors and across broad pedestrian bridges before spilling out onto the elevated concourse. From there they can disperse along a fluid network of roads, trains, subways, canals and parks whose tentacles extend out through the region. (Ouroussoff, 2008, p. 1)

In Kafka's fiction, such movement is relentless, even ominous, yet devoid of ultimate destination or import. (*"There is a destination but no way there,"* Kafka once wrote in his diary; *"what we refer to as way is hesitation."*) For Ouroussoff (2008), too, China's velocity and scope is breathtaking but disconcerting, its future forebodingly uncertain: "Everything is possible here from utopian triumphs of the imagination to soul-sapping expressions of a disregard for individual lives" (p. 14). China, the "great laboratory for architectural ideas," holds within it, intimations of "a vast propaganda machine" (Ourossoff, 2008, p. 14), just as well. Even in the glittering metropolis there are tenements and gaps.

## VI

Writing in his diary under an autobiographical group of entries called "He," Kafka (1971, p. ix) contemplated his destiny and craft:

All that he does seems to him, it is true, extraordinarily new, but also, because of the incredible spate of new things, extraordinarily amateurish, indeed scarcely tolerable, incapable of becoming history, breaking short the chain of the generations, cutting off for the first time at its most profound source the music of the world, which before him could at least be divined. Sometimes in his arrogance he has more anxiety for the world than for himself.

In the modernist/postmodernist world, as R.D. Laing (1962) had informed us, even dissociation becomes part and parcel of normative experience. Looking at himself as if he were another, Kafka dwelled here with fear and trembling on his fateful vocation and prophetic role.

In the *Fourth Blue Octavo Notebook*, the seer of Prague (Kafka, 1954/1999) further elaborated on his calling and path: "I have not been guided into life by the hand of Christianity, admittedly now slack and failing, as Kierkegaard was, and have not caught the hem of the Jewish prayer shawl, now flying away from us as the Zionists have. I am an end or a beginning" (p. 51). Calasso (2005) elaborates on the universal implications in Kafka, man and woman's tenuous place in the modern-become-postmodernist world—a sphere in which, between private and collective realms, no reliable demarcation any longer inheres:

With Kafka a phenomenon burst onto the scene; the *commixture.* There is no sordid corner than can't be treated as a vast abstraction, and no vast abstraction than can't be treated as a sordid corner. This phenomenon isn't a reflection of the writer's personal inclinations. It's a matter of fact. (p. 22)

This *commixture* of elements is precisely what typifies modernist/postmodernist existence and consciousness—what James, always ahead of his time, had called the "blooming buzzing confusion." "Experience is vague," observed Gavin (1992, p. 29), "in the sense of being richer than any formula." This may be good or bad depending on capacity and moment, but privacy and Cartesian clarity are now things of the past.

## VII

In 1922, suffering with tuberculosis and immersed in the writing of his final novel in the Bohemian town of Zurau, Kafka noted in his diary having suffered a nervous breakdown only one week before (Greenberg, 1965). As he pondered his plight, his thoughts turned on two possibilities. First, he imagined, and genuinely feared, that his fanatical inner/modernist "chase" might end in utter isolation or madness. If he was able, however, to "hold up even the littlest bit," letting himself be "borne along by the pursuit," there could exists the possibility of a sort of triumphal "assault against the last earthly frontier," (p. 216) a journey through the vagaries of the modern world and jumbled mind to a forbidding yet new horizon:

> All this writing is an assault upon the frontiers, and if Zionism hadn't intervened might easily have developed into a new secret doctrine, a Kabbalah. There are beginnings in that direction. Of course, it needs an almost inconceivable genius that would be able to strike root again in the old centuries, or would create the old centuries anew without using itself up in doing so, but would only then begin to flower forth. (Greenberg, 1965, p. 216)

Here we are again, with thoughts from James (1950) regarding the quest for a new mythology that does not lose itself in political movement ("if Zionism hadn't intervened") on the one hand nor end in dissolution ("without using itself up") or madness on the other. Awe before mysteries both cosmic and terrestrial, the "reinstatement of the vague" (p. 254).

In a world without revelation, redemption may be gleaned through reverie and the alternating receptive/creative spirit. Although modest in decorum almost to a fault, Kafka realized the enormity of what had been lost and the consequent gravity of his task. "Art like prayer," (as cited in Bauer, 1999, ¶ 4) he once told his youthful friend and admirer Gustav Janouch, "is a hand stretched out in the dark seeking to catch something from grace in order to transform itself into a giving hand"(¶ 4). The ascendancy of imagination, however fleeting, and the act of a genuinely personal expression, thereby rekindling the possibility of encounter, counterposes even the darkest truths. Dark truths have, in turn, their ennobling aspects simply by virtue of being disclosed: there is truth after all. A *"sense of being,* [teaches May (1983)] "the ontological sense" (p. 15).

Kafka did consciously seek to write a kind of "new mysticism, a Kabbalah" for a world shorn of moorings and in alarming disarray, doggedly exposing the extreme states of anxiety and confusion, the augmented self-consciousness ("a sensitivity," John Updike notes, "beyond usefulness") that typifies the collective modernist/postmodernist psyche. Janouch (1971/1985) once suggested to him that his oeuvre constituted, perhaps, "a mirror of tomorrow" (p. 150). Upon hearing these words, Kafka covered his ears with both hands, exclaiming, "Please, don't go on." He then continued himself: "You are certainly right. Probably that's why I can't finish anything. I am afraid of the truth . . . One must be silent, if one can't give any help. No one, through his own lack of hope, should make the condition of the patient worse" (p. 150). Max Brod, Kafka's friend and confidante, thankfully disregarded Kafka's deathbed instructions that his unpublished manuscripts be burned after he had passed away. It was a happy instance of disobedience, noted the Argentinean master Jorge Luis Borges, thereby preserving "the most singular works of our century."

## VIII

It has been said that in Kafka we witness the seamless merging of reality and dream. The oneiric state is itself a merging of realty with the unencumbered mind. One day, my patient Kristina, a multiple personality, set down the following dream about alternate/parallel worlds and selves, dissolution of self/world and engulf-ment by larger bodies and forces—intimations of forthcoming intrapsychic/cataclysmic events, dissociation/escape and resultant macroscopic/global per-spectives. Note here, as in Kafka, the Chinese connection and, also, the vagaries of a world in peril without sure beacons to guide our way:

> I was living way out in the Far East, in China on an island. I was surrounded by all these people who didn't speak the same language as I did except for one person who acted as my translator and guide. I didn't go anywhere without him because I'd get lost or wouldn't be able to communicate with the people around me. I lived in a house with him and a woman who couldn't speak our language either. She was always sitting on a couch in front of a large picture window watching American television, even though she couldn't understand what was being said. I could never figure out why she liked watching it so much. She was older than the man; her hair was already turning grey.
>
> The house that we lived in was small, and it seemed like we lived at the end of a jetty. Three sides of the house looked out upon the ocean. The side of the house with the picture window looked west, so we always saw

the sun setting against the horizon. There was another window that was fairly large, looking out onto the sea.

One day I was sitting with the old woman and the man came in and sat down. He told me that the island was slowly sinking into the ocean and that each day the water came closer and closer to the house. He told me that soon the water would overtake us and the house would be lost to the sea. Eventually the whole island would be buried under the sea. Of course, I was saddened to hear it. It was a beautiful place to live, and I couldn't imagine how we could leave it and travel to another island to live. Days went by and, sure enough, whenever I went to the water's edge, it was closer and closer to my home. If I looked to the west, I could see the horizon, and to the right were enormous cliffs. Maybe we could move there and then we would be safe. The man told me that even these places would eventually be swallowed up. He said we would move to America. I asked him why we had to move so far, and he told me the whole continent would be buried, not just our island.

One day the water reached our steps. It rose and kept on rising. We took everything we had and we moved. We flew to America where we soon settled on the East Coast. We moved into a house right along the water, just as we had in China. Again we lived on a jetty, the water surrounding us on three sides, with one large window looking to the west and the setting sun. I asked the man, still my only companion (for even in America they spoke a language I did not understand), what would happen when the continent drowned. He told me that he did not know, that we would have to wait until it happened to find out. The woman still lived with us, and she still watched television, only now she watched Chinese television! One day the man finally told me that the time had come when the whole continent would be swallowed up. I asked him again what would happen. Surely there would be a massive tidal wave. Would it come all the way to America? Would it swallow us up? Who would survive such a wave? Questions all to which he shrugged his shoulders. We would wait to see.

Then I flew out of my body. At first I hovered over the house and the ocean, and then I hovered over America and then over the whole world. I could see China and Europe and Australia and Africa sinking. It happened slowly at first. Then, as the time grew longer and longer, it happened faster and faster. I knew that when everything had disappeared under the waves, the suction of the sinking would cause a disturbance in the sea. Still I was unsure of exactly what it would do. So, I just hovered in outer space looking at the world. Then it began. The whole globe started to wobble and ripple and fall in upon itself. I watched horrified above the earth, waiting to see what would happen next. It seemed as if the whole earth would collapse upon itself. I was terrified because I knew it meant I would be dead.

Kristina's dream projects upon a planetary canvas an intrapsychic architecture founded on two interior (*altered*) *worlds* or *houses*. Red and blue, blood and tears, action and reaction: an inner sanctuary of makeshift form and *sanity* in the face of overarching chaos from without. As psychotherapy progressed, there was a shift from presenting alters of Kristina's *blue world* of presentation to an earlier *red world* of original pain. Our work together (for, surely, I was the accompanist and guide who had, nonetheless, scant awareness of what exactly would happen next) changed qualitatively as primal trauma is encountered face to face. In Kristina's dream, this shift in alters was mirrored in the relocation from China to the States. Insofar, however, as the precariousness of the outer world continued unabated, the dreamer finally left her body outright as she hovered precariously high above the globe. Dissociation, mastered in early childhood, remained the only means of escape. Yet once the body is abandoned absolutely (just as the nations of the world now abandon Mother Earth), there is no place left to go. All that remains is an apocalyptic flood.

## IX

Louis Sass (1992), in his erudite book *Madness and Modernism,* explores the manner in which modern forms of insanity appear to be epiphenomena (a sensitivity beyond usefulness) of the manifold complexities associated with modern-day existence itself. Mostly, it would seem, there is a retreat from a world of exponentially increasing cacophonies and crosscurrents into a solace afforded by the hypertrophied head. In the *Third Blue Octavo Notebook,* Kafka (1991) wrote:

> In one and the same human being there are cognitions that, however utterly dissimilar they are, yet have one and the same object, so that one can only conclude that there are different subjects in one and the same human being. (p. 34)

And concerning, specifically, the theological connection, Kafka (in Smith, 2008) observed:

> With their posterior legs they were still glued to their father's Jewishness, and with their waving anterior legs they found no new ground. (p. 17)

Here again, the loss of tradition and, as in our dream, the impossibility of effect-tively moving on. Kabbalah, it is interesting to note, meant, literally, *oral-received tradition.* And, so, the complexities not only of the ambiguous postmodernist world but also of the polymorphous postmodernist self.

## X

Yet if revelation is no longer within reach, what then remains? During those contemplative days at Zurau, Kafka (2006) reflected on the possibilities inherent in Exile:

> The Expulsion from Paradise is eternal in its principal aspect; this makes it irrevocable, and our living in the world inevitable, but the eternal nature of the process has the effect that not only could we remain forever in Paradise, but that we are currently there, whether we know it or not. (p. 65)

We are reminded here of Dostoyevsky's observation that we are all happy if we but knew it. Perhaps a Golden Age of perfection is unnecessary. Perhaps it is possible to momentarily rise above what cannot in any case be repaired, finding nobility of spirit, even fleeting triumph, in presence and awareness. Kafka (1954/1999), indeed, seems quite intoxicated with this idea:

> Beyond a certain point there is no return. This point has to be reached.
> The decisive moment in human evolution is perpetual. That is why the revolutionary spiritual movements that declare all former things worthless are in the right, for nothing has yet happened. (p. 16)

And once again:

> There are two cardinal human vices, from which all the others derive their being: impatience and carelessness. Impatience got people evicted from Paradise; carelessness kept them from making their way back there. Or perhaps there is only one cardinal vice: impatience: Impatience got people evicted, and impatience kept them from making their way back. (Kafka, 2006, p. 15)

Even "psychology," suggests Kafka (1954/1999) provocatively, "is hesitation" (p. 15). Perhaps, in other words, we have already what we need.

## XI

One day Janouch brought Kafka a German translation of the *Tao te Ching* popular among mystically inclined westerners at the time. Kafka, familiar with Lao-Tzu's little wisdom book, and contemplating the epigrams within its pages, cautioned the youth still in search of methodology:

> They spell out—as you can see here—transcriptions of reality from translations of ancient Chinese instead of quietly reading the original text of

their own lives and responsibilities. To them the day before yesterday seems more accessible than today. But reality is never and nowhere more accessible than in the immediate moment of one's own life . . . All it guarantees us is what is superficial, the façade . . . [O]ne must break through this. Then everything becomes clear.

But how does one do that? How does one proceed? Is there some sure guide?

"No, there is none," said Kafka, shaking his head. "There is no route map on the way to truth. The only thing that counts is to make the venture of total dedication. A prescription would already imply a withdrawal, mistrust, and therewith the beginning of a false path. One must accept everything patiently and fearlessly. Man is condemned to life, not death." (Janouch, 1985, p. 156)

The immediacy, again, of experience in lieu of traditional comforts afforded once in another time. Kafka's sensibility is, in fact, exceedingly close here to the essence of Taoism, with which he acknowledged being involved "quite deeply and for a long time" (Bauer, 1999, ¶ 5). So much so that the Bulgarian-Jewish novelist Elias Canetti (1974) once cited Kafka as, "the only writer of the Western world who is essentially Chinese" (as cited in Bauer, 1999, ¶ 5). "Knowledge we *have*," mused Kafka (1954/1999) in the *Third Octavo Notebook;* "Anyone who strives for it with particular intensity is suspect of striving against it" (p. 39). Experience no longer mediated by arbiters of the past but written, as we read in Jeremiah (17:1), "upon the tables of [one's] heart....*New*... insights and possibilities," stated May, (1991. p. 86); the ineffable and numinous NOW.

In the *Fourth Octavo Notebook,* Kafka (1954/1999) returned again to the place of reverie in a world of exile:

> Contemplation and activity have their apparent truth; but only the activity radiated by contemplation, or rather, that which returns to it again, is truth. (p. 49)

> There is no need for you to leave the house. Stay at your table and listen. Don't even listen, just wait. Don't even wait, be completely quiet and alone. The world will offer itself to you to be unmasked; it can't do otherwise; in raptures it will writhe before you. (p. 54)

The consolations and, yes, even possibilities, of a world without revelation or gods. "Vagueness," elaborated Gavin (1992) in his excellent book on James, "is not, ontologically speaking, a fall from grace" (p. 179). The secret lies in *attentiveness,* "the natural prayer of the soul" (Benjamin, 1965, p. 134).

And, so, the Great Wall of China will never be complete, just as the Law will never be fully rendered and the Castle walls never breached. Still, there is something holy in it all for the attentive spirit and inspired mind. A secret doctrine, a

Kabbalah, a modernist/postmodernist epiphany in a world without final directives and forms. There is great joy at last in Kafka. The exquisite ecstasy of writing, a concomitant tribulation notwithstanding, is always in evidence just beneath the surface. This new kind of writing with its message of opacity could never have taken root in more coherent times. Kafka's graceful "posture of doubt," reflects Irving Howe (in Kafka, 1930/1992), amid "the vast indifference of the cosmos" (p. xviii). "A word, a glance, a sign of trust," (p. 262) says an official named Burgel in Kafka's final novel. Mysterious yet moving, even hallowed, words.

## XII

It is a unique admixture of horror, grace and courage that allows Kafka to gaze unblinkingly into the Void while succumbing to neither System Replacement nor Nothingness. We find no comforting philosophy in Kafka. What we find, paradoxically, is something both more and less: awareness and the inspired act of creation out of notable decay. Kafka in "his twenty-first-century aspect," stated Smith (2008, p. 17), becomes an "existential prophet" for each one of us, as sinking into the warm bed of the past becomes a quaint yet no longer realistic thought. "These days [Smith (2008) noted] we all find our anterior legs flailing before us" (p. 17). Kafka's message, though never wholly spelled out (it becomes, paradoxically, more difficult to fathom as it is expressed with increasing precision) and (like the myriad villagers of China) interpreted differently by each one who comes to him, seems all the more profound all the same. Wagner (2007), perhaps, stated it as well as anyone:

> And the outcome? Instead of directing his readers to this or that country on the ideological map .., Kafka offers them another attitude toward the complexity of modern knowledge, a new economy of knowing, based on a way of reading his stories: like the Chinese architect, readers are invited to travel through them, across new provinces of knowledge, feeling the risk of the journey and noting the importance of small differences and, occasionally, of laughter, against the backdrop of an age of violent uniformity. (pp. 320-321)

"Only by abandoning all pretended 'groundings,' [Bauer (1999) added] can one attain the freedom out of which authentic existence gives itself a finite meaning" (¶ 8). Reverie is in place of revelation. "The world will not yield to lucidity," [observed Howe—as cited in May, 1991—in his fine essay on Kafka, yet we may find there a kind of metaphysical sublimity nonetheless.] The poignancy of the transient" (, p. 294); a sense of being, the ontological sense.

And only now can we more nearly grasp the observant, indeed worshipful, manner in which Kafka (1949/1988) approached his sacred craft:

The strange, mysterious, perhaps dangerous, perhaps saving comfort that there is in writing: it is a leap out of murderers' row; it is a seeing of what is really taking place. This occurs by a higher type of observation, a higher, not a keener type, and the higher it is and the less within reach of the "row," the more independent it becomes, the more obedient to its own law of motion, the more incalculable, the more joyful, the more ascendant in its course. (p. 423)

The modernist scribe, was, after all, setting down a new mysticism, a Kabbalah, as recompense for a liturgy lost and had, as a consequence, a message at once hallowed and, in a sense, strangely simple to convey.

The Great Wall of China. A new age of radical ambiguity, manifold gaps, and the gathering storm. This storm is what we call progress.

## References

Alter, R. (1991). *Necessary angels: Tradition and modernity in Kafka, Benjamin, and Scholem.* Cambridge, MA: Harvard University Press.

Bauer, J. E. (1999). *Franz Kafka: Power, religious minorities and the inception of existence.* Paper presented at the CESNUR International Conference, Bryn Athyn College, Bryn Athyn, PA.

Benjamin, W. (1969). *Illuminations: Essays and reflections* (H. Arendt, Ed.; H. Zohn, Trans.). New York, NY: Schocken Books.

Calasso, R. (2005). *K* (G. Brock, Trans.). New York, NY: Alfred A. Knopf.

Canetti, E. (1974) *Kafka's other trial: The letters to Felice* (C. Middleton, Trans.) New York, NY: Schocken Books.

Citati, P. (1990). *Kafka* (R. Rosenthal, Trans.). New York, NY: Alfred A. Knopf.

Deleuze, G. & Guattari, F. (1986). *Kafka: Toward a minor literature* (D. Polan, Trans.). Minneapolis, MN: University of Minnesota Press.

Janouch, G. (1985). *Conversations with Kafka* (G. Rees, Trans.) London, UK: Quartet Books.

Gavin, W. J. (1992). *William James and the reinstatement of the vague.* Philadelphia, PA: Temple University Press.

Greenberg, M. (1965). *Kafka: The terror of art.* New York, NY: Horizon Press.

James, W. (1950). *The principles of psychology* (Vol. 1). New York, NY: Dover.

James, W. (1961). *Psychology: The briefer course* (G. Allport, Ed.). New York, NY: Harper Torchbooks.

Kafka, F. (1992). *The castle* ((W. Muir & E. Muir, Trans.). New York, NY: Everyman's Library. (Original work published in 1930)

Kafka, F. (1988). *The diaries of Franz Kafka.* New York, NY: Schoken Books. (Original work published in 1949)

Kafka, F. (1999). *The blue octavo notebooks* (E. Kaiser and E. Wilkins, trans.). Cambridge, UK: Exact Change. (Original work published in 1954)

Kafka, F. (1971). *The complete stories* (N. Glatzer, Trans.). New York, NY: Schocken Books.

Kafka, F. (2006). *The Zurau aphorisms* (M. Hoffman, Trans). New York, NY: Schocken Books.

Kafka, F. (2007). "Building the great wall of China." In *Kafka's selected stories*. (S. Corngold, Ed. & Trans.; pp. 113-124). New York, NY: W. W. Norton & Company.

Kundera, M. (1986). *The art of the novel* (L. Asher, Trans.). New York, NY: Harper & Row.

Laing, R.D. (1962). *The divided self.* New York, NY: Pantheon Books.

May, R. (1983). *The discovery of being.* New York, NY: Norton and Company.

May, R. (1992). *The cry for myth* New York, NY: Norton and Company.

Mendelowitz, E. (2008). *Ethics and Lao-tzu: Intimations of character.* Colorado Springs, CO: University of the Rockies Press.

Ouroussoff, N. (2008). The changing face of Beijing, A look at the new China. In *The New York Times,* 7/13/08.

Sass, L. (1992). *Madness and modernism.* Cambridge, MA: Harvard University Press.

Smith, Z. (2008). "F. Kafka, everyman." In *New York Review of Books,* LV:12, 14-17.

Wagner, B. (2007). No one indicates the direction: The question of leadership in Kafka's later stories. In *Kafka's selected stories* (S. Corngold, Ed. & Trans.; pp. 302-321). New York, NY: Norton & Company.

# Chapter 24

## Kisagotami, Buddha, and Mustard Seeds:
## An Existential Psychological Perspective

Francis Kaklauskas
Elizabeth Olson

**Dew world**
It is a dew world
It is what it is
~ Issa Kobayashi [1]

As interest in Eastern thought continues to increase in Western societies, psychologists and psychology students in India, China, Japan, and other Asian countries are rigorously studying the history and methods of the Western tradition as the use of psychotherapeutic interventions is rapidly expanding there. Cross-cultural dialogue is occurring with greater frequency and the conversations are livelier as clinicians and researchers travel with increasing regularity between cultures than at any time in the past. Curiosity and dynamism continue to hold off the dogmatism that can be present in both traditions, and due to their open-mindedness, Western existential psychology and Eastern Buddhism seem to be at the forefront of this exchange.

In fact, many of the fundamental questions and conclusions of existentialism and Buddhism are analogous. While both traditions value rigorous scientific and philosophical examination, both also use the creative arts and narratives to go beyond reductionist paradigms and engage multiple ways of knowing. This chapter recalls some common stories about *Siddhartha Gautama*, the Buddha, to highlight these similarities and to consider their implications for the practice of psychology and psychotherapy. While some fundamentalist Buddhist scholars prescribe to singular interpretations, or even a literal understanding of these stories, the vast majority of teachers and scholars encourage students to contemplate their meaning not only intellectually, but personally. In fact, the historical information about the actual life of the Buddha, similar to that regarding the life

---

[1] This was written after the death of his two year old daughter. The dew reflects the water covering the grass and vegetation in the morning, the sadness in his heart, and the inevitability and acceptance of death and suffering, all interconnecting in one personal phenomenological moment. Translated by Francis Kaklauskas, 1988.

of Christ, was not codified until after his death. The earliest biographies of the Buddha were written more than five hundred years after his death and most stories have multiple versions, each of which has been influenced by the culture, historical background, and the interests of the writer.

One of the best examples is the multiple versions of a story of Kisagotami. Depending upon the source, Kisagotami can be described as tall, thin, restrained, and unattractive (Hecker, 1982), or pretty, well-spoken, and a cousin of the Buddha (Tisdale, 2006). While these details may carry important information for cultural studies scholars, from a general existential perspective, and particularly for the purpose of this chapter, they are tertiary, as the poignancy of the story transcends these demographic variables. The following summary is drawn from multiple sources in order to capture the essence of the existential messages of the story with particular emphasis placed on the translations from the earliest Pali version (Bhushan, 2008; Gyasto, 1992; Hecker, 1982; Lillie, 1881; Murcott, 2006; Nikaya, 1930; Therigatha, 1883; Tisdale, 2006; Udana, 1948; Weeraperuma, 2006).

## Kisagotami

Kisagotami was from a poor family and, given the culture of ancient India, she was expected to marry and have children. After several false starts and despite her lessening hopes, she eventually married a man from a wealthier class. When she had difficulty bearing a child, her in-laws began planning for their son to find a new bride. Unexpectedly, Kisagotami became pregnant and had a son. She loved her son very much and her wealthy husband and in-laws became supportive. She was relieved, knowing she had secured a financially sound future for both her son and herself.

When her son died unexpectedly in his sleep, Kisagotami was inconsolable. She carried his corpse from home to home asking for a medicine to revive her son. She was eventually directed to the Buddha. By the time she met the Buddha in the forest, she was exhausted, dirty, and becoming physically ill herself and her son's body was decaying badly with maggots running across his flesh. When she approached the Buddha, she told him that she had heard that he was a very special healer and would he cure her son.

Observing the situation, the Buddha told her to put her son down, and he would watch after him. He then instructed her to collect just a small amount of mustard seed from the homes in her village that had not had a death. Kisagotami set off to her village. She thought that because mustard seed is such a common spice that the task of collecting a few seeds would not be difficult.

When she came to the first house, she asked if she could have a few mustard seeds and she was quickly given a few seeds. Then Kisagotami asked whether anyone had died in their home? She was told that the family's father had died in the home just 4 months earlier. Leaving the seeds behind, Kisagotami rushed off to the next home.

In home after home she was told of the parents, the sons and daughters, and the friends who had died in each home. Some had died by falling from a tree or a roof, some from animal attacks or other wounds, others from malnutrition, one from suicide, and still others for reasons no one could name. Everywhere she went she discovered the experience of death. Not only the death of the elderly, but the loss of adults in their prime, children, infants, mothers, fathers, daughters, and sons. Everywhere she went she heard stories of death and grief.

Even before she had finished visiting every home in her village, she returned to the Buddha. She reported that she had been selfish in her grief, that the living are few and the dead many. She brought her dead son to the carnal ground, buried him, and said good-bye. She stood above his grave and said the universal law for all things is impermanence. Change. She then returned to the Buddha and renounced her former life with her husband and in-laws.

Her grief further lifted when she heard the Buddha say that the person who lives 100 years and does not understand the realities of human existence would be better to have lived just one day and beheld the truths. Kisagotami lived the remainder of her long life as a renowned, compassionate nun.

## Existential and Buddhist Themes

The story of Kisagotami is, in many ways, a perfect existential myth. The story is simple, yet leads one to consider many of life's most difficult challenges. The story also outlines many of the existential givens as understood from the Buddhist perspective. Although this story is set over 2,500 years ago and comes from Pali texts of the first century, Kisogotmi's grief, insight, and journey are universal.

### Suffering
Buddha's first teaching was on suffering, pain, or *duhkha* (sanskrit). This is the first noble truth: Pain is the unavoidable companion of existence. Not only is suffering reliable, but it comes in an unlimited variety of flavors. Kisogotami experienced many types of suffering. Prior to marrying, she experienced anxiety about her future, class discrimination, and cultural expectations dictated by her gender. During her marriage, she experienced the pain of being negatively judged by her in-laws and the despair of possibly being infertile. As a mother, she experienced perhaps the greatest suffering one can know, the death of a child, and the resultant despair, confusion, grief, and existential angst.

In many Buddhist traditions, this existential suffering, or all-pervading pain of separation, loneliness, and dissatisfaction, is stressed (Trungpa, 1976). On a cognitive level, one is inevitably uncomfortable with the understanding that life can be difficult, complex, unpredictable, and finite. On the physiological, emotional, and spiritual levels, existence can feel similar to anxiety; as the bubbles of disappointment inevitably rise up to the surface. From both existential and Buddhist psychological perspectives, this experience of dukkha is the uncomfortable foundation of human experience that we defend against and push away. As a consequence of this experience, we can negatively judge both ourselves and our environments as the cause of our suffering, as opposed to directly accepting the inevitability of this experience.

## Impermanence

The story of Kisagotami is filled with change. She experiences the great joy of motherhood and the deep despair of grief. But even the depth of her grief is not permanent. Moreover, her understanding, acceptance, and adaptation to the realities of life also are not permanent. She lived, and like everyone else, she died. Her life, her form, arose and dissipated, leaving only this brief story for the living to consider. Furthermore, for the Buddhist, like the existentialist, the knowledge of the shortness of our lives and the knowledge that our death will come unexpectedly lead to questions concerning life's meaning and our free will (Gyatso, 1984). Kisagotmi chooses a life of spiritual engagement rather than returning to a life designed to meet the expectations of her culture.

In the Buddhist traditions, the truth of impermanence directly flows into the idea of egolessness or no self. On a relative level, this concept is easy to digest. Even if we have the same job, home, and community, at least some in minor way, each day we are different than the day before.

On an absolute level, the self is only an inaccurate construction of reality. In fact, all people and things are dependent upon a limitless network of factors. We only exist because our parents existed, because we have air and food, and because we have an Earth on which to live. The progressive mediation on this topic asks us to contemplate if any part of us represents a continuous enduring self. If we lose a limb or our sight, if we lose our memory or our minds, are we still the same? If we lose our skin, which creates the visual illusion of separateness, are we still a discrete self? If we get an artificial heart, does our essence of selfhood continue? From the Buddhist view, since any singular part of us can be removed, the self has no essence. From the existential-psychology perspective the questions of the self have no dogmatic answer and should be examined not only from a theoretical perspective, but also on a personal level. Everyone should consider one's existence, who they are, and what they believe to be real as part of the journey towards understanding and freedom (May, 1966).

## Phenomenological Consideration

Phenomenology comes from the Greek word meaning *that which appears* (Smith, 2007). In the West, questions about the nature of existence, what is real, and the interplay of the mind and the world are generally the pursuit of academic philosophers, neurologists, and physicists. In Buddhism, however, everyone is encouraged to examine such questions. Through meditative practi-ces, philosophical discourses, myths and stories, one thoroughly absorbs the complexity of these, perhaps, unknowable answers to questions, and becomes comfortable living in a world that is beyond our understanding

If, as Heidegger (1927) asserted, methodology creates phenomenology, in the West the majority of phenomenological explorations are focused on a kind of rationalism. Although Buddhism has a rationalistic and reductionist tradition that at least equals that of Western philosophy (e.g. Nagarjuna, Yogacara), this element has been balanced by the various meditation and yogic practices. The Western dilemmas of subject/object and existential/theoretical have been the common focus of meditative contemplation for thousands of years. The limitation of rationalism and the wisdom of experience were originally addressed and abandoned by Western scholars. Hunt (1994) pointed out that William Wundt and his students tried to journal the experience of consciousness and address the emerging subject-object dyad, but it was felt, given the limits of methodology and scientific instrumentation, that this pursuit was best suited for later psychologists.

Phenomenological philosopher Edward Husserl (as cited in Rollinger, 2008) imagined a philosophy not estranged from everyday life and one that incorporates the existential experience of each person. He sought to understand consciousness not through theoretical reduction, but rather through suspension of judgments. His pursuit of this state of existential consciousness beyond one's thinking was mocked by his contemporaries, including his student, Heidegger. Husserl's pursuit has similarities to the Buddhist view and the mediation experience. But without the support of his culture and an experienced guide, he abandoned this pursuit, but retained the experience of consciousness as a core part of the self.

From the existential and Buddhist philosophical perspectives, a quality of skepticism is essential. In fact, much of psychotherapeutic theory embraces a stance of skepticism for both clients and the clinicians. Whether one seeks to reveal the unconscious motivation of psychodynamic insight or to correct distorted cognitions, the ability to acknowledge that one not may be accurately understanding oneself and the world is a prerequisite for change and growth.

While the Buddhist traditions, particularly Zen, offer stories of immediate enlightenment, such epiphanies may be more the result of an accumulation of experience than an immediate transformation. As seen with Kisagotami, the need to experience grief is necessary to understand and have compassion for others.

### Ambiguity

From a Judeo-Christian point of view, Kisagotami and her son's souls would be everlasting, and depending upon the interpretation of different sects, they may be in hell, purgatory, or heaven. The Buddha, after trying the various Vedic experiential practices and logical arguments of his culture and time, felt that such metaphysical questions could not be answered with certitude. Life must be lived with this ambiguity and tension. The Buddha, however, prompted his followers to consider such questions for themselves and to believe nothing that does not seem to be in accord with common sense and experience. Given such freedom, various Buddhist sects have promoted different tenets. Many Tibetan Buddhists believe in reincarnation, while other Buddhist schools renounce such ideas as unknowable or unimportant (de Bary, 1972). This Buddhist ideal of independent thought has also allowed some of the Judeo-Christian faithful and even atheists to incorporate Buddhist principles that match their own experiences. In both Buddhism and existential thought, dogmatism is scorned in favor of individual exploration and experience.

## Aloneness

From a phenomenological perspective, one's experience of one's life is unique, subjective, and beyond communication. Aloneness is not being without others, but the realization that although we can communicate well, have similar experiences, and have feelings of intimacy and closeness, the phenomenological experience of separateness endures. While Hinduism, Sufism, and even Buddhism promise glimpses of holism in which we transcend the subjective self, the fundamental and relative psychological aloneness returns. To deny this experience is to deny the reality of our lives, and this is as ridiculous as denying our deaths.

While Kisogotami undoubtedly received solace from sharing her grief with others, her grief remained her grief. Not even the experience of her husband or that of other mothers who had lost children can be the same. In the retelling of her story, one can see the struggle against this experience of aloneness. The methods of escape for her are no different than the methods used today. Marriage, children, community, and spiritual exploration can help us feel less lonely, but none can change the fact of our fundamental aloneness.

In both approaches, the path leads to a realization and acceptance of this human predicament. Like all existential and Buddhist givens, only through acknowledgment is there a hope for increased freedom. We are no longer stuck endlessly pursuing escapes from the prison of aloneness, but connect to the world and others more authentically from this experience. Krishnamurti (2005) lived a life that seemed to embody this view. While his ides are similar to those found in both Buddhism and existentialism, he felt his ideas—each of our ideas—transcend the reductionism of labels and are, therefore, soley personal. He stated:

> On the journey of life and death, you must walk alone; on this journey there can be no taking of comfort in knowledge, in experience, in memories. The mind must be purged of all the things it has gathered in its urge to be secure... There must be complete, uncontaminated aloneness. (p. 95)

## Compassion

As Kisagotami's story unfolds, her compassion for others increases. While much of Buddhism strives to be non-metaphysical, the concept of compassion is an exception. Buddha, and most contemporary forms of Buddhism, understands compassion as the base of human experience. One does not develop compassion, but rather one works through obstacles to compassion. Kisagotimi comes to realize that her focus on her own grief limited her openness to the suffering of others. From both Buddhist and Western psychological perspectives, compassion can be seen as a measure of psychological maturity (Gilighan 1982; Kolhberg, 1981), and also a core human competency (Frankl, 1969; May, 1995).

Nietzsche, upon witnessing a horse being beaten by its master, realized the supreme harshness of the world and it inspired him to search for an ethics and ontology that might account for this cruelty (Pearson, 1997). His interpretation, later found in the drive theory of Freud (1923), is that aggression is close to the human soul. Klein (1975) moved this aggression into a frustrated relational drive, while others theorists have abandoned this idea in favor of the ideas of self-actualization (Adler, 1929), meaning (Frankel, 1969), or integration (Schneider, 2007) that might also make sense our experiences. Regardless of how one understands human biological instincts, it is easy to see the external manifestation of multiple beliefs. These theories can be extremely helpful in psychotherapy and in the creation of personal meaning, if tempered. However, the leap from behavior to the latent construct of a specific drive remains filled with holes, which, at this time, cannot be proven.

The concepts of compassion and altruism have gained some support. Both animal and human studies have demonstrated the potential for altruistic and caring behavior (Baron & Burn, 2008). The experience of trauma stirs the heart to help others who are suffering (Batson, 1997), much like Kisogotami was moved to help others after her trauma and hearing of the traumas of others. The scientific case, however, for either aggression empathy/compassion as the core human instinct appears weak. One's personal experience, however, appears to be strongly linked with both the increase of aggressive behavior (Zimbardo, 2007) and compassionate behavior (Schore, 2003). While the Buddhists argue that through meditation and contemplation one comes to understand the encompassing power of compassion, it remains impossible to determine if this understanding is the consequence of uncovering a foundational universal principle or the result of having practiced a specific course of behavior. As Heidegger (1927) concluded, "phenomenology is primarily a certain conception of method" (p. 27). If one practices meditation on compassion, one is apt to feel more compassionate, if one is surrounded by propaganda and authoritarian rule, one can without difficulty become a murderer (Zimbardo, 2007).

## Journey

The Zen teacher Shunyra Suzuki (1973) stressed that while philosophical understanding is good, experience is more important. While philosophical discourse sets forth logical arguments, the personal is often discounted. The personal and the theoretical, and the subject and object examination, can never be fully discrete and never fully explanatory without the other. Buddhist and existential writers have attempted to combine these dualities. The narrative and phenomenological journey is valued and given importance as an essential way of knowing. The core teachings of both traditions repeatedly use myth to help guide the reader or listener to a personal experience of a philosophical message.

The Buddha went through a series of life events that formed the basis of his philosophy. As a young son of a wealthy and over protected father, he was shielded against the painful reality of existence. He eventually snuck away from the grounds of his father's estate. On this journey he encountered individuals that were old, sick, dying, and dead. These experiences became the root of his teaching of suffering. The Buddha then encountered a yogi who was seeking to understand and transcend the suffering in the world. This became Buddha's path as this experience instilled both hope and a life mission in the young Buddha. He left his father's estate and sought the instructions of yogis, philosophers, and spiritual teachers. After years of rigorous training, he became learned and skilled at a variety of spiritual systems and practices, but remained insatiate. He set forth to discover his own path and truths.

Many of the great works of existentialism employ a similar narrative teaching methodology. Nietzsche's (1909/2005) Zarathustra, Camus's (1942/1989) stranger, Sartre's (1947/1992) Mathieu, and a multitude of Kafka characters go through a series of events that inform their philosophies and behavior. This view of the journey is particularly important to the practice of psychotherapy. As the client and clinician review a client's experiences, new meanings and new ways of being emerge. The goal of existential and Buddhist influenced psychotherapy does not have predetermined destination. While valuing symptom reduction, both clinician and client must go beyond in search of meaning and purposeful action.

**Prajna**
In Buddhism, Prajna is the blending of compassion and skillful means. While stories of circuitous teaching methods that shock students into enlightenment abound in the Chinese, Tibetan, and Japanese traditions, the Buddha, himself, is generally understood to have been more direct and less dramatic. In fact, his choice to have Kisogotami search for mustard seeds is not typical of most of his instructions. However, as the story unfolds, this request was perhaps the wisest method. If Buddha had attempted to rationally explain the truths of existence as he understood them to her in her fragile state, the philosophical explanations would have been of little help. Through her search, she learned of the losses of others, released some of the pain of her own loss, and over time made meaning of her son's death.

This journey can be seen as having implications for the practice of therapy. In the legends of the Buddha, we encounter a master who offers various responses depending upon the individual and the circumstances. His approach to personal interactions is not unlike the use of ideographic case conceptualization and treatment planning. In the story of Kisogotami, she embarks on a journey that is filled with empirically supported therapeutic process factors. She catharts about her loss, connects with others, engages in exercise, has a definite goal and course of action, has insight, and uses language and cognition to integrate her experience into new learning.

**Dynamism, Not Dogmatism**

The fundamental questions asked by both Buddhism and existentialism are the timeless ones. What is reality? Who am I? What does it mean to exist? How should I act? While some traditions prescribe a codified belief system to address these questions, which may reduce one's anxiety, the nobler goal is to practice living with these questions. When asked what Buddhism should do if science showed that some aspect of Buddhism was inaccurate, the Gyatso (2005) responded that if that were the case, Buddhism would have to change. He provided an excellent example of a multi-methodological approach towards finding truth. His explorations of Western philosophy, physics, neuroscience, and art suggest a desire to understand reality from multiple diverse cultures and systems.

The same is true for psychological science. The incorporation of multiple data streams allows for the most accurate understanding. Quantitative outcome research should be respected and employed, but balanced against the importance of qualitative depth, an increased focus on process and ideographic research, findings in other fields, personal and mythic narratives, and an openness to new ideas. Through integration, interrogation of previously held beliefs, and new discoveries, psychology moves closer to understanding the complexity of the world and the human psyche. The destination will continue to move and may never be reached, but daytrips and bush-whacking should show us new ground and methods from which to redraw our maps.

## Conclusion

Buddhism and existential psychology are truly compatible. The goals of under-standing the world, acting in a meaningful manner, reducing human and nonhuman suffering are ethical pursuits for this new millennium (Gyatso, 1999). Despite the variables of time and culture, the methodological approaches and resultant findings are shockingly similar and scientifically comforting. While an argument could be made that Buddha was an existentialist, he also could be seen as a scientist of the mind, a spiritual seeker and, by most accounts, a hesitant teacher. The hope in this chapter is that through the stories and comparisons, the reader will become inspired to pursue their own journey towards understanding and to seriously consider the ideas emerging from this and other cross-cultural dialogues.

### References

Adler, A. (1929). *The practice and theory of individual psychology.* New
        York, NY: Harcourt, Brace & World.
Bhushan, N. (2008). Toward an Anatomy of Mourning: Discipline, devotion and
        liberation in a Freudian-Buddhist framework. *Sophia 47*(1), 7-69.
Camus, A. (1942/1989). *The stranger.* (M. Ward, Trans.) New York, NY: Vintage.

de Bary, W. T. (1972). *The Buddhist tradition in India, China, and Japan.* New York, NY: Vintage.

Frankel, V. (1969). *The will to meaning.* Cleveland, OH: World.

Freud, S. (1923). *Introductory lectures on psycho-analysis.* (J. Riviera, Trans.). London, United Kingdom: Allen & Unwin.

Gilligan C. (1982). *In a different voice: Psychological theory and women's development.* Cambridge MA: Harvard University.

Gyatso, K. (1992). *Introduction to Buddhism: An explanation of the Buddhist way of life.* London, United Kingdom : Tharpa.

Gyatso, T. (1999). *Ethics for a new millennium.* New York, NY: Riverhead.

Gyatso, T. (2005). *The universe in a single atom.* New York, NY: Morgan Road.

Hecker, H. (1982). *Buddhist Women at the Time of the Buddha.* (S. Khema, Trans.). Srik Lanka: Buddhist Publication Society.

Heidegger, M. (1927). *Being and time.* (J. Stambaugh, Trans.) New York, NY: State University of New York Press.

Hunt, M. (1994). *The story of psychology.* Landover Hills, MD: Anchor.

Kafka, F. (1971). *The Complete Stories.* (ed. N. Glatzer) New York, NY: Schocken Books.

Klein, M. (1975). *The writings of Melanie Klein.* London, United Kingdom: Hogarth.

Kohlberg, L. (1981). *The philosophy of moral development.* New York, NY: Harper & Row.

Krishnamurti, J. (2004) *On living and dying.* Sandpoint, ID: Morning Light.

Lillie, A. (1881) *Buddha and early Buddhism.* London, United Kingdom: Trubner.

May, R. (1995). *The discovery of being.* Bel Air, CA: Peter Smith.

Murcott, S. (2006). *First Buddhist women: Poems and stories of awakening.* Berkeley, CA: Parallax Press.

Nietzsche, F. (2005). *Thus spoke Zarathustra.* (G. Parkes, Trans.) Oxford: Oxford Press. (Original work published in 1909)

*Samyutta Nikaya.* (1930). Translated by A. F. Rhys Davids & F. L. Woodward. London, United Kingdom: Pali Text Society.

Pearson, A. (1997). *Viroid life: Perspectives on Nietzsche and the transhuman condition.* New York, NY: Routledge.

Rollinger, R. D. (2008). *Austrian Phenomenology: Brentano, Husserl, Meinong, and others on mind and language.* Frankfurt am Main: Ontos-Verlag.

Sartre. J. (1992). *The revival.* (E. Sutton, Trans.). New York, NY: Vintage. (Original work published 1947)

Schneider, K. J. (2007). *Existential-integrative psychotherapy: Guideposts to the core of practice.* New York, NY: Routledge.

Smith, D. W. (2007). *Husserl.* London, United Kingdom: Routledge

Suzuki, S. (1973). *Zen mind, beginner's mind.* Boston, MA: Weatherhill.

*Therigatha.* 1883. H. Oidenberg and R. Pischer (Eds.). London, United Kingdom: Pali Text Society.

Tisdale, S. (2006). *Women of the way: Discovering 2,500 years of Buddhist wisdom.* New York, NY: Harper Collins.

Trungpa, C. (1976). *The myth of freedom.* Boston, MA: Shambhala.

*Udana.* (1948). P. Steithal (Ed.). London, United Kingdom: Pali Text Society.

Weeraperuma, S. (2006). *The first and best Buddhist teachings: Sutta Nipata slelections and insipered writings.* New Delhi, India: New Age.

Zimbardo, P.G. (2007). *The Lucifer effect: Understanding how good people turn evil.* New York, NY: Random House.

# Chapter 25

## Junkanoo: A Bahamian Cultural Myth

Heatherlyn Cleare-Hoffman

> History and culture are inseparable twins. The former conveys to a people a sense of where they have been, and the latter conveys a sense of where they are. If this concept is accepted, it can also be said that the history and culture of any people are essential to their holistic development.
> ~ McCartney, 2004, pp. 1-2

After months of preparation, the day before Junkanoo, Christmas Day, arrives in the Bahamas. The Junkanoo groups have been preparing since the day after the last Junkanoo drum sounded from the previous year's celebration. Families across the Bahamas celebrate Christmas in its usual fashion: church, gifts, food, and time with family. In the early evening, they take naps in preparation for the evening excitement. As it turns from Christmas night to Boxing Day, people begin to venture downtown for the festival.

At 2:00 AM, the first sounds emerge from the darkness. Hearts beat faster in rhythm with the drums, the first sounds heard. Anticipation builds as the sounds of the horns and cowbells soon follow. As the energy nears its height, bodies move to the rhythms and the dazzling colors start to peer through the night. A banner introduces the first Junkanoo group. With sight of the group's leader, the crowds come alive with cheers that fill the islands. The bright, vibrant cardboard costumes adorned with glitter, bright beads, and feathers fill the night with color.

Each of the four main groups—Roots, the Valley Boys, the Saxons, and the Music Makers—have well over 100 members and their own chant. As these groups near, their fans sound off their chant: "Roots! Roots!", "The Valley! The Valley!", "Saxons! Saxons!" The chants dance through the night air with the music, coming together as one. The competition between groups is fierce, and tensions run high as the dawn settles. Later in the morning, the winners are announced to the frustration and celebration of the crowd. For winning groups, they now have a day to revel in their victory before putting on the final touches for the New Year's Day celebration.

## Bahamian Culture

Long before Columbus arrived in the Bahamas, native tribes, such as the Lucayan Indians, thrived in the Bahamas. Although the Lucayans had a rich culture and societal structure, they were not technologically advanced. Various hardships that came with the Europeans caused the indigenous tribes in the Bahamas to become virtually extinct.

The islands were eventually settled by the British who imported many African slaves. Slavery continued in the Bahamas until 1838, when the slaves were finally set free. The Bahamas, however, remained a British colony. On July 10, 1973, the Bahamas gained their independence from Great Britain and became a culture predominantly of African decent, which continues through today. Despite the predominantly African heritage, the British influence remained strong, particularly in regard to religion. Today, the Bahamas is largely a Christian nation.

Although Bahamians of African decent share the history of being brought to the West Indies through the slave trade, there is a significant difference between Bahamian culture and African American culture. While African Americans have been a minority in the United States, those of African decent have been the culture of majority in the Bahamas and have not been subjected to the same extensive history of oppression that African Americans have had to endure.

Bahamian culture is rich in tradition, which is a mixture of African and British influence combined with new Bahamian traditions (McCarthy, 2004). Religion has also been a central influence on the development of Bahamian culture. Early on, the British Anglican influence was the most dominant religious influence; however, this has diversified mostly through the introduction of other forms of Christianity.

The African influence is seen largely in the music and dance of the Bahamas. Junkanoo is just one example of this influence. Traditional African medicine, which includes many bush medicines, herbs, and teas, also continues to be popular in the Bahamas today (McCarthy, 2004).

The most familiar stereotype of the Bahamas, as well as much of the Caribbean, is that Bahamians are very laid back and, potentially, interpreted by observers as lazy. This is an unfortunate misperception. Although Bahamians have a more laid-back approach to time (i.e., not as structured on time), they are a culture that values hard work that tries to improve their lot in life. Many Bahamians go to Europe, Canada, or the United Stats to attend college, and education is prized.

Upon returning from college or graduate education, many Bahamians find employment in the two primary industries of the Bahamas: banking and tourism. Both of these industries cause the Bahamas to be highly dependent upon other countries. In banking, the private bank accounts draw many international customers. In tourism, the beautiful beaches and ocean are the primary draw. However, in the 1920s, the Bahamas Development Board sought to convert Junkanoo into a tourism attraction, which served to help convert the customs into the more elaborate and commercialized form of today. Although Junkanoo remains primarily an attraction to the people of the Bahamas, there are many tourists who travel to the islands for the event.

## The History of Junkanoo

There are many versions of the story how Junkanoo came into existence, but most begin during the time of the slave trade. Junkanoo is thought to stand for *John Canoe*, who is believed to be a successful African merchant in the early 1700s (Thompson, 2006). There are a number of resemblances between aspects of Junkanoo and the Masquerades that were part of West African culture. The link between African celebrations and Junkanoo is evident; however, it has also taken on some variations in form and meaning.

The Junkanoo celebration is also celebrated in other places, such as Jamaica, but the largest and earliest celebrations have been in the Bahamas, where the practice can be seen dating back to the 1600s (Thompson, 2006). Also, there are variations in spelling and culturally derived meaning between the different practices.

Early on, Junkanoo was something that was tolerated, but not embraced, by the authorities (Thompson, 2006). During these times, Junkanoo was described as dangerous and not respected by many. This led to the suspension of Junkanoo for several years by the authorities beginning in 1942. Six years later, in 1948, under pressure from individuals in tourism, Junkanoo returned to the famous Bay Street in Nassau. Since this time, its reputation has changed and the event has grown in size, length, and reputation. Junkanoo has also become an intense mixture of competition and celebration.

## Junkanoo and the Existential Givens

Junkanoo represents the height of Bahamian culture. Beginning with its African origins, Junkanoo has been intimately connected with issues of freedom, survival, and oppression on an individual and cultural level. In this section, I will talk about the way Junkanoo has helped Bahamians face three of the existential givens: freedom, isolation/relationship, and emotions/embodiment.

First, it is important to discuss the place of Bahamian culture in the context of a book dialoguing between the East and the West. Although located in the West and heavily influenced by British culture, *Bahamian culture rightly falls between the East and the West.* This is evident in a number of ways, but most noticeable is the individualism-collectivism dimension. The construct of collectivism is often over-simplified and there are many different types of collectivism. The Bahamas reflects a type of collectivism that is different than those that exist in Southeast Asia, but also noticeably different from the variations of individualism dominant in the United States. In the Bahamas, family and extended family are more central, and often more involved in the decisions and identity of each family member.

Within the Western cultures, Bahamian culture is more similar to the southern European cultures in the expression of emotion. Similar to African American and Latino culture in the United States, Bahamians are much more expressive of their emotions and more open to conflict than most Western subcultures, particularly those originating from northern Europe (Hoffman & Cleare-Hoffman, 2011).

Last, Bahamian culture is located in a paradoxical position in regard to privilege. It is often referred to as a *third world country*, but some Bahamians, including myself, take offense to this classification. We are not as developed in regard to technology and higher education, but have had these commodities readily available through Great Britain, Canada, other Caribbean countries, and the United States. In another form of privilege, Black people have been the culture of majority in the Bahamas; however, as demonstrated in the world's response to Rwanda, the Sudan, Haiti, and other African tragedies, the world seems to be less interested in the rights of Black people around the world. For Bahamians, this has been a collective experience as well as an individual experience. Bahamians have survived as a mixture of privilege and oppression, freedom and subjugation. We have had our cultural pride challenged through a history of slavery, but we remain a proud, celebratory people.

## Freedom

Junkanoo, in the beginning of its history, represented a celebration of freedom while still under the tyranny of slavery. As Frankl (1984) stated in *Man's Search for Meaning*, at the very least, each individual retains the freedom to choose the attitude through which they will face their oppression. In the midst of the horrors of slavery, torture, and oppression, the African slaves celebrated.

It has not been a common narrative for people of European decent to be enslaved because of their group identity. Individuals were enslaved, not groups. For example, some White people *individually* bound themselves as slaves, or what were called indentured servants, to get to the Americas; however, typically this was their individual decision and they were able to earn their freedom through years of service. For the African slaves brought to the Americas and West Indies, slavery was a cultural condition. Political freedom and rights were stripped away as were the clothes that left them bare and exposed to harsh leather of the whips that tried to break them of their personal freedom.

With Junkanoo, the Bahamians demonstrated the difference between political freedom and the more intimate personal and collective freedom to which they firmly held. This stands in stark contrast to the condition of many around the world today who fight hard to maintain and expand their political freedoms all the while remaining unaware of their many levels of personal freedom (see chapter 1). It seems evident that for many born of privilege, they cannot truly understand and embrace their personal freedom until their political freedom has been taken away. Freedom, to them, has more of a symbolic nature than an embodied one.

When one comes from a history of slavery, freedom takes on a new meaning. The Bahamian slaves spent 362 days a year working, bound to the will of their oppressor. Three days a year, December 25, December 26, and January 1, they were allowed to rest or celebrate. It is quite amazing that these Bahamians chose to celebrate two of their three days of rest a year. After enduring so much externally imposed constriction, they spent two days embracing their expansive nature (see Schneider, 2008).

## Isolation/Relationship

Junkanoo has become a solid, unifying part of Bahamian culture. It is a celebration that at once unifies, but often separates, too. The islands as a whole come together to celebrate, yet fierce competition remains between the groups, especially the four main groups previously mentioned.

James F. T. Bugental (1987) discussed the paradox of simultaneously being drawn toward being *a part of* and being *a part from* as part of the existential condition. In other words, human nature places each person in the paradox of continually trying to connect to others or a cultural group while at the same time wanting to remain distinct or separate. Hoffman, Stewart, Warren, and Meek (2014) discussed this as being a basic difference between individualist and collectivist cultures. Although both have to wrestle with this paradox, individualist cultures place more emphasis on the being *a part from* while collectivist cultures emphasize being *a part of* more.

Junkanoo, with its mixture of celebration and competition, emphasizes both aspects of this existential given at once. From an existential perspective, the goal is not to solve the paradox, but to accept it and integrate both aspects. O'Donohue (1998), in his book *Anam Cara*, which means "soul friend' in Gaelic, emphasized that being a part from is an aspect of being a part of. Stated differently, solitude is an essential part of intimacy, and separateness is necessary before coming together.

Being a part of is more central in Junkanoo's function. The individual feels part of the Bahamian culture and part of the group that they are supporting. People unite around shared symbols, which generally represent something that they have in common: a location, a value system, or aesthetic preferences. In Junkanoo, there are various levels of symbolism. Within the group, their colors, costumes, and song unite them. They have different roles, from dancers to those playing the drums and cowbells, but they have a shared purpose, and they move in rhythm to one another. However, the individuals and different roles are functioning in harmony. To win, groups must prioritize this harmony, not individual performance.

Junkanoo groups also spend time together throughout the year building relationship around their shared goal. Family and friends, too, become involved supporting the group in various ways from making costumes to providing food and encouragement. Then, during Junkanoo, they join in the chants with the group so that throughout the route, the fans in the crowd become part of the group.

Even the separateness of *a part from* serves a purpose of uniting, becoming a part of. In sports all around the world competition serves to pull together one team against another. The divisive part of competition can be harmful if competition becomes too intense or the opponent is demonized. The divisiveness of competition that incorporates demonization of the other can be seen in many types of separateness seen all over the world, including racism, gang violence, and even in the behavior of parents who become obsessed with their children's athletic teams. In Junkanoo, the overriding celebration is one focused more on a national uniting, therefore limiting, but not eliminating, the divisive potential.

## Emotions/Embodiment

Individuals of African decent have been integrated into many cultures around the world. One consistent feature in these African threads throughout the world, particularly in the Caribbean and Americas, is that of embodiment. They tend to embrace emotion and to embody it. The colors, sounds, and sights of Junkanoo are but a more pronounced expression of what is present on a daily basis.

Bahamians are often viewed as a gregarious and vibrant culture; we are full of life and energy. This is very different than the British, United States, and Canadian cultures with which we interact regularly. In Schneider's (2008) terminology, Bahamian culture tends to be much more expansive than these other cultures.

The expansiveness of Bahamian culture, which is something shared with African American culture, can create discomfort for those more accustomed to restricted emotion. I wrote the original version of this chapter during the historic 2008 elections, which brings forth a prominent example. Michelle Obama, wife of presidential candidate Barak Obama, is a fairly self-possessed woman, especially for her culture. However, she has been labeled by some as *an angry Black woman*. Although the motivations for this may be political, it brings to light a difficult cross-cultural challenge: It is a common occurrence that people judge different cultures, including their approaches to emotions, based on the norms of their own culture without appreciation of cultural differences. Individuals part of the African diaspora who do not conform to the norms of emotional expression in the culture in which they are living or functioning frequently are pathologized.

Bahamians and African Americans tend to be comfortable with stronger expressions of emotion when compared with most other cultures. This includes being more comfortable with higher levels of conflict and anger. Although this is a matter of culture more relevant to preference than ethics, there are some benefits and liabilities that come with it. This, in itself, is an important point. Although it is often viewed as politically correct to view cultural variations as value neutral, all cultures have their strengths and liabilities from psychological and other perspectives.

Existentially, it is important to integrate one's expansive and constrictive tendencies, finding a place for both of them. The liability in Bahamian culture is to ignore the constrictive tendencies, or to be too expansive. However, in many cultures, the opposite is the liability: being too constrictive. Additionally, and more to the point with the example, individuals more comfortable with the expansiveness often create discomfort in individuals with a preference for a more constricted existence. It is easy to make value judgments about these different preferences that are often culturally influenced.

Junkanoo provides an important, healthy expression for the expansiveness tendencies in the culture. It also provides a particularly important illustration in that it connects the expansiveness to meaning. When a culture has been subjected to hyperconstriction, such as occurred through years of slavery, the need for a healthy expression of the expansive tendencies is needed. As discussed in a previous section, Bahamian slaves chose to celebrate on 2 of the 3 days off of work they had each year. Junkanoo, in its early practice, was a healthy response to the constricted condition of slavery. Today, although the externally imposed constriction has been removed, Junkanoo continues to serve as a healthy expression of the expansive and celebratory tendencies.

## A Bahamian in the West: My Story

I have lived in the United States for many years now; first as a student, now as a professional as well as being a wife and mother to my sons, who were born in the United States and are United States citizens. Before recently becoming a citizen, I often was asked why I did not yet become a citizen. Many in the United States struggled to understand my hesitancy in becoming a United States citizen.

It is often stated in the United States that it is "the greatest country in the world." In my experience, the United States has much to offer and I am thankful for the opportunities I have been given here. There are opportunities for me and for my sons that would not be available in the Bahamas. However, at the same time, I am resistant to the idea of the United States being the greatest country in the world. After all, the Bahamas, with its rich culture, beautiful beaches, and tropical climate, is not such a bad place to live.

Remaining a Bahamian, and not a United States citizen, had a lot to do with the cultural myths and connections. I am proud to be a Bahamian; proud of our legacy and proud of our country. It is important to me that my husband and children, who have been brought up in the United States, know my culture. As part of this, I wanted them to experience Junkanoo and understand its significance in my culture.

In the United States, I am often referred to as an African American and I generally correct this. I am not an African American, and I cannot fully understand what this label means. I have not been through the hardships, struggles, and oppressions that are part of African American heritage. I also have not been part of their victories in the civil rights movements and increased opportunities.

But neither am I African; I have never been to Africa and do not know their struggles or their realities. I refer to myself as being Black, and I do feel a connection with Black people around the world. When watching the aftermath of Hurricane Katrina, it pained me to see that most of the people who were ignored and abandoned looked like me. When watching the movie *Hotel Rwanda,* I grieved at how easy it was for the world to ignore genocide when it involved Black people, knowing full well that the world has generally intervened more quickly when the skin tone of the people suffering is lighter. Today I wonder why it is so easy for many around the world to ignore the atrocities occurring in places in Africa, such as Darfur.

As a Black person, I know what it is like to not be seen when people are looking directly at me; I also know what it is like to be seen too much. In the Bahamas, I had the privilege associated with being a person of majority. I was sheltered from many painful lessons from which I cannot, and should not, protect my sons; they must learn what it means to be African American even though neither their father nor I fit this label. My husband and I both know that our sons will face a reality with which neither of us could fully relate.

Even though I now have become a United States citizen, I will always remain a Bahamian. The Bahamian myths, such as Junkanoo, are meaningful to me. I am not sure as of yet whether I fit with United States myths. The American dream, for all its beauty, has not been my dream. It represents prosperity and the frontier (see May, 1991), but my life has been more about survival, and I am content with that.

## Conclusion

Junkanoo is the most central of all Bahamians myths. It connects us to our African heritage; tells the story of celebrating our freedom even when we were bound to slavery, and unites us as a people. Junkanoo is not just a celebration or parade. It is part of our way of life and our way of being. It is the expression of who we are and what we value. In many ways, no longer living in the Bahamas has deepened my understanding and appreciation of the meaning of Junkanoo.

The greatest threat to Junkanoo is that it could become just another celebration. The commercialization may be beneficial for tourism and the Bahamian economy, but if that replaces the deeper meaning that Junkanoo has served in Bahamian culture it would be tragedy. It is important to retain Junkanoo's mythical nature, and its meaning. If this is done, Junkanoo will continue to unite and inspire Bahamians—including Bahamians living abroad—for many years to come.

## Referneces

Bugental, J. F. T. (1987). *The art of the psychotherapist.* New York, NY: Norton.
Frankl, V. E. (1984). *Man's search for meaning.* New York, NY: Simon & Schuster.
Hoffman, L., & Cleare-Hoffman, H. P. (2011). Existential therapy and emotions: Lessons from cross-cultural exchange. *The Humanistic Psychologist, 39,* 261-267.
Hoffman, L., Stewart, S., Warren, D., & Meek, L. (2014). Toward a sustainable myth of self: An existential response to the postmodern condition. In K. J. Schneider, J. F. Pierson & J. F. T. Bugental (Eds.), *The handbook of humanistic psychology: Theory, research, and practice* (2nd edition; pp. 105-133). Thousand Oaks, CA: Sage.

May, R. (1991). *The cry for myth*. New York, NY: Norton.

McCartney, D. M. (2004). *Bahamian culture and factors which impact upon it: A compilation of two essays*. Pittsburg, PA: Dorrance Publishing.

O'Donohue, J. (1998). *Anam cara. A Celtic book of wisdom*. New York, NY: Harper Collins.

Schneider, K. J. (2008). Theory of the existential-integrative (EI) approach. In K. J. Schneider (Ed.), *Existential-integrative psychotherapy: Guideposts to the core of practice* (pp. 35-48). New York, NY: Routledge.

Thompson, K. (2006). Junkanoo rush. *Caribbean Beat, 82.* Retrieved from http://www.meppublishers.com/online/caribbean-beat/archive/index.php?pid=6001&id=cb82-1-48.

# Appendix:
# Annotated Bibliography of Works
# Related to Existential-Humanistic Psychotherapy

Christopher S. M. Grimes, Ashley Whitaker, Matthew Thelen, Erica Palmer, Michael Moats, J. M. Chavis, Ellen Marsalis, Barbara Dobson, Geneva Shewmaker, Kirk J. Schneider, Victoria Bowers, & Louis Hoffman

This selected annotated bibliography of works related to existential-humanistic psychotherapy contains entries pertaining to scholarly books, journal articles, and popular novels. Although the primary focus is on existential-humanistic therapy, we included a select number of contributions from other schools of existential psychology, particularly the British School of Existential Psychology, which is also known as existential-phenomenological psychology, and Logotherapy/Meaning-Centered Psychotherapy.

## Scholarly Books

Becker, E. (1973). *The denial of death.* New York, NY: Free Press.
Becker provides a re-interpretation of ideas from Freud, Rank, Kierkegaard, and others into an original theory stating that culture and religion are elaborate philosophical systems designed to conceal the overwhelming reality that every individual will die. Humans, according to Becker, are dually comprised of a physical self that is limited by biological determinism and a symbolic self that seeks to either create or endorse symbols that represent immortality in order to prevent an eventual nullification of one's presence on Earth. The goal of the symbolic self is to transcend death through some form of heroism, quest for immortality, or *causa sui* project; all of which can assume an infinite number of forms including the symbolic structures that support modern civilization. Becker explains how religion, sexuality, science, and psychology all attempt to suppress one's anxiety towards death albeit each system is never entirely successful in this accomplishment. Becker hopes increased awareness of how death anxiety is imbedded in all motivations will result in a more effective approach to improving the human condition. *The Denial of Death is* one of the most frequently referred to philosophical works in contemporary existential writing.

Bohart, A. C., Held, B. S., Mendelowitz, E., & Schneider, K. J. (Eds.). (2012). *Humanity's dark side: Evil, destructive experience, and psychotherapy.* Washington, DC: American Psychological Association.
This book began as symposium on the psychology of evil at the American Psychological Association's Annual Convention. The symposium, which was held in one of the larger rooms in the convention center, was completely full. The

psychology of evil is a timely topic, and also one that is foundational in existential psychology. Beginning with the Carl Rogers-Rollo May dialogue on evil (see below), this topic has been foundational for distinguishing humanistic and existential approaches to psychology. In this book, different perspectives on the psychology of evil are discussed by leading scholars.

Bugental, J. F. T. (1987). *The art of the psychotherapist.* New York, NY: Norton.
Bugental outlines his approach to *life-changing psychotherapy,* asserting this approach gives primary attention to the subjective experience of the client. He does not dismiss the usefulness of objective approaches to psychotherapy and clearly states they are necessary and have significant value. However, he argues that objective approaches to therapy are not sufficient to produce major life-changes. Life-changing psychotherapy does not refer to a theoretical orientation, but rather refers to a way of going about the work of depth-oriented therapy. Bugental provides a technical discussion of levels of communication and demonstrates with case examples how the therapist can guide the therapy conversation toward the subjective. He also provides insightful and practical advice on how to work with a client's resistances.

Bugental, J. F. T. (1999). *Psychotherapy isn't what you think: Bringing the psychotherapeutic engagement into the living moment.* Phoenix, AZ: Zeig, Tucker & Theisen.
This volume serves as a companion to Bugental's earlier book, *The Art of the Psychotherapist.* Bugental stresses the importance of understanding the client's immediate subjective experience elucidating the therapeutic opportunities of working in the *living moment.* He proposes to help therapists move away from a historical, information-focused approach to therapy where change occurs as the therapist interprets current behaviors based on past experiences. He encourages therapists to build skills of attunement to the here-and-now experience of the client illustrating how this attunement benefits the therapeutic encounter. Bugental highlights his ideas with segments of client–therapist interaction that provide clear examples of the use of the here-and-now in the context of therapy. The technical examples are less cumbersome than those in *The Art of the Psychotherapist* providing a more user-friendly introduction to Bugental.

Cain, D. J., Keenan, K., & Rubin, S. (Eds.). (2015). *Humanistic psychotherapies: Handbook of research and practice* (2nd ed.). Washington, DC: American Psychological Association.
The second edition of this groundbreaking compilation of research in the field of humanistic psychotherapy represents work done by current leading experts in this area of research and practice. In an attempt to expand and increase awareness of the humanistic approach to therapy, this volume has been created for use primarily in an academic setting. The editors of the work believe this is where change must begin in training humanistic therapists and increasing the presence

of humanistic psychology as a more accepted approach to therapy. This text covers the historical components of humanistic psychology, research on the effectiveness of humanistic psychotherapy, contemporary humanistic therapeutic approaches, modalities with children and families, and other applications of humanistic psychotherapy. With chapters written by accomplished researchers and clinicians, this handbook is a rich source of information and understanding for students or experienced clinicians. The different facets of humanistic psychology covered in this book provide a deep and meaningful understanding of the humanistic approach. The text covers specific models of humanistic psychotherapies, such as Emotion-Focused Therapy (EFT), as well as giving treatment to the core components of humanistic psychotherapy practice such as compassion, positive regard, empathy, and trust.

Cooper, M. (2016). *Existential therapies* (2nd ed.). Thousand Oaks, CA: Sage.
In this comprehensive text, Cooper offers a systematic and accessible answer to the question, "What is existential therapy?" He takes the vast and often confusing landscape of existential philosophy and distils from it a number of key ideas about the nature of existence that apply most directly to the therapeutic approaches described in later chapters. Referencing the *rich tapestry* of existential therapies, Cooper selects five specific approaches and examines the history, influences and core assumptions of each in detail. New for the second edition, the case study of a fictional client, Siân, is woven throughout the text, providing a framework within which the various approaches to therapy are made more concrete. Each of the five approaches is followed by a critical review of its strengths and limitations. Written for both students and professionals, Cooper fulfills his intention to provide a resource that both stimulates interest in existential thought and provides a practical guide to inform clinical work.

Cooper, M., Watson, J. C., & Hölldampf, D. (Eds.). (2010). *Person-centered and experiential therapies work: A review of the research on counseling, psychotherapy and related practices.* Roos-on-Wye, UK: PCCS Books.
Given the contemporary debate about evidence-based practice in psychology and therapy effectiveness, this book by Cooper and his colleagues is an extremely important contribution to the literature. Although the focus is broader than existential psychology, the book complements existential approaches quite well. The research would benefit from an update to include more recent findings; however, *Person-Centered and Experiential Therapies Work* provides a solid foundation for examining the literature supporting the effectiveness of client-centered, experiential, humanistic, and existential therapies.

de Beauvoir, S. (1952). *The second sex.* New York, NY: Vintage. (Original work published in 1949)
The work of de Beauvoir, unfortunately, is often neglected within existential-humanistic psychology. Sartre and de Beauvoir developed much of their

philosophy in conversation with one another. Yet, it is a mistake to assume they are always in agreement or bound by the other's thought. In general, de Beauvoir's thought is more closely aligned with existential-humanistic psychology compared with Sartre. *The Second Sex* is often thought to be her most important contribution. de Beauvoir accomplishes much in this book, including a rethinking of many aspects of gender. She incorporates case studies and application throughout the book to further and clarify her argument. Particularly relevant to existential-humanistic psychology is de Beauvoir's addressing of issues of freedom and the constraints upon freedom, particularly as they are unique to the experience of women. She demonstrates that she is more attuned with and sympathetic to various influences that may limit one's freedom. In particular, she addresses how women, through engagement with their families and culture, often give up their freedom, even if done outside of one's awareness. While her focus on was on women, this line of thinking could be expanded to consider the implication of cultural dynamics on issues of freedom.

Diamond, S. A. (1996). *Anger, madness, and the daimōnic: The psychological genesis of violence, evil, and creativity.* New York, NY: State University of New York Press.

Diamond provides a powerful resource for students and professionals seeking a better understanding of the nature of rage and anger, particularly as it is related to the daimōnic. The United States' plague of violence has left questions regarding how it is possible that society has spiraled so far out of control and who is responsible. Diamond writes of the often-detrimental practices of psychology focused on eliminating the discomfort, minimizing the distressing responsibility for one's actions, or over-pathologizing the presence of anger and rage. He illuminates the overlooked constructive opportunities of anger and rage, and how productively channeling these passions have resulted in creative treasures, as well as personal growth. Diamond draws from Rollo May's work on the daimōnic providing one of the best elucidated overviews of this concept. True to existential and other depth psychologies, Diamond's development of the daimōnic and an existential perspective on anger and rage parallel's May's work to redeem the concept of anxiety.

Elkins, D. N. (2009). *Humanistic psychology: A clinical manifesto.* Colorado Springs, CO: University of the Rockies Press.

David Elkins has been one of the most influential voices in humanistic psychology responding to many of the fundamental threats to the different approaches to humanistic psychology, including existential-humanistic psychology. This book includes a number of Elkin's most influential journal articles critiquing the empirically supported treatment movement and advocating for progressive alternatives to overly restricted approaches to therapy practice.

Elkins, D. N. (2016). *The human elements of psychotherapy: A nonmedical model of emotional healing.* Washington DC: American Psychological Association.

*The Human Elements of Psychotherapy* explores the history of the medical model of psychotherapy, and the ineffectiveness of this model with regard to moving individuals toward emotional healing. Elkins conceptualizes the medical model as consisting of clinical treatment in which there are diagnoses added to a prescriptive treatment, which are expected to result in a cure, thereby making the therapist all but irrelevant in the process. The author attempts to lead the reader away from the medical model and toward a humanistic model wherein the healing is understood to occur through human connection and social interaction. Elkins explores the fields of clinical psychology, attachment theory, social relationships, neuroscience, and evolutionary theory to support his hopes of redirecting therapy from a medical model to a human connection model. He emphasizes the power of human relationships and the notion that the client is the true engine that promotes change and growth, as opposed to notion that the interventions bring about change as is conceived by the medical models of therapy. Finally, Elkins explores the potency of human elements to emotional healing in a therapeutic environment by drawing on scientific evidence that demonstrates humans heal each other through social means, as opposed to diagnoses and prescriptive treatments. Through his writing, Elkins intends to persuade the reader away from outdated and ineffective methods of psychotherapeutic healing, and toward a more effective, humanistic-based method.

Frankl, V. E. (1984). *Man's search for meaning*. New York, NY: Simon & Schuster.
This volume begins with Frankl's autobiographical reflection upon his experience in the Nazi concentration camps during World War II. Frankl begins with obvious, yet profound, observations: Some prisoners were able to maintain hope, others could not; some prisoners endured the camps while maintaining sanity, others did not. From his experiences and observations, Frankl determines there is much truth in Nietzsche's famous quote: "He who has a *why* to live for can deal with almost any *how*" (p. 59). Frankl concluded that those individuals who maintained a reason for surviving managed better emotionally than did those who despaired in meaninglessness and hopelessness. From these observations, Frankl outlines his theory of Logotherapy. Logotherapy focuses on the meaning of human existence and the individual's search for this meaning. Frankl's theory is based on the assumption that the individual's will to meaning is the primary motivation for his or her life, and frustration of the will to meaning can result in neurosis. This is one of the most famous and influential existential books ever written.

Frankl, V. E. (1988). *The will to meaning*. New York, NY: Meridian.
Frankl, a neurologist and psychiatrist and contemporary of Sigmund Freud and Alfred Adler, developed Logotherapy as a result of working with fellow Jewish prisoners during World War II at Auschwitz and Dachau. Written following a series of lectures in 1966, Frankl defines in *The Will to Meaning* and the existential foundations and applications of Logotherapy. The foundations include the freedom of will, the will to meaning, and meaning of life. These foundations may be

applied in mental health treatment for noogenic neurosis, psychogenic neurosis, and somatogenic neurosis.

Frankl, V. E. (2000). *Man's search for ultimate meaning.* Cambridge, MA: Perseus.
The 2000 edition of Frankl's *Man's Search for Ultimate Meaning* is a republication of the text which first appeared in English in 1975. The text presents Frankl's thoughts on existential psychotherapy, and adds to his previous works: *The Will to Meaning* and *Man's Search for Meaning.* He discusses the limitation of a mechanistic view of the human being, and argues for the field of psychotherapy to supplement its traditional emphasis on depth-psychology, as characterized in the psychoanalytic perspective, with a *height-psychology* that recognizes the higher aspirations of the human psyche including the human's search for ultimate meaning. For Frankl, the search for ultimate meaning is spiritual and he presents a model for understanding humans as principally spiritual beings with a psychophysical overlay. This book provides the most complete introduction to Frankl's existential psychology.

Heery, M. (Ed.). (2014). *Unearthing the moment: Mindful applications of
        existential-humanistic and transpersonal psychotherapy.* Petaluma, CA:
        Tonglen Press.
In *Unearthing the Moment*, Heery has compiled over 20 authors' accounts of their application of existential-humanistic and transpersonal psychotherapy principles such as mindfulness, presence, and intentionality. Each author included in this book completed the Unearthing the Moment training program developed in 2000 by Myrtle Heery and James Bugental, and the authors write about how their psychotherapy approaches build bridges between their subjective and objective experiences in order to assist the client in actualizing his or her full potential in how he or she choose to live. The chapters cover experiences with diverse clientele in settings such as homeless shelters, prisons, and hospice settings, to name a few. Specifically, the editor outlines an approach to the existential givens of living: embodiment, choice and responsibility; relatedness and separateness; death; and making meaning in life. This compilation of psychotherapeutic experiences within the existential-humanistic and transpersonal modalities offers the reader an abundance of helpful and inspiring examples of assisting the client to live the life of her or his choosing through mindfulness, intentionality, and presence. Heery hopes that readers answer their personal call to actualize their soul's calling through the process of intentionality.

Heidegger, M. (1996). *Being and time.* (J. Stanbaugh, Trans.). Albany, NY: State
        University of New York Press.
The thesis of Heidegger's book *Being and Time* can be summarized in his words, "Philosophy is universal phenomenological ontology, beginning with a hermeneutic of Dasein which, as an analytic of *existence*, has made fast the guideline for all philosophical questioning at the point where it *arises* and to which

it *returns."* The demanding focus required to abstract concepts from Heidegger's intricate text will likely exclude casual readers, but the essential questions and conclusions contained within his chapters will reward readers who have a persistent curiosity in defining the most primitive foundation of being human. The meaning of being, according to Heidegger, is to care for the future possibility of being, thus implicating the importance of time in the ontic foundation of being. Heidegger, a structural philosopher, investigates the primordial sequence of being through the ontological, phenomenological, and existential intellectual systems. Despite the many profound and sometimes controversial insights contained within, the only absolute truth of all may be that the questions posed are equally as insightful as the answers that may be.

Kierkegaard, S. (1981). *The concept of anxiety* (R. Thomte & A. B. Anderson, Trans.). Princeton, NJ: Princeton University Press. (Original work published in 1844)
Known as the *father of existentialism*, Kierkegaard has written many volumes of philosophical thought uniquely integrated with psychology and Christian theology. In this text, he looks at anxiety from the perspective of its relationship with freedom and original sin. His assertion that anxiety was a forerunner to Adam's fall and is human beings' natural response to his expanse of freedom is followed by a discussion of anxiety as a consequence of sinfulness. The book concludes with the suggestion that this anxiety born of sin can be an individual's salvation and lead the sinner back to God. This circular interconnectedness is a central theme of this writing and speaks of the power of freedom as well as the value of anxiety. A precursor to Rollo May's writings on anxiety and freedom, it could be deduced that Kierkegaard's position regarding these phenomena may have laid the foundation for the subsequent existential writings of May.

Kierkegaard, S. (1985). *Fear and trembling* (A. Hannay, Trans.). New York, NY: Penguin. (Original work published in 1843)
This volume is Kierkegaard's retelling of the biblical story of God's commandment to Abraham to kill his only child, Isaac. During Abraham's journey to Mount Mariah, where he is to sacrifice his son, Kierkegaard explores the moral conflicts that Abraham faced. Commonly the story of Abraham is held as an example of unquestioning faith in God's will. Kierkegaard, however, points out that Abraham's apparently adherent faith in God is actually mixed with fear and trembling towards God. Yet, the magnitude of Abraham's faith in God is increased because he continues to believe despite doubting the intentions of God. In contrast to the existential presupposition that the individual is at the center of his or her own existence, Kierkegaard asserts that God is at the center of human existence. Although Kierkegaard did not intend for the role of God to be interpreted symbolically, non-Christian readers can benefit from his assertion that beneath the self-fulfilling desires of individuals is an eternal consciousness or moral code that functions as a safe-guard from the collapse of civilization.

Krug, O. T. & Schneider, K. J. (2016). *Supervision essentials for existential-humanistic therapy*. Washington, DC: American Psychological Association.
This resource provides readers with a deep understanding of what makes existential-humanistic therapy and supervision transformative for clients and trainees. Krug and Schneider, both highly experienced clinical supervisors themselves, demonstrate through case studies, trainee commentary, and transcripts of supervision sessions, their uniquely experiential training model. The authors begin by providing a concise history of existential-humanistic therapy and a summary of key concepts. Two training models (experiential retreat and individual or group supervision) demonstrate how supervision of existential-humanistic trainees align with the principles and methods of the therapy, itself. Krug and Schneider navigate both the art and the science of existential-humanistic therapy and supervision, bringing to life the difference between a theoretical understanding of existential-humanistic principles, and the embodied knowing that comes from valuing and modeling presence, congruence, and empathy in supervision. This is a guide that offers clinical supervisors and students from any therapeutic orientation an invaluable tool for developing their interpersonal process skills and deepening their level of embodied awareness; it is an essential resource for ushering in the next generation of existential-humanistic teachers and therapists.

May, R. (1969). *Love and will*. New York, NY: Delta.
This volume addresses of the topics of love and eros emerging into awareness during the 1960s and 1970s in Western culture as a more acceptable topic of conversation. By this time, Rollo May had become a leading name in psychology, particularly as a pioneer in existential theory, and this book became a bestseller among professionals as well as the general public. He explores the possibility that to love another within the context of freedom of choice may be an illusion that individuals create for themselves in an attempt to alleviate the pressing anxieties of the modern world, becoming a source of problems rather than the solution. Within this text, May introduces his innovative concept of the daimonic, which has since stimulated much discussion and controversy, but ultimately has come to define May's perceptions of human nature and to steer the course of existential psychotherapy. May also develops his conception of intentionality in this volume.

May, R. (1970). *The meaning of anxiety*. New York, NY: Norton & Company.
        (Original work published in 1950)
May examines the issue of anxiety from multiple viewpoints in this volume. He compiles various theories from the great philosophers and the psychological and sociological schools of thought prior to synthesizing his own theory. May's recognition of the prevalence and significance of anxiety despite the lack of attention on understanding anxiety's purpose led to his assertion that anxiety is not only

brought to our awareness for the purpose of elimination, but is acknowledged as a necessary and meaningful aspect of human existence. Case studies illuminate the application of his integrated theories on anxiety and poignantly display the importance of his endeavor. May postulates that if anxiety is treated as a simple, one-dimensional symptom to be readily alleviated through a few psychothera-peutic techniques, client and therapist alike miss out on a profound experience central to being human.

May, R. (1975). *The courage to create*. New York, NY: Norton & Company.
May, in this volume, introduces creativity as a fluid process of life. The very production of this book was a source of existential angst, which furthered the understanding that overcoming psychological inertia allows one to thrive in life's abundant opportunities to create. May challenges the cornerstone beliefs of logic as a linear process controlled by form, in which he discusses the converse reali-zation that creativity is the basis and catalyst of logical expansion. Whether discussing simple life decisions or Nobel Prize-winning advancements, it is the power of asking *what if* that creates the opportunity for growth, as well as the opportunity for vulnerability. May's inspiration to face one's fears of imperfection, incompletion, and potential displays the power that embracing and encountering latent, ego-bruising discomfort can have toward one's growth.

May, R. (1981). *Freedom and destiny*. New York, NY: Norton & Company.
This volume examines the paradoxical nature of freedom and the importance of accepting one's destiny, or the influences upon humans that cannot be controlled. Through the multi-levels of influence that help to shape one's destiny come the opportunity for existential angst to occur. Only when one accepts his or her desti-ny can he or she begin to find freedom. The West has demonstrated a tendency for attempting to embrace freedom through beliefs that it is found through self-indulgence instead of understanding that destiny is interwoven with transcen-dence of self. Using a case study, Rollo May shares his insights into facing the struggle of attempting to find freedom through living one's destiny and finding comfort in the pause between stimulus and response. It is the emptiness of the pause, as May reflects on Lao Tzu's writings, which give value to the observed form. This volume addresses common misunderstandings of existential views on freedom, particularly through dismissing the idea of absolute freedom.

May, R. (1985). *My quest for beauty*. Dallas, TX: Saybrook.
In a somewhat divergent turn from his previous works, May writes of his experi-ences while teaching in Greece for a 3-year period after graduation from Oberlin College. During this time, he became aware of the physical beauty around him and subsequently interested in how an attunement with beauty and art could enhance mental health. Hearkening back to themes in *The Courage to Create*, May asserts that psychological well-being depends on the ability to create beauty in one's life. The creation of order from chaos, May contends, is the very essence of beauty. In

a personal manner, he relates how his own discovery of art and beauty led him to improved mental health and to his conclusion that recognition of one's individual creative beauty is imperative to social existence. In this way, art is reflective of a culture's design and future direction. Whether with paint, music, language, poetry, or in one's life's work, art is an expression of beauty that is dependent upon the freedom that May has previously defined as one of the ultimate human strivings.

May, R. (1988). *Paulus: Tillich as spiritual teacher* (Rev. ed.). Dallas, TX: Saybrook. In this short book, May honors his teacher and mentor, Paul Tillich. May presents the story of Tillich's life including his professorship at Union Theological Seminary in philosophy and theology. In addition to presenting the biographical information, May also discusses Tillich's person and presence, his way of being, and his manner of impacting others. Tillich significantly influenced his fellow existential adherents, as well. May discusses how Tillich promoted the benefits of doubt and discussed how he sometimes felt it was his mission "to bring faith to the faithless and doubt to the faithful." *Paulus: Tillich as Spiritual Teacher* won the American Psychological Foundation Gold Metal Award in 1987.

May, R. (1989). *The art of counseling* (Rev. ed.). Lake Worth, FL: Gardner Press. The original edition of this text was published in 1939 and, according to May's preface, was the first book on counseling produced in the United States. It provides a concise overview of May's humanistic-existential theory of counseling. *The Art of Counseling* could be classified as a handbook of basic counseling theory. It may be especially helpful for those who find themselves in a position of having to often provide a form of counseling without having the benefit of significant training in the field. Ministers, teachers, physicians, and attorneys, for example, could benefit from adding this text to their reference shelf. May begins with a summation of the underlying principles of counseling and then discusses the practical steps of the counseling process. His definition of empathy and his discussion on the importance of empathy as a key component of the counseling relationship is especially instructive. Of particular interest to clergy is May's discussion of the neurotic tendencies in religion, which he includes in the final section of this book.

May, R. (1991). *The cry for myth.* New York, NY: Delta. May defines myth as "a way of making sense in a senseless world" (p. 15). He promoted and encouraged dialogue among diverse groups and emphasized the importance of seeking to give meaning to one's life. The purpose of myths, according to May, is to provide a sense of identity, to promote a sense of community, to undergird moral values, and to explore the mystery of creation. The first section of the book addresses myth's contribution to the exploration and potential answers to personal crises, the search for one's roots, and mystery. Sections two and three review some United States and Western myths, the voids they fill, and the explanations they offer to Western society. This book also provides the inspiration for section 3 of *Existential Psychology East-West.*

May, R., Angel, E., & Ellenberger, H. F. (Eds.). (1958). *Existence*. Northvale, NJ:
     Jason Aronson, Inc.
May, Angel, and Ellenberger are commonly credited as the first persons to introduce existential psychology to the United States with this volume. In *Existence*, essays written by Ludwig Binswanger, Eugene Minkowski, Roland Kuhn, Erwin Straus, Werner Mendel, and Joseph Lyons are translated into English. Through his own contributions to the book, May asserts his mastery of existential theory and provides an alternative paradigm to the positivistic dominance in Western science and United States psychology. May's idea that even the most empirically based sciences are rested upon philosophical presuppositions regarding the meaning of being human served as inspiration to the first generation of United States existential psychologists.

Mendelowitz, E. (2008). *Ethics and Lao-Tzu: Intimations of character.* Colorado
     Springs, CO: University of the Rockies Press.
This volume is a colorful creation filled with poetic verse, client-originated artistry, and powerful quotes from brilliant minds. Mendelowitz shares his journey with his client, Kristina, as they travel together down a path of acceptance, understanding, and growth. The vulnerability and empathetic frustration Mendelowitz displays in his search for comprehension illuminates the process of existential therapy. The pages are filled with travels through poetry, art, and silence. His ability to collaboratively work with the presenting personalities of Kristina, who suffers from Dissociative Identity Disorder, demonstrates his passion for the person. Mendelowitz boldly challenges traditional approaches to therapy and the *experts* who were unsuccessful in connecting with Kristina. The style and process of this book not only demonstrate existential therapy at its best, but also why Schneider refers to Mendelowitz as the "poet laureate of existential psychology."

Moon, B. L. (2009). *Existential art therapy: The canvas mirror* (3rd ed.) Springfield,
     IL: Charles C. Thomas.
Moon integrates the teachings of the existential tradition with art therapy, suggesting that exploring pieces of client-created art can be a fruitful aspect of the therapeutic process in the course of administering psychological services. He argues that art echoes the existential precept that humans can create meaning in their lives. Moon observes that the act of creation can be a validating force for investigating the personal meaning of one's life through ritual and metaphor, along with audio or visual modalities. Thematic elements arising in therapy that Moon covers include freedom (choice), meaninglessness (purpose), chaos (uncertainty), and isolation (aloneness). The first half of Moon's book introduces existentialism and art therapy while the second half focuses on practical applications and how mental illness may be reframed in a more affirming fashion through considering the ideas Moon proposes in this text.

Moustakas, C. (1994). *Existential psychotherapy and the interpretation of dreams.*
        Northvale, NJ: Jason Aronson.
A leading figure in humanistic psychology, Moustakas is one of the first to conceptualize dream work from an existential perspective. Moustakas attempts to explain the significance of dreams within the context of meaning, existence, anxiety, guilt, and other existential concepts. He examines how all of these are manifest in dreams and how they can be analyzed and processed in therapy. Moustakas begins by establishing a framework for existential psychotherapy, then proceeds to develop a foundation for analysis of dream meaning that incorporates established methods of dream interpretations by Freud and Jung. Although taking a substantial portion of the book to set up this foundational material, his conclusions regarding implementing of existential theory in dream interpretation are innovative. The case examples are highly illuminative in demonstrating the process of existential dream interpretation.

Nietzsche, F. (1954). *Thus spoke Zarathustra: A book for none and all* (W. Kaufmann, Trans.). New York, NY: Penguin. (Original work published 1892)
This volume is a loosely constructed novel that explores several themes through the eyes of the fictitious Zarathustra. These themes include: (a) the overman, a character who has become all-powerful and is nearly omnipresent through self-awareness; (b) the eternal recurrence, the concept that all events have happened and will happen again, repeatedly; (c) the will to power, the essential drive of human nature; (d) the descent and demise of Western religion, including the concepts of good and evil and the *lie* of the afterlife; and (e) the dangers of conformity. This is often conceived as Nietzsche's most important book and one of the best overviews of the central themes of his thought. Many also consider this a great literary work demonstrating both Nietzsche's comprehension of the major religious and philosophical works of his time and his ability to blend fiction and philosophy (non-fiction) in a literary style that later existentialists attempt to replicate.

Nietzsche, F. (1966). *Beyond good and evil: Prelude to a philosophy of future* (W. Kaufmann, Trans.). New York, NY: Vintage Books: (Original work published 1886).
In this sequel to *Thus Spoke Zarathustra*, Nietzsche criticizes various schools of philosophy, both old and new. He finds fault with stoics and scholars, with scientific anti-realism and contemporary religion. Nietzsche explores the concept that religion often is a dangerous and cruel form of control over the masses. Regarding European cultures, Nietzsche honors the Jews and renounces Arian anti-Semitism. He considers France to be culturally spiritual and refined, and he finds particular fault with the English, especially the philosophers Bacon, Hobbes, Hume, and Locke. This provides a basis for an existential perspective on ethics, which goes beyond the morals codes often relied upon in Western culture.

Sartre, J. P. (1956). *Being and nothingness* (H. E. Barnes, Trans.) New York, NY: Washington Square Press. (Original work published in 1943)
Many identify *Being and Nothingness* as the definitive text on existential thought. Although an important contribution, the elevation of this text as the definitive text on existential thought has created a great deal of confusion about the primary tenets of existentialism. It is more helpful to understand this as one important and influential approach to existential thought. According to Sartre, being must be understood in the context of nothingness, an idea that serves as the basis of the title. He discusses his notion of *bad faith*, which essentially delineates his thoughts on self-deception, a tendency most individuals are drawn toward. Next, Sartre develops many of his ideas on relationships, which demonstrate that his individualism is not as unbalanced as often portrayed by many. In the end, Sartre advocates for an extreme approach to self-honesty and overcoming self-deception that many think is too extreme. His approach shows less tolerance of the need for some defenses against the horrors of human condition. Many other existentialists, such as Becker and Nietzsche, provide a more sympathetic understanding of the need for some degree of self-deception while also pursuing greater honesty about the human condition.

Schneider, K. J. (1990). *The paradoxical self: Toward an understanding of our contradictory nature.* Amherst, New York, NY: Humanity Books.
Schneider introduces Kierkegaard's concepts of *infinitize* (expansiveness) and *finitize* (constriction), applying them to psychology, including the concept of spectrums or continuums regarding mental illness and overall human behaviors. Schneider purports that existential-phenomenological theory and practice assumes a mind/body gestalt. Schneider references multiple scholars' writings that endorse the concept that human beings shift between the two poles: expansiveness and constriction. He summarizes the existential agreement that everyone has an individual center or centric (Schneider), also referred to as ego (Freud), centering (Lifton), presence (Bugental), or intentionality (May), depending upon the label provided by the given scholar. Finally, Schneider addresses optimal potentialities: personal, societal, organizational, health-centered, individual developmental, and worship.

Schneider, K. J. (2004). *Rediscovery of awe: Splendor, mystery and the fluid center of life.* St. Paul, MN: Paragon House.
The major threat to humanity, suggests Schneider, is intolerance of paradox. A mass movement towards extreme ideologies in religion, politics, and economics has left many people searching for meaning and happiness in life without success. According to Schneider, the path out of polarized institutions begins with a fluid centered approach to living that is characterized by searching for the mystery, reverie, and splendor in everyday living. The concept of living with a fluid center is based on the impression that the world appears to be an overwhelming and

hostile environment, yet by embracing the paradox, one is able to transform anxiety into excitement, grief into veneration, and despair into hope. Schneider points out social institutions, such as government, school, and business, influence ethical standards for individuals and recommends that a fluid-centered approach be integrated into decision-making processes in social, vocational, and education-al settings. The fluid-filled center is a contentious decision to expand and contract the reciprocity of influence between the environment and oneself for the purpose of enabling intellectual growth and emotional protection. This serves as the most important contemporary application of existential psychology to social issues, including education and ethics.

Schneider, K. J. (2009). *Awakening to awe: Personal stories of profound transformation.* New York, NY: Jason Aronson.
Building from his book the *Rediscovery of Awe*, Schneider offers psychotherapist practitioners and laypersons alike a compilation of personal accounts on how the sensibility of awe transforms lives. Awe, in the sense Schneider advocates, can either be *awful*, illuminating one's deepest dreads, or *awesome*, spotlighting one's most spectacular desires in life. Beginning with personal reflections on trouble-some moments in his life that challenged him to sit with the mystery of life, Schneider provides suggestions for how others can cultivate awe in their lives. Part II delves into six unique case studies; the format is informal dialogue, and the eclectic variety of life events described by each gives a panoramic view of the spectrum of awe. Part III transitions into what Schneider terms the *Experiential Democracy Project*, the thesis that *awe-based* or depth-oriented existential facili-tators working in the public sector and alongside world leaders might enable awe to become more prevalent in major power centers in the world.

Schneider, K. J. (2013). *The polarized mind: Why it's killing us and what we can do about it.* Colorado Springs, CO: University Professors Press.
In *The Polarized Mind*, Schneider builds upon his previous work on awe. In this volume, however, the primary focus is on social and political applications. Polar-ization is defined as "the elevation of one point of view to the utter exclusion of competing points of view" (p. 1). This is distinguished from extremism, which is not necessarily closed off to differing perspectives. Polarization, according to Schneider, is one of the greatest threats in the world today. Connecting to his previous work, Schneider presents awe and openness to the mysteries and unknowns of life as an important part of the solution to the polarized mind. *The Polarized Mind* is an important social applications of existential-humanistic psychology.

Schneider, K. J. (2019). *The spirituality of awe: Challenges to the robotic revolution* (Rev. ed.). Colorado Springs, CO: University Professors Press.
This book takes an existential depth or *awe-based* perspective on one of the most alarming trends of our time—*roboticism*, which is the tendency for humans to act

like and eventually become replaced by machines. This tendency is being spear-headed by a variety of powerful corporate and academic forces and is poised to upend the world, warns Schneider. From the way individuals raise their children, to the work settings, to the government, and even various wars, *the quick fix-instant result* for society is hugely seductive, outwardly successful, and wildly bankable. Yet, what is lost is depth, not just of machines, but of one's own flesh; the capacity to feel and the capacity to dwell in the miracle of the unknown is no longer sought. The chief questions the book raises are: can people preserve awe—the arguable *heart* of humanity—in spite of and even in light of technologies? Or will humans devolve into mechanically driven puppets, numb to their possibilities and blind to their servitude? The book concludes that there is no more critical problem for contemporary times.

Schneider, K. J. (Ed.) (2008). *Existential-integrative psychotherapy: Guideposts to the core of practice.* New York, NY: Routeledge.
This is an essential resource for students and practitioners of virtually any orientation. Schneider has created an important body of information that includes a blend of diversity, student viewpoints, and multiple case illustrations. Schneider has continued the legacy of existential collaboration in his attempt to advance the integration of existential-humanistic psychology with other orientations and diverse clientele. The uniqueness of his work is that he demonstrates a value for various practices, but not without the ever-important significance of the thera-peutic relationship and presence. Schneider begins with an overview of his theory before including several chapters by diverse leading voices in the field of psychol-ogy that address specific types of integration or work with different cultural groups. Undoubtedly, this is a very important contemporary text in existential psychology, especially given its emphasis on the innovative and integrative poten-tial of this approach.

Schneider, K. J., & Krug, O. (2017). *Existential-humanistic therapy.* (2nd ed.). Washington, DC: American Psychological Association.
This is a guide for psychotherapists who wish to implement the principles of existential-humanistic therapy into their professional practice. Ideally drafted for emerging practitioners and graduate students, it provides a comprehensive over-view of theory and practical implications of the existential-humanistic approach to psychotherapy. Numerous case studies demonstrate various scenarios illus-trating the existential-humanistic approach to therapy, including integration of psychosomatic work to bring clients into the present moment. Another theme explored in this book the challenge of clients' capacities to act in the world and navigate the existential responsibilities of daily functioning. This book is part of the American Psychological Association's Theories of Personality Series, which helps position existential-humanistic psychology as one of the most established contemporary approach to therapy.

Schneider, K. J. & May, R. (1995). *The psychology of existence: An integrative, clinical perspective.* New York, NY: McGraw-Hill.
This volume is a concise, yet comprehensive overview of the existential role in today's psychology movement. The text includes a useful overview of existential contributions to literature, philosophy, and psychology. Theoretical and case illustrations provide the foundation of Schneider's more recent book, *Existential-Integrative Psychotherapy: Guideposts to the Core of Practice.* However, the overview of literary and philosophical contributions provides a place of importance for this volume in the literature for psychologists and clinicians.

Schneider, K. J., Pierson, J. F., & Bugental, J. F. T. (Eds.). (2015). *The handbook of humanistic psychology: Leading edges in theory, research, and practice* (2nd ed.). Thousand Oaks, CA: Sage.
This comprehensive, updated volume, concerning the discipline of humanistic psychology ranges over 27 chapters authored by 66 contributors. Schneider, Pierson, and Bugental arranged a textbook meant for intrigued graduate students and practicing psychotherapists desiring more clarity about the central tenets of humanistic psychology. Topics discussed in this book include multiculturalism, gender-identity, ecological psychology, elder-care, neurophenomenology, existential-humanistic and integrative psychotherapy, transpersonal psychology, and the encounter with existential questions of freedom and responsibility. The text acquaints readers with the major thinkers in humanistic psychology. Psychotherapists will appreciate the practical and personal applications of existential-humanism in psychotherapy. This book provides a solid scholarly foundation for humanistic psychology. The success of this book has played an important role in the renewal of humanistic psychology.

Schulenberg, S. E. (Ed.). (2016). *Clarifying and furthering existential psychotherapy: Theories, methods, and practices.* New York, NY: Springer.
This book emerged from a special issue of the *Journal of Contemporary Psychotherapy,* and includes articles by a number of leading existential therapists across different existential schools. As Schulenberg notes in the introduction, part of the impetus for this volume was the First World Congress of Existential Therapy, which was held in London in 2015. It includes research on an important survey on key authors and texts in existential psychology, a chapter on evidence-based practice within existential therapy, and several articles on the different approaches to therapy.

Spinelli, E. (2004). *The mirror and the hammer.* Thousand Oaks, CA: Sage.
Spinelli, representing an existential-phenomenological perspective, challenged the core of commonly accepted psychotherapeutic tenets and techniques from an existential perspective. The intriguing title is meant to convey an image of holding up a mirror to the profession, thereby gaining insights into its present state and taking up a hammer to shatter previously held perceptions to make way for the

creation of something new. Spinelli proceeds to discuss the ways that contemporary psychotherapy has reduced the therapy experience in episodes of short-term problem solving when many problems that individuals face today are not easily solvable and, at times, are irreparable. He proposes that therapists engage with clients in their journey and help them to explore the possibilities and choices available, given that life is unavoidably uncertain at times. Through this framework, Spinelli challenges such icons of therapy as therapist disclosure, the self, the unconscious, the role of childhood experience, sexuality, and the problem of evil. Rather than taking in a skill set to *cure* the client, Spinelli urges that the therapist's role become one who engages in a mutual human experience with another individual, recognizing shared limitations and uncertainty on life's journey.

Spinelli, E. (2015). *Practising existential therapy: the relational world* (2nd ed.).
        Thousand Oaks, CA: Sage.
Ernesto Spinelli's *Practicing Existential Therapy* is a useful guide for existential-phenomenological psychotherapists at any level of experience. Part one of his work explains why existential philosophy is the foundation for a process of thinking that has the potential to result in a new way of thinking. With the therapist's guidance, clients can learn to think with more detail and become adaptive to living in an imperfect world. Spinelli offers his theory on how individuals adapt their worldview by shifting between the dichotomy of sedimentation and dissociation. This theory is in line with existentialists use of paradoxes to represent cognitive flexibility. In Part Two, Spinelli describes the three phases of existential therapy and a few specific concerns common in a client-therapist relationship. Bridging the gap between existential theory and practice, Spinelli engages the client with phenomenological investigation as opposed to humanistic relativeness. Existential-phenomenological psychology and existential-humanistic psychology are complimentary styles of therapy; however, the reader should be aware that Spinelli is solidly rooted in the existential-phenomenological tradition. Following each section of the book are exercises that are intended to provide a lived experience of information Spinelli shares throughout his book. These exercises are not designed to be applied as therapy techniques; rather, the purpose of each exercise is to show that the therapist's own understanding and experiencing of existential therapy facilitates change for the client.

Tillich, P. (1952). *The courage to be.* New Haven, CT: Yale University Press.
Tillich approaches existentialism from a theological perspective and provides valuable insight regarding the interconnectedness of the spirit and mind. In *The Courage to Be,* Tillich addresses the existential dread that all humans encounter and the courage necessary to carry on in the face of dread. Tillich identifies this dread as stemming from awareness of individual guilt, meaninglessness, and the threat of non-being. The courage to overcome this dread, or the courage to despair, requires faith in the Ground of Being, which allows for self-acceptance and self-affirmation in the face of dread. This faith produces courage and allows

the person to transcend fear and carry out his or her existence. Of Tillich's many contributions, this book has been the most influential with regard to existential-humanistic psychology.

Tournier, P. (1957). *The meaning of persons.* New York, NY: Harper & Row.
A medical doctor and general practitioner in Geneva, Switzerland, Tournier was unique in that he recognized the need of some clients for deeper and more personal interventions than those typically offered by the medical establishment. He was a self-proclaimed practitioner of the "medicine of the person," and combined his knowledge of the physical with that of the psychological and spiritual nature of persons. In this text, he addresses basic existential questions of identity and being, one's place in the world, and in relationship with others. Distinguishing the person from personages, Tournier examines the masks that people wear in everyday life and how difficult it often can be to identify the real person within. He explores the ways individuals attempt to interact with the world around them, particularly interpersonal relationships. He also gives examples of how an individual's physical being affects his or her psyche and spirit. Although Tournier speaks from a perspective of Biblical authority, he effectively melds this foundational belief system with scientific evidence and psychological constructs, while not neglecting the importance of spiritual concerns.

van Deurzen, E. (1997). *Paradox and passion in psychotherapy: An existential
      approach to therapy and counseling.* New York, NY: Wiley & Sons.
van Deurzen, the leading figure in the British School of Existential Therapy, or the existential-phenomenological approach, covers a wide range of psychotherapeutic topics and situations in an existential framework. Throughout the book, she challenges therapists to move closer to embracing insecurity as opposed to falling into the trap of false confidence in systematic methods. She reminds readers that excessive grasping for control is not life enhancing but dulling and deadening, and van Deurzen provides vignettes to illustrate this concept.

van Deurzen, E. (2017). *Existential counselling and psychotherapy in practice* (3rd
      ed.). Thousand Oaks, CA: Sage.
This book serves as the most comprehensive overview of the existential-phenomenological approach, or the British School. Van Deurzen begins with an important overview of the philosophical foundations. The book also provides a thorough overview of the British School's theoretical and practice foundations. *Existential Counseling and Psychotherapy in Practice* serves as an important textbook and foundation for existential-phenomenological therapy.

Wong, P. T. P. (Ed.). (2017). *The human quest for meaning: Theories, research, and
      applications* (2nd ed.). New York, NY: Routledge.
Paul T. P. Wong developed what he has called Meaning-Centered Therapy (MCT), which is strongly influenced by Frankl's Logotherapy. This volume provides an

overview of the research and theory that serves as the foundation for contemporary MCT. Additionally, in his chapters within this edited text, Wong provides an introduction to MCT and his dual-systems approach to meaning, which has been influential on the development of dialogues between existential psychology and what Wong labels as second wave positive psychology.

Yalom, I. D. (1980). *Existential psychotherapy*. New York, NY: Basic Books.
*Existential Psychotherapy* has become a standard text for introducing students and therapists to existential psychology. Yalom is clear that the existential orientation is not right for every therapist and will not work for every client. However, for those inclined toward an existential therapeutic orientation, this text is a necessary read because of how Yalom thoughtfully and thoroughly summarizes the existential point of view as it relates to psychotherapy. Yalom begins by outlining the distinction between an existential orientation to therapy and the classical Freudian drive model before focusing on an in-depth exploration of the four ultimate concerns which contribute to existential anxiety in the individual: death, freedom, isolation, and meaninglessness. In his discussion of these ultimate concerns, Yalom lays out a comprehensive theory of existential psychodynamics including a discussion of commonly used defense mechanisms, examples of psychopathology arising from failure to deal with these concerns, and frequent references supporting research and case examples.

Yalom, I. D. (2002). *The gift of therapy: An open letter to a new generation of therapists and their patients*. New York, NY: HarperCollins.
A compilation of Yalom's insights on psychotherapeutic engagement with clients drawn from decades of professional experience, this book spotlights the essence of the psychotherapist-client relationship as sacred. The book is comprised of 83 short chapters of approximately three pages with each chapter focusing on a novel aspect of being with clients and their existential concerns in the therapy room. The book reflects wisdom that Yalom deems beneficial to a new generation of psychotherapists in training. Most poignant is Yalom's emphasis of remaining present at all times in a session, as well as his noting that therapists should be aware of their darker natures and own personal maladies. The first half of the book captures the art of presence, and numerous chapters give accounts of working with issues of death and meaning, as well as dream interpretation.

Yang, M. C. (Ed.). (2017). *Existential psychology and the Way of the Tao: Mediations on the writings of Zhuangzi*. New York, NY: Routledge.
The similarities of existential thought and the writings of Zhuangzi are often recognized by those familiar with both; however, there is little scholarship published relevant to this. Yang's book invited existential scholars and practitioners from the East and the West to engage different short stories or parables by Zhuangzi and then provide an existential reflection inspired by the story. *Existential Psychology and the Way of the Tao* begins providing an important

bridge to deepen the dialogue between Eastern thought and existential psychology, and includes many authors who have been part of the existential psychology dialogues in China, as detailed in this book.

## Journal Articles

This section is very selective in identifying important articles on existential-humanistic psychology that introduce authors not identified in the scholarly books section, important articles distinguishing existential psychology from other approaches, and essential dialogues in the scholarly literature involving existential psychology.

Hoffman, L. (2016). Multiculturalism and humanistic psychology: From neglect
    to epistemological and ontological diversity. *The Humanistic Psychologist,*
    *44,* 56-71. doi: http://dx.doi.org/10.1037/hum0000016
Hoffman shares his story about how seeking to understand human diversity became a major focus of his life, and the relevance of this for humanistic psychology. Hoffman's development of multicultural competency began on a cognitive level and then transitioned to an experiential level leading him to understand how experiential knowledge and scientific knowledge about diversity are equally relevant sources of information. Recognizing that the process of learning is as important as what is learned, Hoffman boldly includes aspects of his personal experience of learning and experiencing diversity. Hoffman observes that while humanistic psychology values diversity on a cognitive level, it is still working to embody diversity in its membership and must be inclusive of multiple epistemologies to expand the knowledge base of humanistic psychology. Hoffman re-imagines humanistic psychology in a manner that is diverse in appearance of its members while also valuing the diverse experiences of its adherents' lives. As Hoffman reflects on missed opportunities to advocate for diversity in his own life, he notes parallel examples of humanistic psychology missing opportunities to be inclusive. This work also provides a history of humanistic psychology's striving to become more diverse, including many layers of resistance encountered. Hoffman provides seven recommendations for action on the inclusive values that humanistic psychology purports.

Hoffman, L., Vallejos, L., Cleare-Hoffman, H. P., & Rubin, S. (2015). Emotion,
    relationship, and meaning as core existential practice: Evidence-based
    foundations. *Journal of Contemporary Psychotherapy, 45,* 11-20. doi:
    10.1007/s10879-014-9277-9.
In this article, Hoffman and colleagues seek to provide a foundation for how existential-humanistic therapists can demonstrate that they are practicing consistently with evidence-based practice in psychology (EBPP). First, they remind readers of the original article by the American Psychological Association Task Force on EBPP, which was not aimed at establishing criteria for therapeutic

modalities to be vetted as being evidence-based, but rather it was focused on how competent clinicians practice consistently with EBPP regardless of theoretical orientation. Second, they maintain that existential therapists should not feel threatened by EBPP, but should engage in the dialogues in the scholarly literature advocating for the importance of a broad and inclusive understanding of EBPP. Third, they identify three core aspects of existential therapy as working with emotion, relationship, and meaning. Finally, they review the research on each of these core aspects demonstrating the evidence-based foundation of each.

Mahrer, A. R. (1989). The case for fundamentally different existential-humanistic
          psychologies. *Journal of Humanistic Psychology, 29,* 249-262.
Mahrer outlines his case for a fundamentally different theory of existential-humanistic psychology. His assertion is based in postmodern thought with respect to previously held definitions of the term *humanistic,* and whether those concepts and constructs typically assigned to humanistic thought are provable truths or if they can be reconstructed based on theories of relativism. Based on this premise, Mahrer provides a foundation on which to build a new definition of humanistic that can exist only if different answers are provided to the fundamental theoretical questions and only if different results or payoffs are offered. In making his case, Mahrer addresses the problem of the tendencies to accept a theory based on preconceived ideas without challenging the boundaries and limitations that may accompany those ideas. He opens up a new door through which existential-humanistic thinkers and practitioners can view their clients and the world.

May, R. (1961). The meaning of the Oedipus myth. *Review of Existential
          Psychology and Psychiatry, 1,* 44-52.
The Oedipus myth is intrinsically connected to the history of psychology. Freud used this to elucidate his theory of sexuality. The psychological literature is replete with reinterpretations of this myth. May provides a reinterpretation of the Oedipal myth that serves as a primary distinction between the psychodynamic and existential perspectives on the core conflict in human nature. For May, the Oedipal conflict illustrates the child's movement toward individuating from the parents and seeking a form of personal freedom. This article initiates May's thoughts on freedom and destiny, which also serve as an important distinguishing factor between existential psychology and the various deterministic schools of psychological thought.

*Rollo May and Carl Rogers on the Problem of Evil*
May, R. (1982). The problem of evil: An open letter to Carl Rogers. *Journal of
          Humanistic Psychology, 22,* 10-21.
Rogers, C. (1982). Notes on Rollo May. *Journal of Humanistic Psychology, 22,* 8-9.
May's article on the problems of evil is in response to a letter published in 1981 by Carl Rogers in a special issue of *Perspectives,* an excerpt of which was published in the *Journal of Humanistic Psychology* in 1982 along with May's response. May

took issue with some of the statements and misinterpretations made by Rogers regarding the problem of evil. He takes this opportunity to clarify several issues, including his use of the term *daimonic*, the necessity of those daimonic urges to be integrated into the whole person to counter potentially destructive forces, and the origin of evil. The primary issue of contention between May and Rogers is on the nature of human beings as intrinsically good and, if it is so, how evil can be explained. While Rogers identifies evil originating in culture and social influences, May contends that there is an inherent potential for evil in all people. This contention sets the stage for an essential debate between existential and humanistic schools of thought, and identifies the psychology of evil as an essential difference between humanistic and existential psychology. May ends the article making a plea for a more realistic view of evil, particularly by those of the humanistic movement, who, in May's opinion, often avoid the confrontation of the reality of evil.

Schneider, J. J. (1999). The revival of the romantic means a revival of psychology. *Journal of Humanistic Psychology, 39*, 13-29.
Schneider elaborates the separation of existential psychology from its romantic roots; traces the progress and process of the theoretical separation from humanities and the arts: the losses resulting from abandoning literary investigation of human psychology; and discusses postmodern psychology as illuminated by romanticism.

Schneider, K. J. (2016). Existential-integrative therapy: Foundational implications for integrative practice. *Journal of Psychotherapy Integration, 26,* 49-55.
This journal article outlines the principles and precepts of existential-integrative psychotherapy practice. Schneider argues that the ability to incorporate existential psychotherapy with other therapy modalities is a basis for the popularity of existential-integrative approach. The article includes a case study of Ellen, who embraced the remarkable aspects of terrifying moments from her past by introducing presence into her consciousness. She, under the existential-integrative model, was able to simmer responses with a richer perspective of her identity at both high and low points in her life. To conclude, Schneider argues that more attention to the cultivation of presence, one stance of employing existential-integrative psychotherapy, is needed in academic literature.

Tillich, P. (1961). Existentialism and psychotherapy. *Review of Existential Psychology and Psychiatry, 1,* 8-16.
Tillich points out that a valid theory of being human is a necessary prerequisite for a valid theory of psychotherapy. One problem with constructing a theory of being human is that it is difficult to separate the difficulties that arise from individuals' essential nature from those arising from their existential predicament. This philosophical problem is explored in-depth and with keen clarity, illuminating important questions and the existential foundation for understanding being.

*Ken Wilber and Kirk Schneider on the Transpersonal Movement*
Schneider, K. J. (1987). The deified self: A "centaur" response to Wilber and the
transpersonal movement. *Journal of Humanistic Psychology, 27,* 196-216.
Schneider, K. J. (1989). Infallibility is so damn appealing: A reply to Ken Wilber.
*Journal of Humanistic Psychology, 29,* 470-481.
Wilber, K. (1989). God is so damn boring: A response to Kirk Schneider. *Journal of
Humanistic Psychology, 29,* 457-469.
Wilber, K. (1989). Reply to Schneider. *Journal of Humanistic Psychology, 29,* 493-
500.
This dialogue serves as an essential guide to distinguishing between existential
and transpersonal psychology, both of which are considered important branches
of humanistic or phenomenological psychology. In particular, Schneider and
Wilber debate the existential and transpersonal perspectives of *ultimate consciousness:* consummate human awareness that transcends time and space to
complete awareness of the universe. Schneider's contributions also serve to
elucidate existential-humanistic perspectives on topics relevant to religion and
spirituality.

Wang, X. (2011). Zhi mian and existential psychology. *The Humanistic
Psychologists, 39,* 240-246. doi: 10.1080/08873267.2011.592465.
Zhi Mian therapy is beginning to be recognized as an indigenous Chinese approach
to existential psychology, and it shares much with existential-humanistic therapy.
However, it is not well-known in the United States. This is the first journal article
to discuss Zhi Mian therapy and serves as an important introduction.

**Novels**

This section, too, is quite select in identifying the novels and works of fiction most
commonly referred to in existential psychology and other works that have influenced existential-humanistic psychology.

Camus, A. (1989). *The stranger* (M. Ward, Trans.). New York, NY: Vintage.
(Originally published in 1942)
Camus' stranger is an anomic man named Meursault who struggles to feel any
emotion while attending his mother's funeral and in many other aspects of his life
experiences. Instead, his attention is focused on the perceptual sensations that
surround him, such as the stifling temperature and his own physical discomfort.
Similarly, he functions in his occupation, friendships, and romantic relationship
with the same emotional detachment that alienates him from his own experiences.
For Meursault, life is an incongruous collection of events that lack both logic and
meaning. His perspective does not change until going through the process of being
convicted of murder and sentenced to death. For the first time, he is forced to
reflect on his responsibility for his actions and his own impending death. In the

end, Meursault denies repentance for his crime and embraces his departure from the world that appears indifferent to human suffering. This illustrates existential concepts of responsibility and the necessity of engaging in self reflections in order to be responsible.

Camus, A. (1991). *The plague* (S. Gilbert, Trans.). New York, NY: Vintage.
       (Originally published in 1947)
This novel is about an Algerian town quarantined due to a plague outbreak. Camus explores the unique paths taken by different townspeople in response to the threat of death and suffering. The extremity of the situation brings the human existential predicament to the forefront in attempts to engage the reader in their own reflections on the existential condition.

Camus, A. (1991). *The fall* (J. O'Brien, Trans.). New York, NY: Vintage. (Original
       work published in 1956)
*The Fall* is the story of Clamence telling his life story. At one time, Clamence was a person appearing beyond reproach, living a life that seemed to represent impeccable character. However, when he did not act to save a woman who died, he began to reflect upon his life and motivations for his many good acts. As he tells the story, he demonstrates that he is, and always has been, guilty. His motivations were always flawed and self-serving when engaging in his many good acts. The reader seems to be invited, too, to examine his or her own motivation for behaviors. As most of Camus's novels, *The Fall* illustrates that to be human is to be guilty; no one is perfect and no one is pure in their motivations. Moreover, through honest self-reflection, the individual is bound to recognize their guilt. This is an important work in understanding ethics from an existential viewpoint.

Dostoevsky, F. (1866/1981). *Crime and punishment.* (C. Garnett, Trans.) New York,
       NY: Bantam Books.
*Crime and Punishment* is a fictional story depicting the multiple causes of murder and the many possible forms of punishment that ensue. Following the murder of two women by a despondent student and the subsequent persecution of an innocent man, the reader is challenged to define the thin lines between perpetrator and victim, guilt and innocence, and lastly between judgment and justice. Through the use of multiple perspectives, Dostoesky meticulously records the self-destruction of a guilty conscious ending in a provoking conclusion regarding the salient consequences of moral guilt and the fallibility of social justice. It seems that any crime will always have two victims, the one who is violated and the one whose conscious is violated. Sadly, after it is too late, Dostoesky's characters realize that fear of the unknown does not exclusively assume tragedy, but that uncertainty for the future contains an equal potentiality for reverence.

Dostoyevsky, F. (1881/2003). *The brothers Karamazov*. New York, NY: Penguin
     Classics
Dostoevsky's last novel, generally considered his masterpiece, follows the tale of
four brothers who are each complicit to varying degrees in the murder of their
father, a scoundrel. Throughout the novel, questions of God and faith, as well as
other ethical questions are wrestled with through the narratives of the brothers,
who each represent a particular aspect of humankind: flesh, intellect, spirit, and
baseness.

Goethe, J. W. (1993). *The sorrows of young Werther.* (E. Mayer & W. H. Auden,
     Trans.). New York, NY: Modern Library. (Original work published in
     1774)
In 1774, Johann Wolfgang von Goethe published his masterpiece novel titled, *The
Sorrows of Young Werther,* which is widely regarded by literary historians as the
first psychological novel. The story is about two young lovers who attempt to
bridge the cultural divide between upper and lower-class membership in 18th
century Europe. The novel inspired a cult following among European youth who
identified with the countercultural message that economic class divisions are
unjust and that every individual should be granted basic civil liberties such as the
right to marriage. Werther, the lower-class protagonist in the story, committed
suicide after he is denied marriage to his upper-class lover Lotte. As a result, some
followers of the novel committed suicide in allegiance to the principals that
Werther appeared to represent: through death all humans become equal. Today,
the Werther Effect refers to the apparent social contagion of suicides following the
suicide of famous individual or when suicide is portrayed as an iconic gesture in
any fictional plot. Existentially, Goethe raises the question whether or not suicide
is the ultimate expression of freedom or the absolute loss of meaning in life.

Kafka F. (1992). *The trial* (W. Muir & E. Muir, Trans.) New York, NY: Schocken
     Books. (Original work published in 1925)
A judicial trial is a powerful metaphor for the daily moral judgments that one must
decide in order to live an authentic and meaningful life. This is the premise for
Kafka, who overloads his morally weak protagonist, K., with the crushing weight
of social judgment and drives him towards his own fatal conclusion that he is, in
fact, guilty. The lesson learned is that if an individual forgoes the responsibility to
make independent moral decisions, then liberty, freedom, and life will be likewise
forfeited resulting in a symbolic if not literal death. The relinquishing of responsibilities for a self-determined life, Kafka warns, is a slow and subtle process that
can deceive the innocent into believing in their own guilt. The simple plot line of
*The Trial* becomes more complex should the reader attempt to name the range of
responsibilities that an individual should assume in relation to the degrees of
freedom that one can deservingly claim. Moreover, who, among all, should be
appointed to judge another; and what, if any, responsibility does one individual
have to another?

Kafka, F. (1926/1998) *The castle.* New York, NY: Schocken. (Original work
        published in 1926)
The type of mindless, convoluted, and ineffective bureaucratic government
depicted in Kafka's novel is increasingly easier to imagine. The premise of the
story is that K., a land surveyor, is mistakenly called into service by the Castle
government but lacking authorization to work. K. voluntarily pauses his life-goals
waiting for permission to proceed, which will never come. For the rest of his life,
K. attempts to gain access to the Castle in order to receive his orders, but he is
continuously refuted by the villagers who assure him that the Castle is a flawless
government that cannot correct a mistake that it did not make. For many, the
Castle is a metaphor for humankind's quest for salvation. Unfortunately, the novel
was never finished by Kafka and many possible interpretations abound.

Sartre, J. P. (1947). *No Exit and three other plays: Dirty hands, The flies, The
        respectful prostitute.* New York, NY: Vintage Books.
"No Exit" is a one act play in which three characters, a man and two women, find
themselves trapped in hell. They discover that they each need and utilize the other
two in order to continue and realize the inevitable consequences of their pre-
death immoral and self-serving behaviors. This illustrates existential themes of
freedom and responsibility, along with the potential for change and facing
suffering. "No Exit" is the most famous of the short plays in this section; however,
the other three plays also illustrate many important existential themes,
particularly of responsibility, morality, and ethics from an existential perspective.

# About the Editors

**Louis Hoffman, PhD,** is a licensed psychologist in private practice in Colorado Springs and teaches at Saybrook University. He is also a co-founder of the International Institute of Existential-Humanistic Psychology (www.iiehp.org), and regularly travels to China to offer teaching and training relevant to existential and humanistic psychology. Dr. Hoffman has been recognized as fellow of the American Psychological Association (APA) and five of its divisions (Divisions 1, 10, 32, 36, & 52) for his contributions to the field of psychology. With 15 books and over 100 articles/book chapters to his credit, he is an avid writer, including poetry, journal articles, book chapters, and books. He serves on the editorial boards of the *Journal of Humanistic Psychology, The Humanistic Psychologist,* and *Janus Head.* Also committed to service, Dr. Hoffman is the current president of the Rocky Mountain Humanistic Counseling and Psychological Association (www.rmhcpa.org), is a past president of the Society of Humanistic Psychology (APA Division 32), and serves of the board of the Humanitarian Alliance. Most importantly, Dr. Hoffman is a husband and father. He enjoys living in beautiful Colorado Springs with his wife, children, and two dogs.

**Mark Yang, PsyD,** is a United States licensed clinical psychologist and co-founder and director of the International Institute of Existential-Humanistic Psychology (www.iiehp.org), whose mission is to promote Existential-Humanistic Psychology and provide counseling skills training to mental health professionals in Asia. He is actively involved in the training and supervision of psychology students from the Existential-Humanistic Perspectives throughout Asia. His professional interests include existential psychology, individual and group psychotherapy, grief and bereavement counseling, legal and ethical issues in clinical practice, and cross-cultural psychology. Dr. Yang is the editor of the book *Existential Psychology and the Way of the Tao: Meditations on the Writings of Zhuangzi.* He is also the co-editor of the books *Existential Psychology: East-West Volumes 1 & 2.* Dr. Yang was born in Taiwan and immigrated with his family to the United States when he was nine years old. He is also a dog and cat lover.

**Francis J. Kaklauskas, PsyD,** is a licensed clinical and organizational consulting psychologist. He has worked in a variety of clinical setting including community mental health, dual diagnosis residential treatment, forensic psychology, and private practice. He is core faculty at Naropa University's Graduate School of Counseling and Psychology and directs the Group Psychotherapy Training Program at the University of Colorado. His publications cover a wide range of topics including the goals and techniques of process groups, spirituality and psychology, and the practical integration of clinical theory and empirical informed approaches. He has served as lead editor and author on several books *Brilliant Sanity: Buddhist Approaches to Psychotherapy, Shadows and Light: Theory,*

*Research, and Practice in Transpersonal Psychology* (Vol. 1 & 2), and *Core Principles of Group Psychotherapy: A Theory-, Practice- and Research-Based Training Manual.*

**Albert Tsun-Hung Chan, PsyD,** is the Head and Professor of the School of Psychology, Gratia Christian College and a Senior Clinical Psychologist of Maggie's Cancer Caring Centre at Tuen Mun Hospital in Hong Kong. In the summer 2018, he was invited as a Visiting Professor for the Department of Counselling Psychology, Faculty of Education, McGill University in Montreal. In addition, he is the founder of the Institute for Family and Psychology. He practices across the fields of social work, clinical psychology, and marriage and family therapy. Since 2012, he has been giving trainings and consultation on clinical psychology and marriage and family therapy to various mental health hospitals and community agencies in the major cities of China including Beijing, Shanghai, Nanjing, Guangzhou, Kunming, and Hong Kong.

**Monica Lily Mansilla, PhD,** is the founder and clinical director of the Relational Path Institute (www.relationalpath.com), whose mission is to promote the Existential-Humanistic approach to couple therapy and mindfulness in the Middle East, Australia, and Spain. Dr. Mansilla holds a doctorate in Psychology and two doctoral level certifications including International Psychology and Existential Humanistic Psychology. She developed the Humanistic-Existential Approach to Relationship Therapy HEART, which she teaches to psychotherapists and psychologists around the world. She also developed the Mindfulness Based Approach to Existential Therapy MBExist, which she utilizes in mindfulness groups, and she teaches to mindfulness group leaders. Dr. Mansilla has been recognized with the Rollo May Scholarship Award for the Advancement of Existential Humanistic Theory. She is currently developing the first HEART Centre in the Middle East, with the mission of exclusively providing Existential-Humanistic counseling and psychotherapy to individuals, families, and groups. Having recently relocated to Canada, she considers herself a citizen of the world, being born and raised in Guatemala, developing her adult years in Canada, having lived, worked, and develop her theories in Qatar, and having traveled over 40 countries while developing her interest in International Psychotherapy.

# Contributor Information

**Zhaohui Bao,** Nanjing University, Nanjing, China.

**Richard Bargdill, PhD,** Teaching Associate Professor, Virginia Commonwealth University.

**Victoria Bowers, MA,** Saybrook University, Oakland, CA.

**Rodger Broomé, PhD,** Assistant Professor, Utah Valley University.

**Kate Calhoon, PsyD,** Private Practice, Denver, CO.

**Cathy Calvert, PsyD,** Gallogly Recreation and Wellness Center, University of Colorado at Colorado Springs.

**Albert Chan, PsyD,** Head and Professor of the School of Psychology, Gratia Christian College; Senior Clinical Psychologist of Maggie's Cancer Caring Centre at Tuen Mun Hospital in Hong Kong.

**J. M. Chavis, MA,** Independent Researcher.

**Heatherlyn Cleare-Hoffman, PsyD,** Gallogly Recreation and Wellness Center, University of Colorado at Colorado Springs.

**Emory G. Cowan, Jr.,** PhD, Retired, Colorado Springs, CO.

**Erik Craig, PhD,** Private Practice.

**Jason Dias, PsyD,** Assistant Professor of Psychology, Pikes Peak Community College, Colorado Springs, CO.

**Barbara Dobson, MSc,** Saybrook University, Oakland, CA.

**Michael M. Dow, PsyD,** Program Manager with Mental Health Partners, and private practice in Boulder, CO.

**J. Christy Thrash, PsyD,** Gallogly Recreation and Wellness Center, University of Colorado at Colorado Springs.

**Steve Fehl, PsyD,** Bereavement Care and Grief Counseling, Colorado Springs, CO.

**Nathaniel Granger, Jr., PsyD,** Saybrook University, Oakland, CA.

**Christine Gregory, PsyD,** Colorado Mental Health Institute-Pueblo, Violence Risk Assessment Specialist, Pueblo, CO.

**Tom Greening, PhD,** Professor Emeritus, Saybrook University, Oakland, CA.

**Christopher S. M. Grimes, PsyD,** Director, Program for Psychology & Religion, St. Louis Behavioral Medicine Institute; Assistant Clinical Professor, Department of Family & Community Medicine, St. Louis University School of Medicine.

**Louis Hoffman, PhD,** Faculty, Saybrook University; International Institute for Existential-Humanistic Psychology, Colorado Springs, CO.

**Anne Hsu, PhD,** Founder and Clinical Psychologist, True Colorado Psychological Clinic (Taiwan); Faculty and Chairperson, Grand Canyon University.

**Francis J. Kaklauskas, PsyD,** Core Faculty, Naropa University.

**Monica Mansilla, PhD,** Founder and Clinical Director, Relational Path Institute.

**Ellen Marsalis, MA,** Retired.

**Ed Mendelowitz, PhD,** Saybrook University, Oakland CA; lecturer, Tuff Medical Center, Boston, MA.

**Michael Moats, PsyD,** Private Practice, Colorado Springs, CO

**Anthony K. Nkyi, PsyD,** Senior Lecturer, University of Cape Coast, Ghana.

**Elizabeth A. Olson, PsyD,** Collective for Psychological Wellness, Boulder, CO.

**Erica Palmer, PsyD,** Psychologist, AspenPointe, Colorado Springs, CO.

**Evone Phoo,** M. Clinical Psychology, HELP University; PhD Candidate, University of Malaya.

**Donadrian L. Rice, PhD,** Professor Emeritus, University of West Georgia.

**Elizabeth Saxon, PsyD,** Independent Researcher, Houston, TX.

**Kirk J. Schneider, PhD,** Saybrook University, Oakland, CA, and the Existential-Humanistic Institute, San Francisco, CA.

**Ilene Serlin, PhD,** Union Street Health Associates.

**Heyong Shen, PhD,** Professor of Psychology (South China Normal University, City University of Macau), Jungian Analyst (International Association of Analytic Psychology), Sandplay Therapist (International Society for Sandplay Therapy).

**Geneva Shewmaker, MEd,** PhD Candidate, Saybrook University, Oakland, CA; Psychology Instructor, Hocking College, Nelsonville, OH.

**Matthew Thelen, PsyD,** Private Practice, Colorado Springs, CO.

**Benjamin Tong, PhD,** Professor Emeritus, Clinical Psychology PsyD Program, California Institute of Integral Studies, San Francisco, CA.

**Alan G. Vaughan, PhD,** Faculty, Saybrook University.

**Wensheng Wang, PhD,** Professor, School of Chinese Language and Culture, Nanjing Normal University, China.

**Xuefu Wang, PhD,** Zhi Mian Institute for Psychotherapy, Nanjing, China.

**Ashley Whitaker, PhD,** University of Alaska Fairbanks.

**Mark Yang, PsyD,** Director, International Institute for Existential-Humanistic Psychology, Beijing, China.

**Bohan Zhang, MA,** Private Practice.

# Index